Social
Cognition
and
Aging

Social Cognition and Aging

WITHDRAWN

Edited by

Thomas M. Hess
Department of Psychology
North Carolina State University
Raleigh, North Carolina

Fredda Blanchard-Fields
School of Psychology
Georgia Institute of Technology
Atlanta, Georgia

ACADEMIC PRESS

San Diego   London   Boston   New York   Sydney   Tokyo   Toronto

Cover photo: © 1999 Digital Stock, Inc., #085.

This book is printed on acid-free paper. ∞

Academic Press
a division of Harcourt Brace & Company
525 B Street, Suite 1900, San Diego, California 92101-4495, USA
http://www.apnet.com

Academic Press
24-28 Oval Road, London NW1 7DX, UK
http://www.hbuk.co.uk/ap/

Library of Congress Catalog Card Number: 98-83121

International Standard Book Number: 0-12-345260-0

PRINTED IN THE UNITED STATES OF AMERICA
99 00 01 02 03 04   MM 9 8 7 6 5 4 3 2 1

CONTENTS

1

THE SOCIAL COGNITIVE PERSPECTIVE AND THE STUDY OF AGING

FREDDA BLANCHARD-FIELDS AND THOMAS M. HESS

SECTION I

FOCUS ON SELF

2

THE SENSE OF CONTROL AND COGNITIVE AGING: TOWARD A MODEL OF MEDIATIONAL PROCESSES

LISA M. SOEDERBERG MILLER AND MARGIE E. LACHMAN

3

BELIEFS ABOUT MEMORY AND AGING

CHRISTOPHER HERTZOG, TARA T. LINEWEAVER, AND CHRISTY L. McGUIRE

4

MEMORY SELF-EFFICACY IN ITS SOCIAL COGNITIVE CONTEXT

JANE M. BERRY

5

POSSIBLE SELVES IN ADULTHOOD: INCORPORATING TELEONOMIC RELEVANCE INTO STUDIES OF THE SELF

KAREN HOOKER

6

SOURCES OF RESILIENCE IN THE AGING SELF: TOWARD INTEGRATING PERSPECTIVES

JOCHEN BRANDTSTÄDTER

7

AUTOBIOGRAPHICAL MEMORY AND SOCIAL COGNITION: DEVELOPMENT OF THE REMEMBERED SELF IN ADULTHOOD

JOSEPH M. FITZGERALD

SECTION II

FOCUS ON OTHERS

8

A SOCIAL COGNITIVE PERSPECTIVE ON AGE STEREOTYPES

MARY LEE HUMMERT

9

AGE AND MEMORY: PERCEPTIONS OF FORGETFUL YOUNG AND OLDER ADULTS

JOAN T. ERBER AND IRENE G. PRAGER

10

SOCIAL SCHEMATICITY AND CAUSAL ATTRIBUTIONS

FREDDA BLANCHARD-FIELDS

11

COGNITIVE AND KNOWLEDGE-BASED INFLUENCES ON SOCIAL REPRESENTATIONS

THOMAS M. HESS

SECTION III

FOCUS ON THE SOCIAL CONTEXT: INTERACTIONS BETWEEN SELF AND OTHER

12

EXPLORING COGNITION IN INTERACTIVE SITUATIONS: THE AGING OF N + 1 MINDS

ROGER A. DIXON

13

MORAL DEVELOPMENT IN MATURITY: LIFE-SPAN PERSPECTIVES ON THE PROCESSES OF SUCCESSFUL AGING

MICHAEL W. PRATT AND JOAN E. NORRIS

14

THE ROLE OF TIME IN THE SETTING OF SOCIAL GOALS ACROSS THE LIFE SPAN

SUSAN TURK CHARLES AND LAURA L. CARSTENSEN

15

SOCIAL COGNITION AND A PSYCHOLOGICAL APPROACH TO AN ART OF LIFE

URSULA M. STAUDINGER

CONTRIBUTORS

Numbers in parentheses indicate the pages on which the authors' contributions begin.

Ronald P. Abeles (xvii) Behavioral and Social Research Program, National Institute on Aging, Office of Behavioral Social Sciences Research, National Institutes of Health, Bethesda, Maryland 20892

Jane M. Berry (69) Department of Psychology, University of Richmond, Richmond, Virginia 23173

Fredda Blanchard-Fields (1, 219) School of Psychology, Georgia Institute of Technology, Atlanta, Georgia 30332

Jochen Brandtstädter (123) Department of Psychology, University of Trier, D-54286 Trier, Germany

Laura L. Carstensen (319) Department of Psychology, Stanford University, Stanford, California 94305

Susan Turk Charles (319) Department of Psychology, Stanford University, Stanford, California 94305

Roger A. Dixon (267) Department of Psychology, University of Victoria, Victoria, British Columbia V8W 3P5, Canada

Joan T. Erber (197) Department of Psychology, Florida International University, Miami, Florida 33199

Joseph M. Fitzgerald (143) Psychology Department, Wayne State University, Detroit, Michigan 48202

Christopher Hertzog (43) School of Psychology, Georgia Institute of Technology, Atlanta, Georgia 30332

Thomas M. Hess (1, 237) Department of Psychology, North Carolina State University, Raleigh, North Carolina 27695

Karen Hooker (97) Department of Human Development and Family Sciences, Oregon State University, Corvallis, Oregon 97330

Mary Lee Hummert (175) Communication Studies Department, University of Kansas, Lawrence, Kansas 66045

Margie E. Lachman (17) Department of Psychology, Brandeis University, Waltham, Massachusetts 02254

Tara T. Lineweaver (43) Joint Doctoral Program in Clinical Psychology, San Diego State University/University of California at San Diego, La Jolla, California 92093

Christy L. McGuire (43) School of Psychology, Georgia Institute of Technology, Atlanta, Georgia 30332

Joan E. Norris (291) Department of Family Studies, University of Guelph, Guelph, Ontario N1G 2W1, Canada

Irene G. Prager (197) Department of Psychology, Florida International University, Miami, Florida 33199

Michael W. Pratt (291) Department of Psychology, Wilfred Laurier University, Waterloo, Ontario N2L 3C5, Canada

Lisa M. Soederberg Miller (17) Department of Psychology, Brandeis University, Waltham, Massachusetts 02254

Ursula M. Staudinger (343) Max Planck Institute for Human Development, Center for Lifespan Psychology, Lentzeallee 94, 14195 Berlin, Germany

FOREWORD

Social psychology, especially as practiced by psychologists, has hardly been influenced by the emergence of life-span perspectives in psychology and sociology since the 1970s (Baltes, 1978; Baltes & Schaie, 1973; Brim & Kagan, 1980; Goulet & Baltes, 1970; Riley, Johnson, & Foner, 1972; Sørensen, Weinert, & Sherrod, 1986). Social psychological theory and research have remained mostly atemporal in that social psychological processes are assumed to be qualitatively constant over the life course and historical time (Gergen, 1973; Gergen & Gergen, 1984). With a few notable exceptions (e.g., Abeles, 1987; Blank, 1982; Rodin & Langer, 1977; Sears, 1981), social psychologists have not considered age-related processes to be of theoretical or substantive interest.

In his book *A Social Psychology of Developing Adults,* Thomas Blank (1982, pp. 11–18) identified four types of critiques of social psychology: assumptions, theories, methods, and areas of interest. Although these critiques were made as far back as 1982, they still ring true. First, in regard to *assumptions,* social psychology embraces positivism by assuming that there are "transpersonal and transsituational regularities of social behavior and cognition" that are "brought about ... by the existence of universal psychological (and/or social structural) mechanisms." Although this assumption could lead to complex models of development, instead rather simplistic models of linear accumulation are adopted. These models rule out the possibility of qualitative changes in underlying processes as people age and across historical epochs. Second, and following from the first, social psychological *theories* tend to emphasize stabilities in behaviors and cognition and to be nondevelopmental. For example, the amount and kinds of attributional bias shown by individuals and the forces shaping attributional processes are presumed implicitly to be constant over the life course. Third, social psychological *methods* rely heavily on research designs that are inadequate to the task of uncovering temporal processes. At best, short-term repeated-measure designs are employed to measure change in variable levels (e.g., attitude change studies) but are unlikely to reveal developmental changes. Following directly from the first assumption, social psychology continues to rely on a restricted segment of the population for its research subjects (Sears, 1987). The almost exclusive use of college students not only raises questions about generalizability to other segments of the population (e.g., their noncollege contemporaries, other age groups) but it rules out the exploration of developmental processes by excluding other age groups. Finally, substantive *areas of interest* are influenced by the restricted subject population and the assumptions of stabilities in behaviors and cognitions. For example, in the area of interpersonal relations, emphasis is placed on initial interpersonal attraction and friendship formation. Almost no attention is given to processes of friendship maintenance and dissolution or to whether the processes of friendship or intimate relationships may change as people move through multiple episodes as they age (cf. Carstensen, 1995).

NATIONAL INSTITUTE ON AGING

Over the past decade or so, while I was associate director for behavioral and social research at the National Institute on Aging (NIA), the NIA engaged in a series of activities designed to bring to bear concepts from social psychology on issues and concerns of aging people. Although the primary goal was to improve understanding of the behavior and cognition of older people, a secondary goal was to draw the attention of *mainstream* social psychology to life-span perspectives. The NIA's first effort was directed toward stimulating research on sense of control (self-efficacy) throughout the life course. The NIA convened workshops, including one on social support and sense of control in cooperation with the MacArthur Foundation Research Program on Determinants and Consequences of Health-Promoting and Health-Damaging Behavior (Judith Rodin, chair). These culminated in the issuance of a call for research (cf. *NIH Guide to Grants and Contracts,* April 1989) and the subsequent awarding of several research grants during the following years.

The NIA's efforts then shifted toward social cognition more generally. Again, the NIH convened a series of workshops and commissioned papers to identify the key concepts, questions, and barriers in applying social cognition to research on aging. Participants in these activities were mainstream social psychologists as well as social psychology researchers on aging, including the editors and many of the authors of this book. (This book is not a direct product of the NIA's initiative, although I would be proud to claim it as one.) These workshops, discussions, and commissioned papers identified six broad issues[1] deserving of more research: (1) knowledge structures or schemas, self-representation, and defense mechanisms; (2) the effects of context (e.g., cultural, cohort, social situational) on cognitive performance and social reasoning; (3) the interface between cognition and emotion; (4) the interface between cognition and motivation; (5) the effect of normative changes in basic cognitive skills on social judgments; and (6) the effect of social cognitive processes on everyday adaptation (e.g., health-related behaviors).

AGE-RELATED CHANGES IN KNOWLEDGE STRUCTURES OR SCHEMAS

A substantial literature exists on mental representations about the self and others, social scripts, stereotypes, implicit theories, and the role of beliefs in health and illness. These knowledge structures play an important role in the interpretation of events, organization of new information, goal setting, and motivation to act in specific ways. However, relatively little empirical evidence exists on possible age differences in the elaboration, consistency, and consequences of knowledge structures or on the ways in which these knowledge structures influence thought and action:

1. How do knowledge structures change as a function of development and changing environments in adulthood and aging? Are some types of social knowledge more likely to change than others? Do individuals' beliefs in a *just world* and needs for consistency change with aging?
2. How do individual differences in knowledge and beliefs facilitate adaptation in old age? How do age-related differences influence the interpretation of events, the motivation to engage in specific behaviors, cognitive performance, health-related behaviors, medical decisions, etc.?
3. How do older adults mentally represent social problems (e.g., in terms of causal attributions, problem interpretation, and importance)? What effect do such representations have on everyday problem solving? Although most people discuss concerns with other people prior to making decisions and resolving problems, a meager amount of research examines decision making as a social process in the middle and later years. In what way do perceptions of problems, self-schemas, and defense mechanisms influence social communication and in what way are such perceptions influenced by social communication?
4. How do stereotypic beliefs about aging and the elderly influence conceptions of self and others? Do individuals' stereotypes change with their own aging, and if they do, with what effects?
5. How are self-efficacy beliefs developed and maintained? How are they accessed and modified? What are the mechanisms by which self-efficacy,

---

[1]These were originally published in Social Cognition and Aging, *NIH Guide to Grants and Contracts, 26* (19), 1997.

once activated, influences behavior? (cf. Sense of Control Throughout the Life Course, *NIH Guide to Grants and Contracts,* 18 (13), 1989).

CONTEXTUAL AND FUNCTIONAL PERSPECTIVES ON SOCIAL COGNITION

Multiple layers of social context—from the immediate environment of the individual to the larger sociocultural context—influence development. So that the individual can be understood in context, both the properties of context and the nature of the individual's representations of those properties need to be considered. For example, how do sociocultural and sociocontextual influences on self-representations and knowledge structures influence memory, decision making, cognition, problem solving, and coping?

1. How does the social environment influence cognitive processing in old age? How do interactions with social partners enhance memory (e.g., collaborative memory)? How do individuals access and use information under particular kinds of situational or environmental demands?
2. Do causal attributions of social interactions change with age? Are these attributions predictive of changes in social behavior? Are there age differences in person perception?
3. Given that cultural transmission of sociocultural information to younger adults has been espoused as a prototypic cognitive task for older adults, how do social cognitive processes operate in the context of group processes, dyadic interactions, etc.? How do mismatches in social knowledge affect communication among older adults and health professionals, caregivers, financial advisers, etc.?
4. As people grow older, how is social knowledge influenced by particular social roles and situations such as gender, birth cohort, culture, socioeconomic status, ethnicity, etc.?

THE INTERFACE BETWEEN COGNITION AND EMOTION

Emotional states importantly influence cognitive performance, and cognitive appraisals influence emotional experience. Although complex models illuminating these issues are beginning to emerge in the social sciences, application to research in gerontology is infrequent:

1. Is the relationship between mood and memory altered with age? Does the relationship between arousal and performance vary across the adult life span?
2. What societal beliefs about emotion influence emotional experience in old age? To what extent do current cohorts of older adults anticipate negative experience in emotional arenas? What is the impact of beliefs about emotion on social attitudes and behaviors?

3. There is some evidence that information processing becomes increasingly "emotional" with age. If so, how do such changes improve or impede social reasoning about, for example, medical decision making or advice giving?

4. What qualitative and/or adaptive changes take place in emotional development and regulation? In contrast to the cognitive representation of emotions, what is the phenomenological experience of emotion (i.e., the current level of functioning of emotional experience) of the older adult?

THE INTERFACE BETWEEN COGNITION AND MOTIVATION

Important reciprocal relations exist between motivation and cognition. On the one hand, various motivational factors may bias the cognitive process, affecting its extent, depth, and directionality. On the other hand, goals (i.e., fundamental motivational constructs) have an important cognitive component. They are formed, activated, and applied in the same way as are other cognitive structures. These issues could be relevant to the aging process in various ways:

1. Does the lowering of energy resources presumably occurring during aging affect the individual's nondirectional cognitive motivations? For instance, is aging positively correlated with a rising need for cognitive closure? Is it negatively correlated with a need for cognition? If these were true, (a) aging could be characterized by a variety of cognitive and social phenomena associated with the workings of these motivations (e.g., stereotyping, insufficient adjustment of initial opinions in light of new information, a preference for similarly minded others), and (b) these effects could be countervailed by appropriate situational conditions instilling in place opposing motivational forces (e.g., a desire for accuracy, accountability, the fear of invalidity).

2. Does aging affect the configuration of the individual's directional motivations? For instance, do achievement or social dominance and power motivations decline—while affiliation motivation, fear of death, and health concerns increase—with aging? What effects might these have on various information-processing biases, such as attribution of (positive or negative) achievement versus health-related outcomes internally or externally?

3. How does the goal-setting process differ, if at all, as people age? Are older people's goals more short term and hence perhaps more specific and concrete than goals set earlier in the life course? Are means to those specific, concrete goals fewer in number than means to more general or abstract goals? As a result, are lives of older people more highly routinized than those of younger individuals? To what extent are the characteristics of goals adopted in old age mediated by their meta-cognitions about, for example, the amount of time left for goal accomplishment?

HOW NORMAL CHANGES IN BASIC COGNITIVE SKILLS
AFFECT SOCIAL COGNITION

Many models of social cognition emphasize the importance of basic information-processing skills in the construction of representations about social events. For example, the formation of impressions of others depends on the activation of appropriate categorical knowledge, the ability to attend to relevant aspects of behavior, the efficiency with which attributes are encoded, and the integration of specific aspects of behavioral information into a coherent representation. Since the nature of representations in memory has a major impact on the types of decisions and judgments people make in reference to specific others or social events, an important issue concerns the extent to which normal (nonpathological) aging-related changes in basic cognitive skills influence the representation of social information and its subsequent use:

1. How is information about specific events represented in memory? Do changes in processing skills influence the type of information represented in memory and, subsequently, the types of decisions and judgments that are made about the event?
2. Are there changes in the ability to access and/or use specific types of social information?
3. Do changes in memory skills have an impact on the ability to acquire new or alter existing social knowledge?

THE EFFECT OF SOCIAL PROCESSES
ON EVERYDAY ADAPTATION

Although basic cognitive processes involved in memory and reasoning have been well illuminated, the determinants of complex cognitive functioning are not well understood. Indeed, predictions based on performance measures are often surprisingly discrepant with the level of adaptive functioning older people display in everyday life. Typically, such measures underestimate performance levels. Because most real-world tasks are complex, there is a need to better understand the ways that motivation, emotion, beliefs, and past experience interact with basic cognitive processes to facilitate adaptive functioning.

1. How do older adults adapt to cognitive and health-related changes with age without showing deteriorated performance in everyday functioning? Similarly, how do people maintain a sense of well-being when age is associated with numerous threats to the self?
2. How are age-related changes in motivation related to social preferences and social goals? What is the role of social motivation in social network composition? Are there motivated changes in qualitative aspects of social relationships? How are age-related changes in motivation related to qualitative differences in processing social information (e.g., interpretation of a problem situation)?

3. In terms of everyday problem solving, how do older adults represent and incorporate knowledge about emotions? Are emotions of self and others over- or underrepresented relative to those of other age groups?
4. What misconceptions do older adults possess regarding specific diseases, the impact of their behavior on health, and medication use? What methods aid in the restructuring of beliefs to encourage adaptive health practices?

CONCLUSION

Clearly, many questions and issues can be better understood from the application of social cognitive approaches to the study of aging. This book and other recent publications (e.g., Blanchard-Fields & Abeles, 1996) demonstrate this amply. For example, researchers in the field of aging and the life course are embracing social cognition as means of adding affect, human fallibility, and social interaction to research on cognitive changes and stabilities as people age. Even though this is to the benefit of research on aging, unfortunately the flow of influence is still almost entirely from mainstream social psychologists to life-span researchers. One sign of hope is that some prominent mainstream social psychologists (e.g., Tory Higgins, Arie Kruglanski, and Abraham Tesser) have expressed interest in aging questions and contributed eagerly and substantially to the NIA's workshops and program announcements. Only time will tell whether efforts such as this book will influence the assumptions, theories, methods, and areas of interest of the social psychological mainstream.

Ronald P. Abeles
Behavioral and Social Research Program
National Institute on Aging
and
Office of Behavioral and Social Sciences Research
Office of the Director
National Institutes of Health

REFERENCES

Abeles, R. P. (Ed.). (1987). *Life-span perspectives and social psychology.* Hillsdale, NJ: Lawrence Erlbaum Associates.

Baltes, P. B. (Ed.). (1978). *Life-span development and behavior.* New York: Academic Press.

Baltes, P. B., & Schaie, K. W. (Eds.). (1973). *Life-span developmental psychology: Personality and socialization.* New York: Academic Press.

Blanchard-Fields, F., & Abeles, R. P. (1996). Social cognition and aging. In J. Birren & K. W. Schaie (Eds.), *Handbook of the psychology of aging* (10th ed., pp. 150–161). New York: Van Nostrand Reinhold.

Blank, T. O. (1982). *A social psychology of developing adults.* New York: Wiley.

Brim, O. G., Jr., & Kagan, J. (Eds.). (1980). *Constancy and change in human development.* Cambridge, MA: Harvard University Press.

Carstensen, L. L. (1995). Evidence for a life-span theory of socioemotional selectivity. *Current Directions in Psychological Science, 4,* 151–156.

Gergen, K. J. (1973). Social psychology as history. *Journal of Personality and Social Psychology, 26,* 309–320.

Gergen, K. J., & Gergen, M. M. (Eds.). (1984). *Historical social psychology.* Hillsdale, NJ: Lawrence Erlbaum Associates.

Goulet, L. R., & Baltes, P. B. (Eds.). (1970). *Life-span developmental psychology: Research and theory.* New York: Academic Press.

Riley, M. W., Johnson, M., & Foner, A. (Eds.). (1972). *Aging and society.* New York: Russell Sage Foundation.

Rodin, J., & Langer, E. (1977). Long-term effects of a control-relevant intervention. *Journal of Personality and Social Psychology, 35,* 897–902.

Sears, D. O. (1981). Life-stage effects on attitude change, especially among the elderly. In S. B. Kiesler, J. N. Morgan, & V. K. Oppenheimer (Eds.), *Aging: Social change* (pp. 183–204). New York: Academic Press.

Sears, D. O. (1987). Implications of the life-span approach for research on attitudes and social cognition. In R. P. Abeles (Ed.), *Life-span perspectives and social psychology* (pp. 17–60). Hillsdale, NJ: Lawrence Erlbaum Associates.

Sørensen, A. B., Weinert, F. E., & Sherrod, L. R. (Eds.). (1986). *Human development and the life course: Multidisciplinary perspectives.* Hillsdale, NJ: Lawrence Erlbaum Associates.

1

THE SOCIAL COGNITIVE

PERSPECTIVE AND THE

STUDY OF AGING

FREDDA BLANCHARD-FIELDS

School of Psychology
Georgia Institute of Technology
Atlanta, Georgia

THOMAS M. HESS

Department of Psychology
North Carolina State University
Raleigh, North Carolina

The study of social cognition and aging has witnessed considerable growth in both breadth and scope since the late 1980s. Historically, the predominant area of research examining social cognitive issues in aging was metacognition in general and self and other beliefs about memory (i.e., control and memory self-efficacy) in particular (see Hertzog & Hultsch, in press, for a review). Yet if we examine the social psychology literature, the study of social cognition is much broader, with interests in such processes and structures as attributions, social schemas, impression formation, attitude change, possible selves, goals, and social communication, to name but a few. More recently, a new wave of studies have begun to examine these mainstream social cognitive domains in an effort to better understand the effects of cognitive aging as well as associated adaptive developmental processes. Along these lines, the National Institute on Aging (NIA) has recently targeted research proposals in this area, reflecting the belief that the study of social cognition and aging will have a stimulating effect on issues of adaptive cognitive functioning in older adulthood. Overall, the focus of the evolving literature in contemporary social cognition and aging literature is two-pronged, including the examination of cognitive mechanisms that underpin social behavior and the issue of social competency in older adulthood.

On the basis of this recent upswing in interest in social cognition and aging research, we thought it important to examine the field more closely. Our primary interest is in identifying the advantages of adopting a social cognitive perspective in the study of aging and illustrating this through current work in the field. The recent proliferation of aging research in this domain is embodied in the chapters in this book, with each written by an active researcher whose work is reflective of and/or contributes to a social cognitive perspective of the aging process. Before the reader delves into these chapters, however, it is necessary to first ask what a social cognitive perspective entails and how it contributes to our understanding of cognitive change as we grow older.

THE SOCIAL COGNITIVE PERSPECTIVE

As with any field, there exists much diversity of opinion regarding the definition of the term *social cognition* (Ostrom, 1984, 1994). Perhaps the best way to define the field is in terms of the goals that researchers set for themselves. To this end, the basic goal of social cognition can reasonably be characterized as understanding how people make sense of themselves, others, and events in everyday life (Fiske & Taylor, 1991). At the heart of this general goal is an emphasis on two interrelated goals: (1) an understanding of the basic cognitive underpinnings that explain such social psychological phenomena (Hamilton, Devine, & Ostrom, 1994; Wyer & Srull, 1994) and (2) an understanding of social competency in terms of the interaction between situational and individual factors that determine the nature of social knowledge (including people's naive conceptions of self, other, and related aspects of the social world) and how it is used (e.g., Cantor & Kihlstrom, 1987).

Consistent with this first goal, social cognitive researchers have been interested in cognitive structures (e.g., beliefs, stereotypes, and representation of person impressions) and processes governing the creation, accessibility, and use of these structures. In studying these factors, researchers have drawn liberally from constructs and models developed in cognitive psychology to better understand how information-processing mechanisms mediate complex, purposive behavior, such as social judgments and decisions. For example, studies have focused on the role of automatic versus controlled processing mechanisms (Bargh, 1994, 1997), implicit cognition (Greenwald & Banaji, 1995), and capacity limitations (Gilbert & Malone, 1995) in determining behavior. The goal of such research, however, is not simply to provide an extension of models of cognition to the social domain but rather to use such models to examine the bases for thinking and behaving in social situations. Of particular importance is an understanding of the processes underlying biases and inaccuracies in processing that might influence subsequent interactions. For example, research by Gilbert and colleagues (see Gilbert & Malone, 1995, for a review) has shown that individuals are more likely to demonstrate a correspondence bias (i.e., judgments that the behavior of an observed actor reflects an underlying disposition of that individual while underestimating extenuating situational factors) if their cognitive resources are taxed than if they are not.

An additional factor that distinguishes such research from traditional work in cognitive psychology is the emphasis on understanding not only the factors associated with the situation that might influence behavior (e.g., concurrent demands on the cognitive system) but also the motivation and goals of the individual. Such factors are thought to play an important role in terms of energizing behavior and influencing the manner in which information is processed in social situations. For example, research has shown that individuals with a high need for cognitive closure are more likely to exhibit the correspondence bias in attribution ratings, consider less information in making judgments about others, and be more resistant to persuasion when presented with prior conclusive information than are those for whom this need is low (Webster & Kruglanski, 1994). Interestingly, these effects mimic those found when need for closure is manipulated through the characteristics of the environment (e.g., when the individual is fatigued or under time pressure to make a decision) (see Kruglanski & Webster, 1996). Of primary importance for the study of social cognition, however, is the idea that goals that are influenced by the situation or by more stable characteristics of the individual may affect the manner in which information is processed and, subsequently, affect outcomes in social situations.

The second goal highlighted in our conceptualization of the social cognitive perspective is associated with understanding social competence. From this perspective, social cognitive research emphasizes the functional importance of social representations and cognitive processes for behavior in context. For example, Cantor and Kihlstrom (1987) conceptualized social competence as one component of an individual's overall intelligence, with associated implications for adaptation. In contrast with more traditional conceptualizations of nonsocial intelligence, however, social intelligence (or competence) is context specific and thus cannot be measured against some global standard that can subsequently be used to discriminate between people. Rather, the emphasis is on the factors that determine an individual's ability to function effectively within his or her current environment.

Within this perspective, major importance is attached to understanding the social tasks associated with specific life contexts and how the characteristics of the individual (e.g., personal goals, stage in life, physical limitations) influence the interpretation of these tasks and the manner with which they are dealt. Central to this understanding is a characterization of knowledge about self, others, and the social world in general, and how such knowledge is used in dealing with everyday behavior in the social world. For example, researchers have investigated the multifaceted nature of self-conceptions in an attempt to understand how these conceptions are related to specific life circumstances and are reflected in an individual's behavior in and adaptation to these circumstances (Kihlstrom & Klein, 1994; Linville & Carlston, 1994). Similarly, social cognitive studies have also focused on representations of the social world and interpretive rules based on the nature of these representations. For example, implicit theories of personality and emotional reactions have been shown to affect impression formation as well as attributional judgments (Epstein, Lipson, Holstein, & Huh, 1992; Skowronski & Carlston, 1989). Fundamental to a social competence perspective is the determination of the circumstances or contexts under which these social knowledge structures are evoked and the real-world consequences of relying on them. From a developmental standpoint, the primary interest is in the individual's ability to adapt to changing life circumstances and in the impact of changing personal and social resources on adaptive functioning.

Obviously, the cognitive process and social competence aspects of the social cognitive perspective are linked. On the one hand, the cognitive processes underlying the acquisition and use of social knowledge directly influence socially competent behavior (e.g., reducing biases in social judgments through attention to significant factors). An understanding of such processes can give us some insight into the manner in which social knowledge is organized and accessed in memory, along with factors that limit effective use of this knowledge. At the same time, social competence factors can be viewed as influencing the way in which cognitive processing proceeds. For example, the sophistication of our social knowledge and interpretive rules can determine the extent to which specific types of social cues that occur in the environment are attended to and processed.

In sum, the social cognitive perspective is multifaceted, with an emphasis on (1) understanding the cognitive mechanisms associated with people's attempts to make sense of and function in the social world and (2) the impact of social knowledge and expertise on how information processing progresses. It is our basic argument that such a perspective can be useful in understanding many aspects of the aging process. We elaborate on this in the next section.

SOCIAL COGNITION AND AGING

COGNITIVE PROCESSES

A rich research literature exists on the study of aging-related changes in cognition (for reviews, see Craik & Salthouse, 1992; Blanchard-Fields & Hess, 1996). A criticism that has been raised about much of this work, particularly those laboratory studies that examine abstract cognitive skills, concerns its external validity. To what extent do findings from the lab translate into understanding behavior in everyday contexts as people grow older? The focus on cognitive mechanisms in the field of social cognition may help address this concern. Specifically, a social cognitive perspective provides a means of placing cognition into context by examining how cognition operates in social situations. In this way, it broadens our understanding of cognitive functioning to include factors such as goals and motivation.

A number of common factors identified in both the cognitive aging and the mainstream social cognition literatures are associated with effective functioning, which in turn may help us understand aging effects on social cognitive behavior. For example, as noted earlier, there is a strong emphasis in the social cognition literature on how processing capacity (e.g., manipulation of cognitive load) is implicated in processing social information (e.g., Gilbert & Malone, 1995). Processing capacity (or resources) has also been a focal point for cognitive aging research, with age-related variations in such capacity assumed to underlie much aging-related variance in cognitive performance (see Salthouse, 1996). Accordingly, changes in such cognitive functions have implications for age-related variation in social cognitive functioning. Given the demands on cognitive resources for elaborative processing of social information (i.e., adjusting the correspondence bias or initial impressions of persons), it may be the case that older adults rely more heavily on easily accessible social representations than do younger adults in making social judgments (e.g., Hess, 1994). Thus, the social cognition and aging literature has effectively encouraged the marriage between traditional cognitive aging literature and mainstream social cognitive issues of effortful versus automatic cognitive processes and cognitive demand.

Perhaps more important for understanding aging and social behavior, however, is the important role that the social cognitive perspective assigns to personal and situational factors that influence information processing. Such factors may influence the types of goals that individuals have in specific situations, which in turn determine what information is accessed and/or attended to and how extensively this information is processed (e.g., resource allocation). For example, situations that encourage cognitive closure or individuals who have a high need for closure or structure are both associated with processing goals that produce biases in social judgments (Kruglanski & Webster, 1996; Neuberg & Newsom, 1993). Importantly, the biases and outcomes associated with these individual and personal factors are also often associated with reductions in capacity. The implication here is that although there may be a relation between available capacity and goals, there is not a simple relationship between outcomes and available capacity.

An examination of goals may also be fruitful in understanding how personal and situational factors associated with aging may influence social information processing, perhaps providing a richer understanding that goes beyond simplistic explanations based in age effects associated with component cognitive processes. Studies on aging suggest that older adulthood is associated with a decrease in cognitive styles such as tolerance for ambiguity and attitudinal flexibility (Blanchard-Fields & Norris, 1994; Schaie, 1996). This has led to research examining the impact of age-related decreases in cognitive flexibility on biases in social judgments (Blanchard-Fields & Hertzog, in press). In addition, there is also some suggestion that goals and resources become more closely linked with aging (Hess, in press), which in turn helps us understand the relationship between processing resources, motivation, and performance. Researchers are also becoming interested in examining how age-related situational factors influence social goals and ultimately how information is processed (e.g., Carstensen & Turk-Charles, 1994). Finally, social cognitive research on stereotype activation and internalization (Steele, 1997) may provide clues as to how negative images of aging influence performance in social and nonsocial contexts (e.g., Levy, 1996; Levy & Langer, 1994). In sum, by focusing on the interaction between motivation and cognition, the social cognitive perspective provides a much richer framework for understanding aging and cognition in context.

SOCIAL COMPETENCE

Our understanding of aging and adaptive functioning may also be enhanced through investigations of social competence that focus on representations of self and the social world, and how these representations change with age. In this case, we are interested in how these changes both reflect the changing life context of the individual and affect adaptation to these changing contexts. The mainstream social cognitive perspective has typically examined changing life context and self-concept within a narrow age range (i.e., within the college years) (Cantor & Fleeson, 1991). Research from an aging perspective has adopted such social cognitive constructs as possible selves and explored how they change throughout the latter half of the life span (Cross & Markus, 1991; Hooker, 1992). This approach, in general, may provide some insight into adaptation processes in aging. For example, one can examine how goals related to possible selves influence social behavior and outcomes, such as health behavior (see Chapter 5). In addition, we can examine how the activation of relevant knowledge structures is related to changes in personal, social, and economic circumstances, which in turn influence interpretation and cognitive appraisals of social events, persons, and self.

Complementary to this perspective is the impact of social cognition on lifespan perspectives of cognitive aging. The social cognition paradigm has offered an enriched understanding of competency in older adulthood. From this perspective, social competence is seen as an important and valid dimension of cognition and intelligence. Thus, social cognitive performance can be explained in terms of adaptation to particular life contexts. This is most evident in areas such as wisdom, practical and social problem solving, and post-formal reasoning Blanchard-Fields, Jahnke, & Camp, 1995; Marsiske & Willis, 1995; Staudinger, Smith, & Baltes, 1992). Examples of such knowledge and strategies include selection, compensation, and optimization; beliefs in self-efficacy and internal control; and flexibility in coping behavior (see Chapter 15). Thus, through examinations of representational systems and the contexts that influence their development and functioning, we may be able to arrive at a better understanding of those factors associated with positive adaptation in later life.

AGING AND SOCIAL COGNITION

As can be seen from the above discussion, principles of social cognition have greatly affected social cognitive research in aging. However, aging research has also broadened our understanding of social cognitive processes. First, aging research provides tests of existing social cognitive models by extending their applicability across adult life span. Second, it has enabled us to identify factors influencing social cognitive processes that were not evident in research using only younger adults. Third, from a developmental perspective, it emphasizes the examination of changes in such constructs as social representations within the context of a changing organism. A number of illustrative examples can be found in the social cognition and aging literature.

For example, there is evidence that attributional processes may operate in different ways depending on the age of the individual and the specific social situation. Blanchard-Fields (1996) found that the correspondence bias is evident in some but not all types of situations. In this case, the relevance of the situation to the particular life stage of the individual mattered. In addition, an adjustment of the correspondence bias was not simply a matter of cognitive load (as discussed in the research by Gilbert and colleagues already mentioned); its occurrence depended on the age group examined and, again, the content of the situations presented. Studies of social inference by Hess and colleagues (Hess, Bolstad, Woodburn, & Auman, 1999; Hess & Pullen, 1994) have also shown that a straightforward extrapolation from research on young adulthood to middle and later adulthood is difficult. This research demonstrated that the use of diagnostic trait information in the construction of social judgments could not be characterized in simple terms. Rather, the use of such information varied with age, and this variation appeared to be related to social experience and changes in the salience of specific behavioral realms as a function of age. Finally, Carstensen's (1993) work suggests that changes in the relative importance of goals across the life span profoundly influence the interpretation of social information as well as the selection and maintenance of intimate relationships.

Overall, the functional approach advocated within a social cognitive perspective requires that models and theories be able to accommodate different groups and life contexts, a goal that is enhanced through the study of individuals of different ages and cohorts. The models developed in mainstream social cognitive research may be too static and unable to incorporate such developmental phenomenon. Incorporating principles derived from the life-span contextual perspective (Baltes, 1987) in the formulation and study of such models should result in greater applicability to understanding social cognition at all points in the lifespan.

ORGANIZATION OF THIS BOOK

The chapters in this book represent a wide range of research topics that are relevant to a social cognitive perspective of adult development. They represent divergent areas of social cognition and aging ranging from self-related metacognition to cognition in a social interactive context. Regardless of these differences, all of the authors accepted the charge to reflect on how mainstream social cognition has influenced their research and theorizing in their respective areas. The result is a book that documents social cognition's current impact on aging research and how it has broadened our understanding of and thinking about the aging process.

Although there are many ways to group these chapters, one salient organizational scheme is related to whether the primary focus is on the self, others, or the social context, including interactions between self and other. Within each of these sections, however, there is clear diversity in terms of the problem focus, the theoretical constructs used to frame research questions, and the methods used to address these questions. The common theme across chapters, however, is the emphasis on representational processes and the social context as a basis for understanding aging-related changes in cognitive performance and social behavior.

FOCUS ON SELF

Chapters 2 through 7 deal with self-representations and their behavioral implications, with a focus on understanding how such representations change with age and influence adaptive functioning. These chapters can be further subdivided into those that examine the impact of belief systems on cognitive performance and those that focus more generally on self-concept.

The first three chapters in this section focus on the self's beliefs about cognitive ability in general and memory ability in particular. Chapter 2 focuses primarily on age-related differences in the control beliefs individuals hold about their abilities and how they influence cognitive performance. Miller and Lachman argue that a sense of control has a positive influence on memory performance despite age-related declines in cognition so well documented in the literature. However, they expand this notion in two ways. First, they present research demonstrating that the influence of control beliefs on cognitive performance varies by cognitive domain (e.g., memory reasoning) and is mediated by background factors such as health and exercise. Second, they argue that performance on cognitive tasks influences self-beliefs. These varying relationships are presented in a conceptual model of sense of control and cognitive aging.

Chapter 3 by Hertzog, Lineweaver, and McGuire, also addresses the role self-beliefs play in memory performance. However, instead of examining how age differences in metacognitive beliefs account for age differences in cognitive performance, the authors focus on beliefs about memory in their own right. They discuss a program of research that attempts to identify the linkages between implicit theories about aging and memory, casual attributions about memory performance, self-referent beliefs about memory, and strategy use. In particular, this research introduces a new methodology for scaling implicit theories about age changes in memory. On the basis of their findings, they challenge the notion that beliefs about the controllability of memory function necessarily result in better memory-related performance and strategy usage.

In the last chapter (Chapter 4) concerning beliefs about cognitive ability, Berry critically examines memory self-efficacy and aging. The research orientation derives primarily from Bandurian self-efficacy theory. Thus, the self-referent beliefs Berry focuses on are task-specific judgments of memory competence and confidence. Similar to Miller and Lachman in Chapter 2, Berry argues that memory self-efficacy predicts memory performance in adulthood and aging. However, she further argues for a developmental perspective in which the predictive validity of memory self-efficacy would vary by task and person over time as well as the social cognitive and personality underpinnings of self-efficacy beliefs.

Chapters 5 and 6 focus on changes in self-concept with increasing age. In Chapter 5, Hooker discusses the development of self in terms of changing goals. In this case, goals are defined as possible selves—that is, one's hopes and fears for the future. Hooker argues that possible selves not only influence one's self-definition but also provide a compelling motivator for self-regulatory behavior. From both a developmental and social cognitive perspective, this research demonstrates both age-related changes in the content of one's representation of possible selves and how they relate to adaptive behavior. For example, health-related selves achieve greater importance in older adulthood and relate to perceived health and health behaviors.

Brandtstädter, in Chapter 6, also focuses on self-concept. The concern addressed here is how individuals preserve a sense of self and integrity in the face of the common losses associated with the process of aging. Of particular interest is the common finding that aging is not consistently associated with declines in well-being or self-esteem. The research presented by Brandtstädter represents attempts by him and his colleagues to understand the adaptive processes (i.e., assimilative, accommodative, and immunizing) that underlie this self-preservation as individuals balance the gains and losses associated with different phases of adulthood.

Chapter 7 also addresses representations of self, but in a somewhat different way. Specifically, the research presented in this chapter deals with autobiographical memory, which Fitzgerald argues provides the basis for a sense of identity as well as a wealth of knowledge about that social world that facilitates our actions therein. Of major developmental interest in this research is an examination of the types of memories that are encoded and retrieved at different stages of life, and how the differential distribution of memories may provide insights into the organization of self knowledge.

FOCUS ON OTHERS

One of the dominant themes in research on social cognition concerns an understanding of how individuals represent information about others, including the mechanisms involved in constructing such representations and the impact of personal and situational factors on this process. A major goal in such research is to understand the factors that influence the accuracy of these representations and their impact on behavior in social contexts (e.g., inferences about and interactions with others). The next four chapters speak to these and related issues.

The first chapter in this section, Chapter 8, addresses a traditional topic in social psychology: stereotypes. Hummert presents research that examines the nature of stereotypes about old age, with a focus on two major concerns. One is understanding the multidimensional structure of age-related stereotypes and how this structure (including positive versus negative conceptions) changes with the age of the perceiver. Consistent with the notion that stereotypes also have social consequences, Hummert also discusses research that examines how stereotype activation may affect attributions about and interactions with older adults.

Chapter 9, by Erber and Prager, extends this line of research by examining how stereotypes influence perceptions of older adults' memory skills. The results of an extensive series of studies are reported that examine how the age of the perceiver interacts with the age of the target and the specific context in which the target is presented in determining inferences about ability. Of primary interest is the finding that these inferences change with age, with younger adults often providing harsher judgments for older adults than for younger adults even though both may be exhibiting the same memory-related behaviors. Such findings have serious implications with respect to the evaluation of older adults' capabilities in real-world situations (e.g., job evaluations).

In Chapter 10, Blanchard-Fields is also concerned about social inference by examining what types of information individuals attend to when making a causal judgment. In her program of research, findings indicate that the nature of social judgment biases differ across the adult lifespan. More importantly, however, she argues that although processing resource capacity may influence age-related differences in judgment biases, one cannot discount the important motivating role that age- and cohort-related differences in underlying social beliefs and values play in determining when more elaborative processing is exercised when making social judgments.

Chapter 11 in this section explores the cognitive underpinnings of social inference. Hess presents a conceptual framework for understanding aging and social information processing that is based on an integration of constructs drawn from the literatures on cognitive aging, social cognition and aging, and mainstream social cognition. This framework emphasizes the multiple determinants of aging-related effects, and research is presented that supports this notion by showing that differences in social representations and inferences can be traced to age-related variations in both goals and cognitive mechanisms, and the interdependency between these two factors.

FOCUS ON THE SOCIAL CONTEXT: INTERACTIONS BETWEEN SELF AND OTHER

Whereas the chapters in the previous two sections emphasized the role of self or other in social cognitive processes, the chapters in this final section all focus on social cognitive functioning as it relates to the dynamic interplay between self, others, and context. In contrast to the chapters in the previous two sections, however, these chapters are more diverse. This diversity is reflected in the degree to which the interplay is examined as process as in collaborative cognition or outcome as in preference for types of social interaction.

Chapter 12 begins this section by examining cognition in social collaborative contexts or the relationship between self and other. Although the reported research has involved cognition in social situations, the primary thrust of Dixon's work in this area has been in terms of the examination of age differences in the benefits or costs of collaboration in cognitive performance (e.g., memory, problem solving). In this chapter, however, Dixon attempts to conceptualize this work using a social cognitive perspective, in part by arguing that collaborative cognitive can be characterized as one aspect of social competence.

Pratt and Norris, who in Chapter 13 discuss moral development during adulthood using ideas drawn from both Kohlberg and Vygotsky, take a different approach. Although not a traditional topic in the mainstream literature on social cognition, moral reasoning is clearly relevant to a social cognitive perspective. Specifically, morality is firmly based in social contexts. People's representations of morality presumably both affect their behavior and are influenced by self–other interactions in these social contexts. The research presented by Pratt and Norris adheres to a social cognitive framework by examining how moral reasoning changes over adulthood and how such changes are linked to the social context and individual variation in experience with such contexts.

Chapter 14, by Turk Charles and Carstensen, examines self–other relations in terms of social partner preferences. They posit a developmental shift in social goals involving the increasing importance of the affective potential of social partners. This in turn influences such social interaction outcomes as selection of partners. However, they also emphasize that this is not simply an age-related phenomenon. An important component of their argument is that perception of time is responsible for this change in social motivation. Overall, they argue that considering changes in social goals recasts age-related decreases in social interaction in terms of its adaptive significance.

Chapter 15, by Staudinger, moves away from self-development as the unit of analysis to that of human life in context. This emphasis reflects the dynamic relationship between the individual and the larger physical and social context. More specifically, knowledge structures and strategies of living are examined as important predictors of adaptive functioning. Such information and strategies are used in composing and managing one's life. Dynamic systems theory is offered as an illustration of how one can examine this adaptive interplay in the relationships among emotion, social context, and cognition.

The chapters in this book represent a broad range of social cognitive approaches to the study of aging ranging from the intrapersonal to the interpersonal. Again, however, we should be reminded that research in social cognition spans an even greater content domain. Current research in social cognition and aging has only scratched the surface. Still, we are optimistic about the growth of the social cognitive approach in research addressing many of the cognitive and socioemotional aspects of behavior that are of interest in the field of adult development. Indeed, this optimism is reflected in the future-direction discussions in each of the chapters.

REFERENCES

Baltes, P. B. (1987). Theoretical propositions of life-span developmental psychology: On the dynamics between growth and decline. *Developmental Psychology, 23,* 611–626.

Bargh, J. A. (1994). The four horsemen of automaticity: Awareness, intention, efficiency, and control in social cognition. In R. S. Wyer, Jr. & T. K. Srull (Eds.), *Handbook of social cognition* (pp. 1–40). Hillsdale, NJ: Lawrence Erlbaum Associates.

Bargh, J. A. (1997). The automaticity of everyday life. In R. S. Wyer, Jr. (Ed.), *Advances in social cognition* (Vol. 10, pp. 1–61). Mahwah, NJ: Lawrence Erlbaum Associates.

Blanchard-Fields, F. (1996). Causal attributions across the adult life span: The influence of social schemas, life context, and domain specificity. *Applied Cognitive Psychology, 10,* 431.1–10.

Blanchard-Fields, F., & Hertzog, C. (in press). Age differences in schematicity. In U. von Hecker, S. Dutke, & G. Sedek (Eds.), *Processes of generative mental representation and psychological adaptation.* Dordrecht, The Netherlands: Kluwer.

Blanchard-Fields, F., & Hess, T. M. (Eds.) (1996). *Perspectives on cognitive change in adulthood and aging.* New York: McGraw-Hill.

Blanchard-Fields, F., Jahnke, H., & Camp, C. (1995). Age differences in problem solving style: the role of emotional salience. *Psychology and Aging, 10,* 173–180.

Blanchard-Fields, F., & Norris, L. (1994). Casual attributions from adolescence through adulthood: Age differences, ego level, and generalized response style. *Aging and Cognition, 1,* 67–86.

Cantor, N., & Fleeson, W. (1991). Life tasks and self-regulatory processes. *Advances in Motivation and Achievement, 7,* 327–369.

Cantor, N., & Kihlstrom, J. F. (1987). *Personality and social intelligence.* Englewood Cliffs, NJ: Prentice-Hall.

Carstensen, L. L. (1993). Motivation for social contact across the lifespan: A theory of socioemotional selectivity. In J. Jacobs (Ed.), *Nebraska Symposium on Motivation* (Vol. 40, pp. 209–254). Lincoln, IL: University of Nebraska Press.

Carstensen, L. L., & Turk-Charles, S. (1994). The salience of emotion across the adult life span. *Psychology and Aging, 9,* 259–264.

Craik, F. I. M., & Salthouse, T. A. (Eds.) (1992). *The handbook of aging and cognition.* Hillsdale, NJ: Lawrence Erlbaum Associates.

Cross, S., & Markus, H. (1991). Possible selves across the lifespan. *Human Development, 34,* 230–255.

Epstein, S., Lipson, A., Holstein, C., & Huh, E. (1992). Irrational reactions to negative outcomes: Evidence for two conceptual systems. *Journal of Personality and Social Psychology, 62,* 328–339.

Fiske, S. T., & Taylor, S. E. (1991). *Social cognition.* New York: McGraw-Hill.

Gilbert, D. T., & Malone, P. S. (1995). The correspondence bias. *Psychological Bulletin, 117,* 21–38.

Greenwald, A. G., & Banaji, M. R. (1995). Implicit social cognition: Attitudes, self-esteem, and stereotypes. *Psychological Review, 102,* 4–27.

Hamilton, D. L., Devine, P. G., & Ostrom, T. M. (1994). Social cognition and classic issues in social psychology. In P. G. Devine, D. L. Hamilton, & T. M. Ostrom (Eds.), *Social cognition: Impact on social psychology* (pp. 1–13). San Diego: Academic Press.

Hertzog, C., & Hultsch, D. F. (in press). Metacognition in adulthood and aging. In Salthouse, T., & Craik, F. I. M. (Eds.), *Handbook of aging and cognition II.* Mahwah, NJ: Lawrence Erlbaum Associates.

Hess, T. M. (1994). Social cognition in adulthood: Aging-related changes in knowledge and processing mechanisms. *Developmental Review, 14,* 373–412.

Hess, T. M. (in press). Aging-related constraints and adaptations in social information processing. In U. Von Hecker, S. Dutke, & G. Sedek (Eds.), *Processes of generative mental representation and psychological adaptation.* Dordrecht, The Netherlands: Kluwer.

Hess, T. M., Bolstad, C. A., Woodburn, S. M., & Auman, C. (1999). Trait diagnosticity versus behavioral consistency as determinants of impression change in adulthood. *Psychology and Aging, 14.*

Hess, T. M., & Pullen, S. M. (1994). Adult age differences in informational biases during impression formation. *Psychology and Aging, 9,* 237–250.

Hooker, K. (1992) Possible selves and perceived health in older adults and college students. *Journal of Gerontology: Psychological Sciences, 47,* P85–P95.

Kihlstrom, J. F., & Klein, S. B. (1994). The self as a knowledge system. In R. S. Wyer, Jr. & T. K. Srull (Eds.), *Handbook of social cognition* (pp. 153–208). Hillsdale, NJ: Lawrence Erlbaum Associates.

Kruglanski, A. W., & Webster, D. M. (1996). Motivated closing of the mind: "Seizing" and "freezing." *Psychological Review, 103,* 263–283.

Levy, B. (1996). Improving memory in old age through implicit stereotyping. *Journal of Personality and Social Psychology, 71,* 1092–1107.

Levy, B., & Langer, E. (1994). Aging free from negative stereotypes: Successful memory in China and among the American deaf. *Journal of Personality and Social Psychology, 66,* 989–997.

Linville, P. W., & Carlston, D. E. (1994). Social cognition of the self. In P. G. Devine, D. L. Hamilton, T. M. Ostrom (Eds.) *Social cognition: Impact on social psychology* (pp. 144–195). San Diego: Academic Press.

Marsiske, M., & Willis, S. (1995). Dimensionality of everyday problem solving in older adults. *Psychology and Aging, 10,* 269–283.

Neuberg, S. L., & Newsom, J. T. (1993). Personal need for structure: Individual differences in the desire for simple structure. *Journal of Personality and Social Psychology, 65,* 113–131.

Ostrom, T. (1984). The sovereignty of social cognition. In R. S. Wyer, Jr., & T. K. Srull (Eds.), *Handbook of social cognition* (Vol. 1, pp. 1–38). Hillsdale, NJ: Lawrence Erlbaum Associates.

Ostrom, T. (1994). Foreword. In R. S. Wyer, Jr. & T. K. Srull (Eds.), *Handbook of social cognition* (pp. vii–xii). Hillsdale, NJ: Lawrence Erlbaum Associates.

Salthouse, T. A. (1996). The processing speed theory of adult age differences in cognition. *Psychological Review, 103,* 403–428.

Schaie, K. W. (1996). *Intellectual development in adulthood: The Seattle Longitudinal Study.* Cambridge, MA: Cambridge University Press.

Skowronski, J. J., & Carlston, D. E. (1989). Negativity and extremity biases in impression formation: A review of explanations. *Psychological Bulletin, 105,* 131–142.

Staudinger, U. M., Smith, J., & Baltes, P. B. (1992). Wisdom-related knowledge in a life review task: Age differences and the role of professional specialization. *Psychology and Aging, 7,* 271–281.

Steele, C. M. (1997). A threat in the air: How stereotypes shape intellectual identity and performance. *American Psychologist, 52,* 613–629.

Webster, D. M., & Kruglanski, A. W. (1994). Individual differences in need for cognitive closure. *Journal of Personality and Social Psychology, 67,* 1049–1062.

Wyer, R. S., & Srull, T. K. (Eds.) (1994). *Handbook of social cognition.* Hillsdale, NJ: Lawrence Erlbaum Associates.

FOCUS ON SELF

2

THE SENSE OF CONTROL AND COGNITIVE AGING

TOWARD A MODEL OF MEDIATIONAL PROCESSES

LISA M. SOEDERBERG MILLER
MARGIE E. LACHMAN

Department of Psychology
Brandeis University
Waltham, Massachusetts

INTRODUCTION

At least since the 1970s, researchers have been interested in the relationship between control beliefs and cognitive performance in later life. Using longitudinal data, Lachman (1983) asked the question whether control beliefs and self-efficacy are antecedents or consequences of cognitive decline. With cognitive behavioral and social learning theories as a conceptual framework (Bandura, 1977; Meichenbaum, 1977; Mischel, 1973), this work built on preliminary evidence that beliefs and performance were related at earlier ages as well as in later life (Cattell, 1971; Costa, Fozard, McCrae, & Bosse, 1976; Lachman, Baltes, Nesselroade, & Willis, 1982; Perlmutter, 1978). Although we are still not fully able to answer the question about directionality, the nature of the question we are asking has changed, and we have made some progress in understanding how beliefs and cognitive aging are related. In this chapter, we review past research investigating the impact of control beliefs on cognitive performance as well as new findings that expand our understanding of control beliefs in relation to other predictors of performance. These findings demonstrate the importance of considering the overlap between control beliefs and background factors when decomposing age-related variance in cognitive performance. We then examine evidence addressing the relationship from another perspective: that cognitive performance has an impact on control beliefs. Last, we describe a conceptual model designed to move us forward in our quest to understand the mediational processes involved in the association between control beliefs and cognitive performance in later life.

THE CONTROL CONSTRUCT

Most conceptualizations of control beliefs use a multidimensional approach (cf. Skinner, 1995) in an attempt to capture the intricacies of the construct. Although there are many overlapping constructs, such as self-directedness, choice, decision freedom, agency, mastery, autonomy, self-determination, and self-efficacy, most working definitions of control include at least two components. Our conceptualization contains two components: (1) beliefs about one's own abilities and capacity to bring about a given outcome and (2) beliefs about the role of factors other than the self that are responsible for outcomes—for example, other people or environmental contingencies (Lachman & Weaver, 1998b). Definitions can also differ in terms of whether they focus on general control beliefs or beliefs that are specific to domains such as memory or health. The domain-specific approach assumes that control beliefs may vary across different spheres of life (Lachman & Weaver, 1998a). We refer to both domain-specific and general conceptualizations of beliefs throughout this chapter.

Very closely related to the notion of control beliefs is the concept of self-efficacy; in fact, the terms are often used interchangeably. Self-efficacy, however, tends to emphasize the component of control that focuses on self-beliefs about one's capability to accomplish a specific task. According to Abeles (1990), self-beliefs about abilities (e.g., skills) and capabilities (e.g., to exert effort) combine with beliefs about the nature of the task (e.g., difficulty) to produce self-efficacy expectations. Cavanaugh and colleagues (Cavanaugh, Feldman, & Hertzog, 1998) emphasize the personal agency aspect of self-efficacy, stating that beliefs about one's ability to use a particular skill effectively are a central component of the construct. Regardless of which term is used, control beliefs are important determinants of well-being. In their analysis of important contributors to successful aging, Rowe and Kahn (1997) identified the sense of control as an important ingredient. The contribution of control beliefs to positive outcomes in later life has been most notably demonstrated in the area of cognitive functioning (Albert et al., 1995; Lachman, Ziff, & Spiro, 1994).

CONTROL OVER COGNITIVE AGING

Consistent with the aforementioned description of a sense of control, control over cognitive aging also includes a constellation of beliefs. These include beliefs about one's own problems, capabilities, or competence (self-efficacy) and the responsiveness of the environment as well as attributions that one makes about the causes of cognitive performance, both successes and failures (Lachman, in press). Not surprisingly, then, there are also a number of constructs that fall under the rubric of control beliefs within the domain of cognitive aging. These include memory complaints or problems, attributions, metamemory, and self-efficacy (e.g., Ryan, 1996). We include each of these constructs in addition to the broader notion of control beliefs in our discussion of how a sense of control may change in later life as well as review evidence that beliefs affect performance. Following this, we present data indicating that the reverse effect is also possible: that performance affects beliefs. However, research investigating the effects of performance successes and failures on subsequent self-beliefs is scant, which limits our discussion to the constructs of self-efficacy and control beliefs.

THE EFFECTS OF BELIEFS ON COGNITIVE PERFORMANCE

One's sense of control is believed to have a variety of effects on cognitive performance (Rodin, 1990). Rodin stated, "People who believe strongly in their problem-solving capabilities are more efficient in their analytic thinking and complex decision-making situations. Those who are plagued by self-doubts are erratic in their analytic thinking. The quality of analytic thinking in turn affects performance accomplishments" (Rodin, 1990, p. 8). People high in perceived control are able to see themselves as successful, and this in turn serves to motivate performance. By contrast, if individuals see themselves as inefficacious, they dwell on failure, which could undermine performance. Perceived control can also affect performance by increasing effort and endurance and by decreasing anxiety and stress (Bandura, 1997).

BELIEFS

As mentioned above, a number of beliefs have been investigated in relation to cognitive performance and aging: memory complaints, attributions, metamemory, self-efficacy, and control. We review findings of age differences and the effects of beliefs on cognitive performance, highlighting the common threads that are closely related to the construct of control.

Memory Complaints

Complaints about memory problems typically include the frequency of memory-problem occurrence as well as the type of concern. They often reflect a concern about perceived decline and the anticipation of further decrement. Although memory complaints appear to be prevalent in later life (Aldwin, 1990; Cutler & Grams, 1988; Jonker, Launer, Hooijer, & Lindeboom, 1996; Zelinski, Gilewski, & Anthony-Bergstone, 1990), recent evidence suggests that the frequency of complaints does not vary throughout adulthood. In a study of adults ranging in age from 25 to 75, memory problems were investigated in the context of 22 other domains of life (Lachman, Maier, & Budner, in preparation). No age differences were found in the reported frequency of general memory problems; 30% of adults at all ages identified problems with memory as occurring several times a week or more. Consistent with findings from other surveys (e.g., Aldwin, 1990; Lachman, 1991), these problems were not rated as highly stressful even though they were one of the most frequently occurring problems identified.

However, some research indicates that the elderly report more problems than do the young with some types of memory—for example, remembering names and telephone numbers (Cohen, 1993). This is consistent with research showing that forgetting names is the most prevalent memory problem reported among older adults given a list of different types of memory problems (e.g., remembering where they parked the car) (Leirer, Morrow, Sheikh, & Pariante, 1990). However, there are some areas in which older adults rate their memory as better than do the young—for example, paying bills, keeping appointments, and taking medicine (Cohen, 1993). These subjective reports have been validated through observations of performance in daily life in which older adults are more likely than are the young to use external memory aids to remember things they need to do (Cohen, 1993).

It has become more common in the late twentieth century for older adults to report concerns about developing Alzheimer's disease. Older adults tend to overestimate the incidence of Alzheimer's disease (Gatz & Pearson, 1988). Furthermore, the Alzheimer's Likelihood Scale (Lachman, Bandura, Weaver, & Elliott, 1995) revealed that those who thought they would be more likely to get Alzheimer's disease had lower perceived memory ability and stronger beliefs about the inevitable decrement of memory. Thus, these fears and concerns about memory loss or Alzheimer's disease may reflect a lack of perceived control over cognitive aging.

Unfortunately, the data at this point are equivocal as to whether memory complaints predict actual memory deficits. For example, data have been reported showing no relationship (Smith, Petersen, Ivnick, Malec, & Tangalos, 1996) and showing a strong relationship (Jonker et al., 1996) between complaints and performance. Some researchers argue that memory complaints are less related to cognitive performance and more to anxiety or depressed affect (Gilewski, Zelinski, & Schaie, 1990; Smith & Earles, 1996; Zarit, Cole, & Guider, 1981). On the basis of findings from the Memory Functioning Questionnaire (MFQ) (Gilewski et al., 1990), the issue remains unclear. This instrument is widely used to assess memory problems and consists of 64 items reduced to 4 factors (frequency of forgetting, seriousness of forgetting, retrospective functioning [memory decline], and mnemonic use). Scores from the MFQ were found to be significantly correlated to word list recall and recognition scores even after controlling for subject background variables, including depression (Zelinski et al., 1990). Thus, although depression and memory complaints appear to be highly correlated in some cases, the overlap is not complete (Lachman et al., 1995).

Although at present the data fail to make a strong case that concerns about memory affect cognitive performance in later life, future work may uncover this association by considering the impact of control beliefs. If one is concerned about performance getting worse and believes that there is little one can do to improve or prevent decline, this could result in fear, anxiety, or depression (Bandura, 1989). These emotional reactions can interfere with performance by limiting effort or even by leading to withdrawal from cognitive tasks because of fear of failure or judgment of incompetence by others (Bandura, 1997). Research also indicates that these emotions can themselves lead to cognitive declines through disruption of thoughts and concentration (cf. Bandura, 1989; Centofanti, 1998). Moreover, attributing isolated incidents of forgetting to internal stable causes such as Alzheimer's disease can be associated with a sense of helplessness (Lachman et al., 1995). Thus, concerns about memory performance may influence actual performance via beliefs about control.

Attributions

Attributions are explanations individuals make regarding successful or unsuccessful performance outcomes (Abramson, Seligman, & Teasdale, 1978). Older adults are more likely to explain outcomes in a disadvantageous way (Lachman, 1990; Lachman & McArthur, 1986; Rodin & Langer, 1980.) For example, Lachman and McArthur (1986) found that when older adults failed to remember something, they blamed it on internal and stable causes, such as their poor memories, whereas young adults blamed failure on internal and unstable factors, such as lack of effort. Younger adults' attributional style is more adaptive because it implies that something can be done to improve functioning the next time, namely, trying harder. Conversely, those who blamed failure on internal stable factors did not improve, perhaps because of feelings of helplessness (Abramson et al., 1978). These perceptions are not held only by older adults. Erber, Szuchman, & Rothberg (1990) found that both younger and older judges were more likely to attribute memory difficulties of older adults to mental difficulties needing treatment, whereas the same mistakes made by younger adults were more likely to be attributed to attentional problems.

Importantly, these beliefs have an impact on subsequent performance. For example, older adults who attributed successful performance to internal and stable factors were more likely to improve over time (Lachman, Steinberg, and Trotter, 1987). Attributions have also been found to have an effect on performance levels of elderly adults through subliminal priming. Older adults who received subliminal priming of words describing positive aspects of aging and who were told that their successful performance was attributable to internal (i.e., modifiable) factors improved their memory scores over two trials (Levy, 1996). On the other hand, older adults who were primed with negative age-stereotypic words and given external (i.e., nonmodifiable) attributions showed decrements in performance. Similarly, cross-cultural work investigating age differences in beliefs indicates that age-related declines that are typically found in memory performance are not found in cultures where age stereotypes are positive (Levy & Langer, 1994). Thus, older adults tend to make less adaptive attributions that may be due in part to cultural values, and these attributions in turn can have negative effects on performance.

Metamemory

Metamemory, or metacognition, examines the knowledge the individual holds about cognitive faculties and how they work, including beliefs about abilities and control (Cavanaugh & Baskind, 1996; Dixon, 1989; Dixon, Hultsch, & Hertzog, 1988; Zelinski et al., 1990). Metamemory knowledge is assessed, for example, by how much an individual knows about circumstances that facilitate or hinder memory and about strategies that support faster learning. One widely used tool to assess metamemory is the Metamemory in Adulthood instrument (MIA; Dixon et al., 1988). This instrument contains seven subscales: self-reported use of strategies, knowledge about basic memory processes, perceived capacity of memory, beliefs surrounding the stability and modifiability of memory, anxiety surrounding memory performance, perceived importance of memory achievement, and locus of control. Factor analyses reveal that there are two higher-order factors, memory knowledge and memory self-efficacy, the latter of which includes perceived capacity of memory and locus of control (Hertzog, Dixon, Schulenberg, & Hultsch, 1987). Reports of age differences in metamemory depend on the specific aspect under investigation. In general, however, younger adults tend to score higher on perceptions of abilities and strategy use (although some research has found no age differences), whereas older adults tend to score higher on perceptions of decline and problems associated with memory (cf. Dixon, 1989).

More importantly, metamemory has been found to be related to memory performance among older adults; those who have higher levels show superior performance on a wide range of memory tasks (e.g., Cavanaugh & Poon, 1989; Hertzog, Dixon, & Hultsch, 1990). The focus of much of this research has used MIA subscales assessing beliefs about one's own cognitive abilities (i.e., self-efficacy beliefs or control beliefs), both of which are described below.

Self-Efficacy

As mentioned earlier, self-efficacy refers to beliefs about one's ability to bring about desired outcomes (Bandura, 1997). Self-efficacy beliefs are assessed in terms of the degree to which individuals expect to be able to perform a particular task as well as their level of confidence in this belief (or prediction). The data suggest that beliefs about cognitive performance, especially memory, tend to be at lower levels among older adults relative to younger adults (cf. Berry & West, 1993). However, both young and older adults tend to become more accurate over time, especially for tasks on which they performed well (Lachman & Jelalian, 1984).

Self-efficacy has been shown to be associated with cognitive performance in a number of different ways. For example, those who believed they had better memories outperformed those with lower self-efficacy scores (Lachman et al., 1987) and they were more likely to improve their performance in response to memory training (Rebok & Balcerak, 1989). Similarly, findings from a longitudinal study of older adults showed that efficacy for influencing everyday tasks was one of four predictors (the others being education, physical activity, and pulmonary functioning) of maintenance of cognitive functioning (Albert et al., 1995).

Self-efficacy predicts not only current performance but also changes in performance (Seeman, McAvay, Merrill, Albert, & Rodin, 1996) and confidence in one's abilities to improve (Bandura, 1997; Lachman et al., 1995). Some work suggests that those who have higher self-efficacy beliefs are likely to exert more effort and to spend more time studying or learning the material (Berry, 1987). Thus, the higher performance levels of individuals with high self-efficacy could be in part attributable to motivational factors (Bandura, 1997).

Control Beliefs

The constructs of self-efficacy and control overlap, with the former being more closely related to beliefs about one's capabilities and the latter being more closely related to beliefs about factors that are responsible for performance outcomes. As mentioned above, however, control is sometimes considered to be a broader concept in that both self-efficacy and outcome expectations are important facets of control (Bandura, 1997). A similar distinction can be made within the locus of control literature between the constructs of internal and external control (Levenson, 1974). In this case, internal control refers to internal causes of behavior, such as self-efficacy, and external control refers to external factors that influence outcomes. Despite these subtle differences, we use the broader conceptualization of control beliefs in the discussion that follows and include both the internal and external dimensions of control.

Although age differences in control beliefs have been reported (Lachman, 1986), more finely grained analyses indicate that these differences are more pronounced for external control than for internal control. This suggests that although older adults are more likely than are the young to believe that external factors are responsible for their cognitive performance, they nevertheless have similar beliefs about their abilities and the role that internal factors such as effort play in achieving outcomes. That is, older adults are more likely to report that external factors contribute to their performance—for example, that they need to rely on others to help them with cognitive tasks. Even though age differences in internal control beliefs are minimal, older adults tend to hold the belief that age-related decrements in performance are inevitable (Lachman, 1986).

A good deal of research is consistent with the notion that control beliefs affect cognitive performance (e.g. Berry, 1987; Cavanaugh & Poon, 1989; Grover & Hertzog, 1991; Lachman et al., 1982; Riggs, Lachman, & Wingfield, 1997; Stine, Lachman, & Wingfield, 1993). This relationship is even stronger for domain-specific control beliefs (e.g., Lachman, 1986) and for older adults (Dixon & Hultsch, 1983; Lachman et al., 1982). Specifically, these data suggest that those with high levels of control beliefs outperform those with lower levels.

For example, Lachman and colleagues (Stine et al., 1991) used the Personality in Context Scale (PIC) (Lachman et al., 1982) to assess the relationship of perceived control to cognitive performance. This instrument contains three control scales regarding everyday cognitive tasks: internal, chance, and powerful others. The internal scale is designed to tap beliefs that improvements are possible through one's own effort and contains items such as "I know if I keep using my memory I will never lose it." The chance scale includes items such as "There's nothing I can do to preserve my mental clarity," which are designed to capture beliefs that performance is controlled by fate or chance. The powerful others scale refers to a reliance on other people for achieving outcomes and includes items such as "I can only understand instructions after someone explains them to me." The external scales of chance and powerful others were negatively correlated to performance on a prose recall task, and interestingly, this relationship was stronger when adults had no control over the speech input (relative to when they could pause the recorded narratives). Thus, these data suggest that perceptions of external control are particularly important when actual control is absent (Stine et al., 1993).

In another study, older adults were divided into "internals" and "externals" on the basis of their scores on the PIC to determine whether these two groups differed in terms of memory monitoring and prose recall (Riggs et al., 1997). Participants were required to select the size of speech input they believed they could accurately recall for both word lists and meaningful passages. Internals showed higher levels of recall for the prose passages and were better able to monitor their memory as indexed by the segment sizes they could accurately recall. These data lend some insight into potential mediational processes in that older adults with high internal control beliefs were better at monitoring their memory capacity, which in turn led to more accurate recall.

Because Lachman and colleagues (Lachman, Weaver, Bandura, Elliott, & Lewkowicz, 1992) were interested in investigating perceptions of ability and controllability that were specific to the domain of memory, the Memory Controllability Inventory (MCI) was developed. This instrument includes items that assess controllability, as does the PIC, but it also attempts to distinguish between perceptions of present and future abilities through the use of four scales: present ability, potential improvement, effort utility, and inevitable decrement. The data thus far indicate that these perceptions are indeed related to cognitive performance. For example, the inevitable decrement scale was correlated with working memory and text recognition, present ability and potential improvement scales were related to name–face recall, and all four scales were correlated with list recall (Lachman et al., 1995).

In their investigation of the psychometric properties of the MCI, Cavanaugh and Baskind (1996) found significant correlations between subscales of the MCI and the MIA. Similarly, Bachrach (1998), using four subscales of the MCI (present ability, potential improvement, effort utility, and inevitable decrement), found significant correlations with MIA subscales, in particular, with the capacity, change, and locus of control subscales. Thus, these data support the notion that the constructs of control and metamemory have a high degree of overlap.

It is interesting, however, that control and self-efficacy do not affect all cognitive abilities uniformly (Gold, Andres, Etezadi, Schwartzman, & Chaikelson, 1995; Lachman & Jelalian, 1984; Miller & Lachman, 1998; Seeman et al., 1996). For example, some work has shown that control beliefs are more highly related to verbal relative to nonverbal tasks (Gold et al., 1995; Lachman & Jelalian, 1984; Seeman et al, 1996). One of the goals of future research, therefore will be to determine which cognitive domains are more closely linked to a sense of control and to uncover the factors responsible for these differences across cognitive domains.

In summary, the evidence presented in this section suggests that the beliefs we hold about our abilities vary by age and influence our performance levels. For older adults, this implies that a sense of control has a positive influence in the face of an age-related decline in cognitive performance (e.g., Salthouse, 1991). Positive attributions, knowledge of memory processes, high self-efficacy, high control beliefs, and perhaps low levels of memory complaints bode well for cognitive outcomes. As we show next, however, the nature of the relationship between beliefs and performance is somewhat complicated by whether background factors, which appear to have an impact on the magnitude of this association, are taken into consideration.

CONTROL BELIEFS IN RELATION TO OTHER PREDICTORS OF COGNITIVE PERFORMANCE

In addition to the literature surrounding control beliefs, there is a large body of research addressing the nature of other sources of individual differences in cognitive performance in later life. Some longitudinal research, for example, has shown that good health and education (e.g., Albert et al., 1995; Katzman, 1997; Schaie, 1990) contribute to cognitive performance. Similarly, other work has shown correlations between cognitive performance and social activity (Hultsch, Hammer, & Small, 1993; Luszcz, Bryan, & Kent, 1997) health (Earles, Connor, Smith, & Park, 1997; Hultsch et al., 1993; Perlmutter & Nyquist, 1990), gender and vocabulary (Luszcz et al., 1997), speed of processing (Earles et al., 1997; Luszez et al., 1997), and exercise (Simonsick, 1997; Dustman et al., 1984). Given that these factors are important contributors of cognitive functioning, we were interested in determining how these variables compared to control beliefs in their ability to predict cognitive performance across the life span. Specifically, our goal was to determine whether the effects of control beliefs on cognitive performance were altered by the presence of other predictors and to explore age–performance relations by decomposing the age-related variance in cognitive ability.

To do this, we categorized predictors (Table 2.1) into noncognitive factors (activity, health problems, exercise, gender), cognitive control (beliefs about control over thinking and learning), distal cognitive ability (vocabulary and educa-

TABLE 2.1   Independent and Dependent Measures

Independent variables	Dependent variables
Noncognitive	**Short-term memory**
Health problems: Self-report scales measuring acute illnesses, chronic illnesses, and number of prescription medications	*Forward digit span:* WAIS subscale
	Backward digit span: WAIS subscale
	Counting backward task: Beginning with 478, the number of times participants correctly subtracted 7 within 30-second interval
Activity: Number of meetings attended per week, hours worked for pay and as a volunteer per week, and student status (none, part time, full time)	**Divided attention**
Exercise: Frequency of engagement in moderate-to-vigorous physical activity	*Letter comparison task* (Salthouse)
Gender	*Counting backward task:* Beginning with 350, the number of times participants correctly subtracted 7 within 30-second interval
Cognitive control beliefs	
Perceptions of control: Learning processes	**Reasoning**
Perceptions of control: Thinking processes	*Raven's Advanced Progressive Matrices*
Distal cognitive	*Schaie–Thurstone letter series*
Vocabulary: WAIS subscale	
Education level: Years of education broken down into 12 levels	
Proximal cognitive	
DSST: WAIS (speed)	
Age	
Age: Years of age	
Age^2: Age squared	

DSST = digit symbol substitution test; WAIS = Wechsler Adult Intelligence Scale.

tion), and proximal ability (speed). This categorization scheme allowed us to evaluate predictors vis-à-vis proximal and distal influences (Salthouse, 1991). Hierarchical regressions were used to predict age-related and total variance in cognitive performance in a representative sample of adults. To have a wide range of cognitive abilities, we selected three domains of cognitive functioning, reasoning, short-term memory, and divided attention. These domains represent areas that typically show (reasoning), fail to show (short-term memory), and sometimes show (divided attention) age-related declines.

Data presented here (based on Miller & Lachman, 1998) are a subset of those from the Midlife in the United States (MIDUS) Survey conducted by the John D. and Catherine T. MacArthur Foundation Network on Successful Midlife Development (MIDMAC). This subset, the Boston In-Depth Study of Management Processes in Midlife, consists of an intentional oversampling of noninstitutionalized, English-speaking adults, between the ages of 25 and 75 ($M = 47.8$, $SD = 13.1$) in the greater Boston area. Of the sample, 41.1% were women and roughly half of the participants had college degree or higher. The sample ($n = 253$) was composed of 83 young adults, 105 middle-aged adults, and 65 older adults (ages 60–75; $M = 65.7$, $SD = 4.1$). Age groups comprised comparable distributions of men and women, and education did not vary as a function of age, gender, or a combination of the two.

Data collection occurred over three time periods, 6–8 months apart. For the cognitive measures, participants were tested individually in their homes at Time 2. Demographic information (gender, age, education) as well as health, activity, and exercise measures were collected through both interview and questionnaire formats at either Time 1 or Time 2. Cognitive control was assessed at Time 3.

We found the expected age-related declines in reasoning abilities such that younger adults outperformed middle-aged adults, who in turn outperformed the oldest group (e.g., Schaie, 1990). The analysis on divided attention also showed significant age differences; however, these were attributable to declines for the oldest relative to the younger two groups, who did not differ from each other. The results of the analysis on short-term memory showed that middle-age group out-performed the older adults; however, the younger adults did not differ from either the middle-aged or older groups. Thus, this pattern of declines in reasoning and divided attention but not in short-term memory among the oldest group relative to the youngest group is consistent with past research (cf. Salthouse, 1991; Smith & Earles, 1996). Furthermore, because the middle-aged group scored above the sample mean on three abilities, these data suggest that midlife is a time of rela-tively high levels of performance across several different abilities.

To examine the degree of overlap among the predictors and outcome mea-sures, we first computed zero-order correlations (Table 2.2) among all variables. The two predictors that appeared to show the greatest number of significant cor-relations to other predictors were exercise, which correlated with all other predic-tors except quadratic age, and speed of processing, which was related to all other predictors except activity. Control beliefs were positively correlated to exercise and to both cognitive predictors (vocabulary, speed) and negatively correlated to health problems and age, however, beliefs were uncorrelated to activity, gender, education, and quadratic age. All three cognitive variables were significantly cor-related to each other and each showed a distinct constellation of correlations with the predictors. Thus, these findings show that although there is some degree of overlap among predictors, the magnitude and the patterns of the correlations var-ied across cognitive factors.

To assess the individual contributions of each category of predictor, we entered them into three hierarchical regressions separately by cognitive outcome variable (Table 2.3, Models 2–5). Noncognitive factors explained between 5% and 15% of the variance in cognitive performance. This is consistent with past research demonstrating that noncognitive factors, such as health and lifestyle, are associ-ated with cognitive abilities in a variety of domains (e.g., Earles et al., 1997; Hultsch et al., 1993; Luszcz et al., 1997; Perlmutter & Nyquist, 1990). Cognitive control beliefs significantly predicted performance on the short-term memory task and reasoning task (3% and 5% of variance, respectively) but not on the

TABLE 2.2 Correlations among Predictors and Outcome Variables

Variable	1	2	3	4	5	6	7	8	9	10	11	12	13	14
1 Activity	1.00													
2 Exercise	0.12	1.00												
3 Health	0.08	-0.18	1.00											
4 Gender	-0.05	-0.12	0.10	1.00										
5 Control—thinking	0.09	0.19	-0.30	-0.08	1.00									
6 Control—learning	0.08	0.12	-0.18	-0.03	0.47	1.00								
7 Education	0.22	0.27	-0.11	-0.05	0.10	0.09	1.00							
8 Vocabulary (WAIS)	0.15	0.16	0.01	-0.12	0.15	0.09	0.55	1.00						
9 DSST (WAIS)	0.09	0.17	-0.19	0.24	0.14	0.14	0.29	0.24	1.00					
10 Age	-0.08	-0.26	0.16	-0.03	-0.09	-0.18	-0.04	0.14	-0.46	1.00				
11 Age squared	-0.07	-0.05	0.03	-0.04	-0.02	-0.10	-0.10	-0.13	-0.18	0.10	1.00			
12 Reasoning	0.13	0.29	-0.25	0.07	0.18	0.20	0.44	0.47	0.63	-0.41	-0.18	1.00		
13 Short-term memory	0.13	0.20	-0.09	-0.18	0.16	0.14	0.29	0.45	0.34	-0.08	-0.16	0.51	1.00	
14 Divided attention	0.09	0.19	-0.11	-0.04	0.04	0.05	0.27	0.26	0.42	-0.20	-0.14	0.46	0.43	1.00

DSST = digit symbol substitution test; WAIS = Wechsler Adult Intelligence Scale. $r > .12$, $p < .05$ (in bold).

TABLE 2.3 Hierarchical Regressions Predicting Short-Term Memory, Divided Attention, and Reasoning

Model Predictor	Short-term memory				Divided attention				Reasoning			
	Cumulative R^2	R^2 change	$F(R^2$ change)	Reduction of age-related R^2	Cumulative R^2	R^2 change	$F(R^2$ change)	Reduction of age-related R^2	Cumulative R^2	R^2 change	$F(R^2$ change)	Reduction of age-related R^2
1 Age/age²	0.03	0.03	3.75*		0.06	0.06	6.93***		0.19	0.19	28.59***	
2 Noncognitive	0.08	0.08	5.26***	25%	0.05	0.05	3.01*	39%	0.15	0.15	11.01***	40%
Age/age²	0.10	0.02	2.95+		0.09	0.04	4.31*		0.26	0.11	18.48***	
3 Cognitive control	0.03	0.03	3.86*	18%	0.00	0.00	0.27 ns	4%	0.05	0.05	6.49**	14%
Age/age²	0.05	0.02	3.04*		0.06	0.06	6.54**		0.21	0.16	24.72***	
4 Distal cognitive	0.21	0.21	32.78***	7%	0.09	0.09	11.49***	2%	0.27	0.27	46.15***	NA
Age/age²	0.23	0.03	4.20*		0.15	0.06	7.50**		0.48	0.21	49.74***	
5 Proximal cognitive	0.12	0.12	33.77***	39%	0.18	0.18	50.76***	91%	0.39	0.39	160.22***	88%
Age/age²	0.14	0.02	2.45+		0.18	0.01	0.64 ns		0.42	0.02	4.69**	
6 Noncognitive	0.08	0.08	5.06***		0.05	0.05	2.97*		0.15	0.15	10.88***	
Cognitive control	0.09	0.01	1.76 ns		0.05	0.00	0.15 ns		0.17	0.02	2.48+	
Distal cognitive	0.24	0.15	24.42***		0.12	0.07	8.16***		0.38	0.21	40.83***	
Proximal cognitive	0.31	0.07	23.62***	82%	0.24	0.12	34.57***	95%	0.56	0.17	92.14***	77%
Age/age²	0.32	0.01	0.81 ns		0.24	0.00	0.44 ns		0.60	0.04	12.58***	

NA resulted in a negative value likely due to suppression.

+$p < .10$ *$p < .05$ **$p < .001$.

divided attention task. Although in past work control beliefs have been associated with memory (Stine et al., 1993) and reasoning performance (Grover & Hertzog, 1991; Lachman & Jelalian, 1984; Lachman & Leff, 1989), we are unaware of work addressing control in relation to divided attention performance. Distal cognitive factors (9–27% of variance) and speed of processing (12–39% variance) significantly predicted cognitive performance on all tasks. This was not surprising given that past research has also shown speed of processing (Earles et al., 1997; Luszcz et al., 1997; Park et al., 1996) and education (i.e., distal cognitive) (Albert et al., 1995; Schaie, 1990) to be important predictors of cognitive performance. These data are consistent with past research showing that both noncognitive and cognitive background variables predict performance across a wide range of abilities and with research showing that control beliefs predict performance for some, but not all, cognitive abilities (e.g., Seaman et al., 1996).

Although these data support the notion that background variables and cognitive control beliefs are both important factors of cognitive performance, two further sets of inquiry are needed to help clarify the relationship between control and cognition and how this relationship may differ with age. First, it is theoretically important to determine the extent to which variance explained by control beliefs and the other predictors is age related (cf. Salthouse, 1996). For example, do beliefs about cognitive control explain variance that is attributable to age alone? Second, given that there was a moderate degree of overlap among the predictor variables (cf. Table 2.2), it is also important to determine whether the relationship between control beliefs and cognitive performance will be diminished or even disappear after background variables are considered.

So that we could investigate the proportion of age-related variance explained by each predictor category, we first calculated the total amount of variance explained by age alone. As shown in Table 2.3, age (Model 1) accounted for 3%, 6%, and 19% of the variance in short-term memory, divided attention, and reasoning performance, respectively. Next, the unique age-related variance was calculated by determining how much variance age explains after partialling out the other predictor variables. The difference between this unique age-related variance and the total age-related variance was then be divided by the total age-related variance. The results of this step, depicted in Models 2–5, indicate the degree to which each category of predictor explained variance in cognitive performance that was attributable to age alone. A comparison of these models shows that cognitive control beliefs were moderately strong in their ability to account for age-related variance. Beliefs attenuated the age-related variance for short-term memory by 18% and for reasoning by 14%.

Last, Model 6 (see Fig. 2.1) shows the total model with all five sets of predictors entered hierarchically to assess the relative strength of factors ranging from distal to proximal (cf. Salthouse, 1991). In this analysis, noncognitive background variables were entered before cognitive control beliefs to assess the effects of beliefs after partialling out gender and individual differences in activity, exercise, and health. This model, summarized in Table 2.3, accounted for between

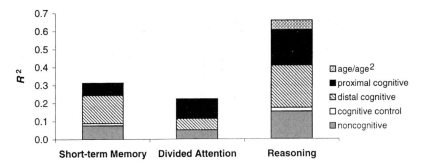

FIGURE 2.1   Total variance accounted for in short-term memory, divided attention, and reasoning performance.

24% and 60% of the variance in cognitive performance. Importantly, when noncognitive factors were controlled for, control beliefs were only marginally significant for reasoning ability and dropped below significance for short-term memory. These data suggest that beliefs about control overlap with some combination of health, activity, exercise, and gender. Significant correlations between control beliefs and health problems and exercise (see Table 2.2) suggest that these two variables may be responsible for this overlap. Further research may be able to shed light on possible mediational processes linking control beliefs, health, exercise, and cognitive performance.

Given that the total variance explained differed across cognitive factors, it is helpful to consider variance explained by each predictor (taken from hierarchical analyses) as a proportion of the total variance. Figure 2.2 shows that control beliefs explain the same proportion of variance in both short-term memory and reasoning. These data beg the question as to why these two variables are associated with beliefs whereas divided attention fails to show this association. It could indicate that our domain-specific measures of control need to be more specific to the cognitive task under investigation. Alternatively, it could be that the divided attention task is too difficult to be influenced by control beliefs and that beliefs are more likely to affect cognitive tasks that are only moderately challenging to older adults.

In summary, this study demonstrated that the strength of each predictor category, whether distal or proximal in nature, varied as a function of cognitive domain and varied in the extent to which it shared age-related variance. Furthermore, beliefs about control predicted cognitive performance within the domains of short-term memory and reasoning but not for divided attention. It is important to note, however, that these significant relationships were attenuated when background variables were taken into consideration. Finally, the large overlap between control beliefs and noncognitive measures suggests that more work is needed to uncover processes underlying these factors so that we can better understand factors contributing to successful cognitive performance.

Before we conclude the sections dealing with the effects of control beliefs on performance, we must point out that not all research has found a link between

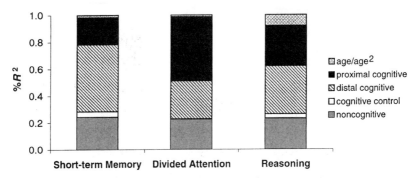

FIGURE 2.2   Relative proportion of variance accounted for across cognitive domains.

beliefs about cognitive ability and cognitive performance. Jonker, Smits, and Deeg (1997) administered both metamemory (MIA) and memory measures within the less-threatening environment of participants' homes. They found little evidence of a relationship between metamemory and immediate recall, delayed recall, and prospective memory performance. In fact, after controlling for age, education, and gender, they found that affective subscales of metamemory (achievement and anxiety) were stronger predictors of memory performance than was the locus of control subscale. Other research, however, argues that the relationship between cognitive performance and affective measures may be moderated by self-efficacy (van den Heuvel, Smits, Deeg, & Beekman, 1996), a possibility that we explore in our model described at the conclusion of this chapter. Thus, although it is possible that moving away from laboratory testing practices will weaken the association between self-efficacy and cognitive performance, the overall pattern of findings suggests that self-efficacy is an important factor associated with cognitive performance among the elderly.

Within a social learning perspective, Bandura (1997) suggested that control beliefs affect performance in part because low efficacy is associated with anxiety and low levels of effort, which lead to decreased levels of performance. An important aspect of this model is that the relationship is reciprocal in that beliefs are influenced by multiple factors, including performance experience. Individuals judge their abilities on the basis of past performance on similar tasks. Moreover, expectancies can be affected vicariously by watching others or through knowledge of aging stereotypes about performance (Bandura, 1997; Levy & Langer, 1994). Thus, we also need to consider the effects of cognitive performance on control beliefs.

THE EFFECTS OF COGNITIVE PERFORMANCE ON CONTROL BELIEFS

In addition to the well-established findings reviewed in the preceding section that beliefs affect performance, Bandura's (1997) notion that performance influences self-efficacy is also supported by research on aging (e.g., Albert et al., 1995; Bachrach, 1998; Berry & West, 1993; Bandura, 1997; Lachman, 1991). Relative to the previous section, however, this perspective is underrepresented within the adult development and aging literature; therefore, we have not attempted to separate the findings into subheadings. Instead, we review the relevant literature on control beliefs and related constructs together.

One example of how cognitive performance influences control beliefs can be found in an experiment in which participants were randomly assigned to one of two instruction groups: memorize a list of activities (e.g., close the window) to pantomime them or to recall them verbally (Bachrach, 1998). Those in the pantomime group showed higher levels of recall than did the other group, and this benefit was greater for older adults, suggesting that encoding instructions can be particularly important to older adults. Importantly, this performance benefit appeared to affect perceptions of memory controllability in that older adults in the pantomime group scored higher on control belief measures than did those in the verbal recall group. Not only did recall performance predict perceptions of memory control immediately following the task (using the MCI), but this difference persisted up to 2 weeks later (using the MIA).

There is also some evidence that prior experience with memory tasks can affect levels of self-efficacy in terms of memory monitoring. That is, past performance can affect self-beliefs about future performance. For example, some research shows that beliefs about performance levels are typically more accurate after the task has been completed and this accuracy increases over trials (Hertzog, Dixon, & Hultsch, 1990; Lachman & Jelalian, 1984). West, Dennehy-Basile, and Norris (1996) assessed both everyday tasks (presumably highly familiar) and laboratory tasks and found that older adults improved memory monitoring over time for only the more familiar tasks. This suggests that knowledge inherent in everyday tasks enables older adults to make better use of actual performance levels to modify their self-beliefs. This line of research showing that past performance can influence self-perception is important because these beliefs can significantly impact learning. Specifically, learning can be compromised if older adults are investing too little or too much of their cognitive resources (Connor, Dunlosky, & Hertzog, 1997). In fact, some evidence suggests that older adults are not as adept as are younger adults in using information regarding past performance, which has the effect of making older adults more confident than they should be on the basis of their recall ability (Dunlosky & Connor, 1997). Not surprisingly, then, this misperception can affect future performance levels, illustrating the cyclical nature of this relationship, a topic that explored in greater detail in the next section.

Finally, data from longitudinal (Lachman, 1983; Lachman & Leff, 1989) and intervention (Caprio-Prevette & Fry, 1996; Dittmann-Kohli, Lachman, Kliegl, & Baltes, 1991; Lachman et al., 1992) studies, also support the notion that cognitive performance influences beliefs. In two short-term longitudinal studies, cognitive performance predicted change in control beliefs. Those who had higher levels of performance were less likely to show declines in control beliefs (Lachman, 1983; Lachman & Leff, 1989). Similarly, cognitive skills training for laboratory tasks led to increases in self-efficacy for these tasks; unfortunately, however, this training failed to transfer to beliefs about abilities in everyday tasks (Dittmann-Kohli et al., 1991).

In a memory intervention study designed to improve both memory performance and control beliefs, individuals who received both cognitive restructuring and memory training showed greater increases in memory control than did those who received only memory skills training (Lachman et al., 1992). In a similar study, memory training that targeted self-beliefs in addition to traditional metamemory training was found to be more effective in improving memory self-efficacy than was traditional metamemory training alone (Caprio-Prevette & Fry, 1996). Thus, performance success as a result of training appears to influence subsequent self-beliefs about performance, especially when the beliefs are directly targeted in the training.

To summarize, the findings surrounding the effects of performance on beliefs support the notion that our past performance has an impact on how we perceive ourselves. Data from both cross-sectional and longitudinal work show that higher levels of performance bode well for subsequent positive self-beliefs. This line of research, however, is somewhat sparse and could benefit from a more in-depth look into feedback mechanisms that are responsible for this link. This may help improve our ability to intervene in cases in which negative performance lowers self-beliefs and help to stem future harmful effects that may result.

The research reviewed in this chapter has drawn from a wide variety of methodologies including correlational, cross-sectional, short-term longitudinal, intervention, and experimental designs. It has also included a comparison of age groups such as young and older adults, or a wide continuum of ages, or only older adults. These studies have also used different measures of control beliefs and related constructs, as well as many different facets of cognitive performance. With all these variations, the bulk of the research supports the notion that the beliefs we hold about our cognitive capabilities have an impact on our subsequent performance levels. Similarly, the little research that has addressed the effects of performance on beliefs suggests that this too occurs; our performance influences our self-beliefs. Although some research suggests that the association between beliefs and performance is stronger among older adults (Dixon & Hultsch, 1983; Lachman et al., 1982), more research is needed to systematically determine specific factors responsible for this relationship as well as which cognitive domains are most closely linked to beliefs. Such background variables as gender, health, activity, and age appear to overlap with beliefs; however, the mechanisms responsible for these links are not well articulated. Nevertheless, the evidence reviewed thus far is consistent with social learning theories (Bandura, 1997) showing that those who have high levels of perceived control actually do show higher levels of performance and that this in turn affects self-beliefs.

A CONCEPTUAL MODEL OF THE
RELATIONSHIP BETWEEN SENSE OF
CONTROL AND COGNITIVE AGING

Research findings reported above are consistent with a reciprocal model of the relationship between control beliefs and cognitive functioning in later life. There is evidence that control beliefs affect performance, and there are also findings suggesting that cognitive functioning affects control beliefs. Moreover, the effects of control beliefs are not isolated; the variance associated with control beliefs overlaps with other noncognitive variables, such as health and exercise, in predicting cognitive functioning. However, more research is needed to uncover the mediational processes involved in linking control beliefs and performance. Using a cognitive social learning theory perspective (Bandura, 1997), we developed a conceptual model to represent this relationship, with the goal of guiding future research on the mediational processes involved (Lachman et al., 1994; Lachman, in press). The model suggests that the mediational processes include behavioral, physiological, motivational, and affective factors.

The conceptual model presented in Figure 2.3 illustrates the interplay of age-related losses and changes in attitudes and motivation and captures the cyclical nature of aging processes (Lachman, Ziff, & Spiro, 1994). Similar to the social breakdown syndrome proposed by Kuypers and Bengtson (1973), this model examines the relationship between internalized negative expectations and age-related declines. To illustrate one possible chain of events (cf. Figure 2.3), age-related losses in cognitive functioning can lead to a lowered sense of control. This may involve a lowered sense of self-efficacy (lack of confidence in abilities), external beliefs (feeling one cannot do something about decling performance because doing so is not under one's own control), and/or attributions to internal stable causes (it is due to aging or poor ability). This lowered control in turn may affect motivation to change, resulting in lower levels of effort and less persistence in the face of difficulties, and may result in affective changes, such as depression and/or anxiety. This process is cyclical in that lowered effort can result in further cognitive decline through disuse, deconditioning, or atrophy.

A similar chain of events can be triggered by beliefs that declines are present rather than the actual presence of declines. For example, if older adults perceive themselves as becoming less capable (low efficacy) and attribute these perceived declines to unchangeable aspects of the aging process (maladaptive attributions), they may feel that nothing can be done (low sense of control) (Lachman et al., 1994). These lowered control beliefs may be associated with decreased motivation to engage in daily activities with cognitive demands and with physiological changes due to increased distress about one's limitations and the potential downward course of aging. The cyclical nature of the model indicates that regardless of where one begins, this is an ongoing process. That is, motivational deficits can trigger memory decrements and, at the same time, memory declines can trigger a lowered sense of control. These dynamics help explain why, for example, mem-

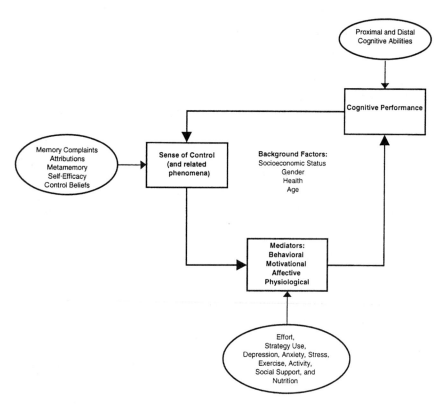

FIGURE 2.3   Mediational model linking control beliefs and cognitive performance.

ory loss may be accepted as inevitable among older adults (e.g., Smith & Earles, 1996), despite the fact that some of these declines are modifiable or even reversible (Schaie & Willis, 1986). Once the process is in motion, therefore, it may continue in a downward path unless interventions are introduced to modify beliefs, affect/motivation, and/or performance (Lachman, in press).

In the cyclical model of age-related loss, the sense of control, motivation, and affective factors are considered as antecedents, consequences, and mediators of age-related losses. Consistent with social cognitive behavioral theory (e.g., Bandura, 1997; Seligman, 1991), the relationship between beliefs and performance is dynamic and reciprocal in nature. Although there has been little empirical work on the mechanisms that link control beliefs and cognitive performance in later life, several classes of mechanisms have been identified (Bandura, 1997): behavioral/motivational (e.g., effort, attention, activity level), affective (e.g. depression, anxiety), or physiological (e.g., stress, exercise, social support). Future research is needed to test the viability of these hypothesized mediators. As data presented here suggest, it is likely that these mediators are not isolated influences but operate together. Ultimately, this work may be useful for refining intervention programs to improve cognitive functioning in the elderly.

The model in Figure 2.3 suggests that intervention programs to improve cognitive functioning should be multifaceted (cf. Lachman, in press). Older adults who improve their cognitive performance do not necessarily improve their beliefs about control which may limit long-term benefits of intervention. Although for younger adults performance experience may be sufficient for changes in self-efficacy, this does not appear to be the case for the elderly (Bandura, 1997). Thus, an intervention that is directly focused on changing beliefs is recommended in conjunction with teaching strategies for improving cognitive performance (Lachman, in press). This multifaceted approach has been successfully applied in two domains: memory enhancement (Lachman et al., 1992) and exercise programs for sedentary adults (Jette et al., in press; Lachman et al., 1997).

SUMMARY AND CONCLUSIONS

The research reviewed in this chapter shows consistently that there is a significant relationship between control beliefs and cognitive performance in later life. Clearly, there is evidence that control beliefs predict changes in cognitive functioning. However, the nature of this relationship is not fully understood. Much of the research has been cross-sectional and correlational in design, limiting the conclusions that can be made about process. Also, when background factors (i.e., health activity, exercise, and gender) are accounted for, the nature of the relationship between control beliefs and performance changes. Thus, future research is needed to investigate which domains of cognitive functioning are most closely linked to both background factors and control beliefs and why.

The findings reviewed in this chapter also indicate that cognitive performance leads to changes in control beliefs, consistent with findings in Bandura's theoretical work (e.g., Bandura, 1997) describing the reciprocal nature of control beliefs and performance. We presented one model linking beliefs and cognitive performance to illustrate the complexity of the relationship and to guide questions for future research. However, more research on the mediational factors linking control beliefs and cognitive aging is needed. For example, it is important to consider the role of biomedical and other psychosocial and behavioral factors as potential mediational processes (cf. Elliott & Lachman, 1989; Lachman, 1991; Lachman, et al., 1992; see also Fillit & Butler, 1997). Additionally, although time (Berry, 1987) and strategy (Stine et al., 1993) have been implicated as factors reflecting effort and performance, we know relatively little about how effort is manifested in cognitive performance. Research of this nature could be used to identify which factors are more or less modifiable and thus could lend themselves to interventions designed to improve the quality of life among older adults.

ACKNOWLEDGMENTS

Support for this chapter was provided by National Institute on Aging (NIA) training grant T32 AG00204 and by the John D. and Catherine T. MacArthur Foundation Network on Successful Midlife Development (MIDMAC). Address correspondence to the Department of Psychology, Brandeis University, Waltham, MA 02454–9110.

REFERENCES

Abeles, R. P. (1990). Schemas, sense of control, and aging. In J. Rodin, C. Schooler, & K. W. Schaie (Eds.) *Self-directedness: Cause and effects throughout the life course.* Hillsdale, NJ: Lawrence Erlbaum Associates.

Abramson, L. Y., Seligman, M. E. P., & Teasdale, J. D. (1978). Learned helplessness: Critique and reformulation. *Journal of Abnormal Psychology, 87,* 49–74.

Albert, M. S., Jones, K., Savage, C. R., Berkman, L. Seeman, T., Blazer, D., & Rowe, J. W. (1995). Predictors of cognitive change in older persons: MacArthur studies of successful aging. *Psychology and Aging, 10,* 578–589.

Aldwin, C. (1990). The elder's life stress inventory: Egocentric and nonegocentric stress. In M. A. P. Stephens, S. E. Hobfoll, J. H. Crowther, & D. L. Tennenbaum (Eds.), *Stress and coping in late life families* (pp. 49–69) New York: Hemisphere.

Bachrach, P. S. (1998). *Prospective memory and aging: Expectations, beliefs, and performance.* Unpublished doctoral dissertation, Brandeis University, Waltham, MA.

Bandura, A. (1977). Self-efficacy: Toward a unifying theory of behavioral change. *Psychological Review, 85,* 191–215.

Bandura, A. (1989). Regulation of cognitive processes through perceived self-efficacy. *Developmental Psychology, 25,* 729–735.

Bandura, A. (1997). *Self-efficacy: The exercise of control.* New York: W. H. Freeman.

Berry, J. M. (1987 August). *A self-efficacy model of memory performance.* Paper presented at the 95th annual convention of the American Psychological Association, New York.

Berry, J. M. & West, R. L. (1993). Cognitive self-efficacy in relation to personal mastery and goal setting across the life span. *International Journal of Behavioral Development, 16,* 351–379.

Caprio-Prevette, M. D., & Fry, P. S. (1996). Memory enhancement program for community-based older adults: Development and evaluation. *Experimental Aging Research, 22,* 281–303.

Cattell, R. B. (1971). *Abilities: Their structure, growth, and action.* Boston: Houghton Mifflin.

Cavanaugh, J. C., Feldman, J. M., & Hertzog, C. (1998). Memory beliefs as social cognition: A reconceptualization of what memory questionnaires assess. *Review of General Psychology, 2,* 48–65.

Cavanaugh, J. C., & Baskind, D. (1996). Relations among basic processes, beliefs, and performance: A lifespan perspective. In D. J. Herrmann, C. McEvoy, C. Hertzog, P. Hertel, & M. K. Johnson (Eds.) *Basic and applied memory research practical applications, vol. 2.* Mahwah, NJ: Lawrence Erlbaum Associates.

Cavanaugh, J. C., & Poon, L. W. (1989). Metamemorial predictors of memory performance in young and older adults. *Psychology and Aging, 4,* 365–368.

Centofanti, M. (1998, June). Fear of Alzheimer's undermines health of elderly patients. *APA Monitor,* p.1.

Cohen, G. (1993). Memory and ageing. In G. M. Davies & R. H. Logie (Eds.) *Memory in everyday life* (pp. 419–459). Amsterdam, North Holland: Elsevier Science Publishers.

Connor, L. T., Dunlosky, J., & Hertzog, C. (1997). Age-related differences in absolute but not relative metamemory accuracy. *Psychology and Aging, 12,* 50–71.

Costa, P. T., Jr., Fozard, J. L., McCrae, R. R., & Bosse, R. (1976). Relations of age and personality dimensions to cognitive ability factors. *Journal of Gerontology, 31,* 663–669.

Cutler, S. J., & Grams, A. E. (1988). Correlates of self-reported everyday memory problems. *Journal of Gerontology, 43,* 582–590.

Dittmann-Kohli, F., Lachman, M. E., Kliegl, R., & Baltes, P. B. (1991). Effects of cognitive training and testing on intellectual beliefs in elderly adults. *Journal of Gerontology: Psychological Sciences, 46,* P162–164.

Dixon, R. A. (1989). Questionnaire research on metamemory and aging: Issues of structure and function. In L. W. Poon, D. C. Rubin, & B. W. Wilson (Eds.). *Everyday cognition in adulthood and late life* (pp. 394–415). Cambridge: Cambridge University Press.

Dixon, R. A., Hultsch, D. F. (1983). Metamemory and memory for text relationships in adulthood: A cross validation study. *Journal of Gerontology, 38,* 689–694.

Dixon, R. A., Hultsch, D. F., & Hertzog, C. (1988). The metamemory in adulthood (MIA) questionnaire. *Psychopharmacology Bulletin, 24,* 671–688.

Dunlosky, J., & Connor, L. T. (1997). Age differences in the allocation of study time account for age difference in memory performance. *Memory and Cognition, 25,* 691–700.

Dustman, R. E., Ruhling, R. O., Russell, E. M., et al. (1984). Aerobic exercise training and improved neuropsychological function of older individuals. *Neurobiology of Aging, 5,* 35–42.

Earles, J., Connor, L., Smith, A. D., & Park, D. (1997). Interrelations of age, self-reported health, speed, and memory. *Psychology and Aging, 12,* 675–683.

Elliot, E., & Lachman, M. E. (1989). Enhancing memory by modifying control beliefs, attributions, and performance goals in the elderly. In P. W. Fry (Ed.), *Psychology of helplessness and control and attributions of helplessness and control in the aged* (pp. 339–367). Amsterdam: North Holland.

Erber, J. T., Szuchman, L. T., & Rothberg, S. T. (1990). Everyday memory failure: Age differences in appraisal and attribution. *Psychology and Aging, 5,* 236–241.

Fillit, H. M., & Butler, R. N. (1997). *Cognitive decline: Strategies for prevention.* London: Oxford University Press.

Gatz, M., & Pearson, C. G. (1988). Ageism revisited and the provision of psychological services. *American Psychologist, 43,* 184–188.

Gilewski, M. J., Zelinski, E. M., & Schaie, K. W. (1990). The memory functioning questionnaire for assessment of memory complaints in adulthood and old age. *Psychology and Aging, 5,* 215–233.

Gold, D. P., Andres, D., Etezadi, J., Arbuckle, T., Schwartzman, A., & Chaikelson, J. (1995). Structural equation model of intellectual change and continuity and predictors of intelligence in older men. *Psychology and Aging, 10,* 294–303.

Grover, D. R., & Hertzog, C. (1991). Relationships between intellectual control beliefs and psychometric intelligence in adulthood. *Journal of Gerontology: Psychological Sciences, 46,* 109–115.

Hertzog, C., Dixon, R. A., & Hultsch, D. F. (1990). Relationships between metamemory, memory predictions, and memory task performance in adults. *Psychology and Aging, 5,* 215–227.

Hertzog, C., Dixon, R. A., Schulenberg, J., & Hultsch, D. F. (1987). On the differentiation of memory beliefs from memory knowledge: The factor structure of the metamemory in adulthood scale. *Experimental Aging Research, 13,* 101–107.

Hultsch, D. F., Hammer, M., & Small, B. (1993). Age differences in cognitive performance in later life: Relationships to self-reported health and activity style. *Journal of Gerontology: Psychological Sciences, 48,* P1–P11.

Jette, A., Lachman, M. E., Giorgetti, M. M., et al. Exercise: It's never too late. *American Journal of Public Health, 89,* 66–72.

Jonker, C., Smits, C. H. M., & Deeg, D. J. H. (1997). Affect-related metamemory and memory performance in a population-based sample of older adults. *Educational Gerontology, 23,* 115–128.

Jonker, C., Launer, L. J., Hooijer, C., & Lindeboom, J. (1996). Memory complaints and memory impairment in older individuals. *Journal of American Geriatrics Society, 44,* 44–49.

Katzman, R. (1997). Education and depression as risk factors for cognitive decline. In H. M. Fillit, & R. N. Butler (Eds.) *Cognitive decline: Strategies for prevention* (pp. 33–38). London: Oxford University Press.

Kuypers, J. A., & Bengtson, V. L. (1973). Social breakdown and competence: A model of normal aging. *Human Development, 16,* 181–201.

Lachman, M. E. (1983). Perceptions of intellectual aging: Antecedent or consequence of intellectual functioning? *Developmental Psychology, 19,* 482–498.

Lachman, M. E. (1986). Locus of control in aging research: A case for multidimensional and domain-specific assessment. *Psychology and Aging, 1*, 34–40.

Lachman, M. E. (1990). When bad things happen to older people: Age differences in attributional style. *Psychology and Aging, 5*, 607–609.

Lachman, M. E. (1991). Perceived control over memory aging: Developmental and intervention perspectives. *Journal of Social Issues, 47*, 159–175.

Lachman, M. E. (in press). Promoting a sense of control over memory aging. In R. D. Hill, L. Bäckman, and A. S. Neely (Eds.). *Cognitive rehabilitation in old age.* New York: Oxford University Press.

Lachman, M. E., Baltes, P. B., Nesselroade, J. R., & Willis, S. L. (1982). Examination of personality-ability relationships in the elderly: The role of the contextual (interface) assessment mode. *Journal of Research in Personality, 16*, 485–501.

Lachman, M. E., Bandura, M., Weaver, S. L., & Elliott, E. (1995). Assessing memory control beliefs: The Memory Controllability Inventory. *Aging and Cognition, 2*, 67–84.

Lachman, M. E., & Jelalian, E. (1984). Self-efficacy and attributions for intellectual performance in young and elderly adults. *Journal of Gerontology, 39*, 577–582.

Lachman, M. E., Jette, A., Tennstedt, S., et al. (1997). A cognitive-behavioural model for promoting regular physical activity in older adults. *Psychology, Health & Medicine, 2*, 251–161.

Lachman, M. E., & Leff, R. (1989). Beliefs about intellectual efficacy and control in the elderly: A five-year longitudinal study. *Developmental Psychology, 25*, 722–728.

Lachman, M. E., Maier, H., & Budner, R. (in preparation). When and what is midlife? Not just problems and crises.

Lachman, M. E., & McArthur, L. Z. (1986). Adulthood age differences in causal attributions for cognitive, physical, and social performance. *Psychology and Aging, 1*, 127–132.

Lachman, M. E., Steinberg, E. S., & Trotter, S. D. (1987). The effects of control beliefs and attributions on memory self-assessments and performance, *Psychology and Aging, 2*, 266–271.

Lachman, M. E., & Weaver, S. L. (1998a). Sociodemographic variations in the sense of control by domain: Findings from the MacArthur Studies of Midlife. *Psychology and Aging, 13*, 553–562.

Lachman, M. E., & Weaver, S. L. (1998b). The sense of control as a moderator of social class difference in health and well-being. *Journal of Personality and Social Psychology, 74*, 763–773.

Lachman, M. E., Weaver, S. L., Bandura, M., Elliott, E., & Lewkowicz, C. (1992). Improving memory and control beliefs through cognitive restructuring and self-generated strategies. *Journals of Gerontology: Psychological Sciences, 47*, 293–299.

Lachman, M. E., Ziff, M. A., & Spiro, A. (1994). Maintaining a sense of control in later life. In R. Abeles, H. Gift, & M. Ory (Eds.), *Aging and quality of life* (pp. 216–232). New York: Sage.

Leirer, V. O., Morrow, D. G., Sheikh, J. I., & Pariante, G. M. (1990). Memory skills elders want to improve. *Experimental Aging Research, 16*, 155–158.

Levenson, H. (1974). Activism and powerful others: Distinctions within the concept of internal–external control. *Journal of Personality Assessment, 38*, 377–383.

Levy, B. (1996). Improving memory in old age through implicit self-stereotyping. *Journal of Personality and Social Psychology, 71*, 1092–1107.

Levy, B., & Langer, E. (1994). Aging free from negative stereotypes: Successful memory in China and among the American deaf. *Journal of Personality and Social Psychology, 66*, 989–997.

Luszcz, M. A., Bryan, J., & Kent, P. (1997). Predicting episodic memory performance of very old men and women: Contributions from age, depression, activity, cognitive ability, and speed. *Psychology and Aging, 12*, 340–351.

Meichenbaum, D. (1977). *Cognitive behavioral modification: An integrative approach.* New York: Plenum.

Miller, L. M. S., & Lachman, M. E. (1998 April). *Health and psychosocial predictors of cognitive performance across adulthood.* Poster presented at the Seventh Cognitive Aging Conference in Atlanta, GA.

Mischel, W. (1973). Toward a cognitive social learning reconceptualization of personality. *Psychological Review, 80*, 252–283.

Park, D. C., Smith, A. D., Lautenschlager, G., et al. (1996). Mediators of long-term memory performance across the life span. *Psychology and Aging, 11*, 621–637.

Perlmutter, M. (1978). What is memory aging the aging of? *Developmental Psychology, 14,* 330–345.

Perlmutter, M., & Nyquist, L. (1990). Relationships between self-reported physical and mental health and intelligence performance across adulthood. *Journal of Gerontology: Psychological Sciences, 45,* P145–155.

Rebok, G. W., & Balcerak, L. J. (1989). Memory self-efficacy and performance differences in young and old adults: The effect of mnemonic training. *Developmental Psychology, 25,* 714–721.

Riggs, K. M., Lachman, M. E., & Wingfield. A. (1997). Taking charge of remembering: Locus of control and older adult's memory for speech. *Experimental Aging Research, 23,* 237–256.

Rodin, J. (1990). Control by any other name: Definitions, concepts and processes. In J. Rodin, C. Schooler, & K. W. Schaie (Eds.) *Self-directedness: Cause and effects throughout the life course.* Hillsdale, NJ: Lawrence Erlbaum Associates.

Rodin, J., & Langer, E. J. (1977). Long-term effects of a control-relevant intervention with the institutionalized aged. *Journal of Personality and Social Psychology, 35,* 897–902.

Rodin, J., & Langer, E. J. (1980). Aging labels: The decline of control and the fall of self-esteem. *Journal of Social Issues, 36,* 12–29.

Rodin, J., Timko, C., & Harns, S. (1985). The construct of control: Biological and psychological correlates. *Annual Review of Gerontology and Genatrics, 5,* 3–55.

Rowe, J. W., & Kahn, R. L. (1997). Successful aging. *The Gerontologist, 37,* 433–440.

Ryan, E. B. (1996, September). *A social cognitive perspective on metacognition in aging.* A workshop on social cognition and aging sponsored by the National Institute on Aging. Bethesda, MD.

Salthouse, T. A. (1991). *Theoretical perspectives on cognitive aging.* Hillsdale, NJ: Lawrence Erlbaum Associates.

Salthouse, T. A. (1996). Constraints on theories of cognitive aging. *Psychonomic Bulletin & Review, 3,* 287–299.

Schaie, K. W. (1990). Intellectual development in adulthood. In J. E. Birren & K. W. Schaie (Eds.), *Handbook of the psychology of aging,* (pp. 291–310). San Diego, CA: Academic Press.

Schaie, K. W. & Willis, S. L. (1986). Can decline in adult intellectual functioning be reversed? *Developmental Psychology, 22,* 223–232.

Seeman, T., McAvay, G., Merrill, S., Albert, M., & Rodin, J. (1996). Self-efficacy beliefs and change in cognitive performance: MacArthur studies of successful aging. *Psychology and Aging, 11,* 538–551.

Seligman, M. E. P. (1991). *Learned optimism.* New York: Knopf.

Simonsick, E. M. (1997). Physical activity and cognitive function in old age. In H. M. Fillit, & R. N. Butler (Eds.) *Cognitive decline: Strategies for prevention* (pp. 39–51). London: Oxford University Press.

Skinner, E. A. (1995). *Perceived control, motivation, and coping.* Thousand Oaks, CA: Sage.

Smith, A, & Earles, J. (1996). Memory changes in normal aging. In F. Blanchard-Fields & T. M. Hess (Eds.), *Perspectives on cognitive change in adulthood and aging* (pp. 192–220). New York: McGraw-Hill.

Smith, G., Petersen, R., Ivnik, R. J., Malec, J. F., & Tangalos, E. G. (1996). Subjective memory complaints, psychological distress, and longitudinal change in objective memory performance. *Psychology and Aging, 11,* 272–279.

Stine, E. A. L., Lachman, M. E., & Wingfield, A. (1993). The roles of perceived and actual control in memory for spoken language. *Educational Gerontology, 19,* 331–349.

van den Heuvel, N., Smits, C. H. M., Deeg, D. J. G., Beekman, A. T. F. (1996). Personality: A moderator of the relation between cognitive functioning and depression in adults aged 55–85? *Journal of Affective Disorders, 41,* 229–240.

West, R. L., Dennehy-Basile, D., & Norris, M. P. (1996). Memory self-evaluation: The effects of age and experience. *Aging, Neuropsychology, and Cognition, 3,* 67–83.

Zarit, S., Cole, K., & Guider, R. (1981). Memory training strategies and subjective complaints of memory in the aged. *The Gerontologist, 21,* 158–164.

Zelinski, E. M., Gilewski, M. J., & Anthony-Bergstone, C. R. (1990). Memory functioning questionnaire: Concurrent validity with memory performance and self-reported memory failures. *Psychology and Aging, 5,* 388–399.

3

BELIEFS ABOUT MEMORY
AND AGING

CHRISTOPHER HERTZOG*,
TARA T. LINEWEAVER†, AND
CHRISTY L. MCGUIRE*

*School of Psychology, Georgia Institute of Technology, Atlanta, Georgia
† Joint Doctoral Program in Clinical Psychology,
San Diego State University–University of California, San Diego, California

INTRODUCTION

We have recently engaged in a series of studies designed to clarify the nature and impact of beliefs individuals have about memory and aging. This chapter describes the status of our work to date and briefly discusses possible future directions for this line of research.

Beliefs about memory are an important part of metacognition, defined as cognitions about cognition (Hertzog & Hultsch, in press). Arguably, the beliefs one has about the self as cognizer and about cognition in the general population have an impact on a number of constructs, including self-concept and self-esteem, anxiety concerning aging, negative affect, life satisfaction, and cognition itself. The relationship of beliefs to cognitive performance has historically been the principal focus of research in this domain (Berry & West, 1993; Cavanaugh, 1996; Hertzog & Hultsch, in press), and it constitutes an important part of our research program. However, metacognitive beliefs are an significant phenomenon in their own right, and in principle, they can influence everyday functioning, irrespective of whether concerns about poor cognitive function are an accurate reflection of cognitive functioning itself (Hertzog & Dixon, 1994). Cognitive psychologists' main interest focuses on whether age differences in metacognition account for age differences in cognitive task performance (Light, 1996; Salthouse, 1991), but this is only one question that can be asked about metacognitive phenomena. From a social cognitive perspective, it may not even be the most interesting question one could ask.

The research we describe in this chapter focuses explicitly on beliefs about memory. There are three major existing areas of research about beliefs and memory function, and all are represented in other chapters in this book. The first area includes implicit theories about aging and memory, including stereotypes about the effects of aging (e.g., Erber & Prager, Chapter 9 this volume; Hummert, 1990; Kite & Johnson, 1988; Ryan & Kwong See, 1993). These beliefs can be conceptualized as generic beliefs about the process of aging as it relates to memory. In principle, these beliefs apply to all persons, although beliefs could be differentiated by some prototypic individual attributes (e.g., exerciser vs couch potato) or situational determinants (e.g., sober vs inebriated). The second area includes self-referent beliefs about memory, or beliefs about oneself as a rememberer. This is perhaps the most widely studied aspect of the metacognitive literature (Berry, Chapter 4, this volume; Berry & West, 1993; Cavanaugh & Green, 1990; Soederberg Miller & Lachman, Chapter 2, this volume). The third area of prior research involves causal attributions about memory task performance (e.g., Devolder & Presley, 1992; Lachman & McArthur, 1986; Lachman, Steinberg, & Trotter, 1987). This research focuses on how individuals construe the causes of their own level of task performance immediately on its completion.

In this chapter, we address all three areas of research on beliefs about memory: implicit theories about aging and memory, causal attributions about memory task performance, and self-referent beliefs about memory. In theory, there are important linkages between these different types of memory beliefs (Cavanaugh & Green, 1990; Elliott & Lachman, 1989). Despite this fact, the three kinds of beliefs are sometimes confused for one another in the literature and are rarely studied as part of an integrated research study. Our research was designed to contribute to the process of identifying and explicating these linkages, adopting in part a social cognitive perspective (see Cavanaugh, Feldman, & Hertzog, 1998).

The empirical results and archival papers summarized in this chapter derive from two master's theses conducted at Georgia Institute of Technology (Georgia Tech) (Lineweaver, 1994; McGuire, 1998). Both studies measured implicit theories, self-referent beliefs, causal attributions, and strategy use during a free-recall memory task. The Lineweaver thesis involved assessment of a cross-sectional sample of unpaid adult volunteers, aged 18 to 93 years. Most of the participants were from two small cities: LaGrange, Georgia, and Springfield, Ohio. Many but not all of the young adults were volunteers from the School of Psychology subject pool at Georgia Tech. The McGuire thesis was conceived as a replication and extension of the Lineweaver thesis, using an oral one-on-one semistructured interview to replace the brief written questions used by Lineweaver to measure casual attributions and strategy use. It used an extreme age groups design (79 young adults, again mostly Georgia Tech students, 80 older paid volunteers from Atlanta, GA). Despite obvious differences in design, sampling procedures, etc., the studies produced similar answers to many of the research questions under study.

The chapter is structured as follows. In the first section, we provide a very brief treatment of the theoretical and empirical literature on implicit theories about memory and aging, then describe new instruments we developed for the purpose of measuring and differentiating implicit theories about memory and aging from self-referent beliefs. We then summarize findings from our recent research studies that fall into five interrelated areas: (1) implicit theories about memory and aging; (2) self-referent beliefs about memory; (3) relationships of implicit theories to self-referent beliefs; (4) causal attributions about memory; and (5) linkages among memory beliefs, strategy use, memory task performance, and attributions about task performance.

IMPLICIT THEORIES OF MEMORY AND AGING

There is a great deal of evidence that adults of all ages have pessimistic stereo-types and beliefs about the effects of aging on cognition, including memory (Camp & Pignatiello, 1988; Hummert, 1990; Kite & Johnson, 1988; Ryan, 1992). Implicit theories about the nature of age-related changes in memory play an important role in several accounts of the relationships between beliefs and cognition (e.g., Elliott & Lachman, 1989). Dweck and colleagues (Dweck & Leggett, 1988; Mueller & Dweck, 1998) have argued that many children maintain an implicit theory that academic performance is determined by a fixed, innate intel-lectual or cognitive ability (entity theory). This implicit theory contrasts with the belief that academic performance reflects learning or attained skill that is deter-mined by effort and practice (skill theory). Different children are conceptualized as being either entity theorists or skill theorists. Skill theorists are thought to be at an advantage over entity theorists because they will work hard to achieve in chal-lenging situations rather than assume that difficult challenges are beyond their fixed capabilities.

This concept has been extended to adulthood in terms of implicit theories about the effects of aging on memory and cognition (Elliott & Lachman, 1989; Langer, 1989; Person & Wellman, 1988). To the extent that older individuals believe in the inevitable, uncontrollable ravages of biological aging, they perceive poor memory to be unavoidable and hence may not behave in ways that maximize everyday memory functioning. On the other hand, older adults who view memory functioning as inherently determined by their own effort and initiative may bene-fit from perceptions of mastery and control and may be more likely to behave strategically and effectively in situations demanding use of memory and related cognitive skills (Levy & Langer, 1994; see Soederberg Miller & Lachman, Chap-ter 2 in this volume).

Studies examining stereotypes about aging and memory have indicated that a belief in memory decline is relatively pervasive. However, these studies focus generically on a wide variety of stereotyped characteristics of older adults (e.g., Hummert, 1990) and are therefore limited in terms of the detail they provide about beliefs concerning different aspects of memory. They also do not necessarily provide much information about how soon and how rapidly age declines are believed to occur (but see Heckhausen, Dixon, & Baltes, 1989).

Ryan developed a method for measuring implicit theories about memory change in adulthood. She adapted existing questionnaires of self-referent beliefs to the measurement of implicit theories about aging and memory. Respondents filled out a memory beliefs questionnaire as if responding for a typical person of a given age, rather than rating themselves. Ryan (1992) found that a cross-sectional sample of adults perceived memory to decline from young adulthood to old age. Ryan and Kwong See (1993) adapted three scales from the Metamemory in Adulthood (MIA) scale (Dixon & Hultsch, 1983) in the same manner. They compared standard self-ratings on the MIA to ratings produced by instructions to respond as if one were a typical person from one of four target ages (25, 45, 65, and 85). Ratings for both self and typical other showed age-related declines from ages 25 to 85. There were apparently no age differences in beliefs about memory and aging in their cross-sectional sample (mostly young and middle-aged adults).

Thus, the existing literature suggests that adults of all ages believe that memory declines during adulthood. Our studies were designed to expand on this understanding of implicit theories about memory and aging while addressing some limitations in the available evidence. Earlier work neither provided an adequate description of the perceived developmental function for memory change over the adult life span nor adequately evaluated whether adults of different ages hold differing beliefs about memory and aging. Moreover, although Ryan's work is a clever adaptation of existing questionnaires, it is not known whether the need to imagine oneself in the role of a typical other person when filling out a personal beliefs questionnaire produces a valid measure of implicit theories of aging and memory.

Lineweaver and Hertzog (in press) developed a method to allow respondents to chart perceived patterns of age-related changes in multiple aspects of memory across a wide age span. The General Beliefs about Memory Instrument (GBMI) asks persons to rate hypothetical target persons of different ages (ages 20–90, in 10-year increments). Items measure perceived memory efficacy (defined as the ability for effective remembering) and perceived control (defined as doing things that influence the likelihood of remembering). In addition to global questions about efficacy and control, the questionnaire also included a number of specific memory efficacy items (e.g., names, faces, telephone numbers just learned). Respondents are asked to use a graphic rating scale, making a mark across a vertical line for each target age to indicate level of perceived efficacy and control. Each item contains eight vertical lines, one for each age decade between 20 and 90. In this way, one can measure each person's perceived developmental function for memory efficacy and control over the life span. Figure. 3.1 shows three representative GBMI items: a global memory efficacy item, an item measuring control

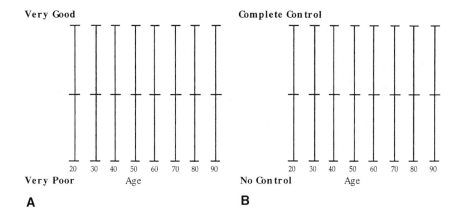

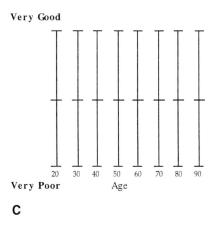

FIGURE 3.1   Illustration of GBMI rating scale method for three items: (A) Global memory efficacy (ability to remember in general), (B) control over memory (amount of control over present memory functioning; the extent to which an adult can do things *now* that will determine how his or her memory works), and (C) one specific memory efficacy item (names).

over memory function (i.e., the amount of control persons of different ages have over their current memory function), and one specific memory efficacy item (ability to remember names).

Figure 3.2 shows mean global memory efficacy developmental curves generated by three separate groups of respondents: younger adults, middle-aged adults, and older adults. All three age groups perceived memory efficacy to decline in a curvilinear fashion across the adult life span. Memory efficacy was perceived to be relatively stable until age 40 and to decline relatively precipitously after age 40. The large sample (about 300 persons), combined with the within-subjects

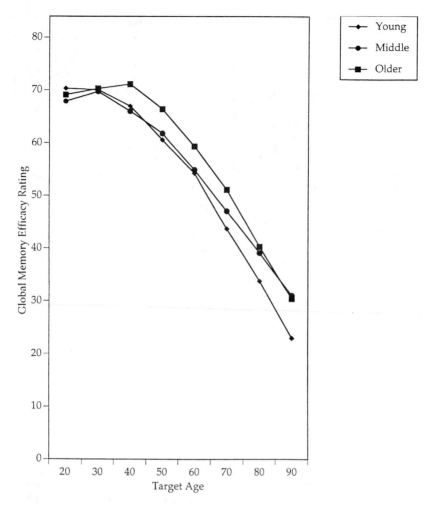

FIGURE 3.2 Developmental curves for GBMI (General Beliefs about Memory Instrument) global memory efficacy.

design on target ages, provided sufficient statistical power to detect a Target Age × Respondent Age interaction. The three respondent age groups produced different patterns of perceived change in global memory efficacy. Older adults perceived memory to improve slightly until age 40, whereas younger and middle-aged adults perceived memory to start declining after age 30.

Figure 3.3 shows the average developmental curve generated for the control over memory item. All three age groups believed that control over memory declines over the adult life span, but, again, there was a significant interaction effect. Younger adults perceived earlier and steeper decline in control than did middle-aged and older adults.

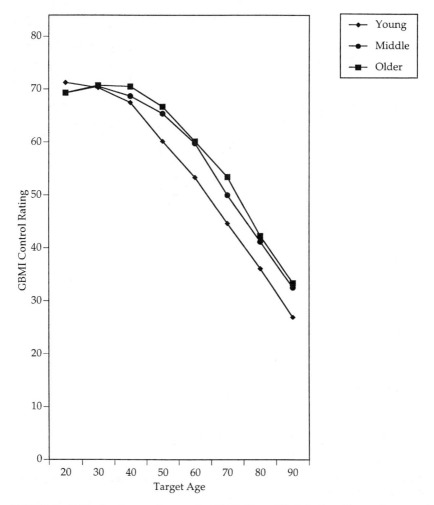

FIGURE 3.3   Developmental curves for GBMI (General Beliefs about Memory Instrument) control over memory.

Figure 3.4   contrasts two complementary specific GBMI items: memory for remote events ("things learned long ago") versus new episodic memory ("things learned recently"). As can be seen from Figure 3.4, there were differences in perceived developmental curves for these two kinds of memory. Decline was seen as beginning earlier and being greater in magnitude for memory for recently learned information, as opposed to things learned long ago. Arguably, these beliefs are accurate reflections of what is known about the effects of aging on episodic and remote autobiographical memory (e.g., Camp, 1989; Craik & Jennings, 1992; Rubin & Wentzel, 1996). Indeed, the GBMI

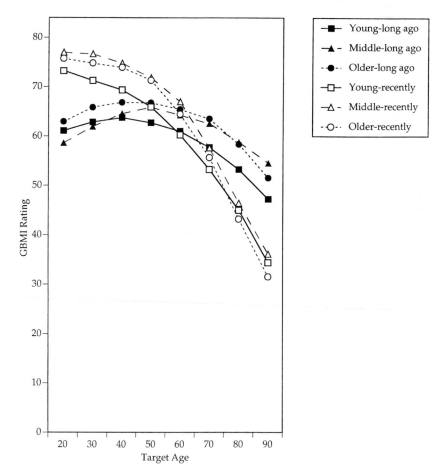

FIGURE 3.4   Developmental curves for two GBMI (General Beliefs about Memory Instrument) specific memory-efficacy items.

revealed several patterns that were broadly consistent with the literature on aging and cognition, such as less decline in remembering faces than in remembering names (see Lineweaver & Hertzog, in press, for more details). In general, then, laypersons' beliefs about memory change showed reasonable correspondence to what scientists have found regarding performance on different kinds of memory tests.

Thus, it appears that adults of all ages believe that memory declines over the life span, consistent with earlier literature. One important question about these implicit theories is whether there is evidence for two types of implicit theories that may be obscured by these developmental functions. Consider the hypothesis that adults are divisible into entity theorists or skill theorists (Elliott & Lachman,

1989). If this hypothesis is true, then one would expect to observe a bimodal distribution in the amounts of perceived age change in memory efficacy and memory control for the typical older adult. The skill theorists should show stable or positive changes in control, whereas the entity theorists should show belief in age-related decline in control and efficacy.

We computed simple difference scores between ages 20 and 90 for rated memory efficacy and rated memory control for the Lineweaver and Hertzog (in press) data. We then examined the frequency distributions for the entire sample, as well as separately for the younger, middle-aged, and older adults. The distributions of perceived change scores for global memory efficacy and memory control were clearly unimodal for all age groups. Figure 3.5 shows a frequency histogram for perceived control over memory for the total sample. The number of persons believing that control over memory functioning is maintained or increased across the life span was relatively small. The difference scores of only about 7.2% of the total sample lay in the interval at or above zero, indicating a belief in stability or improvement. We also checked difference scores from ages 20 to 60, to be sure that perceptions of late-life memory decline did not obscure a bimodal distribution of perceived changes from young adulthood into the beginning phases of old

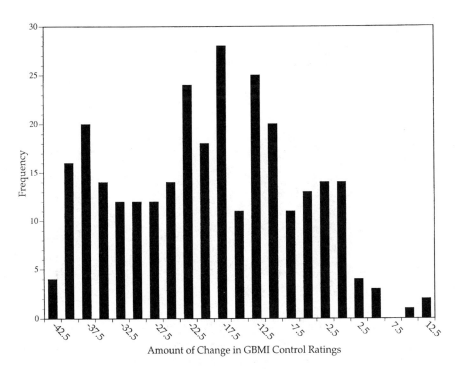

FIGURE 3.5   Frequency distribution for change scores from ages 20 to 90 in General Beliefs about Memory Instrument control for the total sample.

age. As expected, we found lower magnitudes of expected decline from age 20 to 60 but again found no evidence of a bimodal distribution in the data. Thus, the data from the GBMI do not provide strong support for the idea that adults can be divided into those who do and do not believe in age-related decline in control over memory.

SELF-REFERENT MEMORY BELIEFS

Like other researchers in the field, we have been interested in describing beliefs adults of different ages hold about themselves as rememberers. Because we were also interested in directly comparing these beliefs with general stereotypes, Lineweaver and Hertzog (in press) created the Personal Beliefs about Memory Instrument (PBMI). It queries the self-referent aspects of the same beliefs assessed by the GBMI. Like the GBMI, it was constructed to use graphic rating scales for responses, although for the PBMI these responses were placed on a horizontal rather than a vertical scale (Figure 3.6). The scales from the PBMI were based in part on an evaluation of existing questionnaires in the literature,

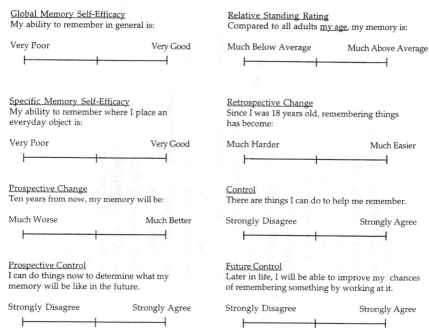

FIGURE 3.6   Sample items on the Personal Beliefs about Memory Instrument.

like the (MIA (Dixon & Hultsch, 1983). The PBMI also included a series of scales measuring perceived and expected change in memory self-efficacy. Perceived change in memory self-efficacy has been shown to produce large age differences, generally larger than those found for current memory self-efficacy (Hertzog & Hultsch, in press).

Lineweaver and Hertzog (in press) found that the self-referent scales from the PBMI had good internal consistency and showed patterns of age differences in self-ratings that were similar to other metamemory questionnaires, like the MIA (Dixon & Hultsch, 1983; Hultsch, Hertzog, & Dixon, 1987). Older adults believed themselves to have lower memory self-efficacy on the global measure, as well as on a specific memory self-efficacy scale that summed ratings for multiple specific PBMI memory items (such as remembering names). Older adults were approximately 0.6 *SD* lower than young adults in global memory self-efficacy and about 0.8 *SD* lower than young adults in specific memory self-efficacy. For both of these scales, middle-aged adults rated themselves lower than younger adults, but the differences were not statistically reliable (differences of 0.2 and 0.3 *SD* on the global and specific scales, respectively).

When respondents were specifically asked to rate their memory relative to persons "my own age" or "persons of all ages," interesting differences emerged. There were no significant age differences in relative standing to one's age peers, but robust age differences occurred between all three age groups when the standard was defined as persons of all ages. Middle-aged adults were about 0.3 *SD* below younger adults on this item, and older adults were about 0.7 *SD* below the middle-aged adults. Thus, specific reference to age eliminated the age differences in memory self-efficacy for ratings relative to peers but accentuated age differences when the explicit standard of persons of all ages was mentioned. This result suggests that explicitly providing the age standard (rating oneself relative to persons of all ages) activates the implicit theory about aging and changes reported self-efficacy, differentially so for older adults (see Schwarz, in press, for possibly related contrast effects with opinion surveys about memory). It also suggests that older adults on average perceive their own level of memory decline as being normative for a person their age.

Older adults also reported themselves to have lower levels of control over memory than middle-aged and younger adults, as would be expected from the literature (Dixon & Hultsch, 1983; Lachman, Bandura, Weaver, & Elliott, 1995). The effect was moderate in magnitude (Cohen, 1988), with older adults falling approximately 0.7 *SD* lower than the younger adults in level of perceived control over memory. Interestingly, the middle-aged and younger adults were quite similar in perceived control over memory. The difference between these two groups was only about 0.1 *SD* in magnitude.

One of the advantages of the PBMI is that it explicitly separates retrospective change (perceptions of change in memory functioning during the past) from prospective change (expectations of change in memory efficacy in the future). A useful feature of the PBMI change scales is that questions are scaled against a midline of 0 (no change), so that the magnitude of the rating is informative about perceived direction of memory change. In rating past changes in memory functioning, young adults reported retrospective improvement, middle-aged adults perceived little retrospective change, and older adults indicated significant memory loss. For prospective change, younger adults anticipated improvement in memory over the next 10 years, middle-aged adults expected small decrements, and older adults anticipated relatively substantial decline. The fact that younger adults anticipated improvement in their own memory functioning is quite interesting, because their GBMI global memory efficacy curves do not reflect an expectation of improvement from age 20 to 30 for the "average" adult (refer to Figure 3.3). This may suggest a discrepancy in expected memory change between oneself and others.

IMPLICIT THEORIES AND SELF-REFERENT BELIEFS

The new procedures provided by the GBMI for measuring implicit theories about memory change provided us with an opportunity to evaluate relationships between implicit theories and self-referent beliefs about memory. Our main focus was on examining relationships between (1) implicit theories about memory efficacy and memory self-efficacy and (2) implicit theories about memory control and beliefs about personal control over memory functioning. To investigate these relationships, we first calculated a linear and quadratic polynomial regression equation *for each person's* GBMI functions. Each person had generated a perceived developmental curve for each GBMI item (like the mean curves shown in Figures 3.2–3.4). The polynomial equation was used to estimate these curves. For each GBMI item, we estimated the intercept, the linear regression coefficient, and the quadratic regression coefficient that best described each person's developmental curve. The intercept represents the initial level of rated memory function. The linear and quadratic coefficients capture the perceived pattern and rate of change in memory function across the adult life span. Because we estimated a separate regression equation for every person on every item, we could use these estimated regression coefficients as variables to relate the GBMI responses to the PBMI responses.

We first correlated the GBMI intercepts and slopes with PBMI items (both for the global and for specific memory self-efficacy items). Correlations with the fitted regression intercepts were generally significant, although roughly .2 in magnitude, on average. In most cases, the fitted linear regression coefficient was not correlated with the PBMI items. These low correlations did not necessarily mean that individuals' implicit theories bore little relationship to their self-referent beliefs about memory control and memory efficacy. We tested an alternative hypothesis about how implicit theories about memory and aging drive personal beliefs. If it is the case that implicit theories are the basis for constructing personal beliefs about memory, then a candidate mechanism for the relationship is that individuals either generate or retrieve from memory an implicit developmental curve and then place themselves on that curve.

To test this hypothesis, we used each person's GBMI polynomial regression equation as a prediction equation. We took each person's current chronological age and substituted it for target age into his or her GBMI regression equation to generate an *age-equivalent rating:*

$$AER = a + b_1{\cdot}AGE + b_2{\cdot}AGE^2,$$

where *AER* is the age-equivalent rating, *a* is the intercept, b_1 is the linear polynomial coefficient, and b_2 is the quadratic polynomial coefficient, and *AGE* is the target age variable from the GBMI developmental function.

We then correlated these age-equivalent ratings with each person's PBMI memory self-efficacy item response. For each PBMI item, there was a significant correlation between the age-equivalent rating from the GBMI and the PBMI item score (see Lineweaver & Hertzog, in press, for complete data). For the GBMI global memory efficacy item, the age-equivalent rating correlated .34 with the PBMI global memory self-efficacy rating and .47 with the aggregate PBMI specific memory self-efficacy scale. The relationship was even more impressive when age-equivalent ratings were summed across all specific GBMI memory efficacy items. The aggregated age-equivalent GBMI scale score correlated .55 with the PBMI specific memory self-efficacy scale. We also estimated age-equivalent ratings for the GBMI control items. The GBMI age-equivalent rating for control over memory correlated .42 with the PBMI control scale. The GBMI age-equivalent rating for control over memory in the future correlated .44 with the corresponding PBMI control scale.

These results support the idea of correspondence between implicit theories and self-referent beliefs in that there are significant relations between where one stands on one's own implicit developmental function and how one rates one's own memory efficacy and control. However, the correlations are sufficiently low to suggest that the self-referent beliefs are not merely a projection, as it were, of implicit theories into the personal realm.

Of course, these analyses are but a first step in evaluating relationships of individual differences in implicit theories about memory change during adulthood to other constructs, including self-referent beliefs. In principle, our approach of using each person's GBMI curves to test hypotheses about relationships of implicit theories about aging and memory to other attributes can be extended to other questions. For example, we are currently involved in using the GBMI efficacy curves to evaluate McFarland, Ross, and Giltrow's (1992) hypothesis that perceived personal memory change in adulthood, as measured by the PBMI, is based on the combination of current memory self-efficacy plus an implicit theory about how memory changes during adulthood.

ATTRIBUTIONS ABOUT MEMORY
TASK PERFORMANCE

One of the major reasons that gerontologists have been interested in perceptions of memory self-efficacy and control over memory functioning is that these control beliefs could affect memory-related behaviors (Bandura, 1989; Lachman et al., 1987). Lachman's pioneering work in this area (see Soederberg Miller & Lachman, Chapter 2, this volume) has shown that older adults become less internal and more external in their locus of control over intellectual function (Lachman & Leff, 1989) and memory (Lachman & McArthur, 1986) as they grow older. Moreover, when older adults do express an internal locus of control, they are more likely to make internally focused attributions based on impaired cognitive ability rather than internal attributions based upon skill or effort (see Devolder & Pressley, 1992; Lachman & McArthur, 1986; Lachman et al., 1987).

In this section of the chapter, we report on the attribution data from the two samples we collected. In the Lineweaver thesis, participants performed a written free-recall task. Individuals had 4 minutes to study a 40-word list and then 4 minutes to write down as many of the words as they could recall. They then reported how many words they had recalled. This performance postdiction was correlated about .9 with actual written recall performance, showing that individuals' perceptions of their recall performance were highly accurate. Immediately after the postdiction, they responded in writing to two open-ended attribution questions: (1) "Why do you think you remembered the number of words that you did?" and (2) "If you were to participate in another memory task like this, what, if anything, would you do differently?" Responses were transcribed and later coded for types of causal attributions made.

Hertzog, McGuire, and Lineweaver (1998) described the attributions found in the written responses. There were significant age differences in the kinds of attributions made about memory performance. The most common type of attributions for all age groups were internal-skill attributions, which included either a generic attribution to effort or, more commonly, a reference to specific kinds of encoding strategies. In this sample, 65% of the younger and middle-aged adults made internal-skill attributions, whereas only 41% of older adults made such attributions. On the other hand, older adults were about twice as likely to make internal-ability attributions for performance (13%) compared to younger (8%) and middle-aged (7%) adults. These age differences were statistically reliable.

The results of the Hertzog et al. (1998) study were limited to a degree by the fact that 37% of older adults made brief written responses that were not codable with respect to type of causal attribution. In the McGuire thesis project, we focused more on using the open-ended questions in the semistructured interview to address self-reports of strategies used in the free-recall task. We approached the causal attribution issue, however, by using an attributional ranking task similar to that used by Lachman et al. (1987), adapted from Devolder and Pressley (1992). After completing the interview, participants in the McGuire thesis project responded to the following instructions: "Please rank how much influence any or all of these had on how many words you remembered today, with `1' meaning `a lot of influence' [and] `7' or the highest number meaning `not as much influence.'" The possible attributions that were explicitly listed included luck, age, task difficulty, task relevance or importance, general effort, effort through a specific strategy, and ability. We also included an open-ended category, other, with a blank line for individuals to write in the cause. There were relatively few "other" responses. A few individuals in both age groups appeared to be rating rather than ranking causes, and their responses were excluded from further analysis. Because individuals rank-ordered only those causes they selected, there were varying numbers of persons ranking each attribute. For example, 68 older adults ranked strategy as a cause, 60 ranked age, and only 42 ranked luck.

One issue of interest was whether older adults were more likely to attribute their performance to uncontrollable causes, such as ability or age, or to a controllable cause, such as effort. To examine this, we compared the responses of the 76 younger adults and the 68 older adults who gave rankings to both ability and effort and the responses of the 63 younger and 60 older adults who ranked both age and effort. Low rankings indicated higher importance. Both younger adults' ($M = 2.84$, $SD = 1.52$) and older adults' ability rankings ($M = 2.85$, $SD = 1.73$) gave ability less importance than effort (young $M = 2.21$, $SD = 1.30$; old $M = 2.59$, $SD = 1.53$). Age differences were not reliable. In the next comparison, we found that both age groups ranked effort as more important than age (young $M = 5.19$, $SD = 1.58$; old $M = 4.18$, $SD = 2.08$), and reliable age group differences were found: $t(121) = 3.03$, $p < .01$.

These results do not control for the overall number of causes that were ranked; therefore, we also classified individuals who ranked ability or age and effort in terms of whether they ranked ability or age as more important than effort, or vice versa. Here, an age difference did emerge. Only 4% of the young adults ranked age as a more important cause than effort, whereas 28% of older adults ranked age as more important than effort. These two categorical variables (age, effort) correlated .34 with each other. A smaller age difference was found between the proportion of younger (35%) and older (46%) adults who ranked ability as more important than effort.

These results were broadly consistent with the findings of Lachman et al. (1987), with the proviso that adults of all ages were more likely to view effort and strategies as being more important than ability. Similar findings held when we evaluated rankings categorized as uncontrollable (luck, age, task difficulty, ability) versus controllable (importance, general effort, and strategies). Young adults and older adults both attributed significantly more importance to controllable factors (overall, $M = 3.07$, $SD = 1.08$ for controllable factors vs $M = 4.02$, $SD = 1.10$ for uncontrollable factors). Uncontrollable factors were ranked as more important by older adults however (young $M = 4.27$, $SD = 0.81$, $N = 75$; old $M = 3.75$, $SD = 1.30$, $N = 70$, $p < .01$). The two age groups differed by approximately 0.5 SD.

CONTROL BELIEFS, STRATEGY USE,
AND ATTRIBUTIONS ABOUT
MEMORY PERFORMANCE

Perceived control may be a critical construct for linking implicit theories and memory task performance (Lachman et al., 1995; Langer, 1989). Older adults who report believing that they have some control over their memory functioning should in theory benefit from these beliefs. They should be more motivated to expend effort to learn, probably by using explicit learning strategies. Conversely, people who do not use strategies for learning may believe that memory is a stable trait and that any attempt to control or guide learning is futile. Similar arguments have been made regarding the relationship of memory self-efficacy to strategic behavior in memory tasks (Bandura, 1989; see Berry, Chapter 4, this volume). Individuals high in self-efficacy may expend more effort and be more persistent in their pursuit of mastery in learning new material.

Causal attributions may indirectly reflect an individual's implicit theory about the nature of memory and how it changes with age, as well as beliefs regarding the potential controllability of memory functioning. Devolder and Pressley (1992) argued that older adults are less strategic and less likely to attribute performance to strategies used during the memory task than are younger adults. They hypothesized that age differences in recall would be reduced, if not eliminated, if comparisons were restricted to younger and older adults who use high-quality strategies and attribute performance to those strategies. Although attributions made after the memory task obviously cannot influence prior task performance, they are argued to be a reflection of stable causal beliefs that were also operating before and during task performance and that act to limit or promote task-specific strategic behavior.

Hertzog et al. (1998) explored the relationships between memory task performance and attributions by comparing the internal-skill and internal-ability groups in free recall. Persons making skill attributions performed much better on the task (marginal means of 19 vs 14 words recalled), controlling for age. Age differences were still robust, however, controlling for attribution type. Thus, although attributions were related to actual memory performance, they could not account for age differences in memory.

In addition to age differences in memory task attributions, there is a large literature suggesting that there are age differences in effective strategy use in episodic memory tasks (Dunlosky & Hertzog, 1998a,b; Kausler, 1994). Older adults may be less likely to use relational processing effectively (Camp, Markley, & Kramer, 1983; Guttentag, 1988; Witte, Freund, & Sebby, 1990). Because there is compelling experimental evidence that relational processing enhances free recall (e.g., Hunt & McDaniel, 1993), we were interested in evaluating whether older adults were deficient in the spontaneous use of relational processes for a free-recall task and, if so, whether this was related to their underlying control beliefs.

The reader may remember that in the Hertzog et al. (1998) study, the modal attribution for all three age groups was to internal-skill causes—that is, attributions to effort, use of skill, or strategies for learning. Indeed, the internal-skill attributions provided by our participants often made specific reference to particular kinds of encoding strategies. Given the large number of internal-skill attributions in all age groups, it was possible to classify participants according to the kinds of strategies they reported. Ultimately, we divided persons into three ordinally ranked strategy categories: optimal, marginal, or none. Optimal strategies included relational processing using semantic meaning, including use of imagery or verbal association. Marginal strategies included association according to structural characteristics as well as other, arguably less effective strategies, such as alphabetization and rote repetition. Persons classified into the "none" group did not provide any written indication of a codable strategy in answer to either question.

There were significant age differences in strategy group assignments, with 48% of the younger adults and 53% of the middle-aged adults reported producing optimal encoding strategies. Only 35% of the older adults did so. Conversely, 39% of the older adults did not report any specific strategy, compared to only 23% of younger adults and 22% of middle-aged adults. Moreover, there were significant effects of self-reported strategy use on free recall.

Do these age differences in the use of relational strategies for organizing the list substantially increase age differences in recall performance? Apparently not. All three age groups showed roughly equivalent effects of the different types of strategies, and there was no Age × Strategy interaction. There were robust age differences in recall performance even when we compared only those younger and older adults who reported using optimal relational strategies. Indeed, the age differences we observed when controlling for strategy use were only slightly smaller than the age differences in recall in the entire sample, ignoring strategy group membership.

The method employed by Hertzog et al. (1998) has a virtue that could also be a liability. Our questions did not explicitly ask about strategies, which should minimize demand characteristics for reporting strategy use. That is, individuals were probably less likely to report strategies merely because they had been asked about them. On the other hand, a rival explanation for the age differences in strategy group membership might be that older adults simply did not provide adequate written responses. The robust effects of the coded strategies on recall argued indirectly for the validity of the coding scheme, but more direct evidence was needed.

McGuire, Hertzog, and Colson (1998) provided those data. In the McGuire thesis, participants completed a free-recall task and then were asked questions about their performance. This time, however, they were given a one-on-one audiotaped interview. Individuals were asked *how* (instead of why) they had remembered as many words as they did, and ambiguous responses regarding strategies were probed with follow-up questions to clarify the exact nature of the strategies being reported. In addition, if individuals made no mention of any strategy, they were explicitly asked about any they might have used. They were also asked to indicate how well they thought they had used the strategy.

As might be expected, overall reports of strategy use dramatically increased. In fact, relatively few older or younger adults failed to mention at least one strategy when probed. We also asked our respondents to rate how effectively they had used each strategy they reported. When persons were coded into strategy groups based on only reports of moderately effective strategy use, a pattern of results similar to Hertzog et al. (1998) emerged. Younger adults reported using more strategies effectively, and these strategies were more likely to be optimal relational strategies. Of the younger adults, 65% reported using optimal strategies, 22% reported using marginal strategies, and 13% reporting using low or poor strategies. In contrast, older adults were more evenly distributed between strategy categories: 39% in the optimal group, 27% in the marginal group, and 34% in the low-quality strategy group. These differences were statistically significant. Thus, age differences in strategic behavior emerged with both self-report methods.

McGuire et al. (1998) also replicated the findings of no Age × Strategy Group interaction, despite the change in method. Figure 3.7 provides the data and shows the effect that the age differences in strategy grouping had on the overall age differences in memory performance between the older and younger samples. Younger adults using optimal strategies recalled about 13% more words than did older adults using optimal strategies. This was smaller than the 16% recall difference between the age groups when strategy use was ignored. Clearly, the inflation in age differences in recall due to age differences in types of strategy employed was relatively small.

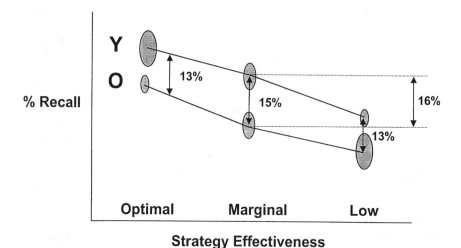

FIGURE 3.7   Free-recall performance for different Strategy × Age groups. Y = young; O = old.

Do these kinds of results indicate that it is fruitless to evaluate relations of memory beliefs to strategy use in older adults? If one is primarily or exclusively interested in finding explanations of the age differences in memory performance (see Salthouse, 1991), perhaps so. However, the fact that strategy use is an important predictor of memory performance for adults of all ages, combined with the fact that older adults are not highly likely to use optimal strategies, suggests the opposite. Remember that only 35–40% of the older adults in both studies reported using optimal strategies. This suggests that a substantial number of older persons were not using optimal strategies, even though they probably would have benefited from them. Therefore, the memory performance of many older adults can in principle be improved by enhancing the quality of strategies they use. Optimizing older adults' effective strategy use could, in effect, compensate for age-related declines in memory. Granted, this argument applies primarily to strategies that are employed to aid remembering in everyday life. Let us accept for the moment, though, the possibility that those persons who use effective strategies for remembering in everyday life are also likely to be the same persons who use effective mnemonic strategies in laboratory tasks. Then increasing the quality of strategy production could assist older adults in achieving higher levels of memory effectiveness—even though strategy production per se is not the cause of their lower levels of memory performance, relative to younger adults.

Of course, another point is that beliefs about memory and strategy effectiveness are of interest in their own right as a way of understanding the system of implicit theories and personalized beliefs individuals develop regarding memory. There were, in fact, some intriguing relationships between implicit theories, personal control beliefs, and strategy use in the two data sets. First, Hertzog et al. (1998) contrasted the three strategy groups (optimal, marginal, and none) in terms of the profile of developmental curves from the GBMI. The curves for memory self-efficacy did not differ, but the strategy groups did differ in perceived developmental changes in control over memory functioning. As would be expected, optimal strategy users perceived slightly less age-related decline in control over memory than did the marginal and no strategy groups, who did not differ (see Hertzog et al., 1998). Inconsistent with expectations, however, the internal-skill and internal-ability attribution groups did not differ in perceived developmental curves for control over memory.

The relationships were somewhat stronger in the domain of personal control beliefs. Here, both a contrast of internal-ability to internal-skill attributors, as well as the contrast comparing different strategy groups, revealed significant strategy group differences in perceived control over memory. Internal-skill attributors reported higher levels of personal control, relative to internal-ability attributors. Individuals who failed to mention any strategies reported lower levels of personal control than did those who reported using either optimal or marginal strategies. Both of these effects were obtained when controlling for age differences in attributions and strategy self-reports. Similar analyses produced no strategy or attribution group differences on any of the memory self-efficacy measures (see Hertzog et al., 1998, for details).

It should be acknowledged that these strategy group differences in perceived control were not large in magnitude. Scaled against the root mean square (the pooled standard deviation), the internal-ability group was 0.4 *SD* lower in perceived control than the internal-skill group. The group reporting no strategies was about 0.7 *SD* lower in perceived control than the optimal and marginal strategy groups.

The effects found in Hertzog et al. (1998) were not fully replicated in the McGuire thesis data. McGuire also measured implicit theories about global memory efficacy and control over memory using a subset of the GBMI items. Older and younger adults both believed that aging causes declines in efficacy and control. However, GBMI curves for control did not vary dramatically as a function of strategy group membership, possibly owing in part to the more liberal strategy elicitation technique in the interview. Moreover, strategy subgroups were also similar in their perceptions of personal control over memory.

There were some relationships between implicit theories, as measured by the GBMI, and the attribution rankings from the McGuire thesis study. One finding was that GBMI curves for control over memory functioning differed for older adults who ranked controllable causes higher than uncontrollable causes as explanations of their memory performance. Figure 3.8 shows that older adults attributing memory performance to controllable factors perceived less age-related decline in control over memory. Similar findings were obtained when the curves were plotted only for those who ranked strategies higher than abilities in the attribution task.

The causal attributions were also related to a sense of personal control over present memory functioning, as measured by the PBMI, but again primarily in the older adult sample. Older adults' personal control ratings were significantly correlated with their attribution of performance to age ($r = .42$) and to strategy ($r = -.25$) in the expected direction. High ratings of personal control were associated with higher age rankings (less importance) and lower strategy rankings (more importance). Personal beliefs in prospective control over memory functioning also showed significant correlations with age ranking ($r = .26$) and strategy rankings ($r = -.37$).

Finally, the importance attributed to age as a causal factor was related to memory task performance. Age rankings were significantly correlated with free-recall scores in the older adults ($r = .29$). A multiple regression showed that both age group and strategy group were significant predictors of recall performance, consistent with previously summarized results on strategy use. Adding the age attribution rankings to the equation resulted in a significant increase in explained variance. The standardized regression weights for age, strategy, and age attribution rankings were $-.39$, $.32$, and $.17$, respectively. Thus, attributing memory performance to one's own age was associated with poorer recall performance, even when controlling for age and type of strategy used.

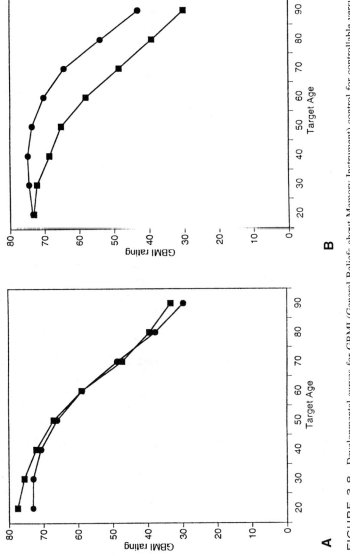

FIGURE 3.8   Developmental curves for GBMI (General Beliefs about Memory Instrument) control for controllable versus uncontrollable attributors from the (A) young and (B) old age groups.

Taken together, the results from the two samples are far from definitive. Strategy group membership was related to implicit theories about change in control and to perceived personal control in Hertzog et al. (1998), but not in the McGuire thesis data. On the other hand, the attribution task in the latter sample revealed some interesting relationships of attributions to implicit theories and to perceived personal control, suggesting some consistency and coherence between the different types of beliefs. Moreover, consistent with findings in Lachman's earlier work, a tendency to attribute memory performance to age was related to recall. Of course, this could be a consequence of perceived poor performance rather than a cause of it (see Soederberg Miller & Lachman, Chapter 2, this volume). Unfortunately, given the method of coding attributions in Hertzog et al. (1998), there was no way for us to attempt to replicate these findings in the Lineweaver thesis data.

SUMMARY AND CONCLUSIONS

We believe the research we described in this chapter has opened new potential avenues for exploration of a number of important issues regarding implicit theories of memory, self-referent beliefs, and related variables. In particular, the new method of scaling implicit theories about age changes in memory used in the GBMI can be extended in several ways. First, it is possible to obtain developmental functions for different kinds of targets. Our research investigated ratings of the "average" adult, but it would be fascinating to manipulate personal characteristics of the hypothetical targets to determine whether perceived developmental functions vary by health status, lifestyle, activity patterns, and other personal characteristics.

Second, it would be possible to address the issue of contextual or situational variance in functioning by asking about developmental functions for the same person but under different situational circumstances. Research on causal attributions in social situations suggests that individuals are prone to make trait-based, dispositional attributions for target individuals' behavior but that they will consider situational information depending on a number of factors (Blanchard-Fields, 1996). Memory functioning is typically considered an internally based and dispositional variable (as indicated by the attribution data summarized earlier in this chapter). Nevertheless, some individuals did make external attributions in our sample, and presumably all individuals would be willing to consider the possibility of situational constraints on memory task performance under some circumstances. At this point, we simply do not know either the extent to which individuals differ in this regard or whether the extent would influence implicit theories about aging and memory.

Consideration of such issues is important because we believe that the available data do not strongly support the argument that older adults can be divided into two types: those who believe in inevitable memory decline and those who do not. Nor do we believe that the available data strongly support the view that individuals who believe in the inherent controllability of memory function are necessarily superior in memory-related performance or in the encoding strategies they employ in memory tasks. Some of our results support this view, but some do not, and in any case the effects were not as large as we had believed they would be, prior to conducting this research, on the basis of our review of the available literature.

Indeed, the data from the GBMI regarding distributions of perceived change in control over memory call the "entity versus skill" view of memory control beliefs into some question. We suggest an alternative hypothesis, one that in principle can be directly examined by a modification of the techniques we have described in this chapter. This hypothesis states that many if not almost all individuals believe that memory decline is in large part inevitable because of effects of biological aging and age-related pathologies. However, it also states that individuals simultaneously vary in the degree to which they believe that memory functioning can be influenced and controlled by their behavior, subject to the constraints imposed by the aging process. That is, laypersons may hold a view of aging that is similar to one offered by Baltes (1987) and others—namely, that there is considerable plasticity in memory performance, both in the laboratory and everyday life, even though there are biologically based age-related changes in the range of possible performance. Moreover, individuals may believe that the control they have is in the degree to which they can compensate for ongoing decline with effortful activity, such as increased use of external aids and routinized procedures to guide remembering and avoid forgetting.

From this point of view, the Lachman et al. (1995) Memory Controllability Inventory scale of Inevitable Decrement might actually be differentiating between (1) those who believe that the inevitable can be postponed and tempered in its impact by the right kinds of behavior and (2) those who do not so believe (rather than between those who believe in inevitable decrement vs those who believe in memory maintenance through exercise of control). In fact, we are currently coding qualitative data from the McGuire thesis interview that asked a series of questions about control over memory and the effects of aging with this hypothesis in mind. We have found some individuals who seem to conform to the simultaneity hypothesis, concurrently holding both entity and skill views of aging and memory.

One participant shared the following statements with us. When asked "In what ways do you have control over memory?" the reply was "I am a firm believer in using it. Just like using your muscles keeps your body fit, using your memory keeps it sharp…You can do your bit to keep it sharp."

Obviously, this person sounds like a skill theorist as defined by Elliott and Lachman (1989), but when asked "In what ways do you *not* have control over memory?" the same person responded:

> I guess the aging process is all. You know, these memory lapses, they go with aging, and I'm in the middle years, and I have all these symptoms of the metamorphosis your body is going through, and sometimes … I'll be blank: "Gosh, what is that guy's name? I

know it as well as my own name." But I just think that goes with the aging process, and that, [I] have no control over, but yet, as far as doing things to keep that memory sharp, I have control.

As we are just beginning the coding process, we do not yet know how prevalent this kind of simultaneous belief in decline and control actually is. It may be far more typical than implied by the typological entity-versus-skill hypothesis. The simultaneity hypothesis leads to some very interesting questions. Is it possible to identify a classic self–other discrepancy (as in other aspects of social cognition), such that, to paraphrase Elisabeth Kübler-Ross, decline happens to thee, and to thee, but control belongs to me? The PBMI prospective change data for younger adults suggests that such an effect might be operating, but more definitive experiments are needed. If individuals simultaneously believe in age-related decline and potential control over memory, under what circumstances can one belief or the other be primed by specific events, such as salient episodes of forgetting? If people believe that different persons decline in different ways and with different outcomes, it seems possible that the fundamental dilemma individuals face is automatic and spontaneous activation of different prototypes of successful and unsuccessful memory aging (e.g., the Alzheimer's patient vs the healthy centenarian), triggered by their interpretation and attributions regarding everyday memory events, and against which they must judge themselves (e.g., Cutler & Hodgson, 1996).

In evaluating such questions, concepts that are currently prevalent in social cognition research (schematicity, accessibility, priming, automaticity) may become extremely important in understanding the dynamics of the belief system regarding memory and aging. These constructs will probably be needed to explain when and how beliefs influence interpretation of everyday memory failures, potentially leading to increased perceptions of threat, anxiety, depressive affect, lowered self-concept, and/or self-protective coping through dissonance reduction, self-enhancement, and so on. It is our hope that future empirical research using and extending the kinds of techniques we have described here can begin to address these issues and provide us with an enriched understanding of the subtle complexities of belief systems adults possess regarding their own and others' memory.

ACKNOWLEDGMENTS

Support for this chapter was provided by research grant R01-AG13148 from the National Institute on Aging (NIA) one of the National Institutes of Health (NIH). Address correspondence to Christopher Hertzog, School of Psychology, 274 5th Street, Georgia Institute of Technology, Atlanta, GA 30332-0170.

REFERENCES

Baltes, P. B. (1987). Theoretical propositions of life-span developmental psychology: On the dynamics between growth and decline. *Developmental Psychology, 23,* 611–626.

Bandura, A. (1989). Regulation of cognitive processes through perceived self-efficacy. *Developmental Psychology, 25,* 729–735.

Berry, J. M., & West, R. L. (1993). Cognitive self-efficacy in relation to personal mastery and goal-setting across the life span. *International Journal of Behavioral Development, 16,* 351–379.

Blanchard-Fields, F. (1996). Social cognitive development in adulthood and aging. In F. Blanchard-Fields & T. M. Hess (Eds.), *Perspectives on cognitive change in adulthood and aging* (pp. 454–487). New York: McGraw-Hill.

Camp, C. J., Markley, R. P., & Kramer, J. J. (1983). Spontaneous use of mnemonics by elderly individuals. *Educational Gerontology, 9,* 57–71.

Camp, C. J. (1989). World-knowledge systems. In L. W. Poon, D. C. Rubin, & B. A. Wilson (Eds.), *Everyday cognition in adulthood and late life* (pp. 457–482). New York: Cambridge University Press.

Camp, C. J., & Pignatiello, M. F. (1988). Beliefs about fact retrieval and inferential reasoning across the adult lifespan. *Experimental Aging Research, 14,* 89–97.

Cavanaugh, J. C. (1996). Memory self-efficacy as a moderator of memory change. In F. Blanchard-Fields & T. M. Hess (Eds.), *Perspectives on cognitive changes in adulthood and aging* (pp. 488–507). New York: McGraw-Hill.

Cavanaugh, J. C., Feldman, J. M., & Hertzog, C. (1998). Memory beliefs as social cognition: A reconceptualization of what memory questionnaires assess. *Review of General Psychology, 2,* 48–65.

Cavanaugh, J. C., & Green E. E. (1990). I believe, therefore I can: Personal beliefs and memory aging. In E. A. Lovelace (Ed.), *Aging and cognition: Mental processes, self-awareness and interventions* (pp. 189–230). Amsterdam, North Holland: Elsevier Science Publishers.

Cohen, J. (1988). *Statistical power analysis for the behavioral sciences* (2nd ed.). Hillsdale, NJ: Lawrence Erlbaum Associates.

Craik, F. I. M., & Jennings, J. M. (1992). Human memory. In F. I. M. Craik & T. A. Salthouse (Eds.), *The handbook of aging and cognition* (pp. 51–110). Hillsdale, NJ: Lawrence Erlbaum Associates.

Cutler, S. J., & Hodgson, L. G. (1996). Anticipatory dementia: A link between memory appraisals and concerns about developing Alzheimer's disease. *The Gerontologist, 36,* 657–664.

Devolder, P. A., & Pressley, M. (1992). Causal attributions and strategy use in relation to memory performance differences in younger and older adults. *Applied Cognitive Psychology, 6,* 629–642.

Dixon, R. A., & Hultsch, D. F. (1983). Structure and development of metamemory in adulthood. *Journal of Gerontology, 38,* 682–688.

Dunlosky, J., & Hertzog, C. (1998a). Aging and deficits in associative memory: What is the role of strategy production? *Psychology and Aging, 13,* 597–607.

Dunlosky, J., & Hertzog, C. (1998b). Training programs to improve learning in later adulthood: Helping older adults educate themselves. In D. J. Hacker, J. Dunlosky, & A. C. Graesser (Eds.), *Metacognition in educational theory and practice* (pp. 251–277). Mahwah, NJ: Lawrence Erlbaum Associates.

Dweck, C. S., & Leggett, E. L. (1988). A social cognitive approach to motivation and personality. *Psychological Review, 95,* 256–273.

Elliott, E., & Lachman, M. E. (1989). Enhancing memory by modifying control beliefs, attributions, and performance goals in the elderly. In Fry, P. S. (Ed.), *Psychology of helplessness and control in the elderly.* (pp. 339–367). Amsterdam, North Holland: Elsevier Science Publishers.

Guttentag, R. E. (1988). Processing relational and item-specific information: Effects of aging and division of attention. *Canadian Journal of Psychology, 42,* 414–423.

Heckhausen, J., Dixon, R. A., & Baltes, P. B. (1989). Gains and losses in development throughout adulthood as perceived by different adult age groups. *Developmental Psychology, 25,* 109–121.

Hertzog, C., & Dixon, R. A. (1994). Metacognition and memory development in adulthood and old age. In J. Metcalfe & A. P. Shimamura (Eds.), *Metacognition: Knowing about Knowing* (pp. 225–251). Boston, MA: MIT Press.

Hertzog, C., & Hultsch, D. F. (in press). Metacognition in adulthood and old age. In F. I. M. Craik & T. A. Salthouse (Eds.), *Handbook of aging and cognition 2.* Mahwah, NJ: Lawrence Erlbaum Associates.

Hertzog, C., McGuire, C. L., & Lineweaver, T. T. (in press). Aging, attributions, perceived control, and strategy use in a free recall task. *Aging, Neuropsychology, and Cognition.*

Hultsch, D. F., Hertzog, C., & Dixon, R. A. (1987). Age differences in metamemory: Resolving the inconsistencies. *Canadian Journal of Psychology, 41,* 193–208.

Hummert, M. L. (1990). Multiple stereotypes of elderly and young adults: A comparison of structure and evaluations. *Psychology and Aging, 5,* 182–193.

Hunt, R. R., & McDaniel, M. A. (1993). The enigma of organization and distinctiveness. *Journal of Memory and Language, 32,* 421–445.

Kite, M. E., & Johnson, B. T. (1988). Attitudes toward older and younger adults: A meta-analysis. *Psychology and Aging, 3,* 233–244.

Kausler, D. H. (1994). *Learning and memory in normal aging.* San Diego: Academic Press.

Lachman, M. E., & Leff, R. (1989). Perceived control and intellectual functioning in the elderly: A 5-year longitudinal study. *Developmental Psychology, 25,* 722–728.

Lachman, M. E., & McArthur, L. Z. (1986). Adulthood age differences in causal attributions for cognitive, physical, and social performance. *Psychology and Aging, 1,* 127–132.

Lachman, M. E., Steinberg, E. S., & Trotter, S. D. (1987). Effects of control beliefs and attributions on memory self-assessments and performance. *Psychology and Aging, 2,* 266–271.

Lachman, M. E., Bandura, M., Weaver, S. L., & Elliott, E. (1995). Assessing memory control beliefs: The Memory Controllability Inventory. *Aging and Cognition, 2,* 67–84.

Langer, E. (1989). *Mindfulness.* Reading, MA: Addison-Wesley.

Levy, B., & Langer, E. (1994). Aging free from negative stereotypes: Successful memory in China and among the American deaf. *Journal of Personality and Social Psychology, 66,* 989–997.

Light, L. (1996). Memory and aging. In E. L. Bjork & R. A. Bjork (Eds.), *Handbook of perception and cognition* (2nd ed., pp. 443–490). San Diego: Academic Press.

Lineweaver, T. T. (1994). *Beliefs about memory in adults of all ages.* Unpublished master's thesis, Georgia Institute of Technology, Atlanta.

Lineweaver, T. T., & Hertzog, C. (in press). Adults' efficacy and control beliefs regarding memory and aging: Separating general from personal beliefs. *Aging, Neuropsychology, and Cognition.*

McFarland, C., Ross, M., & Giltrow, M. (1992). Biased recollections in older adults: The role of implicit theories of aging. *Journal of Personality and Social Psychology, 62,* 837–850.

McGuire, C. L. (1998). *Age differences in recall strategies and estimation accuracy on a free recall task.* Unpublished master's thesis, Georgia Institute of Technology, Atlanta.

McGuire, C. L., Hertzog, C., & Colson, K. F. (1998). *Age differences in performance and strategy use on a free recall task.* Unpublished manuscript, Georgia Institute of Technology, Atlanta.

Mueller, C. M., & Dweck, C. S. (1998). Praise for intelligence can undermine children's motivation and performance. *Journal of Personality and Social Psychology, 75,* 33–52.

Person, D. C., & Wellman, H. M. (1988). *Older adults' theories of memory difficulties.* Unpublished manuscript, University of Michigan, Ann Arbor.

Rubin, D. C., & Wentzel, A. E. (1996). One hundred years of forgetting: A quantitative description of retention. *Psychological Review, 103,* 734–760.

Ryan, E. B. (1992). Beliefs about memory changes across the adult lifespan. *Journal of Gerontology, 47,* P41–P46.

Ryan, E. B., & Kwong See, S. (1993). Age-based beliefs about memory changes for self and others across adulthood. *Journal of Gerontology, 48,* P199–P201.

Salthouse, T. A. (1991). *Theoretical perspectives on aging.* Hillsdale, NJ: Lawrence Erlbaum Associates.

Schwarz, N. (in press). Self-reports of behaviors and opinions: Cognitive and communicative processes. In N. Schwarz, D. Park, B. Knauper, and S. Sudman (Eds.). *Cognition, aging, and self-reports.* Philadelphia: Psychology Press.

Witte, K. L., Freund, J. S., & Sebby, R. A. (1990). Age differences in free recall and subjective organization. *Psychology and Aging, 5,* 307–309.

4

MEMORY SELF-EFFICACY IN ITS SOCIAL COGNITIVE CONTEXT

JANE M. BERRY

Department of Psychology
University of Richmond
Richmond, Virginia

The greatest mistake in modern psychology is to treat the self-in-its-world as a self separated from its surroundings.

(Reed, 1994, p. 278)

...Accounts of memory gain their meaning through their usage, not within the mind nor within the text, but within social relationships.

(Gergen, 1994, p. 89)

This chapter takes a primarily cognitive construct—memory self-efficacy (MSE)—and returns it to its roots—social cognition (Bandura, 1986). This is a natural and obvious move. MSE has evolved since the mid-1980s (Berry, West, & Powlishta, 1986; Hertzog, Dixon, Schulenberg, & Hultsch, 1987) to its present identity and status in the cognitive aging and adult developmental research literature. If it is to avoid becoming a hypothesis in search of data (Light, 1991) or worse, an epiphenomenon to more robust explanations of cognitive aging (e.g., speed) (Salthouse, 1993), its potential and limits must be scrutinized and subjected to rigorous new research agendas. Arguably, MSE has arrived at its present destination via metamemory (Dixon, Hertzog, & Hultsch, 1986; Hertzog, Dixon, & Hultsch, 1990a; Hertzog et al., 1987; Hultsch, Hertzog, Dixon, & Davidson,

1988), thereby acquiring a more cognitive emphasis than its clinical and social underpinnings suggest. This chapter presents MSE research from my lab that has been conducted from the orienting framework of self-efficacy theory and methodology (Bandura, 1977, 1986, 1997; Bandura, Adams, Hardy, & Howells, 1980; Bandura, Reese, & Adams, 1982). The value of this framework lies in its rich theoretical foundation, its unique measurement approach, and its ties to social cognition. The goal of the chapter is to evaluate the present status of MSE research and to suggest new research directions.

WHAT IS MEMORY SELF-EFFICACY?

Memory self-efficacy (MSE) refers to a dynamic, self-evaluative system of beliefs and judgments regarding one's memory competence and confidence (Berry & West, 1993; Cavanaugh, Feldman, & Hertzog, 1998; Cavanaugh & Green, 1990; Hertzog & Dixon, 1994; West & Berry, 1994). In practice, my colleague Robin West and I have adopted a conceptual and methodological approach to the MSE construct that is derived strictly from Bandura's model and methods. In this approach, MSE is a self-judgment about one's ability to perform a given memory task competently and with confidence. Our operationalization of MSE typically yields a summary competence score (MSE level) and a summary confidence score (MSE strength); both are derived from a memory task hierarchy comprising increasingly difficult levels of a given memory task (e.g., remembering 12 words). These two scores are assumed to reflect an individual's appraisal of the relevant features of the task and situation, the relevant ability and affective characteristics of the self, and other stored and concurrent sources of efficacy information. Note, though, that these components of MSE judgments are not measured (directly) and are only *assumed* to be operative when a self-efficacy judgment is made. Our measures of MSE are composed of concrete task-descriptive items with high face validity. Thus, our conception of MSE is intentionally conservative and constrained and does not represent, per se, generalized beliefs or complaints about memory. Our research on MSE is an effort to systematically test tenets of self-efficacy theory, and we argue that the most rigorous and fruitful initial tests of the theory must be based on a strict definition and operationalization of MSE. Other approaches that take a more liberal, encompassing view of the MSE construct and memory beliefs in general are represented in this volume (see Hertzog, Lineweaver, & McGuire, Chapter 3, this volume; Soederberg Miller & Lachman, Chapter 2, this volume); together, the different approaches will help to establish the construct, discriminant, and predictive validity properties of MSE and memory beliefs.

The model of self-efficacy depicted in Figure 4.1 illustrates the causal sources and effects of MSE judgments. The direction of cause to effect in this model is generally from left to right; however, arrows between some constructs are omitted intentionally to indicate the reciprocal nature of some relationships. For example,

SOURCES OF EFFICACY   MEDIATING EFFECTS OF EFFICACY

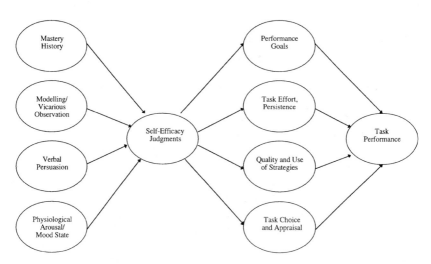

FIGURE 4.1   Sources and effects in self-efficacy theory. (Adapted from Bandura, 1997.)

effort that produces immediate positive performance consequences within a sub-portion of overall task engagement could bolster self-efficacy *during* continued task engagement. Moreover, there are some constructs and paths (e.g., post-task performance attributions that inform future and ongoing efficacy judgments) not depicted in this model in order to keep its explication clear. This model also includes an implied path from task performance back to mastery history (and other variables in the model), which transforms a hitherto *effect* (e.g., task perfor-mance) of a given self-efficacy judgment into a *cause* (source) of future self-effi-cacy judgments. The figure indicates that MSE judgments are formulated from the input of several sources and in turn have specific effects on task-related behaviors. The next two sections provide some details on the measurement and sources of MSE.

MEASUREMENT OF MEMORY SELF-EFFICACY

The approach to MSE measurement has bifurcated into (1) rationally derived sets of items based on Bandurian methodology (Berry, West, & Dennehy, 1989) and (2) factor-analytical scales composed of items from the Metamemory in Adulthood (MIA) questionnaire (Dixon, Hultsch, & Hertzog, 1988) and the Memory Functioning Questionnaire (MFQ) (Gilewski, Zelinski, & Schaie, 1990; Zelinski, Gilewski, & Anthony-Bergstone, 1990). Whereas the former measure-ment approach emphasizes the task-specific nature of MSE (Berry et al., 1989;

West & Berry, 1994), the latter approach emphasizes dispositional and dynamic beliefs about memory capacity and forgetting (Hertzog et al., 1987; Hertzog et al., 1990a; Hultsch et al., 1988). Both groups of researchers have demonstrated adulthood age differences in MSE as well as the predictive utility of MSE in relation to memory performance outcomes. Both groups have also examined the mechanisms by which MSE might influence memory performance, including task-related effort and strategy usage, and individual differences in performance prediction and vocabulary skills.

The primary distinction between these two lines of research, then, is methodological, although there are points of conceptual departure as well. Measures of MSE derived directly from self-efficacy methodology (Bandura et al., 1980; Bandura et al., 1982) have operationalized MSE as a memory evaluation judgment tied to a specific memory task (e.g., remembering names, directions, locations). This approach is based on hierarchically arranged subtask levels that range from low to high levels of mastery of a task goal and is exemplified by the 10-task, 50-item Memory Self-Efficacy Questionnaire (MSEQ) (Berry et al., 1989; West & Berry, 1994). Respondents make binary decisions (Yes or No) and confidence ratings (10–100% confidence) for each task level, as in the following sample items from the MSEQ:

If someone read the list to me twice, I could remember the names of 4 common objects from a list of 12 names.

No   Yes   10%   20%   30%   40%   50%   60%   70%   80%   90%   100%

If someone read the list to me twice, I could remember the names of 6 common objects from a list of 12 names.

No   Yes   10%   20%   30%   40%   50%   60%   70%   80%   90%   100%

If someone read the list to me twice, I could remember the names of 8 common objects from a list of 12 names.

No   Yes   10%   20%   30%   40%   50%   60%   70%   80%   90%   100%

If someone read the list to me twice, I could remember the names of 10 common objects from a list of 12 names.

No   Yes   10%   20%   30%   40%   50%   60%   70%   80%   90%   100%

If someone read the list to me twice, I could remember the names of 12 common objects from a list of 12 names.

No   Yes   10%   20%   30%   40%   50%   60%   70%   80%   90%   100%

The number of yes responses are summed across the 5 items for each of the 10 tasks, and 10 summary scores labeled self-efficacy level (SEL) are retained for analyses. Likewise, the confidence ratings across item and task levels are averaged to yield 10 summary scores labeled self-efficacy strength (SEST). Figure 4.2 displays the MSEQ measurement scheme. For path analyses of the relation of self-efficacy to performance with one or more mediating variables (e.g., Bandura & Jourden, 1991; Bandura & Wood, 1989), SEST scores are the preferred measure because they are based on a larger range of possible responses than are SEL scores, therefore yielding a more sensitive measure (Bandura, personal communication). However, both types of scores are useful indicators of absolute levels of perceived competence and confidence and have been used to examine mean age differences in MSE (Berry et al., 1989; West & Berry, 1994).

In contrast to the MSEQ approach, Hertzog and colleagues have used factor-analytically derived MSE scales from the MIA and MFQ questionnaires (e.g. Hertzog, Hultsch, & Dixon, 1989; Hertzog, Dixon, & Hultsch, 1990b). They define MSE as a "highly schematized system of beliefs regarding one's ability to use multiple types of memory in various contexts" (Hertzog et al., 1990a). This system includes all beliefs that could be brought to bear on memory evaluations, including beliefs about one's own memory abilities and capacity, how the self responds affectively to memory tasks, and how memory changes over time. Perhaps the biggest difference between MSEQ MSE and MIA MSE is that MSEQ items assess self-confidence in one's ability to perform specific memory tasks, whereas MIA items assess self-evaluations of one's general competence or ability across many different memory domains and tasks. The MIA is comprised of 108 items rated on 5-point Likert scales from "agree strongly" to "disagree strongly." A sample item from the MIA capacity subscale (which appears to be the most consistent marker of the MIA MSE subscales) is "I am good at remembering the content of news articles and broadcasts" (Dixon et al., 1988). Note that this item

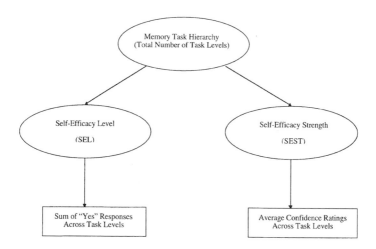

FIGURE 4.2   Self-efficacy measurement.

is combined with such items as "I have no trouble keeping track of my appointments" and "I have no trouble remembering where I have put things" for an aggregate MIA capacity score, illustrating the cross-domain nature of the MIA MSE measure.

Research that combines the two measurement approaches (Gardiner, Luszcz, & Bryan, 1997; Luszcz & Hinton, 1995) indicates that both levels of measurement have predictive utility. Bivariate correlations between MSE and recall reported by Luszcz and Hinton indicate that the Bandurian MSE measure ($r^2 = .52$) accounts for more variance in recall scores than does the MIA MSE (capacity subscale) measure ($r^2 = .06$) by a factor of almost 9. The continued use of both MSEQ and MIA measures in MSE research will help to clarify the meaning and construct validity of MSE and should move MSE research away from a mostly metamemory-measurement emphasis toward the field of social cognition. The Bandurian model employed by Berry and West is particularly amenable to expansion into this territory because we assume that the four sources of efficacy information share conceptual similarities with constructs and methods (e.g., schemata, affect, person perception, stereotypes, in-group biases) from social cognition. This assumption awaits empirical tests in our research programs and is discussed further in the closing section of this chapter "Future Research Directions").

SOURCES AND EFFECTS OF MEMORY
SELF-EFFICACY JUDGMENTS

Self-efficacy judgments for a particular task are constructed from myriad sources (see Figure 4.1), including (1) *mastery,* the structure, content, and pattern of past successes and failures; (2) *modeling,* the observation, adoption, and internalization of the actions of other people; (3) *verbal persuasion,* the encouragement, advice, feedback, ridicule, admonitions, etc., received from other people; and (4) *physiological arousal and mood state,* the internal states of physiological or psychological excitation, inhibition, apathy, anxiety, etc., experienced in a situation (Bandura, 1997, Chapters 3 and 4). These four sources shape self-efficacy judgments, which in turn affect task-engagement processes and outcomes. High self-efficacy is related to high, proximal performance goals (Locke & Latham, 1990), greater persistence toward task completion (Cervone & Peake, 1986), better strategy usage (Bouffard-Bouchard, 1990), greater perceived choice (Betz & Hackett, 1986), and higher task effort (Berry, 1987).

Mastery experiences entail the cumulative history of one's engagement with a particular task, obstacle, or activity. In each successive enactive experience, the organism receives internal and external feedback regarding absolute and relative levels of mastery attainment. Recent empirical work by Sanna and Pusecker (1994) demonstrates self-efficacy can be manipulated by performing difficult versus easy items (on a word-association task) and that self-efficacy interacts with performance feedback (experimenter-provided feedback or no feedback). Specifically, higher self-efficacy expectations were obtained from subjects who worked on easier (vs harder) word-association items in a pretest phase. Moreover, performance scores on the word-association test were predicted by a Self-Efficacy × Feedback Condition interaction, such that high self-efficacy subjects in the experimenter-provided feedback condition answered more items correctly than did low self-efficacy subjects in the experimenter-provided feedback condition. These results suggest that self-efficacy judgments can be predicated on task experience and, further, that self-efficacy interacts with self-evaluative concerns about performance: Efficacy effects on performance were greatest in the condition in which subjects were led to expect explicit feedback on performance. This research supports the influence of mastery experience as an important source of efficacy information. The overall valence of performance evaluations can be positive, negative, or neutral, but appraisal of the stored, cumulative record of experiences will depend on the subjective state of the individual approaching and during task engagement. Moreover, temporal, social, and affective variables influence interpretations of mastery records: An individual might be quite pleased privately with his or her work accomplishments on one day but view them more harshly and self-critically on another day in a public setting.

Each of the four sources of efficacy information comprise some form of social or situational information. Mastery experiences are often judged in relation to a social-referent standard, such as peer groups or age groups. Arousal may be heightened or attenuated positively or negatively in the presence of onlookers/observers to performing a memory task. Modeling (or vicarious observation) and verbal persuasion are the most directly social sources of self-efficacy information. Modeling involves the discernment and adaptation or rejection of other people's relevant behavior. (It could be argued that the self serves as a model, either at a younger age or as a self "ideal," but this argument is not developed here.) Verbal persuasion (or dissuasion) comes directly from others, although again, one could talk oneself into or out of attempting a challenging task. These two sources probably share common variance as sources of external feedback. For example, one might look to one's immediate social group (i.e., friends) for memory modeling information as well as attend closely to the verbal feedback it offers.

Physiological arousal is a fourth source of efficacy information. The effects of anxious arousal or mood state may operate only initially on self-efficacy judgments at points of task appraisal and performance anticipation, or the effects may be operative throughout a memory task and fluctuate as a function of ongoing performance feedback. However, the effects of anxiety on MSE may be more reactive if an initially nonanxious person becomes anxious during performance of a challenging, difficult memory task. In research settings, it is also possible that self-corrective or experimenter feedback over multiple trials would enhance or decrease anxiety, depending on the valence of the feedback.

SUMMARY

Self-efficacy theory and methods provide a rich theoretical network of testable, falsifiable hypotheses. Some hypotheses have received strong empirical support, such as those applied to achievement domains, including mathematics (e.g., Pajares & Miller, 1995), reading (e.g., Schunk & Rice, 1987), and writing (e.g., Zimmerman & Bandura, 1994). Research on mediational effects supports the reciprocal nature of self-efficacy and goal setting/attainment, although not equivocally (Mathieu & Button, 1992). The theoretical strengths and empirical yield of mainstream self-efficacy research have guided our MSE research efforts. This work, along with other MSE research, is described in the next section ("Status and Critique of Memory Self-Efficacy Research"). Research on questionnaire measures of memory control, complaints, concerns, and subjective memory beliefs (e.g., Lachman, Weaver, Bandura, & Elliott, 1995; Hermann, 1982) is not reviewed here. Although a large body of research is related derivatively (memory predictions), tangentially (memory complaints, memory beliefs, memory controllability), or superordinately (metamemory, metacognition, self-regulation) to MSE, the focus in this chapter is on work with close conceptual and/or methodological ties to self-efficacy theory. Thus, the work to date can be characterized as having two major emphases: (1) description of age differences in MSE and (2) the predictive and explanatory validity of MSE as a mediator of adulthood age differences on memory performance tasks. MSE is important because of its influence on how memory tasks are perceived, evaluated, and enacted. Empirical work has demonstrated that MSE declines in adulthood and has a positive effect on memory performance (Berry et al., 1989; Hertzog et al., 1990b; Luszcz & Hinton, 1995). The next section presents and critiques research on MSE in relation to age, predictive validity, and mediating effects.

STATUS AND CRITIQUE OF MEMORY SELF-EFFICACY RESEARCH

One of the most established conclusions in the cognitive aging literature is that memory declines with age (see Salthouse, 1991; Verhaeghen, Marcoen, & Goossens, 1993). This conclusion holds across diverse laboratory tasks (e.g., words, texts, pictures, drawings, object locations, numbers, names–faces, activities), encoding conditions (strategy instruction, incidental and intentional orienting tasks), and retrieval instructions (recall and recognition, implicit and explicit, free and cued recall). The *explanatory* mechanisms by which age influences memory functioning have been discussed from MSE, metamemory, and metacognitive perspectives (Berry & West, 1993; Berry, Acosta, Baldi, Burrell, & Rotondi, 1994; Cavanaugh & Green, 1990; Cavanaugh, Morton, & Tilse, 1989; Hertzog & Hultsch, in press; Hertzog & Dixon, 1994) and in the field of social cognition (Cavanaugh, Feldman, & Hertzog, 1998). These approaches examine knowledge and beliefs about memory; self-regulation of memory skills and affect; age differences in knowledge, beliefs, self-regulation, and self-knowledge; and the relation of these factors to overt memory behavior.

AGE DIFFERENCES AND PREDICTIVE VALIDITY OF MEMORY SELF-EFFICACY

Most studies on MSE and aging have used samples of young and old adults and have found negative age differences between these two groups (Berry et al., 1989; Berry, West, & Cavanaugh, 1996; Gardiner et al., 1997; West, Dennehy-Basile, & Norris, 1996). Conclusions about the developmental nature of MSE, such as its relative salience and impact at different ages, are tenuous because although middle-aged adults have been included in MSE research designs (Berry, Thompson, Bryant, Hambrick, & Drew, 1998; Hertzog et al., 1990a; Hultsch, Hertzog, & Dixon, 1987; Ryan & See, 1993), curvilinear age effects have not been given as much explanatory emphasis as have the negative linear age effects obtained. For example, Berry et al. (1998) found that middle-aged adults reported higher MSE SEST for text recall than did younger and older adults who had comparable text MSE SEST scores. On a word-recall task, however, younger and middle-aged adults had comparable and higher MSE SEST scores than those of older adults. Figure 4.3 displays these results.

Differential patterns of age effects on MSE SEST scores were also obtained by Berry et al. (1996). Age differences for MSEQ MSE and for MIA MSE were all generally negative but not always linear. On some scales, younger adults reported higher MSE than did middle-aged and older adults, but on other scales, younger and middle-aged adults reported higher scores than did older adults. The eight memory tasks displayed in Figure 4.4 all yielded significant negative linear effects, but for some tasks (e.g., Grocery—recalling items from a grocery list), younger and middle-aged adults had comparable scores; both were higher than older adults' scores. Moreover, on the phone number recall task (Phone), all three age groups had significantly different MSE SEST scores. In the same study, Berry et al. reported that the factor structure of MSE may not be age invariant. In exploratory research on a sample of 489 adults between the ages of 18 and 90 years, factor analyses of the eight MSEQ subscales and the seven MIA subscales yielded a first factor composed of all eight MSEQ subscales for all age groups. The MIA subscales that loaded on the first factor (i.e., with the MSEQ scales) varied by age group: Anxiety, for younger adults; Change and Capacity for middle-aged adults; and Change, Capacity, Locus, and Anxiety for older adults. Table 4.1 displays these factor loadings for MSEQ and MIA subscales by age group. For the total sample, all eight MSEQ MSE subscales and MIA Change and MIA Capacity subscales showed good convergence of factor loadings on the first factor (MSE) of the solution (see Table 4.2).

In other research, West et al. (1996) found that MSE–performance relationships were higher among younger than older adults, particularly for laboratory memory tasks, but Berry, Geiger, Visocan, and Siebert (1987) found that MSE

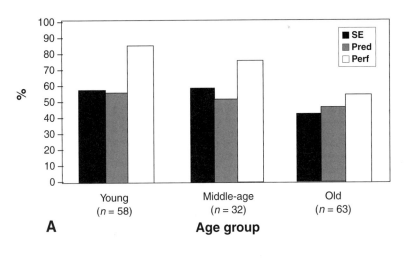

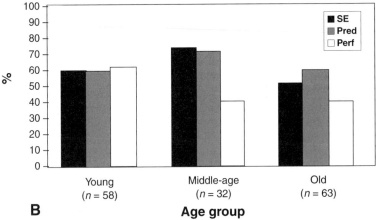

FIGURE 4.3   Age differences on self-efficacy strength (SEST) ratings of (A) word and (B) text recall. SE = self-efficacy; Pred = prediction; Perf = performance.

and recall were significantly correlated among older but not younger women. Luszcz and Hinton (1995) reported results that corroborated those of Berry et al. (1987) in that MSE scores explained more variance in the memory scores of older than younger adults. Similarly, Berry et al. (1994) found that models of the mediating effects of study time and strategy use on MSE–performance correlations were stronger for older than younger adults, as indicated by the overall variance explained by the models. Elsewhere, Berry and West (1993) have argued that MSE–performance relationships *should* be strongest for older adults as a group

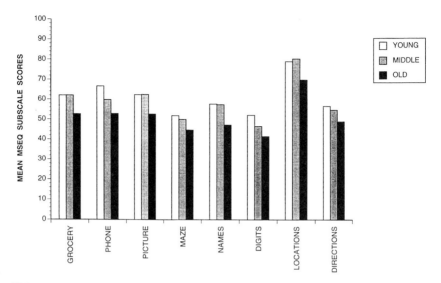

FIGURE 4.4   Age differences on self-efficacy strength (SEST) ratings of eight memory tasks. MSEQ = Memory Self-Efficacy Questionnaire.

because they are more concerned with memory functioning and losses than are younger adults. Perhaps older adults are more "memory schematic" (Cavanaugh et al., 1998) than are younger adults, which would suggest that memory functioning carries more personal importance for older adults and yields more accurate indicators of memory self-knowledge and evaluation.

The variable magnitude and patterning of MSE correlations with performance and performance mediators across age groups should be addressed in systematic, controlled research designed to determine when, why, and for which age groups MSE predicts performance. A memory system in flux at midlife seems particularly worthy of research attention, as middle-aged individuals begin facing the task of balancing losses and gains in cognitive (and other) domains (Baltes, 1987). How the individual compensates for or adapts to developmental changes, including fluctuating memory abilities, will depend partly on his or her beliefs about the nature of aging in general and his or her own experience of it in particular. To the extent that memory ability is important to the sense of self, adapting to a changing system will become a central developmental issue (Allport, 1955).

Definitive empirical work on MSE and aging has provided persuasive evidence that MSE is a developmentally relevant construct that predicts memory performance in adulthood (Berry et al., 1989; Cavanaugh & Poon, 1989; Dixon & Hultsch, 1983a, 1983b; Hertzog et al., 1987; Hertzog et al., 1989; Hertzog et al., 1990b; Hultsch et al., 1988; Rebok & Balcerak, 1989; West & Berry, 1994). This

TABLE 4.1   MSE and Knowledge Factor Loadings for MSEQ and MIA Scales by Age Group

Factor	Young		Middle		Old	
	MSE	KNW	MSE	KNW	MSE	KNW
MSEQ						
Names	.847	.084	.802	.171	.820	.168
Directions	.765	−.001	.718	−.210	.689	.167
Maze	.746	.042	.761	.022	.774	.079
Grocery	.734	.120	.784	−.019	.720	.062
Pictures	.692	.070	.652	.151	.654	−.085
Digits	.651	−.056	.778	−.098	.759	.127
Locations	.622	.013	.588	−.089	.661	−.061
Phone	.606	.106	.625	.068	.691	.225
MIA						
Anxiety	−.313	−.047	−.434	.614	−.721	.331
Locus	.053	.722	.351	.550	.420	.416
Achievement	.106	.717	.116	.787	.049	.787
Change	.189	.611	.474	−.238	.682	−.146
Task	.001	.542	−.159	.589	.107	.475
Capacity	.468	.487	.541	−.283	.681	.063
Strategy	−.259	.417	−.044	.594	−.223	.605

KNW = knowledge; MIA = Metamemory in Adulthood; MSE = memory self-efficacy; MSEQ = Memory Self-Efficacy Questionnaire.

TABLE 4.2   MSE and Knowledge Factor Loadings for Total Sample

Factor	MSE	KNW
MSEQ		
Name	.825	.079
Maze	.756	−.001
Grocery	.755	.012
Directions	.730	−.080
Digits	.718	−.047
Pictures	.674	.048
Phone	.662	.121
Locations	.637	−.056
MIA		
Capacity	.613	.052
Change	.541	.156
Achievement	.128	.775
Task	.063	.643
Strategy	−.142	.615
Locus	.330	.531
Anxiety	−.438	.473

KNW = knowledge; MIA = Metamemory in Adulthood; MSE = memory self-efficacy; MSEQ = Memory Self-Efficacy Questionnaire.

relationship holds for word, text, and digit span recall tasks, but future research should identify the memory tasks for which MSE has the greatest and least predictive utility. If self-efficacy (Berry & West, 1993) and social cognitive (Cavanaugh et al., 1998) theories of MSE are viable and robust, the predictive validity of MSE should vary by task, from person to person, and over time (i.e., developmentally).

MEDIATING EFFECTS OF MEMORY SELF-EFFICACY

Research on the processing mechanisms by which MSE influences memory performance has lagged behind that of age differences, MSE–performance correlational research, and MSE measurement. This is understandable given the need to establish valid and reliable measures of MSE that yield consistent age differences and are significantly related to memory performance processes. Bandura's hypothesis that self-efficacy operates through effort and persistence (see Figure 4.1) has been tested in a series of studies by Berry and colleagues. The results of these studies are mixed: Berry (1987) found that task study time mediated the MSE–performance (word recall) relationship among older women ($N = 120$) with complaints of memory. The women completed a word-recall MSEQ and then studied concrete nouns, each word printed separately on a small white card. The size of the word set for each participant was determined by a baseline measure taken before the performance trial; the performance word-recall sets ranged in size from 14 to 35 words. Subjects were instructed to study the words for as long as they wished (up to a maximum of 20 minutes) in order to recall as many as possible. Following study, subjects informed the experimenter when they were ready to attempt recall, at which time the experimenter recorded study time, collected the word set, and recorded the participants' responses (i.e., words recalled aloud). A path analysis of the data indicated that when study time (task effort) was added to the regression equation that predicted word recall from MSE, the standardized beta coefficient for the path from MSE to word-recall performance decreased from .42 to .19, indicating a partial but not total mediating effect. Overall, study time ($pr^2 = .30$) and MSE ($pr^2 = .17$) explained significant and unique proportions of total memory variance: $R^2 = .48$, $p < .0001$. Berry concluded that MSE has indirect effects on word-recall performance through study time but may also have direct effects on word-recall performance and/or additional indirect effects on variables (e.g., strategy use) that were not measured in this study.

In a follow-up study to Berry (1987), younger and older women without memory complaints (Berry et al., 1987) were tested, with less conclusive effects observed regarding the mediation of MSE and word-recall performance by task effort. Specifically, MSE and performance were significantly correlated in the older sample ($r = .58$, $n = 30$), but not the younger sample ($r = .10$, $n = 30$). For younger adults, study time was significantly related to MSE ($r = .40$) and to memory performance ($r = .66$), but neither of these relationships was significant for the older adults (for both, $r < .09$). Taken together, the results of Berry (1987) and Berry et al. (1987) suggest that individual differences and age differences in self-reported concerns of memory ability differentially affect MSE and its effects. As suggested by Cavanaugh et al. (1998) and Berry and West (1993), and consistent with self-efficacy theory, the strongest effects of self-efficacy on task engagement and performance outcomes should be obtained among individuals for whom memory functioning (and concomitant worries) is important and integral to their sense of self.

In other tests of mediation effects, Berry et al. (1994) reported significant effects of MSE on study time and strategy use as mediators of word-recall performance, but these relationships varied as a function of age group and effort type: Stronger mediating effects were obtained overall for study time versus strategy use measures of task effort, and more overall variance in recall scores was explained in the path models for older (e.g., $R^2 = .60$ for study time mediation model) than for younger (e.g., $R^2 = .25$ for study time model) adults. Finally, Berry et al. (1998) found differential effects of MSE on recall across domains: MSE was significantly related to word recall but not text recall in a sample of 156 adults between the ages of 17 and 86 years. For word recall (see Figure 4.5), MSE and memory ability (Wechsler Memory Scale—Revised [WMS-R]) predicted performance scores initially, but in the final equation with task study time and self-reported strategies partialled, MSE became nonsignificant, suggesting that it operates through task-engagement variables (study time and strategy use).

Other process-oriented MSE research includes the "upgrading effect," wherein correlations between predictions and performance are higher following task experience than those calculated on pretest prediction data (Hertzog et al., 1990b; Hertzog, Saylor, Fleece, & Dixon, 1994; West et al., 1996). These data revive arguments found in earlier research literature that self-efficacy beliefs are not antecedent to but, rather, are consequent to performance outcomes (Lachman & Jelalian, 1984; Lachman & Leff, 1989; Luszcz & Hinton, 1995). The positive effects of task experience on MSE ratings are not inconsistent with self-efficacy theory. Self-efficacy judgments are formed from several sources, including immediate and distal past performance experiences and trials (see Bandura, 1997). It is critical to remember, however, that self-efficacy is not simply a dispositional reflection of past mastery: It is situationally determined and has its greatest impact for tasks that are overly challenging, anxiety provoking, and *unfamiliar.* Strict empirical tests of this theoretical claim must be made in order to answer the chicken–egg question that won't go away: Does self-efficacy predict performance or does performance predict self-efficacy? This question is simplistic and its answer is yes. The direction of causality depends on the situation, the person, and the task, as well as the time frame. The temporal patterning of efficacy-performance-efficacy relationships in short-term (multiple trials within one test session) and long-term (longitudinal analyses of change data) research designs warrants further study. It is encumbent on

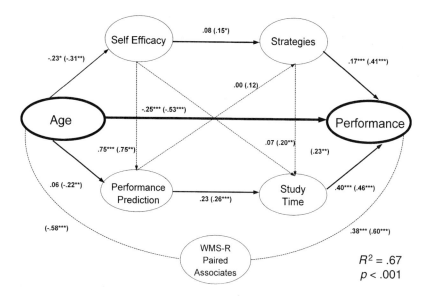

FIGURE 4.5   Path analysis model of age, self-efficacy, ability, task-engagement, and word recall. WMS-R = Wechsler Memory Scale—Revised.

MSE researchers to clearly specify when MSE is a cause and when it is an effect of memory ability and performance.

To my knowledge, research on physiological task arousal during MSE-performance trials has not been conducted. Questionnaire measures of anxiety yield mixed results (Davidson, Dixon, & Hultsch, 1991; Drew & Berry, 1996; Hertzog et al., 1990b). Davidson et al. found that state and trait anxiety predict memory performance, and Hertzog et al. reported significant correlations between metamemorial trait anxiety and MSE. Drew and Berry found that both MSE and a state measure of anxiety correlated significantly with word recall but that metamemorial trait anxiety and generalized trait anxiety did not. In a hierarchical regression analysis that predicted word recall from age, MSE, and state and trait measures of general anxiety and memory-specific anxiety, only age (age range, 53–88 years) and MSE significantly predicted word-recall performance at the final step in the regression. Although it is tempting to suggest from these results that age and MSE effects on performance were mediated by anxiety, the statistical power of this study was limited by a small sample size (N = 61). Clearly, questionnaire measures of anxiety and mood are important sources of data, but this line of research would be more informative if physiological measures of anxiety (e.g., skin conductance, heart rate) were collected concurrently with multiple measures of state and trait anxiety, general and specific memory anxiety, MSE, and memory performance throughout an entire testing session. Although enactive experiences are the strongest sources of efficacy information (Bandura, 1997), the anxiety and arousal that accompany each masterful or failure experience may become coregistered or encoded with the outcome itself, becoming transformed into a multiplicative source of efficacy information.

In summary, solid headway has been made in measuring age differences in MSE and in documenting the effects of MSE on memory-related behaviors, including effort and strategy use, but particularly memory performance. The next section examines the potential of social cognition research methods for moving the field of MSE research even farther ahead.

SOCIAL COGNITION AS A CONTEXT FOR MEMORY SELF-EFFICACY RESEARCH

Self-efficacy theory (Bandura, 1977; 1986; 1997) squarely places the individual in his or her social milieu, yet empirical tests of MSE and aging (Berry et al., 1989; Gardiner et al., 1997; Hertzog et al., 1990b; Hertzog et al., 1994; Luszcz & Hinton, 1995; Rebok & Balcerak, 1989; West & Berry, 1994; West et al., 1996) have extracted the individual from the social and instead examined the contents in the head (and, to be fair, various task and timing characteristics). This practice has shortchanged the field by neglecting the *social processes* inherent in self-efficacy judgments, behavior, and outcomes. Moreover, most conceptions of MSE are devoid of personality structure, process, and content. This is a mistake, given what is known about personality–situation interactions as determinants of behavior (e.g., Cervone, 1997; Funder & Ozer, 1983; Mischel & Shoda, 1995; Shoda, Mischel, & Wright, 1993; Thorne, 1987). Social cognitive psychologists have implored us to put the person back in (the study of) behavior (Carlson, 1984). The resurgent interest in people in context and "ordinary personology" (Gilbert, 1998) provides a timely framework for reconsidering the social and personal nature of memory functioning and self-efficacy in adulthood and old age.

Social cognitive approaches to studying persons offer compelling suggestions regarding the return of MSE to its social context. Generally speaking, social cognition is how we make sense of self and others (Fiske & Taylor, 1991; see also Blanchard-Fields & Hess, Chapter 1, this volume). MSE judgments involve "making sense of" one's own changing and dynamic memory system and integrating this with social information regarding age-normative memory decline. Social cognitive research emphasizes mentalistic explanations, process analyses, and the cross-fertilization of cognitive and social psychological methodologies (Fiske & Taylor, 1991). These areas provide some connections between MSE and the broader field of social cognition.

Mentalistic explanations of behavior include two cognitive constructs—*attributions* and *schemas*—that have dominated the field of social psychology in the twentieth century (Heider, 1958; Kelley & Michela, 1980; Weiner, 1985). The explanations that people give for their own and others' behavior are cognitive representations that allow them to make sense of cause-effect-cause sequences of behavior. In the memory domain, one might offer different explanations for self-forgetting ("I'm tired") versus other-forgetting ("She's slipping"). Causal attributions for forgetting (or remembering) vary by age and subject matter (Erber, Szuchman, & Rothberg, 1990), and depend on the individual's level of interest and skill (Blanchard-Fields, 1996).

Schemas are cognitive constructs that serve to organize and filter information (Alba & Hasher, 1983; Hastie, 1981; Markus, 1977). Implicit theories and stereotypes of aging constitute schemas for "old age" that can affect whether, how, and what kind of information is processed (Hummert, 1990, 1993; Levy, 1996; Levy & Langer, 1994; McDonald-Miszczak, Hertzog, & Hultsch, 1995; McFarland, Ross, & Giltrow, 1992). Positive or negative views of aging should have an impact on memory and MSE judgments—information about memory functioning should be processed in a manner consistent with schemas about self and others.

Social cognitive research also emphasizes process analyses. In MSE terms, appraisal of the demands of a memory task will be influenced by the individual's analysis of relevant information, as well as by the feedback received from coappraisers of the situation. For example, if a woman claims she cannot remember directions to a destination, her ability to retrieve or reconstruct that information will depend on whether she receives encouragement and tips from a sympathetic other or is admonished and criticized for her faulty memory. Analysis of the socially reciprocal processes that produce the outcome (destination remembered or not) in this example give insight into the facilitative and inhibitory functions of social feedback.

Finally, social cognitive research has adopted methodologies from cognitive and social psychology that could be applied fruitfully in MSE research. For example, reaction time and latency data are used routinely to measure the structure, contents, and processing outcomes of self-schems (e.g., Fekken & Holden, 1992; Mueller, Wonderlich, & Dugan, 1986; Neubauer & Malle, 1997; Siem, 1996; Strube, Berry, Lott, et al., 1986). These methods could be used to analyze the impact of memory self-schemas, aging self-schemas, and competency self-schemas on MSE (see Cavanaugh et al., 1998).

MEMORY SELF-EFFICACY AS A SOCIAL CONSTRUCT

The processes, contents, and expressions of memory are often social in nature. This notion was formalized by Bartlett (1932) who, after conducting a series of experimental social psychological studies on memory, claimed that "social organisation gives a persistent framework into which all detailed recall must fit, and it very powerfully influences both the manner and matter of recall" (p. 296). Dixon, Gagnon, & Crow (1998) have argued persuasively for the view that much of our cognitive activity is collaborative and occurs in social dyads (e.g., married couples), and that this characteristic has special relevance for cognitive aging. If memory is to be taken as a socially constructed phenomenon, then when it serves as the referent for reflection and evaluation, as in the case of self-efficacy judgments and ruminations about memory phenomena, MSE *by definition* must be a social construction.

How is memory self-efficacy a *social* process? How is social information weighted differentially by individuals to yield self-efficacy judgments? The social contexts (groups, individuals, interpersonal relationships) that more or less shape the experience and storage of self-relevant events will depend on the goals and dispositions of the individual. Carlson (1980) showed that the bipolar personality dimensions of introversion/extraversion and thinking/feeling (from Jungian type theory) influence the affective tone and the interpersonal distance attached to remembered social interactions. In other work, "introverted-thinking" women had better digit span recall than did "extraverted-feeling" women who performed at a superior level on a face memory task (Carlson & Levy, 1973). Fong and Markus (1982) found that extravert and introvert schematics were more likely to choose schema-consistent questions from a list of extraverted, introverted, and neutral questions for the purpose of interviewing another person. These studies suggest that personality dimensions of "sociability" influence the content of memory recall, as well as the attentional focus to both self and other personality information that bears on social interactions (e.g., an interview with a stranger). In a related vein, Cohen and Ebbesen (1979) described the effects of goals and schema activation on person perception. Subjects were asked to either "form an impression" or to "describe the details" of the same target person. Those in the former group recalled larger units from the stream of behavior (displayed by the target) than did the latter group. This research demonstrates that the goals of the perceiver influence attention to different dimensions of a person/situation (i.e., part vs whole) with consequences for the nature and content of memory retrieval.

In a similar manner, personality probably interacts with the sources of information that yield MSE judgments. For those who look routinely to others as sounding boards for advice, feedback, and direction, information from the social realm will be processed differently (i.e., given more weight) than for those who are more inner-directed and self-reliant. Introspective individuals may engage more naturally and comfortably in temporal-comparative self-evaluations than in social-comparative evaluations. Classic social comparison theory (Festinger, 1954) states that individuals derive the most meaningful data for self-evaluations from similar others. Later research (Gastorf & Suls, 1978) refined this position by providing empirical support for the hypothesis that individuals compare themselves to similar others only to the extent that those others possess traits relevant to task performance. A review of reattribution training research (Forsterling, 1985) indicates that higher perceived similarity with models has a greater impact on receptivity to modeling information (e.g., attributions of lack of effort for failure).

MEMORY SELF-EFFICACY AS
A DEVELOPMENTAL CONSTRUCT

MSE has particular relevance for midlife and older adults whose memory abilities may not be as good as they were in younger adulthood. When memory failures begin to occur repeatedly in the same situation, for the same task; when failures begin to have a familiar feeling; when they annoy, constrain, fluster, or worry us, they become data that can no longer be explained away as unsystematic error variance or noise but rather as possibly reliable (i.e., stable) indicators of a system in flux. This argument maps well onto a self-efficacy analytical template, but MSE analyses are not simply analyses of increasing, more regular failures of the operating system and its regulation. With age and development come self-knowledge and awareness, such that one selects those domains and contexts for which the behavioral repertoire is well suited—where one can thrive and perform capably and competently (Baltes, Dittman-Kohli, & Dixon, 1984; Carstensen, 1992; Hoyer & Rybash, 1994; Rybash, Hoyer, & Roodin, 1986). A social cognitive analysis of memory development and aging must account for negative and positive developmental changes as well as selection and compensation processes (Staudinger, Marsiske, & Baltes, 1993) as the organism experiences shifting operations and capacities in adulthood. The memory domains for which MSE explanations are most relevant and robust need to be identified: There may be universal domains (e.g., memory for proper nouns) that invoke MSE appraisals in all individuals at some point in development. Moreover, a differential model that identifies problematic memory domains at both intraindividual and interindividual levels would complement the universal approach, for a more complete developmental model of MSE appraisal.

MEMORY SELF-EFFICACY AS
A PERSONALITY CONSTRUCT

In his classic treatise on the self as "the proprium," Allport (1955) made a distinction between facts about the self versus matters of importance to the self. He argued that habitual modes of behavior (or facts about the self) do not surface as matters of importance unless they are disrupted. At that time (i.e., when they become threatened as no longer automatically "self"), they become consciously important and attended to. Allport gives as example the use of one's native language as an habitual, unconscious part of the self that if suddenly threatened by "some foreign invader ... who forbid us to use our native language" (p. 40) would become a central, conscious, and utterly important aspect of the self. By analogy, this reasoning can be applied to the operation of MSE, especially when placed in a developmental framework. Specifically, MSE may lie relatively dormant as part of the proprium and personality during young adulthood, but if or when memory functioning becomes unreliable—less "habitual"—and thereby threatened, this may provoke self-efficacy appraisals of the system, and the seeds of "memory as a matter of importance" are sown. At times, MSE is a conscious process as the self sizes up a situation and its ability to tackle it, but at other times, MSE operates with less awareness, as in situations in which the task is perceived as less challenging. In sum, MSE may operate on a continuum of consciousness, both over time (i.e., appearing as a more conscious part of the self in middle adulthood) and between domains of memory ability (i.e., some parts of memory functioning may never falter over a lifetime, remaining relatively "unconscious").

MEMORY SELF-EFFICACY ROOTS IN SOCIAL AND TEMPORAL COMPARISON PROCESSES

A social cognitive perspective on MSE encompasses the bidirectional flow of information between context and self over time. The self is organizer, reactor, and writer of its experience. This self takes into account the temporal components of memory functioning and the social milieu in which it operates, asking comparative questions such as "How am I doing relative to others?" and "How am I doing relative to my former (younger) self?" Suls and Mullen (1982) have argued that older adults may be more likely to engage in temporal than social comparisons (cf. Heckhausen & Krueger, 1993). McFarland et al. (1992) have issued a call for empirical analyses of temporal versus social reference points for older adults' characterizations of self. These questions and issues reflect the intraindividual and interindividual contexts of life-span development (Baltes, 1987). This line of self-reflective questioning probably also includes musings (and worries) about the future and possible selves (Baltes & Carstensen, 1991; Markus & Nurius, 1986) couched in goal-directed language such as "Where do I want (and not want) to be and how will I get there?" These past, present, and future characterizations of self-as-rememberer surely comprise components of a memory self-efficacy schema.

SUMMARY

A social cognitive MSE framework could integrate findings from developmental, personality, and sociotemporal comparison research in order to assess systematically the degree to which perceivers identify with models and others. Such a paradigm would entail detailed analyses of self, model, task, and situation characteristics, from the perspective of the dispositions, goals, standards, and needs of the self in a memory problem domain. Task demands should be analyzed in concert with an inventory of the skills of the individual who is to perform the task. Is there a match between task requirements and competencies of the individual? Do new skills need to be learned? To what features of a model does an individual attend: motivation? ability? skills? effort? age? attitude? Which models are available to the individual and which are rated as most important, instructive, and useful to him or her? Does a "previous" self at a younger age serve as a model, as in temporal comparisons? Are self-standards of performance realistic or unrealistic, given present levels of ability and opportunity? Is the social environment supportive or prohibitive toward attaining memory goals (Welch & West, 1995)? Self-schema research methods could be applied to answer these questions. For example, research participants could be instructed to respond to a variety of hypothetical models and/or real models in real situations using Like Me/Not Like Me endorsement rating and reaction time procedures (Markus, 1977; Markus, Crane, Bernstein, & Siladi, 1982; Strube et al., 1986). These data would assess the degree to which perceivers identify with and learn from others. Moreover, various "prototypes" of aging (ranging from competent/positive to incompetent/negative) could be developed and assessed with reaction-time endorsements to determine the extent to which subjects hold stereotypic views of aging of themselves. This approach is highly compatible with the modelling (vicarious observation) source of efficacy information.

FUTURE RESEARCH DIRECTIONS

Memory self-efficacy (MSE) has been investigated primarily among adults from the perspective of normative memory functioning, although little is known about the initial appearance of MSE concerns in midlife, or even younger adulthood, and its developmental course in later adulthood. This knowledge gap suggests that careful longitudinal, cross-sectional, and case history investigations of the emergence, evolution, and impact of memory concerns and reappraisals during adult development are needed to move the field forward. These methodological efforts will be most productive if they are driven by theory. MSE theory and methodology provide a good orienting framework for this goal, especially when integrated with compatible approaches from the fields of social cognition and life-span development.

Empirical studies of MSE have been rather mentalistic in nature and have focused on the internal process of judgments of efficaciousness from which behavioral action flows (Berry, 1987; Hertzog et al., 1990b; West & Berry, 1994). The antecedent and on-line processes comprising self-efficacy judgments are much more complex than what is apparent in single-occasion self-reports of efficacy given before or after memory tests in psychologists' laboratories. These MSE judgments are constructed contemporaneously in response to a demand on memory and they reflect current feelings of efficacy. What remains latent in these assessments is the schematic representation of the self-as-rememberer, constructed over years of experiences with a memory system used in myriad social, achievement, personal, and occupational settings. Surely this memory self-schema is activated when situational appraisals of memory ability are called for and drives "in-the-moment" self-efficacy judgments. The social-situational sources of MSE must be incorporated into a more holistic research approach to MSE.

Just as we accept the notion that memory is a constructive process (Bruner, 1994; Gergen, 1994; cf. Brewer, 1988), so must we consider MSE. In theory, MSE, like memory proper (cf. Alba & Hasher, 1983), is schematically based in its architecture, materials, and functionality. Although this claim awaits empirical test, a conceptual argument could be made for recasting the classic sources and effects of self-efficacy judgments as schematically structured and driven. The sources, in particular, may be construed as filters that enable the processing of efficacy-relevant information. The premise that MSE is active and dynamic—driven by stored experience (past), immediate task context (present), and the goals and hopes of the individual (future)—is highly amenable to verification or disconfirmation via empirical analyses.

Insights regarding the verbal persuasion source of self-efficacy may be found in the anxious concerns of older adults about quotidia-forgetting as an incipient signpost of Alzheimer's disease (Cutler & Hodgson, 1996). Methods that systematically classify such concerns and their sources could inform MSE research. For example, the various sources of social feedback could be cast as a hierarchy of persons who provide verbal feedback to individuals about their memory functioning. The input of close peers, casual acquaintances, spouses/partners, siblings, offspring, doctors, other professionals, etc., are potentially salient sources of memory evaluation and should be examined closely, to test the validity of this component of self-efficacy theory. The verbal persuasion source of self-efficacy may be selected and weighted differentially, depending on the predisposition of the perceiver toward a particular persuader/dissuader. Different individuals will have different verbal feedback hierarchies.

Systematic, process-oriented studies of MSE that employ multimethod/multimeasure research designs that include developmental, personality, and social variables are called for. Most MSE research has focused on measurement issues to the exclusion of process issues. Research on the social, interpersonal, and intrapersonal sources of MSE is needed, together with the more cognitive, self-regulatory, and schema-driven processing effects that connect MSE judgments to memory-performance outcomes. The MSE-relevant attributions that people make for long-term memory changes (e.g., temporal comparisons) and contemporaneous memory functioning (e.g., "post-test" performance attributions in the lab and causal explanations/excuses in everyday life) should be investigated.

Studies of intraindividual changes in MSE are virtually nonexistent. Research on individuals whose MSE holds steady through adulthood versus those whose MSE becomes highly sensitive and reactive to even benign memory lapses would yield important insights. Such research would identify those individuals for whom memory functioning is intact and nonthreatening, and in turn, these individuals could be followed closely using case study methods in order to develop prototypes of "sucessful memory aging." This knowledge could serve as the basis for modeling interventions designed to allay serious concerns and negative affect attached to memory functioning among midlife and older adults. Questions regarding individual performance/competence standards and goals, versus those regarding normative memory functioning imposed by memory researchers, should be explored. The person who states that "I want to be the best in my social group—I pride myself on my memory" is suggesting a different sort of memory self-schema than one who simply wants to maintain his or her own status quo regarding memory abilities.

A "PERSONS IN PLACES IN PROCESS" APPROACH TO MEMORY SELF-EFFICACY

MSE researchers might take their cue from Gilbert's (1998) argument to return to the study of "the ordinary" in people's lives. Do we really believe that when people are confronted with a memory-demanding task (e.g., retrieving a word, name, place, location, object, thought) and fail, they pause at the moment of task presentation and assess their abilities? (No.) Just how aware of self- and task-appraisal states are they? Is it important that they be aware? How conscious or unconscious are these processes? Are memory tasks really as "threatening" as self-efficacy purists would claim? When people fail to remember—when they forget—their reaction is probably more benign and they probably do *not* make a self-efficacy judgment per se (e.g., "This task would require all of my concentration with no distractions for the next 10 minutes for me to get it right and to be happy with my performance"). Rather, their reaction is probably more diffusely affective in nature, and possibly reflective as well.

CONCLUSIONS

To realize the full potential of MSE as an important adult developmental and cognitive aging research construct, MSE researchers need to move beyond their emphases on measurement and modeling. Questions about people in places in process—not methodology—should drive the research. It seems the most promising questions would center on the individual's sense of self immersed in his or her social world (Reed, 1994) and the meaning that memory in social relationships imparts (Gergen, 1994).

ACKNOWLEDGMENTS

Support for this chapter and the empirical work reported herein was provided in part by National Institute on Aging grant (NIA) R01 AG13508-02. I thank John Cavanaugh, Christopher Hertzog, and Robin West for being sources of intellectual inspiration for this chapter.

REFERENCES

Alba, J., & Hasher, L. (1983). Is memory schematic? *Psychological Bulletin, 93,* 203–231.
Allport, G. W. (1955). *Becoming* (pp. 36–56). New Haven, CT: Yale University Press.
Baltes, P. B. (1987). Theoretical propositions of life-span developmental psychology: On the dynamics between growth and decline. *Developmental Psychology, 23,* 611–626.
Baltes, M. M., & Carstensen, L. L. (1991). "Possible selves across the life span": Comment. *Human Development, 34,* 256–260.

Baltes, P. B., Dittman-Kohli, F., & Dixon, R. A. (1984). New perspectives on the development of intelligence in adulthood: Toward a dual-process conception and a model of selective optimization with compensation. In P. B. Baltes & O. G. Brim (Eds.), *Life-span development and behavior* (vol. 6, pp. 33–76). New York, NY: Academic Press.

Bandura, A. (1977). Self-efficacy: Toward a unifying theory of behavior change. *Psychological Review, 84,* 191–215.

Bandura, A. (1986). *Social foundations of thought and action: A social cognitive theory.* Englewood Cliffs, NJ: Prentice-Hall.

Bandura, A. (1997). *Self-efficacy: The exercise of control.* New York: W. H. Freeman

Bandura, A., Adams, N. E., Hardy, A. B., & Howells, G. N. (1980). Tests of the generality of self-efficacy theory. *Cognitive Therapy and Research, 4,* 39–66.

Bandura, A., & Jourden, F. J. (1991). Self-regulatory mechanisms governing the impact of social comparison on complex decision making. *Journal of Personality and Social Psychology, 60,* 941–951.

Bandura, A., Reese, L., & Adams, N. E. (1982). Microanalysis of action and fear arousal as a function of differential levels of perceived self-efficacy. *Journal of Personality and Social Psychology, 43,* 5–21.

Bandura, A., & Wood, R. (1989). Effect of perceived controllability and performance standards on self-regulation of complex decision making. *Journal of Personality and Social Psychology, 56,* 805–814.

Bartlett, F. C. (1932). *Remembering: A study in experimental and social psychology.* New York: Cambridge University Press.

Berry, J. M. (1987, August). *A self-efficacy model of memory performance.* Paper presented at the annual American Psychological Association meeting, New York.

Berry, J. M. (1989). Cognitive efficacy across the lifespan: An introduction to the special series. *Developmental Psychology, 25,* 683–686.

Berry, J., Acosta, M., Baldi, R., Burrell, C., & Rotondi, J. (1994, July). *Age differences in memory processing, outcome, and appraisal: A self-efficacy analysis.* paper presented at the Third Practical Aspects of Memory Conference, University of Maryland, College Park, MD.

Berry, J. M., Geiger, H., Visocan, K., & Siebert, J. (1987, November). *Age differences on subjective measures of memory.* Paper presented at the annual Gerontological Society of America meeting, Washington, D.C.

Berry, J., Thompson, J., Bryant, D., Hambrick, J., & Drew, M. (1998, April). *Age- and domain-specific effects of memory self-efficacy on word and text recall performance.* Paper presented at the seventh Cognitive Aging Conference, Atlanta, GA.

Berry, J. M., & West, R. L. (1993). Cognitive self-efficacy in relation to personal mastery and goal setting across the life span. *International Journal of Behavioral Development, 16,* 351–379.

Berry, J. M., West, R. L., & Cavanaugh, J. C. (1996, April). *Construct validity analyses of memory self-efficacy in adulthood.* Paper presented at the Sixth Cognitive Aging Conference, Atlanta, GA.

Berry, J. M., West, R. L., & Dennehy, D. (1989). Reliability and validity of the Memory Self-Efficacy Questionnaire (MSEQ). *Developmental Psychology, 25,* 701–713.

Berry, J. M., West, R., & Powlishta, K. K. (1986, November). *Self-efficacy and performance differences on laboratory and everyday memory tasks.* Paper presented at the annual Gerontological Society of America meeting, Chicago.

Betz, N. E., & Hackett, G. (1986). Applications of self-efficacy theory to understanding career choice behavior. *Journal of Social and Clinical Psychology, 4,* 279–289.

Blanchard-Fields, F. (1996). Causal attributions across the adult life span: The influence of social schemas, life context, and domain specificity [Special issue]. *Applied Cognitive Psychology, 10,* S137–S146.

Bouffard-Bouchard, T. (1990). Influence of self-efficacy on performance in a cognitive task. *Journal of Social Psychology, 130,* 353–363.

Brewer, W. F. (1988). Memory for randomly sampled autobiographical events. In U. Neisser & E. Winograd (Eds.), *Remembering reconsidered: Ecological and traditional approaches to the study of memory* (pp. 21–90). New York: Cambridge University Press.

Bruner, J. (1994). The "remembered" self. In U. Neisser and R. Fivush (Eds.), *The remembering self: Construction and accuracy in the self-narrative* (pp. 41–54). Cambridge, MA: Cambridge University Press.

Carlson, R. (1984). What's social about social psychology? Where's the person in personality research? *Journal of Personality and Social Psychology, 47,* 1304–1309.

Carlson, R. (1980). Studies of Jungian typology: II. Representations of the personal world. *Journal of Personality and Social Psychology, 38,* 801–810.

Carlson, R., & Levy, N. (1973). Studies of Jungian typology: I. Memory, social perception, and social action. *Journal of Personality, 41,* 559–576.

Carstensen, L. L. (1992). Selectivity theory: Social activity in life-span context. *Annual Review of Gerontology and Geriatrics, 11,* 195–217.

Cavanaugh, J. C., Feldman, J. M., & Hertzog, C. (1998). Memory beliefs as social cognition: A reconceptualization of what memory questionnaires assess. *Review of General Psychology, 2,* 48–65.

Cavanaugh, J. C., & Green, E. E. (1990). I believe, therefore I can: Self-efficacy beliefs in memory aging. In E. A. Lovelace (Ed.), *Aging and cognition: Mental processes, self-awareness, and interventions. Advances in psychology, 72,* 189–230. Amsterdam, North Holland: Elsevier Science Publishers.

Cavanaugh, J. C., Morton, K. R., & Tilse, C. S. (1989). A self-evaluation framework for understanding everyday memory aging. In J. D. Sinnott (Ed.), *Everyday problem solving: Theory and applications.* New York: Praeger.

Cavanaugh, J. C., & Poon, L. W. (1989). Metamemorial predictors of memory performance in young and older adults. *Psychology and Aging, 4,* 365–368.

Cervone, D. (1997). Social-cognitive mechanisms and personality coherence: Self-knowledge, situational beliefs, and cross-situational coherence in perceived self-efficacy. *Psychological Science, 9,* 43–50.

Cervone, D., & Peake, P. K. (1986). Anchoring, efficacy, and action: The influence of judgmental heuristics on self-efficacy judgments and behavior. *Journal of Personality and Social Psychology, 50,* 492–501.

Cohen, C. E., & Ebbesen, E. B. (1979). Observational goals and schema activation: A theoretical framework for behavior perception. *Journal of Experimental Social Psychology, 15,* 305–329.

Cutler, S. J., & Hodgson, L. G. (1996). Anticipatory dementia: A link between memory appraisals and concerns about developing Alzheimer's disease. *The Gerontologist, 36,* 657–664.

Davidson, H. A., Dixon, R. A., & Hultsch, D. F. (1991). Memory anxiety and memory performance in adulthood. *Applied Cognitive Psychology, 5,* 423–433.

Dixon, R. A., Gagnon, L. M., & Crow, C. B. (1998). Collaborative memory accuracy and distortion: Performance and beliefs. In M. J. Intons-Peterson & D. Best (Eds.), *Memory distortions and their prevention* (pp. 63–88). Mahwah, NJ: Lawrence Erlbaum Associates.

Dixon, R. A., Hertzog, C., & Hultsch, D. F. (1986). The multiple relationships among Metamemory in Adulthood (MIA) scales and cognitive abilities in adulthood. *Human Learning, 5,* 156–177.

Dixon, R. A., & Hultsch, D. F. (1983a). Structure and development of metamemory in adulthood. *Journal of Gerontology, 38,* 689–694.

Dixon, R. A., & Hultsch, D. F. (1983b). Metamemory and memory for text relationships in adulthood: A cross-validation study. *Journal of Gerontology, 38,* 689–694.

Dixon, R. A., Hultsch, D. F., & Hertzog, C. (1988). The Metamemory in Adulthood (MIA) questionnaire. *Psychopharmacology Bulletin, 24,* 671–688.

Drew, M. R., & Berry, J. M. (1996, November). *Strategy, affect, and self-efficacy predict memory performance in older adults.* Paper presented at the 49th annual meeting of the Gerontological Society of America, Washington, D. C.

Erber, J. T., Szuchman, L. T., & Rothberg, S. T. (1990). Age, gender, and individual differences in memory failure appraisal. *Psychology and Aging, 5,* 600–603.

Fekken, G. C., & Holden, R. R. (1992). Response latency evidence for viewing personality traits as schema indicators. *Journal of Research in Personality, 26,* 103–120.

Festinger, L. A. (1954). A theory of social comparison processes. *Human Relations, 7,* 117–140.

Fiske, S. T., & Taylor, S. E. (1991). *Social cognition* (2nd ed.). New York: McGraw-Hill.

Fong, G. T., & Markus, H. (1982). Self-schemas and judgments about others. *Social Cognition, 1,* 191–204.

Forsterling, F. (1985). Attributional retraining: A review. *Psychological Bulletin, 98,* 495–512.

Funder, D. C., & Ozer, D. J. (1983). Behavior as a function of the situation. *Journal of Personality and Social Psychology, 44,* 107–112.

Gardiner, M., Luszcz, M., & Bryan, J. (1997). The manipulation and measurement of task-specific memory self-efficacy in younger and older adults. *International Journal of Behavioral Development, 21,* 209–227.

Gastorf, J. W., Suls, J. (1978). Performance evaluation via social comparison: Performance similarity versus related-attribute similarity. *Social Psychology, 41,* 297–305.

Gergen, K. J. (1994). Mind, text, and society: Self-memory in social context. In U. Neisser and R. Fivush (Eds.), *The remembering self: Construction and accuracy in the self-narrative* (pp. 78–104). Cambridge, MA: Cambridge University Press.

Gilbert, D. T. (1998). Ordinary personology. In D. T. Gilbert, S. T. Fiske, & G. Lindzey (Eds.), *The handbook of social psychology* (4th ed., pp. 89–150). Boston: McGraw-Hill.

Gilewski, M. J., Zelinski, E. M., & Schaie, K. W. (1990). The memory functioning questionnaire for assessment of memory complaints in adulthood and old age. *Psychology and Aging, 5,* 482–490.

Hastie, R. (1981). Schematic principles on human memory. In T. E. Higgins, D. Herman, and M. P. Zanna (Eds.), *Social cognition: The Ontario symposium on personality and social psychology,* Vol. 1. Hillsdale, NJ: Lawrence Erlbaum Associates.

Heckhausen, J., & Krueger, J. (1993). Developmental expectations for the self and most other people: Age grading in three functions of social comparison. *Developmental Psychology, 29,* 539–548.

Heider, F. (1958). *The psychology of interpersonal relations.* New York: Wiley.

Hermann, D. J. (1982). Know thy memory: The use of questionnaires to assess and study memory. *Psychological Bulletin, 92,* 434–452.

Hertzog, C., & Dixon, R. A. (1994). Metacognitive development in adulthood and old age. In J. Metcalfe & A. P. Shimamura (Eds.), *Metacognition: Knowing about knowing* (pp. 227–251). Cambridge, MA: MIT Press.

Hertzog, C., Dixon, R. A., Hultsch, D. F. (1990a). Metamemory in adulthood: Differentiating knowledge, belief, and behavior. In T. M. Hess (Ed.), *Aging and cognition: Knowledge organization and utilization. Advances in psychology, 71,* 161–212. Amsterdam, North Holland: Elsevier Science Publishers.

Hertzog, C., Dixon, R. A., & Hultsch, D. F. (1990b). Relationships between metamemory, memory predictions, and memory task performance in adults. *Psychology and Aging, 5,* 215–227.

Hertzog, C., Dixon, R. A., Schulenberg, J., & Hultsch, D. F. (1987). On the differentiation of memory beliefs from memory knowledge: The factor structure of the Metamemory in Adulthood scale. *Experimental Aging Research, 13,* 101–107.

Hertzog, C., & Hultsch, D. F. (in press). Metacognition in adulthood and old age. In F. I. M. Craik & T. A. Salthouse (Eds.), *Handbook of aging and cognition, II.* Malwah, NJ: Lawrence Erlbaum Associates.

Hertzog, C., Hultsch, D. F., & Dixon, R. A. (1989). Evidence for the convergent validity of two self-report metamemory questionnaires. *Developmental Psychology, 25,* 687–700.

Hertzog, D., Saylor, L. O., Fleece, A. M., & Dixon, R. A. (1994). Metamemory and aging: Relations between predicted, actual and perceived memory task performance. *Aging and Cognition, 1,* ˙203–237.

Hoyer, W. J., & Rybash, J. M. (1994). Characterizing adult cognitive development. *Journal of Adult Development, 1,* 7–12.

Hultsch, D. F., Hertzog, C., & Dixon, R. A. (1987). Age differences in metamemory: Resolving the inconsistencies [Special issue: Aging and cognition]. *Canadian Journal of Psychology, 41,* 193–208.

Hultsch, D. F., Hertzog, C., Dixon, R. A., & Davidson, H. (1988). Memory self-knowledge and self-efficacy in the aged. In M. L. Howe & C. J. Brainerd (Eds.), *Cognitive development in adulthood: Progress in cognitive development research* (pp. 65–92). New York: Springer.

Hummert, M. L. (1990). Multiple stereotypes of elderly and young adults: A comparison of structure and evaluations. *Psychology and Aging, 5,* 182–193.

Hummert, M. L. (1993). Age and typicality judgments of stereotypes of the elderly: Perceptions of elderly versus young adults. *International Journal of Aging and Human Development, 37,* 217–226.

Kelley, H. H., & Michela, J. L. (1980). Attribution theory and research. *Annual Review of Psychology, 31,* 457–501.

Lachman, M. E., & Jelalian, E. (1984). Self-efficacy and attributions for intellectual performance in young and elderly adults. *Journal of Gerontology, 39,* 577–582.

Lachman, M. E., & Leff, R. (1989). Perceived control and intellectual functioning in the elderly: A 5-year longitudinal study. *Developmental Psychology, 25,* 722–728.

Lachman, M. E., Weaver, S. L., Bandura, M., & Elliott, E. (1995). Assessing memory control beliefs: The Memory Controllability Inventory. *Aging and Cognition, 2,* 67–84.

Levy, B. (1996). Improving memory in old age through implicit self-stereotyping. *Journal of Personality and Social Psychology, 71,* 1092–1107.

Levy, B., & Langer, E. (1994). Aging free from negative stereotypes: Successful memory in China and among the American deaf. *Journal of Personality and Social Psychology, 66,* 989–997.

Light, L. L. (1991). Memory and aging: Four hypotheses in search of data. *Annual Review of Psychology, 42,* 333–376.

Locke, E. A., & Latham, G. P. (1990). *A theory of goal setting and task performance.* Englewood Cliffs, NJ: Prentice-Hall.

Luszcz, M., & Hinton, M. (1995). Domain- and task-specific beliefs about memory in adulthood: A microgenetic approach. [Special issue: Cognitive development]. *Australian Journal of Psychology, 47,* 54–59.

Markus, H. (1977). Self-schemata and processing information about the self. *Journal of Personality and Social Psychology, 35,* 63–78.

Markus, H., Crane, M., Bernstein, S., & Siladi, M. (1982). Self-schemas and gender. *Journal of Personality and Social Psychology, 42,* 38–50.

Markus, H., & Nurius, P. (1986). Possible selves. *American Psychologist, 41,* 954–969.

Mathieu, J. E., & Button, S. B. (1992). An examination of the relative impact of normative information and self-efficacy on personal goals and performance over time. *Journal of Applied Social Psychology, 22,* 1758–1775.

McDonald-Miszczak, L., Hertzog, C., & Hultsch, D. F. (1995). Stability and accuracy of metamemory in adulthood and aging: A longitudinal analysis. *Psychology and Aging, 10,* 553–564.

McFarland, C., Ross, M., & Giltrow, M. (1992). Biased recollections in older adults: The role of implicit theories of aging. *Journal of Personality and Social Psychology, 62,* 837–850.

Mischel, W., & Shoda, Y. (1995). A cognitive-affective system theory of personality: Reconceptualizing situations, dispositions, dynamics, and invariance in personality structure. *Psychological Review, 102,* 246–268.

Mueller, J. H., Wonderlich, S., & Dugan, K. (1986). Self-referent processing of age-specific material. *Psychology and Aging, 1,* 293–299.

Neubauer, A. C., & Malle, B. F. (1997). Questionnaire response latencies: Implications for personality assessment and self-schema theory. *European Journal of Psychological Assessment, 13,* 109–117.

Pajares, M., & Miller, D. (1995). Mathematics self-efficacy and mathematics performances: The need for specificity of assessment. *Journal of Counseling Psychology, 42,* 190–198.

Rebok, G. W., & Balcerak, L. W. (1989). Memory self-efficacy and performance differences in young and old adults: The effect of mnemonic training. *Developmental Psychology, 25,* 714–721.

Reed, E. S. (1994). Perception is to self as memory is to selves. In U. Neisser and R. Fivush (Eds.), *The remembering self: Construction and accuracy in the self-narrative* (pp. 278–292). New York: Cambridge University Press.

Ryan, E. B., & See, S. K. (1993). Age-based beliefs about memory changes for self and others across adulthood. *Journals of Gerontology, 48,* P199–P201.

Rybash, J. M., Hoyer, W. J., & Roodin, P. A. (1986). *Adult cognition and aging: Developmental changes in processing, knowing, and thinking.* New York: Pergamon Press.

Salthouse, T. A. (1991). *Theoretical perspectives on cognitive aging.* Hillsdale, NJ: Lawrence Erlbaum Associates.

Salthouse, T. A. (1993). Speed mediation of adult age differences in cognition. *Developmental Psychology, 29,* 722–738.

Sanna, L. J., & Pusecker, P. A. (1994). Self-efficacy, valence of self-evaluation, and performance. *Personality and Social Psychology Bulletin, 20,* 82–92.

Schunk, D. H., & Rice, J. M. (1987). Enhancing comprehension skill and self-efficacy with strategy value information. *Journal of Reading Behavior, 19,* 285–302.

Shoda, Y., Mischel, W. & Wright, J. C. (1993). The role of situational demands and cognitive competencies in behavior organization and personality coherence. *Journal of Personality and Social Psychology, 65,* 1023–1035.

Siem, F. M. (1996). The use of response latencies to enhance self-report personality measures. *Military Psychology, 8,* 15–27.

Staudinger, U. M., Marsiske, M., & Baltes, P. B. (1993). Resilience and levels of reserve capacity in later adulthood: Perspectives from life-span theory [Special issue: Milestones in the development of resilience]. *Development and Psychopathology, 5,* 541–566.

Strube, M. J., Berry, J. M., Lott, C. L., Fogelman, R., Steinhardt, G., Moergen, S., & Davison, L. (1986). Self-schematic representation of Type A and B behavior patterns. *Journal of Personality and Social Psychology, 51,* 170–180.

Suls, J., & Mullen, B. (1982). From the cradle to the grave: Comparison and self-evaluation across the life-span. In J. Suls (Ed.), *Psychological perspectives on the self* (pp. 97–125). Hillsdale, NJ: Lawrence Erlbaum Associates.

Thorne, A. (1987). The press of personality: A study of conversations between introverts and extraverts. *Journal of Personality and Social Psychology, 53,* 718–726.

Verhaeghen, P., Marcoen, A., & Goossens, L. (1993). Facts and fiction about memory aging: A quantitative integration of research findings. *Journal of Gerontology, 48,* P157–P171.

Weiner, B. (1985). An attributional theory of achievement motivation and emotion. *Psychological Review, 92,* 548–573.

Welch, D. C., & West, R. L. (1995). Self-efficacy and mastery: Its application to issues of environmental control, cognition, and aging. *Developmental Review, 15,* 150–171.

West, R. L., & Berry, J. M. (1994). Age declines in memory self-efficacy: General or limited to particular tasks and measures? In J. D. Sinnott (Ed.), *Interdisciplinary handbook of adult lifespan learning.* Westport, CT: Greenwood.

West, R. L., Dennehy-Basile, D., & Norris, M. P. (1996). Memory self-evaluation: The effects of age and experience. *Aging, Neuropsychology, and Cognition, 3,* 67–83.

Zelinski, E. M., Gilewski, M. J., & Anthony-Bergstone, C. R. (1990). The Memory Functioning questionnaire: Concurrent validity with memory performance and self-reported memory failures. *Psychology and Aging, 5,* 388–399.

Zimmerman, B. J., & Bandura, A. (1994). Impact of self-regulatory influences on writing course attainment. *American Educational Research Journal, 31,* 845–862.

5

POSSIBLE SELVES IN ADULTHOOD

INCORPORATING TELEONOMIC RELEVANCE INTO STUDIES OF THE SELF

KAREN HOOKER

Department of Human Development and Family Sciences
Oregon State University
Corvallis, Oregon

Social cognition depends on the complex construct of *self.* There has been increased recognition of the role that the self plays in directing attentional resources, perceptions, memory, and attributions of self and others (see Fiske & Taylor, 1991, for a review). Self-characteristics are important for understanding cognitive processes because people are more likely to pay attention to information relevant for a crucial domain of self, more likely to remember the information, and more likely to be able to resist counter schematic information in such a domain (Hess, 1994; Kihlstrom & Klein, 1994). Also, the self is important for understanding behaviors because it is the source of human agency. Volitional processes, or goals, must be tied to something central to the person engaging in behaviors and the self is critical to understanding these processes. As stated recently by Blanchard-Fields and Abeles (1996), more research on the self in adulthood, and especially links to functional outcomes, is necessary.

Successful aging and development can be viewed as dynamic processes of adaptation between the self and the environment. How do we become who we are? How is who we are influenced by our goals? How are our goal hierarchies generated, and how do they evolve and change over the course of our lives? These questions are partially and independently addressed in the literature on development (e.g., Schulz & Heckhausen, 1996), personality (e.g., McAdams, 1993), and motivation (e.g., Deci & Ryan, 1991). Previous research on anticipated outcomes for later life reveal that people have a preponderance of negative expectations—that is, that they perceive future losses will outweigh future gains (e.g., Heckhausen, Dixon, & Baltes, 1989; Ryff, 1991). This research was not focused explicitly on views of the self-concept from the personal perspective of the older adult, however. Research described in this chapter, and a study of self-descriptions generated by older adults (Freund & Smith, 1999), suggest a view of the late-life self as one with many positive attributes and functions.

As humans, we must navigate among various challenges, demands, and expectations, many of which are *socially* defined. Social cognitive researchers interested in personality and self in later life study domains in which growth and development are possible even into advanced old age. Development in adulthood poses special challenges for researchers because changes that adults undergo often do not happen in limited time frames as in childhood and adolescence. This is true in part because development is not so closely linked with such biological phenomena as physical maturation. A major challenge for developmental theory, especially in adulthood, has been to distinguish *change in general* from *development,* with some theorists seeing potential for loss as well as gain in every developmental process (e.g., Baltes, 1987) and others arguing that change must be adaptive to the individual, or "elaborative," to be considered a developmental change (see Ford & Lerner, 1992; Kaplan, 1983).

One strategy to assess whether a change in adulthood is adaptive for the individual is to determine if it is *teleonomically relevant* for that individual. *Telic* means tending toward a definite goal or purpose. Allport (1937) coined the term *teleonomic trend* to refer to behaviors that capture the individual's intention, or meaning—"in short, what does the individual seem to be `trying to do'?" (p. 204). Allport argued that the discovery of teleonomic trends requires an intraindividual approach. Many of his arguments foreshadow modern-day treatment of personality research with its emphasis on goals (e.g., Cantor & Zirkel, 1990; Pervin, 1983), idiographic methods (e.g., Lamiell, 1987), and the "doing" side of personality (e.g., Cantor, 1990). If we can measure what adults are *trying to do* and whether they are successful at their purposive strivings, then there is some basis for arguing that development has taken place. There is a growing literature documenting the positive relationship between progress toward identity-relevant goals and well-being (e.g., Brunstein, 1993; Hooker & Siegler, 1993; Emmons, 1986; Emmons & King, 1988; McGregor & Little, 1998; Ogilvie, 1997; Omodei & Wearing, 1990; Sheldon & Kasser, 1995).

An examination of the theoretical and empirical literature on adult development in several domains suggests that self-directed choices and selection processes are the linchpins for understanding aging processes. Baltes (1997) described development as an evolutionary process involving *selection* with *optimization and compensation.* In the cognitive domain, there is striking evidence that abilities are preserved in chosen areas of expertise (e.g., Rybash, Hoyer, &

Roodin, 1986; Salthouse, 1991); socially, Carstensen's (1995) socioemotional selectivity theory provides a framework for interpreting the increasing evidence that people select and manage their social environments to regulate positive affect; and in terms of health, it appears that people cognitively manage their expectations and social comparison processes so that they are, in general, no less satisfied with their health status despite increasing physical limitations (e.g., Idler, 1993).

This selection process, also known as specialization, canalization, or chanelized experience (e.g., Kelly, 1955; Waddington, 1975), is widely recognized as a crucial element of development. Consistent with the notion of operative selection processes, there is evidence that individual trajectories become increasingly differentiated over the life span (e.g., Nelson & Dannefer, 1992). There is relatively scant attention paid, however, to how these selection processes actually operate. It is posited that in adulthood it is increasingly the *self*—specifically, the motivational goal-oriented aspects of the self—that is relevant for understanding these processes.

In this chapter, these goals are viewed in terms of possible selves—the hopes and fears for the future that are tied to one's self-definitions (Markus & Nurius, 1986). A compelling aspect of viewing goals in terms of possible selves is that it provides a concrete link of the cognitive system with the emotional system. The self is linked to emotion in part through its ability to generate goals, which in turn drive the emotions in our day-to-day transactions. According to Lazarus (1991), "Goal relevance has to do with what if anything is at stake, and on this depends whether there is the potential for any emotion in the encounter" (p. 827).

In later life, adults may have the psychological resources to more closely regulate their emotions (Labouvie-Vief, 1997; Labouvie-Vief & DeVoe, 1991) on the basis of their thoughts about self and others. Older adults may also have more coping strategies for approaching problems that are high in emotional salience (Blanchard-Fields, Jahnke, & Camp, 1995) than do younger adults. Additionally, older adults adopt "front end" regulation strategies (Turk-Charles & Carstensen, Chapter 14, this volume) through selection of social partners to enhance positive emotions. Management of one's possible self repertoire, and regulatory strategies to enact one's hoped-for selves and successfully avoid feared selves, may also become more focused with age (Cross & Markus, 1991; Frazier, Hooker, Johnson, & Kaus, 1998; Hooker, 1992; Hooker & Kaus, 1994; Hooker, Fiese, Jenkins, Morfei, & Schwagler, 1996).

THEORETICAL FRAMEWORK

The research presented here is grounded in developmental systems theory (Ford & Lerner, 1992). Virtually all current theories of self-regulatory processes are based on some variant of living systems theory or control theory, in which negative feedback functions and feed-forward functions play important roles in regulating goals and, ultimately, behaviors. In developmental systems theory, emphasis is placed on the creative feed-forward processes associated with goal setting and self-directed behavior. Feed-forward processes are proactive, anticipatory, and selective in preparing humans for future action. We believe this function is crucial in organizing the individual's current life and determining whether development occurs.

FEED-FORWARD PROCESSES

The self, throughout the life span, can be characterized as generative rather than reactive (e.g. Brandtstädter, 1989; Breytspraak, 1984; George, 1990). That is, to a large extent, we guide, create, and re-create our life histories (Whitbourne, 1985). The construct of *possible selves* (Markus & Nurius, 1986) has evoked considerable theoretical interest among researchers interested in understanding the self from a life-span perspective (e.g., Baltes & Carstensen, 1991; Brandtstädler & Greve, 1994; Cross & Markus, 1991; Hooker, 1992; Hooker & Kaus, 1994; Hooker et al., 1996; Markus & Herzog, 1992). Possible selves include positive images of self in the future, or hoped-for selves, as well as negative images of self, or feared selves. They are the personal embodiment of one's life goals. As such, they are inherently malleable and thus useful for those who view development as personally guided, dynamic, and contextually sensitive (e.g., Brandstädter, 1989; Lerner, 1978). Possible selves provide a useful way to think about how it is that people, in their infinite diversity, can be working on similar life tasks at certain life stages yet manifest these life tasks in vastly different ways (Cross & Markus, 1991; Markus & Ruvolo, 1989).

Consistent with the idea that selection is a universal developmental process, studies have shown possible selves exist in fewer domains in later life than in young adulthood (e.g., Cross & Markus, 1991; Hooker, 1992) but that activities to *support* these selves are better elaborated than in young adulthood. Furthermore, possible selves in early and middle adulthood "map onto" age-graded developmental tasks more tightly than do possible selves in later adulthood (Hooker, Kaus, & Morfei, 1993), suggesting that goals for the self may be more individually guided than earlier in the life span.

Another important function of possible selves is that self-regulatory processes initiated in response to a specific possible self may serve as a segue to the more microanalytical theories of "action control" (e.g., Atkinson & Birch, 1970; Carver & Scheier, 1982; Heckhausen, 1986; Kuhl, 1985), which attempt to explain how thoughts about the self are transformed into action. For example, the activation of *specific* future self-images, rather than general persuasive messages, has been shown to be more useful in influencing subsequent behavior (e.g., Ewart, 1991; Gregory, Cialdini, & Carpenter, 1982; Ruvolo & Markus, 1992). The cognitive consequences of thinking about a specific self-relevant image is that information is selectively processed (Klinger, 1975), people are better able to make plans (e.g., Klinger, Barta, & Maxeiner, 1980), and they are more persistent in pursuing those plans (e.g., Bandura, 1977; Kuhl, 1985). Indeed, a proposed function of possible selves is to motivate current behavior (Markus & Nurius, 1986). Other theorists have put forth similar arguments that having a goal in a particular domain organizes and regulates behaviors (e.g., Allport, 1961; Bandura, 1989).

Such cognitive expectations as *self-efficacy* and *outcome expectancy*—often referred to as *self-regulatory processes* (Bandura, 1977, 1982, 1989; Carver & Scheier, 1982; Heckhausen, 1986; Kuhl, 1985)—determine the action plans set in motion to accomplish one's goals. Self-efficacy refers to the level of confidence individuals have in personally effecting an outcome. Outcome expectancy is the expected attainability of a given outcome. These two cognitive expectations are related, but not perfectly so, because there are outcomes not totally under one's own control.

The few studies that have examined the motivational consequences of possible selves have supported these ideas. For example, Oyserman and colleagues (Oyserman & Markus, 1990; Oyserman & Saltz, 1993) found that the balance of positive to feared expected selves in particular domains discriminated delinquent from officially nondelinquent boys. Similarly, in two studies using a sample of older adults (Hooker & Kaus, 1992) and young and middle-aged adults (Hooker & Kaus, 1994), it was found that having a possible self in the realm of health was more strongly related to reported health behaviors than was a global measure of health values. Thus, there is some evidence that possible selves do motivate current behaviors.

OVERVIEW OF STUDIES

In my laboratory, my students and I have conducted a series of studies on possible selves and various developmental outcomes across the adult life span. For these data sets of young, middle-aged, and older adults, we have examined both the content of possible selves and the extent to which self-regulatory processes associated with specific possible selves are related to current outcomes (e.g., psychological well-being) and behaviors (e.g., health behaviors). We have examined possible selves and relations to health (Hooker, 1992) and health behaviors (Hooker & Kaus, 1992, 1994) among college students and young, middle-aged and older adults. We have also studied how possible selves in the transition to parenthood are related to self-concept and well-being both concurrently (Hooker, et al., 1996) and prospectively (Morfei, Hooker, & Fiese, 1994). Other projects have as their focus examination of possible selves in relation to tasks of later life, such as caregiving (e.g., Hooker, Monahan, Frazier, DeHart, & Lamp, 1997) and living with chronic illness (Cotrell & Hooker, 1998; see also Frazier & Hooker, 1993). Although this chapter focuses on studies that have involved older adults, Table 5.1 shows a complete listing of our studies, samples, and foci of these studies.

Discussion of the results from these studies first requires understanding how data on possible selves are collected. Our standard procedure for measuring pos-

TABLE 5.1   Possible Selves Studies

Author(s)/date	Samples	Focus of study
1. Hooker, 1992	College students and older adults	Health-related possible selves and perceived health
2. Hooker & Kaus, 1992	Older adults	Health-related possible selves and health behaviors
3. Hooker, Kaus, & Morfei, 1993	Young, middle-aged, and older adults	How possible selves "map onto" developmental tasks
4. Frazier & Hooker, 1993	Older adults with Parkinson's disease and healthy older adults	Perceived health and health locus of control
5. Hooker & Kaus, 1994	Young and middle-aged adults	Health-related possible selves and health behaviors
6. Morfei, Hooker, & Fiese, 1994	Young and middle-aged parents of infants and preschoolers	Continuity and change in parenting possible selves over a 2-year period
7. Hooker, Fiese, Jenkins, Morfei, & Schwagler, 1996	Young and middle-aged parents of infants and preschoolers	Parenting possible selves and gender differences
8. Morfei & Hooker, 1997	Middle-aged parents with children aged 15–22 years	Possible selves for self and child; gender differences; generativity, agency, communion
9. Hooker, Monahan, Frazier, DeHart, & Lamp, 1997	Older adult caregivers of spouses with Alzheimer's disease or Parkinson's disease	Caregiving selves and mental health
10. Frazier, Hooker, Johnson, & Kaus, in press	Older adults measured at two time points	5-year stability of possible self domains in later life
11. Willard & Hooker, 1998	College students	Possible selves in relation to traits (agency, communion) and personal projects
12. Hooker, Lanning, Edwards, Derryberry, & Reed, 1998	College students	Possible selves in relation to several personality (e.g., ego integrity, big 5 traits) and social cognitive measures
13. Cotrell & Hooker, 1999	Older adults with Alzheimer's disease and healthy older adults	Conceptions of self and future among Alzheimer's patients; awareness deficits

Studies can be broadly grouped into four thematic areas. Health: 1, 2, 4, 5, 10; life events, tasks, transitions: 3, 7, 8, 9, 13; interrelationships among possible selves and personality: 3, 11, 12; intraindividual stability of possible selves: 6, 10.

sible selves is modeled after the procedure described in Cross and Markus (1991) as follows:

> This part of the questionnaire [or interview] addresses how you see yourself in the future. We all think about our futures to some extent. When doing so, we usually think about the kinds of experiences that are in store for us and the kinds of people we might possibly become. Sometimes we think about what we *hope* we will be like—selves we hope to become in the future, or *"hoped-for possible selves."* Some hoped-for possible selves seem quite likely, like becoming a homeowner or [interviewer mentions or questionnaire lists one appropriate for group under study]. Other future selves seem quite far-fetched but are still possible for example, winning the lottery. Things that we do are not possible selves but are usually part of a possible self. For example, to write books is not a possible self; to be a writer is a possible self. Please take a few minutes and think about all of your *hoped-for possible selves*. You may have just a few, or you may have many.

Next, participants are asked to identify their three most important hoped-for selves (e.g., "to be a good father"; "to continue caring for my husband at home"; "to save enough to retire at age 60"). For each hoped-for self identified, participants are asked *why* the possible self identified is important. Finally, a series of self-regulatory questions (e.g., "How capable do you feel of achieving this possible self?") are rated on 7-point Likert scales for each possible self. A similar procedure is followed for eliciting and rating individuals' three most dreaded selves.

METHODOLOGICAL ISSUES IN THE MEASUREMENT OF POSSIBLE SELVES

The appendix to this chapter is the measuring instrument we are currently using in most of our ongoing possible selves studies. It is based on the Cross and Markus (1991) instrument, with some changes (discussed in the "Format" section) that improve the measurement procedure.

In our studies of possible selves, we have usually been interested in both *content* of the possible selves and the self-regulatory *processes* brought to bear on those specific possible selves. Thus, we typically take a two-pronged approach. Our first goal is to identify the hoped-for and feared possible selves that people in the sample possess. If the study is designed to explore and test hypotheses in a specific domain (e.g., health, parenting), then we are usually quite interested in the following simple questions: How many people in our sample have a possible self in the domain of interest? Are these possible selves typically framed positively, as a hoped-for self? Are they framed negatively, as a feared self? Or does balance (a hoped-for and countervailing feared self in the same domain) exist?

A second goal in our studies has been to determine the extent to which self-regulatory processes operate in service of a specific possible self. For each of the possible selves provided, we ask the person to rate a series of statements on a Likert scale (from 1 [low] to 7 [high]; see Appendix). These statements are designed to assess importance, "distance" from current self, perceived efficacy, outcome expectancy, and amount of time spent thinking about this self. Thus, the instrument we use measures both product (content) and processes of the self. For researchers interested in collecting data on possible selves, there are several decisions to be considered.

FORMAT

Spontaneous ("Open-Ended") versus Provided

One of the strengths of using the measurement system of possible selves is that it allows the respondent to provide the relevant categories of self. This ensures that the possible selves provided have psychological centrality for the individual and implicitly acknowledges the expertise that the person has about what is important to himself or herself, now and into the future. These are important strengths that in our view outweigh the negative aspects of this format.

A significant drawback to this open-ended format is that there is no guarantee that people will provide a possible self in a category relevant for one's specific research question (e.g., a health-related self; parenting self; exercise-related self). Thus, if one of the goals of the study is to assess self-regulatory processes in relation to a specific possible self (which is typically a focus in our studies), one inevitably ends up with data from some people that do not speak to the self-regulatory question. This is because some subset of individuals in any sample would not spontaneously provide a self in the category of interest (for the researcher); thus, they would not rate the self-regulatory items in relation to the self category of interest for the researcher's question. One way to circumvent this problem would be to specifically *ask* the respondent about a self in the area of interest for one's research question, perhaps at the end of the interview or questionnaire (e.g., Whaley, 1997). This procedure would enhance the data set in terms of numbers of subjects but might be suspect in terms of keeping to the spirit of the open-ended, totally self-generated process of possible selves measurement.

Another approach, one mentioned in the original Markus and Nurius (1986) article, is to provide a checklist of possible selves to which people can respond. The advantage of the checklist approach is that everyone rates every possible self. The disadvantage is that this procedure does not ensure that each self on the checklist is psychologically meaningful for every person in the sample. As researchers begin to amass more data on what possible selves are typical for what ages and samples, however, this may become more feasible.

In our more recent studies, we have opted to probe for the three most important hoped-for selves and three most dreaded selves for each participant. This allows for self-regulatory items to be scored in reference to six possible selves. The probe for three hoped-for selves and three feared selves also serves to enhance comparability across individuals. For example, in a previous study (Hooker, 1992) some people spontaneously mentioned only one hoped-for and one feared self, whereas others provided as many as 18 hoped-for selves and 14 feared selves. We allow those people who have many possible selves to mention or list them, but we do not collect self-regulatory data on any selves more than three hoped-for and three feared selves. Limiting possible selves does reduce some potentially interesting variability, but the increase in standardization is an important strength, and for our research purposes, probing for six possible selves has been adequate.

Interview versus Questionnaire

We have collected data on possible selves using both interview methods and pencil-and-paper questionnaires. The advantages to collecting data on possible selves in a face-to-face interview are that one can ascertain that the individual fully understands the task and encourage him or her to complete the task. The disadvantages are lack of anonymity and the time and expense involved in conducting the interviews. Interview length varies greatly depending on the individual, but it is not unusual for the possible selves interview to last close to an hour.

We have used the possible selves questionnaire with good results in several studies. The questionnaire format is somewhat less successful in samples of older adults, however, thus, for older adults, we recommend the interview format be used whenever feasible. Problems with missing data exist when questionnaires for collecting data on possible selves are used with older adults. It is unclear whether the instrument appears too burdensome for some (this may be especially true if it is part of a questionnaire packet that contains many measures) or whether older adults do not want to report thoughts about their future selves. Future research to assess the reasons behind missing data with older adults would be illuminating.

CODING

There are two primary coding issues: (1) establishing the possible selves content categories and (2) determining the reliability of those categories. The possible selves coding categories that we use were originally based on the Cross and Markus (1991) categories, with some modifications. Specifically, we separate out *health* from a category labeled *physical* because we believe there may be important differences underlying motivations to look good and motivations to be healthy, especially among older adults. The basic coding scheme consists of 16 categories (see descriptions of each in the appendix): *personal, physical, abilities and education, lifestyle, family, relationships, occupation, material, success, social responsibility, leisure, health, independence/dependence, death, bereavement,* and *threats.* Then, depending on the research question being addressed, we typically include another specific category. For example, in recent studies (Hooker et al., 1996, 1997), we created *parenting* and *caregiving* as separate categories because these were the domains for which we had made specific theoretical predictions with the samples. Because there are numerous categories, it may make sense to establish a minimum percentage of the sample (e.g., 5%) that identifies a possible self in a category for it to be included in reporting of results.

Another salient change from the Cross and Markus (1991) protocol is that we probe for the underlying motivation for the possible self by asking *why* the self is important. We have found that it is necessary to include this question to obtain an accurate portrayal of the person's goals (Morfei, Hooker, & Fiese, 1994).

Reliability of the categories are established through inter-rater reliability procedures. A statistical method, such as Cohen's kappa, that adjusts for the extent to which raters would agree on categories based on chance alone should be used. In our studies, interreliability for each category has ranged from .75 to .94. Since possible selves comprise the part of the self that theoretically is expected to be malleable (Markus & Nurius, 1986), one might not expect test–retest reliability to be very high. Studies have shown that there is substantial stability, however, in possible self repertoires over time frames ranging from 6 months (Oyserman & Markus, 1990) to 5 years (Frazier et al., in press).

RESEARCH FINDINGS

HEALTH

Health is a domain of presumed importance across the adult life span. The process by which possible selves can influence health is described in control theory (Carver & Scheier, 1982; Miller, Galanter, & Pribram, 1960). According to control theory models, people have internal standards (i.e., goals) that are compared with their current state. If a discrepancy exists between a goal and a current state, people will engage in behaviors aimed at narrowing such a discrepancy. For example, good health may be a goal that is partially perceived as attainable on the basis of one's own health behaviors and decisions. If this goal were present, then self-regulatory processes associated with such a goal would predict the likelihood of engaging in health-protective behaviors. Thus, self-efficacy and outcome expectancy of achieving a hoped-for health-related self or preventing a feared health-related self should be related to health behaviors. Health—like many domains—is multiply determined, however, and negative health outcomes could occur despite one's actions. For example, one could feel efficacious in enacting health behaviors to promote health, yet not have a high level of outcome expectancy for a health goal if one were convinced that hereditary factors were important for a particular disease.

Control theory explains how goals are met, but it is relatively silent about how goals for the self are generated or developed. Similarly, though increasingly arguments are made for incorporating the self-system into models of health and health behaviors (e.g., Ewart, 1991; Heidrich & Ryff, 1993; Leventhal & Hirschman, 1982), these models leave out the developmental perspective that health and health behaviors may have different meanings at different points in the life span (see Siegler, 1989).

Our work in this area is explicitly developmental. Possible selves are created from one's basis of self-knowledge, which includes past and current experiences as well as future scenarios (Markus & Herzog, 1992). Contextual influences associated with midlife make it likely that people will have at least one possible self related to health by the time they reach their forties.

Our studies have shown that health becomes increasingly incorporated into the self over the life span (Frazier et al., in press; Hooker, 1992; Hooker & Kaus, 1992; Hooker & Kaus, 1994). This growth in salience of health-related selves (Figure 5.1) has importance because of its implications for how people think and plan for their future, the degree to which health behaviors can be motivated by these health-related selves, and the role health-related selves may play in bolstering and protecting psychological and physical well-being.

Our data indicate that by midlife, health often is part of a crucial *feared* self—most likely triggered by life experiences more common in midlife than earlier in adulthood. One's parents may be failing physically and the incidence of serious illnesses (e.g., cardiovascular disease, cancers) begins to be high enough that it is likely one personally knows peers with these illnesses and thus can more easily construct a significant feared self in the area of health. Actual health problems or even "health scares" (being tested for a potentially serious condition and having test results indicate no problem) could trigger a feared self in the realm of health. These logically would seem to strengthen motivation for health behaviors. If one holds an image of oneself as someone with heart disease, one would be more likely to control diet and exercise. Indeed, Hooker and Kaus (1992) showed that older adults with a health-related possible self were more likely to report engaging in more positive health behaviors and fewer negative ones.

Self-regulatory processes associated with a health-related self have been shown to be related to perceived health (Hooker, 1992). Specifically, in a sample

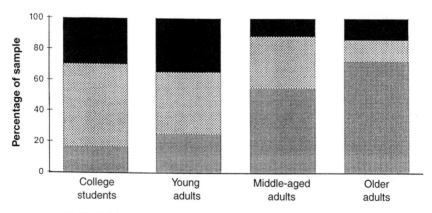

FIGURE 5.1   Cross-sectional view of health-related possible selves across the adult life span.

of older adults, perceived efficacy and outcome expectancy of a most important hoped-for self was positively related to perceived health. The relationship between these self-regulatory variables and perceived health was not, however, related to a feared health-related self. This asymmetry is intriguing and suggests that positive self-images and negative self-images, even in the same domain, relate differentially to life outcomes. The amount of time spent thinking about either a positively framed or negative framed health-related self was negatively related to perceived health, probably indicating that people who ruminate on their health are more likely to rate it negatively.

Self-regulatory processes associated with a health-related self have been shown to be related to such health behaviors as smoking, exercising, and other commonly measured behaviors (Hooker & Kaus, 1992, 1994), even after controlling for people's global health values as measured by a standardized instrument. Thus, information on self-regulation related to a health-focused possible self provides unique data that could be clinically relevant. For example, those who have a health-related possible self but are not strongly efficacious in their thinking about avoiding (or becoming) this self might need extra support to remain in compliance with an exercise or medication regimen. Additionally, if people could cognitively construct a health-related possible self in an attempt to motivate better health behaviors, our data indicate that a hoped-for self might be more powerful than a feared self (cf. Buirs & Martin, 1997).

Cross-sectional data show that by later life, older people are equally likely to have a *hoped-for* health-related self as they are a *feared* health-related self. Generally these hoped-for selves have to do with being able to maintain the relatively good health older adults already have. The Frazier et al. (in press) longitudinal study of possible selves of older adults showed that health-and physical-related possible selves were the domains most likely to emerge over a 5-year period in later life. The accommodative cognitive strategies captured in exploring possible selves longitudinally show that people may shift goals in response to what Whitbourne (1996) called threshold events. For example, one person who had experienced a heart attack stated that "health is my most important hope for the future." This research provided longitudinal evidence to support and extend earlier work (Hooker, 1992) showing that health becomes more incorporated into the self-system in later life.

Ironically, one study (Frazier & Hooker, 1993) indicated that people living with a difficult chronic illness (Parkinson's disease) were less likely to have a health-related possible self than were healthy older adults. These findings validate the future orientation that possible selves is meant to capture. People with Parkinson's disease already have a health problem and so may not focus on health as a fear for the future. At present, the disease is incurable, so a hope to be disease free may be a fantasy more than a feasible possibility. Older adults especially seem to have possible selves that are more realistic and grounded in current realities than do young adults (Cross & Markus, 1991; Hooker, 1992), which makes sense given the more limited future (time) available to them.

Although older adults report fewer possible selves than do younger adults (Hooker, 1992), the ones reported tend to be better cognitively elaborated. Older adults report more activities than do younger adults to support achievement of a hoped-for self or prevent a feared self. Interestingly, though older adults do not spend as much time thinking about their most important possible selves, they do report feeling just as capable of achieving a hoped-for self or preventing a feared self as do college students. That control in general is compromised in later life seems almost axiomatic (e.g., Rodin, 1986; Schulz & Heckhausen, 1996). How-ever, perhaps one way in which older adults strive to preserve their sense of auton-omy and maintain well-being is by *choosing at least one important goal for the self* that they are confident of being able to manage (Brandtstädter & Wentura, 1995; Brim, 1992). Since control is domain specific (Lachman, 1986), people could have a diminished sense of overall control yet still maintain a sense of con-trol and perceived efficacy over domains that have particular relevance for the self.

LIFE EVENTS, TASKS, AND TRANSITIONS

The possible selves construct is key to understanding changes in self. Life-span developmentalists have argued that changes in self are more likely to occur during transition periods or important life events (Hagestad & Neugarten, 1985; Havighurst, 1972; Hooker, 1991; Kling, Ryff, & Essex, 1997).

To the extent that these events are socially structured (Havighurst, 1972; Neu-garten & Datan, 1973) one would expect to see more similarity in possible selves earlier in the life span than later, assuming that roles and tasks are less structured in later life (Rosow, 1985). We tested this idea by using Havighurst's (1972) developmental task framework and "mapping" possible selves onto that frame-work for a sample of young adults, middle-aged adults, and older adults (Hooker, Kaus, & Morfei, 1993). Our young-adult sample was from our study on the tran-sition to parenthood (Hooker et al., 1996) and was composed of 228 men and women primarily in their late twenties to midthirties. Havighurst identified eight developmental tasks for this period of life. One of them, *selecting a mate,* was precluded from being represented in this sample because the sample consisted of married adults. The other seven tasks, however, were well represented in the pos-sible self repertoires—four of them were present in over half of the sample. The developmental tasks of *starting a family, raising children,* and *learning to live with a marriage partner* were relevant for the 73% of the sample who listed a hoped-for self in the domain of *family* and the 65% of the sample who listed a feared self in this domain. The developmental task of *getting started in an occu-pation* was also a major issue for this group, as *occupation* was the next most common possible self domain, with 66% of the sample listing it as a hoped-for self and 31% listing it as a feared self. The developmental tasks of *taking on civic responsibility* and *finding a congenial social group* were less relevant but still rep-resented in the 25% of the sample who listed a hoped-for self in the *leisure* domain. The task of *managing a home* could be construed as a relevant self in the *material* domain (e.g., selves related to financial security and specific posses-sions), listed as a hoped-for self and a feared self by 27% of the sample. Thus, our data indicated that age-graded developmental tasks of early adulthood provided a fairly accurate framework for understanding which domains of possible selves were likely to be relevant for most individuals during this period of life. Cantor (1990) also found that among a sample of college students, normative task cate-gories captured most task concerns.

Our middle-aged sample was from a study (Hooker & Kaus, 1994) of 84 adults between the ages of 40 and 59. Of the seven developmental tasks identified by Havighurst (1972) of this age, six seemed to be present in the possible selves of this sample. The tasks of *assisting teenage children to become responsible and happy adults, relating oneself to one's spouse as a person,* and *adjusting to aging parents* were clearly present in the possible selves of this sample, as 52% had a hoped-for self in the *family* domain. The tasks of *reaching and maintaining satis-factory performance in one's occupational career* was reflected by 56% of the sample who had a hoped-for self in the *occupational* domain. *To accept and adjust to the physiological changes of middle age* seemed like a very relevant task for this sample, as 67% had a feared self in the domain of *health* and 21% had a hoped-for self in this domain; 38% had a *dependent* feared self and 25% had a hoped-for self in the *physical* domain. *Developing adult leisure-time activities* was a task represented for the 43% of the sample who listed a hoped-for self in the *leisure* domain and also seemed a likely task associated with the *abilities* domain, listed by 27% of the sample as a hoped-for self. The developmental task of *achieving social and civic responsibility* was not prominently represented for this sample of middle-aged adults. Similarly, the possible selves that seemed to "slip through the normative sieve" included *material, personal,* and *relationship* selves, each listed by more than 20% of the sample. Thus, most possible selves do appear to be related to developmental tasks of this phase of life, with some notable exceptions.

The older adult sample is from a study (Hooker, 1992) composed of 114 adults over the age of 60. It was in this older adult group that the matchup of normative developmental tasks to possible selves was the most uncertain. Of the six devel-opmental tasks listed for this period, we could find evidence that only three were represented in the possible self repertoires of this sample. The developmental task of *adjusting to decreasing physical strength and health* was present for most older adults, as 55% had a hoped-for self in the *health* domain and 49% had a feared self in that domain. One could also construe the domain of *dependence* as relevant here; 50% of the sample had a feared self in this domain. The tasks related to *establishing satisfactory living arrangements* and *adjusting to retire-ment* seemed well represented in the possible self repertoires, with *leisure* and *lifestyle* (primarily fear of living in a nursing home) domains listed by 49% and 21% of the sample, respectively. However, the remaining developmental tasks (*adjusting to death of a spouse; establishing an explicit affiliation with one's age group; adopting and adapting social roles in a flexible way*) were not clearly discernible in the goals for the self. As individual development becomes increasingly guided by unique characteristics of the self, the relationship between possible selves and normative developmental tasks become less closely linked.

Goals in later life may be less normatively structured than early and midlife, which makes sense if differences between individuals increase with age. Thus, social cognition researchers interested in goals and self-directedness would be well advised to examine older adults because their activities are the most likely to be motivated by their own personal agendas. These agendas, though personal, are not always chosen and are structured by the social context. For example, in a study of spouse caregivers for people with Alzheimer's disease and Parkinson's disease (Hooker et al., 1997), approximately half of the sample (49%) had caregiving represented in their possible self repertoire. A future self related to caregiving was the most frequently listed hoped-for self and second only to health for feared selves. Interestingly, those with a caregiving possible self showed a trend toward more positive mental health outcomes. Thus, for older adult caregivers, incorporating caregiving into their goal structures may be a cognitive adaptation that allows them to find meaning and challenge in their efforts to support their spouses. This incorporation of teleonomic relevance into daily tasks is posited to be a benchmark for development in later life. The decrease in normative goal structure with age and increasing salience of one's personal agenda speaks to the integration of life tasks with identity and to the self-directed nature of aging well.

FUTURE DIRECTIONS

There are several gaps in the possible selves research literature that future work could address. Studies that examine relationships between possible selves and important life outcomes across the life span should be conducted. There is a paucity of data (but see Oyserman & Markus, 1990; Oyerserman & Saltz, 1993) on outcomes that are independently verified or measured by someone other than the respondent. Similarly, there are few studies that have examined possible selves longitudinally (but see Frazier et al., in press) and none that have explicitly tested the motivational aspect of possible selves in a design (longitudinal or experimental) where cause could be definitively established. The importance of this for applied work with older adults is enormous. If we could work with adults to construct possible selves in domains where behavioral changes were desired (e.g., health behaviors, medication compliance, affective changes) and could establish that cognitive changes in self translated to behavioral changes, we could devise a plethora of positive interventions. Clinical psychologists who capitalize on clients' ability to imagine future possibilities in effecting changes in their lives would be well equipped to help with these types of intervention goals (e.g., see Buirs & Martin, 1997). Future studies should be designed to determine the conditions under which specific possible selves can be induced and what the consequences are for associated behaviors.

Another topic in the possible self literature that deserves more attention is the distinction of hoped-for versus feared selves, as these distinct sets of selves may generate distinct patterns of affect (cf. Higgins, 1997). For example, Higgins (1987) proposed a theory in which discrepancies between one's current perception of self and one's "self-guides" result in different patterns of psychopathology. Discrepancies between one's perceived current self and one's "ideal" self result in depressive disorders, whereas discrepancies between one's current self and one's "ought" self lead to anxiety disorders. These distinctions seem relevant for the hoped-for selves ("ideal") and feared selves ("ought") distinction; we have found different patterns between relationships of outcome variables and hoped-for versus feared selves. A recent study (Allen, Woolfolk, Gara, & Apter, 1996) showed depressed patients to be more likely than nondepressed controls to have feared selves similar to their actual selves. Clearly, the distinction of hoped-for from feared possible selves is an area that is ripe for research.

A third direction for future research is to study possible selves in large, representative samples. Most studies have relied on relatively small "convenience" samples, or samples targeted to a specific population. We need to increase ethnic and cultural diversity and include people from all socioeconomic strata in order to enhance scientific understanding of the construct and, of course, to increase generalizability of results.

SUMMARY AND CONCLUSIONS

The ability to orchestrate one's life so that activities support meaningful aspects of the self—that is, creating high teleonomic relevance—is posited to be an aspect of development. The processes associated with goal setting and life organization, however, must be examined from an intraindividual perspective. It is important for life-span developmental researchers interested in social cognition and aging to incorporate an awareness of the perceivers' goals. We have shown in several studies that possible selves can be measured with a high degree of interrater reliability and thus can serve as a way of operationalizing important self goals. An understanding of what is teleonomically relevant for aging individuals would allow researchers to distinguish change from development in later life and to better grasp the adaptation inherent in successful aging.

REFERENCES

Allen, L. A., Woolfolk, R. L., Gara, M. A., & Apter, J. T. (1996). Possible selves in major depression. *Journal of Nervous and Mental Disease, 184,* 739–745.

Allport, F. H. (1937). Teleonomic description in the study of personality. *Character and Personality, 5,* 202–214.

Allport, G. W. (1961). *Pattern and growth in personality* (2nd ed.). New York: Holt, Rinehart, & Winston.

Atkinson, J. W., & Birch, D. (1970). *The dynamics of action.* New York: Wiley.

Baltes, M. M., & Carstensen, L. L. (1991). Commentary on possible selves across the life span. *Human Development, 34,* 256–260.

Baltes, P. B. (1987). Theoretical proposition of life-span developmental psychology: On the dynamics between growth and decline. *Developmental Psychology, 23,* 611–626.

Baltes, P. B. (1997). On the incomplete architecture of human ontogeny: Selection, optimization, and compensation as foundation of developmental theory. *American Psychologist, 52,* 366–380.

Bandura, A. (1977). Self-efficacy theory: Toward a unifying theory of behavior change. *Psychological Review, 84,* 191–215.

Bandura, A. (1982). Self-efficacy in human agency. *American Psychologist, 37,* 122–147.

Bandura, A. (1989). Regulation of cognitive processes through perceived self-efficacy. *Developmental Psychology, 25,* 729–778.

Blanchard-Fields, F. & Abeles, R. P. (1996). Social cognition and aging. In J. E. Birren & K. W. Schaie (Eds.), *Handbook of the psychology of aging* (4th ed., pp. 150–161). New York: Academic Press.

Blanchard-Fields, F., Jahnke, H., & Camp, C. (1995). Age differences in problem solving style: The role of emotional salience. *Psychology and Aging, 10,* 173–180.

Brandtstädter, J. (1989). Personal self-regulation of development: Cross-sequential analyses of development-related control beliefs and emotions. *Developmental Psychology, 25,* 96–108.

Brandtstädter, J., & Greve, W. (1994). The aging self: Stabilizing and protective processes. *Developmental Review, 14,* 52–80.

Brandstädter, J., & Wentura, D. (1995). Adjustment to shifting possibilities in later life: Complementary adaptive modes. In R. A. Dixon & L. Backman (Eds.), *Psychological compensation: Managing losses and promoting gains* (pp. 83–106). Hillsdale, NJ: Lawrence Erlbaum Associates.

Breytspraak, L. M. (1984). *The development of self in later life.* Boston: Little, Brown.

Brim, O. G., Jr. (1992). *Ambition: How we manage success and failure throughout our lives.* New York: Basic Books.

Brunstein, J. C. (1993). Personal goals and subjective well-being: A longitudinal study. *Journal of Personality and Social Psychology, 65,* 1061–1070.

Buirs, R. S., & Martin, J. (1997). The therapeutic construction of possible selves: Imagination and its constraints. *Journal of Constructivist Psychology, 10,* 153–166.

Cantor, N. (1990). From thought to behavior: "Having" and "doing" in the study of personality and cognition. *American Psychologist, 45,* 735–750.

Cantor, N., & Zirkel, S. (1990). Personality, cognition, and purposive behavior. In L. A. Pervin (Ed.), *Handbook of personality research* (pp. 135–164). New York: Guilford Press.

Carstensen, L. L. (1995). Evidence for a life-span theory of socioemotional selectivity. *Current Directions in Psychological Science, 4,* 151–156.

Carver, C. S., & Scheier, M. F. (1982). Control theory: A useful conceptual framework for personality-social, clinical, and health psychology. *Psychological Bulletin, 92,* 111–135.

Charles, S. T., & Carstensen, L. L. (in press). The role of time in the setting of social goals across the life span. In F. Blanchard-Fields, & T. Hess (Eds.), *Social cognition and aging.* New York: Academic Press.

Cotrell, V., & Hooker, K. (1999). Self-perceptions in individuals with Alzheimer's disease. Unpublished data. Oregon State University, Corvallis, OR.

Cross, S., & Markus, H. (1991). Possible selves across the lifespan. *Human Development, 34,* 230–255.

Deci, E. L., & Ryan, R. M. (1991). A motivational approach to self: Integration in personality. *Nebraska Symposium on Motivation, 40,* 209–254.

Emmons, R. A. (1986). Personal strivings: An approach to personality and subjective well-being. *Journal of Personality and Social Psychology, 51,* 1058–1068.

Emmons, R. A., & King, L. A. (1988). Conflict among personal strivings: Immediate and long-term implications for psychological and physical well-being. *Journal of Personality and Social Psychology, 54,* 1040–1048.

Ewart, C. K. (1991). Social action theory for a public health psychology. *American Psychologist, 46,* 931–946.

Fiske, S. T., & Taylor, S. E. (1991). *Social cognition* (2nd ed.). New York: McGraw-Hill.

Ford, D. H., & Lerner, R. M. (1992). *Developmental systems theory: An integrative approach.* Newbury Park, CA: Sage.

Frazier, L. D., & Hooker, K. (1993). *The relationship between possible selves and health locus of control: A comparison of chronically ill and healthy older adults.* Unpublished manuscript.

Frazier, L. D., Hooker, K., Johnson, P., & Kaus, C. R. (in press). *Continuity and change in possible selves in later life: A 5-year longitudinal study. Basic and Applied Social Psychology* (Special Issue on Social Psychology and Aging).

Freund, A. M. & Smith, J. (1999). Content and function of the self-definition in old and very old age. *Journal of Gerontology: Psychological Sciences, 54B,* P55–P67.

George, L. K. (1990). Social structure, social processes, and social-psychological states. In R. H. Binstock & L. K. George (Eds.), *Handbook of aging and the social sciences* (3rd ed., pp. 186–204). New York: Academic Press.

Gregory, W. L., Cialdini, R. B., & Carpenter, K. M. (1982). Self-relevant scenarios as mediators of likelihood estimates and compliance: Does imagining make it so? *Journal of Personality and Social Psychology, 43,* 89–99.

Hagestad, G. O., & Neugarten, B. L. (1985). Age and the life course. In R. H. Binstock & L. K. George (Eds.), *Handbook of aging and the social sciences* (2nd ed., pp. 35–61). New York: Van Nostrand Reinhold.

Havighurst, R. H. (1972). *Developmental tasks and education* (3rd ed.). New York: David McKay.

Heckhausen, H. (1986). Achievement and motivation through the life span. In A. B. Sorenson, F. E. Weinert, & L. R. Sherrod (Eds.), *Human development and the lifecourse: Multidisciplinary perspectives* (pp. 445–466). Hillsdale, NJ: Lawrence Erlbaum Associates.

Heckhausen, J., Dixon, R. A., & Baltes, P. B. (1989). Gains and losses in development throughout adulthood as perceived by different age groups. *Developmental Psychology, 25,* 109–121.

Heidrich, S. M., & Ryff, C. D. (1993). Physical and mental health in later life: The self-system as mediator. *Psychology and Aging, 8,* 327–338.

Hess, T. M. (1994). Social cogntion in adulthood: Aging related changes in knowledge and processing mechanisms. *Developmental Review, 14,* 373–412.

Higgins, E. T. (1987). Self-discrepancy: A theory relating self and affect. *Psychological Review, 94,* 319–340.

Higgins, E. T. (1997). Beyond pleasure and pain. *American Psychologist, 52,* 1280–1300.

Hooker, K. (1991). Change and stability in self during the transition to retirement: An intraindividual study using P-technique factor analyses. *International Journal of Behavioral Development, 14,* 209–233.

Hooker, K. (1992). Possible selves and perceived health in older adults and college students. *Journal of Gerontology: Psychological Sciences, 47,* P85–95.

Hooker, K., Fiese, B. H., Jenkins, L., Morfei, M. Z., & Schwagler, J. (1996). Possible selves among parents of infants and preschoolers. *Developmental Psychology, 32,* 542–550.

Hooker, K., & Kaus, C. R. (1992). Possible selves and health behaviors in later life. *Journal of Aging and Health, 4,* 390–411.

Hooker, K., & Kaus, C. R. (1994). Health-related possible selves in young and middle adulthood. *Psychology and Aging, 9,* 126–133.

Hooker, K., Kaus, C. R., & Morfei, M. Z. (1993, November). *The function of possible selves in linking personal goals to developmental tasks.* Paper presented at the 46th annual Scientific Meetings of the Gerontological Society of America, New Orleans.

Hooker, K., Lanning, K. Edwards, J., Derryberry, D., & Reed, M. (1998). Cognitive parameters of personality functioning. Unpublished data. Oregon State University, Corvallis, OR.

Hooker, K., Monahan, D. J., Frazier, L. D., DeHart, K., & Lamp, D. (1997 November). *Caregiving possible selves.* Paper presented at the 50th annual Scientific Meeting of the Gerontological Society of America, Cincinnati.

Hooker, K., & Siegler, I. C. (1993). Life goals, satisfaction, and self-rated health: Preliminary find-ings. *Experimental Aging Research, 19,* 97–110.

Idler, E. L. (1993). Age differences in self-assessments of health: Age changes, cohort differences, or survivorship? *Journal of Gerontology, 48,* S289–S300.

Kaplan, B. (1983). A trio of trials. In R. M. Lerner (Ed.), *Developmental psychology: Historical and philosophical perspectives* (pp. 185–228). Hillsdale, NJ: Lawrence Erlbaum Associates.

Kelly, G. A. (1955). *A theory of personality: A psychology of personal constructs.* New York: W. W. Norton.

Kihlstrom, J. F., & Klein, S. B. (1994). The self as a knowledge structure. In R. S. Wyer & T. K. Srull (Eds.), *Handbook of social cognition: Vol. 1: Basic processes* (pp. 153–208). Hillsdale, NJ: Lawrence Erlbaum Associates.

Kling, K. C., Ryff, C. D., & Essex, M. J. (1997). Adaptive changes in the self-concept during a life transition. *Personality and Social Psychology Bulletin, 23,* 981–990.

Klinger, E. (1975). Consequences of commitment to and disengagement from incentives. *Psychological Review, 82,* 1–25.

Klinger, E. (1977). *Meaning and void: Inner experice and the incentives in people's lives.* Minneapolis: University of Minnesota Press.

Klinger, E., Barta, S. G., & Maxeiner, M. (1980). Motivational correlates of thought content, frequency, and commitment. *Journal of Personality and Social Psychology, 39,* 1222–1237.

Kuhl, J. (1985). Volitional mediators of cognition-behavior consistency: Self-regulatory processes and action versus state orientation. In J. Kuhl & J. Beckmann (Eds.), *Action control: From cognition to behavior* (pp. 101–128). New York: Springer-Verlag.

Labouvie-Vief, G. (1997). Cognitive-emotional integration in adulthood. In K. W. Schaie & M. P. Lawton, (Eds.), *Annual Review of Gerontology and Geriatrics* (vol. 17, pp. 206–237). New York. Springer.

Labouvie-Vief, G. & DeVoe, M. (1997). Emotional regulation in adulthood and later life: A developmental view. In K. W. Schaie & M. P. Lawton (Eds.), *Annual Review of Gerontology and Geriatrics* (vol. 11, pp. 172–194). New York: Springer.

Lachman, M. E. (1986). Locus of control in aging research: A case for multidimensional and domain-specific assessment. *Psychology and Aging, 1,* 34–40.

Lamiell, J. T. (1987). *The psychology of personality: An epistemological inquiry.* New York: Columbia University Press.

Lazarus, R. S. (1991). Progress on a cognitive-motivational-relational theory of emotion. *American Psychologist, 46,* 819–834.

Lerner, R. M. (1978). Nature, nurture, and dynamic interactionism. *Human Development, 21,* 1–20.

Leventhal, H. & Hirschman, R. S. (1982). Social psychology and prevention. In G. S. Sanders & J. Suls (Eds.) *Social psychology of health and illness* (pp. 183–226). Hillsdale, NJ: Lawrence Erlbaum Associates.

Markus, H. & Nurius, P. (1986). Possible selves. *American Psychologist, 41,* 954–969.

Markus, H., & Herzog, A. R. (1992). The role of the self-concept in aging. In K. W. Schaie & M. P. Lawton (Eds.), *Annual Review of Gerontology and Geriatrics* (vol. 11, pp. 110–143). New York: Springer.

Markus, H., & Ruvolo, A. (1989). Possible selves: Personalized representations of goals. In L. A. Pervin (Ed.), *Goal concepts in personality and social psychology* (pp. 211–241). Hillsdale, NJ: Lawrence Erlbaum Associates.

McAdams, D. P. (1993). *Stories we live by: Personal myths and the making of the self.* New York: William Morrow & Co.

McGregor, I., & Little, B. R. (1998). Personal projects, happiness, and meaning: On doing well and being yourself. *Journal of Personality and Social Psychology, 74,* 494–512.

Miller, G. A., Galanter, E., & Pribram, K. (1960). *Plans and the structure of behavior.* New York: Holt, Rinehart, & Winston.

Morfei, M. Z., Hooker, K., & Fiese, B. H. (1994). *Possible selves among parents of young children: A longitudinal follow-up.* Unpublished manuscript.

Morfei, M. Z., & Hooker, K. (1997 May). *Generative possible selves in the parents of young adults.* Paper presented at the annual meeting of the Midwestern Psychological Association, Chicago.

Nelson, E. A., & Dannefer, D. (1992). Aged heterogeneity: Fact or fiction? The fate of diversity in gerontologicall research. *The Gerontologist, 32,* 17–23.

Neugarten, B. L., & Datan, N. (1973). Sociological perspectives on the lifecycle. In P. B. Baltes & K. W. Schaie (Eds.), *Life-span developmental psychology* (pp. 53–69). New York: Academic Press.

Ogilvie, D. M. (1987). Life satisfaction and identity structure in late middle-aged men and women. *Psychology and Aging, 2,* 217–224.

Omodei, M. M., & Wearing, A. J. (1990). Need satisfaction and involvement in personal projects: Toward an integrative model of subjective well-being. *Journal of Personality and Social Psychology, 59,* 762–769.

Oyserman, D., & Markus, H. R. (1990). Possible selves and delinquency. *Journal of Personality and Social Psychology, 59,* 112–125.

Oyserman, D., & Saltz, E. (1993). Competence, delinquency, and attempts to attain possible selves. *Journal of Personality and Social Psychology, 65,* 360–374.

Pervin, L. A. (1983). The stasis and flow of behavior: Toward a theory of goals. In M. M. Page (Ed.), *Nebraska Symposium on Motivation 1982: Personality—current theory and research* (pp. 1–53). Lincoln NE: University of Nebraska Press.

Rodin, J. (1986). Health, control, and aging. In M. M. Baltes & P. B. Baltes (Eds.), *The psychology of control and aging* (pp. 139–167). Hillsdale, NJ: Lawrence Erlbaum Associates.

Rosow, I. (1985). Status and role change through the life cycle. In R. H. Binstock & E. Shanas (Eds.), *Handbook of aging and the social sciences* (2nd ed., pp. 62–93). New York: Van Nostrand Reinhold.

Ruvolo, A. P., & Markus, H. R. (1992). Possible selves and performance: The power of self-relevant imagery. *Social Cognition, 10,* 95–124.

Rybash, J. M., Hoyer, W. J., & Roodin, P. A. (1986). *Adult cognition and aging: Developmental changes in processing, knowing, and thinking.* New York: Pergamon Press.

Ryff, C. D. (1991). Possible selves in adulthood and old age: A tale of shifting horizons. *Psychology and Aging, 6,* 286–295.

Salthouse, T. A. (1991). *Theoretical perspectives on cognitive aging.* Hillsdale, NJ: Lawrence Erlbaum.

Schulz, R., & Heckhausen, J. (1996). A life-span model of successful aging. *American Psychologist, 51,* 702–714.

Sheldon, K. M., & Kasser, T. (1995). Coherence and congruence: Two aspects of personality integration. *Journal of Personality and Social Psychology, 68,* 531–543.

Siegler, I. C. (1989). Developmental health psychology. In M. Storandt & G. R. Vanden Bos (Eds.), *The adult years: Continuity and change* (pp. 119–142). Washington, D. C.: American Psychological Association.

Waddington, C. H. (1975). *The evolution of an evolutionist.* Edinburgh, Scotland: Edinburgh University Press.

Whaley, D. E. (1997). *An investigation of possible selves across stages of exercise involvement with middle-aged women.* Unpublished doctoral dissertation. Corvallis, OR: Oregon State University.

Whitbourne, S. K. (1985). The psychological construction of the life span. In J. E. Birren & K. W. Schaie (Eds.), *Handbook of the psychology of aging* (2nd ed., pp. 594–618). New York: Van Nostrand Reinhold.

Whitbourne, S. K. (1996). *The aging individual: Physical and psychological perspectives.* New York: Springer.

Willard, W. A., & Hooker, K. (1998, April). *Personality is as personality does: A contextual analysis.* Paper presented at the 70th annual meeting of the Eastern Psychological Association, Baltimore.

Appendix

- This questionnaire addresses how you see yourself in the future. We all think about our future to some extent. When doing so, we usually think about the kinds of experiences that are in store for us and the kinds of people we might possibly become. Sometimes we think about what we hope we will be like—selves we *hope* to become in the future, or *"hoped-for possible selves."*
- Some hoped-for possible selves seem quite likely, like becoming a homeowner or achieving higher status at work. Other future selves seem quite far-fetched but are still possible—for example, winning the lottery. Things that we do are not possible selves but are usually part of a possible self. For example, to write books is not a possible self; to be a writer is a possible self.
- Please take a few minutes and think about all of your *hoped-for possible selves.* You may have just a few, or you may have many.
- The following questionnaire asks you to identify 3 *hoped-for selves* that are currently most important to you and then to respond to a series of 6 questions about each possible self you identify.

POSSIBLE SELVES QUESTIONNAIRE

Hoped-for self #1: (Describe in this space)

Why is this hoped-for self important to you? (Answer in this space)

1. To what extent does this possible self describe you now?

   1   2   3   4   5   6   7
Not at all   Somewhat   Very much

2. To what extent would you like this possible self to describe you in the future?

   1   2   3   4   5   6   7
Not at all   Somewhat   Very much

3. How important is it to you to achieve this possible self?

   1   2   3   4   5   6   7
Not at all   Some what   Very
important   important   important

4. How capable do you feel of achieving this possible self?

   1   2   3   4   5   6   7
Not at all   Some what   Very
capable   capable   capable

5. How likely do you think it is that this possible self will be achieved?

   1   2   3   4   5   6   7
Not at all   Some what   Very
likely   likely   likely

6. How much time do you spend thinking about this possible self?

   1   2   3   4   5   6   7
Rarely   Sometimes   Often

Hoped-for self #2: (Describe in this space)

Why is this hoped-for self important to you? (Answer in this space.)

1. To what extent does this possible self describe you now?

   1   2   3   4   5   6   7
Not at all   Somewhat   Very much

2. To what extent would you like this possible self to describe you in the future?

   1   2   3   4   5   6   7
Not at all   Somewhat   Very much

3. How important is it to you to achieve this possible self?

   1   2   3   4   5   6   7
Not at all   Some what   Very
important   important   important

4. How capable do you feel of achieving this possible self?

   1   2   3   4   5   6   7
Not at all   Some what   Very
capable   capable   capable

5. How likely do you think it is that this possible self will be achieved?

   1   2   3   4   5   6   7
Not at all   Some what   Very
likely   likely   likely

6. How much time do you spend thinking about this possible self?

   1   2   3   4   5   6   7
Rarely   Sometimes   Often

Hoped-for self #3: (Describe in this space)

Why is this hoped-for self important to you? (Answer in this space.)

1. To what extent does this possible self describe you now?

   1   2   3   4   5   6   7
Not at all   Somewhat   Very much

2. To what extent would you like this possible self to describe you in the future?

   1   2   3   4   5   6   7
Not at all   Somewhat   Very much

3. How important is it to you to achieve this possible self?

   1   2   3   4   5   6   7
Not at all   Some what   Very
important   important   important

4. How capable do you feel of achieving this possible self?

   1   2   3   4   5   6   7
Not at all   Some what   Very
capable   capable   capable

5. How likely do you think it is that this possible self will be achieved?

   1   2   3   4   5   6   7
Not at all   Some what   Very
likely   likely   likely

6. How much time do you spend thinking about this possible self?

   1   2   3   4   5   6   7
Rarely   Sometimes   Often

- In addition to having hoped-for possible selves, we may have images of ourselves in the future that we fear, dread, or don't want to happen. Some of these *feared possible selves* may seem quite likely, like fear of dependency on another person. Other *feared possible selves* may seem quite unlikely—for example, becoming a homeless person. Some of us may have a large number of *feared possible selves* in mind, whereas others may have only a few.
- Take a few minutes to think about all of your *feared possible selves.* Again, please identify 3 *feared selves* that are currently *most dreaded* by you, and then respond to the 6 questions about each possible self you identify.

POSSIBLE SELVES QUESTIONNAIRE

Feared self #1: (Describe in this space)

Why is this feared self of concern to you? (Answer in this space)

1. To what extent does this possible self describe you now?

1	2	3	4	5	6	7
Not at all			Somewhat			Very much

2. To what extent would you like to avoid having this possible self to describe you in the future?

1	2	3	4	5	6	7
Not at all			Somewhat			Very much

3. How important is it to you to prevent the occurance of this possible self?

1	2	3	4	5	6	7
Not at all important			Some what important			Very important

4. How capable do you feel of preventing this possible self?

1	2	3	4	5	6	7
Not at all capable			Some what capable			Very capable

5. How likely do you think it is that this possible self will be prevented?

1	2	3	4	5	6	7
Not at all likely			Some what likely			Very likely

6. How much time do you spend thinking about this possible self?

1	2	3	4	5	6	7
Rarely			Sometimes			Often

Feared self #2: (Describe in this space)

Why is this feared self of concern to you? (Answer in this space)

1. To what extent does this possible self describe you now?

1	2	3	4	5	6	7
Not at all			Somewhat			Very much

2. To what extent would you like to avoid having this possible self to describe you in the future?

1	2	3	4	5	6	7
Not at all			Somewhat			Very much

3. How important is it to you to prevent the occurance of this possible self?

1	2	3	4	5	6	7
Not at all important			Some what important			Very important

4. How capable do you feel of preventing this possible self?

1	2	3	4	5	6	7
Not at all capable			Some what capable			Very capable

5. How likely do you think it is that this possible self will be prevented?

1	2	3	4	5	6	7
Not at all likely			Some what likely			Very likely

6. How much time do you spend thinking about this possible self?

1	2	3	4	5	6	7
Rarely			Sometimes			Often

Feared self #3: (Describe in this space)

Why is this feared self of concern to you? (Answer in this space)

1. To what extent does this possible self describe you now?

1	2	3	4	5	6	7
Not at all			Somewhat			Very much

2. To what extent would you like to avoid having this possible self to describe you in the future?

1	2	3	4	5	6	7
Not at all			Somewhat			Very much

3. How important is it to you to prevent the occurance of this possible self?

1	2	3	4	5	6	7
Not at all important			Some what important			Very important

4. How capable do you feel of preventing this possible self?

1	2	3	4	5	6	7
Not at all capable			Some what capable			Very capable

5. How likely do you think it is that this possible self will be prevented?

1	2	3	4	5	6	7
Not at all likely			Some what likely			Very likely

6. How much time do you spend thinking about this possible self?

1	2	3	4	5	6	7
Rarely			Sometimes			Often

POSSIBLE SELVES CODING CATEGORIES

Personal: Included references to personal attributes or attitudes ("independent," "intelligent," "harried," or "dissatisfied with my life") and to philosophical or spiritual issues.

Physical: Included references to fitness ("in good shape"), attractiveness ("thin" or "fat"), or a physical problem (e.g., "disabled").

Abilities and education: Included references to creative or artistic expression ("to be a good artist"), to education ("to have an advanced degree," "flunking out of school"), and to general knowledge ("becoming fluent in another language," "being well read").

Lifestyle: Included geographical references ("to live on the East Coast"), references to living in a nursing home, and references to quality of life ("living a simpler lifestyle," "having children move far away").

Family: Included all references to marriage or divorce, spouse, grandparenting, relating to one's own parents, and family illness. Refers to anything family related.

Relationships: Included references to friendship ("being a sympathetic friend," "being alone and lonely") and personal relationships not clearly indicated as family.

Occupation: Included all references to jobs ("having a job I truly enjoy," "having a boring job"), careers ("to be an effective therapist"), and retirement.

Material: Included references to financial security ("self-supporting," "poor") and to specific possessions ("having a medium-size comfortable home").

Success: Included references to achieving goals ("to finish the story of my family," "to be a failure") and to recognition or fame ("becoming a dominant authority in my field").

Social responsibility: Included all references to volunteer work, community involvement, and activity relating to other social issues ("a leader in eliminating the threat of nuclear war").

Leisure: Included references to travel or vacations ("traveling with my husband as semiretirees"), hobbies and recreational sports ("a good tennis player and runner"), and other leisure activities ("someone who appreciates music").

Health: Included references to general health ("in poor health," "long-lived"), specific diseases ("having Alzheimer's disease"), or substance abuse ("being an alcoholic").

Independence/dependence: Included references to being dependent on others for activities of daily living ("couldn't take care of myself," "maintaining my independence").

Death: Included any references to personal death ("having a prolonged death," "terminal illness").

Bereavement: Included references to death of a loved one ("losing my spouse," "widowed," "child's death").

Threats: Included references to events that were perceived to be threatening to the individual ("being raped," "having my house broken into").

6

SOURCES OF RESILIENCE IN THE AGING SELF

TOWARD INTEGRATING PERSPECTIVES

JOCHEN BRANDTSTÄDTER

Department of Psychology
University of Trier
Trier, Germany

It's time to be old,
To take in sail:
The god of bounds,
Who sets to seas a shore,
Came to me in his fatal rounds,
And said: "No more!
No farther shoot
Thy broad ambitious branches, and thy root.
Fancy departs: No more invent;
Contract thy firmament
To compass of a tent.
There's not enough for this and that,
Make thy option which of two;
Economize the failing river,
Not the less revere the giver,
Leave the many and hold the few.

Ralph Waldo Emerson, Terminus

Emerson's poem, written in the 19th century, reflects a view of aging that may not gain much applause among developmentalists today. It is *en vogue* to dismiss as obsolete views of aging that bear connotations of loss, constraint, and acceptance and to propagate an expansive concept of active, "successful" aging that is modeled on ideals of youthful vigor and attractiveness. Neither traditional "deficit views" of aging nor their optimistic counterparts, however, can do justice to the multifaceted and to some extent even counterintuitive picture of development in later life that has emerged since the late 1980s from research on resilience and vulnerability in the elderly.

There can be no doubt, on the one hand, that the biological, social, and psychological processes of aging involve a multitude of aversive and irreversible changes in many domains of life and functioning. The fading of physiological and adaptive resources is an outstanding feature of biological aging, although, because of advances in medical care and prevention, morbidity is increasingly "compressed" into the terminal phases of life (e.g., Fries & Crapo, 1981). The social resources of the elderly person are undermined by role losses as well as by social isolation and marginalization; as one grows old, the convoy of agemates with whom one shares a similar biographical and experiential background is gradually extenuated. Furthermore, aging inherently involves a shrinking of temporal resources of action. Time, as time yet to be lived, is not only required for the attainment of plans and goals that extend into the future but is also a resource for resolving goal conflicts; goals that cannot be simultaneously accomplished may eventually be arranged in a temporal sequence, as far as there remains enough time to do so. A common aversive experience in the life of elderly persons is the recognition that personally important goals may remain unachieved and that some projects have to be abandoned for the sake of others. With the fading of action reserves in many domains, the efficient use and allocation of remaining resources becomes an increasingly urgent concern (cf. Brandtstädter & Wentura, 1994). These adaptive problems are potentiated by the processes of sociohistorical change. The dynamics of cultural acceleration increasingly impede extrapolation and transfer of personal biographical knowledge to the future; wisdom and life experience tend to be devalued when older generations increasingly have to learn from the younger in order to keep in stride with cultural change.

This somewhat bleak scenario has to be qualified in important respects, of course. The processes of aging are not uniform; there are wide margins for variation and modification, and thus also for prevention and optimization (cf. Baltes, 1987; Brandtstädter & von Eye, 1982; Rowe & Kahn, 1987). Elderly people certainly differ in their capacity to draw sense and meaning from their aging (Staudinger & Dittmann-Kohli, 1992). Furthermore, aging involves not only resource decrements but also gains, such as increases in life experience, expertise, or—in fortunate cases—even the attainment of virtues and competences as they are addressed in old and new conceptualizations of "wisdom" (cf. Sternberg, 1990). When adults of different age groups are asked to balance perceived developmental losses against gains, both aspects are commonly reported. However, it appears that with advancing age, the balance tips toward the negative; people feel that they drift away from their desired self in many attributes, and this negative tendency increases with age (cf. Brandtstädter, Wentura, & Greve, 1993; Heckhausen, Dixon, & Baltes, 1989).

Losses and constraints of action resources tend to promote further loss and are a central source of stress (Hobfoll, 1989). Consistent with this assumption, physical, temporal, or social resources (e.g., health, social integration, extension of future perspectives) are positively related to measures of self-esteem, coping competence, and the like (e.g., Perrig-Chiello, 1997). Given this backdrop, it is remarkable that there is no evidence for a consistent or general decline in measures of well-being and subjective quality of life. At least until the terminal phases of life, there is no consistent evidence for an increased incidence in depression or self-esteem problems. Contrary to widespread assumptions, it also appears that prevailing negative stereotypes of aging do not generally undermine the integrity of the aging self (cf. Blazer, 1989; Lawton, 1991; Stock, Okun, Haring, & Witter, 1983). Briefly, the resilience and adaptive flexibility of elderly persons seem far greater than hitherto assumed. Indeed, the themes of vulnerability and resilience of the aging self gained priority on the agenda of developmental and gerontological researchers in the 1990s (cf. Brandtstädter & Greve, 1994; Staudinger, Marsiske, & Baltes, 1995).

This chapter looks at the different types of adaptive and protective processes that help the elderly person to maintain personal continuity and integrity despite the aversive and irreversible losses that often accompany the transition to old age. The model of assimilative, accommodative, and immunizing processes (AAI model) (Brandtstädter & Greve, 1994; Brandtstädter & Renner, 1990) will be discussed as a framework that integrates different types of protective mechanisms and spells out their developmental implications and constraints.

ADAPTIVE RESOURCES OF THE SELF-SYSTEM IN LATER LIFE: ASSIMILATIVE, ACCOMMODATIVE, AND IMMUNIZING PROCESSES

How do individuals construe the balance of gains and losses in later life? Through which activities do they try to keep this balance positive? What kind of processes—intentional or automatic—help mitigate or neutralize experiences of loss?

First, it should be noted that gains and losses over the life course do not occur in a fortuitous fashion. The developing individual continuously tries to optimize the balance of positive and negative changes in development through preventive, corrective, and compensatory efforts. Such efforts are part and parcel of intentional self-development over the life span; explications of successful development are often framed in terms of the individual's factual or perceived efficacy to maximize gain and minimize loss (e.g., Baltes & Baltes, 1990). The processes of aging, however, not only involve a shrinking of valued resources but likewise curtail the potential to compensate this loss. In other words, preventive, corrective, or compensatory efforts are in turn constrained by available resources and thus can be effective only within margins that may themselves shrink with advancing age (cf. Brandtstädter & Wentura, 1995). Furthermore, developmental changes are not positive or negative in or by themselves but gain particular valence only in relation to the person's goals, preferences, and self-definitions. These are not inherently stable but can change over the life course, and it seems plausible to assume that they tend to change in ways that contribute to resilience and personal continuity in the lives of elderly persons.

Experiences of developmental loss generally involve discrepancies between desired and actual self-states. How individuals respond to such discrepancies crucially depends on whether they feel capable of eliminating them; feelings of hopelessness and depression will be more likely when individuals expect that they can no longer be or become what they want to be or become. Here, the "possible self" (Markus & Nurius, 1986) that delineates the individual's action resources and developmental potentials comes into play. In later life, individuals may also have to come to terms with their "counterfactual" self—that is, with those options of personal development that have remained unrealized. Explicating the sources of resiliency and vulnerability in later life thus translates into the task of delineating the activities or mechanisms through which actual, desired, potential, and counterfactual self-representations—all of which are themselves subject to developmental change—are coadjusted and permanently readjusted in ways that reduce or minimize personal discontinuity and distress.

In the AAI model, three different but interrelated ways to accomplish that basic aim are distinguished (cf. Brandtstädter & Greve, 1994; Brandtstädter & Renner, 1990). Self-discrepancies may be eliminated first by intentionally transforming the actual situation so that it comes into a closer fit with personal goals, identity projects, or self-definitions. This we have termed the *assimilative* mode of coping. Not only may assimilative interventions be targeted on external circumstances but as purposeful actors, individuals can also try to eliminate self-discrepancies by making themselves—or their own behavior—the object of corrective intervention. Second, perceived self-discrepancies, and the emotional distress that they involve, may be neutralized by adjusting goals and preferences to situational constraints. We denote this as the *accommodative* mode of coping. Accommodative processes alter the individual's evaluation of a problem rather than the factual situation itself; this mode will dominate in situations that are—factually or subjectively—impervious to active change.

Assimilative and accommodative processes both presuppose some recognition of an aversive self-discrepancy. There is an inherent tendency of the self-system, however, to shield itself against self-discrepant evidence or feedback. In our terminology, such tendencies belong to the *immunizing* mode. Immunizing mechanisms negotiate self-referent evidence in self-serving ways, and they may engage processes of dissonance reduction as well as processes of self-enhancement.

Going beyond a mere taxonomy of sources of resiliency or coping strategies, the AAI model specifies functional linkages and interdependencies between these different types or families of protective processes and spells out relevant personal and contextual conditions that affect their interplay in concrete episodes of coping. A core assumption of the model is that assimilative, accommodative, and immunizing processes are antagonistic and tend to inhibit each other, although all three modes may work together on different functional levels in a synergistic and complementary fashion.

ASSIMILATIVE ACTIVITIES

Assimilative activities aim at shaping processes and outcomes of personal development so that they converge with personal goals and self-definitions. In early adulthood, assimilative efforts may predominantly strive for an expansion of action resources and for an achievement of identity goals and personal projects that extend into the future. In later life, however, assimilative efforts increasingly tend to center on maintaining resources and avoiding skill–demand mismatches. To keep a desired level of competence, to minimize health risks, or to maintain a desired bodily self, individuals may change their eating habits, engage in bodily exercise, select particular environments, shift daily routines, and more. Assimilative efforts can be targeted on any domain of life and functioning that is perceived as open to intentional modification; they will primarily center, however, on those areas of life and functioning that are of personal significance.

Assimilative efforts centering on compensatory goals gain particular importance in later life. Generally, mental or physical skills involve a multitude of functional components and allow for alternative ways of implementation. Accordingly, performance deficits that are caused by a decrease in particular subfunctions can often be offset by selective strengthening of unimpaired functions or by the development or use of latent skills. Compensatory strategies may range from the use of external aids and prosthetic means (e.g., visual or hearing aids, self-help devices in the house) to the use of mnemonic techniques to maintain desired levels of cognitive performance in later life (see Bäckman & Dixon, 1992; Baltes & Baltes, 1990; Salthouse, 1987).

Assimilative (preventive, corrective, compensatory) activities reflect the individual's identity goals and basic life design; they are characterized by a continuing commitment and tenacious adherence to the goals and self-evaluative standards that one has set for oneself. Under scarce action reserves, the tenacious pursuit of goals may eventually involve auxiliary efforts to enhance personal efficiency and optimal resource allocation. To the extent that corrective efforts aim at changing entrenched habits that are maintained by their immediate rewarding effects, self-discipline and self-regulatory skills may become important ingredients of assimilative action (cf. Baumeister, Heatherton, & Tice, 1994).

The pursuit of self-corrective and compensatory activities crucially hinges on self-beliefs of control and efficacy. Under particular circumstances, however, assimilative efforts may persist even when action-outcome expectancies are low. Provided that the expected outcome is important enough, it may be rational to try a solution even when the odds of succeeding are unfavorable. In the extreme, assimilative efforts may even border on superstition. People tend to grasp at straws to prevent or mitigate functional loss in later life when other means are exhausted or not available, and it may become difficult to draw a rigid boundary between reasoned action and self-serving illusions in such cases.

Although assimilative (corrective, preventive, compensatory) activities generally aim at maintaining functional resources, they also depend on and deplete available resources. Older athletes, for example, may try to compensate for physiological decrements through intensified training; however, the increased investment of time and energy may eventually conflict with other personal or social goals, so that the costs of assimilative activities may come to outstrip their benefits. Assimilative activities thus are subject to a principle of diminishing returns. Under such conditions, it may become increasingly difficult to maintain desired standards, and individuals may be forced to accommodate their goals in order to find a new equilibrium between personal aspirations and functional resources.

ACCOMMODATIVE PROCESSES

According to the AAI model, assimilative efforts will be inhibited when goals or self-evaluative standards drift outside the feasible range; to the same degree, accommodative processes will be activated. As defined above, the accommodative mode involves a restructuring of preferences and self-evaluative standards. A key characteristic of accommodation, then, is the flexible adjustment of barren goals and ambitions, rather than the persistent effort to maintain them, which characterizes the assimilative mode. The accommodative process overrides assimilative tendencies by destroying or neutralizing the valuations and cognition that support these tendencies. The accommodation of goals prevents or mitigates feelings of frustration or helplessness that tend to persist as long as the individual holds on to a blocked goal, and it helps to economize action reserves by channeling them to a "feasible set" of options (Elster, 1989).

The adaptive importance of accommodative processes has been seriously underrated in the past. Clearly, the disengagement from goals and the downscaling of aspirations may constrain developmental potentials as long as there are objective chances to alter the situation (e.g., Bandura, 1986). On the other hand, assimilative persistence may become maladaptive under constrained resources and in situations of irreversible loss that are typical in later life. It is increasingly recognized that besides the loss of control over personally important goals, the inability to let go of blocked goals is a potent etiological factor in reactive depression (cf. Brandtstädter & Renner, 1990; Carver & Scheier, 1990).

The process of disengagement from barren goals and attachments is not necessarily a smooth one, and it generally cannot be set into operation by an intentional act or decision. Any intentional resolution to dissolve a commitment
would already presuppose what it is purported to bring about—a downgrading
of the given goal; a decision to disengage thus would be the result rather than
the initial cause of accommodative processes. Rather than being voluntarily
enacted, accommodative processes are differentially enhanced or impeded by
personal and contextual factors over which the individual has limited personal
control. For example, individuals will find it most difficult to disengage from
goals that are central to their identity and life design and for which substitutes
are not easily available. A complex self-structure that embraces a diversity of
goals and identity projects will often enhance disengagement from blocked
goals and commitment to new goals and may thus protect individuals from
emotional turmoil in situations of loss (cf. Linville, 1987). Sociocultural contexts differ as to the degree to which they support an age-related rescaling of
goals and performance standards; cultures in which notions of successful aging
are dominated by ideals of youthful strength will presumably offer less leeway
in that regard. As individuals move through the life cycle, they enter different
informational and symbolic contexts that may provide different standards and
comparison perspectives for self-evaluation (e.g., Frey & Ruble, 1990), and that
may thus impede or enhance the flexible accommodation of personal goals to
changed action resources.

IMMUNIZING MECHANISMS

The immune system responds to an antigenic agent by the formation of anti-
bodies that are capable of rendering it harmless or suppressing its pathological
effects. Similar mechanisms tend to protect the self-concept—or the theory one
holds about oneself—from discrepant evidence. People tend to actively avoid situations in which they are likely to be confronted with self-discrepant feedback,
and they also tend to negotiate self-referential information in ways that protect
their preferred and entrenched self-definitions (e.g., Pyszczynski & Greenberg,
1987; Steele, 1988; Swann, 1983; Tesser, 1986). The notion of immunizing mechanisms, as it is used here, refers to this self-protective negotiation of evidence,
which we consider a third mode of self-maintenance in later life (see also Greve,
1990).

Immunizing processes protect in particular those elements of the self-system
that are central or most relevant to the individual's identity. In contrast to assimilative activities (but similar in that respect to accommodative processes), immunization mechanisms should not be equated with intentionally chosen coping
strategies. The assumption that one could intentionally adopt a belief for the purpose of soothing oneself is incoherent, quite apart from the fact that such a
maneuver would ironically undermine its intended effect (cf. Johnston, 1995). We
hold a belief because it seems plausible to us, not because we consider it useful to

have that belief, although of course the motive to check the validity of a belief may be compromised when the belief in question has strongly positive implications for the individual's self-view.

Generally, the degree to which empirical data can affect a self-referential belief is jointly dependent on the strength of the particular belief and on the strength or diagnostic relevance of the evidence. Strong or well-entrenched self-beliefs tend to resist discrepant evidence and to raise the individual's susceptibility for arguments that discredit the corresponding sources of evidence (e.g., Markus & Wurf, 1987). Immunization can involve a variety of mechanisms, ranging from self-serving attributions to subtle shifts in the semantic structure of self-descriptive attributes. Elderly individuals may respond to perceived losses in specific skills by downgrading the diagnostic relevance of the corresponding performances for valued self-attributes; for example, difficulties in retaining items in short-term memory may be attributed to a temporary indisposition or to external disturbances rather than to an enduring functional loss (cf. Greve, 1990). Such self-serving attributions are not always irrational; within the limits of rationality, there is often leeway for negotiating evidence in ways that preserve personal continuity and self-esteem.

In particular cases, however, the motives of cognitive consistency and self-enhancement may pose conflicting demands on the processing of information (cf. Swann, Griffin, Predmore, & Gaines, 1987); aversive or self-threatening evidence may become too strong to be negotiated in self-serving ways. The self-system may then alter the criteria or reference points for ascribing some self-attribute, thus establishing a second line of defense, as it were. For example, when elderly people evaluate their health or physical fitness, they often tend to apply more lenient standards than do younger people. (To some extent, this phenomenon may also be accounted for by accommodative processes.) This age-related rescaling of attributional criteria often reflects shared notions of what is "normal" and can be legitimately expected from a person of a given age. The interesting point here is that this process contributes to preserved stability of self-descriptions in spite of perceived changes or losses on the level of actual performance.

On a rear line of defense, the "immune response" of the self-system may even involve a shift in the semantic structure of attributes. The fuzziness of concepts in everyday language fosters this type of immunization. For example, elderly persons may change their notions of cognitive competence in a self-protective way by putting more emphasis on such intellectual capacities or skills that do not decrease, or even show increases, with age, such as wisdom or expertise (cf. Ryff, 1991).

Through raising the individual's recognition thresholds for self-discrepant evidence, immunizing mechanisms inhibit problem-focused, assimilative activities as well as accommodative readjustments of goals. Accordingly, self-discrepant evidence must become sufficiently strong or salient to override immunizing tendencies and to activate assimilative counteractions or accommodative processes. I do not suggest here, however, that the self-system is generally geared to reject or neutralize aversive information. As long as resources to actively cope with the problem are available, the individual will tend to respond in a more vigilant or sensitive way to problems. Immunizing tendencies should be most strongly displayed when the individual sees no chances to alter the situation, and when the barren commitments or attachments are too strong or important to be relinquished.

Figure 6.1 summarizes the functional interrelations and constraints of AAI processes that have been discussed so far. These modes are depicted as antagonistic or mutually exclusive, which means that the conditions or mental sets that specifically enhance a particular mode will generally inhibit the other two modes. This does not preclude a synergy between these modes in concrete episodes of crisis or loss. First, crises and losses in later life typically entail a diversity of adaptive tasks and accordingly may call for different modes of coping in different phases or on different levels. In bereavement situations, for example, accommodative flexibility may enhance the finding of new, meaningful life perspectives; assimilative persistence may help in establishing a new routine of life; and immunization-like processes, such as imagining the presence of the deceased loved one, may contribute to psychological readjustment (cf. Börner, 1997). Furthermore, one should consider the possibility that each of the three modes may

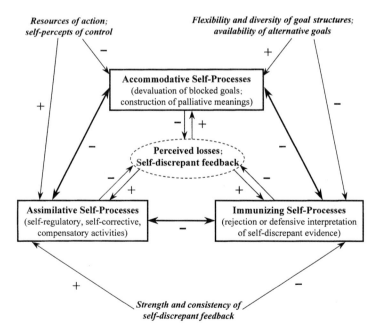

FIGURE 6.1   Sources of resilience in the aging self: assimilative, accommodative, and immunizing self-processes. Enhancing and inhibiting effects are marked by + or –, respectively.

engage the other two as auxiliary subfunctions. For example, assimilative persistence in the face of obstacles and drawbacks may be enhanced by an "implementative" mind-set (Gollwitzer, 1990) that temporarily immunizes self-percepts of efficacy against discrepant feedback. Likewise, the tenacious pursuit of some assimilative (corrective, compensatory) goal may be facilitated by disengaging, temporarily or permanently, from other commitments in order to focus available resources on that goal. (To some extent, such "instrumental" forms of disengagement are basic to any goal-related action.)

EMPIRICAL SCOPE OF THE MODEL OF ASSIMILATIVE, ACCOMMODATIVE, AND IMMUNIZING PROCESSES

In its explanatory scope, the AAI model covers a diversity of phenomena that seem central to the stability and resilience of the self-system in later life. The following illustrations center primarily on accommodative processes. This emphasis seems justified for two reasons: First, accommodative processes appear to be strongly underresearched in comparison to active-compensatory and immunizing-defensive modes of coping; second, empirical evidence underscores the particular importance of this variant of adaptive processes in later life.

ACCOUNTING FOR THE POTENTIALLY NEGATIVE EFFECTS OF PERCEIVED CONTROL

Although self-beliefs of internal control generally predict better coping with situations of crises and loss, many studies have not found the predicted negative relationship between measures of control and depression, or even have reported converse results (for an overview, see, e.g., Coyne & Gottlib, 1983). In light of these inconsistencies, the need for a more balanced view of the functional and dysfunctional implications of perceived control has drawn increasing attention (e.g., Thompson, Cheek, & Graham, 1988). The AAI model posits that self-percepts of efficacy should enhance the intensity and persistence of active, problem-focused efforts; in that respect, it partly converges with traditional formulations of control. However, the model also posits that a strong sense of personal control may impede the flexible adjustment of goals and ambitions to situational constraints. When individuals are confronted with factually irreversible loss, a delayed shift toward accommodative modes of coping may even result in prolonged depressive rumination (cf. Brandtstädter, Rothermund, & Schmitz, 1998). In line with these assumptions, there is evidence that the effect of internal control on measures of well-being is moderated by contextual variables and can even become negative in refractory situations that resist active modification (e.g., Renner, 1990; Wolk, 1976).

THE SHIFT TOWARD ACCOMMODATIVE MODES OF COPING IN LATER LIFE

Related to the last point in the previous section, it should be noted that situations involving factually irreversible and uncontrollable loss are quite typical for old age. According to the AAI model, the cumulation of irreversible aversive changes, together with the fading of action resources in many domains of life and functioning, should lead to an increasing predominance of accommodative over assimilative modes of functioning. Brandtstädter and Renner (1990) have designed scales to assess dispositional differences in assimilative persistence and accommodative flexibility (Tenacious Goal Pursuit [TGB], Flexible Goal Adjustment [FGA]). Both scales are positively related to indicators of well-being and subjective life quality, but at the same time, they exhibit opposite regressions on chronological age. In line with theoretical expectations, there is an age-related increase in FGA, indicating a growing capacity or readiness to adjust ambitions and preferences to situational constraints (cf. Brandtstädter, 1992; Heckhausen & Schulz, 1998). These findings, however, should not be taken to imply that assimilative modes of coping generally tend to vanish in later life. By continually adjusting preferences to constraints and resources, the accommodative process rather establishes new reference points for assimilative activities. Channeling assimilative energies to the feasible range even serves to maintain a sense of personal control and efficacy; this point is discussed in more detail later in this chapter.

COPING WITH AGE-TYPICAL LOSSES AND CONSTRAINTS

Evidence suggests that with advancing age, accommodative flexibility becomes increasingly important as a resource of resiliency. With the narrowing of future perspectives, most individuals will face the problem that some valued goals cannot be accomplished in the remaining time or have to be relinquished to allow concentration of scarce resources on some selected domains of high priority. Accommodative flexibility should mitigate such adaptive strains. Consistent with this assumption, individuals with high accommodative flexibility seem to be less negatively affected by the inexorable fading of temporal reserves in later life (cf. Brandtstädter & Wentura, 1995). Furthermore, accommodative flexibility (as measured by the FGA scale) apparently tones down the emotional impact of age-typical problems. For example, moderated regression analyses hint that for individuals scoring high in FGA, the negative regression of well-being or life satisfaction on such variables as health problems, chronic pain, or physical impairments is less expressed or vanishes (Brandtstädter et al., 1993; Schmitz, Saile, & Nilges, 1996). Such interactive buffering effects tend to be weaker or absent for assimilative persistence as measured by the TGP scale.

An interesting asymmetry also appears in the relationship of accommodative flexibility and assimilative persistence to health status measures. Findings from ongoing studies suggest a slight but significant negative relation of FGA with morbidity, which seems most clearly expressed with respect to diabetes, cardiovascular disorders, and genitourinary problems. By contrast, the TGP scale seems unrelated to actual health status; longitudinal comparisons, however, suggest that negative changes in health status are initially accompanied by an increase in assimilative tendencies. Though it seems premature yet to draw causal conclusions, these findings further testify to the potential of accommodative flexibility as a protective resource in later life.

MAINTAINING A SENSE OF CONTROL THROUGH ACCOMMODATION OF GOALS

Such age-related changes as decreasing action resources and adaptive reserves, role losses, and social marginalization are generally deemed to undermine a sense of control; accordingly, efforts to counteract losses in perceived control have been a focal concern in intervention studies with elderly people (e.g., Schulz, 1980). Given this backdrop, it is all the more surprising that research has failed to provide evidence for a general or pervasive age-related decline of control in later adulthood (cf. Brandtstädter & Baltes-Götz, 1990; Lachman, Ziff, & Spiro, 1994). The AAI model suggests that accommodation of goals should contribute to maintaining a sense of control in later life. At first glance, this hypothesis may seem to conflict with the proposition that accommodative processes are induced by the experience of losing control over particular goals. Notions of control and efficacy, however, conceptually imply the capacity to reach goals of personal importance; this apparently implies that downgrading the importance of goals that have drifted beyond the individual's span of control may protect a global sense of control. Findings by Brandtstädter and Rothermund (1994) support this assumption. With respect to a list of goals, participants at this study were asked to rate the extent of personal control over each goal as well as the personal importance of that goal. These data were repeatedly assessed from a sample of 735 adults (initial age range: 30–59 years) over a longitudinal interval of 8 years. A global index of control was formed by aggregating domain-linked ratings. Moderated multiple-regression techniques indicated that the impact of differential longitudinal change in domain-linked control on global control beliefs was dependent on the importance of the particular goal domain; in particular, longitudinal decreases in domain-specific control affected the individual's general sense of control to a lesser degree when the importance of the respective domain was downgraded within the same longitudinal interval. This again indicates that accommodative flexibility may help maintain a self-assured, confident outlook and counteract feelings of helplessness and depression in later life.

ACCOMMODATING MEANING PERSPECTIVES
IN LATER LIFE

Goals and plans that extend into the future are potent sources of meaning, but they tend to lose their motivating potential when future perspectives narrow down in later life. The loss of "future meaning" (Reker, Peacock, & Wong, 1987) may raise the vulnerability for depression and alienation in later life. Psychological problems of this kind may be mitigated if meaning perspectives shift toward themes that are less dependent on lifetime reserves. First, sense and meaning may increasingly be found in the biographical past, or in the "having been" rather than in the "becoming" (Raynor, 1982). Furthermore, goals and existential orientations that are timeless or transcend a limited temporal horizon may gain dominance over instrumental projects aiming at some future return. Brandtstädter, Wentura, & Schmitz (1997) have provided evidence for age-related shifts in meaning perspectives that conform with these assumptions. In a study involving 896 participants in the age range of 58–82 years, they found evidence for an age-related shift from time-immanent meaning perspectives centering on investment-oriented, consummatory, or maintenance activities toward sources of meaning such as retrospection and life review, expression of personal ideals, and "transcendent" orientations (such as charity goals or a commitment to religious ideas). An orientation toward time-transcendent values also was found to reduce the negative emotional impact of health problems in later life.

NEUTRALIZING THE IMPACT OF NEGATIVE AGE
STEREOTYPES

Negative age stereotypes are commonly thought to undermine the elderly person's self-esteem. Age-comparative and longitudinal studies, however, have revealed the considerable stability and integrity of the aging self (e.g., Costa & McCrae, 1986; Kaufman, 1986); this suggests that the presumptively negative impact of aging stereotypes on the older person's self-definition is, at least to some extent, buffered by protective mechanisms. Two processes seem relevant in this regard, both of which involve an accommodation of self-evaluative standards. First, stereotyped expectations about age may serve as an anchor point for self-enhancing downward comparisons; in fact, most elderly people tend to compare themselves positively to the generalized image that they have of their agemates (e.g., Schulz & Fritz, 1987). Related to this point, studies on age identification have commonly found that adults tend to "feel" themselves younger than they are (e.g., Baum & Boxley, 1983); this tendency apparently reflects the negative connotations of the concept of old and a corresponding reluctance to categorize oneself as old. Rejecting a self-description as old, however, tends to become more difficult with advancing age. The AAI model would suggest that under such conditions, older people may increasingly include positive meanings into their personal concept of being old. Rothermund, Wentura, and Brandtstädter (1995) used a semantic priming technique to analyze this process on a microanalytical level. In this study, the word *old* was presented on a computer monitor, followed by such positively valued target words as *good, happy, confident,* and *influential* (stimulus onset asynchrony: 1000 milliseconds). Priming effects were measured by a lexical decision procedure. The results in fact hint that *old* takes on increasingly positive connotations with age. This effect might also be accounted for by immunizing processes as defined earlier in this chapter; there was, however, no evidence for a corresponding inhibiting effect on the processing of negatively valued target words. In addition, the tendency to enrich the meaning of *old* with positive connotations was more strongly displayed by participants who scored high in accommodative flexibility (as assessed by the FGA scale), whereas it was absent in "inflexible" individuals.

SUMMARY AND CONCLUSIONS

The self is not stable or invulnerable in any simple empirical sense; rather, the self-system permanently produces and selects conditions that foster and serve to maintain personal continuity and self-esteem across the life span. Three basic types of protective self-processes have been discussed in this chapter.

Through *assimilative* activities, individuals try to shape themselves, their development, and their personal aging so that it conforms with the goals and self-definitions that they have construed for themselves and their life. Assimilative activities are a basic ingredient of intentional self-development; across the life span, the basic themes of assimilative activity may gradually change from the growth and expansion of resources to concerns of maintenance and of compensating for developmental losses.

Accommodative processes, by contrast, adjust goals and self-definitions so that they conform with the action resources and developmental potentials that individuals have or believe they have. This adaptive mode becomes relevant and functionally predominant when assimilative efforts turn out to be futile or to drift beyond the possibility frontiers delineated by functional resources and self-percepts of control. In accounting for phenomena of resilience in later life, accommodative processes deserve much more attention than they have hitherto received. Available evidence suggests that the readiness or capability to relinquish barren goals and to adjust ambitions to the feasible range is a potent adaptive resource in later life that seems to mitigate the aversive impact of losses and constraints. Far from being symptoms of resignation and depression, accommodative processes are functional in maintaining a sense of control and a positive self-perspective in later life.

Immunizing processes have been considered as a third group of protective processes. These processes interact with assimilative and accommodative functions insofar as they tend to suppress a recognition of self-discrepancies. Immunizing processes are not simply illusionary maneuvers that impede flexible adjustment to developmental changes; rather, they serve positive adaptive functions. Any adaptive system must come to terms with what Grossberg (1987) called the "stability–plasticity dilemma": It has to remain stable enough in response to potentially irrelevant events, and it has to remain plastic and vigilant in response to potentially significant changes. In synergy with assimilative and accommodative modes, immunizing processes apparently play a significant part in resolving this dilemma. Within the constraints posed by personal knowledge, beliefs, and identity constructions, these functions will generally converge toward some individualized resolution of the dilemma to maintain personal continuity and to adjust to developmental changes and losses. Though this is somewhat speculative, it seems plausible to assume that the self-system may become more prone to engage in more extreme forms of immunization (denial, self-deception, and the like) when coping resources of the assimilative or accommodative variant are exhausted, so that a "realistic" orientation has lost its particular adaptive function.

The AAI model challenges theoretical notions that have been and continue to be influential in the domains of social cognition and aging. It replaces the opposition of activity-theoretical and disengagement notions of successful aging by a more balanced and integrated approach that highlights the functionality both of self-regulatory activities that aim at maintaining valued skills and competences and of processes that rescale goals and ambitions so that they fit with changing resources of action. This approach also renders questionable the current lopsided emphasis on active-offensive modes of coping with losses; the arguments presented caution us that the tendency to tenaciously maintain youthful goals and identity projects may become a source of frustration and depression in later life.

Adaptive resilience and resourcefulness in later life apparently stems from a balanced interplay between assimilative, accommodative, and immunizing functions. These do not, however, always and automatically prevent discontinuity, distress, and depression. The AAI model delineates conditions that impede the interplay between the different adaptive modes and may lead to a dysfunctional predominance of one or the other mode. These conditions are differentially related to personal factors, such as self-complexity, self-efficacy beliefs, or the availability of palliative meanings; they likewise depend on contextual conditions, such as available resources of action, stereotyped notions of development, or social representations of successful aging. Assimilative, accommodative, and immunizing functions thus are inherently tied to the historical and sociocultural matrix within which individuals construe their self-understandings, shape their development, and manage their aging.

Though empirical applications of the present theoretical model have primarily centered on development in later adulthood, the model's explanatory scope is not limited to any particular period of the life span. Rather, the model provides a general and integrated account of the processes through which identity is realized, maintained, defended, and transformed in personal development across the life span. At the same time, it marks points of convergence where research on social cognition and the self may coalesce with conceptualizations of optimal development and successful aging.

ACKNOWLEDGMENTS

The research reported in this chapter was supported by grants from the German Research Foundation (DFG).

REFERENCES

Bäckman, L. & Dixon, R. A. (1992). Psychological compensation: A theoretical framework. *Psychological Bulletin, 112,* 259–283.

Baltes, P. B. (1987). Theoretical propositions of life-span developmental psychology: On the dynamics between growth and decline. *Developmental Psychology, 23,* 611–626.

Baltes, P. B. & Baltes, M. M. (1990). Psychological perspectives on successful aging: The model of selective optimization with compensation. In P. B. Baltes & M. M. Baltes (Eds.), *Successful aging: Perspectives from the behavioral sciences* (pp. 1–34). New York: Cambridge University Press.

Bandura, A. (1986). *Social foundations of thought and action: A social cognitive theory.* Englewood Cliffs, NJ: Prentice-Hall.

Baum, S. K. & Boxley, R. L. (1983). Age identification in the elderly. *The Gerontologist, 23,* 532–537.

Baumeister, R. F. & Heatherton, T. F., & Tice, D. M. (1994). *Losing control: How and why people fail at self-regulation.* San Diego, CA: Academic Press.

Blazer, D. (1989). Depression in late life: An update. *Annual Review of Gerontology and Geriatrics, 9,* 197–215.

Börner, K. (1997). *The grieving process and continuing ties to the deceased.* Diploma thesis, University of Trier, Trier, Germany.

Brandtstädter, J. (1992). Personal control over development: Some developmental implications of self-efficacy. In R. Schwarzer (Ed.), *Self-efficacy: Thought control of action* (pp. 127–145). New York: Hemisphere.

Brandtstädter, J. & Baltes-Götz, B. (1990). Personal control over development and quality of life perspectives in adulthood. In P. B. Baltes & M. M. Baltes (Eds.), *Successful aging: Perspectives from the behavioral sciences* (pp. 197–224). New York: Cambridge University Press.

Brandtstädter, J. & Greve, W. (1994). The aging self: Stabilizing and protective processes. *Developmental Review, 14,* 52–80.

Brandtstädter, J. & Renner, G. (1990). Tenacious goal pursuit and flexible goal adjustment: Explication and age-related analysis of assimilative and accommodative strategies of coping. *Psychology and Aging, 5,* 58–67.

Brandtstädter, J. & Rothermund, K. (1994). Self-percepts of control in middle and later adulthood: Buffering losses by rescaling goals. *Psychology and Aging, 9,* 265–273.

Brandtstädter, J., Rothermund, K., & Schmitz, U. (1998). Maintaining self-integrity and self-efficacy through adulthood and later life: The adaptive functions of assimilative persistence and accommodative flexibility. In J. Heckhausen & C. Dweck (Eds.), *Motivation and self-regulation across the life span* (pp. 365–388). New York: Cambridge University Press.

Brandtstädter, J. & von Eye, A. (1982). *Psychologische Prävention: Grundlagen. Programme, Methoden.* Bern: Huber.

Brandtstädter, J. & Wentura, D. (1994). Veränderungen der Zeit- und Zukunftsperspektive im Übergang zum höheren Erwachsenenalter: entwicklungspsychologische und differentielle Aspekte. *Zeitschrift für Entwicklungspsychologie und Pädagogische Psychologie, 26,* 2–21.

Brandtstädter, J. & Wentura, D. (1995). Adjustment to shifting possibility frontiers in later life: Complementary adaptive modes. In R. A. Dixon & L. Bäckman (Eds.), *Compensating for psychological deficits and declines: Managing losses and promoting gains* (pp. 83–106). Mahwah, NJ: Lawrence Erlbaum Associates.

Brandtstädter, J., Wentura, D., & Greve, W. (1993). Adaptive resources of the aging self: Outlines of an emergent perspective. *International Journal of Behavioral Development, 16,* 323–349.

Brandtstädter, J., Wentura, D. & Schmitz, U. (1997). Veränderungen der Zeit- und Zukunftsperspektive im Übergang zum höheren Alter: quer- und längsschnittliche Befunde. *Zeitschrift für Psychologie, 205,* 377–395.

Carver, C. S. & Scheier, M. F. (1990). Origins and foundations of positive and negative affect: A control-process view. *Psychological Review, 97,* 19–25.

Costa, P. T., Jr., & McCrae, R. R. (1989). Personality continuity and the changes of adult life. In P. T. Costa, M. Gatz, B. L. Neugarten, T. A. Salthouse, & I. Ziegler (Eds.), *The adult years: Continuity and change* (pp. 41–77). Washington, D. C.: American Psychological Association.

Coyne, J. C. & Gotlib, I. H. (1983). The role of cognition in depression: A critical appraisal. *Psychological Bulletin, 94,* 472–505.

Elster, J. (1989). *Nuts and bolts for the social sciences.* New York: Cambridge University Press.

Fries, J. F. & Crapo, L. M. (1981). *Vitality and aging.* San Francisco, CA: Freeman.

Frey, K. S. & Ruble, D. N. (1990). Strategies for comparative evaluation: Maintaining a sense of competence across the life span. In R. J. Sternberg & J. Kolligian, Jr. (Eds.), *Competence considered* (pp. 167–189). New Haven, CT: Yale University Press,

Gollwitzer, P. M. (1990). Action phases and mind-sets. In E. T. Higgins & R. M. Sorrentino (Eds.), *Handbook of motivation and cognition: Foundations of social behavior* (vol. 2, pp. 53–92). New York: Guilford Press.

Greve, W. (1990). Stabilisierung und Modifikation des Selbstkonzeptes im Erwachsenenalter: Strategien der Immunisierung. *Sprache & Kognition, 9,* 218–230.

Grossberg, S. (1987). Competitive learning: From interactive activation to adaptive resonance. *Cognitive Science, 11,* 23–63.

Heckhausen, J. & Schulz, R. (1998). Developmental regulation in adulthood: Selection and compensation via primary and secondary control. In J. Heckhausen & C. Dweck (Eds.), *Motivation and self-regulation across the life span* (pp. 50–77). New York: Cambridge University Press.

Heckhausen, J., Dixon, R. A., & Baltes, P. B. (1989). Gains and losses in development throughout adulthood as perceived by different adult age groups. *Developmental Psychology, 25,* 109–121.

Hobfoll, S. E. (1989). Conservation of resources: A new attempt at conceptualizing stress. *American Psychologist, 44,* 513–524.

Johnston, M. (1995). Self-deception and the nature of mind. In C. Macdonald & G. Macdonald (Eds.), *Philosophy of psychology: Debates on psychological explanation* (vol. 1, pp. 433–460). Oxford: Blackwell.

Kaufman, S. (1986). *The ageless self.* New York: Meridian.

Lachman, M. E., Ziff, M. X., & Spiro, A. (1994). Maintaining a sense of control in later life. In R. P. Abeles, H. C. Gift, & M. G. Ory (Eds.), *Aging and quality of life* (pp. 216–232). New York: Springer.

Lawton, M. P. (1991). A multidimensional view of quality of life in frail elders. In J. E. Birren, J. E. Lubben, J. C. Rowe, & D. E. Deutchman (Eds.), *The concept and measurement of quality of life in the frail elderly* (pp. 3–27). San Diego, CA: Academic Press.

Linville, P. W. (1987). Self-complexity as a cognitive buffer against stress-related illness and depression. *Journal of Personality and Social Psychology, 52,* 663–676.

Markus, H. & Nurius, P. (1986). Possible selves. *American Psychologist, 41,* 954–969.

Markus, H. & Wurf, E. (1987). The dynamic self-concept: A social psychological perspective. *Annual Review of Psychology, 38,* 299–337.

Perrig-Chiello, P. (1997). *Wohlbefinden im Alter: Körperliche, psychische und soziale Determinanten und Ressourcen.* Weinheim, Germany: Juventa.

Pyszczynski, T., & Greenberg, J. (1987). Depression, self-focused attention, and self-regulatory perseveration. In C. R. Snyder & C. E. Ford (Eds.), *Coping with negative life-events* (pp. 105–129). New York: Plenum.

Raynor, J. O. (1982). A theory of personality functioning and change. In J. O. Raynor & E. E. Entin (Eds.), *Motivation, career striving, and aging* (pp. 13–82). Washington, D. C.: Hemisphere.

Reker, G. T., Peacock, E. J., & Wong, P. T. (1987). Meaning and the purpose in life and well-being: A life-span perspective. *Journal of Gerontology, 42,* 44–49.

Renner, G. (1990). *Flexible Zielanpassung und hartnäckige Zielverfolgung: Zur Aufrechterhaltung der subjektiven Lebensqualität in Entwicklungskrisen.* Doctoral thesis, University of Trier, Trier, Germany.

Rothermund, K., Wentura, D., & Brandtstädter, J. (1995). Selbstwertschützende Verschiebungen in der Semantik des Begriffs "alt" im höheren Erwachsenenalter. *Sprache & Kognition, 14,* 52–63.

Rowe, J. W. & Kahn, R. L. (1987). Human aging: Usual and successful. *Science, 237,* 143–149.

Ryff, C. D. (1991). Possible selves in adulthood and old age: A tale of shifting horizons. *Psychology and Aging, 6,* 286–295.

Salthouse, T. A. (1987). Age, experience, and compensation. In K. Schooler & K. W. Schaie (Eds.), *Cognitive functioning and social structure over the life course* (pp. 142–150). Norwood, NJ: Ablex.

Schmitz, U., Saile, H., & Nilges, P. (1996). Coping with chronic pain: Flexible goal adjustment as an interactive buffer against pain-related distress. *Pain, 67,* 41–51.

Schmitz, R. (1980). Aging and control. In J. Garber & M. E. P. Seligman (Eds.), *Human helplessness* (pp. 261–277). New York: Academic Press.

Schulz, R. & Fritz, S. (1987). Origins of stereotypes of the elderly: An experimental study of the self–other discrepancy. *Experimental Aging Research, 13,* 189–195.

Staudinger, U. M. & Dittmann-Kohli, F. (1992). Lebenserfahrung und Lebenssinn. In P. B. Baltes & J. Mittelstraß (Ed.). *Zukunft des Alterns und gesellschaftliche Entwicklung* (pp. 408–436). Berlin: de Gruyter.

Staudinger, U. M., Marsiske, M., & Baltes, P. B. (1995). Resilience and reserve capacity in later adulthood: Potentials and limits of development across the life span. In D. Cicchetti & D. Cohen (Eds.), *Developmental psychopathology. Vol. 2: Risk, disorder, and adaptation* (pp. 801–847). New York: Wiley.

Steele, C. M. (1988). The psychology of self-affirmation: Sustaining the integrity of the self. In L. Berkowitz (Ed.), *Advances in experimental social psychology. Vol. 21: Social psychological studies of the self: Perspectives and programs* (pp. 261–302). New York: Academic Press.

Sternberg, R. J. (1990). *Wisdom: Its nature, origin, and development.* New York: Cambridge University Press.

Stock, W. A., Okun, M. A., Haring, M. J., & Witter, R. A. (1983). Age and subjective well-being: A meta-analysis. In R. J. Light (Ed.), *Evaluation studies: Review annual* (vol. 8, pp. 279–302). Beverly Hills, CA: Sage.

Swann, W. B. (1983). Self-verification: Bringing the social reality in harmony with the self. In J. Suls & A. G. Greenwald (Eds.), *Psychological perspectives on the self* (vol. 2, pp. 33–66). Hillsdale, NJ: Lawrence Erlbaum Associates.

Swann, W. B., Griffin, J. J., Predmore, S. C., & Gaines, B. (1987). The cognitive–affective crossfire: When self-consistency confronts self-enhancement. *Journal of Personality and Social Psychology, 52,* 881–889.

Tesser, A. (1986). Some effects of self-evaluation maintenance on cognition and action. In R. M. Sorrentino & E. T. Higgins (Eds.), *Handbook of motivation and cognition: Foundations of social behavior* (pp. 435–464). New York: Guilford.

Thompson, S. C., Cheek, P. R., & Graham, M. A. (1988). The other side of perceived control: Disadvantages and negative effects. In S. Spacapan & S. Oskamp (Eds.), *The social psychology of health* (pp. 69–93). Newbury Park, CA: Sage Publications.

Wolk, S. (1976). Situational constraint as a moderator of the locus of control–adjustment relationship. *Journal of Consulting and Clinical Psychology, 44,* 420–427.

7

AUTOBIOGRAPHICAL
MEMORY AND SOCIAL
COGNITION

DEVELOPMENT OF THE REMEMBERED
SELF IN ADULTHOOD

JOSEPH M. FITZGERALD

Psychology Department
Wayne State University
Detroit, Michigan

Research on social cognition asks questions about the representation and processing of knowledge about social objects and events (Kihlstrom, 1993). Although the majority of social cognition research is concerned with knowledge about others, autobiographical memory is a topic that clearly fits within the domain of social cognition. As Kihlstrom pointed out, the self is a social topic of particular interest to humans and, I would argue, autobiographical memory is a central topic in any consideration of the self. Throughout the life span, we have many opportunities to think and rethink who we have been, who we are, and who we might become in the future—a variety of self-representations. In this chapter, the focus is on how we think about our various selves in the context of the remembered self, which is defined as representations of who we have been at various points in the past.

Several aspects of autobiographical memory highlight its central location in a life span developmental account of social cognition. First, autobiographical memory provides individuals with a sense of who they are. As has been noted by several authors (Bruner, 1986; Cohler, 1982; Fitzgerald, 1988, 1996a; McAdams,

---

1988, 1994), our memories provide us with a sense of identity in narrative form. Second, knowledge about others, relationships, successful and unsuccessful social behaviors, and a host of other social information is represented in the auto-biographical memory system. In this sense, autobiographical memory enables adaptive social behavior and our ability to monitor that behavior (metacognition) through representations of the past. Third, autobiographical memories provide an important basis for social interaction. Telling stories allows us to reveal ourselves, manage impressions, let others know what we think about them, teach lessons we feel are valuable, and a variety of other tasks that allow us to sustain and develop our cultures. In sum, autobiographical memory can be thought of as enabling identity, representing knowledge and playing a role in social interactions.

Although these assertions reflect my enthusiasm about the key role of autobio-graphical memory in social cognition, it is not case that one can readily locate a large body of research on these various topics. In fact, the corpus of autobio-graphical memory research is best described as embryonic. The long historical tradition of memory research in psychology has taught us much about memory for word lists and brief textual materials but much less about the complex domain of autobiographical memory. In fairness, the decision of Ebbinghaus (1885) to study carefully controlled materials in the laboratory was appropriate for a young and uncertain science. The problem is that once psychology grew comfortable in the laboratory, it not only was reluctant to move back into the less controlled set-tings of everyday life but developed the view that the study of everyday cognition was folly.

An autobiographical memory may put the issue of the scientific status of auto-biographical memory research in context. I once had a conversation with a col-league from Physics. He asked me what I studied. I replied that I studied autobio-graphical memory and went on to briefly described some of the methodologies autobiographical memory researchers employ. As a good lab scientist, he seemed truly astonished (or appalled). He said that what I was trying to do was like trying to explain why one particular apple fell from a tree instead of why apples fall from trees. With so many uncontrolled variables, how could I ever draw any solid conclusions? I thought for a moment and replied that I really was not interested in one why one apple fell from a tree, although horticulturists probably view that as an interesting question. Rather, I hoped that by observations of real-world mem-ory activities I would learn something about them that scientists working in labo-ratories might have missed. After all, is that not how Newton started his scientific discipline?

I tell this story whenever attempting to explain to students what it is that I do. I tell it here because I want readers of this chapter to know something about the general motivating force behind research on autobiographical memory. If one reads collected reviews of the literature in this area (Rubin, 1986; 1996), one will discover that most autobiographical memory researchers are quite interested in the same basic questions as laboratory researchers are, including how memory is organized, what factors influence the accuracy of memory, and how emotion affects memory. What distinguishes their efforts, however, is a desire to develop models of memory and its development that can adequately reflect how people use memory in daily life (Bruce, 1985).

AN OUTLINE

This chapter provides an overview of those issues in autobiographical memory research and theory that seem most germane to issues of concern to social cognition theory and research. The main sections of the chapter are concerned with definitions of autobiographical memory, retrieval and organizational processes, and the temporal distribution of memories. Much of the research discussed is not explicitly developmental, but every effort has been made to explore developmental implications and the potential of autobiographical memory research and theory for adult development and aging.

DEFINITIONS

What are autobiographical memories? The identification of a memory as autobiographical tells us something about the content of the memory but does not clearly specify the type of memory system that might be involved in the encoding, storage, or retrieval of the memory. The term *autobiographical* tells us that the memory has something to do with the individual who is remembering. The form of the memory may be procedural, semantic, or episodic, to use the nomenclature of contemporary cognitive psychology (Tulving, 1983). That is, the person may be remembering how to do something (procedural), remembering that he or she knows something to be true (semantic), or recollecting (reexperiencing) some particular experience (episodic). As is clarified in the coming paragraphs, the restriction of the term *autobiographical memory* to only episodic memory would seriously underestimate the range of phenomena of interest to autobiographical memory researchers.

Brewer (1986, 1996) has written extensively on definition issues in autobiographical memory, as have Conway (1992) and Nelson (1992, 1993). Definitions are important for considering the relationship of autobiographical memory to social cognition, because different forms of autobiographical memory may play different roles in understanding the self and its relationship to others. In his 1986 article, Brewer noted four types of autobiographical memory: personal memory, autobiographical facts, generic personal memories, and self-schema.

Personal memories are defined as the phenomenal reexperiencing of a single episode. For example, I have a clear personal memory of my wedding ceremony. When I recollect that ceremony, many of the sensory experiences of that memory flood into consciousness. In his 1996 discussion, Brewer referred to this category as recollective memories to emphasize the fundamental role of imagery in this form of memory. Recollective memory is noteworthy for its singularity and the sense of reexperiencing the event entailed. Wheeler, Stuss, and Tulving (1997) discussed such experiences as episodic memory. Like Brewer, they placed a heavy emphasis on the sense of reexperiencing the event reported by subjects during episodic remembering. From their review of psychological, neuropsychological, and brain imaging research, they conclude that there are distinctive features of this form of memory. Further, they link it to the functioning of the frontal lobes and the processes of self-awareness, which previously have been limited to models of executive functioning tasks. We will return to their argument shortly, but note that the phenomenal, subjective nature of these personal memories—which psychology has long ignored—have become a defining feature.

According to Brewer (1996), autobiographical facts are nonphenomenally experienced products of a single episode. By *nonphenomenal* Brewer means that there is no sense of reexperiencing the event. Thus, there is neither the sensory aspect of remembering nor the sense of singularity connected with episodic/recollective experience. For example, I know *that* I am married, but when I check *married* on a credit card application, I do not reexperience my wedding day. The key here is the phrase *know that*. Autobiographical facts of this sort are qualitatively different from episodic personal memories. Experimentalists have recently paid more attention to this distinction in what is termed the remember/know paradigm. In these experiments, subjects are presented with a recognition memory task; for each word they recognize, they are asked if they actually remember the word or if they simply know that the word was on the list they viewed. Wheeler et al. (1997) used this paradigm to illustrate how performance on an episodic memory task may be influenced by both episodic and semantic memory systems.

Hyman and Pentland (1996) have shown that the difference between remembering and knowing is also an important one in the domain of autobiographical memory and that individuals sometimes confuse what they remember and what they know. For example, subjects might report remembering an event even though they have never experienced it but instead have been given false information by a researcher that they did experience it. For example, if my wife falsely told me that I choked on my wedding cake and I later reported reexperiencing a memory of this event, I would be in error. I might well be imagining that this took place. This would not be an episodic memory even though it would most likely involve the same neurological structures and mechanisms (Wheeler et al., 1997). Our inability to detect such differences is one of the issues at the heart of the false-versus-recovered memory debate (Pezdek & Banks, 1996). Indeed, a limitation of many studies of autobiographical memory is that our methods have tended to downplay this distinction. Frequently, instructions ask participants to report specific events and we treat the data as if they were reporting personal/recollective memories, but they may well report a significant proportion of autobiographical facts (or fictions) that happen to take event form.

According to Brewer (1986), generic personal memories are phenomenally experienced products of multiple episodes. In his account, these would involve recollective experience without reference to a specific event. For example, I may recall driving to work as a generic memory without actually recollecting any of the details of a specific commute. I may recall driving past a series of expressway exits being surrounded by a generic set of cars, trucks, exit signs, and bleary-eyed commuters. The construct of generic memories is similar to other constructs discussed later in this chapter, such as general event memories (Conway, 1992), repisodes (Neisser, 1986), and scripts (Schank & Abelson, 1977, 1995). These constructs all refer to the role of memory in such complex processes as comprehension, planning, and the recollection of complex experiences. As such, this form of memory plays a central role in social cognition. In fact, for Schank and Abelson (1995), these generic memories form the basis for all significant human knowledge. An interesting but uninvestigated issue is the relative involvement of the episodic and semantic memory systems in this form of memory. On the one hand, the nonspecific nature of these memories would imply the involvement of semantic processes, the *knowing that* form of memory, but the claim by Brewer that they involve phenomenally reexperiencing the memory would appear to involve the self-awareness that Wheeler et al. (1997) regard as the hallmark of the episodic system.

The fourth category proposed by Brewer, the self-schema, is no doubt the most familiar to readers of a volume devoted to social cognition. Brewer defines *self-schema* as nonphenomenally experienced products of multiple experiences. According to a variety of different theories, people possess more or less complex views of who they are and their behavior in various situations (Cantor & Kihlstrom, 1987). Self-schema may include physical and psychological traits, assessments of health and well-being, and a variety of other self-descriptors. As a form of memory, these self-schema have some basis in experience, although at some point the schematic information become independent of specific experiences (Klein & Loftus, 1993), and the relation of the contents of self-schema to other forms of autobiographical memory is anything but simple (Srull & Wyer, 1993). Understanding the role of these self-schema is integral to models of actual and possible selves across the lifespan (see Brandtstädter, Chapter 6; Hooker, Chapter 5; and Turk-Charles & Carstensen, Chapter 14, all in this volume).

Brewer (1996) and Baddeley (1992) would prefer that psychologists not use the term *autobiographical memory* because of the complexity of the issues discussed in the preceding paragraphs. *Autobiographical memory* is a classic example of a term inherited by scientific psychology from natural language. The term identifies the domain of concern but lacks the precision needed in science. In this chapter, *autobiographical memory* is used to refer to Brewer's category of recollective memory with the emphasis placed on phenomenal reexperiencing and singularity. I note, however, that in many studies the data may not have been evaluated for how well the memories studied met those criteria. Thus, some studies of recollective experience may have mixed recollective experience with generic memories. When I use the term *episodic memory* in the following sections, I refer not to a specific type of task but to the memory system characterized by self-awareness, the capacity of humans to mentally represent and become aware of their subjective experiences of past, present, and future (Wheeler et al., 1997). When discussing other aspects of autobiographical memory, I use Brewer's specific terms.

RETRIEVAL AND RECONSTRUCTION

What takes place when an individual deliberately attempts to retrieve an auto-biographical memory or when one spontaneously comes to mind? The answer is intimately bound to the question of how autobiographical memory is organized. Most contemporary autobiographical memory theorists reject the model of a sim-ple copy theory in which the brain records events in detail and then stores them in a massive, elaborately organized database that is accessed with blinding speed during retrieval. The reasons for rejecting such a model are both empirical and theoretical, including the well-known research of Bartlett (1932) and others on the pliability of human memory. This work demonstrates the inconsistency of human memory with copy theories but does not specify the best replacement.

Alternatives to copy theories rely on some constructivist interpretation of the data (Vico, 1948). The most radical perspective suggests that each act of retrieval is actually an act of total construction. In such accounts, some stimulus in either the environment or private experience triggers a set of constructive processes. These stimuli may be associated with an activity or an action. Thus, the sight of a grocery bag may be associated with the activity of shopping. The memory con-struction process then assembles a set of specific actions, objects, and actors on the basis of probabilities to create the experience of remembering the trip to the grocery store last Sunday. From a radical constructivist position, everything about such a memory is based on such mental schema as scripts and self-schema, along with general knowledge representations such as the probability level that I would have gone shopping on Sunday, the location where I usually shop, and a variety of other information, such as whether there was actually food in the house. A key subset of that information is knowledge about the self concerning psychological characteristics: goals, expectancies, behavioral tendencies, traits, competencies, attitudes, and self-assessments, such as metamemory. One of the major contribu-tions of developmental psychology to the study of memory development is to build and test models of how those aspects of the self develop over time. To the extent there are either normative or nonnormative developmental differences in the content of the self-as-me, these are likely to be reflected in autobiographical memory processes.

The reconstructive view was articulated by Barclay in a series of studies in which subjects kept diaries and were then tested for their memories for the events they had recorded. In the recognition procedure, actual event records are mixed with a variety of lures (foils) in which some aspect of the event has been changed or the experimenter has substituted a completely fictitious event (Barclay, 1986; Barclay & Wellman, 1986; Barclay & DeCooke, 1988). Collectively, the results of these studies suggest that college-age subjects correctly recognize most actual events, but their false-alarm rates for foils are very high and that those rates increase as a function of the time, rising to as high as 73% after 1 year. As Barclay (1986) summarized, "subjects were more confident about the exact nature of their lives than they should have been" (p. 291).

This type of methodology has not been employed with middle-aged or older adults to determine whether the false-alarm rates to various forms of foils is similar. The rates for younger adults are very high, but it may be that this is partly a function of their limited life contexts. Students living at a residential college lead largely routine schedules and although they were instructed to record memorable events, they may have had a limited range from which to select and what seemed memorable at the time may have turned out to be trivial. Wagenaar (1986) did an intense study of his own memories over several years and found that many of the events he regarded as significant 2 or 3 years later could not be remembered at all, even with extensive cues. This raises the prospect that adults leading more varied lives may perform somewhat better on such tasks, while those leading a more routine lifestyle of a tedious job or a congregate living situation might perform at a low level. From the standpoint of laboratory tasks, the generally strong performance of older adults on recognition memory tasks might work in their favor.

Although radical constructivism has some appeal, the notion that there are no enduring records of specific experiences is not accepted by all autobiographical memory theorists. Two prominent theorists, Brewer (1996) and Conway (1992) suggested a more moderate or partial reconstructive position. In essence, they claimed that at least some base or skeletal representation is available in memory. These representations are thought to contain some essential elements of the event that serve as the basis of the experienced memory. The core representation may contain pointers that refer the memory system to knowledge, goals, scripts, and schema that are relevant to reconstructing that particular event.

Figure 7.1 presents a prototypic recall protocol and how that protocol might be reconstructed. This memory was retrieved by a 71-year-old man who was asked to report memories that belonged in a book about his life (Fitzgerald, 1996b). He recalled a distant memory about a job interview. His protocol may be decomposed into a core plus details supplied by reference to a variety of his self-as-me at age 22. These details include where he lived at the time, his employer, as well as significant goals and self-schema during that era. In this example, the details represent a variety of aspects of the self-as-me, including the physical and the affective.

Not all recollective memories include the same slots or components, which may be a function of the availability of some piece of general knowledge, the frequency with which a memory has been rehearsed, the goals of the individual in telling the memory, or the operation of defenses of the self-as-I at the time of encoding or recall. For example, when asked to recall significant events, individuals vary considerably in terms of whether they report their age at the time of an event. This could reflect the lack of available information needed to reconstruct that aspect of the memory, the teller's assumption that listeners can infer his or her age from the nature of the event, or the subject's unwillingness to acknowledge the fact that

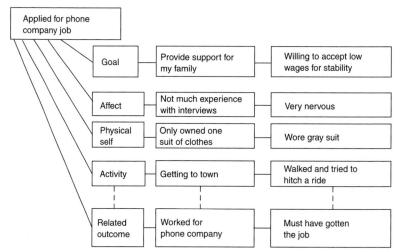

Recall text: I remember the day I applied for a job at the phone company. I was really nervous because I had never actually been interviewed for a job. I had to walk several miles to get to the bus line. I tried to hitch a ride, but no one would pick me up. I dressed in my best (only) gray suit. The job didn't pay much, but I was just starting out and my wife wanted to start a family. It worked out okay. I got the job and stayed with that company for 30 years.

FIGURE 7.1   Decomposition of recall protocol into phenomenal record and elements provided by autobiographical knowledge.

such a long time has passed since the event. One of the limitations of many models of retrieval has been their tendency to regard it as a solitary rather than social process. Although a small number of studies have examined the interactive (McFarland & Ross, 1987) and collaborative (Gould & Dixon, 1993) aspects of memory, our understanding of autobiographical memory is limited by the limited variety of contexts in which it has been studied. Methodologies are needed that allow us to examine autobiographical memory in a variety of social contexts that differ along such dimensions as intimacy, power, and perceived importance. Such methods would allow us to address issues related to the functional aspects of auto-biographical memory. For example, in studies of self-disclosure, it would be inter-esting to note when are individuals likely to recall and express specific versus generic autobiographical memories or when they restrict themselves to revealing autobiographical facts. These functional issues in autobiographical memory research may be of great interest to social cognition researchers.

ORGANIZATION

How are the various elements of autobiographical memory organized? This is a difficult issue to address methodologically because the number of memories people can report is exceedingly large and the classification and categorization of any corpus of memories is not something that psychologists can readily agree on.

One of the early findings related to organization was provided by Robinson (1976). Robinson employed Galton's cue-word method, in which subjects are asked to report the first memory to come to mind in association with a specific stimulus, usually a word. He found that some cues prompted memories more quickly than others. Specifically, words describing object and actions were responded to more quickly than those describing affective states. A related series of studies was derived from the work of Schank and Abelson (1977) on script theory and memory organization. In these studies, experimenters provided a variety of different cues and combinations of cues related to activities (going to weddings) and actions (sitting). Reisser, Black, and Abelson (1985) found support for the primacy of activities in memory organization. Schank and Abelson (1995) appear to hold a partial reconstructive view that depends on people telling stories about the events as part of the encoding process. In their model, it is the stories that are actually encoded into memory. If we do not tell or rehearse the story, then bits and pieces of the event may be absorbed into general knowledge, but otherwise the event will be forgotten. If, however, the event becomes a story, then it will take on a stable form that will be indexed by such key words as *activities, places,* and *characters.* Their indexing process appears to be somewhat decontextualized. Although they alluded to social goals in the telling of stories, the actual indexing process is not clearly specified and reflects a rationalist perspective on cognition. That is, their model seems to imply that there is some preset categorization system that will be used consistently across individuals. Such a system would seem more descriptive of a computer database rather than a human cognitive system designed to be adaptive and flexible.

More contextualized perspectives on organization are provided by Neisser (1986) and Conway (1992, 1996; Conway & Berkerian, 1987; Conway & Rubin, 1993). Neisser (1986) proposed that memory is organized in a set of nested hierarchies. At the top of these hierarchies are self-schema and "repisodes," which are a form of generalized event knowledge similar to the generic personal memories of Brewer (1986). The content of self-schema and repisodes derive from specific events and are then used in the reconstruction of those events in memory. Neisser first developed the notion of repisodes in his analysis of John Dean's testimony in the Watergate hearings (Neisser, 1981). Using the Richard Nixon tapes, Neisser was able to check the accuracy of Dean's testimony. Dean made many errors of fact, but, Neisser argued, his testimony was nevertheless truthful and reflected the accurate consolidation of many specific memories into repisodes. Thus, according to Neisser, memory representations of general knowledge are more a function of specific experiences than seems true in the Schank and Abelson model.

Conway put forth a model that seems even more rooted in individual experiences. Conway and Berkerian (1987) provide support for the hypothesis that autobiographical memory has a hierarchical organization with lifetime periods at the top of the hierarchy, followed by general events/event knowledge, and then detailed records of specific events that Conway (1992) termed the phenomenal record.

According to this view, lifetime periods are represented as knowledge about common features of the period and temporal knowledge about the duration of the period. This is more than a simple slicing of the life course into 5-year periods. In fact, lifetime periods not only overlap but might actually be completely coincidental in time. For example, an individual may consider the chronological time frame of 12–14 years as "my middle school period," "adolescent rebellion," and "the Bobby Smith–was-my-constant-companion period." These three lifetime periods would most likely share some common elements, but because they focus on different aspects of the self—student, child, and friend—they may involve distinct organizing themes: achievement and affiliation. General events in the Conway system may either be repeated events of the sort identified by Neisser as repisodes or be a single event composed of a sequence of minor subevents. Thus, attending several retirement parties may give rise to a general event structure for such events, whereas the retirement party of a given individual may consist of a series of specific events linked together by the temporal framework of the party.

The most detailed autobiographical knowledge, event-specific information, seems the least clearly modeled in Conway (1992). The phenomenal record is temporally specific. An individual viewing a list of words in a laboratory experiment would have a phenomenal record of each word and a general event memory for the entire experience. The phenomenal record may not be very accurate or persist very long, as witnessed by the rather poor performance of even young subjects in most list-learning experiments. Conway envisions a large capacity storage device that retains information linked to lifetime periods and overwrites those that are not. What seems unclear is how the passage of time is incorporated into the model. We know from a variety of different studies that autobiographical memory for specific events declines in a regular fashion over time (Brewer, 1986; Linton, 1975; Wagenaar, 1986), but how is that to be incorporated into a hierarchical model? Perhaps it is strictly a matter of storage requirements. If the storage capacity for such memories is limited, the memory system may have some criterion that it employs on a period basis to purge phenomenal records from the system. If a memory has not been rehearsed, mentally or verbally, or if its connections to salient themes is not sufficiently strong, then it may be that the system will seize the space, delete the record, and write a new record in its place. From a lifespan perspective, this may reflect the operation of selection and optimization. Individuals may optimize their recollection of significant events by selectively investing resources in those events that contain important lifetime period information.

Finally, in considering the organizational nature of autobiographical memory, it should be noted that the phenomenal records apparently have a very strong temporal organization. That is, it appears that the closest associates of most phenomenal records are those that occur closest in time. Although there is evidence from list-learning experiments that words presented in close proximity are recalled in close proximity, the more relevant question is whether this takes place in autobiographical memory. Brown (1993) reported an experiment in which subjects provided a set of autobiographical memories that were then used as stimuli to collect additional memories. For example, if I recalled "talking about how World War I influenced Freud's theory in class," this would be used as a prompt for the retrieval of another memory. In the large majority of cases, individuals recall events that come from the same general event. Thus, I might recall "having a discussion after class about how the Vietnam War influenced psychology in the 1970s and 1980s." Temporal organization in storage, however, is not always reflected in temporal organization in recall. Thus, in a list-learning experiment, if the words are members of semantic categories, those categories are used to organize at least some of the words recalled. In autobiographical memory, other links, such as central figures, actions, and affect, serve as links between autobiographical memories (Brown, 1993; Fitzgerald, 1980); time, however, seems the best predictor.

Unfortunately, there is no research that really tells us much about how these organizational principles operate over time or how aging influences organizational aspects of the autobiographical memory systems of adults. Laboratory research has established that older adults have difficulty at the level of creating phenomenal records (encoding deficits) and substantial difficulties accessing those records created during retrieval. The phenomenal records of autobiographical memory are likely to be richer than those of single words, however, and this may enhance the probability of recall. Older adults may also compensate for the limitations by devoting resources differentially. As will be seen below, they are clearly doing something that allows them to remember many events from their daily lives. In addition, the constructive nature of memory may play much more of a role in autobiographical memory than in list-learning experiments. As Winograd (1988) has noted, there is a need to integrate laboratory and ethological/observational data and theory. There are methodologies available to study organizational features of autobiographical memory in adulthood and aging; this section suggests the utility of doing so.

ORGANIZATION AND SOCIAL COGNITION

In the context of the study of social cognition, the organization of autobiographical memory is a crucial element. The significance of these issues is highlighted in the model of Schank and Abelson (1977, 1995). Although their extreme position that all significant human knowledge is represented as stories is inconsistent with what is known about autobiographical memory (Brewer, 1995; Rubin, 1995), their general point that much work in social cognition suffers from a lack of attention to *storied* representation seems valid. In the introduction to this chapter, the social nature of cognition about the self was noted. If we are to fully understand self-related cognition, then we must include autobiographical memory in both the narrow sense of recollective experiences and the broader conceptualization of autobiographical knowledge.

Conway (1992) emphasized that the self was actively involved in autobiographical memory processes. Some of the central themes in contemporary discussions of the self include the formation of goals (Cantor & Kihlstrom, 1987), the formation of possible selves (Markus & Nurius, 1986), and the role of discrepancies in self-representation in affect (Higgins, 1987). Some of these treatments of the self have been reflected in discussions of the life-span developmental aspects of self and are discussed in other chapters in this volume (Brandtstädter, Chapter 6, and Turk-Charles & Carstensen, Chapter 14). From the standpoint of autobiographical memory, a limiting feature of many of these discussions has been their focus on rather abstract or generalized trait representations. In prototypic methodology, individuals are presented with lists of traits or general attributes and asked to make judgments about their descriptive value for some aspect of the self, such as the past, current, or future self.

This sort of methodology tells us only about one form of self-knowledge, the paradigmatic, while ignoring narrative forms. Also, it is implicit in these conceptualizations that what people tell us about each of these selves ought to be consistent. If people appear to embrace views of themselves or others that are contradictory, then this is regarded as a flaw in either the method or the subjects. Very few social cognition researchers have embraced inconsistency, contextualism, and qualifications as meaningful (Sande, Goethals & Radloff. 1988), and even then, the emphasis has been on explaining the inconsistencies with regard to traits rather than viewing the inconsistencies as an integral part of successful adaptation to the complexities of filling multiple roles.

The view here is that the hierarchical nature of human memory allows for the construction of narrative representations of the self, of which any individual will have many. A more open view of the varieties of self-knowledge regards traits and their organization into self-schema as one form of self-knowledge with adaptive value for some circumstances, whereas narrative representations have adaptive value in others. The dual nature of human knowledge representation as paradigmatic and narrative has been proposed and discussed in several contexts (Bruner, 1986; Fitzgerald, 1996; McAdams, 1988; Robinson & Hawpe, 1986). Science has a distinct bias toward the paradigmatic and an aversion to narrative, or storied, forms of knowledge. The former form holds, in principle, the promise of distinguishing truth from fiction, or at least "the currently most likely account" from "less likely accounts." The narrative form, in contrast, is much more contextualized and more personal. There are good and bad stories, but using truth criterion to evaluate narratives misses their point. Stories are created by people for many purposes and their value to their authors must be studied in the context of those purposes.

A few theories in the developmental literature have emphasized the value of the narrative form. Primary among these is that of Erikson (1958, 1959), who relied on a variety of sources, including autobiographical materials, to construct biographical accounts of well-known individuals, such as Martin Luther and Gandhi. From his analysis of these lives and the many lives he encountered as a therapist, Erikson created a sweeping account of the life span centered on life themes. In the Conway model, Erikson can be seen as providing an analysis of the highest level of the hierarchy. Thus, the narratives of older adults are hypothesized to be organized around issues of integrity and despair. For Erikson, the emergence of life themes is hypothesized to reflect the unfolding of an epigenetic sequence, but one need not limit the emergence of such themes to those developed in Erikson's stages.

In fact, one need not limit this form of analysis to strictly normative themes. Life-span models have long noted the important influence of both historically normative and nonnormative events. What the narrative perspective offers is a way to model how such influences are incorporated into the lives of people. For example, in the generation of older American adults alive in the late 1990s, there are many military service veterans. How does veteran status influence cognitions about the self? The traditional methodology in psychology would involve contrasting the performance of older adults who either were or were not veterans on a series of self-descriptive measures, such as personality tests. Such a study might report that being a veteran accounts for X% of the variance in personality. This has normative value, but the narrative methodology would ask a different set of questions. It would ask, for example, how being in the military influenced the themes that organized the young adulthood of these women and men. How does their status as veterans influence the overall organization of their autobiographical memory? Have they carried through those themes throughout adulthood? Is there adaptive significance attached to the extent to which individuals keep distinct their soldier narratives and their nonsolider narratives? Within the autobiographical memory literature, the work of Schuman and his colleagues on the influence of cultural forces on autobiographical memory provides perhaps the best example of how we might frame research questions to understand such issues (Schuman, Rieger, & Gaidy, 1994).

The most explicitly autobiographical model in developmental psychology is represented by McAdams (1988, 1994). His theory derives from the normative flow of Erikson, the personology of Murray (1938), the motivational theories of McClelland (1985), and the archetype of Jung (1961). McAdams proposed that people develop life narratives that not only give meaning to present and prior experience but also have a generative component that guides the emergence of new behaviors. McAdams (1994) centered a discussion of the narrative of Margaret Mead's life around the theme of exploration. At any one moment, Mead could look back over her life decisions and behavior and interpret them in accordance with this theme. At the same time, according to McAdams, when she encountered choice points in her life, the pathways she chose were most consistent with the exploration theme.

McAdams (1988) demonstrated the value of using such dimensions as agency and communion (intimacy) to code earliest memories, peak and nadir experiences, and a variety of other textual material. His strategy is to apply taxonomies to narrative output, a solution that follows from McClelland's analysis of Thematic Apperception Test protocols, in which individuals invent narratives to match drawings of people in a variety of situations. The limiting feature of this approach is that the narrative representation of the self can be lost to the interpretive framework of the particular taxonomy employed. If, for example, one were to code the memories of soldiers from World War II, it might well be that agency and communion would be common themes, but would one fully capture those events with such a scheme? This brings up two related questions: First, can the motivations that drive scientific psychology be reconciled with the contextualized nature of narrative representations? Second, can psychological understanding of individual behavior be complete without an understanding of contextualized narratives? I believe that the answer to the second question is no. The answer to the first question is yes, but significant work needs to be done to achieve that objective. That work begins with developing a more complete understanding of the how and why of narrative representations of the self-as-me. If we knew more about how the narratives were constructed, we would know more about what they were telling us about individual lives. McAdams stressed the development of the narrative self. This is a large entity, equivalent in many ways to asking about an individual's personality in terms of the big five personality factors (Costa & McCrae, 1985). That is, the unit of analysis is an entity that integrates a great many behaviors that occur over long periods of time. In some cases, such as Margaret Mead's, psychologists have available autobiographical materials representing enough behavior that one can talk meaningfully about the *narrative self*. Even in those cases in which we have such materials, though, before we can ask about such a large construct as the *narrative self*, it seems we need to know more about *self-narratives*, which are representations of the individual in the small everyday events of our lives. These smaller constructions are the contents of our recollective experience, stories about the self-as-me constructed by the self-as-I. I now turn to what we know about the developmental history of such accounts.

THE DISTRIBUTION OF MEMORIES OVER TIME

Most of what we know about the development of recollective experience has to do with how much people remember about various parts of their lives. Using a variety of different methodologies, researchers have attempted to characterize the contents of autobiographical memory by their chronological characteristics. As the reader might expect, the method used to elicit memories can strongly influence the outcome. For example, if individuals report only memories satisfying some particular criterion for imagery, affect, or importance, the outcome might be very different than if subjects are simply free to report the first memory that comes to mind.

When Sir Francis Galton first addressed the issue of the chronological distribution of autobiographical memories, he did so by using himself as a subject. He attempted to recall a specific memory associated with a given word, typically an unusual word. Nearly 100 years later, Crovitz and Schiffman (1974) revisited the Galton method with a study of memory sampling in college students. The methodology is very simple. Subjects are instructed to report the first memory that comes to mind in association with a specific word. The only criteria for memories is that they refer to a specific experience. For example, subjects might be presented with the word *desk*. They would be instructed that remembering that they had a desk in their room would not be a specific memory but that remembering that they had studied for an exam in history would qualify. Subjects of all ages readily understand these instructions; for the most part, they report specific memories, although depressed individuals have a tendencies to report general memories, such as "I often sit at my desk thinking" (Williams, 1996). Typically, subjects are asked to report one memory per prompt and are not asked to date or rate characteristics of the memories until the experimenter has finished collecting a set of memories. The memories reported in this form of cue-word study range from the significant to the mundane; subjects describe the memories in a few words and researchers have not been interested in the accuracy of such memories or in the issues of deception or self-censorship. Thus, the situation in which the memories are collected is designed to be as neutral as possible. The model is that subjects are randomly sampling from a pool of available memories.

Crovitz and Schiffman (1974) reported that a straightforward power function accounted for the data of college students. In this function, the log of memory strength declines as a function of the log of time. Their primary finding was that the power function is a useful model for retention of autobiographical memories; it has been replicated for several variations of the basic Galton paradigm, including the use of olfactory cues (Rubin, Groth, & Goldsmith, 1984) and no cues at all (Rubin, 1982). The slope of the retention function bears a strong resemblance to that of retention functions generated from laboratory studies of memory for word lists (Rubin & Wenzel, 1996), even though those studies typically involve much shorter retention intervals. In both laboratory and autobiographical memory studies, the functions account for 98% or 99% of the empirical data. Thus, for all its lack of control, the Galton technique produces remarkably clear data. The function is robust and changes very little even when subjects are given instructions that might bias them to produce older memories (Rubin & Schulkind, 1997a).

There are, however, two exceptions to the predictive power of the power function. The first of these is for memories from birth to roughly 3 or 4 years of age. For this era, most individuals report few—if any—memories. This phenomenon has long been noted and has been replicated using the cue-word technique with college students (Rubin, Wetzler, & Nebes, 1986) and children as young as 6 (Fitzgerald, 1991). The phenomena has been termed *infantile amnesia* or *early childhood amnesia*. Various theoretical mechanisms have been advanced to account for the data, including Freudian accounts centered around repression and

more contemporary models based on the emergence of a distinctive autobiographical memory system (Nelson, 1993) or the emergence of the self (Howe &
Courage, 1997). Although this phenomenon is not directly related to this review,
it is noteworthy that most current explanations have at least acknowledged the
social aspects of development during childhood in explaining the emergence of
autobiographical memory. For example, Tessler and Nelson (1996) have shown
that the narrative style of mothers leads to individual differences in the emergence
of the autobiographical memory system.

The second exception to the predictions of the power function was reported by
Fitzgerald and Lawrence (1984). They found that when older adults responded to
the cue-word task, their data were very consistent with the power function except
for the early childhood amnesia component and a small but statistically significant overproduction of memories from the period of late adolescence and early
adulthood. This finding has received the inelegant but descriptive label of *the
bump*. In the following five sections, we discuss the two most striking aspects of
this data: the high number of very recent memories and the bump.

RECENCY

Regardless of age, all adults in the Fitzgerald and Lawrence study (1984) had
almost exactly the same retention function. This finding has been replicated several times (Rubin et al., 1986). In a study in which each subject reported 125
memories, Rubin and Schulkind (1997b) conducted a detailed analysis on memories reported for the most recent 10 years and confirmed the equivalent performance of older adults and college students. This finding certainly counters the
stereotype that older adults are somehow living in the past or that they do not
remember much of their current lives. This recency data seems very important for
our understanding of the self-related cognition of older adults.

Fitzgerald (1996a) calculated that typically, 50% of cue-word-prompted memories are from the most recent 12 months and a total of 80% are from the most
recent decade. Although there are clearly some contexts, such as family reunions,
in which we might expect adults to retrieve a larger proportion of memories from
earlier in life, we might expect similar behavior from individuals of any age over
25. The only difference was the size of the gap between now and "earlier in life."
The evidence seems to suggest that on a daily basis, the internal psychological
context provided by autobiographical memory will be formed from recent events.
This pattern has implications for disclosure about the self to others and for self-
evaluation that have not been fully explored.

Autobiographical memories serve many functions in social interactions.
According to self-reports, Rotter (1997) found that subjects stated that the most
frequent (79% of the time) reason that they had recalled memories in the past was
to make conversation. Subjects also reported, however, that they frequently recall
autobiographical memories to receive feedback from others, become close to others, and make a good impression. Hyman and Faries (1992) use a different

methodology but essentially replicate the finding that most autobiographical memory recall is social in nature. One of the interesting findings in Rotter's study was that dysphoric individuals report making less use of opportunities to disclose negative memories to others, thereby minimizing their opportunities to obtain support, advice, or feedback from others. It is intriguing to ponder what role autobiographical memory plays in the sustenance of affective well-being across the lifespan.

One of the least studied aspects of social behavior in older adults has been self-disclosure. Much of the literature in this area relates to reminiscence. The available data suggest that most characteristics of reminiscence change very little in adulthood (Fitzgerald, 1996a; Webster, 1993), although there may be some differences in motivation in later adulthood. Clearly, older adults do recall and discuss events in their conversations. The recency data suggest that most events that will be recalled will be recent rather than temporally distant events—that is, that their remembered self is largely a *now self,* not a *distant self.* Dramatic departures from recency may be regarded by peers and family as diagnostic of cognitive impairment. As noted above, there may be contexts in which departures from recency are normative, such as family reunions, but we actually understand the norms for such behavior very poorly.

How autobiographical memory is used in self-evaluation is just beginning to attract attention in contemporary social cognition research. In the simplest model, individuals respond to such questions as "How happy are you?" by attempting to retrieve a happy memory. According to this model, respondents to such survey items evaluate how easy or difficult it is to find relevant memories, then make a self-evaluation (Conrad, Brown, & Cashman, 1988). This model accounts for self-evaluations regarding the frequency of affect (Fitzgerald, Slade, & Lawrence, 1988), but it may not work as well for trait ratings (Klein & Loftus, 1993). Even in trait ratings, however, the availability of autobiographical memories may be salient for self-evaluation when individuals are in a transitional period. Klein and Loftus (1993) report that when adolescents were making the transition to college, recalling trait-relevant autobiographical memories facilitated trait evaluations. In adulthood, transitions associated with changes in marital status, work, the loss of loved ones, and changes in residence are all times in which the self-as-me is open to question. Such moments may represent the onset of new lifetime periods, such as those proposed by Conway (1996). At these times, we are more reliant on the evidence of daily experience to answer the questions of who we are and how we are coping. As we settle into new roles and environments, themes become established and the abstract self-schema become more independent from the evidence of specific events. Older adults are clearly similar to younger adults in their ability to access recent memories, and their self-reports indicate that they access those memories at the same frequency as do younger adults (Fitzgerald, 1996a). What we now need is research to clarify whether they access them in the same manner and to the same end as younger adults.

THE BUMP

Although the recency effect and the standard retention function clearly account for the largest share of the variance in autobiographical memory behavior in older adults, the overproduction of memories from the young adult period has attracted more theoretical and empirical attention. This reflects psychology's love of a good anomaly as well as the particular fascination with the notion that someone claims to remember an event from 40 years ago but cannot remember what he or she had for breakfast last week. Although I do not totally agree with the generality that things learned in early adulthood are remembered best (Rubin, Rahhal, & Poon, 1998), it does seem that more things learned in early adulthood are remembered better than standard memory models predict.

Rubin et al. (1986) reported that in addition to Fitzgerald and Lawrence, several other laboratories have replicated the basic phenomenon of the bump. They also reviewed several hypotheses that might explain the phenomenon. They concluded at the time that some characteristic of older adults must account for the phenomenon, but that view has not been supported by subsequent research. Much of the attention now centers on what takes place at the time of encoding rather than the time of retrieval.

Fitzgerald (1988) introduced the self-narrative hypothesis, based on the psychological activities and processes at time of encoding. The notion was that late adolescence and young adulthood were periods of intense psychological activity related to the self that might favor the retention of autobiographical memories from this period. The hypothesis was built, in part, on the finding that individuals reliably designate certain memories as highly vivid and personally important, so-called flashbulb memories (Rubin & Kozin, 1984), even if such memories may not be accurate records of the event. From the standpoint of the hypothesis, the important point is not that events are remembered accurately but that individuals believe that the memory accurately reflects who he or she was at the time of the event. Such events have been portrayed by Neisser (1982, 1988) as providing us with benchmarks in organizing our life record. To test the hypotheses, adults were asked to report events for which they had vivid flashbulb memories. The data indicated that subjects readily understood the instructions and had little difficulty reporting such memories.

The distribution of flashbulb memories from Fitzgerald (1988) along with those of younger subjects (age range, 31–46) is presented in Figure 7.2. The recency effect found when memories are obtained using the Galton cue-word method virtually disappears for this class of memory reports. The distribution for both age groups is heavily biased toward the period of the bump. Given that the older adults were sampling from almost twice as many years of experience, it is not surprising that their proportion from the bump era is somewhat lower. A categorical analysis indicated that subjects reported a wide variety of events. Many of the events might have been rated as trivial by an "objective" rater but were rated as very important to the individual. Life events in the sense of graduations, wed-

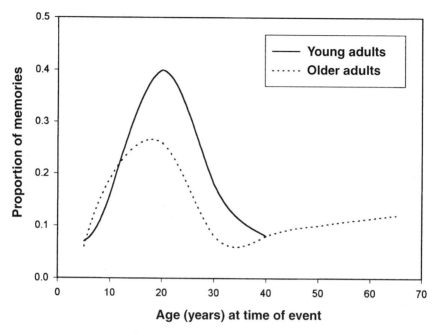

FIGURE 7.2 The distribution of flashbulb memories produced by younger and older adults. For the older sample, the last two decades of life have been combined because few older subjects were older than 65. (Modified from Fitzgerald, 1996a.)

dings, and so forth constituted only 14% of the bump-era memories. The memories were often intensely personal and reported in well-formed stories. Although most memories had been rehearsed frequently, there were some that subjects claimed they had never before told to anyone.

The self-narrative hypothesis seemed to fit this data well. The notion was that people accumulate a set of stories that communicate who they are to both an internal audience (self) and external audiences. Although the recency effects with cue-word memories indicate that the autobiographical memory system is capable of adding new memories to this self-narrative, it may be that the stable nature of self-representations across adulthood operates to maintain a core set of stories about events from the late adolescence and early adulthood periods. In the context of reconstructive models of memory, this would imply that the autobiographical knowledge needed to construct these memories remains available with greater strength than any traditional memory model would predict.

In support of the self-narrative hypothesis, two further studies were conducted in which adults were asked to report memories that they would include in a book about their life story. They reported these stories in either a free-form monologue (Fitzgerald, 1992) or in the form of four written stories (Fitzgerald, 1996b). In both studies, the distribution of memories was very similar to that presented in Figure 7.2. Those studies also indicated that the memories reported with such instructions frequently are reported as well-formed, well-rehearsed narratives. The basic pattern has also been replicated by Benson et al. (1992) in both Midwestern American and Japanese subjects and by Cohen and Faulkner (1988) in a British sample. In both of these studies, the subjects were reporting vivid or important memories. The timing of the bump was slightly different in each sample, with more memories from the first decade in the British sample and more from the third decade in the Japanese sample. These discrepancies may reflect small differences in methodology or cultural differences in the underlying phenomenon. The shape of the distribution is also somewhat flatter if the data are coded into 5-year intervals rather than decades (Jansari & Parkin, 1996). The bump is also present in many autobiographies, including those of famous psychologists who have written autobiographies of their professional careers, even though their careers did not actually begin until after the bump period (Mackevay, Malley, & Stewart, 1991).

The finding of the bump has also been found in a sample of moderately impaired people with Alzheimer's disease (Fromholt & Larsen, 1991). The methodology used for that sample resembled that of Fitzgerald (1992) in that subjects were asked to recall important events from their lives in a monologue with no cue words or interrogation by the interviewer. Although subjects reported fewer memories overall, the distribution of memories conformed to the bump distribution of normal age-matched controls. This distribution does not fit with the standard views of amnesia that focus on a smooth temporal gradient of declining memory strength. Although people with Alzheimer's disease clearly do not add memories to their life story, the recall of predisease memories reflects a preserved ability to either recall or reconstruct memories from the bump era.

Two studies indicate that the bump phenomenon may not be as pronounced in older adults who are depressed. In the first, reported in Fitzgerald (1992), hospitalized depressed older adults reported significantly fewer memories from the bump era using the Galton technique of cueing memories with words. In the second study, Fromholt, Larsen, and Larsen (1995) asked depressed older adults to talk about important events in their life. They report that the depressed adults reported significantly fewer memories from the bump than did either control subjects or the Alzheimer's sample already discussed. These findings cannot tell us whether the depressed individuals are unable to access or reconstruct memories from this era, or if the data simply reflect these individuals' preoccupation with their current problems. It may be noteworthy, however, that even after they had recovered, depressed subjects in the study by Fromholt et al. continued to report fewer memories from the bump period. This may reflect greater discontinuities in representations of the self that relate to their affective disturbance.

OTHER BUMP PHENOMENA

A number of other empirical findings suggest that the bump era has some unique effects. One set of findings might be grouped under the heading of "arts and leisure." These include a study by Larsen (in press) who surveyed older adults in Scandinavia regarding the age at which they read memorable books of their own selection. The distribution closely followed the bump. Holbrook and Schindler (1989) reported that individuals rated songs from their bump era as more desirable. Sehulster (1996) surveyed adults ranging in age from 26 to 67 concerning their preferences for films, asking them to list five films that defined or captured their era. Although the concept of *era* may seem rather vague, subjects displayed consensus that their era falls right in the middle of the bump because on average, subjects were 22 when their era-defining films were released.

Another category of studies relates to the emergence of the collective social and political consciousness of a generation. Schuman and his colleagues (Schuman & Rieger, 1992; Schuman, Rieger, & Gurdy, 1994; Schuman & Scott, 1989) have reported a series of studies related to the emergence of a generational identity. Schuman hypothesizes that each generation frames its political identity around the first set of sociopolitical events that it faces on reaching maturity. The data (Schuman & Scott, 1989) for identification of important political events support their hypotheses, although it should be noted that in their methodology subjects were not actually asked if they remembered anything about the events. Belli, Schuman, and Johnson (1997), however, did find greater accuracy for identifications of people and events from the bump era.

Rubin et al. (1998) reported the development of a new set of questionnaires for memory for public events. Prior studies using such methodologies have not provided a consistent pattern because of a host of methodological problems in constructing such measures. Their new instruments use a multiple-choice format, thus relying on recognition memory, and were developed using stringent criteria with regard to foils (incorrect alternatives). Data for two cohorts of older adults tested in 1984 and 1994 are of most interest here. In both cohorts, older adults performed better for events from their chronological age range of 11–30 than for 31–50. This was true for current events and Academy Award winners. Only data for the World Series questionnaire failed to conform to the pattern, perhaps due to the domination of the New York Yankees for a prolonged period in baseball history. Clearly, then, the data from a variety of domains support the notion that the bump phenomenon extends beyond the type of recollective memory tapped by autobiographical memory tasks.

CUE WORDS REVISITED

Two studies by Rubin and Schulkind (1997a, 1997b) replicated the bump phenomenon for cue-word memories. Rubin and Schulkind (1997b) attempted to evaluate several hypotheses that might account for the phenomenon. Subjects were asked to rate memories for vividness, pleasantness, significance, novelty, and frequency of rehearsal. Subjects reported 125 memories but related only a subset of them. They also reported five important memories. Consistent with earlier work, the distribution of important memories differed significantly from that for memories prompted with cue words.

The results from analysis of the rating scales did not succeed in identifying any characteristic that distinguished between memories from the bump era and memories from other eras. Thus, memories from the bump were not rated as more important, more significant, more frequently rehearsed, more vivid, or more emotional than nonbump memories. Rubin and Schulkind concluded that "it remains possible that memories from the bump are encoded in a way that makes them easier to retrieve in later life other than by the factors considered here" (1997b, p. 533)." They believed that the data were inconsistent with the self-narrative hypothesis because they claimed it predicts differences in rehearsal, importance, and significance for bump memories.

Rubin et al. (1998) discussed several alternative explanations. One is a cognitive account of the mnemonic advantages for events that occur during a period of rapid change that is followed by a period of stability. In their account, items and events are easier to remember if cues are available at retrieval that uniquely identify them from among all other items in memory. In such an account, traditional factors, such as encoding specificity (Tulving, 1983), form the basis of predicting that the novel events of late adolescence and early adulthood are better recalled because of their novelty. They gain further advantage from spaced practice; that is, they will be recalled on multiple occasions far apart in time. Although this cognitive account fits with several laboratory phenomena, it does not fit well with some of the conclusions drawn by Rubin and Schulkind (1997b). For example, the cognitive account of Rubin et al. predicts the same differences in rehearsal, novelty, and importance that Rubin and Schulkind associate with the self-narrative hypothesis. For example, in both their view and the self-narrative hypothesis, memories that take place during the bump are likely to be the object of frequent rehearsal and may be regarded as more novel, since the individual must put forth more effort to comprehend them. Although Rubin and Schulkind failed to find such differences, their application of rating methodology to memories elicited with cue words might not fairly evaluate either their cognitive account or the self-narrative hypothesis. If the mechanisms involved work on a broader level than memories for specific events, then the ratings of specific events could be misleading. This possibility is discussed in the following section.

SELF-NARRATIVES AND ADAPTATION

The self-narrative hypothesis was developed to account for a cognitive phenomenon at a sociocontextual level. As such, it is compatible with a variety of cognitive and neuropsychological explanations of the memory phenomena involved. As Rubin et al. (1998) noted psychology needs to integrate different levels of explanation to be a successful science. If their account of the bump is correct, then the self-narrative hypothesis clearly needs to be evaluated in terms of consistency with those mechanisms they described.

The self-narrative hypothesis centers around the type of recollective experiences that Tulving defines as episodic memory. Why do humans have such a memory system? If we understand something about the adaptive role of such a system in human cognition, then we might illuminate the issue of why one period of the life span would be favored over others. Shallice (1998) and Baddeley (1992) provided similar characterizations of the adaptive purpose of episodic memory. The gist of their argument is that our survival as a species depends on or is enhanced by our ability to plan in accordance with the information contained in a single event. Baddeley gives the example of how the human memory system might respond to an expected encounter with a predator on a particular path. Although the semantic memory system is capable of incorporating such information into our knowledge base, that system is biased to update slowly, abstracting commonalties from a series of similar events. If it updates too quickly, then it may put the organism in harm's way with false generalizations—but there is value to developing the capacity to alter behavior on the basis of a single experience. Such capacity requires an episodic system that can encode events in sufficient detail to distinguish one event from another. We know that humans can and do encode and retain many events; we also know that it seems they do not encode all events and that they retain even fewer over time. Baddeley stated that "any adequate theory of memory must take into account the central role of the rememberer who has goals and emotions rather than as a straightforward and impartial system for recording events" (1992, p. 17). In a similar vein, Shallice emphasized that episodic memory is designed to serve a supervisory system, a set of mechanism and/or processes responsible for executive functions. When it encounters a situation for which no existing routine seems appropriate, the supervisory system needs memories for specific events that match its current needs on appropriate criteria.

From this, we would imply that the episodic memory system is tuned to selectively operate during periods of change, growth, and novelty. For that reason, any event that occurs during periods of such change is likely to be the target of cognitive activities that enhance the probability of retrieval for recollective experience at a later time. Although postulating a distinct mechanism such as Shallice's may not be necessary, his general point about a governing adaptive principle for episodic memory seems well taken. Thus, we would expect that it is not necessarily novel events per se that are favored for recall, but rather events that occur during periods of novelty, change, or development. Rubin et al. (1998) emphasized that single novel events may be better recalled, but the self-narrative hypothesis emphasizes broad periods of change. Some events during those periods will be regarded in retrospect as novel, but some events from the self-narrative era will not be rated as novel and may not be frequently rehearsed. Because they took place during periods of change, however, they may be better recalled. For example, in addition to the bump phenomena, there is research suggesting that the transition to college is also marked by the enhanced recall a wide variety of events (Pillemer, Reichman, 1996). Thus, the memory system responds both to single novel events and to prolonged periods of change. Once the system senses that it has enough of any sort of information, there is a lower probability that the effort for complex processing will be expended or that storage space will be dedicated to retaining specific event records. In the case of college, that might be a few weeks. In terms of the transition to adult status, the transition period may be much longer. The bump may reflect the accumulated impact of several such transitions compressed into a relatively short period of time. Some of these transitions may occur simultaneously.

The temporal organization of autobiographical memory proposed by Conway explicitly includes the possibility that a number of lifetime periods, corresponding to different aspects of the self, may take place during the same chronological period. When individuals report important memories, they tend to report about events from these periods that have come to play a significant role in defining, directing, and evaluating the self. These memories are reported in the form of well-articulated stories. On the remember/know dimension, these memories are likely to be rated toward the remember end of the scale, because the rich narratives will provide the opportunity for recollective experience. On the other hand, in cue-word studies, individuals report many memories that are not rated as novel, important, significant, or well rehearsed. If they ever were regarded as memorable, they are no longer regarded as such. These events happened at the right time in the life course and so they are reported in greater numbers than expected. The autobiographical knowledge needed to reconstruct those events likely overlaps with many events that appear significant, novel, or important. The intense processing of "important" events that take place during transitional periods is likely to produce elaborated and well-learned semantic memories in the form of repisodes and self-schema that Neisser placed at the top of the autobiographical memory hierarchy. Such knowledge is likely to be preserved by the spaced practice (rehearsal) of our significant memories, the self-narratives we employ to guide, direct, comprehend, and communicate about our selves throughout life.

SUMMARY AND CONCLUSIONS

Autobiographical memory poses a number of challenges to life-span researchers. It is a complex area that does not always lend itself to the traditional models of human memory. For example, the reader may note that the word *decline* has not been used in this chapter, even though laboratory research has clearly established that as people grow older, they do not perform as well on most memory tasks. The fact that this chapter has not discussed declines in autobiographical memory does not mean that older adults do not experience memory failures in remembering everyday life events. Rather, I think it means that human memory probably retains sufficient capacity that the declines experienced in memory functioning may not significantly affect memory in daily life. The fact is that when people do experience such declines, it is regarded as a symptom of some pathological state.

Most of what we have learned about autobiographical memory and aging, we have learned since the 1980s. We have learned two things that have significant implications for social cognition. The first is that most older adults are encoding daily experiences at about the same rate as are younger adults. We do not know much about the details of that encoding, but we do know—at least using the methodologies available to us—that older adults perform very similarly to younger adults. Thus, when interacting with others, older adults have their recent past available. This would seem to have important implications for their ability to sustain social interactions, to be interesting conversation partners, and to maintain a sense of connectedness to their social world. We should note, however, that if the content of their experience is highly routinized and becomes dull to them, it is likely that their interest in what is available to encode and retrieve might affect social interaction.

The second major finding has been the bump. This phenomenon has grabbed the attention of those autobiographical memory researchers with an interest in aging. The next findings will probably tell us more about why the bump is there. The bias of this chapter has been to suggest that some social cognitive and socio-cultural factors are involved in developing the bump. What has not yet been researched is what it means for older adults to have bump memories available to them and what it might mean for cultural groups to have those older adults. It is hoped that we will soon learn more about how older adults use their bump memories. Are there social rules for when it is appropriate to evoke the past? Are there sanctions applied for overuse of the past? These are different questions than memory researchers are accustomed to asking, but one of the advantages of the field of aging is that it has a rich interdisciplinary history. Already, the study of autobiographical memory has attracted the interest of anthropologists, sociologists, historians, and students of literature. The study of autobiographical memory must move from the embryonic to the newborn stage.

REFERENCES

Baddeley, A. D. (1992). What is autobiographical memory? In M. A. Conway, D. C. Rubin, H. Spinnler, & W. A. Wagenaar (Eds.), *Theoretical perspectives on autobiographical memory* (pp. 13–29). Boston: Kluwer Academic Publishers.

Barclay, C. R. (1986). Schematization of autobiographical memory. In D. C. Rubin (Ed.), *Autobiographical memory*. New York: Cambridge University Press.

Barclay, C. R., & DeCooke, P. A. (1988). Ordinary everyday memories: Some of the things of which selves are made. In U. Neisser & E. Winograd (Eds.), *Remembering reconsidered: Ecological approaches to the study of memory* (pp. 91–125). New York: Cambridge University Press.

Barclay, C. R., & Wellman, H. M. (1986). Accuracies and inaccuracies in autobiographical memory. *Journal of Memory and Language, 25,* 93–103.

Bartlett, F. C. (1932). *Remembering: A study in experimental social psychology.* Cambridge, MA: Cambridge University Press.

Belli, R. F., Schuman, H., & Jackson, B. (1997). Autobiographical misremembering: John Dean is not alone. *Applied Cognitive Psychology, 11,* 187–209.

Benson, K. A., Jarvi, S. D., Arai, Y., Thiebar, P. R. S., Fiye, K. J., & Cohen, B. L. (1992). Socio-historical context and autobiographical memories: Variations in the reminiscence phenomenon. In M. A. Conway, D. C. Rubin, H. Spinnler, & W. A. Wagenaar (Eds.), *Theoretical perspectives on autobiographical memory* (pp. 313–322). Boston: Kluwer Academic Publishers.

Brewer, W. F. (1986). What is autobiographical memory? In D. C. Rubin (Ed.), *Autobiographical memory* (pp. 25–49). New York: Cambridge University Press.

Brewer, W. F. (1995). To assert that essentially all human knowledge and memory is represented in terms of stories is certainly wrong. In R. S. Wyer (Ed.), *Knowledge and memory: The real story: Advances in Social Cognition* (vol. 8., pp. 109–120), Hillsdale, NJ: Lawrence Erlbaum Associates.

Brewer, W. F. (1996). What is recollective memory? In D. C. Rubin (Ed.), *Remembering our past: Studies in autobiographical memory* (pp. 19–66). New York: Cambridge University Press.

Brown, N. R. (1993). Response time, retrieval strategies, and the investigation of autobiographical memory. In T. K. Srull, & R. S. Wyer, Jr. (Eds.), *The mental representation of trait and autobiographical knowledge about the self: Advances in Social Cognition* (vol. 5., pp. 61–68). Hillsdale, NJ: Lawrence Erlbaum Associates.

Brown, R., & Kulik, J. (1977). Flashbulb memories. *Cognition, 5,* 73–99.

Bruce, D. (1985). The functional explanation of memory. In L. W. Poon, D. C. Rubin, & B. A. Wilson (Eds.), *Everyday cognition in adulthood and late life* (pp. 44–58). New York: Cambridge University Press.

Bruner, J. (1986). *Actual minds, possible worlds.* Cambridge, MA: Harvard University Press.

Cantor, N., & Kihlstrom, J. F. (1987) *Personality and social intelligence.* Englewood Cliffs, NJ: Prentice-Hall.

Cohen, G., & Faulkner, D. (1988). Lifespan changes in autobiographical memory. In M. E. Gruenberg, P. E. Morris, & R. N. Sykes (Eds.), *Practical aspects of memory: Vol. 1: Memory in everyday life* (pp. 277–282). New York: Wiley.

Cohler, B. J. (1982). Personal narratives and life course. In P. Baltes & O. Brim (Eds.), *Life-span development and behavior* (vol. 4) (pp. 205–241). New York: Academic Press.

Conrad, F. G., Brown, N. R., & Cashman, E. R. (1998). Strategies for estimating behavioral frequencies in survey interviews. *Memory, 4,* 339–366.

Conway, M. A. (1992). A structural model of autobiographical memory. In M. A. Conway, D. C. Rubin, H. Spinnler, & W. A. Wagenaar (Eds.), *Theoretical perspectives on autobiographical memory* (pp. 167–194). Boston: Kluwer Academic Publishers.

Conway, M. A. (1996). Autobiographical knowledge and autobiographical memories. In D. C. Rubin (Ed.), *Remembering our past: Studies in autobiographical memory* (pp. 67–93). New York: Cambridge University Press.

Conway, M. A., & Berkerian, D. A. (1987). Organization in autobiographical memory. *Memory and Cognition, 15,* 119–132.

Conway, M. A., & Rubin, D. C. (1993). The structure of autobiographical memory. In A. C. Collins, S. E. Gathescote, M. A. Conway, & P. E. M. Morris (Eds.) *Theories of memory* (pp. 103–137). Sussex, New Brunswick, Canada: Lawrence Erlbaum Associates.

Costa, Jr., P. T., & McCrae, R. R. (1985). *The NEO Personality Inventory* (manual). Odessa, FL: Psychological Assessment Resources.

Crovitz, H. F., & Schiffman, H. (1974). Frequency of episodic memories as a function of their age. *Bulletin of the Psychonomic Society, 4,* 517–518.

Ebbinghaus, H. (1885/1964). *Memory.* New York: Dover.

Erikson, E. (1958). *Identity: Youth and crisis.* New York: W. W. Norton.

Erikson, E. (1959). *Identity and the life cycle.* New York: International University Press.

Fitzgerald, J. M. (1980). Sampling autobiographical memory reports in adolescence. *Developmental Psychology, 16,* 675–676.

Fitzgerald, J. M. (1986). Autobiographical memory: A developmental perspective. In D. C. Rubin (Ed.), *Autobiographical memory* (pp. 122–133). New York: Cambridge University Press.

Fitzgerald, J. M. (1988). Vivid memories and the reminiscence phenomenon: The role of a self narrative. *Human Development, 31,* 261–273.

Fitzgerald, J. M. (1991). A developmental account of early childhood amnesia. *Journal of Genetic Psychology, 152,* 159–171.

Fitzgerald, J. M. (1992). Autobiographical memory and conceptualizations of the self. In M. A. Conway, D. C. Rubin, H. Spinnler, & W. A. Wagenaar (Eds.) *Theoretical perspectives on autobiographical memory.* (pp. 99–114). Boston: Kluwer Academic Publishers.

Fitzgerald, J. M. (1996a). Intersecting meanings of reminiscence in adult development and aging. In D. C. Rubin (Ed.), *Remembering our past: Studies in autobiographical memory* (pp. 360–383). New York: Cambridge University Press.

Fitzgerald, J. M. (1996b). The distribution of self-narrative memories in younger and older adults: Elaborating the self-narrative hypothesis. *Aging, Neuropsycholgy, and Cognition, 3,* 229–236.

Fitzgerald, J. M., & Lawrence, R. (1984). Autobiographical memory across the life-span. *Journal of Gerontology, 39,* 692–699.

Fitzgerald, J. M., Slade, S., & Lawrence, R. (1988). Memory availability and judged frequency of affect. *Cognitive Therapy and Research, 12,* 379–390.

Fromholt, P., Larsen, P., & Larsen, S. F. (1995). Effects of late-onset depression and recovery on autobiographical memory. *Journal of Gerontology: Psychological Sciences, 46,* 85–91.

Fromholt, P., & Larsen, S. F. (1991). Autobiographical memory in normal aging and primary degenerative dementia (dementia of Alzheimer type). *Journal of Gerontology: Psychological Sciences, 46,* 85–91.

Gould, O. N., & Dixon, R. A. (1993). How we spent our vacation: Collaborative storytelling by young and old adults. *Psychology and Aging, 8,* 10–17.

Higgins, E. T. (1987). Self discrepancy theory: A theory relating self and affect. *Psychological Review, 94,* 319–340.

Holbrook, M., & Schindler, R. M. (1989). Some exploratory findings on the development of musical taste. *Journal of Consumer Research, 16,* 119–124.

Howe, M. L., & Courage, M. L. (1997). The emergence and early development of autobiographical memory. *Psychological Bulletin, 104,* 499–523.

Hyman, I. E., & Faries, J. M. (1992). The function of autobiographical memory. In M. A. Conway, D. C. Rubin, H. Spinnler, & W. A. Wagenaar (Eds.) *Theoretical perspectives on autobiographical memory* (pp. 207–221). Boston: Kluwer Academic Publishers.

Hyman, Jr., I. E., & Pentland, J. (1996). Guided imagery and the creation of false childhood memories. *Journal of Memory and Language, 35,* 101–117.

Jansari, A. M., & Parkin, A. J. (1996). Things that go bump in your life: Explaining the reminiscence bump in autobiographical memory. *Psychology and Aging, 11,* 85–91.

Jung, C. (1961). Memories, dreams, reflections. New York: Vintage.

Kihlstrom, J. (1993). What does the self look like? In T. K. Srull, & R. S. Wyer, Jr. (Eds.), *The mental representation of trait and autobiographical knowledge about the self: Advances in social cognition* (vol. 5, pp. 79–90). Hillsdale, NJ: Lawrence Erlbaum Associates.

Klein, S. B., & Loftus, J. (1993). The mental representation of trait and autobiographical knowledge about the self. In T. K. Srull, & R. S. Wyer, Jr. (Eds.), *The mental representation of trait and autobiographical knowledge about the self: Advances in social cognition* (vol. 5, pp. 1–50). Hillsdale, NJ: Lawrence Erlbaum Associates.

Larsen, S. F. (In press). Memorable books: Recall of reading in its personal context. In M. S. MacNealey & R. Kreuz (Eds.), *Empirical approaches to literature and aesthetics: Advances in discourse processes* (vol. 52). Norwood, NJ: Ablex.

Linton, M. (1975). Memory for real-world events. In D. A. Norman & D. E. Rumelhart (Eds.), *Explorations in cognition* (pp. 376–404). San Francisco: Freeman.

Mackavey, W. R., Malley, J. E., & Stewart, A. J. (1991). Remembering autobiographically consequential experiences: Content analysis of psychologists' accounts of their lives. *Psychology and Aging, 6,* 50–59.

Markus, H., & Nurius, P. (1986). Possible selves. *American Psychologist, 41,* 954–969.

McAdams, D. P. (1988). *Power, intimacy, and the life-story: Personological inquiries into identity.* New York: Guilford.

McAdams, D. P. (1994). *The person: An introduction to personality psychology.* New York: Harcourt Brace.

McClelland, D. C. (1985). *Human motivation.* Glenview, IL: Scott Foresman.

McFarland, C., & Ross, M. (1987). The relation between current memories and memories of self and dating partners. *Personality and Social Psychology Bulletin, 13,* 228–238.

Murray, H. (1938). *Explorations in personality.* New York: Oxford University Press.

Neisser, U. (1981). John Dean's memory: A case study. *Cognition, 9,* 1–22.

Neisser, U. (1982). Snapshots or benchmarks? In U. Neisser (Ed.), *Memory observed: Remembering in natural contexts* (pp. 43–48). San Francisco: Freeman.

Neisser, U. (1986). Nested structure in autobiographical memory. In D. C. Rubin (Ed.), *Autobiographical memory* (pp. 77–81). New York: Cambridge University Press.

Neisser, U. (1988). Commentary. *Human Development, 31,* 271–273.

Nelson, K. (1992). The emergence of autobiographical memory at age four. *Human Development, 35,* 172–177.

Nelson, K. (1993). The psychological and social origins of autobiographical memory. *Psychological Science, 4,* 7–14.

Pezdek, K., & Banks, W. P. (Eds.) (1996). *The recovered memory/false memory debate.* New York: Academic Press.

Pillcmer, D. B , Piçariello, M. L., Law, A. B., Reichman, J. S. (1996). In D. C. Rubin (Ed.), *Remembering our past: Studies in autobiographical memory* (pp. 318–337). New York: Cambridge University Press.

Reisser, B. J., Black, J. B., & Abelson, R. P. (1985). Knowledge structures in the organization and retrieval of autobiographical memories. *Cognitive Psychology, 17,* 89–117.

Robinson, J. R. (1976). Sampling autobiographical memory. *Cognitive Psychology, 8,* 578–595.

Robinson, J. R., & Hawpe, L. (1986). Narrative thinking as a heuristic process. In T. R. Sarbin (Ed.), *Narrative psychology: The storied nature of human conduct* (pp. 111–125). New York: Praeger.

Rotter, A. M. (1997). Patterns of self-disclosure: Implications of dysphoria, gender, and topic. Unpublished dissertation, Wayne State University, Detroit, MI.

Rubin, D. C. (1982). On the retention function for autobiographical memory. *Journal of Verbal Learning and Verbal Behavior, 21,* 21–38.

Rubin, D. C. (Ed.), (1986). *Autobiographical memory.* New York: Cambridge University Press.

Rubin, D. C. (1995). Stories about stories. In R. S. Wyer, Jr. (Ed.) *Knowledge and memory: The real story: Advances in Social Cognition* (vol. 8, pp. 153–164). Hillsdale, NJ: Lawrence Erlbaum Associates.

Rubin, D. C. (Ed.) (1996). *Remembering our past: Studies in autobiographical memory.* New York: Cambridge University Press.

Rubin, D. C., Groth, L., & Goldsmith, D. (1984). Olfactory cueing of autobiographical memory. *American Journal of Psychology, 97,* 493–507.

Rubin, D. C., & Kozin, M. (1984). Vivid memories. *Cognition, 16,* 81–95.

Rubin, D. C., Rahhal, T., & Poon, L. W. (1998) Things learned in early adulthood are remembered best: Effects of a major transition on memory. *Memory and Cognition, 26,* 3–19.

Rubin, D. C., & Schulkind, M. D. (1997a). The distribution of autobiographical memories across the lifespan. *Memory and Cognition, 25,* 859–866.

Rubin, D. C., & Schulkind, M. D. (1997b). Distribution of important and word-cued memories in 20-, 35-, and 70-year-old adults. *Psychology and Aging, 12,* 524–535.

Rubin, D. C., & Wenzel, A. E. (1996). One hundred years of forgetting: A quantitative description of retention. *Psychological Review, 103,* 734–760.

Rubin, D. C., Wetzler, S. E., & Nebes, R. D. (1986). Autobiographical memory across the adult life span. In D. C. Rubin (Ed.), *Autobiographical memory.* New York: Cambridge University Press.

Sande, G. N., Goethals, G. R., & Radloff, C. E. (1988). Perceiving one's own traits and others: The multifaceted self. *Journal of Personality and Social Psychology, 59,* 229–241.

Schank, R. C., & Abelson, R. P. (1977). *Scripts, plans, goals, and understanding.* Hillsdale, NJ: Lawrence Erlbaum Associates.

Schank, R. C., & Abelson, R. P. (1995). Knowledge and memory: The real story. In R. S. Wyer (Ed.) *Knowledge and memory: The real story: Advances in Social Cognition* (vol. 8, pp. 1–86). Hillsdale, NJ: Lawrence Erlbaum Associates.

Schuman, H., & Rieger, C. (1992). Collective memory and collective memories. In M. A. Conway, D. C. Rubin, H. Spinnler, & W. A. Wagenaar (Eds.), *Theoretical perspectives on autobiographical memory.* Boston: Kluwer Academic Publishers.

Schuman, H., Rieger, C., & Gaidy, V. (1994). Collective memories in the United States and Lithuania. In N. Schwartz & S. Sudman (Eds.), *Autobiographical memory and the validity of retrospective reports* (pp. 313–333). New York: Springer-Verlag.

Schuman, H., & Scott, J. (1989). Generations and collective memories. *American Sociological Review, 54,* 359–381.

Sehulster, J. R. (1996). In my era: Evidence for the perception of a special period of the past. *Memory, 4,* 145–158.

Shallice, T. (1988). *From neuropsychology to mental structure.* New York: Cambridge University Press.

Srull, T. K., & Wyer, Jr., R. S. (Eds.) (1993). *The mental representation of trait and autobiographical knowledge about the self: Advances in Social Cognition,* vol. 5. Hillsdale, NJ: Lawrence Erlbaum Associates.

Tessler, M., & Nelson, K. (1996). Making memories: The influence of joint encoding on later recall by young children. In K. Pezdek & W. P. Banks (Eds.), *The recovered memory/false memory debate* (pp. 101–120), New York: Academic Press.

Tulving, E. (1983). *Elements of episodic memory.* New York: Oxford University Press.

Vico, G. (1948). *The new science* (T. G. Bergin & M. H. Fisch, Trans.). Ithaca, NY: Cornell University Press.

Wagenaar, W. A. (1986). My memory: A study of autobiographical memory over six years. *Cognitive Psychology, 18,* 225–252.

Webster, J. D. (1993). Construction and validation of the reminiscence functions scale. *Journal of Gerontology: Psychological Sciences, 48,* P256–P262.

Wheeler, M. A., Stuss, D. T., & Tulving, E. (1997). Toward a theory of episodic memory: The frontal lobes and autonoetic consciousness. *Psychological Bulletin, 121,* 331–354.

Williams, J. M. G. (1996). Depression and the specificity of autobiographical memory. In D. C. Rubin (Ed.), *Remembering our past: Studies in autobiographical memory* (pp. 244–270). New York: Cambridge University Press.

Winograd, E. (1988). Continuities between ecological and laboratory approaches to memory. In U. Neisser & E. Winograd (Eds.), *Remembering reconsidered: Ecological and traditional approaches to the study of memory* (pp. 11–20). New York: Cambridge University Press.

FOCUS ON OTHERS

8

A SOCIAL COGNITIVE PERSPECTIVE ON AGE STEREOTYPES

MARY LEE HUMMERT

Communication Studies Department
University of Kansas
Lawrence, Kansas

Most of us would readily acknowledge that age stereotypes permeate our culture. This is evident in the extended media coverage of the baby boomers' turning 50 (Will they change the meaning of aging?) and former President George Bush's parachute jump on his 70th birthday (amazing feat *at his age*). Humorous birthday cards for middle-aged and older persons capitalize on negative expectations about aging: Too bad you are turning 40 (or 50 or 60); you will start to forget things, become grouchy, lose your physical stamina and sexual abilities, etc. Paradoxically, positive expectations about aging apparently coexist with these negative expectations. Again, birthday cards provide evidence. Those for grandmothers and grandfathers celebrate their loving behavior toward their grandchildren, while those specifically for 70-, 80- and 90-year-olds refer to the accomplishments of age: wisdom, generosity, self-acceptance. Perhaps more important from a social cognitive perspective, these age stereotypes also influence our attributions for our own and others' behaviors. For instance, in Chapter 9 of this book Erber and Prager focus on how forgetting carries different implications for perceptions of a young person than of an older one.

The personal consequences of negative stereotypes about aging can be serious. Recently, an 80-year-old relative of mine received the following advice from his physician (himself over 60): "Well, of course, you're tired. You just need to slow down. After all, you're getting older and you can't expect to do what you could when you were younger." Although my relative knew to look for a second opinion, many older patients may accept this type of advice even though it is based on age stereotypes as opposed to medical research. This chapter is based on the premise that social cognitive processes provide the key to understanding both the complex nature of age stereotypes and their impact on our self-perceptions and interpersonal interactions. Three issues are considered: (1) age stereotypes as person perception schemas, (2) activation of age stereotypes in interpersonal interaction, and (3) developmental processes and age stereotyping.

AGE STEREOTYPES AS PERSON PERCEPTION SCHEMAS

From a social cognitive perspective (Ashmore & Del Boca, 1981; Hamilton & Trolier, 1986), age stereotypes are seen as person perception schemas that use age as a categorization principle. As schemas, age stereotypes represent organized, prior knowledge structures that facilitate interpretation of new information (Fiske & Taylor, 1991). From this perspective, age stereotypes are not seen as inherently negative, even though they may at times have negative consequences. Instead, age stereotypes are knowledge structures that people use to help them process the mass of information in a typical social interaction. This social cognitive perspective on age stereotypes stands in contrast to two other perspectives on stereotypes described by Ashmore and Del Boca (1981), the sociocultural and the psychodynamic, both of which emphasize the negative apsects of stereotyping. A brief overview of these contrasting perspectives helps to illuminate the unique characteristics and benefits of viewing age stereotypes as person perception schemas.

SOCIOCULTURAL AND PSYCHODYNAMIC PERSPECTIVES ON AGE STEREOTYPES

The sociocultural perspective highlights the cultural roots and shared nature of stereotypical beliefs. Age stereotypes, from this perspective, are beliefs about the characteristics of older people that are widely held by members of a particular culture. Initial research on age stereotypes adopted a sociocultural approach, employing questionnaires and adjective checklists to assess beliefs about older people (e.g., Harris, 1975; Palmore, 1977; Tuckman & Lorge, 1953). This approach still generates much interest today as researchers attempt to map current perceptions of aging (e.g., Giles, Harwood, Pierson, Clément, & Fox, in press; Silverstein & Parrott, 1997; Speas & Obenshain, 1995). To stereotype theorists from the sociocultural school, stereotypes about older people are negative in that they are unconsciously adopted by individuals within the society, often incorrect, and applied equally to all over 65 years of age. Further, age stereotypes serve to reinforce such discriminatory cultural practices as mandatory retirement and isolation of older individuals. The concept of age prejudice or ageism (Butler, 1969) thus had its genesis in the sociocultural perspective.

Whereas the sociocultural perspective looks to society as the source of negative age stereotypes, the psychodynamic perspective looks to the individual's personality (Ashmore & Del Boca, 1981) and the psychological function that stereotypes may serve for that individual. For instance, Adorno, Frenkel-Brunswik, Levinson, and Sanford (1950) suggested that individuals with an authoritarian personality were predisposed to categorize or stereotype others. In the case of age stereotypes, researchers have tried to identify whether such individual characteristics as aggressiveness (Katz, 1990; Thorson & Perkins, 1981) and a deterministic cognitive system (Klemmack & Roff, 1983) are related to negative stereotypes about older people. These efforts have been largely unsuccessful to date (Hummert, Shaner, & Garstka, 1995).

WHAT CAN A SOCIAL COGNITIVE PERSPECTIVE OFFER?

The sociocultural perspective and the psychodynamic perspective each focus on questions that are important to understanding age stereotypes. In the former case, that question is What are the age stereotypes within a culture?, whereas in the latter, it is Who is most likely to use age stereotypes? Yet both ignore the equally important questions of *when* and *how* stereotypes influence our perceptions of and behaviors toward others. Further, the sociocultural and psychodynamic perspectives each cannot account for important psychological realities related to age stereotypes. In the case of the sociocultural perspective, it is the fact that not every individual within a culture has exactly the same set of stereotypical beliefs about older people, as evidenced by several studies (Kite, Deaux, & Miele, 1991; Hummert, Garstka, Shaner & Strahm, 1994; Rothbaum, 1983; Schmidt & Boland, 1986). For the psychodynamic perspective, it is the assumption that a propensity to stereotype is driven by a need to find a socially acceptable outlet for unconscious aggressive impulses (Ashmore & Del Boca, 1981). If this were the case, only younger people should hold negative stereotypes of older people, a conclusion that is not supported by the research on age stereotypes (Brewer & Lui, 1984; Hummert, et al., 1994; Rothbaum, 1983; Schulz & Fritz, 1987). Finally, by classifying age stereotyping as flawed thinking (the sociocultural perspective) or as evidence of psychological inadequacy (the psychodynamic approach), these two perspectives discourage us from acknowledging the ways in which age stereotypes influence our own perceptions and behaviors. Instead, we see age stereotyping as deviant behavior in which others engage but that we ourselves avoid at all costs.

Viewing stereotypes as person perception schemas—that is, from a social cognitive perspective—overcomes these limitations of the sociocultural and psychodynamic approaches. The social cognitive perspective encompasses the important questions of the sociocultural and psychodynamic researchers but also considers issues of how age stereotypes become salient during interaction, when they affect perceptions and behaviors, and how they both develop and change. By acknowledging that age stereotypes have a basis in cultural beliefs yet exist only as cognitive representations within individuals, this perspective, unlike the sociocultural, can account for both the similarity and differences among individuals' age stereo-type schemas. By considering age stereotypes as knowledge structures possessed and employed at some level by all perceivers, the social cognitive perspective, unlike the psychodynamic, can account for why even older people sometimes stereotype their peers. Further, by identifying stereotyping as a normal part of the perceptual process, the social cognitive perspective removes the stigma that may interfere with our acknowledging the ways in which age stereotypes may affect our own perceptions and behaviors.

THE NATURE AND CONTENT OF AGE STEREOTYPE SCHEMAS

One focus of social cognitive research on age stereotypes has been to describe the content and organization of stereotype schemas. This goal parallels that of the sociocultural perspective—that is, answering the question What are age stereo-types within a culture? However, it adds an emphasis on the structure, interrela-tionships, and variability of beliefs that is absent from the sociocultural approach.

Categorization of others by age appears to be a fundamental principle in per-son perception (Brewer, 1988; Brewer & Lui, 1989; Milord, 1978), with the cate-gory *older adult* functioning as a superordinate category that subsumes several more specific subcategories. This is analogous to the way in which *bird* functions as a superordinate category including such members as *cardinal, blue jay,* and *crow,* as reported by Rosch (1978). Members of different subcategories share many of the same general features—for example, wings and feathers in the case of birds and gray hair and wrinkles (Hummert et al., 1994; Schmidt & Boland, 1986) in the case of older adults. At the same time, members of each subcategory have features that distinguish them from members of other ones; for example, cardinals have red plumage and crows have black.

In the case of age stereotypes, research (Brewer, Dull & Lui, 1981; Brewer & Lui, 1984; Hummert, 1990; Hummert et al., 1994; Schmidt & Boland, 1986) has documented both positive and negative subcategories or stereotypes of older adults (For a detailed review of the multiple stereotype research see Hummert, Shaner & Garstka, 1995). These stereotypes consist of clusters of personality, cognitive, and general physical traits. For instance, Hummert et al. (1994) first asked one group of young, middle-aged, and older adults to generate a list of traits they associated with the category *older adult*. A second group of adults represent-ing the same three age groups sorted the resulting 97 traits into groups describing individual older persons. Cluster analysis of these groupings showed that although the two older groups had more complex stereotype sets than did the young, the participants shared seven powerful cultural archetypes of aging: the *golden ager, John Wayne conservative, perfect grandparent, shrew/curmudgeon, recluse, despondent,* and *severely impaired.* The nature and extent of stereotype differences across the age groups is considered later in this chapter in relationship to developmental issues in age stereotyping.

TABLE 8.1   Traits Associated with Stereotypes of Older Adults

Stereotype	Traits
Negative	
Severely impaired	Slow-thinking, incompetent, feeble, inarticulate, incoherent, senile
Despondent	Depressed, sad, hopeless, afraid, neglected, lonely
Shrew/curmudgeon	Complaining, ill-tempered, demanding, stubborn, bitter, prejudiced
Recluse	Quiet, timid, naive
Positive	
Golden ager	Active, capable, sociable, independent, happy, interesting
Perfect grandparent	Loving, supportive, understanding, wise, generous, kind
John Wayne conservative	Patriotic, conservative, determined, proud, religious, nostalgic

From Hummert et al., 1994.

Representative traits that distinguish these stereotypes are presented in Table 8.1. Note that this group includes almost the same number of positive and negative stereotypes, and only one that describes a physically and cognitively impaired older adult or the traditional stereotype of old age. Whereas the samples in this and the earlier multiple stereotype studies were predominantly white, recent research shows that African Americans have similar stereotypes (Adams & Hummert, under review). Further, attitudes toward the stereotypes vary consistently with the valence of the traits, and both positive and negative stereotypes are viewed as equally representative of the general older adult population (Hummert, 1990; Hummert, Garstka, Shaner & Strahm, 1995; Schmidt & Boland, 1986).

Two questions are suggested by the multiple stereotype research: (1) What features and/or behaviors of older persons result in their being categorized positively or negatively? (2) If perceivers view both positive and negative stereotypes as equally representative of the older population, why do behaviors (e.g., patronizing talk; Caporael, 1981; Hummert, Shaner, Garstka, & Henry, 1998; Ryan, Giles, Bartolucci & Henwood, 1986) and attitudes (Speas & Obenshain, 1995; Crockett & Hummert, 1987; Harris, 1975; Kite & Johnson, 1988) reflect the negative stereotypes more than the positive ones? Answering these questions requires a focus on age stereotyping as a *social cognitive process* in which age stereotype schemas are accessed as knowledge sources, often unconsciously, to guide social judgments and behavior (Leyens, Yzerbyt, & Schadron, 1994).

ACTIVATION OF AGE STEREOTYPES IN INTERPERSONAL INTERACTION

Journalist Walter Lippmann, who first introduced the term *stereotype* into social scientific discourse in his 1922 book *Public Opinion,* characterized stereotypes as "pictures in our heads." Reflecting this view, a major emphasis in the research on age stereotypes has been on the association between physical features and the stereotypes (Brewer et al., 1981; Brewer & Lui, 1984; Hummert, 1994b; Hummert, Garstka, & Shaner, 1997). Brewer (Brewer et al., 1981; Brewer, 1988; Brewer & Lui, 1989) and her colleagues have suggested that facial features may be prototypic of particular stereotypes, and, in fact, the primary way in which stereotypes are activated.

Sorting tasks that invite participants to pair photographs and stereotype traits support this view. For instance, Hummert et al. (1997) used a two-part study to examine the role of target facial cues (physiognomic cues to age, sex, and facial expression) in stereotyping of older persons, as well as how perceiver age and sex may affect sensitivity to these cues. Forty-five older men and women (age range, 60–95) volunteered to have their photographs taken, using both smiling and neutral facial expressions. In the first part of the study, young, middle-aged, and older participants sorted either the smiling or neutral photographs into one of five age groups: under 60, 60–69, 70–79, 80–89, 90 and over. On the basis of those judgments, a set of 18 photographs was constructed consisting of 3 men and 3 women consistently perceived to be either in their sixties (young-old), in their seventies (middle-old), or 80 and over (old-old) by participants of all ages. In the second part of the study, additional young, middle-aged, and older participants were asked to pair the photographs with trait sets describing 6 age stereotypes (3 positive and 3 negative) identified in Hummert et al. (1994). Stereotype labels were not included with the trait sets. Results showed a strong association between the perceived age of the individuals in the photographs and negative stereotyping: those who appeared to be in their eighties and nineties were more likely to be paired with traits of negative stereotypes than were those who appeared to be in their sixties. Supporting a double standard of aging, facial expression played a stronger role in judgments of female targets than of male targets, and women were stereotyped negatively at a younger age (70–79) than were men. On the other hand, photographs of the old-old (80 and over) men were stereotyped more negatively than were those of the old-old females. Although participant age moderated these judgments slightly, as is discussed later in this chapter, participant sex was unrelated to perceptions. Of the various factors affecting the stereotyping process considered in this study, however, the physiognomic cues to age played the strongest role. Apparently, it is not facial features per se that are prototypic of positive and negative stereotypes, as implied by Brewer and colleagues (Brewer, 1988; Brewer et al., 1981; Brewer & Lui, 1989), but those facial features that are linked to perceptions of age.

Two subsequent stereotype activation studies (Hummert & Garstka, 1997, 1998), however, suggest that the physical cues to age alone may not be sufficient to activate the more extreme positive and negative stereotypes of older persons in a social judgment task. In these studies, young, middle-aged, and older participants were randomly assigned to one of three cue conditions: traits, photograph, or traits + photographs. Traits and photographs were selected to represent the stereotypes of golden ager, despondent, and severely impaired. In the first study, photographs were all of women perceived to be in their eighties. The photographs used had been identified as good representatives or prototypes of the three stereotypes in prior research (Hummert et al., 1997). Participants were asked to give a recommendation to each target about a dilemma the target was facing (e.g., whether to move to a congregate living setting) and to provide assessments of the target's traits and abilities.

Results from this study pointed to the importance of trait information in perceptions of old-old targets. Without trait information, judgments of the three old-old targets did not differ significantly on most measures, eliciting neither extremely negative nor extremely positive assessments. When significant differences among targets emerged in the photo-only condition, they were as a rule less marked than in the other two conditions. For instance, more recommendations to the golden ager target in all three cue conditions were consistent with positive stereotypes (e.g., stay in your own home) than were recommendations to the other two targets. The differences in the percentage of positive recommendations to the golden ager versus the other two targets was higher in the trait-only (82% vs 53.3% to the despondent and 15.6% to the severely impaired) and trait + photo (80% vs 46.7% and 24.4%) conditions, however, than in the photo-only condition (65% vs 50% and 56.5%).

One explanation for the greater importance of trait than physical information in perceptions of the targets may stem from the fact that all photographs were of women over 80. Given the strong association of the 80+ age range with negative stereotypes (Hummert et al., 1997), it is reasonable that participants given only the physical information viewed the targets similarly, whereas those who also had trait information distinguished among the targets. As a result, the second activation cue study employed target photographs that varied in age (golden ager, sixties; despondent, seventies; severely impaired, eighties). With this one change in the design of the study, participants showed a greater willingness to make dispositional inferences distinguishing the three targets in the photo-only condition. Results on the decision recommendation in the photo-only condition, for example, showed that positive recommendations to the golden ager were significantly greater (73.3%) than those to the despondent (62.2%) and severely impaired (40%) targets, but again, significant differences in judgments of targets in this condition were less extreme than when trait information was included. Unlike the first study, however, the most extreme differences in judgments of the targets emerged in the photo + trait condition, with over 91% of the participants making positive recommendations to the golden ager versus 82% in the trait-only condition and under 7% making positive recommendations to the severely impaired (vs 16% in the trait-only condition). As in Hummert et al. (1997), participant age differences also had an impact on judgments and are considered in relationship to developmental issues in age stereotyping later in this chapter.

Considering these two studies together, we see that participants were unwilling to make dispositional inferences at the positive and negative extremes based on the physical cue information (photographs) alone when the women in the photographs were similar in perceived age (all over 80). Only when the women in the photographs differed in perceived age did impressions and advice in the photo-only condition approach the valence of the judgments in the trait-only and trait + photo conditions. Even in this second study, though, trait information was required to produce the most extreme judgments.

The social judgeability theory of Leyens et al. (1994) offers a possible explanation for these results. According to this theory, because of the social proscription against stereotyping, perceivers apply stereotypes in their judgments of others only when they believe that they have individuating information that *justifies* that application. Applied to the activation cue studies, social judgeability theory suggests that only those perceivers who received trait information about the old-old women felt justified in making recommendations consistent with the most positive or most negative age stereotypes. By contrast, when the photographs themselves varied in age, that variation was viewed as individuating information that justified more extreme positive judgments of the woman in her sixties and more extreme negative judgments of the woman in her eighties in comparison to judgments of the woman in her seventies. When this individuating physical information was combined with individuating trait information, judgments in the second study became even more extreme than when only trait information was provided.

This does not mean that people consciously draw on the stereotypes in their judgments or that the information must be relevant to the stereotypes. As Yzerbyt, Schadron, Leyens, and Rocher (1994) showed in two studies, simply believing that one has individuating information is sufficient to induce stereotypic judgments. Participants in those studies first viewed a target on videotape, learning the target's name and occupation (comedian or archivist). Next they engaged in a dichotic listening task that involved attending to input in one ear. Following this task, half the participants were told that they had received additional information about the target in the unattended ear, although this was not true. This manipulation was sufficient to induce stereotype-consistent (comedian/archivist) judgments of the extroversion/introversion of the target in that group of participants, whereas those in the no-information condition rated the targets similarly on extroversion/introversion. Further, participants in the information condition insisted that their judgments were based not on stereotypes but on the "information" they had received.

The findings of Yzerbyt et al. (1994) illustrate the operation of implicit stereotypes. Greenwald and Banaji (1995) defined implicit stereotypes as "the introspectively unidentified (or inaccurately identified) traces of past experience that mediate attributions of qualities to members of a social category" (p. 15). In a sense, the stereotypes operate automatically—that is outside, conscious awareness (Bargh, 1994). Implicit gender (Banaji & Greenwald, 1995; Banaji, Hardin, & Rothman, 1993) and race (Devine, 1989; Gaertner & McLaughlin, 1983; Greenwald, McGhee, & Schwartz, 1998) stereotypes have been identified. Implicit age stereotypes have received less attention, although Perdue and Gurtman (1990) demonstrated automatic operation of age stereotypes and Levy (1996) reported implicit self-stereotyping by older adults.

Perdue and Gurtman (1990) conducted two studies of the automaticity of age stereotypes. In the first, participants remembered more negative traits when the traits had been encoded in reference to an older person but more positive traits when the traits were encoded in reference to a young person. In the second study, participants made semantic judgments about negative traits more quickly after being unobtrusively primed with *old* than with *young,* whereas the opposite pattern was found for positive traits. These types of automatic associations with stereotypes can be found even in participants who disavow negative stereotypes for a particular group, as illustrated in the study of race stereotypes (Devine, 1989; Gaertner & McLaughlin, 1983; Greenwald et al., 1998) and gender stereotypes (Banaji & Greenwald, 1995).

Implicit age stereotypes may provide the key to understanding the types of information that warrant the application of positive versus negative age stereotypes in judgments of and behavior toward older individuals in interpersonal interaction, as well as to understanding why negative stereotypes seem to predominate in those judgments. A consideration of the nature of the interpersonal communication process illustrates how implicit age stereotyping may occur.

IMPLICIT AGE STEREOTYPING AND INTERPERSONAL COMMUNICATION

As Gilbert and Hixon (1991) showed, stereotypes affect social perception only when they are relevant to goals of the perceiver—that is, when the "cognitive busyness" of the perceiver involves the stereotypes. When the social perception task is communication, perceivers' cognitive resources are directed toward constructing the most effective message to accomplish their ends. This task involves a consideration of the target's special characteristics, needs, or interests (Higgins, McCann, & Fondacaro, 1982), so that the message can be accommodated to that individual (Giles, Coupland, & Coupland, 1991; Giles, Mulac, Bradac, & Johnson, 1987). Age stereotypes, with their associated beliefs about age-related deficits in communication skills (Hummert, Garstka, & Shaner, 1995), will be relevant, then, to most perceivers faced with communicating with an older person. This is not to say that perceivers consciously draw on aging stereotypes. Rather, it is more likely that age stereotypes affect impressions of and communication behavior toward older persons implicitly, in that the speaker is concentrating not on applying age stereotypes but on creating an effective message.

OLDER ADULTS' COMMUNICATION BEHAVIORS AND
ACTIVATION OF AGE STEREOTYPES

Consider first the interpretation of older adults' communication behaviors in the impression formation process. In natural settings, individuals do not present perceivers with a specific list of their personal traits as in the activation cues studies described earlier (Hummert & Garstka, 1997, 1998). Instead, traits must be inferred from behaviors during interaction—that is, from communication, both verbal and nonverbal. Given the communication implications of traits associated with negative (e.g., slow-thinking, inarticulate, sad) and positive (e.g., sociable, proud, supportive) stereotypes, communication behaviors may be particularly influential in generating dispositional inferences consistent with age stereotypes. Further, naturalistic studies have documented unique features of older adults' conversational style that may serve as stereotype cues. These practices include age disclosure (working one's age into the conversation; Coupland, Coupland, & Giles, 1989), verbosity or prolonged off-target talk (Arbuckle & Gold, 1993; Arbuckle, Gold, & Andres, 1986; Gold, Arbuckle, & Andres, 1994), passive responses to patronizing talk (Harwood, Giles, Fox, Ryan & Williams, 1993; Harwood, Ryan, Giles, & Tysoski, 1997; Hummert & Mazloff, 1998) and "painful self-disclosures" of bereavement, ill health, immobility, and assorted personal and family problems (Coupland, Coupland, Giles, Henwood, & Wiemann, 1988; Coupland, Coupland, Giles & Wiemann, 1988; Coupland, Henwood, Coupland, & Wiemann, 1990). Each of these has the potential to activate negative age stereotypes.

Painful self-disclosures provide an example. Although such disclosures may serve self-presentational or emotional goals of older communicators, they also reinforce negative stereotypes about older persons as weak and disabled (Shaner, 1996; Shaner & Hummert, 1997). Coupland et al. (1990) reported that young women find these behaviors difficult to deal with in conversation and associate them with negative aspects of aging, such as loneliness. Certainly, these behaviors violate norms for self-disclosure between strangers by revealing personal, negative, and excessive information (Berger & Bradac, 1982). Conversational practices unique to older individuals that may be associated with positive stereotypes are less easy to identify, although stories told by older individuals are perceived as more interesting than those told by younger ones (Kemper, Rash, Kynette, & Norman, 1990). This disparity in the number of negative and positive conversational behaviors that are uniquely identified as old may be one factor underlying the prevalence of negative age stereotypes in social judgments.

Communication behaviors of older persons, then, may play a powerful role in the age stereotyping process. They are likely to operate on an implicit level, however. That is, perceivers believe the conversational behaviors constitute a warrant for dispositional inferences (Leyens et al., 1994) consistent with negative age stereotypes (e.g., painful self disclosures indicate loneliness), without realizing (1) that such inferences may be inaccurate (perhaps the disclosures indicate resiliance) or (2) that the inferences involve applying age stereotypes (loneliness is a particular problem of the old).

COMMUNICATION BEHAVIORS TOWARD OLDER
INDIVIDUALS AS IMPLICIT STEREOTYPING

One focus of my prior research has been the ways in which negative age stereotypes may be related to patronizing talk toward older adults. Patronizing talk is characterized by the presence of simplification strategies (e.g., slow speech, simple vocabulary), clarification strategies (e.g., careful articulation and simple sentences), a demeaning emotional tone (overbearing, or alternatively, overly familiar), and a low quality of talk (i.e., superficial conversations) (Hummert & Ryan, 1996; Ryan et al., 1986; Ryan, Hummert, & Boich, 1995). An extreme form of patronizing talk is secondary baby talk addressed to institutionalized adults (Caporael, 1981; Caporael & Culbertson, 1986; Caporael, Lukaszewski, & Culbertson, 1983). Other patronizing talk may take the form of a disapproving or controlling message (Hummert et al., 1998). Theoretical explanations for patronizing talk have identified negative age stereotypes as a primary cause (Caporael, 1981; Giles et al., 1991; Hummert, 1994a; Ryan et al., 1986), although empirical verification of that hypothesis has been achieved only recently, and then only through the use of explicit manipulations of target stereotype (Hummert, Garstka, & Shaner, 1995; Hummert & Shaner, 1994; Hummert, et al., 1998; Kemper, Ferrell, Harden, Finter-Urczyk, & Billington, 1998).

Evaluative studies of patronizing talk have shown consistently that observers view this type of talk to older adults as disrespectful and demeaning (Ryan, Bourhis, & Knops, 1991; Ryan, Hamilton, & Kwong See, 1994; Ryan, Meredith, & Shantz, 1994). At the same time, widespread use of patronizing talk has been documented through observation in nursing homes (Caporael, 1981; Caporael & Culbertson, 1986; Grainger, 1993), interviews with older persons (Hummert & Mazloff, 1998; Ryan & Cole, 1990; Shadden, 1988), and analysis of informative talks to older persons (Kemper, 1994). Participants freely offer patronizing messages to older adults even in laboratory settings, where one might expect them to avoid a talk style that might be viewed negatively (Hummert & Shaner, 1994; Hummert et al., 1998; Kemper et al., 1998). As suggested earlier, implicit stereotyping and the nature of the communication process may account for why persons engage in a communication style that as an observer, they themselves might view as less than optimal. That is, in order to be effective communicators, people attempt to accommodate their talk to the needs of their partners (Giles et al., 1987; Giles et al., 1991). What they may not realize is that their assessment of necessary accommodations may be grounded in age stereotypes (Hummert, 1994a; Ryan et al., 1986). Hummert, Garstka, and Shaner (1995), for example, found that perceivers believe that individuals fitting negative age stereotypes are more likely to experience increased conversational difficulty related to declines in memory and hearing abilities than are those fitting positive stereotypes. This was true even though the traits of the negative stereotypes (e.g., sad, greedy) carried no implication of memory or hearing problems. In other words, patronizing talk may be evidence of implicit stereotyping of older persons.

FUTURE STUDY OF ACTIVATION CUES

As suggested by the literature reviewed in this section, the nature of the interpersonal interaction process may encourage persons to rely implicitly on age stereotypes in two ways: first, as aids to interpreting the behaviors of older individuals and second, as guidelines for constructing effective messages to those individuals. Extending the study of activation cues for age stereotypes from physical age cues to behavioral cues thus offers the promise of new insights into the age stereotyping process. Further, study of the relationship between behavioral cues to age stereotypes and subsequent communication to older individuals may illuminate aspects of how age stereotypes operate implicitly to affect not only judgments of older persons but also behaviors toward them.

DEVELOPMENTAL PROCESSES
AND AGE STEREOTYPING

Age is a unique social category in that individuals progress unavoidably from one category level (i.e., young) to another (i.e., middle-aged) to yet another (i.e., old) over time: What is an in-group at age 20 becomes an out-group at age 60. As a result, we might expect that age stereotypes reflect not only in-group/out-group categorization processes (Linville, 1982; Tajfel & Turner, 1979) but also developmental differences related to individuals' position in the life course (Whitbourne, 1986). That is, as individuals negotiate the aging process, their ideas about aging should reflect their experiences and their age schemas should become more elaborated as those experiences are integrated into those schemas (Baltes, 1987; Whitbourne, 1986). Developmental processes may affect age stereotypes both in terms of content of stereotype schemas and operation of stereotypes in interpersonal interaction.

DEVELOPMENTAL DIFFERENCES
IN AGE STEREOTYPE SCHEMAS

As noted earlier in this chapter, prior research has shown that young and older persons share some quite similar age stereotypes (Brewer et al., 1981; Brewer & Lui, 1984; Hummert et al., 1994). This basic level of agreement on age stereotypes, however, coexists with evidence that the complexity of age stereotype schemas increases with age. In terms of traits associated with age stereotypes, Heckhausen, Dixon, and Baltes (1989) found that older individuals identified more traits (both positive and negative) that show developmental increases with age than did younger ones. Likewise, older persons associate more subcategories with the superordinate category *older adult* than do younger ones (Brewer & Lui, 1984; Hummert et al., 1994). For example, analogous subcategories to six of the stereotypes in Table 8.1 were reported in earlier research with young samples

(Brewer et al., 1981; Hummert, 1990; Schmidt & Boland, 1986). Only when middle-aged and older persons were included in the Hummert et al. (1994) study did the subcategory golden ager emerge, demonstrating the importance of examining perceptions of persons across the adult age range in the study of age stereotypes.

A legitimate question, however, is whether the complexity differences in age stereotype schemas are due to developmental processes or to in-group/out-group categorization processes. As established by Linville (1982), persons have more complex representations of their in-group than of an out-group. Since the specific representations investigated by Linville were young men's perceptions of older men, that research is applicable to age stereotype research at a content as well as conceptual level. In-group/out-group processes would suggest that young and middle-aged adults should view older persons similarly—that is, as members of an out-group. Developmental processes, in contrast, would suggest that the greater experience and personal encounters of middle-aged people with aging individuals and their own development should be reflected in more varied and rich age schemas in comparison to those of young persons. The same should hold true for the age schemas of older people in comparison to those of middle-aged people. The inclusion of middle-aged participants in the Heckhausen et al. (1989) and Hummert et al. (1994) research on age stereotypes provides evidence supporting this developmental view.

Heckhausen et al. (1989) reported that judgments of middle-aged participants about developmental increases with age fell midway between those of young and older participants. Hummert et al. (1994) found that middle-aged participants had more age stereotype subcategories than did younger participants but fewer than did the older participants. Whereas both in-group/out-group and developmental explanations for age group differences would predict that young and old individuals would differ in the complexity of age stereotype schemas, only the developmental explanation can account for the finding that middle-aged individuals have more complex age schemas than do younger persons but less complex schemas than do older persons (Hummert et al., 1994).

From a social cognitive perspective on age stereotypes, age stereotypes become more elaborated across the life span as individuals integrate their life experiences into their conceptions of aging (Baltes, 1987; Whitbourne, 1986). In particular, as they observe the heterogeneity of aged individuals, the elaboration occurs at both the trait level (Heckhausen et al., 1989) and at the subcategory level (Hummert et al., 1994) of stereotype schemas. Certainly, in-group/out-group categorization processes may affect perceptions of those in other age groups, but the research involving participants across the adult age range suggests that developmental processes serve to modify in-group/out-group perceptions. Although this research has been cross-sectional whereas a complete test of developmental processes requires a longitudinal design, no obvious cohort differences among young, middle-aged, and older participants in these studies would account for the pattern of results obtained.

DEVELOPMENTAL PROCESSES, AGE STEREOTYPING,
AND INTERPERSONAL INTERACTION

There are two ways in which prior research suggests that developmental processes may moderate the operation of implicit age stereotypes in interpersonal interaction. First, whereas young people may associate behaviors such as age disclosure and painful self-disclosure with negative age stereotypes, older persons may view them instead as normal ways of sharing information about important events in one's life (Shaner, 1996; Shaner & Hummert, 1997). Blanchard-Fields (1994; Chapter 10, this volume) has found that older adults are more likely to integrate dispositional and situational explanations in their attributions about others. In evaluating conversations, older adults may thus be less likely than younger ones to attribute painful self-disclosures and age telling to negative dispositional characteristics (sad, complaining, bitter) and more likely to see them as coherent responses to the unique challenges of aging. Further, differences in perception of these behaviors may vary within the older adult age range, just as do perceptions of the problems of older adults (Seccombe & Ishii-Kuntz, 1991). With the increase in health problems with advancing age, old-old persons (over age 75) may see such conversational practices as even more appropriate than do young-old persons.

It must be noted that these predictions reinforce the idea that older and younger persons may process the same information differently on the basis of their goals (Carstensen, 1992) and schemas (Blanchard-Fields, 1994). As Hess and colleagues (Hess, Bolstad, Woodburn, & Auman, 1999; Hess & Pullen, 1994; Hess & Tate, 1991; Chapter 11, this volume) have established, older and younger persons exhibit different patterns of impression change that reflect qualitative differences in processing rather than simple differences in cognitive resources, such as working memory. In particular, Hess et al. noted the increased use of inferential, knowledge-based processing with age. The differences in the content and salience of age stereotype schemas across young, middle-aged, and older age groups may thus be particularly important in impression formation and change processes.

Second, and similarly, older individuals may be less likely than younger ones to see a need for the accommodations of patronizing talk to negatively stereotyped others. For instance, Hummert, Garstka and Shaner (1995) found that older participants were less likely than were younger ones to associate negative trait information with communication problems in memory and hearing. In turn, Hummert et al. (1998) found that older participants were less likely than were younger ones to use a patronizing talk style with a negatively stereotyped target. In that study, young, middle-aged, and older participants provided persuasive oral messages to two older targets, one fitting a negative (despondent) and one a positive (golden ager) stereotype, in a counterbalanced design. As expected, analysis of the messages revealed both affirming (normal adult) and patronizing message types. Two distinct types of patronizing messages, however, were evident: (1)

patronizing/nurturing, containing the varied pitch and compassionate, simple content associated with secondary baby talk; and (2) patronizing/directive, containing a tone of exasperation and highly directive content. As predicted, older participants gave more affirming messages than did middle-aged and young participants. Of particular import, however, is that the older participants, unlike the young and middle-aged participants, gave predominantly affirming messages to both targets, despondent (75% of messages) as well as golden ager (65% of messages). Middle-aged participants and young participants, by contrast, gave significantly more affirming messages to the golden ager (young, 63% of messages; middle-aged, 58%) than to the despondent target (young, 42%; middle-aged, (40%). Young and middle-aged participants differed, however, in the type of patronizing message they used with the targets. For example, with the despondent target, young participants provided more directive messages (35%) than nurturing messages (22%), whereas middle-aged participants gave more nurturing messages (40%) than directive ones (15%). Developmental differences, then, were evident both (1) in the greater sensitivity of young and middle-aged participants in comparison to older ones to the negative stereotype and (2) in the type of patronizing talk produced by young participants in comparison to middle-aged participants.

Developmental differences also emerged in the two studies investigating the relative importance of trait and physical information in the activation of age stereotypes discussed earlier (Hummert & Garstka, 1997, 1998). Older and middle-aged participants in those studies considered trait information more than did young participants, particularly in judgments of the severely impaired target. These results are consistent with the report of Hess et al. (1999) of an age-related increase in reliance on trait diagnosticity and knowledge-based processing in impression judgments.

Some age differences in judgments, however, appear to reflect intergroup processes more than developmental ones. For instance, in the activation cue studies (Hummert & Garstka, 1997, 1998), the oldest participants provided more moderate judgments of the targets than did young and middle-aged participants, suggesting a complexity-extremity effect (Linville, 1982). Further, when issues of personal versus group identity are involved, older persons may provide more negative judgments of peers than do younger ones. Results from the Hummert et al. (1997) study of associations between the positive and negative stereotypes and facial features indicating young-old, middle-old, and old-old age illustrate this fact. In that study, older participants were more likely than were young and middle-aged participants to pair negative stereotype traits with the photographs of those who looked the oldest (80 and over in perceived age). This seemed to constitute a *black sheep effect* (Branscombe, Wann, Noel, & Coleman, 1993; Marques, Yzerbyt, & Leyens, 1988) in which the older participants, as in-group members, derogated unfavorable representatives of the group, the oldest-old, as a way of protecting their self-identity. That is, by assigning the old-old photographs to the negative stereotypes, the older participants in this study, who were primarily in their sixties and seventies, may have been distancing themselves from the negative aspects of aging.

Thus, prior research suggests that age stereotyping in interpersonal interaction may differ depending on the age of the participant. Young, middle-aged, and older individuals differ in both the content of implicit positive and negative age stereotypes (representation) and in the relative strength of those stereotypes (salience), and both types of differences appear to affect the age stereotyping process in interpersonal interaction. Developmental and intergroup processes may jointly account for these differences, although developmental processes appear to be more predominant than intergroup ones. In particular, the prior research points to a developmental increase in the richness and complexity of age stereotype schemas that reflects the integration of life experiences into those schemas.

SUMMARY AND CONCLUSIONS

This chapter presented a social cognitive perspective on age stereotypes. The application of social cognitive principles and methods to age stereotype research has contributed to the quality of that research in several ways. First, social cognitive theories have provided a conceptual framework that can account both for age stereotypes as *knowledge structures* and for age stereotyping as an *impression formation process* with both inferential and behavioral outcomes. Second, a social cognitive perspective links age stereotype research to the larger social psychological literature so that the similarities, as well as differences, between age stereotyping and other forms of stereotyping can be examined. Third, by emphasizing the social aspect of social cognition, this perspective centers research on age stereotypes in interpersonal perception, the arena in which all forms of stereotypes have a major impact. Finally, the social cognitive literature has provided productive directions for prior research on age stereotypes (e.g., Brewer et al.'s 1981 investigation of age stereotypes as prototypes) and should serve as a continued source of research questions in the future.

A brief consideration of current issues in general social cognitive research on stereotypes indicates several promising areas for future age stereotype research, including representational issues (e.g., exemplar vs abstract representational models, Hilton & von Hippel, 1996; Sherman, 1996; subgroup vs subtype models, Hamilton & Sherman, 1994; Hewstone, Macrae, Griffiths, Milne, & Brown, 1994; Maurer, Park, & Rothbart, 1995), stereotyping processes (e.g., implicit stereotyping, Greenwald, & Banaji, 1995; Hense, Penner, & Nelson, 1995; Levy, 1996; multiple social category information, Macrae, Bodenhausen, & Milne, 1995; Stangor, Lynch, Duan, & Glass, 1992; effects of inhibition and cognitive busyness, Gilbert & Hixon, 1991; Macrae et al., 1995), affect and motivation in stereotyping (Krueger, 1996; Oakes, Haslam, & Turner, 1994; Pendry & Macrae, 1996; Stangor, Sullivan, & Ford, 1991; Williams & Giles, 1996), intergroup processes (Harwood, Giles, & Ryan, 1995; Oakes et al., 1994; Tajfel & Turner, 1979; Turner,

1985), developmental issues (Blanchard-Fields, 1994; Higgins & Brendl, 1995; Hess, Pullen & McGee, 1996), and stereotype change (Hess & Pullen, 1994; Hewstone & Brown, 1986; Higgins & Winter, 1993; Smith, Stewart, & Buttram, 1992). Not only will our knowledge of age stereotypes be enriched by a consideration of the social cognition research issues outlined above but the investigation of those issues may benefit from a focus on age stereotypes. Age stereotypes are strongly embedded in our culture, consist of both positive and negative beliefs, embody behavioral elements, and carry important applied implications. Further, as the only major group classification that changes over time—outside the control of the individual—age stereotypes offer the unique advantage of allowing the study of developmental as well as intergroup perception processes in stereotyping.

REFERENCES

Adams, V. H., & Hummert, M. L. (under review). African American stereotypes of older adults.

Adorno, T. W., Frenkel-Brunswik, D. J., Levinson, D. J., & Sanford, N. H. (1950). *The authoritarian personality.* New York: Harper & Row.

Arbuckle, T. Y., & Gold, D. P. (1993). Aging, inhibition, and verbosity. *Journal of Gerontology: Psychological Sciences, 48,* P225–P232.

Arbuckle, T. Y., Gold, D. P., & Andres, D. (1986). Cognitive functioning of older people in relation to social and personality variables. *Psychology and Aging, 1,* 55–62.

Ashmore, R. D., & Del Boca, F. K. (1981). Conceptual approaches to stereotypes and stereotyping. In D. L. Hamilton (Ed.), *Cognitive processes in stereotyping and intergroup behavior* (pp. 1–35). Hillsdale, NJ: Lawrence Erlbaum Associates.

Baltes, P. B. (1987). Theoretical propositions of life-span developmental psychology: On the dynamics between growth and decline. *Developmental Psychology, 23,* 611–626.

Banaji, M. R., & Greenwald, A. G. (1995). Implicit stereotyping in judgments of fame. *Journal of Personality and Social Psychology, 68,* 181–198.

Banaji, M. R., Hardin, C., & Rothman, A. J. (1993). Implicit stereotyping in person judgment. *Journal of Personality and Social Psychology, 65,* 272–281.

Bargh, J. A. (1994). The four horsemen of automaticity: Awareness, intention, efficiency, and control. In R. S. Wyer & T. K. Srull (Eds.), *Handbook of social cognition, vol. 1: Basic Processes* (2nd ed.) (pp. 1–40). Hillsdale, NJ: Lawrence Erlbaum Associates.

Berger, C. R., & Bradac, J. J. (1982). *Language and social knowledge.* London: Edward Arnold.

Blanchard-Fields, F. (1994). Age differences in causal attributions from an adult development perspective. *Journal of Gerontology: Psychological Sciences, 49,* P43–P51.

Branscombe, N. R., Wann, D. L., Noel, J. G., & Coleman, J. (1993). In-group or out-group extremity: Importance of the threatened social identity. *Personality and Social Psychology Bulletin, 19,* 381–388.

Brewer, M. B. (1988). A dual process model of impression formation. In T. K. Srull & R. S. Wyer (Eds.), *Advances in social cognition, vol. 1: A dual process model of impression formation* (pp. 1–36). Hillsdale, NJ: Lawrence Erlbaum Associates.

Brewer, M. B., Dull, V., & Lui, L. (1981). Perceptions of the elderly: Stereotypes as prototypes. *Journal of Personality and Social Psychology, 41,* 656–670.

Brewer, M. B., & Lui, L. (1989). The primacy of age and sex in the structure of person categories. *Social Cognition, 7,* 262–274.

Brewer, M. B., & Lui, L. (1984). Categorization of the elderly by the elderly. *Personality and Social Psychology Bulletin, 10,* 585–595.

Butler, R. N. (1969). Ageism: Another form of bigotry. *The Gerontologist, 9,* 243–246.

Caporael, L. R. (1981). The paralanguage of caregiving: Baby talk to the institutionalized aged. *Journal of Personality and Social Psychology, 40,* 876–884.

Caporael, L. R., & Culbertson, G. H. (1986). Verbal response modes of baby talk and other speech at institutions for the aged. *Language and Communication, 6,* 99–112.

Caporael, L. R., Lukaszewski, M. P., & Culbertson, G. H. (1983). Secondary baby talk: Judgments by institutionalized elderly and their caregivers. *Journal of Personality and Social Psychology, 44,* 746–754.

Carstensen, L. L. (1992). Social and emotional patterns in adulthood: Support for socioemotional selectivity theory. *Psychology and Aging, 7,* 331–338.

Coupland, J., Coupland, N., & Giles, H. (1989). Telling age in later life: Identity and face implications. *Text, 9,* 129–151.

Coupland, N., Coupland, J., Giles, H., Henwood, K., & Wiemann, J. (1988). Elderly self-disclosure: Interactional and intergroup issues. *Language and Communication, 8,* 109–133.

Coupland, J., Coupland, N., Giles, H., & Wiemann, J. (1988). My life in your hands: Processes of self-disclosure in intergenerational talk. In N. Coupland (Ed.), *Styles of discourse* (pp. 201–253). London: Croom Helm.

Coupland, N., Henwood, K., Coupland, J., & Giles, H. (1990). Accommodating troubles-talk: The young's management of elderly self-disclosure. In G. M. McGregor & R. White (Eds.), *Reception and response: Hearer creativity and the analysis of spoken and written texts* (pp. 112–144). London: Croom Helm.

Crockett, W. H., & Hummert, M. L. (1987). Perceptions of aging and the elderly. *Annual Review of Gerontology and Geriatrics, 7* 217–241.

Devine, P. G. (1989). Stereotypes and prejudice: Their automatic and controlled components. *Journal of Personality and Social Psychology, 56,* 5–18.

Fiske, S. T., & Taylor, S. E. (1991). *Social cognition* (2nd ed.). New York: McGraw-Hill.

Gaertner, S. L., & McLaughlin, J. P. (1983). Racial stereotypes: Associations and ascriptions of positive and negative characteristics. *Social Psychology Quarterly, 46,* 23–30.

Gilbert, D. T., & Hixon, J. G. (1991). The trouble of thinking: Activation and application of stereotypic beliefs. *Journal of Personality and Social Psychology, 60,* 509–517.

Giles, H., Coupland, N., & Coupland, J. (1991). Accommodation theory: Communication, context, and consequence. In H. Giles, J. Coupland, & N. Coupland (Eds.), *Contexts of accommodation: Developments in applied linguistics* (pp. 1–68). Cambridge, MA: Cambridge University Press.

Giles, H., Harwood, J., Pierson, H. D., Clément, R., & Fox, S. (in press). Stereotypes of the elderly and patronizing speech: A cross-cultural foray. In R. K. Agnihotri & A. L. Khanna (Eds.), *Research in applied linguistics* IV: *The social psychology of language.* New Delhi: Sage.

Giles, H., Mulac, A., Bradac, J. J., & Johnson, P. (1987). Speech accommodation theory: The first decade and beyond. In M. L. McLaughlin (Ed.), *Communication yearbook 10* (pp. 13–48). Newbury Park, CA: Sage.

Gold, D. P., Arbuckle, T. Y., & Andres, D. (1994). Verbosity in older adults. In M. L. Hummert, J. M. Wiemann, & J. F. Nussbaum (Eds). *Interpersonal communication in older adulthood: Interdisciplinary theory and research* (pp. 107–129). Thousand Oaks, CA: Sage.

Grainger, K. (1993). "That's a lovely bath dear": Reality construction in the discourse of elderly care. *Journal of Ageing Studies, 7,* 247–262.

Greenwald, A. G., & Banaji, M. R. (1995). Implicit social cognition: Attitudes, self-esteem, and stereotypes. *Psychological Review, 102,* 4–27.

Greenwald, A. G., McGhee, D. E., & Schwartz, J. L. K. (1998). Measuring individual differences in implicit cognition: The implicit association test. *Journal of Personality and Social Psychology, 74,* 1464–1480.

Hamilton, D. L., & Sherman, J. W. (1994). Stereotypes. In R. S. Wyer, Jr., & T. K. Srull (Eds.) *Handbook of social cognition, vol. 2: Applications* (2nd ed.) (pp. 1–68). Hillsdale, NJ: Lawrence Erlbaum Associates.

Hamilton, D. L., & Trolier, T. K. (1986). Stereotypes and stereotyping: An overview of the cognitive approach. In J. F. Dovidio & S. L. Gaertner (Eds.), *Prejudice, discrimination and racism* (pp. 127–163). Orlando, FL: Academic Press.

Harris, L. (1975). *The myth and reality of aging in America.* Washington, D. C.: National Council on Aging.

Harwood, J., Giles, H., Fox, S., Ryan, E. B., & Williams, A. (1993). Patronizing young and elderly adults: Response strategies in a community setting. *Journal of Applied Communication Research, 21,* 211–226.

Harwood, J., Giles, H., & Ryan, E. B. (1995). Aging, communication, and intergroup theory: Social identity and intergenerational communication. In J. L. Nussbaum & J. Coupland (Eds.), *Handbook of communication and aging research* (pp. 133–159). Hillsdale, NJ: Lawrence Erlbaum Associates.

Harwood, J., Ryan, E. B., Giles, H., & Tysoski, S. (1997). Evaluations of patronizing speech and three response styles in a non-service-providing context. *Journal of Applied Communication Research, 25,* 170–195.

Heckhausen, J., Dixon, R. A., & Baltes, P. B. (1989). Gains and losses in development throughout adulthood as perceived by different adult age groups. *Developmental Psychology, 25,* 109–121.

Hense, R. L., Penner, L. A., & Nelson, D. L. (1995). Implicit memory for age stereotypes. *Social Cognition, 13,* 399–415.

Hess, T. M., Bolstad, C. A., Woodburn, S. M., & Auman, C. (1999). Trait diagnosticity versus behavioral consistency as determinants of impression change in adulthood. *Psychology and Aging, 14.*

Hess, T. M., & Pullen, S. M. (1994). Adult age differences in impression change processes. *Psychology and Aging, 9,* 237–250.

Hess, T. M., Pullen, S. M., & McGee, K. A. (1996). Acquisition of prototype-based information about social groups in adulthood. *Psychology and Aging, 11,* 179–190.

Hess, T. M., & Tate, C. S. (1991). Adult age differences in explanations and memory for behavioral information. *Psychology and Aging, 6,* 86–92.

Hewstone, M., & Brown, R. (1986) (Eds.) *Intergroup contact.* Oxford: Blackwell.

Hewstone, M., Macrae, C. N., Griffiths, R., Milne, A. B., & Brown, R. (1994). Cognitive models of stereotype change: 5. Measurement, development, and consequences of subtyping. *Journal of Experimental Social Psychology, 30,* 505–526.

Higgins, E. T., & Brendl, C. M. (1995). Accessibility and applicability: Some "activation rules" influencing judgment. *Journal of Experimental Social Psychology, 31,* 218–243.

Higgins, E. T., McCann, C. D., & Fondacaro, R. (1982). The "communication game": Goal-directed encoding and cognitive consequences. *Social Cognition, 1,* 21–37.

Higgins, E. T., & Winter, L. (1993). The "acquisition principle": How beliefs about a behavior's prolonged circumstances influence correspondent inference. *Personality and Social Psychology Bulletin, 19,* 605–619.

Hilton, J. L., & von Hippel, W. (1996). Stereotypes. *Annual Review of Psychology, 47,* 237–271.

Hummert, M. L. (1990). Multiple stereotypes of elderly and young adults: A comparison of structure and evaluations. *Psychology and Aging, 5,* 183–193.

Hummert, M. L. (1994a). Stereotypes of the elderly and patronizing speech style. In M. L. Hummert, J. M. Wiemann, and J. F. Nussbaum (Eds.), *Interpersonal communication in older adulthood: Interdisciplinary theory and research* (pp. 162–185). Newbury Park, CA: Sage.

Hummert, M. L. (1994b). Physiognomic cues and the activation of stereotypes of the elderly in interaction. *International Journal of Aging and Human Development, 39,* 5–20.

Hummert, M. L., & Garstka, T. A. (1997, November). Activation cues for stereotypes of older adults. Paper presented at the annual meeting of the Gerontological Society of America, Cincinnati.

Hummert, M. L., & Garstka, T. A. (1998). Target age and activation cues for stereotypes of older adults. Unpublished manuscript; University of Kansas, Lawrence, KS.

Hummert, M. L., Garstka, T. A., & Shaner, J. L. (1997). Stereotyping of older adults: The role of target facial cues and perceiver characteristics. *Psychology and Aging, 12,* 107–114.

Hummert, M. L., Gartska, T. A., & Shaner, J. L. (1995). Beliefs about language performance: Adults' perceptions about self and elderly targets. *Journal of Language and Social Psychology, 14,* 235–259.

Hummert, M. L., Garstka, T. A., Shaner, J. L., & Strahm, S. (1994). Stereotypes of the elderly held by young, middle-aged, and elderly adults. *Journal of Gerontology: Psychological Sciences, 49,* P240–P249.

Hummert, M. L., Garstka, T. A., Shaner, J. L., & Strahm, S. (1995). Judgments about stereotypes of the elderly: Attitudes, age associations, and typicality ratings of young, middle-aged, and elderly adults. *Research on Aging, 17,* 168–189.

Hummert, M. L., & Mazloff, D. (1998). Elderly adults' perceptions of patronizing speech: Situations and responses. Unpublished manuscript.

Hummert, M. L., & Ryan, E. B. (1996). Toward understanding variations in patronizing talk addressed to older adults: Psycholinguistic features of care and control. *International Journal of Psycholinguistics, 12,* 149–169.

Hummert, M. L., & Shaner, J. L. (1994). Patronizing speech to the elderly as a function of stereotyping. *Communication Studies, 45,* 145–158.

Hummert, M. L., Shaner, J. L., & Garstka, T. A. (1995). Cognitive processes affecting communication with older adults: The case for stereotypes, attitudes, and beliefs about communication. In J. F. Nussbaum & J. Coupland (Eds.), *The handbook of communication and aging research* (pp. 105–132). Hillsdale, NJ: Lawrence Erlbaum Associates.

Hummert, M. L., Shaner, J. L., Garstka, T. A., & Henry, C. (1998). Communication with older adults: The influence of age stereotypes, context, and communicator age. *Human Communication Research, 25,* 124–151.

Katz, R. S. (1990). Personality trait correlates of attitudes toward older people. *International Journal of Aging and Human Development, 31,* 147–159.

Kemper, S. (1994). "Elderspeak": Speech accommodations to older adults. *Aging and Cognition, 1,* 17–28.

Kemper, S., Ferrell, P., Harden, T., Finter-Urczyk, A., & Billington, C. (in press). The use of elderspeak by young and older adults to impaired and unimpaired listeners. *Aging, Neuropsychology, and Cognition, 5,* 43–55.

Kemper, S., Rash, S. R., Kynette, D., & Norman, S. (1990). Telling stories: The structure of adults' narratives. *European Journal of Cognitive Psychology, 2,* 205–228.

Kite, M. E., Deaux, K., & Miele, M. (1991). Stereotypes of young and old: Does age outweigh gender? *Psychology and Aging, 6,* 19–27.

Kite, M. E., & Johnson, B. T. (1988). Attitudes toward older and younger adults: A meta-analysis. *Psychology and Aging, 3,* 233–244.

Klemmack, D. L., & Roff, L. L. (1983). Stimulus evaluation and the relationship between a deterministic cognitive system and cognitive differentiation. *The Journal of Psychology, 113,* 199–209.

Krueger, J. (1996). Personal beliefs and cultural stereotypes about racial characteristics. *Journal of Personality and Social Psychology, 71,* 536–548.

Levy, B. (1996). Improving memory in old age through implicit self-stereotyping. *Journal of Personality and Social Psychology, 71,* 1092–1107.

Leyens, J-P., Yzerbyt, V., & Schadron, G. (1994). *Stereotypes and social cognition.* London: Sage.

Linville, P. W. (1982). The complexity-extremity effect and age-based stereotyping. *Journal of Personality and Social Psychology, 42,* 193–211.

Lippmann, W. (1922). *Public opinion.* New York: Harcourt, Brace, Jovanovich.

Macrae, C. N., Bodenhausen, G. V., & Milne, A. B. (1995). The dissection of selection in person perception: Inhibitory processes in social stereotyping. *Journal of Personality and Social Psychology, 69,* 397–407.

Marques, J. M., Yzerbyt, V. Y., & Leyens, J. P. (1988). The "black sheep effect": Extremity of judgments towards ingroup members as a function of identification. *European Journal of Social Psychology, 18,* 1–16.

Maurer, K. L., Park, B., & Rothbart, M. (1995). Subtyping versus subgrouping processes in stereotype representation. *Journal of Personality and Social Psychology, 69,* 812–824.

Milord, J. T. (1978). Aesthetic aspects of faces: A (somewhat) phenomenological analysis using multidimensional scaling methods. *Journal of Personality and Social Psychology, 36,* 205–216.

Oakes, P. J., Haslam, S. A., Turner, J. C. (1994). *Stereotyping and social reality.* Oxford: Blackwell.

Palmore, E. B. (1977). Facts on aging: A short quiz. *The Gerontologist, 17,* 315–320. *Research on Aging, 4,* 333–348.

Pendry, L. F., & Macrae, C. N. (1996). What the disinterested perceiver overlooks: Goal-directed social categorization. *Personality and Social Psychology Bulletin, 22,* 249–256.

Perdue, C. W., & Gurtman, M. B. (1990). Evidence for the automaticity of ageism. *Journal of Experimental Social Psychology, 26,* 199–216.

Rosch, E. H. (1978). Principles of categorization. In E. Rosch & B. B. Lloyd (Eds.), *Cognition and categorization.* Hillsdale, NJ: Lawrence Erlbaum Associates.

Rothbaum, F. (1983). Aging and age stereotypes. *Social Cognition, 2,* 171–184.

Ryan, E. B., Bourhis, R. Y., & Knops, U. (1991). Evaluative perceptions of patronizing speech addressed to elders. *Psychology and Aging, 6,* 442–450.

Ryan, E. B., and Cole, R. L. (1990). Evaluative perceptions of interpersonal communication with elders. In H. Giles, N. Coupland, & J. Wiemann (Eds.), *Communication, health and the elderly,* Fulbright Series #8 (pp. 172–190). Manchester, England: Manchester University Press.

Ryan, E. B., Giles, H., Bartolucci, G., & Henwood, K. (1986). Psycholinguistic and social psychological components of communication by and with the elderly. *Language and Communication, 6,* 1–24.

Ryan, E. B., Hamilton, J. M., & Kwong See, S. (1994). How do younger and older adults respond to baby talk in the nursing home? *International Journal of Aging and Human Development, 39,* 21–32.

Ryan, E. B., Hummert, M. L., & Boich, L. H. (1995). Communication predicaments of aging: Patronizing behavior toward older adults. *Journal of Language and Social Psychology, 14,* 144–166.

Ryan, E. B., Meredith, S. D., & Shantz, G. B. (1994). Evaluative perceptions of patronizing speech addressed to institutionalized elders in contrasting conversational contexts. *Canadian Journal on Aging, 13,* 236–248.

Schmidt, D. F., & Boland, S, M, (1986) The structure of impressions of older adults. Evidence for multiple stereotypes. *Psychology and Aging, 1,* 255–260.

Schulz, R., & Fritz, S. (1987). Origins of stereotypes of the elderly: An experimental study of the self–other discrepancy. *Experimental Aging Research, 13,* 189–195.

Seccombe, K., & Ishii-Kuntz, M. (1991). Perceptions of problems associated with aging: Comparison among four older age cohorts. *The Gerontologist, 31,* 527–533.

Shadden, B. B. (1988). Perceptions of daily communicative interactions with older persons. In B. Shadden (Ed.), *Communication behavior and aging: A sourcebook for clinicians* (pp. 12–40). Baltimore: Williams & Wilkins.

Shaner, J. L. (1996). *Painful self-disclosures of older adults: Judgments of disclosure characteristics, discloser traits, and perceived motivation.* Unpublished doctoral dissertation, University of Kansas, Lawrence, KS.

Shaner, J. L. & Hummert, M. L. (1997, November). Painful self-disclosures of older adults in relation to aging stereotypes and and perceived motivations. Top Four Paper in Communication and Aging, National Communication Association, Chicago.

Sherman, J. W. (1996). Development and mental representation of stereotypes. *Journal of Personality and Social Psychology, 70,* 1126–1141.

Silverstein, M., & Parrott, T. M. (1997). Attitudes toward public support of the elderly: Does early involvement with grandparents moderate generational tensions? *Research on Aging, 19,* 108–132.

Smith, E. R., Stewart, T. L., & Buttram, R. T. (1992). Inferring a trait from a behavior has long-term, highly specific effects. *Journal of Personality and Social Psychology, 62,* 753–759.

Speas, K., & Obenshain, B. (1995). *Images of aging in America: Final report.* Washington, D. C.: American Association of Retired Persons.

Stangor, C., Lynch, L., Duan, C., & Glass, B. (1992). Categorization of individuals on the basis of multiple social features. *Journal of Personality and Social Psychology, 62,* 207–218.

Stangor, C., Sullivan, L. A., & Ford, T. E. (1991). Affective and cognitive determinants of prejudice. *Social Cognition, 9,* 359–380.

Tajfel, H., & Turner, J. C. (1979). An integrative theory of intergroup conflict. In W. G. Austin & S. Worchel (Eds.), *The social psychology of intergroup relations.* Monterey, CA: Brooks/Cole.

Thorson, J. A., & Perkins, M. L. (1981). An examination of personality and demographic factors on attitudes toward old people. *International Journal of Aging and Human Development, 12,* 139–148.

Tuckman, J., & Lorge, I. (1953). Attitudes toward old people. *Journal of Social Psychology, 37,* 249–260.

Turner, J. C. (1985). Social categorization and the self-concept: A social cognitive theory of group behaviour. In E. J. Lawler (Ed.). *Advances in group processes* (vol. 2). Greenwich, CT: JAI Press.

Whitbourne, S. K. (1986). The psychological construction of the life span. In J. E. Birren & K. W. Schaie (Eds.), *Handbook of the psychology of aging* (pp. 594–618). New York: Van Nostrand Reinhold.

Williams, A., & Giles, H. (1996). Inergenerational conversations: Young adults' retrospective accounts. *Human Communication Research, 23,* 220–250.

Yzerbyt, V. Y., Schadron, G., Leyens, J.-P., & Rocher, S. (1994). Social judgeability: The impact of meta-informational cues on the use of stereotypes. *Journal of Personality and Social Psychology, 66,* 48–55.

9

AGE AND MEMORY

PERCEPTIONS OF FORGETFUL YOUNG AND OLDER ADULTS

JOAN T. ERBER AND IRENE G. PRAGER

Department of Psychology
Florida International University
Miami, Florida

When we were conducting research on age and memory performance, older adults were often hesitant to participate in our studies. Yet, the same older individuals who were so reluctant to be tested were willing, and in many instances eager, to relay anecdotes about their forgetfulness. They frequently made light of their own memory failures, but at the same time, they were worried about how such failures would make them look to others. Partly because of these experiences with older adults' concerns about their memory, our research turned to the question of how forgetful individuals are perceived. What intrigued us most, though, was whether the age of forgetful individuals makes any difference in this regard. In addition, we were curious about what other factors might play a role, either separately or in conjunction with age. For example, it seemed reasonable to suppose that some types of everyday memory failure might be perceived differently from others. Also, it was conceivable that the age of the perceivers might have some bearing on how forgetful individuals are viewed.

Our perceptions of other people are influenced by the cognitions and representations we hold. The research program described in this chapter takes a social cognitive approach to investigating how we view people who are forgetful. The studies deal with factors, including age, that may influence our cognitions, representations, impressions, and ultimately, our propensity to behave in certain ways toward others who forget.

A person perception paradigm was ideal for investigating our questions about how forgetful individuals are viewed. This paradigm, frequently used by social cognition researchers, makes use of scenarios, or vignettes, in which an individual (i.e., target person, or target) is described. After being presented with a vignette, research participants (i.e., perceivers) are asked to make judgments about the target. The person perception paradigm has many elements in common with the experimental approach, since the characteristics of the target person and/or the content of the vignette can be manipulated. For the purpose of our research, we could make use of vignettes to describe a target who experiences everyday memory failures. The age and possibly other characteristics of the target could be varied, as could the number and type of memory failures experienced by the target. Finally, judgments about a young or old target who is described in a vignette could be made by both young and older perceivers. Perceivers' judgments would reveal something about their cognitions and representations about the target.

SERIOUSNESS OF FORGETTING

In an early study (Erber, 1989), judgments were made about the seriousness of memory failures experienced by young or old targets. A group of young perceivers read a series of brief vignettes, each of which described a young or old target who experiences a single incident of everyday memory failure. The vignettes included little individuating information, since the goal of this study was to determine whether perceivers' judgments would differ solely on the basis of the target's age.

Fourteen pairs of vignettes were devised, with one member of each pair describing a more serious incident and the other a less serious incident of the same type of memory failure. For example, forgetting the name of someone you have known for a long time would probably be considered more serious than forgetting the name of someone to whom you have just been introduced. The distinction in degree of seriousness for this pair of vignettes, and for the other 13 pairs as well, was corroborated in pilot work with vignettes in which the age of the target was not specified.

For the actual study, young perceivers read all 28 vignettes. At the outset, they were told either that the target person in each vignette ("Mrs. X") is age 30 or that the target person in each vignette ("Mrs. X") is age 70. Each perceiver was given vignettes either with young targets or with old targets. Making target age a between-groups rather than a within-subjects variable was considered a more conservative approach, since the "demand character" of the target age variable would be minimized (Kogan, 1979).

After reading each vignette, young perceivers rated how serious they thought the target's failure was on a 7-point Likert scale (1 = *not at all serious—it could happen to anyone*; 7 = *very serious—it could be a sign the person is suffering from mental difficulty*). It was not surprising that the average rating for the 14 more serious memory failures was higher ($M = 4.73$) than the average rating for the 14 less serious memory failures ($M = 2.98$). But of particular importance was the fact that the young perceivers gave higher ratings (i.e., they considered memory failures more serious) when the targets were old than they did when the targets were young ($Ms = 3.99$ and 3.72 for the old and young targets, respectively). Moreover, the nonsignificant interaction between target age and memory failure seriousness illustrated that, regardless of degree of seriousness in general, the young perceivers considered memory failures more serious when they were experienced by old targets rather than by young targets. These results lend some credence to the apprehensions expressed by older adult research participants about how their memory failures would make them look to others.

Next, we asked older perceivers to rate the identical 28 vignettes. Again, the targets in the vignettes were either young (age 30) or old (age 70). As with the young perceivers, the older perceivers' ratings were higher for the more serious memory failures ($M = 3.85$) than for the less serious memory failures ($M = 2.99$). Unlike the young perceivers, however, the older perceivers did not rate the failures any differently for the young and old targets ($Ms = 3.44$ and 3.40, respectively). In addition to the disparate target age findings for the young and older perceivers, there was also a difference in the average seriousness rating given by the two perceiver age groups ($Ms = 3.86$ and 3.42 for the young and older perceivers, respectively). Compared with the young perceivers, the older perceivers considered memory failures less serious overall.

The results of this study provided several important insights. First, perceivers' metacognitive schemas differed for the more serious and the less serious memory failures; both young and older perceivers thought that the less serious memory failures were more likely to happen to anyone and that the more serious memory failures were a greater sign of mental difficulty. Second, the age of the target made a difference, although only for young perceivers, who thought that memory failures were more serious when experienced by old targets than by young targets. Third, perceiver age was a factor with regard to overall judgments: Older perceivers were more lenient than were young perceivers for forgetful targets of both ages. One explanation for this finding is that older adults' self-concept may affect their judgments about others (Markus, Smith, & Moreland, 1985). Older adults report themselves as experiencing a higher frequency of everyday memory failures than do young adults (Cavanaugh, Grady, & Perlmutter, 1983; Erber, Szuchman, & Rothberg, 1992) and therefore may view themselves as having more in common with forgetful targets. Kerr, Hymes, Anderson, and Weathers (1995) proposed the similarity-leniency hypothesis, which has been applied in the context of jury selection. According to this hypothesis, the more similar a juror's life experiences are to those of the defendant, the greater the chance that juror will be more understanding of the defendant's actions. In the context under discussion here—judgments about the seriousness of memory failures—it is conceivable that older perceivers' more lenient ratings stem from a tolerance for memory failures that could be explained, at least in part, by their own tendency to experience memory failures.

ATTRIBUTIONS FOR FORGETTING

From a social cognitive perspective, people often try to understand what causes someone else to behave in a particular way. Attribution theory, which has its roots in Heider's naive psychology, deals with the inferences people make about the causes of observed behavior. In Erber's study (1989), the anchor for the high end of the seriousness rating scale was "very serious—could be a sign the person is suffering from mental difficulty," which alluded to one possible cause, or attribution, for the target's memory failure. Since attributions might be related to how others are perceived, the next step in our program of research was to expand on what perceivers might consider to be the cause(s) for a young or old target's memory failures. Weiner and his associates (e.g., Weiner et al., 1971) have conducted research on attributions made in achievement-related situations, and their model provided a framework for our investigation.

In a study by Erber, Szuchman, and Rothberg (1990a), perceivers were asked to make attributions for everyday memory failures experienced by young or old female targets. In that study, eight different memory failure vignettes were devised, which corresponded with the empirically derived everyday memory factors (memory for names, memory for people, memory for conversation, memory for errands, memory for place, retrieval, rote memory, and absentmindedness) of Herrmann and Neisser (1978). In the names vignette, the target was introduced to someone but shortly afterward forgot the person's name. In the people vignette, the target did not recognize someone whom she had seen numerous times in another context. In the conversation vignette, the target forgot what her friend had said and what she herself was about to say in a group discussion. In the errands vignette, the target forgot to buy one of three items that she had intended to purchase at the grocery store. In the place vignette, the target hid money in her house and the next day could not remember where it was. In the retrieval vignette, the target recognized someone but could not remember where she had seen this person before. In the rote vignette, the target looked up a number in the telephone book but after dialing three digits could not remember the rest. In the absentmindedness vignette, the target went upstairs to get a postage stamp but, once upstairs, forgot why she was there.

All eight vignettes were read by young and older perceivers, and the target was given a different chronological age in each vignette as a means of ensuring that perceivers would view the target as someone different each time. For half the young and half the older perceivers, targets in all eight vignettes were young (age range 23–32 years); for the other half of the young and older perceivers, targets in all eight vignettes were old (age range 63–74 years). As in Erber's study (1989) target age was a between-groups variable and the vignettes provided minimal individuating information.

After reading each vignette, perceivers made ratings on 7-point Likert scales to indicate possible causes, or attributions, for the young or old target's memory failure (1 = not at all a cause; 7 = very much a cause). These scales were derived from the two-dimensional framework of Weiner et al. (1971) for perceived causes of behavioral outcomes: locus (internal vs external) and stability (stable over time vs. unstable over time). This 2×2 framework, which yields four possible types of attribution (internal stable, internal unstable, external stable, and external unstable), has been used in a number of studies in which young perceivers have made attributions for the successes and failures of young versus old targets in achievement-related situations (e.g., Banziger & Drevenstedt, 1982; Locke-Conner & Walsh, 1980; Reno, 1979). As in those studies, we asked perceivers to rate the following causes for a target's memory failure: lack of ability (internal stable), lack of effort (internal unstable), task difficulty (external stable), and bad luck (external unstable). In addition, our perceivers rated two other causes: mental difficulty (considered to be an internal stable attribution) and lack of attention (considered to be an internal unstable attribution).

The results of the Erber et al. (1990a) study demonstrated that perceivers use an age-based double standard in their attributions for memory failures: Memory failures were attributed more to an internal stable cause (i.e., mental difficulty) for old targets, and more to an internal unstable cause (i.e., lack of attention) for young targets.

In another attribution study (Erber, Szuchman, & Rothberg, 1990b), which included male as well as female targets, perceivers again attributed old targets' failures more to an internal stable cause (mental difficulty) and young targets' failures more to internal unstable causes (lack of effort, lack of attention) regardless of the target's gender. In addition, perceivers completed an objective memory test (recalling a 16-item grocery list), as well as self-report measures on depression, frequency of everyday memory failure, and discomfort/annoyance with memory failure. Neither their objective memory performance nor their responses on the self-report measures were significantly related to perceivers' attributions for the targets' memory failures. These results corroborated what Erber et al. (1990a) had reported earlier: Perceivers use an age-based double standard when making attributions for targets' memory failures.

In addition to the attribution rating scales, perceivers in the studies by Erber et al. (1990a, 1990b), as well as those in a study by Erber and Rothberg (1991), rated the point at which they would recommend evaluation in order to determine whether the target's failure was caused by medical and/or psychological problems (1 = *I see no need for evaluation no matter how often it happens*; 2 = *I recommend evaluation if it happens several times a day*; 3 = *I recommend evaluation if it happens once a day*; 4 = *I recommend evaluation if it happens several times a week*; 5 = *I recommend evaluation if it happens once a week*; 6 = *I recommend evaluation if it happens once a month*; 7 = *I recommend evaluation the first time this type of failure happens*). In one of the studies (Erber & Rothberg, 1991), higher ratings were given to the old targets, who were recommended for evaluation after fewer occurrences of memory failure. Thus, there was some evidence that old targets' memory failures are seen as calling for medical and/or psychological evaluation at an earlier point.

TYPE OF MEMORY FAILURE

As described previously, young and older perceivers in Erber's study (1989) made the anticipated distinction between examples of more serious memory failures and examples of less serious memory failures; they gave higher seriousness ratings to failures that fell into the more serious category. However, they did so for both young and old targets. Overall, the findings from the attribution studies also indicate that young and older perceivers hold similar metacognitive schemas about different types of memory failure. In the study by Erber et al. (1990a), the young and older perceivers showed parallel variation in the attributions they made for the eight failures, which were modeled after the everyday memory factors of Herrmann and Neisser (1978). Also, the pattern of perceivers' attributions was similar whether memory failures were experienced by young targets or old targets.

In subsequent attribution studies by Erber et al. (1990b) and Erber and Rothberg (1991), the targets' memory failures were derived from an information-processing model, in which memory is conceptualized in terms of short-term and long-term stores (Atkinson & Shiffrin, 1968) as well as an additional very-long-term store (Botwinick, 1984). Short-term memory (STM) involves immediate forgetting; long-term memory (LTM) involves forgetting information at a later time (e.g., from 30 minutes to several hours after encoding); and very-long-term memory (VLTM) involves forgetting highly familiar and presumably overlearned information. For example, in one STM vignette, the target looks up a phone number and then forgets it in the few seconds it takes to dial the phone; in one LTM vignette, the target calls to find out the times a particular movie would be showing at the theater, but then forgets this information an hour later; in one VLTM vignette, the target forgets the phone number of an often-called relative.

Perceivers in the studies by Erber et al. (1990b) and Erber and Rothberg (1991) made similar attribution ratings for memory failures in the STM and LTM categories. Their attributions for the STM and LTM failures differed from their attributions for memory failures in the VLTM category, however. The STM and LTM failures were seen as being due more to lack of effort and lack of attention compared with the VLTM failures. By contrast, the VLTM failures were seen as being more indicative of mental difficulty compared with the STM and LTM failures. Also, perceivers recommended medical and/or psychological evaluation after fewer occurrences for VLTM failures than was the case for STM and LTM failures. Thus, perceivers made different attributions as well as different evaluation recommendations when memory failures involved information exposed a limited number of times (regardless of the retention interval) as opposed to information that is likely to be well rehearsed and highly familiar. Again, this pattern of findings was the same regardless of the target's age.

AGE OF PERCEIVERS

In the studies by Erber and Rothberg (1991) and by Erber et al. (1990a, 1990b), young and older perceivers both used an age-based double standard when making attributions. There were some differences between the two perceiver age groups, however, in the absolute level of their attribution ratings. Compared with the young perceivers, the older perceivers in the attribution study by Erber et al. (1990a) gave lower mental difficulty ratings and higher task difficulty ratings ("these kinds of things are hard to remember"). In the attribution study by Erber et al. (1990b), the older perceivers gave lower mental difficulty ratings and higher task difficulty ratings for memory failures that fell into the VTLM category. The lower ratings for mental difficulty and higher ratings for task difficulty signify that older perceivers are more likely than are young perceivers to attribute targets' forgetting to external causes and less likely than are young perceivers to attribute targets' forgetting to internal causes. Jones and Nisbett (1972) described an attributional bias called the actor–observer effect, whereby people see their own behavior as caused by external factors but other people's behavior as caused by internal factors. It is possible that older perceivers, who may view themselves as forgetful, tend to identify more with forgetful targets than do young perceivers. Perhaps closer identification with forgetful others could be one reason why older perceivers tend to attribute targets' memory failures more to external causes.

With regard to their evaluation recommendations, older perceivers saw a less urgent need than did young perceivers for medical and/or psychological evaluation in response to a target's memory failure (Erber & Rothberg, 1991; Erber et al., 1990a, 1990b). This finding is congruent with Erber's report (1989) that older perceivers consider memory failures less serious than do young perceivers. The lower seriousness ratings, coupled with the lesser degree of urgency in recommending evaluation, suggest that older perceivers are more willing to give forgetful targets the benefit of the doubt. Further investigation might establish whether the above findings are related to older perceivers' tendency to identify more with forgetful targets.

Overall, the findings of the attribution studies have been highly consistent. First, it is clear that the attributions perceivers make for everyday memory failures are influenced by the age of the target person who experiences those failures. Compared with a young target's forgetting, an old target's forgetting is attributed more to internal stable causes, such as mental difficulty and poor memory ability. Also, and consistent with their higher internal stable attributions for the old targets, perceivers recommend medical and/or psychological evaluation at an earlier point for old targets than they do for young targets. Second, there are definite distinctions in the attributions made for different types of memory failure, which suggests perceivers hold different metacognitive schemas for the various types, or categories, of memory failure. These schemas seem to be independent of the age of the target experiencing the failures, since the pattern of attributions is similar for young and old targets. Finally, young and older perceivers differ in the absolute level of their attributions. Older perceivers are less likely than are young perceivers to attribute everyday memory failures to internal stable causes, such as mental difficulty. Also, older perceivers feel that there is less need for medical and/or psychological intervention in response to memory failure.

CAPABILITY IMPRESSIONS

When perceivers form impressions of a target's cognitive capability, they may take a number of factors into account. One factor is the target's memory behavior. Both the number and type of memory failures experienced by the target could be important when perceivers are forming capability impressions. The greater the number of failures experienced by the target, the higher the likelihood that failures could have a negative impact with regard to perceivers' impressions. Also, the type of memory failures could make a difference; forgetting highly familiar, overlearned information could have a greater negative impact than forgetting information exposed only a limited number of times. Furthermore, given the age-based double standard perceivers use when making attributions for memory failures, it seemed reasonable to suppose that perceivers would form different impressions about the cognitive capability of a forgetful young target versus a forgetful old target. Initially, we predicted that the negative impact of forgetful behavior on perceivers' impression of cognitive capability would be greater for old targets, whose failures are attributed more to internal stable causes, than for young targets, whose failures are attributed more to internal unstable causes. However, it was not clear whether the number and/or type of memory failures would make a greater difference for perceivers' impressions of the cognitive capability of young versus old targets.

Thus, we set out to investigate the effect of young and old targets' memory failures on perceivers' impressions of their cognitive capability. For this purpose, we continued to use a person perception paradigm. However, instead of the brief vignettes, each describing a single instance of memory failure experienced by a young or an old target (e.g., Erber, 1989; Erber & Rothberg, 1991; Erber et al., 1990a, 1990b), we adopted an interview format. With interviews, it was possible to manipulate not only the target's age but also the number and type of the target's memory failures. Thus, we could determine how these factors, in conjunction with age, would affect perceivers' impressions of the target's cognitive capability.

TASK ASSIGNMENT

For the initial study on capability impressions (Erber, Etheart, & Szuchman, 1992), we made tape recordings of a female target being interviewed for a school volunteer position. We used a volunteer rather than a paid work context to obviate hiring issues and to minimize any concerns perceivers might have about benefits and retirement; yet, a volunteer position could entail tasks of varying levels of difficulty, and perceivers could be asked to evaluate a target's capability of performing each of these tasks.

At the outset, perceivers in the study by Erber, Etheart, and Szuchman (1992) were instructed to imagine themselves as the head of the school volunteer program. They were told that some of the tasks performed by school volunteers are easy and require only a low level of cognitive capability, whereas other tasks are more challenging and require a higher level of cognitive capability. Perceivers were told that the school uses volunteers from the community because of financial constraints but that there could be difficulties for the operation of the school if a target is given tasks that are too challenging. Then perceivers listened to the tape-recorded interview, on the basis of which they were asked to form an impression of the target's cognitive capability.

During the interview, the target (who states that she is 32 or 67 years old) either experienced no incidences of forgetting (i.e., was nonforgetful), forgot four items of information (was moderately forgetful), or forgot eight items of information (was highly forgetful). Thus, the young and old targets varied in the number of memory failures they experienced, with the moderately and highly forgetful targets experiencing a mixture of two types of memory failure: episodic and semantic. Episodic failures involve forgetting information to which one has been exposed at some specific point in time, whereas semantic failures involve forgetting information that is not temporally identified (Squire, 1987) and is likely to be highly overlearned. One example of episodic failure was that the interviewer introduces herself to the target at the beginning of the interview, but at the end of the interview the target says, "Oh, I forgot your name." One example of semantic failure was that the interviewer asks the target to supply the phone number of someone who could be called in an emergency. The target cannot remember her sister's phone number even though she says she calls her sister all the time.

We chose to index perceivers' impressions of the target's cognitive capability with a potential behavioral response. That is, how would perceivers act toward or treat (or at least *say* they would treat) the target? Our index was the likelihood with which perceivers would allow the target an opportunity to perform challenging tasks. We assumed perceivers would allow the target to perform challenging tasks if the target were considered to be capable. Alternatively, perceivers would not allow the target to perform these tasks if the target were considered to be incapable.

Perceivers were given descriptions of 12 different tasks that volunteers can perform at the school. Two of the 12 tasks fell into each of 6 categories (e.g., filing, attendance, exams, supervision, library, and teaching). In pilot work, we verified that within each category, one task was considered easy and the other was considered difficult. For example, in the filing category, the easy task was "organize 10 papers according to the number grade, putting the highest grade first"; the difficult task was "Fifty papers from the files that were examined yesterday need to be refiled in 1 of 20 different categories." For the actual study, perceivers rated the likelihood with which they would assign each of the 12 tasks to the target whose interview they had just heard (1 = *not at all likely*; 7 = *very likely*). Not surprisingly, task assignment ratings were higher, overall, for the easy tasks (M = 5.80) than for the difficult tasks (M = 3.30).

The results of this study confirmed that memory behavior is an important factor in perceivers' impressions of a target's capability. This was illustrated by the higher average task assignment ratings given to nonforgetful targets (M = 5.26) than to forgetful targets (*Ms* = 4.49 and 3.89 for moderately and highly forgetful targets, respectively). Task assignment ratings for the moderately and highly forgetful targets differed, though not significantly, in the expected direction.

Initially, we had predicted that after listening to the tape-recorded interview, perceivers would have a particularly negative impression of a forgetful old target's capability. That is, we thought that memory failures would have a stronger negative impact on perceivers' capability impressions of old targets than of young targets. We anticipated that the more negative capability impressions would be reflected in lower task assignment ratings for forgetful old targets than for forgetful young targets. Indeed, memory failures did have a negative impact on perceivers' impressions, as illustrated by the lower task assignment ratings given to forgetful targets than to nonforgetful targets. However, task assignment ratings did not differ for the young and old targets. Thus, our prediction that forgetful old targets would be differentially disadvantaged was not supported.

CONFIDENCE

In another study (Erber, Prager, Williams, & Caiola, 1996), we also investigated perceivers' capability impressions of young versus old targets. This time, perceivers read an interview script rather than listening to a tape-recorded interview. In the script, the targets experienced four memory failures that were either all episodic or all semantic rather than a mixture of the two types of failure, as in Erber, Etheart, and Szuchman (1992). In this study, targets were male and female rather than all being female, as in in the study by Erber, Etheart, and Szuchman (1992). Also, the target was interviewed for a museum volunteer position rather than for a school volunteer position. It was specifically mentioned by the interviewer that museum volunteer work could be done evenings and weekends so that the museum volunteer context would be viewed as more gender neutral than the school volunteer context used by Erber, Etheart, and Szuchman (1992).

Rather than the "easy" versus "difficult" categorization used by Erber, Etheart, and Szuchman (1992) for the school volunteer tasks, the museum volunteer tasks were categorized as to how much memory was required (i.e., task memory load). Compared with task difficulty, task memory load seemed more directly relevant to the targets' forgetfulness. Of the 12 tasks, 4 fell into a low task memory load category, 4 fell into a medium task memory load category, and 4 fell into a high task memory load category.

An example of a low memory load task was "Stand by the door of the gift shop and greet patrons as they enter and bid them a good day as they exit." A medium memory load task was "In the gift shop, know what is contained in each of 10 storage cabinets under the display cases." A high memory load task was "Each of 15 gift shop display cases can be opened with different 3-digit combinations that are changed every month. Without looking up the combination, be able to open each cabinet on the first try." Pilot work verified that perceivers made the anticipated distinction between the degree of memory load that was required to perform tasks in the low, medium, and high memory load categories.

In the study by Erber, Etheart, and Szuchman (1992), task assignment ratings were used to index perceivers' impressions about a target's cognitive capability. In the museum volunteer study by Erber et al. (1996), perceivers rated how confident they would feel that the target could perform a task both accurately and efficiently (1 = not at all confident; 7 = very confident). Compared with task assignment ratings, confidence ratings were a less direct way of indexing perceivers' potential behavioral response toward a forgetful target. For that reason, confidence ratings might be a more subtle, and possibly a more sensitive, means of accessing any differences in perceivers' views of forgetful young versus forgetful old targets.

Nonetheless, contrary to what was anticipated, perceivers' level of confidence was equivalent for young and old targets. This outcome paralleled the egalitarian task assignment ratings given to young and old targets in the study by Erber, Etheart, and Szuchman (1992). Thus, regardless of the way perceivers' capability impressions were indexed (task assignment or confidence ratings) and regardless of the specific nature of the volunteer context (school vs. museum), there was no evidence that perceivers judged young and old targets any differently.

With regard to type of memory failures, perceivers in the study by Erber et al. (1996), as well as those in a subsequent study by Erber and Prager (1997), were more confident in targets who experienced episodic failures rather than in those who experienced semantic failures. Also, there was a significant two-way interaction between the type of memory failure and the memory load of the tasks. For tasks in the low memory load category, perceivers had an equally high level of confidence in targets who experienced episodic failures and semantic failures. For tasks in the high memory load category, perceivers had an equally low level of confidence in targets who experienced episodic failures and semantic failures. It was only when tasks posed a moderate level of memory demand (i.e., tasks in the medium memory load category) that perceivers' confidence was sensitive to the type of memory failure experienced by both young and old targets. Although perceivers' confidence ratings were not high in an absolute sense, their ratings for the medium memory load tasks were higher for young and old targets who experienced episodic failures ($M = 2.94$) than for young and old targets who experienced semantic failures ($M = 2.57$). Neither type of memory failure nor task memory load interacted with target age, indicating that regardless of the targets' age, perceivers made the same distinctions between episodic and semantic failures, and between tasks that were low, medium, and high in memory load.

Thus far, our data have not supported the prediction that perceivers' tendency to attribute old targets' failures to internal stable causes would have greater negative implications for their capability judgments of forgetful old targets rather than forgetful young targets. On the contrary, perceivers reported themselves as equally likely to assign tasks to old and to young targets, and they were just as confident that tasks could be performed accurately and efficiently by old targets as by young targets.

There may be several explanations as to why perceivers' capability judgments do not reflect the age-based double standard found with their attributions for memory failures. The egalitarian task assignment and confidence ratings for young and old targets could have been due, at least in part, to the increased amount of individuating information given for targets in the capability studies. In the earlier attribution studies, little or no individuating information was provided, other than the target's age. In the capability studies (Erber, Etheart, & Szuchman, 1992; Erber et al., 1996), however, perceivers listened to or read an interview narrative in which targets disclose not only their age but also their education level, their previous work experience, and their interest in the volunteer position. When individuating information is available, people may rely less on stereotypes about age (Crockett & Hummert, 1987). In the study by Erber et al. (1996), perceivers not only made confidence ratings but they also made attributions for the target's memory failures. Evidence for the age-based double standard was weaker than in prior attribution studies, in which targets were less individuated. This also suggests, though indirectly, that individuating information may reduce perceivers' tendency to use stereotypes when making judgments about others.

Another possible explanation for the equivalent capability ratings for young and old targets is that perceivers' task assignment and confidence ratings could be based on a constellation of factors, each of which may be weighted differently for the young and the old targets. Undoubtedly, the target's memory behavior is taken into consideration, and the attributions perceivers make for the target's memory failures could also play a role. When forming impressions about a target's capability, however, perceivers may consider other factors as well. For instance, they may hold schemas about traits as being characteristic of members of a particular age group. Responsibility is one trait that is perceived to increase with age (Heckhausen, Dixon, & Baltes, 1989). Erber, Szuchman, and Etheart (1993) reported that young perceivers consider old targets to be not only more responsible but also more reliable, dependable, and helpful than young targets. When capability is being judged, having a higher degree of such traits could compensate for forgetfulness, thus resulting in an allowance for forgetful targets who are old rather than young.

One further consideration is that perceivers' judgments may depend not only on the target but also upon the context in which they are made (Eagly & Steffen, 1986). Even though older targets' memory failures may be attributed more to internal stable causes, the volunteer role may be viewed as more suitable for old targets. If so, then old targets could be at an advantage when their capability is being judged in a volunteer context. It is possible that old targets could lose this advantage in a nonvolunteer context. For example, in a study by Erber and Danker (1995), perceivers read a narrative that described incidences of a young or an old target worker's forgetfulness which were causing problems for the operation of the company. Prior to the narrative, perceivers read either a low-pressure memo or a high-pressure memo to convey the atmosphere of the company for which the target worked. The high-pressure memo referred to possible downsizing to increase company efficiency, whereas the low-pressure memo merely consisted of announcements about company-sponsored activities. Perceivers who read the downsizing memo were less likely to recommend training workshops for the forgetful old worker than for the forgetful young worker. Thus, in a paid work context with high bottom-line pressure, perceivers make different judgments about forgetful young and old targets. Perhaps perceivers' task assignment and confidence ratings were similar for young and old targets in the studies by Erber, Etheart, and Szuchman (1992) and Erber et al. (1996) because the type of pressure in volunteer situations is not equivalent to the bottom-line pressure in a paid work context as conveyed in the study by Erber and Danker (1995).

MEMORY OPINION

Not only did the perceivers in the studies by Erber, Etheart, and Szuchman (1992) and Erber et al. (1996) give task assignment or confidence ratings but they also rated their opinion of the target's memory (1 = *very poor*; 7 = *very good*). Not surprisingly, perceivers' memory opinion was sensitive to both the number and the type of memory failures experienced by the target. In the school volunteer study by Erber, Etheart, and Szuchman (1992), targets who experienced eight memory failures were given the lowest memory opinion rating ($M = 1.81$), targets who experienced four memory failures were given higher ratings ($M = 2.98$), and targets who experienced no memory failures were given the highest ratings ($M = 5.71$). In the museum volunteer study by Erber et al. (1996), perceivers' memory opinion ratings were lower for targets whose memory failures were semantic ($M = 2.23$) than for targets whose memory failures were episodic ($M = 2.58$). Of particular interest for our investigation, however, was that despite the egalitarian capability ratings (i.e., task assignment and confidence) for young and old targets, the old targets received higher ratings on the memory opinion scale. The less negative memory opinion for a forgetful old target than for a similarly forgetful young target was corroborated in a study by Erber, Caiola, and Pupo (1994) as well.

One way to interpret perceivers' relative leniency in their memory opinion of old targets is based on the expectancy-violation theory, which postulates that responses to expected behaviors tend to be less extreme than responses to unexpected behaviors (Jackson, Sullivan, & Hodge, 1993; Jussim, Coleman, & Lerch, 1987). With regard to memory behavior, people may associate older adulthood with forgetfulness (e.g., Ryan, 1992; Ryan & Kwong See, 1993), so memory failures may be more expected for older adults than for young adults. Deaux and Emswiller (1974) suggested that expected behaviors are attributed to stable causes, whereas unexpected behaviors are attributed to unstable causes. Accordingly, the age-based double standard used by perceivers in our attribution studies (i.e., old targets' memory failures were attributed more to internal stable causes) may reflect an expectation that old targets will experience memory failures. This expectation could translate into an allowance for old targets, which could explain why perceivers have a less negative opinion of forgetful old targets' memory. For young targets, memory failures may be less expected, which could be the reason why young targets' memory failures are attributed more to internal causes that are unstable (i.e., lack of effort, lack of attention). Also, since young targets' memory failures may violate expectancy, young targets may be judged harshly when they do forget.

Another—though related—interpretation of perceivers' less negative opinion of old targets' memory is based on the shifting-standards model (Biernat, Manis, & Nelson, 1991). In this model, it is postulated that judgments about another individual's behavior are made in reference to the perceived range, or variation, in that behavior for the group to which that individual belongs. Thus, an old target who forgets may be considered average in reference to the perceived range of memory functioning for an older adult group. By contrast, a young target who forgets may be considered less than average in reference to the perceived range of memory functioning for a young adult group. Another test of the shifting-standards interpretation of our memory opinion findings might be to pose the question "How many times would a target have to forget before you would think he or she had a poor memory?" A response indicating a higher number of times for an old target than for a young target would offer additional support for the possibility that perceivers adjust their standards depending on the target's age group.

In addition to expectancy violation and shifting standards, the attribution-of-contrast model (Krueger, Heckhausen, & Hundertmark, 1995) could also help explain our memory opinion findings. According to the attribution-of-contrast model, people's expectations about a group are the background against which individual members are judged. Not only may people associate older adulthood with forgetfulness but they may also hold a generalized stereotype of older adults as having a dependent lifestyle (see Krueger et al., 1995). Describing an old target with an old lifestyle should reinforce a generalized stereotype of old age, whereas describing an old target with a young lifestyle should minimize such a generalized stereotype. Forgetfulness may be more expected for old targets whose lifestyle is congruent with their membership in an older age group than for old targets whose lifestyle is inconsistent with membership in an older age group. Thus, a forgetful old target with an old lifestyle should be congruent with expectations for that age group and that target's memory failures should be judged leniently. However, a forgetful old target with a young lifestyle should be inconsistent with expectations and therefore could lose the leniency accorded to forgetful age peers who have an old lifestyle. A study by Erber, Szuchman, and Prager (1997) tested this idea. Perceivers rated their memory opinion of a forgetful young or old target who was described as having an age-congruent versus an age-incongruent lifestyle. The lifestyle description made no difference for perceivers' memory opinion of young targets, but it did for old targets: Both young and older perceivers had a less negative memory opinion of the old target with the old lifestyle than they did of the old target with the young lifestyle. Thus, older adults who act young may be held to higher standards with regard to memory. An increasing proportion of today's older adults are in good health and may have lifestyles similar to those of younger adults. The findings of Erber et al. (1997) suggest, however, that older adults who act young may have to be more concerned about how their memory failures make them look to others.

IMPRESSION MANAGEMENT

The results of our studies indicate that perceivers form similar impressions about the capability of young and old targets and that they may even be somewhat more lenient in judging old targets' memory. However, there is little question that perceivers form more negative capability impressions of forgetful targets than of nonforgetful targets. They are less likely to give forgetful targets than they are nonforgetful targets the opportunity to perform challenging tasks; they are less confident in forgetful targets' ability to perform tasks accurately and efficiently; and they have a lower opinion of forgetful targets' memory.

Little is known about managing impressions that are formed on the basis of cognitive behavior such as memory (Gentry & Herrmann, 1990), but it is important to determine whether anything can be done to moderate perceivers' impressions. Therefore, in two different studies, we tested the effect of strategies that could ameliorate perceivers' negative impressions of forgetful targets.

Initially, we thought that it might be more difficult to moderate perceivers' negative impressions of forgetful old targets than of forgetful young targets. This assumption was based on our prior findings that memory failures are attributed more to internal stable causes for old targets. Behavior that is attributed to an internal stable cause, such as mental difficulty, is likely to be considered invariable over time (Weiner, Figueroa-Muñoz, & Kakihara, 1991) and thus more difficult to distance from the target's central self (Snyder & Higgins, 1988).

In one impression management study (Erber et al., 1994), we introduced positive information about the target in the form of a reference letter. Young perceivers read a somewhat positive letter or a strongly positive letter written by the target's previous supervisor. The letter was read either before or after perceivers listened to one of the tape-recorded interviews used by Erber, Etheart, and Szuchman (1992) with either a moderately forgetful (four memory failures) or a highly forgetful (eight memory failures) young or old female target who was applying for a school volunteer position. The somewhat positive letter listed traits that had been verified in pilot work as being both positive and relevant to the job-related tasks for which the target was being considered (e.g., "Kathryn was *cooperative* and *helpful*."). The strongly positive letter mentioned the same traits and elaborated by giving relevant examples of the target's behavior (e.g., "Kathryn was *cooperative* and *helpful;* she always seemed to be right there to lend a hand no matter what task needed to be done."). The young perceivers were more likely to assign tasks when moderately and highly forgetful young and old targets were described with a strongly positive rather than a somewhat positive letter. However, the strongly positive letter was beneficial only when it was read *after* perceivers listened to the interview tape with the forgetful target.

To determine whether perceiver age would make a difference, we asked older perceivers to read the strongly positive letter either before or after they listened to a tape-recorded interview with the moderately forgetful or highly forgetful young or old female target. Our findings were similar to those obtained with young perceivers (i.e., perceivers were more likely to assign tasks to the target when the letter was read after rather than before listening to the tape). However, older perceivers were influenced by the strongly positive letter only when judging the moderately forgetful old target, which suggests that capability impressions may be somewhat less malleable in older perceivers than in young perceivers. A similar finding was obtained in a study by Guo, Erber, and Szuchman (in press), in which young and older perceivers read a brief written article stating that memory declines with age. After reading the article, perceivers rated the extent to which a forgetful young or old target's memory failures were caused by lack of ability. Young perceivers gave higher lack of ability attributions for the forgetful old target than for the forgetful young target, but older perceivers' lack of ability attribution ratings did not differ for the two target age groups. Thus, older perceivers seemed less susceptible than did young perceivers to the influence of written information about memory and age. Additional research is needed to broaden our understanding of the conditions under which young and older perceivers' judgments are swayed by written information from an outside source.

In a second impression management study (Erber & Prager, in press), we investigated whether an excuse given by a forgetful target him- or herself would be effective in ameliorating negative impressions. Perceivers read the same interview scripts used by Erber et al. (1996), in which a young or old (male or female) target experiences episodic or semantic memory failures. In Erber and Prager's study, however, the target gave an excuse for forgetting (an attempted car break-in that occurred prior to the interview). This excuse, which would be considered "good" according to the criteria of Weiner et al. (1987) of being external and unstable, was given by the target either before or after the interview. Perceivers reported being more confident that targets could perform memory-related tasks when the excuse was given after rather than before the interview. This was the case regardless of the type of memory failure the target experienced (episodic or semantic) and regardless of the target's age. Furthermore, subsequent analyses that included a no-excuse control group (data from Erber et al., 1996) indicated that giving the excuse before the interview was no better than giving no excuse at all.

A reference letter and an excuse were both effective for managing perceivers' impressions of forgetful targets. However, these strategies worked only when used after the target's memory failures had occurred. This recency effect may relate to the fact that the interview, during which the target experienced memory failures, was lengthier than either the letter or the excuse and for that reason may have exerted a stronger influence on perceivers' impressions of the target. The stronger influence of the interview could have weakened any schema initially instilled by the letter or the excuse. However, the reference letter and excuse might have been more salient when presented after the interview and immediately prior to perceivers' ratings. Indeed, our findings indicate that under this condition, the reference letter and the excuse were successful in modifying perceivers' impressions of both forgetful young and forgetful old targets.

SUMMARY AND CONCLUSIONS

Memory has received a great deal of attention in the study of aging. Indeed, there is considerable evidence for the existence of age-related changes/differences in memory. Moreover, older adults often complain about memory failures. However, memory failures can happen to anyone, regardless of age. The research program described in this chapter used a social cognitive approach to investigate factors that may influence the cognitions and representations that we hold about everyday memory failures and the people who experience them.

It is clear that perceivers use an age-based double standard when making attributions for memory failures. Even so, perceivers seem to be egalitarian in their judgments about the capability of forgetful young and forgetful old targets to perform various volunteer tasks. That young and old targets are perceived as having equivalent capability could be related to a number of factors, including individuating information about the target, schemas perceivers may hold about compensating traits considered more typical of older than of young adults, and the context in which capability judgments are made. With regard to their opinion of a target's memory, perceivers make an allowance (i.e., have a less negative memory opinion) when the target is old rather than young. This leniency as far as their memory opinion of old targets may be a factor contributing to perceivers' overall equivalent capability ratings for young and old targets.

Despite their equivalent capability judgments of young and old targets, there is no question that memory failures have a negative effect, overall, on perceivers' capability impressions; perceivers view forgetful targets as being less capable than nonforgetful targets. Moreover, targets who experience semantic failures are considered less capable than targets who experience episodic failures. We tested two different strategies (presenting positive written information about a target in the form of a reference letter and having the target give an excuse for his or her own forgetting) that could be used to moderate the negative impact of forgetting on perceivers' capability impressions. When applied after memory failures occur, both strategies had an ameliorative effect on perceivers' capability judgments for both forgetful young and forgetful old targets. If the frequency of everyday memory failures does increase with age (Cavanaugh et al., 1983; Erber, Szuchman, &

Rothberg, 1992), however, then strategies for countering the negative effects of forgetting could have particular relevance for older adults, who may have particular concerns about maintaining a positive image when they experience memory failures.

With regard to the age of the perceivers, our findings suggest that older perceivers are more lenient when judging others who experience memory failures. Compared with young perceivers, older perceivers consider memory failures less serious in an absolute sense, they attribute memory failures less to internal stable causes and more to causes outside the target, and they see a less urgent need for medical and/or psychological evaluation for forgetful targets. However, perceiver age has not been studied as systematically as has target age, and further investigation is certainly needed.

The program of research described thus far has not focused on emotional, or affective, reactions perceivers may have toward forgetful targets. Yet, there may be a connection between the cognitive schema perceivers hold as to what caused a memory failure and the affective responses perceivers direct toward a forgetful target. According to Weiner's model (1993) of social motivation, failures attributed to internal stable causes are considered less controllable than are failures attributed to internal unstable causes. When failures are considered less controllable, then those who fail may be held less responsible and may also elicit greater sympathy from others than would be the case if failures were considered more controllable.

Given the age-based double standard our perceivers have used when making attributions for memory failures, it is reasonable to postulate that an old target's memory failures would be considered less controllable than a young target's memory failures. Accordingly, an old target may be held less responsible for memory failures and might elicit more sympathy.

In the only study to touch upon affect (Erber et al., 1997), perceivers read a narrative in which a young or old target forgot to bring a discount coupon when meeting a friend at a restaurant, thus causing both the target and her friend to pay twice as much for their meals. Perceivers rated how sympathetic they thought the friend would be with the target for forgetting the coupon. Young perceivers thought that the friend would have greater sympathy if the forgetful target were old rather than young. However, this greater sympathy extended only to the old target who was described as having an old lifestyle. Thus, young perceivers thought the friend would be particularly sympathetic when the old target was clearly identified as a member of an old age group. The pattern of results was the reverse for the older perceivers, who thought the friend would be more sympathetic toward the old target with the young lifestyle than toward the old target with the old lifestyle. The older perceivers in this study were active community-living members of a walking and exercise group. Perhaps they identified more with the old target who had a young lifestyle and thus were more willing to give that target the benefit of the doubt. Possibly, the lower degree of sympathy the older perceivers thought the friend would have for the old target with the old lifestyle could be explained by the black sheep hypothesis (Marques, Yzerbyt, & Leyens, 1988), which postulates that people derogate unfavorably described in-group members as a way of maintaining positive social identity. The older perceivers in this study may have viewed the old lifestyle as an unfavorable one for age peers (in-group members); therefore, they may have been more willing to derogate the old target with the old lifestyle in terms of having less sympathy with that target's failure. In any case, the results of this study suggest that older perceivers may not be so lenient when judging an age peer whose forgetting has immediate negative consequences, particularly when that age peer has a lifestyle that differs from their own. Additional research is underway to explore the nature of young and older perceivers' affective responses toward forgetful targets who are the same or different in age. Such affective responses could have implications for the self-image, and possibly the mental health, of the individuals who are forgetful.

ACKNOWLEDGMENTS

Support for the research reported in this chapter was provided by National Institute on Aging (NIA) grant RO1 AG06268.

REFERENCES

Atkinson, R. C., & Shiffrin, R. M. (1968). Human memory: A proposed system and its control processes. In K. W. Spence and J. T. Spence (Eds.), *The psychology of learning and motivation,* Vol. 2. (pp. 89–195) New York: Academic Press.

Banziger, G., & Drevenstedt, J. (1982). Achievement attributions by young and old judges as a function of perceived age of stimulus person. *Journal of Gerontology, 37,* 468–474.

Biernat, M., Manis, M., & Nelson, T. E. (1991). Stereotypes and standards of judgment. *Journal of Personality and Social Psychology, 60,* 485–499.

Botwinick, J. (1984). *Aging and behavior* (3rd ed). New York: Springer.

Cavanaugh, J. D., Grady, J. G., & Perlmutter, M. (1983). Forgetting and use of memory aids in 20 to 70 year olds everyday life. *International Journal of Aging and Human Development, 17,* 113–122.

Crockett, W. H., & Hummert, M. L. (1987). Perceptions of aging and the elderly. *Annual Review of Gerontology and Geriatrics, 7,* 217–241.

Deaux, K., & Emswiller, T. (1974). Explanations of successful performance on sex-linked tasks: What is skill for the male is luck for the female. *Journal of Personality and Social Psychology, 29,* 80–85.

Eagly, A. H., & Steffen, V. J. (1986). Gender stereotypes, occupational roles, and beliefs about part-time employees. *Psychology of Women Quarterly, 10,* 252–262.

Erber, J. T. (1989). Young and older adults' appraisal of memory failures in young and older adult target persons. *Journal of Gerontology: Psychological Sciences, 44,* P170–P175.

Erber, J. T., Caiola, M. A., & Pupo, F. A. (1994). Age and forgetfulness: Managing perceivers' impressions of targets' capability. *Psychology and Aging, 9,* 554–561.

Erber, J. T., & Danker, D. C. (1995). Forgetting in the workplace: Attributions and recommendations for young and older employees. *Psychology and Aging, 10,* 565–569.

Erber, J. T., Etheart, M. E., & Szuchman, L. T. (1992). Age and forgetfulness: Perceivers' impressions of targets' capability. *Psychology and Aging, 7,* 479–483.

Erber, J. T., & Prager, I. G. (1997). Age and forgetfulness: Absolute versus comparative decisions about capability. *Experimental Aging Research, 23,* 355–367.

Erber, J. T., & Prager, I. G. (in press). Age and excuses for forgetting: Self-handicapping versus damage-control strategies. *International Journal of Aging and Human Development.*

Erber, J. T., Prager, I. G., Williams, M., & Caiola, M. A. (1996). Age and forgetfulness: Confidence in ability and attribution for memory failures. *Psychology and Aging, 11,* 310–315.

Erber, J. T., & Rothberg, S. T. (1991). Here's looking at you: The relative effect of age and attractiveness on judgments about memory failure. *Journal of Gerontology: Psychological Sciences, 46,* P116–P123.

Erber, J. T., Szuchman, L. T., & Etheart, M. E. (1993). Age and forgetfulness: Young perceivers' impressions of young and older neighbors. *International Journal of Aging and Human Development, 37,* 91–103.

Erber, J. T., Szuchman, L. T., & Prager, I. G. (1997). Forgetful but forgiven: How age and lifestyle affect perceptions of memory failure. *Journal of Gerontology: Psychological Sciences, 52B,* P303–P307.

Erber, J. T., Szuchman, L. T., & Rothberg, S. T. (1990a). Everyday memory failure: Age differences in appraisal and attribution. *Psychology and Aging, 5,* 236–241.

Erber, J. T., Szuchman, L. T., & Rothberg, S. T. (1990b). Age, gender, and individual differences in memory failure appraisal. *Psychology and Aging, 5,* 600–603.

Erber, J. T., Szuchman, L. T., & Rothberg, S. T. (1992). Dimensions of self-report about everyday memory in young and older adults. *International Journal of Aging and Human Development, 34,* 311–323.

Gentry, M., & Herrmann, D. J. (1990). Memory contrivances in everyday life. *Personality and Social Psychology Bulletin, 16,* 241–253.

Guo, X., Erber, J. T., & Szuchman, L. T. (in press). Age and forgetfulness: Can negative age stereotypes be modified? *Educational Gerontology.*

Heckhausen, J., Dixon, R. A., & Baltes, P. B. (1989). Gains and losses in development throughout adulthood as perceived by different adult age groups. *Developmental Psychology, 25,* 109–121.

Herrmann, D. J., & Neisser, U. (1978). An inventory of everyday memory experiences. In M. M. Gruneberg, P. E. Morris, & R. N. Sykes (Eds.); *Practical aspects of memory* (pp. 35–51). New York: Academic Press.

Jackson, L. A., Sullivan, L. A., & Hodge, C. N. (1993). Stereotype effects on attributions, predictions, and evaluations: No two social judgments are alike. *Journal of Personality and Social Psychology, 65,* 69–84.

Jones, E. E., & Nisbett, R. E. (1972). The actor and the observer: Divergent perceptions of the causes of behavior. In E. E. Jones, D. Kanouse, H. H. Kelley, R. E. Nisbett, S. Valins, & B. Weiner (Eds.), *Attribution: Perceiving the causes of behavior* (pp. 79–94) Morristown, NJ: General Learning Press.

Jussim, L., Coleman, L. M., & Lerch, L. (1987). The nature of stereotypes: A comparison and integration of three theories. *Journal of Personality and Social Psychology, 52,* 536–546.

Kerr, N. L., Hymes, R. W., Anderson, A. B., & Weathers, J. E. (1995). Defendant–juror similarity and mock juror judgments. *Law and Human Behavior, 19,* 545–567.

Kogan, N. (1979). Beliefs, attitudes, and stereotypes about old people: A new look at some old issues. *Research on Aging, 1,* 11–36.

Krueger, J., Heckhausen, J., & Hundertmark, J. (1995). Perceiving middle-aged adults: Effects of stereotype-congruent and -incongruent information. *Journal of Gerontology: Psychological Sciences, 50B,* P82–P93.

Locke-Conner, C., & Walsh, P. (1980). Attitudes toward the older job applicant: Just as competent but more likely to fail. *Journal of Gerontology, 35,* 920–927.

Markus, H., Smith, J., & Moreland, R. L. (1985). Role of the self-concept in the perception of others. *Journal of Personality and Social Psychology, 49,* 1494–1512.

Marques, J. M., Yzerbyt, V. Y., & Leyens, J. P. (1988). The 'black sheep' effect: Extremity of judgments towards ingroup members as a function of group identification. *European Journal of Social Psychology, 18,* 1–16.

Reno, R. (1979). Attribution for success and failure as a function of perceived age. *Journal of Gerontology, 34,* 709–715.

Ryan, E. B. (1992). Beliefs about memory changes across the adult life span. *Journal of Gerontology: Psychological Sciences, 47,* P41–P46.

Ryan, E. B., & Kwong See, S. (1993). Age-based beliefs about memory changes for self and others across adulthood. *Journal of Gerontology: Psychological Sciences, 48,* P199–P201.

Snyder, C. R., & Higgins, R. L. (1988). Excuses: Their effective role in the negotiation of reality. *Psychological Bulletin, 104,* 23–35.

Squire, L. R. (1987). *Memory and brain.* New York: Oxford University Press.

Weiner, B. (1993). On sin versus sickness: A theory of perceived responsibility and social motivation. *American Psychologist, 48,* 957–965.

Weiner, B., Figueroa-Muñoz, A., & Kakihara, C. (1991). The goals of excuses and communication strategies related to causal perceptions. *Personality and Social Psychology Bulletin, 17,* 4–13.

Weiner, B., Frieze, I., Kukla, A., Reed, L., Rest, S., & Rosenbaum, R. M. (1971). *Perceiving the causes of success and failure.* Morristown, NJ: General Learning Press.

10

SOCIAL SCHEMATICITY AND CAUSAL ATTRIBUTIONS

FREDDA BLANCHARD-FIELDS

School of Psychology
Georgia Institute of Technology
Atlanta, Georgia

Every day, we encounter events that require an explanation. We attempt to identify what factors gave rise to specific outcomes. For example, consider the following situation:

> Jennifer had been dating Don for three years. She wanted to marry Don, but he felt that the relationship was fine just the way it was. Jennifer gave Don an ultimatum: Marry me or else. Still uncertain about the whole idea, Don agreed to marry her. During the 2 years of their marriage, they fought constantly; they recently divorced.

Social psychologists have been interested in what types of information an individual processes when presented with such a situation and how this information is combined to form a causal judgment (Fiske, 1993; Gilbert & Malone, 1995). Two types of information typically used to determine causality include (1) dispositional information, such as personality characteristics, that exacerbate the main character's role in producing the negative outcome and (2) situational information that presents extenuating circumstances surrounding the main character's involvement in the negative outcome. In addition, the ambiguity of such information and whether someone is reasoning about her- or himself or others will also influence whether a dispositional or situational attribution will be made. In the above example, the following question could be asked: What influences the extent to which an individual attributes the cause of the divorce to something about Jennifer's dispositional characteristics and/or to external extenuating circumstances (factors involving Don or society's social rules)? In addition, Jennifer could have foreseen the outcome, yet she most likely did not intend the outcome. Given the ambiguity as to what caused the negative outcome, the negative outcome itself and the fact that the situation involved a hypothetical other as opposed to oneself should increase the likelihood that individuals will hold Jennifer responsible for the divorce. The dispositional attribution made about Jennifer could subsequently influence social interactions, behavior, and/or feelings about Jennifer and the divorce situation.

As we can see from the above example, causal attributions or causal explanations of behavior play an important role in our everyday reasoning. If someone rebuffs us or an event results in a negative outcome, we look for explanations as to what caused the behavior or negative outcome, respectively. If we are failing at a task, we need to understand why to know how to proceed next. If an interpersonal dilemma (as in the divorce example above) emerges in our lives, we need to understand why to know what to do next and/or how to effect a change. In situations such as these, people consistently demonstrate the desire to predict the future and control events that impinge on their daily functioning, hoping to control the likelihood that an event will or will not occur (Fiske & Taylor, 1991). In addition, causal attributions are tied to attitudes and fundamental values that can be the basis of future behavior, thoughts, and emotion (Fiske & Taylor, 1991). Given that a major goal of aging research is to identify areas of adaptive functioning, it is important to study the underlying reasoning, such as causal attributions, that drives older adults' behavior. More specifically, understanding the nature of and changes in attributional reasoning may help identify the types of responses an older adult will select to solve a problem, cope with a stressful event, or make a social judgment.

The social psychology literature on causal attributions is replete with studies that demonstrate the nature of attributions individuals make and the biases and distortions inherent in these types of social judgments (Gilbert & Malone, 1995; Ross & Nisbett, 1991). In particular, the correspondence bias has been a well-documented outcome of attributional processing (Gilbert & Malone, 1995; Schneider, 1991). This bias involves the tendency to make dispositional, trait-based attributions for causally ambiguous events and underestimate the powerful influences of situational constraints. Research has revealed a number of social and cognitive factors that influence when the correspondence bias is likely to occur, as indicated in the example at the beginning of this chapter, from the availability of cognitive resources (Gilbert & Malone, 1995) to motivational factors (Fiske, 1993). Studies concerning the existence of attributional biases and the way in which social cognitive factors operate on them have been conducted primarily on college-aged subjects, however (Blanchard-Fields & Abeles, 1996; Sears, 1987).

In this chapter, I examine the extent to which social cognitive factors shown to influence whether attributional processing biases occur apply equally well across the latter half of the life span. In other words, under what conditions and/or contexts are age-related differences in attributional biases likely or not likely to occur? Attributional processing studied within a life-span developmental context not only will expand our understanding of the nature of attributional biases but will add to a growing literature on the nature of social cognitive change as we grow older (Blanchard-Fields, 1994; Blanchard-Fields & Abeles, 1996; Blank, 1987; Sears, 1987).

My colleagues and I have conducted a number of studies examining the extent to which attributional biases are observed across the adult life span. In brief, the method was to present adults with situations resulting in a negative outcome. They were to rate the degree to which something about the main character was the cause of the negative outcome. Using this method, we have repeatedly found an increase in the correspondence bias in older adults (i.e., greater dispositional attributions). However, we were also intrigued by the consistent finding that the degree and quality of dispositional biases were influenced by the content specificity of the problem situations presented to the participants. For example, in negative relationship vignettes similar to the one described earlier (Jennifer and Don), older adults are more likely than are younger adults to assign responsibility for the divorce to something about Jennifer. In other types of situations (e.g., health and work), though, age differences were not found (Blanchard-Fields, 1996). Given these findings, we have taken a contextual and differential approach to the study of attributions in adulthood and aging.

To address the issue of contextual variability, we turned to specific principles of social cognition theory to help provide a basis for more systematically predicting individuals' attributional responses (Blanchard-Fields, 1996; Blanchard-Fields & Abeles, 1996). The fundamental premise is that beliefs and values that are well instantiated in the individual are systematically related to attributions. Thus, the content specificity in responding across situations arises because of individual differences in the content of such beliefs and value systems. For example, when we asked adults of varying ages to generate a main theme for numerous types of social problem scenarios, there were age differences in the types of schematic beliefs produced (Blanchard-Fields, 1996; Chen & Blanchard-Fields, 1997). In a scenario depicting problems for a relationship when two individuals live together before marriage, older adults produced such schematic beliefs as "People are obligated to uphold society's morality" (i.e., "One should not cohabitate before marriage"). By contrast, young adults simply produced themes reflecting the importance of outside pressure in these types of situations. From this perspective, we suggest that age-related differences in attributional processes are mediated by age-related differences in background, values, and belief systems. I will come back to this point after addressing the research leading to this conclusion as well as alternative explanations for its occurrence.

There are four goals for this chapter: (1) review of research examining developmental differences in attributional processing, (2) consideration of knowledge-based and processing perspectives as possible explanations for these findings, (3) review of current and ongoing research addressing these two perspectives, and (4) consideration of implications for social cognitive changes in adulthood from a life-span developmental perspective.

DEVELOPMENT AND ATTRIBUTIONAL PROCESSING

In an ongoing program of research, we explored age differences in attributional processing from both a developmental and a traditional social cognitive paradigm. The extant literature on social cognition examining the correspondence bias has specified a number of factors that identify the conditions under which individuals are susceptible to this bias. These factors include (1) the ambiguity of information presented with respect to the relative contribution of the main character and extenuating circumstances in producing the final outcome (Blanchard-Fields, 1994; Trope, 1986); (2) the positive or negative valence of the outcome (Gilbert, Taforodi, & Malone, 1993; Skowronski & Carlston, 1989); (3) the motivation to provide an accurate or objective portrayal of the situation (Fiske & Neuberg, 1990); and (4) the amount of background information provided suggesting a situational explanation (Krull, 1993; Lupfer, Clark, & Hutcherson, 1990).

On the basis of these findings, we conducted a number of studies using a causal attribution paradigm that presents socially ambiguous situations, such as the Jennifer and Don vignette presented earlier, to adults ranging in age from adolescence through older adulthood (Blanchard-Fields, 1994; Blanchard-Fields & Norris, 1994). In this procedure, adults make attributions about vignettes varying in level of ambiguity. Level of ambiguity refers to either a high degree of uncertainty as to whether the primary character is responsible for the outcome of the situation or a high degree of certainty as to the intentions of the primary character and the causal link between her or him and the final outcome. Action situations also involve either a relationship situation or an achievement situation and have a negative or positive outcome. Participants rated the extent to which the outcome of the vignette was due (1) to dispositional factors (something about the primary actor), (2) to situational factors (extenuating circumstances or factors external to the main character), and (3) to an interaction of factors (an interactive attribution consisting of a combination of dispositional and situational factors).

On the basis of social cognitive principles of attributional processing, we expected that ambiguous situations with a negative outcome would produce a greater degree of dispositional attributions than would situations that were low in ambiguity and reflected a positive outcome. Overall, this hypothesis was supported.

We also argued, from a life-span developmental perspective, that attributional biases and distortions should decrease with increasing age. For example, from a post-formal developmental perspective, increasing age in adulthood is associated with a corresponding increase in relativistic thinking (Blanchard-Fields, 1986; Labouvie-Vief, 1992; Staudinger, Smith, & Baltes, 1992). Thus, we hypothesized that with increasing age, adults would rely less on dispositional attributions as the primary cause of negative event outcomes and, in turn, rely more on a combination of factors (both dispositional and situational: interactive attributions).

However, this hypothesis was only partially supported. When situations were ambiguous with respect to the main character's role in causing the event outcome and reflected negative interpersonal content, older adults made both higher dispositional and interactive attribution ratings than did young and middle-aged adults (Blanchard-Fields, 1994). To further examine developmental differences in causal attributions, we also examined dialectical attributional processing in adolescence through older adulthood using a qualitative analysis. In addition to the attribution rating scales, participants gave explanations as to why they made their respective attribution ratings. We found that middle-aged adults scored higher on dialectical attributional reasoning (considering dispositional and situational factors in relation to each other, mutually determined and co-defined) than did adolescents, youth, young adults, and older adults. In this case, however, older adults (in particular older women) and adolescents scored lowest on dialectical reasoning (Blanchard-Fields & Norris, 1994).

From these findings, it appears that older adults tend to make snap attributional judgments and do not engage in conscious, deliberate, well-thought-out causal analyses. Is it simply the case that older adults are deficient in their causal analysis of the situation, however, or are there other possible explanations for this finding? So that these questions can be answered, two other findings from the above research need to be considered. First, Blanchard-Fields and Norris (1994) found that age was not necessarily the best predictor of causal attributions. Instead, individual differences in trait measures of flexibility in thinking (i.e., tolerance for ambiguity, ego level) demonstrated greater variability in older adulthood. This, in turn, predicted dialectical causal explanations above and beyond the effect of age. Individual differences in attitudes and beliefs may help explain the conditions under which adults of varying ages and of different personological and developmental characteristics are likely to produce relativistic causal attributions.

Second, we have consistently found that the domain of the problem situation (i.e., achievement vs relationship situations) is important in determining whether age differences in dispositional attributions are found. Older adults are more likely to show a correspondence bias when making attributions for relationship vignettes with negative outcomes (e.g., divorce). In addition, age differences in attributions vary as a function of the specific type of situation within the domain (e.g., a situation involving divorce produced age differences, whereas a situation involving a father not spending enough time with his children did not [Blanchard-Fields, 1996]).

These two phenomena are consistent with an individual differences explanation of the age effects in dispositional attributions (i.e., the dispositional bias found with older adults). That is, we suggest that across all age groups, individuals differ in the extent to which the content of particular negative relationship vignettes may trigger automatic, rule-based social schemas and/or beliefs relevant to how an actor should behave in such situations (Blanchard-Fields, 1996; Chen & Blanchard-Fields, 1997). If specific social schemas were violated in a vignette, this might influence the extent to which we would observe a dispositional bias. Before pursuing this explanation further, I will contrast this schema-based explanation for the dispositional biases observed in older adults with a processing resource explanation.

PROCESSING RESOURCES AND ATTRIBUTIONAL PROCESSING

Current research in social cognition and aging suggests that both age-related variations in basic information processing mechanisms and knowledge-based mechanisms affect the processing of social information, which may in turn influence age differences in dispositional judgments (Blanchard-Fields, 1996; Chen & Blanchard-Fields, 1997; Hess, 1994). The mainstream social cognition literature provides a framework for examining these mechanisms in an aging population. For example, Gilbert and colleagues (e.g., Gilbert, Pelham, & Krull, 1988) advanced a sequential stage model of attributional processing: (1) categorization (e.g., identifying actions), (2) characterization of the action (i.e., trait-based and dispositional attributions), and (3) a correction procedure in which situational information is used to adjust for the initial dispositional attribution. Gilbert considered the first two stages to be relatively automatic and spontaneous but the correction procedure to require more effortful processing. Although there is no consensus on whether these stages are sequential or concurrent, category-based trait inferences appear to be made without awareness (though they are in principle controllable). It should be noted that there are other social cognitive processes that fall into the first two relatively automatic stages, such as stereotypes or schema activation (Gilbert & Malone, 1995). A number of studies do indicate that dispositional attributions are made more spontaneously because they require less effort and are more efficient than situational attributions (Gilbert, McNulty, Giuliano, & Benson, 1992; Lupfer, et al., 1990; Osborne & Gilbert, 1992). To demonstrate this phenomenon, Gilbert and colleagues contrasted individuals' dispositional judgments made under high cognitive load (i.e., a divided attention condition) with those made under low cognitive load (i.e., a full attention condition). It was assumed that in the high cognitive load condition individuals do not have the capacity to make an attributional correction and thus rely more heavily on their initial dispositional attribution. In fact, this is what Gilbert found (Gilbert et al., 1988) to be the case. Individuals in the high cognitive load condition made higher trait-based dispositional attributions when observing the behavior of another. Individuals in the low cognitive load condition appeared to correct this initial trait-based inference by taking into account situational constraints. Accordingly, they made lower trait-based dispositional attributions.

Whereas the social cognitive literature has manipulated cognitive capacity, aging research has treated it as an individual difference variable. There is a long history of research that has interpreted age-related declines in cognition as the reluctance or inability on the part of older adults to engage in high levels of cognitive effort when processing information (see Salthouse, 1996, for a recent review). Given the demands on cognitive resources for a correction or adjustment procedure, it may be the case that older adults rely more heavily on easily accessible dispositional judgments than do younger adults in making social judgments.

There are a number of studies in the literature that suggest that a processing approach can explain older adults' biases in social judgment. For example, Hess and colleagues found that older adults tend not to use newly presented trait information when forming impressions (Hess & Follett, 1994; Hess, Follett, & McGee, in press). Overall, they found that older adults fail to integrate novel and inconsistent behavioral or trait information into initial trait-based impressions of a target person. They suggest that retrieval and use of such information demand more processing effort. On the other hand, they found few age differences when adults processed evaluative information. For example, when descriptions contained evaluative information there were no age differences in the ability to abstract prototype information (see Hess, Chapter 11, this volume, for more details). Given that the social cognitive literature argues that evaluative information is more easily accessible (e.g., as in affective priming [Fazio, Sanbonmatsu, Powell, & Kardes, 1986]), this further supports the notion that more cognitively demanding presentations of information (such as a list of traits) pose more difficulty for older adults.

Overall, a processing perspective to understanding social judgment biases in older adults suggests that age-related decline in cognitive functioning limits the ability of older adults to override the impact of more easily accessible information. For example, Schwarz, Park, Knauper, Davidson, and Smith (1998) argued that it may not be the case that older adults become less traditional in their stereotypes but that because of processing constraints, they rely on them more heavily than do young adults, given that stereotypes are spontaneous and automatically accessed. I suggest that social information processing (i.e., making social judgments) is not sufficiently explained, however, by processing constraints identified in the cognitive aging literature (e.g., inhibition, speed, working memory). Although these mechanisms play a role in social information processing and are indeed necessary in an integrative theory of social cognition, they do not sufficiently explain our findings.

THE INFLUENCE OF ATTITUDES, VALUES, AND SOCIAL BELIEFS ON ATTRIBUTIONAL PROCESSING

Much like the work on expertise, such as Charness's work (1981, 1983, 1987) on memory for chessboard positions, processing capacity alone is not necessarily the best explanation of performance on the part of older adults. Ability to use expertise plays a central role. In the context of social cognition, knowledge or expertise must be more broadly defined to include attitudes, values, and social belief systems, along with other factors, such as motivations, goals, and emotions. If such factors are considered, it may not simply be the case that only older adults are more susceptible to the influence of easily accessible schema information; it may be that all age groups are if we can tap into their strong evaluative belief systems. Imagine a 20-year-old fundamentalist Christian who has been asked to make a trait judgment about a woman getting an abortion. An immediate negative trait-based dispositional attribution may *not* be corrected given extenuating, situational information, not because the young person lacks the cognitive resources to do so but because she lacks the desire or motivation to do so, given her belief system.

As noted earlier, I have consistently found that older adults make higher dispositional attribution ratings when explaining a negative outcome in relationship situations. This form of the correspondence bias suggests that it may be due to reduced cognitive resources to devote to elaborative thought concerning other causes. Thus, if age-related increases in capacity limitations impair elaborative cognition of older adults, one would predict that older adults would engage in more trait-based (i.e., dispositional) and schema-driven processing. Again, this should lead to the correspondence bias (e.g., Gilbert et al., 1988).

However, there are other rival explanations for older adults' higher dispositional ratings. First, it could be that there is limited motivation for elaborative processing on the part of the older adult. For example, if older adults would have positively identified with the main character, they might have actively inhibited emotion-laden automatic evaluative mechanisms and engaged in elaborative processing of alternative explanations for the negative outcomes. Second, dispositional biases may be a function of a particular personality or cognitive style. For example, Kruglanski (1990) found that individuals with a high need for structure are more likely to rely on spontaneous or immediate dispositional judgments than are individuals with a low need for structure. Finally, it may be the case that person and belief schemas were automatically activated during vignette comprehension, priming trait/dispositional information, as suggested earlier in this chapter. In this case, if strong emotional reactions are above threshold, elaborative processing will be inhibited and dispositional attributions are more likely (Epstein, Lipson, Holstein, & Huh, 1992). Under these rival hypotheses, older adults have sufficient processing capacity to engage in elaborative social information processing but do not do so in certain contexts because of overriding considerations as those listed above. Let us now turn to some empirical work addressing these alternative explanations for older adults' dispositional biases in social judgments.

AGE DIFFERENCES IN ATTRIBUTIONAL
PROCESSING: FURTHER EVIDENCE

Three initial studies examining age-related differences in social schemas evoked by the attributional paradigm vignettes and their relationship to dispositional attributions are discussed in this section. In the first study, we were interested in determining whether the findings from previous research (i.e., Blanchard-Fields, 1994; Blanchard-Fields & Norris, 1994) could be further explained in terms of age differences in evoked social schemas. In the second study, we pursued this notion further to examine both a processing resource and a social schema explanation for the dispositional bias. In the third study, we initiated a methodology to assess not only the content of one's social schemas but also the strength of the social schema for the particular individual. In other words, two individuals could agree with the social schema that "marriage comes before career," yet for one individual it is a strongly held belief that drives behavior and for the other it is less relevant to his or her daily life.

AGE DIFFERENCES IN SOCIAL SCHEMAS

We hypothesized that the dispositional bias found in older adults could be a function of a particular type of situation, such as a negative relationship situation, that might have triggered relatively automatic trait and rule-based schemas relevant to the actor in the problem situation. Social schemas are easily accessible knowledge structures that consist of a set of interrelated propositions (including rules on how to operate in particular social situations, traits, and attributes) about categories of self, other, or events. They can reflect individualized and normative (i.e., to a particular society or culture) goals and rule systems that guide decision making, problem solving, and problem interpretation.

In the context of our earlier work, we believed that it was the case that generational differences in the content and accessibility of relationship schemas contributed to the higher dispositional ratings of older persons, relative to middle-aged and younger adults. In an initial attempt to explore this hypothesis, we conducted post hoc content analyses on our original qualitative data. These qualitative protocols contained written justifications for attributional ratings made by each of the participants. From the written justifications, we were able to extract social schemas, which appeared to be evoked as a function of the value-laden content of several of the negative relationship vignettes (Blanchard-Fields, 1996). An example of a social schema is "Marriage comes before one's career." In this case, older adults and adolescents produced this schema more often than did young and middle-aged adults (Blanchard-Fields, 1996). The social schemas might have been particularly salient for older cohorts, given their years of accumulated experience, stage in life, and the particular cohort in which they were socialized, and might have triggered a different orientation and approach to the task for older compared to young adults. Furthermore, previous work on aging suggests that the relationship between information schemas and judgments is particularly great in older adults (Hess, 1994; see Hess, Chapter 11, this volume).

In a recent study, we probed further the hypothesis that older adults' propensity to make more dispositional attributions than do younger age groups is connected to social schemas that are evoked by reading the social dilemma vignettes (Blanchard-Fields, Chen, Schocke, & Hertzog, in press). First, young, middle-aged, and older adults made causal attribution ratings (dispositional, situational, interactive) for 12 vignettes representing both relationship and achievement situations (similar to the method already described in earlier work). Second, the qualitative analysis used by Blanchard-Fields and Norris (1994), described earlier, was used to assess the degree to which participants used dialectical reasoning in their written explanations of their attribution ratings. Finally, a second qualitative analysis of these written protocols was used to extract social schemas from the written justifications. Consistent with previous findings, older adults made greater dispositional attribution ratings (i.e., blaming the main character for the negative outcome) than did younger age groups.

Of particular interest, however, is the qualitative assessment of social schemas evoked by the problem situations. First, similar to the post hoc analysis just described (Blanchard-Fields, 1996), we extracted the social schemas embedded in the written explanations of participants for each of the vignettes. To perform the content analysis of these schemas, we first segmented each essay protocol into statement units that reflected different types of social rules used to explain the negative outcome. For each of the vignettes, distinct types of social schema statements elicited across age groups were recorded. Number of statements per vignette ranged from 10 to 17. To determine the extent to which there were age and gender differences in the type of attribution/schema statement made, a log linear analysis was conducted on statements that were elicited by at least 10% of the participants across age groups. Age and/or gender differences were found for attributional statements for 8 of the 12 vignettes.

For example, let us examine the following vignette:

> Margie and Amanda have been good friends for 7 years. Margie started seeing Brad and spending less time with Amanda. Amanda warned Margie that if she didn't make time to see Amanda more frequently, their friendship would be at risk. Margie continued to neglect Amanda, and the friendship ended.

Five statements extracted from this vignette reflected a minimum of 10% responses from our sample and thus were analyzed. Each of these five statements yielded significant age effects. For example, for the statements "Margie should not take her friendship with Amanda for granted" and "One should not take friendships for granted," young adults generated significantly more of these statements (50%) than did middle-aged (31%) or older adults (20%). Young adults also generated the statement "Amanda didn't understand Margie's situation" significantly more often (36%) than did middle-aged (13%) or older adults (8%). By contrast, the statements "The friendship wasn't that strong to start with" and "A strong friendship can weather any storm" yielded different age effects. Older adults generated these statements more often (25%) than did young adults (4%), with middle-aged adults in the middle (21%). The theme of "One should talk things out" or "Drifting apart is a natural process" showed up significantly more often in older adults' protocols. These "interactive" statements (as opposed to blaming Margie or Amanda) correspond well with the increase in interactive attributional ratings on the part of older adults.

Second, this study examined profiles of individuals with qualitatively different patterns of social schemas and the degree to which these social schema patterns relate to dispositional attribution ratings. For this analysis, each of the extracted schema statements just described was categorized as dispositional target (having to do with the main character in the story), dispositional other (having to do with other characters in the story), situational (having to do with factors in the story outside of the characters), and interactive (involving both the main character and other factors). Ratios were computed for each category indicating the degree to which each individual produced a specific type of social schema statement (e.g., dispositional target) relative to the total number of statements that the individual produced.

Next, we computed correlations between the dispositional ratings (rating scale scores) and the ratios of dispositional target and dispositional other. Overall, we found that individuals' ratios of dispositional target social schemas and dispositional other social schemas were significantly correlated with their dispositional ratings. The mean correlation between dispositional ratings and ratios of dispositional target was significant for relationship situations (.32) and nonsignificant for achievement situations (.16). The mean correlation between dispositional ratings and ratios of dispositional other was significant for relationship situations (–.26) and nonsignificant for achievement situations (–.10). Thus, there were positive significant relationships between dispositional target schemas and dispositional ratings, and significant negative relationships between dispositional other schemas and dispositional ratings, for relationship situations only. In other words, in the relationship domain, there were individual differences in whether people held the main character or other characters involved responsible for the outcomes. Accordingly, the focus of an individual's social schemas related to a specific character was associated with high dispositional ratings for that character. In addition, this pattern applied to relationship situations and not achievement situations.

However, this analysis does not tell the complete story about the relationship between social schemas and ratings. We conducted a cluster analysis to identify underlying qualitative differences in patterns of the content of social schemas. We also examined the relationship between these social schema patterns and attributional ratings. For example, consider the vignette in which the boss overheard Marcia (the main character) talking on the phone to her coworker and friend Amy (another character). Amy had called in sick to work because she had stayed out too late at a party the previous night. One cluster of individuals, who focused their statements on the main character, Marcia shared a common social rule: "Don't talk about personal matters at work." By contrast, individuals in a second cluster focused on the other character, Amy. This cluster produced the social rule "You should be responsible in your job." Individuals in a third cluster focused on both characters and stated that "When two people are involved in a problem, both are always responsible for the outcome—that is, it takes two to tango." If the cluster analysis provides a valid classification of individuals, then we would expect to find cluster differences in both dispositional ratings and dialectical reasoning scores. That is, to the extent that individuals focus exclusively on one character and blame her or him for violating a certain social rule, they ought to make high dispositional ratings if the main character violated the rule and low dispositional ratings if the other character did. In addition, to the extent that individuals focus on more than one character, then they should be more likely to produce higher dialectical reasoning scores. (High dialectical scores reflect a consideration of the role both characters play in producing the negative outcome.) Analyses examining the relationship of cluster membership to both the dispositional ratings and the dialectical reasoning scores conducted across all relationship vignettes supported this hypothesis. For example, the cluster that focused on the main character, Marcia, was significantly higher on dispositional ratings than the cluster that focused on the other character, Amy. The third cluster was in the middle but was the highest in dialectical reasoning scores. These differentiated patterns of cluster responses were replicated across all vignettes.

In sum, it appears that there are age and cohort differences in the accessibility of strong relationship schemas related to specific social dilemmas, and they appear to be related to dispositional attributions. Qualitatively different clusters of individuals were clearly identified who produced varying patterns social rules about relationship situations. In turn, these clusters of persons systematically differed in the degree to which a dispositional attribution rating was made about characters in the relationship situations. There was a tendency to focus blame on the character that violated a sanctioned social rule: either the main character or another character involved in the relationship dilemma.

There are limitations to this study, however. We did not directly elicit social schemas. Instead, social schemas were inferred from the written statements participants produced to justify their attributional ratings. In addition, we did not examine the strength of the schemas associated with specific vignettes. Thus, we can only infer that differential attributions are made as a function of the type and strength of the schema elicitation associated with a particular problem situation. We began to remedy this problem in the next two studies.

STAGES OF ATTRIBUTIONAL PROCESSING
AND SCHEMAS

In a study by Chen and Blanchard-Fields (1997), we asked the following question: would older adults engage in a correction procedure if they were given more time? Increased time would provide fewer cognitive processing demands and produce higher dispositional attributions. Alternatively, would social schemas or beliefs about a certain type of person or event presented in a vignette result in less correction, again resulting in a higher degree of dispositional attributions?

In this study, we again presented vignettes similar in structure as those already described (Blanchard-Fields, 1994; Blanchard-Fields & Norris, 1994). However, all vignettes represented an uncertain level of ambiguity, had a negative outcome, and were categorized within a romantic relationship domain. It should be noted that within each vignette there were a number of representative social schemas or rules about what is appropriate social behavior in the specific type of situation. The main character and/or other characters violated the social rules or schemas. Thus, we could explore whether the negative affect related to a violated social belief or schema is activated for older adults (as well as for younger adults). In that case, they may attribute more causality to the main character. Alternatively, can older adults adjust their dispositional attribution, given other information provided in the vignette (i.e., Gilbert's correction stage)? A sample vignette follows:

> Allen had been dating Barbara for over a year. At Barbara's suggestion, they moved in together. Everyone kept asking when they were getting married. Allen found it extremely uncomfortable to live with Barbara and not be married to her. Even though Barbara disagreed, Allen kept bringing up the issue of marriage. Eventually, they broke up.

We directly measured a correction stage that was differentiated from the dispositional inference stage and compared performance of younger and older adults. We assessed the correction stage by including the following conditions. First, participants read vignettes and answered comprehension questions to calculate reading speed. Vignettes for the study were presented to each individual on a computer at their own reading speed rate. We assessed the correction stage by including the following conditions. In Condition 1, participants made a causal dispositional rating immediately after they finished reading a vignette. In Condition 2, they had a 30-second delay after reading the vignette before making the rating. For the delayed period, it was expected that if given enough time, participants would not make a strong dispositional attribution (i.e., holding the main character responsible for the outcome of the problem situation) but would engage in a correction procedure that takes into consideration situational information.

We found that older adults made higher dispositional ratings than did young adults in the immediate rating condition only (Figure 10.1). Older adults made fewer dispositional attributions (i.e., corrected more) if they were given more time to think about the situations than in the immediate judgment condition. In addition, there was a slight tendency for younger adults to increase their dispositional attributions given more time. These findings address the processing issue in that if given more time, older adults will adjust their attributions. However, it should be noted that we could only infer this, given that it was a between-subjects

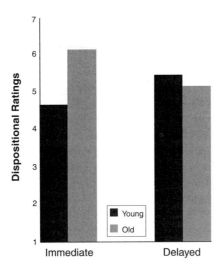

FIGURE 10.1   Dispositional ratings as a function of age group and condition. (Copyright ©
1997 by the American Psychological Association. Adapted with permission.)

design. These findings also suggest that "correction" does not always work in the
same way (i.e., correcting for dispositional attributions). As seen in younger
adults, it is more of an adjustment that can occur in the direction of higher dispositional or situational attributions (Krull, 1993).

However, this is not the complete story. In this study, we also assessed social
schemas that were evoked as a function of the different vignettes. Thus, in addition to the on-line rating assessment of dispositional attributions, we asked participants to write brief essays revealing the main theme they perceived in each
vignette. We were interested in whether age-related differences in attributional
processing were related to age-related differences in social schemas. First, in the
immediate condition, older adults made more social schemas than young adults
did in the form of evaluative rule statements about the main character in the
immediate rating condition. For example, in the Allen and Barbara vignette, Allen
was seen as "more obligated to society's morality, so he felt uncomfortable living
with Barbara and not being married!"

Second, high dispositional attributional ratings were correlated with
social/evaluative schema statements about the main character. Finally, and most
important, we found that age-related differences in schematic beliefs about the
relationship dilemmas accounted for age differences in dispositional biases. In
other words, the ratio of content-evoked social schema/evaluative rule statements
about the main character mediated the relationship between age and dispositional
ratings about the main character in the immediate rating condition. Overall, it
may be the case that people will correct their initial attributions only to the extent
that their values and beliefs and the characteristics of the task (time constraints)
provide the motivational goals to do so.

AGE DIFFERENCES IN SCHEMATICITY

The above two studies are limited in that they both extracted social schemas and beliefs post hoc to the attribution task. In an ongoing study that I am conducting in collaboration with Christopher Hertzog, we are assessing preexisting belief systems and their affect on causal attributions in young, middle-aged, and older adults. One of the major problems in past work on age differences in stereotypes, social knowledge, and social schemas is that the major focus has been on content only and how these content differences influence social information processing. We argue that age differences in the content of the schemas do not tell the whole story. It may be the strength of the social belief systems that determines when and how accessible social schemas will influence social judgment and behavior.

We have identified sets of social schemas related to particular vignettes in various everyday domains (e.g., relationship, friendship, health, and family). Each has a specific content-related theme, such as the one found in the Allen and Barbara vignette already described: "One should not cohabitate before marriage." Again, within each vignette, a character in the story violated a schema like this one. We have developed not only a method to assess whether individuals of differing ages agree or disagree with these sets of schemas but also a reaction time method to assess the strength of the schema, or "schematicity." In addition to a "schematicity" assessment (agree/disagree and strength), we are administering individual difference measures of cognitive style and values and beliefs (e.g., intolerance for ambiguity, need for closure, family values, gender roles). Individuals may not correct their initial social judgments unless their personal styles afford such a correction. Recall that Kruglanski (1990) demonstrated that high need for closure is associated with less correction. Finally, we are assessing working memory. After this initial assessment, participants are brought back 4–5 months later for a causal attribution assessment (i.e., causal attributions—dispositional, blame, responsibility) for vignettes related to the social schemas previously assessed. In this way, we can directly contrast the potential explanations for age differences in the correspondence bias. The overall hypothesis is that social schematicity (content and strength) will be the prepotent predictor of the correspondence bias in social vignettes. It will mediate the effects of variables such as religiosity while predicting dispositional attributions independently of working memory and constructs such as need for closure. More specifically, we are seeking to determine whether individuals overestimate dispositional-type attributions and do not correct because

1. A particular social behavior is inconsistent with their beliefs/values (both in content and strength) to overcome the predisposition to adjust initial judgments (Gilbert et al., 1988)
2. A particular social behavior is inconsistent enough with their cognitive style to overcome a predisposition to adjust their initial judgments
3. Working memory, as a measure of cognitive capacity, influences whether they can adjust their initial judgments.

We expect that explanations suggesting that the individual does not take information stored in memory into account to correct her or his initial judgment because of the processing demands of the task (i.e., a resource limit view) will not account for age differences in dispositional biases. This processing view suggests that values and beliefs do not interfere with the motivation to produce an accurate response. Preliminary evidence suggests that this is not so. This suggests that a premature cognitive commitment to a resource deficit interpretation when other viable interpretations are available is risky. We need more research that explicitly compares and contrasts processing resource explanations with knowledge-based and motivational explanations. This is not yet evident in the literature.

SUMMARY AND CONCLUSIONS

In this chapter, I began by presenting some puzzling findings with respect to an adult developmental perspective on changes in attributional processing. Instead of finding that older adults were more post-formal in that they were more relativistic and dialectical in the types of attributions they made, my colleagues and I found that they displayed a dispositional bias. The purpose of our ongoing program of research is to reveal possible explanations for these findings. If we go back to the original finding that older adults (women in particular) are more predisposed to specific schematic beliefs when reading specific negatively valenced relationship vignettes, we should be able to identify the beliefs and the strength of activation. If so, we can predict when these older adults will and when they will not be prone to a dispositional bias. To accomplish this goal, we bring both social cognitive theory and a life-span developmental perspective to bear on this problem. Cognitively mature responding is difficult to demonstrate, as illustrated in the post-formal literature (Labouvie-Vief, 1992; Baltes & Smith, 1990). In addition, a major problem in past research assessing problem interpretations and styles in real-world dilemmas is that the strategies and interpretations appear to be driven by the content variation in the different problem situations presented. The context specificity of responding makes it difficult to assess systematic age differences in attributional processing, for example. A differential approach may help identify conditions under which adults of different ages and different schematic beliefs are likely to engage in elaborative reasoning and relativistic forms of causal attributions and when they are not. By further developing methods of measuring age and or cohort differences in schematicity, we can examine more complex social judgment processes, such as attributions and everyday problem solving. Age/cohort and other individual differences in attitudes, beliefs, and social knowledge representation should particularly affect these processes.

This research approach also shows how a developmental perspective to the study of causal attributions expands on the generic rules advanced by mainstream social cognition in predicting the correspondence bias. For example, although level of ambiguity was validly reflected in the vignettes used in the above research, individual vignettes did not behave consistently. Whereas the generic rules of attribution theory tend to be context free in their application, our approach suggests that a closer examination of the content of the target problem situation is warranted.

Finally, I have highlighted the importance of considering social factors in explanations of social cognitive functioning. Such factors as schematic beliefs and values, stereotypes, and motivational goals, among others, influence social information processing in important ways. Thus, it is important not to limit our explanations of social cognitive change to cognitive processing variables even though seasoned with a social flavor. There are important social factors influencing how and when an individual will attend to specific information and when this information will influence social cognitive functioning. These factors include those I listed earlier: motivational goals, cognitive style, attitudes, and values. It is hoped that the quality and subtlety of our ideas will be limited only by our processing resources and not co-opted by our preexisting beliefs and values.

ACKNOWLEDGMENTS

Support for the research reported in this chapter was provided by National Institute on Aging (NIA) research grant AG-7607 awarded to Fredda Blanchard-Fields. Address correspondence to Fredda Blanchard-Fields, School of Psychology, Georgia Institute of Technology, Atlanta, GA 30332-0170; e-mail: fb12@ prism.gatech.edu.

REFERENCES

Baltes, P. B., & Smith, J. (1990). Toward a psychology of wisdom and its ontogenesis. In R. J. Sternberg (Ed.), *Wisdom: Its nature, origins, and development.* New York: Cambridge University Press.

Blanchard-Fields, F. (1986). Reasoning in adolescents and adults on social dilemmas varying in emotional saliency. *Psychology and Aging, 1,* 325–333.

Blanchard-Fields, F. (1994). Age differences in causal attributions from an adult developmental perspective. *Journal of Gerontology: Psychological Sciences, 49,* 43–51.

Blanchard-Fields, F. (1996). Causal attributions across the adult life span: The influence of social schemas, life context, and domain specificity. *Applied Cognitive Psychology, 10,* 431.1–10.

Blanchard-Fields, F., & Abeles, R. P. (1996). Social cognition and aging. In J. E. Birren & K. W. Schaie (Eds.), *Handbook of psychology and aging* (4th ed., pp.) San Diego: Academic Press.

Blanchard-Fields, F., & Norris, L. (1994). Causal attributions from adolescence through adulthood: Age differences, ego level, and generalized response style. *Aging and Cognition, 1,* 67–86.

Blanchard-Fields, F., Chen, Y., Schocke, M., & Hertzog, C. (in press). Evidence for content-specificity of causal attributions across the adult life span. *Aging, Neuropsychology, and Cognition.*

Blank, T. O. (1987). Attributions as dynamic elements in a lifespan social psychology. In R. P. Abeles (Ed.), *Life-span perspectives and social psychology.* Hillsdale, NJ: Lawrence Erlbaum Associates.

Charness, N. (1981). Aging and skilled problem solving. *Journal of Experimental Psychology: General, 110,* 21–38.

Charness, N. (1983). Age, skill, and bridge bidding: A chronometric analysis. *Journal of Verbal Learning and Verbal Behavior, 22,* 406–416.

Charness, N. (1987). Component processes in bridge bidding and novel problem-solving tasks. *Canadian Journal of Psychology, 41,* 223–243.

Chen, Y., & Blanchard-Fields, F. (1997). Age differences in stages of attributional processing. *Psychology and Aging,* 694–703.

Epstein, S., Lipson, A., Holstein, C., & Huh, E. (1992). *Journal of Personality and Social Psychology, 62,* 328–339.

Fazio, R. H., Sanbonmatsu, D. M., Powell, M. C., & Kardes, F. R. (1986). On the automatic activation of attitudes. *Journal of Personality and Social Psychology, 50,* 229–238.

Fiske, S. (1993). Social cognition and social perception. *Annual Review of Psychology, 44,* 155–194.

Fiske, S. T., & Neuberg, S. L. (1990). A continuum of impression formation, from category-based to individuating processes: Influences of information and motivation on attention and interpretation. In M. P. Zanna (Ed.), *Advances in experimental social psychology,* (vol. 23, pp. 1–74). New York: Academic Press.

Fiske, S., & Taylor, S. (1991). *Social Cognition.* New York: McGraw-Hill.

Gilbert, D. T., & Malone, P. S. (1995). The correspondence bias. *Psychological Bulletin, 117,* 21–38.

Gilbert, D. T., McNulty, S. E., Giuliano, T. A., & Benson, J. E. (1992). Blurry words and fuzzy deeds: The attribution of obscure behavior. *Journal of Personality and Social Psychology, 62,* 18–25.

Gilbert, D. T., Pelham, B. W., Krull, D. S. (1988). On cognitive busyness: When person perceivers meet persons perceived. *Journal of Personality and Social Psychology, 54,* 733–740.

Gilbert, D. T., Tafarodi, R. W., & Malone, P. S. (1993). You can't not believe everything you read. *Journal of Personality and Social Psychology, 65,* 221–233.

Hess, T. M. (1994). Social cognition in adulthood: Age-related changes in knowledge and processing mechanisms. *Developmental Review, 14,* 373–412.

Hess, T. M., & Follett, K. J. (1994). Adult age differences in the use of schematic and episodic information in making social judgments. *Aging and Cognition, 1,* 54–66.

Hess, T., Follett, K., & McGee, K. (in press). Aging and impression formation: The impact of processing skills and goals. *Journal of Gerontology: Psychological Sciences.*

Kruglanski, A. W. (1990). Motivations for judging and knowing: Implications for causal attribution. In E. T. Higgins & R. M. Sorrentino (Eds.), *Handbook of motivation and cognition: Foundation of social behavior* (vol. 2, pp. 333–368). New York: Guilford Press.

Krull, D. S. (1993). Does the grist change the mill? The effect of the perceiver's inferential goal on the process of social inference. *Personality and Social Psychology Bulletin, 19,* 340–348.

Labouvie-Vief, G. (1992). A neo-Piagetian perspective on adult cognitive development. In R. J. Sternberg and C. A. Berg (Eds.), *Intellectual development* pp. 52–86. New York. Cambridge University Press.

Lupfer, M. B., Clark, J. F., Hutcherson, H. W. (1990). Impact of context on spontaneous trait and situational attributions. *Journal of Personality and Social Psychology, 58,* 239–249.

Osborne, R. E. & Gilbert, D. T. (1992). The preoccupational hazards of social life. *Journal of Personality and Social Psychology, 62,* 219–228.

Ross, L., & Nisbett, R. E. (1991). *The person and the situation: Perspectives of social psychology.* New York: McGraw-Hill.

Salthouse, T. A. (1996). The processing speed theory of adult age differences in cognition. *Psychological Review, 103,* 403–428.

Schneider, D. J. (1991). Social cognition. *Annual Review of Psychology, 42,* 527–561.

Schwarz, N., Park, D., Knauper, B., Davidson, N., & Smith, P. (1998, April). Aging, cognition, and self-reports: Age-dependent context effects and misleading conclusions about age differences in attitudes and behavior. Paper presented at the Bi-Annual Cognitive Aging Conference, Atlanta.

Sears, D. O. (1987). Implication of life-span approach for research on attitudes and social cognition. In R. P. Abeles (Ed.), *Life-span perspectives and social psychology,* pp. 17–60. Hillsdale, NJ: Lawrence Erlbaum Associates.

Skowronski, J. J., & Carlston, D. E. (1989). Negativity and extremity biases in impression formation: A review of explanations. *Psychological Bulletin, 105,* 131–142.

Staudinger, U. M., Smith, J., & Baltes, P. B. (1992). Wisdom-related knowledge in a life review task: Age differences and the role of professional specialization. *Psychology and Aging, 7,* 271–281.

Trope, Y. (1986). Identification and inferential processes in dispositional attribution. *Psychological Review, 93,* 239–257.

11

COGNITIVE AND KNOWLEDGE-BASED INFLUENCES ON SOCIAL REPRESENTATIONS

THOMAS M. HESS

Department of Psychology
North Carolina State University
Raleigh, North Carolina

> *Prosecutor:* *"Doctor, can you give the court your impression of Mr. Striker?"*
>
> *Witness:* *"I'm sorry. I don't do impressions. My training is in psychiatry."*
>
> *—from the movie Airplane II, The Sequel*

Contrary to the punchline, we all "do" impressions. When we encounter someone within the context of everyday life, we create a mental representation of that person. The process associated with formation of this representation may be rather simple, as when a single, easily perceived characteristic (e.g., dark skin) is used to align someone with an existing schematic structure (e.g., a stereotype of African Americans). In other cases, the process may be relatively complex, reflecting an integration of specific physical and behavioral features into a relatively unique structure. The representation that we construct about another guides our social interactions in that it forms the basis for inferences about the person's likes and dislikes, the motives behind past actions, and the direction of future behaviors. Thus, at an intuitive level, more accurate representations should be associated with better understanding of the individual and hence more successful interactions with him or her. In other words, representations have consequences for our adaptation to the social world.

In this spirit, a primary focus of work in social cognition has to do with the study of such mental representations, including their formation, structure, modification, and use. This interest is based not only on the just-described common-sense relationship with social functioning but also on the assumption that our impressions of others reflect the cognitive processing underlying social interactions. By examining the cognitive underpinnings of impression formation, we can understand not only how individuals achieve accurate representations of the social world but also the factors that result in less than optimal representations. To accomplish these goals, we must understand how the information-processing system operates in social situations. Obviously, the nature of any representation has something to say about the complexity of the cognitive operations involved in its construction, as well as the efficiency with which those operations are performed, but an understanding of impression formation is more than an extension of current models of information processing to the social realm. For example, although accuracy may reflect the use of efficient information-processing mechanisms, inaccuracies do not necessarily reflect inefficient processing. In fact, they may in some respects reflect overly efficient, top-down processing that is inappropriately applied (e.g., through automatic schema activation) or biased toward achieving a specific goal. Implicit in the social cognitive approach is the notion that the past experience and goals of the perceiver as well as specific situational factors also influence the operation of the information-processing system. This emphasis on the "hot" aspects of cognition (e.g., goals, motivation) distinguishes it from the "cold" approach typical of many studies of cognition, in which the primary interest is in understanding the mechanics of the system.

An understanding of representational processes within social contexts is critical in examining developmental processes across the life span. If we accept the notion that representations have real-world consequences in social situations, then these representations should provide us with a window that allows an examination of how individuals adapt to specific social contexts at different points in the life span. For example, the increased experience in the social world that accompanies the process of aging could result in more sophisticated theories regarding the trait implications associated with specific behaviors. Age differences in the nature and operation of such theories could then be identified through the examination of the differential emphasis given to specific types of information in the construction of representations and judgments about a person. At the same time, a developmental focus also requires an understanding of age-related constraints on social information processing that may reflect developing or deteriorating cognitive systems. For example, examinations of the limitations imposed by aging-related reductions in working memory functions may enable us to better understand problems that arise for older adults in social contexts.

Despite the important implications of such a developmental focus, however, research on representational processes has been largely restricted to the study of young adults in the mainstream social cognition literature. This may reflect the belief that aging-related changes simply mimic those of specific experimental manipulations and that the mechanisms underlying representational processes do not change in any fundamental way. Unfortunately, the absence of aging research does not allow an evaluation of this viewpoint, limiting external validity of models developed with young adults (Blank, 1987; Sears, 1987). The focus on young adulthood also does not allow us to understand how changes in life circumstances influence the operation of social cognitive models, limiting their usefulness for understanding developmental changes in adaptational processes. Finally, if existing models lack external validity, research on aging could contribute to model construction in a meaningful way by identifying mechanisms that may emerge only with development and thus are ignored in studies of young adults.

A GENERAL FRAMEWORK FOR UNDERSTANDING AGING AND REPRESENTATIONAL PROCESSES

How might the nature of impression formation change with aging, and what might account for these changes? In an initial attempt to deal with these questions, I proposed a simple conceptual framework (Hess, 1994) that attempted to capture the multidimensional/multidirectional nature of aging-related influences on representational processes. The framework uses prototypical features of existing models of impression formation (e.g., Brewer, 1988; Fiske & Neuberg, 1990; Hilton & Darley, 1991) as a starting point for understanding potential aging effects. Within these models, it is generally agreed that individuals use different types of operations across situations in constructing representations. These operations can be divided into two general categories: category-based and piecemeal processing (see also Asch, 1946). In the former case, impressions are based in simple categorization processes whereby the target person is identified as a member of a specific category (e.g., college professor), and the attributes associated with the category (e.g., scholarly, absentminded) as well as corresponding affective associations are then attributed to the target. In contrast, piecemeal processing is more of a bottom-up process, in which the perceiver attempts to construct a unique representation for the target by attending to and integrating individual pieces of information (e.g., physical characteristics, observed behaviors).

One general characteristic that distinguishes between these two types of operations relates to the cognitive resources necessary for their performance. Categorization is thought to occur in a relatively effortless and spontaneous fashion, placing few demands on processing resources. Piecemeal processing, however, is assumed to require more cognitive resources, owing to the active, self-initiated processing associated with construction of the impression. A simple extrapolation based on these different resource requirements suggests that individual differences in cognitive resources (e.g., working memory capacity) should be related to the type of processing operations used, and there is some rudimentary evidence that this is so (Conway, Carroll, Pushkar, Arbuckle, & Foisy, 1996). Differential cognitive resource demands associated with the two types of processing are also implicated by studies examining competing demands on resources. When situational constraints (e.g., time, mental fatigue, secondary tasks) limit the amount of resources available for processing, individuals are likely to engage in simple, relatively undemanding category-based processing (e.g., Kruglanski & Freund, 1983; Srull, Lichtenstein, & Rothbart, 1985; Webster, Richter, & Kruglanski, 1996). Piecemeal processing is more likely (although not always observed) under conditions in which external resource demands are minimal.

Cognitive resource availability and/or demands, however, are not the sole determinants of impression formation. The operations used in constructing representations also can be affected by the goals of the perceiver and the knowledge that he or she brings to the situation. Even if cognitive resources are sufficient for using piecemeal processing, models of impression formation assume that the willingness to engage these resources is dependent on the goals of the perceiver. If accuracy in representation is of high importance, then the perceiver will be more motivated to use piecemeal processing, particularly if initial attempts at category-based processing prove inadequate in characterizing the target (e.g., Neuberg, 1989; Srull et al., 1985; Thompson, Roman, Moskowitz, Chaiken, & Bargh, 1994). Perceiver goals are also associated with the activation of specific knowledge structures in memory, thereby leading to heightened accessibility of these structures. This can influence impressions in terms of the information on which they are based (e.g., Bargh & Pratto, 1986; Bargh, Bond, Lombardi, & Tota, 1986). For example, someone with strong beliefs regarding the importance of honesty in determining the character of others will tend to use that trait dimension to characterize a behavior that might otherwise be interpreted in a number of different ways. Accessibility could also influence the probability of engaging in piecemeal processing, depending on the goodness of fit between those accessible structures and the observable characteristics of the target.

Using this characterization of the impression formation process, my conceptual framework (Hess, 1994) identified two specific types of aging-related influences, which were termed *processing* and *knowledge-based*. The processing component relates to both (1) the types (e.g., complexity) of operations used, which is associated with available resources, and (2) the efficiency of these operations. Research suggests that cognitive aging may have an impact on both these aspects of processing. Many conceptions of cognitive change in adulthood center around an aging-related reduction in processing resources (see Salthouse, 1988), which is thought to limit the initiation of specific operations and the complexity of these operations. These resource limitations are often conceptualized in terms of constraints on working memory functions. Other views also center on working memory but suggest that aging may limit the efficiency with which specific functions (e.g., inhibition of extraneous thoughts, speed of processing) are carried out (e.g., Mackay & Burke, 1990; Salthouse, 1997; Zacks & Hasher, 1994). Although somewhat different in focus, both conceptions lead to the straightforward prediction that normative age differences in working memory processes should have an impact on the processing component of impression formation. Thus, for example, increasing age in adulthood should be associated with less use of piecemeal processing and a decrease in the efficiency with which it is carried out.

Recent work on the construction of mental models provides some evidence for the just-described negative impact of aging on representational processes. Mental models are representations of specific situations that are constructed by individuals to reflect their current level of understanding (Johnson-Laird, 1983). They represent an integration of the elements within these contexts with general knowledge about the world, resulting in a coherent, conceptual representation that is independent of the specific surface structure of incoming information. Such models are useful because they allow one to make inferences and predictions regarding specific events that occur within these contexts, thereby facilitating comprehension of and adaptation to one's environment. Examinations of aging and mental model construction suggest that age differences in working memory (i.e., resource limitations) and inhibitory functions (i.e., operational efficiency) have a negative effect on the ability to construct, update, and access mental models (e.g., Gerard, Zacks, Hasher, & Radvansky, 1991; Morrow, Leirer, & Altieri, 1992; Radvansky, Zacks, & Hasher, 1990). If impressions are thought of as situational models that perceivers create on the basis of the specific behaviors and characteristics of a target person and of the inferences associated with such information (e.g., Wyer & Srull, 1989), aging-related problems similar to those observed with mental model construction should be expected in the creation of "person models."

The second component of potential age-related influence on impression formation was characterized as factors that have their impact in terms of the experience and knowledge base, broadly defined, that an individual brings to a given social situation. In contrast to the aging-related effects associated with processing components, such factors may be associated with an increase in the accuracy of representations with age. For example, the accumulation of experience in the social world that accompanies aging could lead to well-elaborated theories of trait-behavior relations, affecting the interpretation of the behavior of others. These, in turn, could facilitate the adaptational outcomes of impressions to the extent that they lead to more accurate inferences about others. Developmental forces may also have an impact on the nature of representation because of changes that reflect adaptations to the social world rather than increased proficiency. For example, transitions through age-related roles might alter one's interactional goals (e.g., Carstensen, 1991), which in turn may influence the construction of representations as individuals judge the relevance of specific social situations in relation to these goals and make decisions about the allocation of cognitive resources. Goals may also affect the activation of, and automaticity of application associated with, specific knowledge structures that subsequently organize incoming information. As noted before, research in impression formation (e.g., Bargh et al., 1986; Sedikides, 1990) has noted the importance of the perceiver's chronic and situational goals as well as associated chronically and temporally accessible knowledge structures in determining what information is attended to and how the information is incorporated into one's impression. Developmental changes in goals might affect the accuracy with which we form representations because of qualitative changes in the ways in which we process social information. Thus, to the extent that age in adulthood is systematically related to goals and/or available and accessible knowledge, age differences should also be expected in the construction of mental models representing others.

In the original conceptualization of this framework, no crossover was depicted between the processing and knowledge-based sources of age-related variation. This implies that goal-based effects on processing operations operate independently (or at least have independent effects) from resource-based factors. It is clear, however, that resources will be tied to the impact of goals on performance. Specifically, goal-based effects related to processing complexity are associated with the amount of resources that are available. For example, individuals use simpler operations and consider fewer pieces of information when processing capacity is limited by the amount of time available, by performance of a concurrent task, or by level of energy (e.g., Kruglanski & Freund, 1983; Webster et al., 1996). Thus, even if an individual's goals are consistent with a more piecemeal approach to mental model construction, the ability to create such a representation is limited by available resources (see also Bar-Tal, Kishon-Rabin, & Tabak, 1997). This further suggests that to the extent that goals lead to rather than are reflective of specific types of processing, some older adults may be limited in their ability to take advantage of their motivation because of working memory limitations. This would lead to the more complete characterization of age effects presented in Figure 11.1, in which processing resources are not only influenced by goals but also affect goals.

In our research on impression formation and person memory, my colleagues and I have attempted to elucidate the mechanisms underlying age differences in performance using this simple conceptualization of age effects as a guide. In the next two sections, I discuss the results of several studies that my colleagues and I have conducted. The emphasis in this discussion is on identifying age-related differences in performance associated with (1) processing mechanisms and (2) knowledge-based factors, such as goals and construct accessibility.

COGNITIVE CONSTRAINTS ON REPRESENTATION

On the basis of existing theory and research in cognitive aging, my colleagues and I have hypothesized that social representational processes will be most affected by aging-related changes in the efficiency of working memory functions.

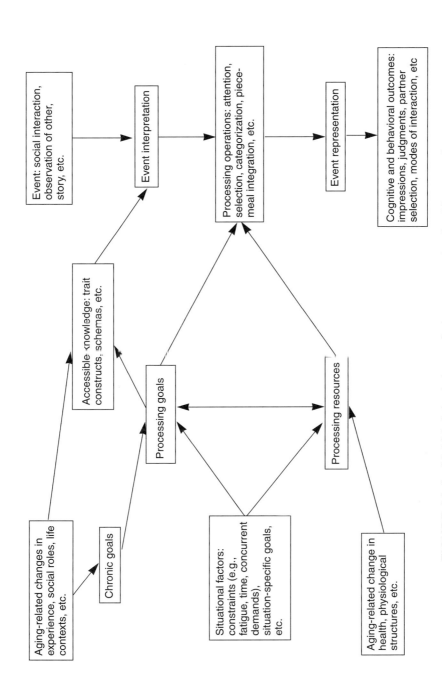

FIGURE 11.1   Model depicting the impact of aging on construction of social representations.

There is substantial research that suggests a decline in functions associated with working memory with increasing age in adulthood, and most models of impression formation assume that working memory functions play an important role in the construction of representations. Although several mechanisms have been proposed to account for such age-related changes (e.g., Craik, 1986; Salthouse, 1997; Zacks & Hasher, 1994), we have focused more on the form that such changes take in terms of specific behaviors. In doing so, we have adopted a position similar to that of Bargh (1994) by using the distinction between automatic and controlled processing mechanisms in thinking about soccial cognitive functioning. Automatic and controlled processes traditionally were thought to vary simultaneously along four dimensions that reflect awareness, intentionality, controllability, and resource demands, with automatic functions being low on each of these dimensions. Bargh argued, however, that it makes sense to consider the dimensions separately, asserting that most complex social cognitive tasks consist of a combination of automatic and controlled features. For example, although individuals may be unable to prevent processing of certain types of information (e.g., evaluative content), they can become aware of its influence and attempt to control it.

For our purposes, we have assumed that the features associated with controlled processing reflect working memory efficiency and thus are likely to be negatively affected by aging. By contrast, automatic aspects of processing should remain relatively invariant across adulthood. Thus, aging should have its greatest impact when performance relies on controlled processing mechanisms. For example, we might expect to find age differences when individuals must initiate specific processing operations, control the influence of irrelevant information, monitor the contents of working memory, or deal with high resource demands. In this section, we consider the role of aging-related constraints on processing mechanisms by examining automatic and controlled processing mechanisms associated with different aspects of representation.

PERSON MEMORY

Most models of impression formation propose that our representations of others are multifaceted, consisting of information about specific behaviors organized around trait inferences and evaluations (e.g., Wyer & Srull, 1989). Whereas working memory resources and functions are assumed to play a role in the construction of these representations, the demand placed on them appears to vary depending on the task and type of information being processed. This further suggests that age differences in performance will also vary across information types.

Our initial investigations of social representations concentrated on examining memory for specific behaviors attributed to a target person. This work was guided by our previous research on memory for script-related narratives (Hess, 1985, 1992; Hess, Donley, & Vandermaas, 1989; Hess & Tate, 1992), which revealed three relevant findings with respect to aging effects on representational processes.

First, adults of all ages exhibited sensitivity to script structure when remembering narratives, with recall and recognition of individual script actions varying systematically as a function of their typicality and relevance to the scripted activity. This suggests that the use of generic script knowledge to construct situational models is common across age groups in adulthood. Second, age differences in memory were revealed as a function of typicality and relevance, with age differences in performance increasing as these two factors decreased. This suggests that older adults are more dependent than younger adults on the script structure to support their construction of a situational model. That is, aging has less of an impact on memory for information that can be easily integrated into a representation using preexisting slots or links with the generic script than it does on information for which no such linkages exist. In the latter case, the individual needs to construct an association, which may be limited by aging-related changes in processing resources. Hess and Tate (1992) supported this interpretation by demonstrating that (1) age differences in memory for novel information were eliminated when performance was not dependent on retrieval links associated with integrative processing and (2) a measure of working memory efficiency predicted recall performance in older adults. Finally, age differences were also found in generic script representations, with the nature of these differences relating to current life circumstances. For example, when asked to describe what happens when one gets up in the morning, younger adults spent more time than did older adults discussing personal grooming, whereas older adults spent more time discussing breakfast than did younger adults, for whom eating this meal seemed to be almost an after thought. This suggests that even relatively common, socially shared schemas vary depending on one's experience.

For present purposes, these findings are interesting for at least two reasons. First, they are consistent with our bipartite conceptualization of age-related influences on the construction of social representations, with cognitive resources appearing to account for age-related variation in memory and at least the potential existing for age differences due to the organization of knowledge. Second, they have direct relevance to our understanding of mental model construction in the social domain, since many scripted activities have an interpersonal focus. We expanded our program of research to specifically focus on the applicability of these results to a more traditional social cognitive domain: person memory.

Consistent with our emphasis in the studies of script memory, our initial investigations examined memory for behavioral information as a function of its consistency with a dominant personality trait attribution or evaluative characterization (e.g., positive vs negative) of a target person. We reasoned that cognitive constraints similar to those assumed to underlie aging effects on script memory might affect memory for specific behaviors. Investigations of young adults have shown that recall of behavioral information is dependent on the consistency between such information and the dominant impression of the target (e.g., Hastie & Kumar, 1979; Srull, 1981). For example, if a target is depicted as honest and then performs both honest (e.g., told a store clerk he was undercharged) and dishonest (e.g., cheated while playing a game) behaviors, perceivers tend to remember the dishonest behaviors more than the honest ones. The difference in recall as a function of consistency is assumed to reflect the nature of the underlying representation and the cognitive operations engaged in constructing it. For example, Wyer and Srull (1989) argued that people organize individual behaviors in memory around a general evaluative impression of the target and that the links or associations between this evaluation and individual behaviors vary in strength as a function of consistency (Figure 11.2). Thus, impression-consistent behaviors have stronger linkages with the central impression than do inconsistent or irrelevant behaviors. By contrast, inconsistent behaviors have more linkages with other behaviors, creating more potential retrieval routes to these items in memory. These linkages are thought to be constructed as the perceiver engages in more extensive processing of inconsistencies and attempts to reconcile the unexpected nature of these behaviors by examining them in the context of other behavioral information. An illustration of such processing was obtained by Hastie (1984), who found that people were more likely to provide causal explanations for inconsistent behaviors than for consistent behaviors. For example, if the behavior "he invited the neighbors over for dinner" was attributed to an unfriendly person, the perceiver might reconcile the apparent inconsistency by noting that the target extended the invitation because his wife forced him to do it. Thus, young adults appear to be motivated to understand unexpected events by seeking out potential causes, a form of self-initiated processing. This extended processing, in turn, accounted for the observed discrepancy in recall across levels of consistency.

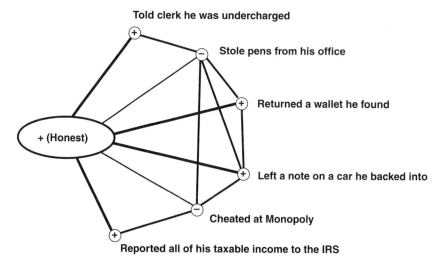

FIGURE 11.2   Hypothetical representation of behavioral information about target initially represented as honest. The thickness of the lines represents the strength of association between nodes, and + and − represent the valence of the node. IRS = Internal Revenue Service.

To examine the possibility that aging-related changes in working memory might have a negative affect on such self-initiated processing, we (Hess & Tate, 1991) essentially duplicated the procedure used by Hastie (1984) with groups of young and older adults. Consistent with our hypothesis—and with the previously discussed work on script memory—age differences in recall were greater for inconsistent behaviors than for consistent behaviors. In addition, age differences were also evident in the probability of participants producing causal explanations for inconsistencies, with younger adults being more likely to try to reinterpret these behaviors in a manner that resolved the apparent inconsistency. Importantly, these between-group differences in production of explanations accounted in part for the difference in recall patterns across age groups. When behavior recall was conditionalized on production of an explanation, both young and older adults exhibited superior recall for inconsistencies, indicating that adults of all ages benefit from the production of causal explanations.

A similar result was obtained by Hess (1995, Experiment 1) using a somewhat different procedure in which different-aged adults read pairs of sentences that varied in their degree of causal relationship (see Keenan, Baillet, & Brown, 1984; Myers, Shinjo, & Duffy, 1987) and then attempted to recall the second sentence in each pair using the first as a cue. Age differences in sentence recall as a function of causality implied that younger adults were more likely than were older adults to construct causal linkages between sentences. Older adults relied more on explicitly stated causal connections between sentences to support recall.

One way to think of the pattern of results from these two studies is in relation to the intentionality dimension of the automatic-controlled processing distinction. Elaborative processing is a form of self-initiated (and thus controlled) processing, which Craik (1986) has argued will be negatively affected by aging-related changes in processing resources. Thus, for example, the results of Hess and Tate (1991) can be explained in terms of the probability of older adults engaging in inconsistency resolution rather than in their ability to do so. Craik (1986) has argued that problems in self-initiated processing can be overcome if appropriate environmental supports are provided, which reduce the demands placed on working memory. This hypothesis was supported in a second experiment by Hess (1995) in which instructions to generate causal linkages between the two sentences resulted in disproportionate memory benefits for older adults relative to the other age groups. This suggested that such linkages were not being produced spontaneously and that structuring of the environment to facilitate their production reduced age-related deficits.

In sum, there are age differences in what is remembered about people, and these differences appear to reflect aging-related problems in controlled processing mechanisms. The functional impact associated with these problems is most likely to occur when behavioral information is necessary for making decisions. These situations are referred to as memory based (e.g., Hastie & Park, 1986), in that they involve the construction of new inferences from information stored in memory and occur after one's initial encounter with the target. This might occur, for example, when you are asked whether a coworker might make a good addition to your weekly poker game. Since no ready inference regarding acceptability within this role exists, you have to search your memory to identify relevant behaviors or traits that would assist in making a decision. To the extent that aging negatively affects the accessibility or availability of relevant information in memory, age differences will exist in memory-based judgment processes. In addition, aging effects on the efficiency of working memory functioning may also create problems in constructing such judgments. Indeed, Hess, Follett, and McGee (1998, Experiment 2) found that older adults were less systematic in their use of existing behavioral information in memory when making memory-based impression judgments, suggesting problems in retrieval and integration processes.

PROCESSING OF DESCRIPTIVE
AND EVALUATIVE INFORMATION

Our representations of other people do not, however, simply consist of lists of behaviors. Rather, we go beyond the information given and make inferences about people on the basis of their behavior. For example, a perceiver may try to identify the reasons behind a target's behavior by attempting to infer the specific trait that underlies the behavior. If a person backs into a parked car and then drives away without attempting to notify the owner of the damaged vehicle, we might reasonably infer that the driver is dishonest and inconsiderate. This dispositional inference then forms the basis for the attribution process, whereby individuals attempt to understand the causal mechanisms underlying another person's behavior by considering dispositional and situational information. Most current views of attribution assume that one of the primary pieces of information used in constructing theories of causation is a dispositional, or trait, inference made by the perceiver based on the behavior. Recent reviews of the literature (Bargh, 1994; Uleman, Newman, & Moskowitz, 1996; Wyer & Carlston, 1994) have indicated that these trait-based inferences are made so often that they become relatively spontaneous in younger adults, requiring little in the way of cognitive resources (although the degree of spontaneous trait inference may be affected by the goals of the perceiver, [Uleman et al., 1996]). In fact, many recent models of attribution argue for a multistage process, consisting of relatively effortless dispositional attribution followed by correction if time and resources permit (e.g., Gilbert, Pelham, & Krull, 1988; Quattrone, 1982). What is less clear from this literature is the extent to which the use of such information in constructing impressions is effortless (Wyer & Carlston, 1994). For example, some research has demonstrated that the use of traits in organizing an impression is dependent on the perceiver's goals, with trait-based organization being more likely with an impression-formation goal than with other types of goals, such as memorization (e.g., Bassili & Smith, 1986). This suggests that the use of trait inferences in the creation of person representations may be under the conscious control of the perceiver. Consistent with views that suggest that aging is associated with decreased ability to effectively allocate resources and control processing (e.g., Craik & Byrd, 1982; Jennings & Jacoby, 1993), we might then expect that older adults would be less likely than younger adults to organize their representations around specific traits.

At least two pieces of evidence from our research are consistent with this hypothesis. In one study (Hess & Follett, 1994), young and older participants read either a positive or negative description of a target person. For example, the positive description characterized the target as hard working, successful, family oriented, and sociable. Participants then read a list of 75 traits purportedly generated by other judges. This list included 45 positive traits and 30 negative traits, with one third of each type of trait being presented either two, five, or eight times. When we examined frequency estimations for individual traits, it was found that both young and older adults were equally accurate in assessing the number of times each trait was presented. This indicates that participants in both age groups had similar types of trait-based information available to them in memory.

Participants were then presented with a series of behaviors that were reflective of the individual traits presented in the list (e.g., "She selfishly refused to consider lending her sister the money"). For each behavior, participants judged the probability with which the target was likely to perform a specific behavior given the trait list with which they were previously presented. Both young and older adults indicated a bias in their responses that was consistent with the initial description that was read about the target. Thus, even though all participants saw exactly the same trait list, participants who read the positive description rated the target as being more likely to perform positive behaviors than negative ones, whereas the participants who read the negative description did just the opposite. In other words, both age groups were influenced by previously presented evaluative information (i.e., the positive or negative description) that they were told to ignore. Age differences were observed, however, in the extent to which the behavioral judgments corresponded with the specific trait information presented to participants. Younger adults were significantly more likely to use the frequency information associated with individual traits in making their probability judgments than were the older adults. For example, younger adults were more likely to rate the above-described behavior as probable if the trait *selfish* was presented 8 times than if it was presented 5 times; older adults were less likely to make such discriminations. This suggests that increasing age is associated with less use of specific trait information in constructing judgments about people.

In another study (Hess, Follett & McGee, 1998), young and older participants formed impressions of a target based on a set of six positive and three negative behaviors. They were then presented with a list of traits and asked to judge the extent to which each characterized the target. These traits represented either positive (e.g., confident, friendly) or negative (e.g., dishonest, friendly) characteristics, and they varied in the degree to which they were descriptively consistent with individual behaviors in the set. In general, all participants were more likely to attribute positive than negative traits to the target, reflecting the impact of the dominant valence associated with the behavior set. In addition, regardless of trait valence, participants were more likely to attribute a specific trait to the target if a behavior referring to that trait had been presented, indicating that specific trait inferences were being constructed for individual behaviors. Age differences existed, however, in the extent to which participants used this referential informa-tion. Specifically, younger adults were more likely than were older adults to dis-tinguish between traits with and without behavioral referents. Once again, this suggests that older adults are less likely than are young adults to use specific trait information in forming impressions. To the extent that the retrieval and use of such information uses processing resources, this finding is consistent with the hypothesis that age differences in impression formation are tied to aging effects in working memory efficiency.

In spite of the differences observed in the use of specific trait information, the just-described results suggest an aspect of impression formation that is relatively constant across age groups: the processing of evaluative information. When we view a specific behavior, we not only spontaneously encode trait information; we also represent information regarding our evaluation of the behavior, as reflected in our positive or negative reactions. This evaluative information is then used in form-ing our impression. That is, the extent to which we like a person's behavior will be used in determining whether we like him or her. This evaluative information appears to be processed in an effortless fashion without intent of the individual, as indicated by priming studies showing that the processing of an event is facilitated by prior processing of an event for which the individual holds a similar evaluation (Bargh, Chaiken, Govender, & Pratto, 1992; Fazio, Sanbonmatsu, Powell, & Kardes, 1986). In addition, evaluative information appears to spill over into other situations, resulting not only in the facilitation of processing similar events but also in "attaching" itself to previously neutral events (e.g., Murphy & Zajonc, 1993), at least when the individual is unaware of its contaminating influence.

As mentioned in the foregoing discussion of the studies by Hess and Follett (1994) and Hess, Follett, & McGee (1998), whereas age differences were observed in the use of specific trait information in constructing impressions, both young and older adults appear to process and use evaluative information in the same manner. This finding is consistent with the hypothesis that the processing of evaluative information is not dependent on cognitive resources and thus should not be affected by aging-related declines in such resources. Several other studies that we conducted provided results that are consistent with this hypothesis.

In one set of experiments (Hess, Pullen, & McGee, 1996), we examined the ability of young and older adults to abstract a group prototype from descriptions of individual group members. When the prototype was based on a specific but arbitrarily determined set of traits, older adults were significantly poorer than younger adults at abstracting and using the group prototype. We attributed this age effect to the working memory demands associated with learning the arbitrary prototype (e.g., organizing trait information in memory, formulating and testing hypotheses about group membership). This interpretation was bolstered when independent measures related to processing resources were found to partially account for the age effects. By contrast, when prototype abstraction and membership judgments could be based solely on evaluative information, both young and older adults could abstract prototype information. In fact, age effects were observed in favor of the older adults in this condition, perhaps reflecting the younger adults' greater ability to control automatically processed evaluative information, which would actually interfere with performance. In general, however, these findings are consistent with the hypothesis that evaluative information is processed in a relatively automatic fashion and thus should not be affected by resource limitations associated with aging. The fact that independent measures of processing efficiency did not predict performance in this condition provided further supported for this view.

In another set of studies (Hess & Bolstad, 1998), we presented different-aged adults with a series of brief descriptions about people. Each description consisted of some general categorical information (e.g., the target's job) followed by a list of more specific attributes (e.g., personality traits). In some cases, the attribute information was consistent with the category (i.e., the traits were commonly associated with the job), whereas in other cases, the two types of information were inconsistent with each other. Fiske and Neuberg's (1990) model of impression formation predicts that category-based processing should be dominant in the first case, since the specific attribute information simply reinforces the applicability of the category. Thus, impressions should be primarily based on the perceiver's affective reaction to the target's job. By contrast, inconsistency between category and attribute information is predicted to encourage piecemeal processing, with impressions being based more on the integration of affective information associated with specific traits. In three separate studies, we found that adults of all ages modified their likability judgments in response to situational information (i.e., category–attribute consistency) in a manner consistent with Fiske and Neuberg's model. Thus, we once again have a situation in which the processing of evaluative information is unaffected by aging.

Although the age constancy implied by these results is an important finding, it should not be used to suggest that null age effects will be obtained in all situations involving the processing of evaluative information. In the just-described research, the spontaneous encoding and use of evaluative information supported the ability to make accurate judgments about other people. In other words, little control over processing was necessary for a positive influence of evaluative information on performance to be observed. In other cases, however, this information may bias representations, requiring the perceiver to control its influence to preserve accuracy. For example, Murphy and Zajonc (1993) demonstrated that young adults' likability ratings for Chinese ideograms were consistent with the emotion depicted in a smiling or frowning face that was presented suboptimally just prior to the ideogram. Presumably, the unintentional activation of affective information by the faces influenced responses toward a previously neutral stimulus. Consistent with the ideas of Bargh (1994), however, Murphy and Zajonc (1993) also demonstrated that the impact of previously activated affective information was reduced if the participant was aware of the potential bias. Thus, awareness allowed the individual to bring an unintentionally initiated response under conscious control. Similar findings have been observed using other procedures (e.g., Higgins, Rholes, & Jones, 1977; Martin, Seta, & Crelia, 1990). If aging is associated with problems in controlled processing functions (e.g., monitoring and controlling cognitive processes), older adults should be more susceptible to unintended sources of bias.

We investigated this hypothesis in two separate studies (Hess, McGee, Woodburn, & Bolstad, 1998). In each one, different-aged adults were presented with either positive or negative trait information in an initial task. This was followed by a supposedly unrelated impression formation task, in which participants read a descriptively and evaluatively ambiguous description about a target. In addition, awareness of the potential biasing effects of the trait information from the initial task on this latter task was manipulated within age groups. In line with previous research, young adults tended to produce descriptors of the target that were consistent with the primed trait information (i.e., assimilation), unless they were aware of the priming source, in which case they corrected their judgments for the perceived prime influence. By contrast, older adults produced assimilation effects in every condition, even when circumstances highlighted the awareness of the potentially biasing information.

These findings are once again consistent with our conceptualization of age differences using the automatic-controlled processing distinction. Adults of all ages spontaneously processed trait and evaluative information, but increasing age was associated with decreased ability to control the impact of this information. What is interesting in this case is the observation that older adults exhibited greater use of trait-based and evaluative information in forming impressions, a finding in direct contrast to the previously discussed research in which young adults were more likely to use trait-based information and minimal age differences were observed in the processing of evaluative information. Thus, variations in representational processes cannot be predicted solely in terms of general age differences in the processing of trait and evaluative information. Rather, obtained age effects also appear to depend on the ability to control the use of this information in constructing representations and judgments in response to situational demands.

In sum, these results are consistent with the notion that aging has a negative impact on the processing mechanisms associated with the construction of person representations. When all the just-described findings are taken together, it appears reasonable to characterize these differences using the distinction between automatic and controlled processing, with aging being associated with problems in the latter. That is, older adults are more likely than are younger adults to have problems when effective processing requires monitoring, initiating, and/or controlling specific operations, or when the operations used place demands on processing resources. A general inference is that such differences reflect aging-related changes in general biological mechanisms that support processing. As will be seen in the next section, however, such explanations may be too simplistic.

KNOWLEDGE-BASED INFLUENCES
ON REPRESENTATION

The just-described research suggests that the accuracy and efficiency of social representational processes in adulthood may be negatively affected by changes in cognitive skills associated with age. Consistent with the life-span perspective (Baltes, 1987), however, these losses may be accompanied by compensations or gains in other aspects of functioning. In our research, we have identified at least two possible ways in which this may occur. The first is through adjustments in the attention to specific pieces of behavior as a function of their diagnosticity with respect to specific dispositional qualities. The second is an adjustment in the allocation of cognitive resources devoted to constructing representations as a function of task meaningfulness.

As suggested by our previous discussion, the construction of representations about other people goes beyond simply encoding and storing information picked up from the environment. It also involves interpretive processes, which presumably are based in one's knowledge about the social world. Thus, the types of inferences we make about a particular behavior relate to our prior social experience involving similar types of behavior and the meaning attached to them. It seems reasonable to assume that as we accumulate such experiences with age in adulthood, the knowledge that we have about the world would also change and be reflected in the meaning attached to specific behaviors.

One way that we have investigated this hypothesis is by examining age differences in the use of trait-diagnostic information in constructing social judgments. In an initial set of studies (Hess & Pullen, 1994), we were interested in examining how people's impressions of others changed as a function of the type of information that was presented to them. Young and older adults first read a positive or negative description of a target person and then provided impression ratings. Participants were subsequently presented with a new set of behaviors attributed to the target, with instructions to incorporate this new information into their impressions of the target. Some of these behaviors were inconsistent with the initial depiction of the target. For example, a behavior suggesting dishonesty might be attributed to a target originally characterized as a good person. Impression ratings were once more collected, then there was an unexpected recall test of the new set of behaviors.

On the basis of our work examining cognitive constraints, we initially hypothesized that impression change would be greater in the younger adults than in the older ones, reflecting age-related differences in the extent to which unexpected information is integrated into the memory representation. This was not found. Instead, we observed that the extent of age differences in impression change was moderated by the manner in which the target was depicted. When the target was initially portrayed in negative terms, the subsequent presentation of inconsistent information resulted in the predicted effect, with younger adults changing their impressions more than older adults did. The opposite pattern of performance was observed, however, when the initial portrayal was positive in nature. This is clearly at odds with a hypothesis based on straightforward age differences in the efficiency of integration operations.

Instead, these results suggest that there are age differences in the use of negative information in modifying impressions. This was indicated by the older adults' greater willingness to change positive impressions when presented with negative behavioral information than to change negative impressions when presented with positive information. This performance pattern was not as evident in the younger adults. The age-related variation in the emphasis on negative information is important in that it appears to reflect differential attention to diagnostic information in constructing impressions. Specifically, negative information is thought to be more diagnostic than is positive information for morality-related traits (Skowronski & Carlston, 1989). For example, a dishonest behavior typically allows greater certainty in terms of where an individual falls on the dishonest–honest trait dimension than does an honest behavior. This is because we generally believe that only dishonest people perform dishonest deeds, whereas honest deeds can be performed by both honest and dishonest types. Thus, in essence, we can be more confident in making a trait inference of dishonest on the basis of the observation of a dishonest behavior than we can in making a inference of honesty based upon an honest behavior. Given that the characterizations of the targets in our study were primarily in terms of morality-related behaviors, the performance patterns suggest that older adults were more likely than were younger adults to take into account diagnosticity in changing their impressions.

We have hypothesized that the apparent age difference in attention to diagnostic information may reflect a general age-related trend in the degree to which people attempt to attach meaning to information in their environment. Similar to findings by Adams (1991; Adams, Labouvie-Vief, Hobart, & Dorosz, 1990), these data suggest that older adults are more likely than are younger adults to interpret events in terms of their past experience. Thus, inconsistent behaviors were not encoded just in terms of their congruence with previous information about the target but also in terms of whether this new information was significant in relation to participants' implicit theories of social behavior. By contrast, younger adults appeared to process information primarily in terms of its situational consistency, with implicit theories having little impact on performance.

One potential problem with this explanation relates to the fact that diagnosticity was confounded with valence in the Hess and Pullen (1994) research. That is, diagnostic behaviors were also negative, making it uncertain as to whether older adults were being influenced by the valence or informativeness of specific behaviors. From a cognitive efficiency view, it could be argued that negative information is processed in a relatively automatic fashion (e.g., Pratto & John, 1991) and that the greater impact of negative information with age may be based in cognitive efficiency mechanisms. To address this concern, we (Hess, Bolstad, Woodburn, & Auman, 1999) conducted another study in which an attempt was made to disentangle the effects of diagnosticity and valence. This was done by examining impression change in the domains of morality and ability. In this latter domain, positive behaviors are thought to be more diagnostic than are negative behaviors (Skowronski & Carlston, 1989). For example, both a smart person and a stupid person could fail a calculus test, but only a smart person would get an A on one. If participants are attending to negative information, then impression change should be greater whenever negative information is presented after an initial positive characterization, regardless of the trait domain. By contrast, if diagnosticity is being attended to, then impression change in the ability domain should exhibit the opposite pattern of performance to that observed in Hess and Pullen (1994). That is, impression change should be greater when positive behaviors follow a negative portrayal. We also included a middle-aged group to get a better feel for the developmental progression associated with the obtained effects.

The results of this study were interesting and added another potential twist to our understanding of representational processes. The young adults performed in a consistent manner across domains, with impression change being similar regardless of valence of the initial description or trait domain. Thus, as in Hess and Pullen (1994), although younger adults did appear to integrate the new behavioral information with the old, there was little attempt to interpret this information beyond the current context. By contrast, the middle aged adults based their impression change primarily on diagnosticity factors. This suggests that they were adding an additional layer of meaning to the behavior information beyond that having to do with consistency. Finally, the older adults once again attended to diagnosticity in altering their impressions in the morality domain. In the intelligence domain, however, impression change was similar across levels of diagnosticity. These results provide support for our general notion that increased age in adulthood is associated with greater interpretive processing. They also appear to argue against a simple cognitive efficiency explanation of age differences in terms of the use of negative information. The findings created, however, an additional piece of data to be explained: Why were the older adults attending to diagnosticity only in the morality domain?

One potential explanation may be that the diagnostic value attributed to individual behaviors varies with age in adulthood. For example, Heckhausen and Baltes (1991) found that increasing age was associated with perceptions of decreased control over negative traits. Thus, older adults might perceive stupid behaviors to reflect a basic aspect of intellectual functioning, thereby changing the diagnosticity associated with positive and negative behaviors in the intellectual domain. When we examined diagnosticity in a manner similar to that used by Skowronski and Carlston (1987), however, age differences were found to be minimal for both morality and ability-related behaviors. Even if perceptions of diagnosticity do not change, the accessibility of such information may increase with age. Consistent with this explanation, Skowronski and Carlston (1992) found that diagnosticity was most likely to have an impact on younger adults' impressions when the target's behaviors were extreme reflections of a trait dimension. This suggests a weaker linkage between diagnosticity and trait schemas than occurs in middle-aged and older adults, who appear to access diagnostic information even in behaviors that are only moderate exemplars of a given trait.

The obtained age effects may also be based in the meaning or personal significance attached to traits underlying specific behaviors. The differential use of diagnosticity in constructing impressions may reflect reactions to certain behaviors in terms of their meaningfulness to the individual's current life circumstances, which in turn may be reflected in affective responses to those behaviors. It is reasonable to assume that behaviors construed as meaningful by the perceiver will elicit stronger affective responses and in turn will be processed more extensively than those that do not. Within a developmental context, the hypothesis could be made that the intellectual domain holds more meaning for younger and middle-aged adults, who are more likely to be focused on individual achievement, than for older adults. By contrast, morality-related behaviors, such as those associated with honesty, may increase in relative importance with age in adulthood, particularly since such behaviors typically have an interpersonal focus. This hypothesis fits with Carstensen's characterization (Carstensen, 1991; Turk-Charles and Carstensen, Chapter 14, this volume) of changing goals in adulthood, in terms of an aging-related shift toward emphasizing the affective outcomes of social interactions. We obtained some support for this hypothesis by showing that the intensity of affective responses to the honest and dishonest behaviors used in our study increased with age across young, middle-aged, and older adults. By contrast, affective responses to intelligent and stupid behaviors remained relatively stable with age and were significantly lower than those toward morality-related behaviors in the older adult group. Thus, these data suggest that differential attention to diagnostic information across age groups may reflect affective responses associated with specific behavioral information that are tied to age-related goal structures.

One interesting general implication that arises from this conclusion is that age differences in the meaning attached to a situation may influence the extent to which the individual is willing to engage limited cognitive resources in processing operations. As noted before, this general motivational factor is incorporated in many models of impression formation (e.g., Fiske & Neuberg, 1990). What is of particular interest with respect to aging is the possibility that such motivational differences may underlie some of the age effects observed elsewhere that were attributed to cognitive deficits. For example, it may be possible that the lower probability of older adults engaging in elaborative processing (e.g., Hess & Tate, 1991) is based in part on the low personal meaning attached to the task by these participants, resulting in a reduced probability of resource engagement.

We (Hess, Follett, & McGee, 1998) examined this possibility by varying the instructions provided to different-aged adults in an impression formation task.

Participants were presented with lists of behaviors in which the majority of the behaviors were descriptively and evaluatively consistent with each other. In some cases, participants were given standard impression formation instructions; in other cases, participants were asked to evaluative the target's fitness for a job, such as teacher. We then examined subsequent recall of the behaviors. With standard impression formation instructions, younger adults exhibited a recall advantage for inconsistent behaviors over consistent behaviors, whereas no such effect was observed for older adults. This finding is consistent with other research demonstrating age differences in the processing of unexpected information. With job evaluation instructions, recall levels of all participants were elevated. In addition, young adults exhibited a similar pattern of recall to that observed with standard instructions. For the older adults, these instructions also resulted in better recall for inconsistent behaviors than for consistent ones, but only for those adults with high scores on a test of working memory efficiency (i.e., reading span).

These results have two interesting implications. First, age differences in elaborative processing will be minimized if task meaningfulness is increased. Thus, when the standard impression formation task was reframed in a more specific, everyday form, older adults appeared more willing to us cognitive resources and engaged in integrative processing similar to that observed in younger adults. Second, such motivational manipulations may be effective for only those who have sufficient cognitive resources. Older participants with limited cognitive resources may be unable to engage in efficient processing, even if the goal structure of the task encourages.

Taken together, these studies highlight the importance of considering processing goals in understanding aging effects on impression formation, as well as considering their interaction with cognitive skills. Whereas this research is still in its initial stages, the findings presented in this section suggest that age-related changes in goals will influence the importance attached to specific situations and types of information. This is turn affects how such information is processed and ultimately what is represented in memory. Importantly, the impact of processing goals—and associated age differences therein—may be moderated by available cognitive resources. This highlights the importance of considering age differences in representational processes in a broader context that emphasizes multiple influences and interactions between these influences, as depicted in Figure 11.1.

SUMMARY AND CONCLUSIONS

In this chapter, I have presented a general framework for understanding the nature of developmental changes associated with social representational processes in adulthood. This framework identifies at least two sets of influences on such processes that are affected by aging and highlights their independent as well as interactive effects. I have also discussed a series of studies that my colleagues and I have conducted examining representational processes using this framework as a guide. Taken together, this research presents a somewhat complex picture. For example, it is evident that aging is associated with constraints on impression formation through normative changes in cognitive skills. These changes affect the efficiency of operations and the resources available for processing social information. At the same time, changes in goals and belief systems influence the characteristics of other people to which we attend and the nature of processing in which we engage.

This latter conclusion highlights perhaps the most important point associated with this framework. Specifically, a complete understanding of age differences in representational processes will not come from an examination of processing and knowledge-based factors in isolation. Rather, the interplay between these factors needs to be considered. For example, our research has suggested that age differences in the content and complexity of representations are based in variations in socially relevant goals. This conclusion is supported by other research showing that increasing age in adulthood is associated with consideration of more sources of information in making causal attributions (Blanchard-Fields, 1994; Blanchard-Fields & Norris, 1994), greater attention to the emotional content of social interchanges (Carstensen & Turk-Charles, 1994), and an increased focus on how events relate to personal experience (Adams, 1991; Adams et al., 1990). These findings point to the important role that goals play in determining the cognitive operations associated with constructing representations and to the need for consideration of goals as a potential explanatory mechanisms for age differences in processing.

It is also important to consider the extent to which cognitive factors influence goals. Our research has suggested that aging-related declines in cognitive functioning might limit the ability of individuals to process social information in a manner consistent with situational goals. This finding is consistent with research in younger adults that has examined such relationships, where situational demands on cognitive resources bias specific processing goals (e.g., Webster et al., 1996) and available skills have been shown to limit one's ability to engage in the cognitive operations normally associated with a specific goal (e.g., Bar-Tal et al., 1997). These findings have two implications for understanding aging processes. First, declining cognitive skills may limit the ability to achieve certain goals. Second, cognitive changes may also influence chronic processing goals in that such goals may change to become more consistent with current levels of functioning (see also Brandtstädter & Greve, 1994). For example, we (Hess, Follett, & McGee, 1998) have speculated that aging is associated with an increase in the selectivity surrounding the individual's willingness to engage cognitive resources, perhaps to conserve diminishing physical resources. Carstensen (1991) has also discussed this within the context of her socioemotional selectivity theory. We believe, however, that selectivity may be a more general phenomenon that manifests itself across a variety of situations.

These findings have important implications for understanding social functioning in adulthood. For example, changes in cognitive functioning may have a negative effect on one's ability to form accurate representations and thus to make decisions in everyday situations. To illustrate, one common ploy in advertising is to use a well-known and well-liked actor or athlete as a spokesperson for a particular product. The hope is that the affective responses associated with the spokesperson will be associated with the product, thereby positively affecting the consumer's attitude toward and increasing the probability that it will be bought. It is easy to see how this could happen, particularly if the perceiver is unaware of the intended outcome. Our characterization of controlled processes in social information processing, however, suggests that the impact of such information may be brought under the control of the perceiver, who can correct his or her impression of the product to control for this affective bias. If aging is associated with a decrease in the efficiency of such controlled processing, however, older people may be more susceptible to these ploys than are younger adults, not only in commercials but also in other types of face-to-face interactions (e.g., a friendly insurance salesperson). This susceptibility may increase to the extent that circumstances (e.g., physical frailty) make one more dependent on others.

There are also positive implications, however, as changes in social goals and knowledge may make one more accurate in making inferences about others. This is suggested by our studies of diagnosticity. Thus, the experience associated with living longer may benefit one's ability to understand others, either through the availability of specific knowledge or the ease of access associated with such knowledge. This could be thought of as one component of wisdom, which has been characterized as expertise in the pragmatics of life (Smith, Dixon, & Baltes, 1989).

The results of our studies also have general implications for the study of cognitive change in adulthood. Most perspectives in cognitive aging have focused on deficit-related explanations to account for age differences in performance in memory and other cognitive tasks. There is no doubt that age-related declines in cognitive functioning exist; our research suggests, however, that certain aspects of age-related performance may reflect changing goals and knowledge bases. These variables should be considered in our examinations of cognitive ability in adulthood, particularly as they relate to performance within everyday contexts. I would argue that adoption of a social cognitive framework, in which knowledge-based factors are considered, not only will contribute to our understanding of functioning in social situations but will also enhance our understanding of aging effects on cognitive performance.

Finally, our research has implications for the study of social cognition in general. Obviously, the focus and design of our studies have benefited from research and theory from the mainstream social cognitive literature. Indeed, as noted before, this literature may have much to offer in our examinations of many aspects of cognitive and social functioning in adulthood. At the same time, it is clear that the focus on younger adults limits our understanding of the mechanisms underlying social information processing. For example, our work on diagnosticity effects in impression change suggests that the use of diagnostic information is not an all-or-none process and may be moderated by specific conditions that are asso-ciated with development. Thus, the work conducted by social psychologists (e.g., Skowronski & Carlston, 1987, 1992; Wojciszke, Brycz, & Borkenau, 1993) iden-tifying the importance of the diagnostic value of trait-related behaviors in con-structing impressions is expanded by our research highlighting the circumstances associated with the use of this information. Similar benefits should be obtained in understanding other aspects of social cognitive functioning when age is included as a variable in research (e.g., Chen & Blanchard-Fields, 1997; Sears, 1987).

ACKNOWLEDGMENTS

Support for this chapter was provided by National Institute on Aging (NIA) grant AG05552.

REFERENCES

Adams, C. (1991). Qualitative age differences in memory for text: A life-span developmental perspec-tive. *Psychology and Aging, 6,* 323–336.

Adams, C., Labouvie-Vief, G., Hobart, C. J., and Dorosz, M. (1990). Adult age group differences in story recall style. *Journal of Gerontology: Psychological Sciences, 45,* P17–P27.

Asch, S. E. (1946). Forming impressions of personality. *Journal of Abnormal and Social Psychology, 41,* 1230–1240.

Baltes, P. B. (1987). Theoretical propositions of life-span developmental psychology: On the dynam-ics between growth and decline. *Developmental Psychology, 23,* 611–626.

Bargh, J. A. (1994). The four horsemen of automaticity: Awareness, intention, efficiency, and control in social cognition. In R. S. Wyer, Jr. & T. K. Srull (Eds.), *Handbook of Social Cognition* (pp. 1–40). Hillsdale, NJ: Lawrence Erlbaum Associates.

Bargh, J. A., Bond, R. N., Lombardi, W. L., & Tota, M. E. (1986). The additive nature of chronic and temporary sources of construct accessibility. *Journal of Personality and Social Psychology, 50,* 869–878.

Bargh, J. A., Chaiken, S., Govender, R., & Pratto, F. (1992). The generality of the automatic attitude activation effect. *Journal of Personality and Social Psychology, 62,* 893–912.

Bargh, J. A., & Pratto, F. (1986). Individual construct accessibility and perceptual selection. *Journal of Experimental Social Psychology, 22,* 293–311.

Bar-Tal, Y., Kishon-Rabin, L., & Tabak, N. (1997). The effect of need and ability to achieve cognitive structuring on cognitive structuring. *Journal of Personality and Social Psychology, 73,* 1158–1176.

Bassili, J. N., & Smith, M. C. (1986). On the spontaneity of trait attribution: Converging evidence for the role of cognitive strategy. *Journal of Personality and Social Psychology, 50,* 239–245.

Blanchard-Fields, F. (1994). Age differences in causal attributions from an adult developmental per-spective. *Journal of Gerontology: Psychological Sciences, 49,* P43–P51.

Blanchard-Fields, F., & Norris, L. (1994). Causal attributions from adolescence through adulthood: Age differences, ego level, and generalized response style. *Aging and Cognition, 1,* 67–86.

Blank, T. O. (1987). Attributions as dynamic elements in a life-span social psychology. In R. Abeles (Ed.), *Life-span perspectives and social psychology* (pp. 61–84). Hillsdale, NJ: Lawrence Erlbaum Associates.

Brandtstädter, J., & Greve, W. (1994). The aging self: Stabilizing and protective processes. *Develop-mental Review, 14,* 52–80.

Brewer, M. B. (1988). A dual process model of impression formation. In T. K. Srull & R. S. Wyer, Jr. (Eds.), *Advances in social cognition* (vol. 1, pp. 1–36). Hillsdale, NJ: Lawrence Erlbaum Associates.

Carstensen, L. L. (1991). Socioemotional selectivity theory: Social activity in life-span context. *Annual Review of Gerontology and Geriatrics, 11,* 195–217.

Carstensen, L. L., & Turk-Charles, S. (1994). The salience of emotion across the adult life span. *Psychology and Aging, 9,* 259–264.

Chen, Y., & Blanchard-Fields, F. (1997). Age differences in stages of attributional processing. *Psychology and Aging, 12,* 694–703.

Conway, M., Carroll, J. M., Pushkar, D., Arbuckle, T., & Foisy, P. (1996). Anticipated interaction, individual differences in attentional resources, and elaboration of behavior. *Social Cognition, 14,* 338–366.

Craik, F. I. M. (1986). A functional account of age differences in memory. In F. Klix & H. Hagendorf (Eds.), *Human memory and cognitive capabilities, mechanisms, and performances* (pp. 409–422). Amsterdam: Elsevier Science Publishers.

Craik, F. I. M., & Byrd, M. (1982). Aging and cognitive deficits: The role of attentional resources. In F. I. M. Craik & S. Trehub (Eds.), *Aging and cognitive processes* (pp. 191–211). New York: Plenum.

Fazio, R. H., Sanbonmatsu, D. M., Powell, M. C., & Kardes, F. R. (1986). On the automatic activation of attitudes. *Journal of Personality and Social Psychology, 50,* 229–238.

Fiske, S. T., & Neuberg, S. L. (1990). A continuum of impression formation, from category-based to individuating processes: Influences of information and motivation on attention and interpretation. In M. P. Zanna (Ed.), *Advances in experimental social psychology* (vol. 23, pp. 1–74). San Diego: Academic Press.

Gerard, L., Zacks, R. T., Hasher, L., & Radvansky, G. A. (1991). Age deficits in retrieval: The fan effect. *Journal of Gerontology: Psychological Sciences, 46,* P131–P136.

Gilbert, D. T., Pelham, B. W., & Krull, D. S. (1988). On cognitive busyness: When person perceivers meet persons perceived. *Journal of Personality and Social Psychology, 54,* 733–740.

Hastie, R. (1984). Causes and effects of causal attribution. *Journal of Personality and Social Psychology, 46,* 44–56.

Hastie, R., & Kumar, P. (1979). Person memory: Personality traits as organizing principles in memory for behaviors. *Journal of Personality and Social Psychology, 37,* 25–38.

Hastie, R., & Park, B. (1986). The relationship between memory and judgment depends on whether the judgment task is memory-based or on-line. *Psychological Review, 93,* 258–268.

Heckhausen, J., & Baltes, P. B. (1991). Perceived controllability of expected psychological change across adulthood and old age. *Journal of Gerontology: Psychological Sciences, 46,* P165–P173.

Hess, T. M. (1985). Aging and context influences on recognition memory for typical and atypical script actions. *Developmental Psychology, 21,* 1139–1151.

Hess, T. M. (1992). Adult age differences in script content and structure. In R. L. West & J. D. Sinnott (Eds.), *Everyday memory and aging: Current research and methodology* (pp. 87–100). New York: Springer-Verlag.

Hess, T. M. (1994). Social cognition in adulthood: Aging-related changes in knowledge and processing mechanisms. *Developmental Review, 14,* 373–412.

Hess, T. M. (1995). Aging and the impact of causal connections on text comprehension and memory. *Aging and Cognition, 2,* 310–325.

Hess, T. M., & Bolstad, C. A. (1998). Category-based versus attribute-based processing in different-aged adults. *Aging, Neuropsychology, and Cognition, 5,* 27–42.

Hess, T. M., Bolstad, C. A., Woodburn, S. M., & Auman, C. (1999). Trait diagnosticity versus behavioral consistency as determinants of impression change in adulthood. *Psychology and Aging.*

Hess, T. M., Donley, J., & Vandermaas, M. O. (1989). Aging-related changes in the processing and retention of script information. *Experimental Aging Research, 15,* 89–96.

Hess, T. M., & Follett, K. J. (1994). Adult age differences in the use of schematic and episodic information in making social judgments. *Aging and Cognition, 1,* 54–66.

Hess, T. M., Follett, K. J., & McGee, K. A. (1998). Aging and impression formation: The impact of processing skills and goals. *Journal of Gerontology: Psychological Sciences, 53B,* P175–P188.

Hess, T. M., McGee, K. A., Woodburn, S. M., & Bolstad, C. A. (1998). Aging-related priming effects in social judgments. *Psychology and Aging, 13,* 127–137.

Hess, T. M., & Pullen, S. M. (1994). Adult age differences in informational biases during impression formation. *Psychology and Aging, 9,* 237–250.

Hess, T. M., Pullen, S. M., & McGee, K. A. (1996). The acquisition of prototype-based information about social groups in adulthood. *Psychology and Aging, 11,* 179–190.

Hess, T. M., & Tate, C. S. (1991). Adult age differences in explanations and memory for behavioral information. *Psychology and Aging, 6,* 86–92.

Hess, T. M., & Tate, C. S. (1992). Direct and indirect assessments of memory for script-based narratives in young and older adults. *Cognitive Development, 7,* 467–484.

Hess, T. M., Vandermaas, M. O., Donley, J., & Snyder, S. S. (1987). Memory for sex-role consistent and inconsistent actions in young and old adults. *Journal of Gerontology, 42,* 505–511.

Higgins, E. T., Rholes, W. S., & Jones, C. R. (1977). Category accessibility and impression formation. *Journal of Experimental Social Psychology, 13,* 141–154.

Hilton, J. L, & Darley, J. M. (1991). The effects of interaction goals on person perception. In M. P. Zanna (Ed.), *Advances in experimental social psychology* (vol. 24, pp. 235–267). San Diego: Academic Press.

Jennings, J. M., & Jacoby, L. L. (1993). Automatic versus intentional uses of memory: Aging, attention, and control. *Psychology and Aging, 8,* 283–293.

Johnson-Laird, P. N. (1983). *Mental models.* Cambridge, MA: Harvard University Press.

Keenan, J. M., Baillet, S. D., & Brown, P. (1984). The effects of causal cohesion on comprehension and memory. *Journal of Verbal Learning and Verbal Behavior, 23,* 115–126.

Kruglanski, A. W., & Freund, T. (1983). The freezing and unfreezing of lay-inferences: Effects of impressional priming, ethnic stereotyping, and numerical anchoring. *Journal of Experimental Social Psychology, 19,* 448–468.

MacKay, D. G., & Burke, D. M. (1990). Cognition and learning: A theory of new learning and the use of old connections. In T. M. Hess (Ed.), *Aging and cognition: Knowledge organization and utilization* (pp. 213–263). Amsterdam: Elsevier Science Publishers.

Martin, L. L., Seta, J. J., & Crelia, R. A. (1990). Assimilation and contrast as a function of people's willingness and ability to expend effort in forming an impression. *Journal of Personality and Social Psychology, 59,* 27–37.

Morrow, D. G., Leirer, V. O., & Altieri, P. A. (1992). Aging, expertise, and narrative processing. *Psychology and Aging, 7,* 376–388.

Murphy, S. T., & Zajonc, R. B. (1993). Affect, cognition, and awareness: Affective priming with suboptimal and optimal stimulus. *Journal of Personality and Social Psychology, 64,* 723–739.

Myers, J. L., Shinjo, M., & Duffy, S. A. (1987). Degree of causal relatedness and memory. *Journal of Memory and Language, 26,* 453–465.

Neuberg, S. L. (1989). The goal of forming accurate impressions during social interactions: Attenuating the impact of negative expectancies. *Journal of Personality and Social Psychology, 56,* 374–386.

Pratto, F., & John, O. P. (1991). Automatic vigilance: The attention-grabbing power of negative social information. *Journal of Personality and Social Psychology, 61,* 380–391.

Quattrone, G. A. (1982). Overattribution and unit formation: When behavior engulfs the person. *Journal of Personality and Social Psychology, 42,* 593–607.

Radvansky, G. A., Gerard, L. D., Zacks, R. T., & Hasher, L. (1990). Younger and older adults' use of mental models as representations for text materials. *Psychology and Aging, 5,* 209–214.

Salthouse, T. A. (1988). Resource-reduction interpretations of cognitive aging. *Developmental Review, 8,* 238–272.

Salthouse, T. A. (1997). The processing speed theory of adult age differences in cognition. *Psychological Review, 103,* 403–428.

Sears, D. O. (1987). Implications of the life-span approach for research on attitudes and social cognition. In R. P. Abeles (Ed.), *Life-span perspectives and social psychology* (pp. 17–60). Hillsdale, NJ: Lawrence Erlbaum Associates.

Sedikides, C. (1990). Effects of fortuitously activated constructs versus activated communication goals on person impressions. *Journal of Personality and Social Psychology, 58,* 397–408.

Skowronski, J. J., & Carlston, D. E. (1987). Social judgment and social memory: The role of cue diagnosticity in negativity, positivity, and extremity biases. *Journal of Personality and Social Psychology, 52,* 689–699.

Skowronski, J. J., & Carlston, D. E. (1989). Negativity and extremity biases in impression formation: A review of explanations. *Psychological Bulletin, 105,* 131–142.

Skowronski, J. J., & Carlston, D. E. (1992). Caught in the act: When impressions based on highly diagnostic behaviors are resistant to contradiction. *European Journal of Social Psychology, 22,* 435–452.

Smith, J., Dixon, R. A., & Baltes, P. B. (1989). Expertise in life planning: A new research approach to investigating aspects of wisdom. In M. L. Commons, J. D. Sinnott, F. A. Richards, & C. Armon (Eds.), *Adult development* (vol. 1, pp. 307–331). New York: Praeger.

Srull, T. K. (1981). Person memory: Some tests of associative storage and retrieval models. *Journal of Experimental Psychology: Human Learning and Memory, 7,* 440–463.

Srull, T. K., Lichtenstein, M., & Rothbart, M. (1985). Associative storage and retrieval processes in person memory. *Journal of Experimental Psychology: Learning, Memory, and Cognition, 11,* 316–345.

Thompson, E. P., Roman, R. J., Moskowitz, G. B., Chaiken, S., & Bargh, J. A. (1994). Accuracy motivation attenuates covert priming: The systematic reprocessing of social information. *Journal of Personality and Social Psychology, 66,* 474–489.

Uleman, J. S., Newman, L. S., & Moskowitz, G. B. (1996). People as flexible interpreters: Evidence and issues from spontaneous trait inference. M. P. Zanna (Ed.), *Advances in experimental social psychology* (vol. 29, pp. 211–279). San Diego: Academic Press.

Webster, D. M., Richter, L., & Kruglanski, A. W. (1996). On leaping to conclusions when feeling tired: Mental fatigue effects on impressional priming. *Journal of Experimental Social Psychology, 32,* 181–195.

Wojciszke, B., Brycz, H., & Borkenau, P. (1993). Effects of information content and evaluative extremity on positivity and negativity biases. *Journal of Personality and Social Psychology, 64,* 327–336.

Wyer, R. S., Jr., & Carlston, D. E. (1994). The cognitive representation of persons and events. In R. S. Wyer, Jr. & T. K. Srull (Eds.), *Handbook of social cognition* (vol. 1, pp. 41–98). Hillsdale, NJ: Lawrence Erlbaum Associates.

Wyer, R. S., Jr., & Srull, T. K. (1989). *Memory and cognition in its social context.* Hillsdale, NJ: Lawrence Erlbaum Associates.

Zacks, R. T., & Hasher, L. (1994). Directed ignoring: Inhibitory regulation of working memory. In D. Dagenbach and T. H. Carr (Eds.), *Inhibitory processes in attention, memory, and language* (pp. 241–264). San Diego: Academic Press.

FOCUS ON THE SOCIAL CONTEXT

INTERACTIONS BETWEEN SELF AND OTHER

12

Exploring Cognition in Interactive Situations

The Aging of N + 1 Minds

Roger A. Dixon

Department of Psychology
University of Victoria
Victoria, British Columbia, Canada

The topic of social cognition as investigated developmentally throughout adulthood represents a promising convergence of theoretical traditions, research questions, and investigative methods. Like perhaps several contributors to this volume, I do not come directly to this emerging combination of emphases. Of the three principal terms in the title of the book—*social, cognition, aging*—my interests have been traditionally lodged in the latter two. That is, I have focused primarily on the field of cognitive aging—the study of cognitive changes throughout adulthood. Moreover, as is apparent in this chapter, my approach to social cognition and aging derives far more from the literature of cognitive than from that of social psychology. Nevertheless, as many observers have noticed, it is equally apparent that as one pushes the boundaries of cognition and aging, one quickly approaches the territory of such topical and antipodal neighbors as neuroscience and social psychology (Dixon & Hertzog, 1996). Thus, it is reasonable that such emphases as cognitive neuroscience and aging (e.g., Woodruff-Pak, 1997) and social cognition and aging (e.g., Blanchard-Fields, 1996) are growing rapidly. The prevailing assumption seems to be that research in cognitive aging can benefit both from reaching "up" to the social context of cognition and "out" to social aspects of cognitive functioning, and from reaching "down" to the neurological substrate and "out" to biomedical aspects of cognitive functioning. Indeed, broad-

Copyright © 1999 by Academic Press.
All rights of reproduction in any form reserved.

based, integrative scholarship has long been a hallmark of attempts to understand the complexities of human psychological aging.

Accordingly, in recent research, I have attempted to examine cognition in a selected set of situations, each of which could be characterized *provisionally* as a social context. I emphasize *provisionally* because I examine only a small portion of activities and characteristics that bona fide social psychology researchers may use, address, or define. Specifically, I examine cognition in interactive situations and cognition as it occurs in groups of two or more individuals. Thus, the goal of this chapter is to describe my perspective on collaborative cognition and aging. By way of introduction, I describe the origin of my own perspective on social cognition and aging. Following this, I summarize the rationale and selected theoretical issues and methodological challenges of exploring adult cognitive performance in collaborative, interactive, or communicative situations. Next, I review briefly some recent research on collaborative cognition and aging. I conclude with an initial effort to link further collaborative cognition with social cognition.

STEPPING FROM COLLABORATIVE COGNITION TO SOCIAL COGNITION

As described in more detail elsewhere (e.g., Dixon, 1992, 1996), my view of collaborative cognition follows that of numerous neighboring areas of research; that is, it is cognitive activity occurring in the context of more than one individual, when that activity is directed at solving an objectively common task and performed together. Such a definition typically requires some elaboration, if not qualification, as many of the neighboring literatures are organized by terms that imply less neutrality than is commonly desired by scholars, or even merited by research. For example, if rendered literally, the following terms employed by active literatures could imply some degree of interaction or cooperation, if not effectiveness: *collaborative cognition, cooperative cognition, interactive cognition, interactive minds, transactive cognition, tutorial cognition,* and *socially shared cognition.* (To be sure, relatively neutral terms, such as *situated cognition* and *situated learning,* are also available.) In any event, it is fair to characterize the most common elaborations and qualifications as focusing on the well-known notions that the group activities may not be commonly defined, that the goals may be inexplicit and changing, and that the cognitive activity of the unit may be, for a variety of reasons, less than optimally efficient (e.g., Andersson & Rönnberg, 1997; Meudell, Hitch, & Kirby, 1992; Steiner, 1972). Unsurprisingly, I typically underscore the point that the expression *collaborative cognition* is neutral with respect to the products and processes of the activity. As is true with all the literatures captured by the above terms, far from assuming a positive outcome to collaborative activities, the effects of collaboration are examined empirically.

Therefore, collaboration describes the fact that cognition is occurring in an interactive context of more than one individual, but it does not imply anything about any other characteristics or qualities of the interaction. Cognitive activity in groups of more than one individual can be cooperative and effective, leading to or promoting "process gain" (Steiner, 1972), but such collaborative cognitive activity can also be discoordinated and ineffective, leading to or promoting "process loss" (Steiner, 1972). Thus, cognitive activity may or may not benefit from the presence of collaborators, depending in part on the quality of the processes through which the group members interact and engage the problem (Hill, 1982). The definition of *collaborative cognition* is based on three sources of information, including anecdotal, previous research literature, and new empirical data.

Anecdotal examples of collaborative activity leading to either gains or losses (or stasis) are legion for most socially or professionally active individuals. Collaborations sometimes occur through efficient and thoroughly pleasant and strategic interactions, culminating in products arguably superior to those that could have in principle been produced by any given individual in the group. A symbiosis, a meeting of minds, teamwork: Cooperative, coordinative interactions may lead to correct, functional, and perhaps optimal solutions. Simply put, sometimes two (or more) people produce more than does one alone. On the other hand, some collaborations may occur through relatively inefficient, unpleasant, or nonstrategic processes, culminating in suboptimal, if not inferior, products. Disruptive or divisive individuals, discontinuity in skills or effort (e.g., social loafing), discooperative groups with individuals working at cross-purposes, or disoriented and unfocused assemblages—all can lead to ineffective collaborative processes and products. Some things are better done alone; Too many cooks may spoil some broths. Naturally, the lessons contained in these anecdotes reflect a wide range of pertinent research (e.g., Andersson, 1996; Galegher, Kraut, & Egido, 1990; Paulus, 1989; Steiner, 1972). Put colloquially, the principal research issues include the following: (1) How many cooks does it take to spoil (or improve) the broth? (2) What are the processes through which the broth is spoiled (or enhanced)? (3) What characteristics of cooks lead to spoiling or improving broth created collaboratively? (4) What is the broth and how should its quality be measured? In extant research on group cognition with children, students, and adults, the answers to these research questions often involve the social aspect or context of collaborative processes (e.g., Paulus, 1989; Resnick, Levine, & Teasley, 1991; Staudinger, 1996; Steiner, 1972).

At the very least, collaborative cognition is social in the simple sense that it occurs in social communicative settings through the medium of language and in the context of relationships and expectations (Goodnow, 1996). It is cognitive in that many tasks rendered collaboratively by social groups require individual cognitive activity as well as cooperative remembering, joint problem solving, tutorial learning, and so forth. Indeed, most research on collaborative cognition and aging thus far has been conducted with tasks conceptually and procedurally quite close to individual-level cognitive tasks. Therefore, no cognitive processes that are distinctly *social* cognitive are as yet necessarily involved. In the field of psychological aging, it remains to be seen how closely collaborative cognition will shift to or be influenced by social cognition (see Blanchard-Fields, 1996) or contextual cognition (see Berg & Klaczynski, 1996). At least in my own recent research, tasks have included collaborative episodic word memory, story memory, story telling, and problem solving. Thus far, my work in collaborative cognition and aging research has been social cognitive in nature not because of the content of the tasks but because of inherent features of the experimental situation. In the following section, the rationale and principle procedures for research on collaborative cognition and aging are presented.

WHY EXAMINE COGNITIVE AGING IN (SOCIAL) COLLABORATIVE SITUATIONS?

Although the aging-related changes associated with social cognitive performance have not yet been sufficiently charted, prodigious evidence pertaining to cognitive aging has accumulated. For understanding why cognitive aging could be studied profitably in collaborative situations, it is useful to review briefly the general profile of cognitive development in adulthood.

COGNITIVE AGING IN BRIEF

Several volumes presenting reviews of various aspects of cognitive development in adulthood have been published recently (e.g., Blanchard-Fields & Hess, 1996; Craik & Salthouse, 1992). For the most part, cognitive changes associated with aging are decremental in nature. Episodic memory—memory for personally experienced events—is an apt illustration, for it is one of the most extensively studied aspects of cognitive aging. Across a wide range of episodic tasks in literally hundreds of empirical reports, both cross-sectional and longitudinal studies have revealed patterns reflecting general decline in performance with advancing age (e.g., Bäckman, Small, & Larsson, in press; Craik & Jennings, 1992). Some discussion occurs regarding how dramatic the changes may be, but no one argues that people get better in episodic memory as a function of normal aging. Recent longitudinal studies have revealed that the decline in late life is more gradual than is indicated by cross-sectional comparisons of younger with older adults, but the profile is still one of decline (e.g., Small, Dixon, Hultsch, & Hertzog, 1999). Furthermore, prominent explanations for the descriptive observations associate the decline with inevitable and universal changes occurring in the neurological and sensory substrates (e.g., Salthouse, 1991).

With some exceptions, the picture of cognitive aging is one of generalized decline. The exceptions are indeed of interest, however, and considerable research has focused on them. Indeed, some cognitive aging researchers have examined the mechanisms and conditions under which facets of knowledge, skills, and everyday competence may be maintained, buffered from precipitous decline, or even improved throughout adulthood. Such diverse conditions as practice in a particular domain of expertise, contextual support, and compensatory mechanisms may operate selectively to promote continued cognitive competence (e.g., Baltes, 1987; Dixon & Bäckman, 1995; Perlmutter, 1990; Salthouse, 1990). For example, in his classic article on "self-management" in late life, B. F. Skinner (1983) lamented that older adults' memory failures could be associated with deficits in the environment. Obviously, his recommendations included several ways of remediating the environment, both social and physical. At one point, for example, Skinner related how he used his immediate social environment (i.e., his spouse) to supplement his failing everyday memory skills.

More recently, Charness and Bosman (1995) have addressed numerous ways that older adults experiencing aging-related cognitive and sensory deficits may compensate by modifying their environment. These authors focus on modifications to the physical environments of older adults, such as implementing architectural changes and assistive devices to counteract mobility impairments, redesigning the aural environment to reduce ambient noise levels and bolster social integration, and improving transportation access and automobile design to counter for aging-related sensory changes that affect driving safety. Nevertheless, some social environment issues are occasionally mentioned. Thus, the discussion regarding maintenance of cognitive competence in late life has attended to managing both the physical and social environments of aging and managing the individual sensory and cognitive changes associated with aging. Although not linked directly to aging issues, the situativity perspective of cognitive science provides similar ideas (e.g., Greeno, 1998).

In one sense, then, the focus has been on managing losses: What about identifying, if not promoting, gains with aging? Both gains and losses are viewed as part of life-span development (Baltes, 1987). Although most research has uncovered evidence for losses, some researchers have attempted to examine possible cognitive gains with aging. To date, however, the evidence for gains in cognitive aging is not yet substantial and persuasive. As I have noted elsewhere (Dixon, 1998), the evidence for maintenance, or lack of compelling decline, has been in the form of the following four categories: (1) more-slowly-than-expected declines in select functions, (2) losses of a lower-than-expected magnitude in some domains, (3) greater-than-expected benefits from practice or especially training, and (4) losses potentially balanced by compensatory mechanisms (e.g., Baltes, 1987; Schaie, 1996). Research targeting gains *qua* gains has not yet produced unequivocal evidence that cognitive advancement per se characterizes late life (Dixon, 1998).

COLLABORATION AND COGNITIVE LOSSES

How does collaborative cognition fit into this picture of losses, management of losses, and hoped-for gains with cognitive aging? Many observers from a wide variety of perspectives have noted the frequency with which everyday adult cognitive activity occurs in interactive contexts (e.g., Clancey, 1997; Greeno, 1998;

Greeno & Moore, 1993; Lave & Wenger, 1991; Vygotsky, 1978). A collaborative context frequently envelops cognitive performance in everyday life. Everyday examples of collaborative cognition include (1) scientific colleagues attempting to solve thorny methodological problems together; (2) medical colleagues consulting about diagnoses based on complex patterns of test results and symptomatology; (3) student study groups preparing themselves for examinations or constructing projects on challenging course material; (4) family groups or lineages attempting to reconstruct stories from their shared past; (5) spouses enlisted to help remember important appointments, duties, dates, or where the car is parked; and (6) strangers in unknown cities consulted in order to solve way-finding or map-reading problems (Dixon, 1996). Lurking behind the fact that much everyday cognition is collaborative in nature and the fact that several observers have exclaimed its theoretical relevance is the assumption that collaboration may lead to functional performance outcomes.

Collaborative cognition may represent a form of cognitive activity that is practical, leading to effective or improved solutions in some circumstances. Mechanisms leading to improved memory performance include internal mnemonic devices and external memory aids. The former include memory strategies, such as method of loci, and have been shown to greatly enhance an individual's skill in particular domains of memory. The latter include notes, calendars, diaries, tags, and the proverbial string around the finger. One form of external memory aids may also be other humans, who act as passive or active contributors to a given individual faced with a memory task. Whereas internal mnemonic devices may be limited in their scope of applicability, external memory aids may be more generalizable, more applicable to a wide range of domains and memory demands. Both may be useful in improving memory skills in memory impaired individuals (e.g., Wilson & Watson, 1996), but external memory aids may be practically useful for ameliorating performance for normal aging-related decline. Of particular relevance at present is the possibility that external memory aids in the form of human collaborators may be a means of overcoming individual-level losses or deficits.

COLLABORATION AND COMPENSATION

One general (and long-term) goal is to investigate the extent to which collaboration may be a means of compensation in cognitive aging. Put in simple social cognitive terms, the issue is whether an aging individual may benefit cognitively from collaborating with others in his or her social world. How could such a social compensatory mechanism operate? In general, compensation occurs when an individual uses an alternative mechanism for performing a given task when the previously used mechanism is unavailable because of an injury-related deficit or a aging-related decline (Bäckman & Dixon, 1992; Salthouse, 1990). Despite the loss of a typical or even principal means of performing a complex task, a compensatory mechanism can support continued high levels of performance on skill-related tasks. Most examples of compensatory mechanisms in cognitive aging are substitutions, involving a latent component taking over the task previously performed by the declining component (Salthouse, 1995). Other forms of compensation, however, are possible and may in fact be more likely to occur in interactive settings (e.g., Dixon, 1992; Dixon & Bäckman, 1995; Dixon & Gould, 1996).

As implied in the brief section on cognitive aging above, many older adults are working (cognitively) at the receding edge of their individual abilities. Such individuals may have experienced aging-related decrements in fundamental mechanisms that contribute to memory performance (e.g., speed of processing, processing resources, sensory capacities). Could they be able to compensate for such individual-level decline by pooling their available resources with cooperating individuals? Combining resources in some cooperative fashion may promote successful performance on complex and demanding cognitive-based tasks of daily living, many of which are social cognitive in nature. These include such tasks as decision making, life planning, advice giving, collective remembering, intellectual teamwork, and storytelling. Successful combinations of resources may be additive (e.g., in the sense of combining like skills and domains across cooperating individuals), complementary (e.g., in the sense of combining different skills or domains from the cooperating individuals), or emergent (e.g., performing at levels that are qualitatively different or higher than would have been possible for only one of the cooperating individuals).

The principal medium of such collaboration is language or, more functionally, communication. Through conversation, collaborators construct a mutual set of meanings or interpretations concerning the nature, purpose, goals, procedures, and conventions of the interaction (e.g., Clark, 1996; Schegloff, 1991). Notably, communication is a competence generally maintained with aging (Ryan, Giles, Bartolucci, & Henwood, 1986). If older adults interacting conversationally may carry out the mutual construction of meanings competently, then conversation may be a mechanism through which some compensation could occur. Because the medium of collaboration is (observable) conversation and the focus of collaboration is cognitive problems, an opportunity to view metacognitive (e.g., strategic) processes *in situ* is presented. Individual participants are obliged to make some metacognitive efforts explicit, manifesting through their deliberations their intentions, strategies, plans, reviews, and even ongoing performance monitoring. From this perspective, the emphasis is less on the individual and group level performance (e.g., memory and metamemory) and more on the processes through which the group accomplishes its activities. These processes are both verbal and nonverbal but are nearly always symbolic, communicative, interactive, and social.

To the extent that communication is involved—and to the extent that communication is a skill—the probability of successful collaboration may be enhanced by experience. At the individual level as well, the probability of compensation is increased as a function of experience or, especially, domain-relevant expertise. At the group level, compensation may be a function of successful communication, which may be related to experience with the problem domain, the processes of interaction, or the particular interactants participating. This leads to two main theoretical issues posed by collaboration and cognition research.

TWO THEORETICAL ISSUES IN COLLABORATIVE COGNITION AND AGING RESEARCH

The principal descriptive issue in collaborative cognition and aging research pertains to the extent to which and how well older groups of adults use collaborators to perform complex cognitive tasks. Descriptive targets include the products (how many, how fast) and processes (communicative characteristics) of collaboration. This basic issue is of considerable interest, for very little empirical evidence has been gathered concerning whether, at what level, and under what conditions older adults may collaborate with colleagues successfully (or unsuccessfully). In addressing theoretical issues, however, it is useful to assume that older adults will collaborate at some level of effectiveness with colleagues. It is not necessary to assume that the collaboration will be optimal, only that it will occur through observable processes that lead to measurable products. Although there are numerous theoretical issues in collaborative or interactive research (e.g., Baltes & Staudinger, 1996; Greeno, 1998), I discuss only two in this section, both of which have already been broached.

Collaborative Expertise

The first theoretical issue to highlight is whether there are experience-based differences in collaborative effectiveness. Although addressed in other literatures (e.g., Andersson & Rönnberg, 1997; Engeström, 1992; Gagnon, 1995; Galegher et al., 1990; Wegner, Erber, & Raymond, 1991), it is not widely developed in aging. The issue is as follows: For individuals, experience at the level of expertise may lead to sustained performance in domain-specific cognitive activities. Could such experience operate—and influence performance—at the group level? With aging, an intriguing set of questions emanate from the hypothesis that collaborative or interactive expertise may develop with practice (Engeström, 1992). If interactive expertise may be characterized similarly to individual expertise, then researchers might expect better performance for experienced collaborating groups than for inexperienced groups. For example, interactive expert groups might perform cognitive tasks relatively fast, efficiently, accurately, and with some degree of self-monitoring. These characteristics are signs of expertise at the individual level. If expertise at a social group level exists, then the suggestion is that one of the conditions under which collaborative effects may be observed relates to a fundamental characteristic of the group itself.

For collaborative cognition theory in general, this perspective suggests that one issue to consider is the extent to which the individual participants are acquainted with one another. Beneficial effects of collaboration may be more or less observed depending on the experience of the collaborative group. For example, from the situativity viewpoint (Greeno, 1998) it may be possible that *affor-*

dances—aspects of the systems that support interactions—and *attunements*—or adjustments—to constraints may be more readily available for experienced inter-actants. More specifically, for collaborative cognition and aging theory, such an approach provides a potential explanation for the performance boost that may ensue from collaboration. It also provides clues regarding the interactive processes that support or detract from efficient collaborative functioning.

Along with a long life, socially active older adults may participate in several longstanding collaborative groups. Many older adults have participated in bridge clubs, service clubs, religious organizations, hobby-related groups (e.g., garden-ing clubs, golf clubs), professional or retirement committees, and teams of vari-ous sorts. As a function of their membership in such groups, they may have par-ticipated in a variety of activities requiring communication in the service of group decision making and the like. In addition, many older adults—especially of the current cohort—have been members of a longstanding dyad, one that is typified by frequent interaction, much collaborative cognitive activity, and the develop-ment of a high degree of knowledge about one another's strengths and weak-nesses. Perhaps more than before in history, many older adults are one half of a long-term married couple, where *long term* means more than 40 years of marriage (Carstensen, Gottman, & Levensen, 1995; Dixon, 1996, Gagnon, 1995). Indeed, because of sociohistorical characteristics of the life course in the 20th century, long-term married couples provide a unique and naturally available experimental resource. It may be possible, therefore, to begin the investigation of interactive expertise and its relevance for cognitive aging with older married couples, com-paring their collaborative products and processes to those of younger couples, younger and older unacquainted dyads, as well as to individuals. As it is for indi-vidual cognitive aging, expertise—in this case, interactive expertise—may pro-vide a mechanism through which group cognitive competence may be maintained into late life.

Collaborative Compensation

A second highlighted theoretical issue is closely related to the first. As noted earlier, older individual adults may compensate for decline in skill-related com-ponents through several mechanisms. A well-researched example in cognitive aging is that of transcription typing, in which skilled older typists compensate for losses in reaction time and finger-tapping speed by using large hand–eye previews (Bosman, 1993; Salthouse, 1987). Is it possible for a group of older individuals to compensate for aging-related losses in components of particular skills by recruit-ing other individuals who possess relatively preserved components or who have developed alternative mechanisms?

The compensation issue provides a theoretical framework in which to under-stand such patterns of results (e.g., Bäckman & Dixon, 1992; Dixon, 1996; Dixon & Gould, 1996). In addition, however, compensation may be linked to expertise; that is, collaborative compensation may be linked to collaborative expertise. As it may be at the individual level, the probability of compensation may be enhanced by experience. If collaborative compensation is linked to communication—as was discussed earlier—then it may be hypothesized that effective and successful communication may be at least partly a function of interactive experience. Aging collaborative experts may be more likely to compensate for declining individual-level cognitive skills through interactive-level adjustments, strategies, monitoring, support, and queries. Thus, long-term married couples—to continue the example of collaborative expertise—may be more likely to benefit from collaboration in everyday life—and the lab—than are other collections of older adults.

Summary

Two prominent theoretical issues are noted—collaborative expertise and collaborative compensation. Highlighting the potential linkage between these two issues allows attention to turn to selected methodological challenges in collaborative cognition and aging research.

RESEARCH ISSUES IN COLLABORATION AND AGING

There are four interesting categories of research challenges in collaboration and aging: (1) group size and composition issues, (2) comparison indicators, (3) alternative comparison units or groups, and (4) temporal or dynamic sampling of group performances and process. One purpose of conducting collaborative cognition research in aging populations is to investigate whether older groups perform some cognitive tasks better than do older individuals, whether two or more heads are better than one, and if so, what the conditions are under which this obtains. Thus, it is important to identify and characterize the principal dimensions along which the data are being selected.

Group Composition

The first of the research issues focuses on the construction of the groups themselves, including the size (individual, dyad, triad, tetrad, and so forth) and various features of the composition of the groups. These compositional features include such social status characteristics as age of the members, gender, perceived social power or status, culture or ethnicity, and language (e.g., Baltes & Staudinger, 1996; Resnick et al., 1991; Steiner, 1972). Initial studies described in the next major section of this chapter have proceeded conservatively, in that each group has been homogeneous with respect to age, gender, and language, with social status remaining undefined and unmeasured, although participants have been drawn from a common population. When the groups have not been homogeneous, the manipulation of group composition factors has been modest, such as using two-gender dyads (married couples and controls). Future research from a social cognitive perspective may find many of these selection factors to be interesting grouping variables. Manipulating age or social status characteristics within a group may be of interest for some interactive research. An additional composition issue concerns the relationships among the group members. Although it is reasonable to begin a research program by examining unacquainted groups, supplementing that strategy with theory-driven selections of experienced dyads may be useful. All groups are not alike, and they are not alike in some detectable, controllable, theoretically meaningful, and manipulable ways. Researchers should attend carefully to group composition.

Tasks

The second issue focuses on the tasks administered and the measures derived to represent the group performance: What variables should researchers compare across factors related to group composition? For several reasons, my own research plan began by maximizing the comparability to individual-level cognitive aging performance (Dixon, 1992). Thus, tasks continuous with individual cognition literature were selected. This is not necessary, however, for researchers can adapt tasks from other neighboring literatures, and specific tasks representing practical or social cognition may hold special promise (e.g., Berg & Klaczynski, 1996; Blanchard-Fields, 1996; Staudinger, 1996). Apart from this dimension, the focus is on both products and processes of collaboration. In cognitive aging—and perhaps social cognitive aging—research, it is not always sufficient to compare age groups in terms of the most typical or simplest single product, such as the number of items remembered. Several other theoretically and practically relevant performance measures should be considered. However, even a relatively rich selection of product variables may not capture the potential richness available in this paradigm. Thus, I recommend that researchers consider videotaping the interactions and examining a variety of variables pertaining to the communicative process—the process through which group members interact in performing their group task. The collaborative cognition paradigm provides a unique window into the manner (and efficiency) in which social cognitive tasks are solved.

Comparisons

The third research issue concerns the key comparisons required and available to the researcher (Paulus, 1989; Steiner, 1972). Assuming a principal interest in cognitive aging, the performance of older groups may be compared with a series of possible alternatives: (1) older individuals (including other individuals or themselves as baseline), (2) older groups of different sizes, (3) older groups of different compositions, (4) younger individuals (including other individuals or, in a longitudinal design, themselves as younger individuals), (5) younger groups of same or different sizes, (6) younger groups of same or different compositions, (7) nominal groups (which are not actual groups but are aggregations of data from lower-size experimental units), or (8) predicted performance (which is derived from a variety of mathematical formulas). Certainly, not all possible combinations of these comparison groups may be generated in a single research program, much less a single experiment. Nevertheless, it is useful to know that these options exist, that the population of comparison groups is much broader than simply (say) individuals versus dyads. Researchers are necessarily selecting along this dimension when they decide their comparison groups, so it is better to be more than less aware of this fact. Arguably, it is best to sample systematically among these options.

Intragroup Variability

The fourth issue concerns the dynamic characteristics of groups and collaborative episodes. Two senses of within-group (across time) dynamics or variability may be noted. First, more evidence pertaining to the extent to which individuals may vary in their own performance on similar tasks and ratings over multiple assessments is accumulating (e.g., Dixon, Hertzog, Friesen, & Hultsch, 1993; Nesselroade, 1988, 1991). This fact has been noted as especially relevant to theoretical issues in cognitive aging (Dixon & Hertzog, 1996) and may apply to social cognitive aging. The fluctuation across seemingly stable characteristics is not only a function of measurement error, but also reflects genuine intraindividual variability. If individuals vary across time in episodic memory performance (Dixon et al., 1993), then it is quite possible that a given occasion of assessment of group memory performance may reflect the individuals' contributions that are at different points in their fluctuating intraindividual profiles. Thus, it is a simple speculation that groups, too, may vary "intraindividually." That is, it may be worthwhile investigating the extent to which one-shot estimates of group or social cognition result in stable estimates of a group's "true" score. On the other hand, the presence of multiple partners may serve as a reliability control, such that multiple indicators may produce a more stable estimate of the true score.

A second form of intraindividual variability in group performance is that occurring within a given session or collaborative conversation. We have seen that the relative proportion of contributions from various categories, including products and processes, varies as a function of such methodological considerations as (1) when (i.e., at what point in time) in the conversation the researcher observes and (2) what part of the conversation the researcher samples (Gould, Kurzman, & Dixon, 1994). We have also seen that examining social cognitive conversations dynamically may reveal much about the processes that occur, as well as the functions of those processes. Indeed, a dynamic analysis may shed light on the interpretation regarding collaborative benefits, as has been revealed in one recent study (see the next major section in this chapter and Gould et al., 1994). Dynamic characteristics cannot be observed—or at least not in compelling fashion—if simple summary scores of product or process variables are used. Overall, some attention to the fact that groups, like individuals, are changing, dynamic, adaptive "organisms" may be justified for social cognitive approaches.

Summary

The purpose of this section is not to review a daunting set of methodological complications derived from only four categories of methodological issues but to note that all researchers conducting studies on collaborative cognition will, whether they consider it explicitly or not, make selections among these four methodological dimensions. For the most part, such selections can be justified, but until the territory is thoroughly explored, it may be premature to generate strongly worded conclusions about the benefits (or lack thereof) of collaborative cognition. At the very least, this review of the methodological signposts may encourage both modesty in interpreting completed research and ambition in constructing new research in collaborative cognition and aging.

EXAMPLES OF RESEARCH ON COGNITION IN (SOCIAL) COLLABORATIVE SITUATIONS

In this section, I note briefly several studies on collaborative cognition and aging, especially as they pertain to one or more of the issues described above. The purpose is not to review these studies—or this growing literature—comprehensively but rather to demonstrate selectively that (1) some of the principal substantive issues have been addressed and (2) many substantive, methodological, and theoretical issues remain to be explored. Although studies of situativity in cognition are increasing (e.g., Greeno, 1998), much remains to be done, especially in furthering our understanding of the aging mind in social group situations. Thus, this section provides only highlights, but interested readers may consult primary sources or other reviews for further information. It is organized into three subsections, corresponding to the products, processes, and metacognitive aspects of collaborative cognition and aging.

PRODUCT STUDIES

A variety of cognitive tasks have been employed in collaborative cognition research in general and collaborative cognition and aging research in particular. The tasks have included memory tasks (e.g., word, digit, story, and working memory; world fact knowledge; and autobiographical recall), problem solving (e.g., practical problems, wisdom), storytelling, and neuropsychological assessment (e.g., fluency and card sorting). Some of the aging-related work is reviewed in several sources (e.g., Baltes & Staudinger, 1996; Dixon, 1996). Other reviews may be found in Clancey (1997) and Resnick et al. (1991).

As it has been most extensively studied in aging-related literatures, I focus here on collaborative story remembering. Based in part on the extant neighboring story memory literature (e.g., Clark & Stephenson, 1989; Middleton & Edwards, 1990), several studies pertaining to aging have been completed. For example, a basic study explored (1) whether younger and older unacquainted adults could perform better in a story memory task when working in groups of two (dyads) or four (tetrads) as compared to working alone and (2) whether younger or older adults benefited differentially from the presence of acquainted collaborators (see Dixon & Gould, 1998). In the first of two experiments, younger and older adults recalled more information from the stories when performing as groups than as individuals, but neither group benefited differentially. The recall difference between tetrad and individual performance was 7% for younger adults and 9% for older adults. In the spirit of scrutinizing multiple performance measures to reach conclusions regarding the effectiveness of collaboration, we also inspected the quality of the recall. It would be in principle possible for the groups to be recalling more of the original story information than individuals, where that additional information is relatively disordered or composed of lower-level details. Such ancillary evidence would not support an inference of benefits to collaboration. Typically, individuals (both younger and older) recall a greater proportion of main ideas from stories, followed by successively subordinate ideas (or details). In the discourse processing literature, this is considered a well-structured retold story. Would the unacquainted dyads and tetrads of this study produce a qualitatively well-structured recall protocol? We observed that indeed they did: The structures of the collaboratively retold stories by both groups of two and four were indistinguishable from those of the individuals working alone. Furthermore, younger and older groups' story structures were indistinguishable from one another.

The second experiment in this study was designed to initiate the examination of collaborative expertise. Complementing the earlier testing of unacquainted dyads on story memory, Dixon and Gould (1998) recruited younger and older married couples. The rationale was that members of married couples would offer extensive experience of collaborating cognitively with one another, especially perhaps in retelling stories. Interestingly, the older couples, who had been married at least 40 years, performed as well as the younger married couples in the collaborative story recall task. Comparing their performance to that of the groups in the first experiment made for some interesting conjectures: Most notably, the older dyads performed better than the older tetrads and older dyads of the previous experiment. Following the recommendation to inspect multiple indicators of performance, we embedded a metamemory evaluation in the collaborative story recall procedures. Specifically, just prior to performing the recall task, we asked the couples to predict how much (in percent) they would recall from the original story, and just after they performed the recall task, we asked them to postdict how much information they had indeed recalled from the story. The younger and older couples tended to overestimate their performance, both before and after their actual collaborative recall effort. Although the magnitude of performance estimates is of interest, the extent of their accuracy is more indicative of the quality of performance monitoring (e.g., Hertzog & Dixon, 1994). Examining the accuracy of their predictions and postdictions, we found that the couples were understandably less accurate before than after the collaborative recall episode. However, the older couples especially upgraded their predictions from one story to the next; by the second story their prediction accuracy was virtually the same as their postdiction accuracy (see Dixon & Gould, 1998).

The results of this particular study confirm the premise that older adult groups can collaborate on cognitive tasks. Their performance is indeed quantitatively better than the average of same-age individuals and is qualitatively similar to that of younger groups. In addition, older couples seemed to be especially effective at collaborating with one another in performing such complex cognitive tasks. Rarely are older individual adults as cognitively effective as younger individual adults, so the potential social cognitive benefit is at least worth exploring further. Indeed, other product variables have been examined, with converging results. Studies examining elaborations produced during recall (Gould, Trevithick, & Dixon, 1991), everyday problem-solving performance (Dixon, Fox, Trevithick, & Brundin, 1997), and other aspects of story memory (Gagnon, 1995) have led to similar interpretations. These are product-centered studies: What about the processes of collaboration?

PROCESS STUDIES

Process studies typically focus on the collaborative episode as a conversation or communication (e.g., Clark & Wilkes-Gibbs, 1986; Hupet, Chantraine, & Nef, 1993; Ryan et al., 1986). Using tasks identical in design to the product studies, the goal of process studies is to examine explicitly the processes through which groups accomplish whatever it is they accomplish. In one highlighted study, Gould et al. (1994) recorded and transcribed the entire collaborative recall conversations of younger and older unacquainted dyads and married couples. All statement clauses were assigned to one of four categories: (1) individual based recall, or correctly recalled information or inferences based on the story and produced by one of the individuals; (2) collaborative story-based recall, or correctly recalled information or inferences produced as a function of the group effort; (3) task discussion, or statements referring to the performance of the task and strategies for improving, and (4) sociability and support statements, or personal elaborative commentary and verbal indications of agreement and harmony.

When comparing only the overall proportions of total statements in each of these categories, we observed similar levels of individual-based recall across the four groups, as well as similar levels of collaborative-based recall across the groups. However, younger and older married couples produced more task and strategy discussion statements than did the younger and older unacquainted dyads. Instead, the latter groups produced more sociability and support statements. Although such simple comparisons characterize the overall process of communication in the collaborative episode, they do not yet do so optimally. To approximate a more dynamic analysis, we divided the conversations into three parts and examined the relative proportions of these four categories of statements at the beginning and the end of the conversations (Gould et al., 1994). All groups, but especially the older couples and dyads, began with a spurt of individual-based recall statements, which dropped off substantially by the final third of their conversations. Older couples and dyads showed very different patterns of conversations in the final third. Increasing from the first to final third for older couples were statements regarding the task and strategies for solving it. Seemingly, the effort was to wrench every last bit of possible recall from their collaborative episode. In so doing, they might have recognized that their actual recall production was declining as a function of time in the conversation—and time since the exposure to the story. By contrast, the older unacquainted dyads showed no change in this variety of statements, increasing instead their production of sociability and support statements. Seemingly, they had no particular motivation or no particular knowledge on which to base strategy comments and thus resorted to personal commentary and social support. Whereas younger couples had a pattern similar, but less pronounced, to that produced by older couples, younger dyads showed no evidence of compensatory efforts (Gould et al., 1994).

Overall, it is conceivable that the long-term married couples were experienced enough with one another that they could bypass the sociability concern and concentrate on strategic efforts to improve their performance. Naturally, unacquainted dyads do not have the luxury of such knowledge and so concentrate on other aspects of the interaction. This research is, of course, not yet definitive, but it does point to several potentially intriguing avenues of future studies, many of which are social cognitive in nature.

METACOGNITIVE STUDIES

Metacognition refers to awareness (i.e., self-representations, beliefs, knowledge, monitoring) of one's own cognitive functioning, including influences, predilections, performance, skills, vulnerabilities, and mnemonic techniques. Metacognition has been widely studied in developmental psychology, cognitive psychology, and in cognitive aging (e.g., Cavanaugh, 1996; Metcalfe & Shimamura, 1994). As noted earlier, some aspects of metacognition are closely related to social cognition; these include memory self-efficacy beliefs and aspects of memory performance occurring in or affected by social situations.

Until recently, virtually no research has been conducted on metacognitive characteristics of collaborating groups of older adults, although several related reasons for investigating such phenomena may be noted. First, given the integration of the cognitive and the metacognitive, if collaborating groups produce cognitive phenomena, they may also produce metacognitive phenomena. Such phenomena may be of interest to researchers in that they characterize, in a way not available through standard cognitive measures, the cognitive functioning of groups. Second, on the individual level, some aspects of metacognition—such as accuracy of performance awareness—are linked to individual expertise. The question is raised, therefore, whether such characteristics are linked to group or interactive expertise. Third, in cognitive aging, several aspects of metacognition are of interest insofar as they reflect phenomena pertaining to cognitive activities, interests, performance, and changes therein in late life (Hertzog & Dixon, 1994). Thus, research in memory self-efficacy, memory beliefs, and memory monitoring have been actively pursued in this area (Berry, Chapter 4, this volume; Cavanaugh, 1996; Hertzog & Dixon, 1994). The notion is that beliefs may function to determine whether an older adult engages in cognitive activity, the extent and breadth of such engagement, the effort invested in performing well, the attribution made for successful performance, and the accommodation made for unsuccessful performance.

Two aspects of collaborative metacognition and aging have been explored recently. The first is collaborative memory monitoring, or collaborating on producing performance estimates both before (prediction) and after (postdiction) collaborative cognitive performance. I briefly summarized this study above and will not address it further in this section (see Dixon & Gould, 1998). The second aspect refers to beliefs about collaboration, as held by individuals and collaborating groups. We explored this aspect recently in several different ways (see Dixon, Gagnon, & Crow, 1998; Gagnon, 1995), two of which I summarize in this section.

In the first effort to investigate collaborative beliefs, we asked younger and older married couples, as well as younger and older unacquainted dyads, to rate their general memory separately as individuals and as (their current) dyads. Both younger and older adults rated their couple-level memory performance to be better than their individual-level memory performance. Furthermore, older couples rated their couple-level performance higher than older dyads rated their dyad-level performance. One tentative interpretation was that older adults implicitly support the linked hypotheses that there are beneficial collaborative effects especially for interactive experts (Dixon et al., 1998).

Another aspect of collaborative metacognition was explored in this study (Dixon et al., 1998). We asked a set of questions concerning participants' comparative beliefs about collaborative memory effectiveness (see also Staudinger, 1996). For example, participants were asked to rank-order the effectiveness (regarding memory performance) of the following recall conditions: working alone, working with a spouse, working with a friend (same gender), working with a friend (other gender), working with a stranger (same gender), and working with a stranger (other gender). For both younger and older adults, collaborating with a spouse was believed to be the most effective mechanism of memory performance. Following this, in order, the participants believed that memory performance would be more effective when collaborating with friend (same gender), friends (other gender), working alone, stranger (same gender), and stranger (other gender). Both gender and relationship experience appear to matter to these expectations. Notably, although the rank orders were the same, the patterns were slightly different for the two age groups. Whereas younger adults seemed to cluster spouses with friends (of both genders) as the better bets for collaborative memory performance, older adults appeared to place couples substantially above a second cluster, consisting of friends (of both genders) and working alone.

In sum, these data are consistent with the hypothesis that interactive expertise is believed by adults to play a role in the extent of benefits accruing to collaboration. It is not known how much these beliefs may generalize to other tasks; the potential cohort and gender specificity has not been explored adequately. The three major points of this section are that (1) metacognitive phenomena exist at the collaborative level of analysis, (2) collaborative metacognitive phenomena may be measured, and (3) metacognitive phenomena may provide useful information about group expectations and functioning.

SUMMARY AND CONCLUSIONS:
MERGING SOCIAL COGNITION
AND COLLABORATIVE COGNITION

I began with the premise that collaborative cognition may be one form of social cognition. At least in the simple sense of cognition occurring in social interactive circumstances, this premise appears to be safe. In deeper senses, it is cognition that is (1) frequent in its everyday appearance; (2) practical and seemingly functional in its everyday effects; (3) operating through the prism of communication, including verbal and nonverbal manifestations; (4) measurable in terms of a wide range of group products and interactive processes; and (5) theoretically linked to interactive (or social) phenomena, such as collaborative expertise and compensation, with parallel processes at the individual level.

Insofar as social cognitive competence is reflected in collaborative cognitive competence, similar criteria for research progress may be elucidated. That is, social cognitive aging may be examined in multiple domains of performance as indicated by multiple tasks, ranging from cognitive tasks administered or performed in social situations to social cognitive tasks administered and performed in individual laboratory situations. As noted above, both products and processes are important in evaluating the extent of collaborative benefits and in evaluating social cognitive competence. Finally, the individual is not lost in social cognitive research, just as this unit of analysis is not replaced in collaborative cognition research. Social cognitive competence may be evaluated in both individual and interactive contexts. Collaborative competence must be evaluated in interactive contexts, but individually produced phenomena are relevant, as are various comparisons of group-level to individual-level performance.

The brief research examples represent only a small fraction of potential research questions in collaborative cognition and aging. When each of the dimensions tapped by the research program are considered, it is possible to stipulate others that could be of interest to social cognition researchers. Selected illustrations will suffice. First, although I have used primarily "laboratory" cognitive tasks, adapted for interactive performance, it is possible to apply a much wider range of tasks. Such new tasks could include explicitly social cognition tasks, everyday competence tasks, and professional or leisure pursuit tasks (e.g., Blanchard-Fields, 1996; Dixon et al., 1997; Staudinger & Baltes, 1997; Streufert, Pogash, Piasecki, & Post, 1990). Second, it is possible to expand the range of performance indicators. I have argued that a shortcoming of some extant collaborative cognition research is that only single products (e.g., number of words or digits recalled) are used to evaluate group performance. Given that many cognitive tasks are complex, such an approach may insufficiently represent the wide range of behaviors that accompany correct performance and that may yield valuable insights into group functioning. For example, elaborations, inferences, macrostatements, metastatements, errors, and other products may, if analyzed and compiled, contribute to a more accurate profile of the strengths and weaknesses of group memory performance. Some of these product indicators may be useful, as well, for other tasks, such as social or practical problem solving.

Third, as indicated in earlier research, interaction patterns—or process indicators—are of crucial importance to understanding the productivity and efficiency of collaborating groups. Some research on affect in long-term married couples has been conducted, including both verbal and nonverbal indicators of affective expressions in problem-discussing interactions (e.g., Carstensen et al., 1995). Affect expression in interaction, however, is rarely related to interactive cognitive performance, although it is reasonable to assume that the quality of the interaction—and perhaps the quality of the relationship—could affect the quality of performance. Thus, incorporating affect in social cognitive research could be profitable. Other process-oriented work has been accomplished in collaborative memory and aging research, with indicators such as strategy negotiations, social support, sharing, and cross-cuing considered by several authors (e.g., Dixon & Gould, 1998; Gould et al., 1994; Meudell, Hitch, & Boyle, 1995). For the most part, little importation of interaction analyses on interactive cognition has as yet been accomplished (see Greeno, 1998, for suggestions). Further merging of these approaches should be of immense interest to social cognitive researchers.

A fourth area for further development in social cognitive approaches to collaborative cognition includes an expansion of individual- and group-level correlates of group performance. Perhaps the most relevant at this juncture are the group-level correlates. Relatively little research has investigated "group differences" characteristics of older adult groups and related these characteristics to group-level performance. Our initial effort at beginning such work was in examining dyad-level metacognitive beliefs, including memory confidence, memory self-efficacy beliefs, and implicit theories of collaborative effectiveness (Dixon et al., 1998). Relating such social cognitive indicators to social group performance will be an interesting next step. In addition, measuring aspects of the group itself, such as cohesion and quality, may lead to interesting predictions about performance measures. In this regard, married couples have been evaluated for marital satisfaction and even collaborative working memory, and group-level scores have been initially related to group-level cognitive performance (Gagnon, 1995). Much more can be done in this regard.

A fifth area for further expansion includes exploration of a greater variety of naturally occurring groups. Unacquainted groups have been the most frequently examined unit, although older married couples have received growing attention. Of particular relevance for social cognitive aging research could be such groups as caregiving dyads (e.g., Cavanaugh et al., 1989; Fox, 1997), work or hobby teams, families or lineages, and committees or clubs. How well would such groups perform in domains relevant to their collaborative experience? How much experience is required for older adults to develop or benefit from collaborative expertise?

Finally, a sixth area for further research should be noted. Virtually no research has been conducted on groups of individuals from diverse ethnic or racial backgrounds. This is potentially a valuable source of information about social cognition, as cultures may more or less emphasize collaborative versus individual ethics (Cole, 1996). In cultures emphasizing the group (over the individual), group-level cognitive performance may be quite impressive indeed. No universal claims about the effectiveness of collaboration can be made until groups of different constellations and backgrounds are systematically explored.

The purpose of this conclusion is to focus on several interesting possibilities for future research that could merge even more closely the growing social cognitive emphasis and the inchoate collaborative cognition program. The focus, of course, is on how these potentially interesting new directions of research may make contributions to understanding psychological aging. In general, the argument is a simple one: Much adult cognitive activity occurs in the context of other individuals, and much of this activity is collaborative in nature, with two or more individuals working together to solve a particular set of problems. For adults experiencing individual-level decline or impairment, such collaborative activities hold potential for promoting effective solutions to everyday cognitive problems. In this sense, aging individuals may be able to compensate for some cognitive decline through the strategic use of collaborators, via the mechanism of communication. Notably, many older adults believe that they may benefit selectively from at least close collaborative relationships (Dixon et al., 1998). Unlike researchers investigating younger adults only (primarily university students; e.g., Andersson & Rönnberg, 1996), we have found some evidence, from examining a wide range of product and process variables, that such a performance benefit may be observed in at least select circumstances. I have tried to offer a sense of how much more (in both quantity and refinement) collaborative (social) cognitive work there is to do—but also how auspicious it appears at this juncture. The continued merging of social cognition and collaborative cognition in the study of human aging is a promising direction of future progress.

ACKNOWLEDGMENTS

Support for this chapter and most of the research described herein was provided by a grant from the Natural Sciences and Engineering Research Council of Canada. Some research summarized in this chapter was supported by grant AG08235 from the National Institute on Aging (NIA) and a grant from the Canadian Aging Research Network.

REFERENCES

Andersson, J. (1996). *Two is one too many: Dyadic memory collaboration effects on encoding and retrieval of episodes.* Unpublished doctoral dissertation, Department of Education and Psychology, Linköping University, Linköping, Sweden.

Andersson, J., & Rönnberg, J. R. (1996). Collaboration and memory: Effects of dyadic retrieval on different memory tasks. *Applied Cognitive Psychology, 10,* 171–181.

Andersson, J., & Rönnberg, J. R. (1997). Cued memory collaboration: Effects of friendship and type of retrieval cue. *European Journal of Cognitive Psychology, 9,* 273–287.

Bäckman, L., & Dixon, R. A. (1992). Psychological compensation: A theoretical framework. *Psychological Bulletin, 112,* 259–283.

Bäckman, L., Small, B. J., & Larsson, M. (in press). Memory. In J. G. Evans, T. F. Williams, B. L. Beattie, J.-P. Michel, & G. K. Wilcock (Eds.), *Oxford textbook of geriatric medicine* (2nd ed.). Oxford: Oxford University Press.

Baltes, P. B. (1987). Theoretical propositions of life-span developmental psychology: On the dynamics between growth and decline. *Developmental Psychology, 23,* 611–626.

Baltes, P. B., & Staudinger, U. M. (Eds.). (1996). *Interactive minds: Life-span perspectives on the social foundation of cognition.* Cambridge, UK: Cambridge University Press.

Berg, C. A., & Klaczynski, P. I. (1996). Practical intelligence and problem solving: Searching for perspectives. In F. Blanchard-Fields & T. M. Hess (Eds.), *Perspectives on cognitive change in adulthood and aging* (pp. 323–357). New York: McGraw-Hill.

Blanchard-Fields, F. (1996). Social cognitive development in adulthood and aging. In F. Blanchard-Fields & T. M. Hess (Eds.), *Perspectives on cognitive change in adulthood and aging* (pp. 454–487). New York: McGraw-Hill.

Blanchard-Fields, F., & Hess, T. M. (Eds.). (1996). *Perspectives on cognitive change in adulthood and aging.* New York: McGraw-Hill.

Bosman, E. A. (1993). Age-related differences in the motoric aspects of transcription typing skill. *Psychology and Aging, 8,* 87–102.

Carstensen, L. L., Gottman, J. M., & Levenson, R. W. (1995). Emotional behavior in long-term marriage. *Psychology and Aging, 10,* 140–149.

Cavanaugh, J. C. (1996). Memory self-efficacy as a moderator of memory change. In F. Blanchard-Fields & I. M. Hess (Eds.), *Perspectives on cognitive change in adulthood and aging* (pp. 488–507). New York: McGraw-Hill.

Cavanaugh, J. C., Dunn, N. J., Mowery, D., Feller, C., Niederehe, G., Frugé, E., & Volpendesta, D. (1989). Problem-solving strategies in dementia patient-caregiver dyads. *The Gerontologist, 29,* 156–158.

Charness, N., & Bosman, E. A. (1995). Compensation through environmental modification. In R. A. Dixon & L. Bäckman (Eds.), *Compensating for psychological deficits and declines: Managing losses and promoting gains* (pp. 147–168). Mahwah, NJ: Lawrence Erlbaum Associates.

Clancey, W. J. (1997). *Situated cognition.* Cambridge, UK: Cambridge University Press.

Clark, H. H. (1996). *Using language.* Cambridge, UK: Cambridge University Press.

Clark, H. H., & Wilkes-Gibb, D. (1986). Referring as a collaborative process. *Cognition, 22,* 1–39.

Clark, N. K., & Stephenson, G. M. (1989). Group remembering. In P. B. Paulus (Ed.), *Psychology of group influence* (pp. 357–391). Hillsdale, NJ: Lawrence Erlbaum Associates.

Cole, M. (1996). Interacting minds in a life-span perspective: A cultural-historical approach to culture and cognitive development. In P. B. Baltes & U. M. Staudinger (Eds.), *Interactive minds: Life-span perspectives on the social foundation of cognition* (pp. 59–87). Cambridge, UK: Cambridge University Press.

Craik, F. I. M., & Jennings, J. M. (1992). Human memory. In F. I. M. Craik & T. A. Salthouse (Eds.), *Handbook of aging and cognition* (pp. 51–110). Hillsdale, NJ: Lawrence Erlbaum Associates.

Craik, F. I. M., & Salthouse, T. A. (Eds.). (1992). *Handbook of aging and cognition.* Hillsdale, NJ: Lawrence Erlbaum Associates.

Dixon, R. A. (1992). Contextual approaches to adult intellectual development. In R. J. Sternberg & C. A. Berg (Eds.), *Intellectual development* (pp. 350–380). Cambridge, UK: Cambridge University Press.

Dixon, R. A. (1996). Collaborative memory and aging. In D. Herrmann, C. McEvoy, C. Hertzog, P. Hertel, & M. K. Johnson (Eds.), *Basic and applied memory research: Theory in context* (vol. 1, pp. 359–383). Mahwah, NJ: Lawrence Erlbaum Associates.

Dixon, R. A. (1998). The concept of gains in cognitive aging. In N. Schwarz, S. Sudman, B. Knäuper, & D. Park (Eds.), *Cognition aging and self-reports* (pp. 71–92). Philadelphia, PA: Psychology Press.

Dixon, R. A., & Backman, L. (Eds.). (1995). *Compensating for psychological deficits and declines: Managing losses and promoting gains.* Mahwah, NJ: Lawrence Erlbaum Associates.

Dixon, R. A., Fox, D. P., Trevithick, L., & Brundin, R. (1997). Exploring collaborative problem solving in adulthood. *Journal of Adult Development, 4,* 195–208.

Dixon, R. A., Gagnon, L. M., & Crow, C. B. (1998). Collaborative memory accuracy and distortion: Performance and beliefs. In M. J. Intons-Peterson & D. Best (Eds.), *Memory distortions and their prevention* (pp. 63–88). Mahwah, NJ: Lawrence Erlbaum Associates.

Dixon, R. A., & Gould, O. N. (1996). Adults telling and retelling stories collaboratively. In P. B. Baltes & U. M. Staudinger (Eds.), *Interactive minds: Life-span perspectives on the social foundation of cognition* (pp. 221–241). Cambridge, UK: Cambridge University Press.

Dixon, R. A., & Gould, O. N. (1998). Younger and older adults collaborating on retelling everyday stories. *Applied Developmental Science, 2,* 160–171.

Dixon, R. A., & Hertzog, C. (1996). Theoretical issues in cognition and aging. In F. Blanchard-Fields & T. M. Hess (Eds.), *Perspectives on cognitive change in adulthood and aging* (pp. 25–65). New York: McGraw-Hill.

Dixon, R. A., Hertzog, C., Friesen, I. C., & Hultsch, D. F. (1993). Assessment of intraindividual change in text recall of elderly adults. In H. H. Brownell & Y. Joanette (Eds.), *Narrative discourse in neurologically impaired and normal aging adults* (pp. 77–101). San Diego: Singular Press.

Engeström, Y. (1992). Interactive expertise: Studies in distributed working intelligence. *Research Bulletin, 83,* Department of Education, University of Helsinki, Finland.

Fox, D. P. (1997). *Effects of collaboration on problem solving performance in healthy elderly couples and Parkinsonian-caregiver dyads.* Unpublished doctoral dissertation, University of Victoria, British Columbia, Canada.

Gagnon, L. M. (1995). *Collaborative remembering: Are there age-related differences in working with a stranger or a spouse?* Unpublished master's thesis, University of Victoria, British Columbia, Canada.

Galegher, J., Kraut, R. E., & Egido, C. (Eds.). (1990). *Intellectual teamwork.* Hillsdale, NJ: Lawrence Erlbaum Associates.

Goodnow, J. J. (1996). Collaborative rules: How are people supposed to work with one another? In P. B. Baltes & U. M. Staudinger (Eds.), *Interactive minds: Life-span perspectives on the social foundation of cognition* (pp. 163–197). Cambridge, UK: Cambridge University Press.

Gould, O. N., & Dixon, R. A. (1993). How we spent our vacation: Collaborative storytelling by young and old adults. *Psychology and Aging, 8,* 10–17.

Gould, O. N., Kurzman, D., & Dixon, R. A. (1994). Communication during prose recall conversations by young and old dyads. *Discourse Processes, 17,* 149–165.

Gould, O. N., Trevithick, L., & Dixon, R. A. (1991). Adult age differences in elaborations produced during prose recall. *Psychology and Aging, 6,* 93–99.

Greeno, J. G. (1998). The situativity of knowing, learning, and research. *American Psychologist, 53,* 5–26.

Greeno, J. G., & Moore, J. L. (1993). Situativity and symbol: Response to Vera and Simon. *Cognitive Science, 17,* 49–59.

Hertzog, C., & Dixon, R. A. (1994). Metacognitive development in adulthood and old age. In J. Metcalfe & A. P. Shimamura (Eds.), *Metacognition: Knowing about knowing* (pp. 227–251). Boston: MIT Press.

Hill, G. W. (1982). Group versus individual performance: Are N+1 heads better than one? *Psychological Bulletin, 91,* 517–539.

Hultsch, D. F., Hertzog, C., Dixon, R. A., & Small, B. J. (1998). *Cognitive change in the aged.* Cambridge, MA: Cambridge University Press.

Hupet, M., Chantraine, Y., & Nef, F. (1993). References in conversation between young and old normal adults. *Psychology and Aging, 8,* 339–346.

Lave, J., & Wenger, E. (1991). *Situated learning: Legitimate peripheral participation.* Cambridge, UK: Cambridge University Press.

Metcalfe, J., & Shimamura, A. P. (Eds.). (1994). *Metacognition: Knowing about knowing.* Boston: MIT Press.

Meudell, P. R., Hitch, G. J., & Boyle, M. M. (1995). Collaboration in recall: Do pairs of people cross-cue each other to produce new memories? *Quarterly Journal of Experimental Psychology, 48A,* 141–152.

Meudell, P. R., Hitch, G. J., & Kirby, P. (1992). Are two heads better than one? Experimental investigations of the social facilitation of memory. *Applied Cognitive Psychology, 5,* 525–543.

Middleton, D., & Edwards, D. (Eds.). (1990). *Collective remembering.* Newbury Park, CA: Sage.

Nesselroade, J. R. (1988). Some implications of the trait-state distinction for the study of development over the life span: The case of personality. In P. B. Baltes, D. L. Featherman, & R. M. Lerner (Eds.), *Life-span development and behavior* (vol. 8, pp. 163–189). Hillsdale, NJ: Lawrence Erlbaum Associates.

Nesselroade, J. R. (1991). Interindividual differences in intraindividual change. In L. M. Collins & J. L. Horn (Eds.), *Best methods for analyzing change* (pp. 92–105). Washington, D.C.: American Psychological Association.

Paulus, P. B. (Ed.). (1989). *Psychology of group influence.* Hillsdale, NJ: Lawrence Erlbaum Associates.

Perlmutter, M. (Ed.). (1990). *Late life potential.* Washington, D. C.: Gerontological Society of America.

Resnick, L. B., Levine, J. M., & Teasley, S. D. (Eds.). (1991). *Perspectives on socially shared cognition.* Washington, D. C: American Psychological Association.

Ryan, E. B., Giles, H., Bartolucci, G., & Henwood, K. (1986). Psycholinguistic and social psychological components of communication by and with the elderly. *Language and Communication, 6,* 1–24.

Salthouse, T. A. (1987). Age, experience, and compensation. In C. Schooler & K. W. Schaie (Eds.), *Cognitive functioning and social structure over the life course* (pp. 142–137). Norwood, NJ: Ablex.

Salthouse, T. A. (1990). Cognitive competence and expertise. In J. E. Birren & K. W. Schaie (Eds.), *Handbook of the psychology of aging* (3rd ed., pp. 310–319). San Diego: Academic Press.

Salthouse, T. A. (1991). *Theoretical perspectives on cognitive aging.* Hillsdale, NJ: Lawrence Erlbaum Associates.

Salthouse, T. A. (1995). Refining the concept of compensation. In R. A. Dixon & L. Bäckman (Eds.), *Compensating for psychological deficits and declines: Managing losses and promoting gains* (pp. 21–34). Mahwah, NJ: Lawrence Erlbaum Associates.

Schaie, K. W. (1996). *Intellectual development in adulthood: The Seattle Longitudinal Study.* Cambridge, UK: Cambridge University Press.

Schegloff, E. A. (1991). Conversation analysis and socially shared cognition. In L. B. Resnick, J. M. Levine, & S. D. Teasley (Eds.), *Perspectives on socially shared cognition* (pp. 150–171). Washington, D. C.: American Psychological Association.

Skinner, B. F. (1983). Intellectual self-management in old age. *American Psychologist, 38,* 239–244.

Small, B. J., Dixon, R. A., Hultsch, D. F., & Hertzog, C. (1999). Longitudinal changes in quantitative and qualitative indicators of word and story recall in young-old and old-old adults. *Journal of Gerontology: Psychological Sciences, 54B,* P107–P115.

Staudinger, U. M. (1996). Wisdom and the social-interactive foundation of the mind. In P. B. Baltes & U. M. Staudinger (Eds.), *Interactive minds: Life-span perspectives on the social foundation of cognition* (pp. 276–315). Cambridge, UK: Cambridge University Press.

Staudinger, U. M., & Baltes, P. B. (1997). Interactive minds: A facilitative setting for wisdom-related performance? *Journal of Personality and Social Psychology, 71,* 746–762.

Steiner, I. D. (1972). *Group process and productivity.* New York: Academic Press.

Streufert, S., Pogash, R., Piasecki, M., & Post, G. M. (1990). Age and management team performance. *Psychology and Aging, 5,* 551–559.

Vygotsky, L. S. (1978). *Mind in society: The development of higher psychological processes.* Cambridge, MA: Harvard University Press.

Wegner, D. M. (1986). Transactive memory: A contemporary analysis of the group mind. In B. Mullen & G. R. Goethals (Eds.), *Theories of group behavior* (pp. 185–208). New York: Springer-Verlag.

Wegner, D. M., Erber, R., & Raymond, P. (1991). Transactive memory in close relationships. *Journal of Personality and Social Psychology, 61,* 923–929.

Wilson, B. A., & Watson, P. C. (1996). A practical framework for understanding behavior in people with organic memory impairment. *Memory, 4,* 456–486.

Woodruff-Pak, D. S. (1997). *The neuropsychology of aging.* Malden, MA: Blackwell.

13

MORAL DEVELOPMENT IN MATURITY

LIFE-SPAN PERSPECTIVES ON THE PROCESSES OF SUCCESSFUL AGING

MICHAEL W. PRATT

Department of Psychology
Wilfrid Laurier University
Waterloo, Ontario, Canada

JOAN E. NORRIS

Department of Family Studies
University of Guelph
Guelph, Ontario, Canada

INTRODUCTION

I have lived in the pursuit of a vision, both personal and social. Personal: to care for what is noble, for what is beautiful, for what is gentle; to allow moments of insight to give wisdom at more mundane times. Social: to see in imagination the society that is to be created, where individuals grow freely, and where hate and greed and envy die because there is nothing to nourish them. These things I believe, and the world, for all its horrors, has left me unshaken.

Bertrand Russell (1991),
"Reflections on My Eightieth Birthday" (p. 45)

Russell, admittedly, was an exceptional individual in many ways. Nevertheless, his writings provide examples of some of the issues that we explore in this chapter, as he faced later life with the sense of moral courage and integrity conveyed here. Russell's personal journey can be traced through the formal logic of his early scholarship to the autobiographical musings of an older adult deeply committed to social justice. The profound events of the first and second world wars in Europe, followed by the uncertain times of the Cold War, appeared to spur this development; as he aged, he became more concerned with the social and moral context and consequences of his thinking (Pratt & Norris, 1994).

In our research and writing in recent years, we have focused on how older adults. perceive and understand their social and moral worlds. In this chapter, we review what is known of adult moral reasoning and decision making from the traditional cognitive developmental framework of Kohlberg (1969) as well as consider issues of social collaboration in thinking about personal moral issues from the perspective of Vygotsky (1978) and others. Throughout, we focus on mechanisms by which adults may achieve a measure of "successful aging" within this central life domain of sociomoral functioning.

THEORETICAL FRAMEWORKS AND ISSUES

Probably because of its roots in the biological sciences, the study of aging began as a study of loss (Cole, 1996). As many authors have noted, this decremental view continues to be prevalent in much of the theorizing and research on old age (Ferraro, 1990). Older adults are typically characterized as a burden to both society and to families and friends. Medical scientists writing in journals from 31 countries (e.g., journals of the American, Canadian, and British medical associations) have recently cautioned that health-care systems in the West are becoming overwhelmed with the needs of an increasing number of frail older adults (Elash, 1997). Psychological researchers, too, have focused on age-related declines in almost all areas of sensation, perception, and cognition (see Birren & Schaie, 1996, for reviews).

A decremental view of aging may persist, at least in part, because we lack theoretical models to guide thinking and questioning about development in later life. Recently, Bengtson, Burgess, and Parrott (1997) reviewed contributions to gerontological theory and found that most social scientists still rely on a "happily atheoretical" approach, content to gather more and more data with little thought to an explanatory framework. Thus, Bengtson et al. recommended the use of "third generation" theories: those which are multidisciplinary but specifically focused on aging-related phenomena. We made efforts in this regard in our work on later life social cognition. Using a life-span paradigm, we integrated traditional developmental and social psychological theories to provide such a third-generation framework for understanding how older adults think about their social worlds (Pratt & Norris, 1994).

Adopting a life-span orientation appears useful both in countering the decremental view of aging predominant in the research literature and in encouraging researchers to go beyond the simple cataloguing of phenomena. Life-span theorists, most notably Baltes and his colleagues (Baltes 1987; Baltes & Baltes, 1980), have emphasized the plasticity of human development well into advanced old age. Although the life-span framework has been criticized as too broad to be considered a true theory or even a paradigm (Bengtson et al., 1997), a number of useful third-generation theories have followed from this conceptual framework. Perhaps the most notable of these is Baltes's metatheory (Baltes, 1997; Marsiske, Lang, Baltes, & Baltes, 1995) of "selective optimization with compensation," developed as a way of understanding growth, loss and coping in later adulthood. This framework explicitly provides a model for conceptualizing "successful aging," and we will use it throughout this chapter as an heuristic for thinking about the meaning of moral development in later life.

The first component of this framework, *selection,* refers to the choices that individuals make—either consciously or unconsciously—to focus on domains of personal development in which they are likely to be successful. The second, *optimization,* refers to maintaining skills or competencies that have already been acquired. The third, *compensation,* is perhaps the most complex component; it refers to efforts that an individual makes to maintain competencies when losses have occurred, goals have become incompatible, or new constraints have been imposed (e.g., lessened energy) (Baltes, 1997).

As an example of how these processes work within an individual life course, consider jazz violinist Stephane Grappelli, who died at the age of 89. As a teenager, with a love of jazz—but no horn—he consciously chose to adapt the popular music of his day for the violin, an instrument at which he was already skilled (selection). Throughout his adulthood, he strove to extend and perfect his technique by performing with all manner of other musicians who played a variety of instruments (optimization). He continued to play into advanced old age, noting that music was his "fountain of youth," by becoming more selective in his repertoire and restrictive in his venues and partners (compensation).

UNDERSTANDING THE MEANING OF SUCCESSFUL AGING

Built into Baltes's metatheory (1997) is the belief that individuals are active participants in their own development. Thus, understanding the meaning of a change is not the sole responsibility of the researcher. At least as important are the views of older adults themselves. This perspective leads us away from the mechanistic view of aging, in which the old are seen to react, with losses, to biologically determined change. Instead, aging is seen as a process in which development is influenced by competence, preferences, and social and environmental forces or "press" (Ferraro & Farmer, 1996; Lawton, 1987). Observers might well have viewed Grapelli's smaller repertoire as a personal loss for the aging musician. He, on the other hand, may well have regarded honing his skills on a restricted selection of pieces as the gains of a mature artist. Cole (1996), in a *Journal of Gerontology* editorial marking 50 years of social science research on aging, speculated that the future of gerontological research lies precisely in exploring the meaning of *successful aging* to older adults themselves. He further argued that this study of success must focus directly on the moral and spiritual dimensions of growing older.

Carstensen, Hansen, and Freund (1995) noted that because of the decrement perspective that most researchers adopt, it is tempting to regard gains in later life as "compensation" rather than as mastery. The goal of successful aging then becomes compensating for loss rather than optimizing current functioning and acquiring new skills. In our examination of moral reasoning, however, we take the position that both optimization and compensation must be considered. Furthermore, we regard it as essential to study later moral development from both the point of view of others and the self. What are the various paths of development for older adults as they cope with moral issues? How do they respond when some paths are blocked and they must seek other avenues to understanding?

Several areas of theorizing and research have considered compensatory mechanisms in the social functioning of older people. Studies of social support, social consultation, and socioemotional selectivity have the greatest relevance for our purposes here. Social gerontologists have had a longstanding interest in the compensatory effects of social support for older adults. In 1968, Lowenthal published her widely cited study on mental illness in later life. This study provided evidence for the protective, or buffering, effect of social relationships, suggesting that the presence of a confidant was enough to compensate for other social deficiencies in an older person's life. It appears that being able to talk things over with just one person has powerful mental-health benefits. More recent work by Antonucci (Antonucci & Akiyama, 1995; Kahn & Antonucci, 1980) has described the "social convoys" that move with individuals through their lives, providing support, self-definition, and identity. The most intimate of these appear to provide compensatory functions during both early and later adulthood (Davey & Norris, in press).

A recent area of more specifically cognitive research, "distributed" or "collaborative" cognition, also offers promising insights into successful aging and compensation (Dixon, 1992). For example, researchers have noted the adaptive function of reminiscence as a means of achieving ego integrity (Butler, 1963; Wong & Watt, 1991). A few have also mentioned the central role of a receptive and involved audience. Apparently, co-creating one's life story with the help of others can lead to a more balanced view of events (Gould & Dixon, 1993), as well as to greater satisfaction with past and current life (Marshall, 1980).

Finally, a further useful perspective on compensation comes from Carstensen's socioemotional selectivity theory (1993). Carstensen has found evidence that as adults grow older, more distant relationships are shed in favor of intimate connections, which, in turn, become more rewarding. Carstensen et al. (1995) believe that this process is selection, not compensation, arguing that older adults proactively choose those relationships that are likely to be most successful and rewarding. Regardless of the specifics of how these processes are categorized, however, this framework provides an interesting model for successful coping with the difficult contingencies of later adulthood.

Despite the usefulness of these perspectives on aging to theoreticians and researchers, they have not been widely applied in the study of moral development. Missing from much of this literature is a consideration of the life-span implications of moral reasoning and the relationship of moral development in maturity to other features of successful aging. How, for example, can one optimize the experiences of later life for the maximum impact on thinking about values and beliefs? How might an older person compensate for restrictions in social contacts that previously have kept views on moral issues current and complex?

In this chapter, we have attempted to consider moral development in maturity from a life-span developmental perspective, fully integrated into other aspects of successful aging and inextricably linked to the social context. First, using Rest's four-component model (1983) of moral actions, and some of our own data, we explore older adults' sensitivity to moral situations, their capacities for moral judgment, their processes of decision making, and, finally, issues of consistency between moral reasoning and behavior. We then consider, from the perspective of the sociocultural theory of Vygotsky (1978), the possible roles of social collaboration and consultation with others in later life moral problem-solving. Finally, we describe some research on adults' own perspectives regarding their moral development.

MORAL REASONING DEVELOPMENT IN MATURITY: A REVIEW

Since the late 1960s, research on moral development in psychology has been heavily influenced by the cognitive-developmental perspective of Kohlberg (e.g., 1969). Kohlberg, drawing on the pioneering research of Piaget (1932), suggested a sequence of developmental levels in thinking about morality, proposing a progression through six stages of increasingly sophisticated reasoning and taking account of more and more complex issues. These stages were firmly based within Piaget's developmental framework and focused on growth from early childhood into the midlife period (e.g., Kohlberg, 1969). Although Kohlberg speculated about development in moral reasoning in later life (e.g., Kohlberg, 1973), including a possible seventh stage, this work was never systematically pursued.

Kohlberg's theory continues to be influential, but it has also been increasingly criticized for its almost exclusive emphasis on cognitive factors in morality (e.g., Walker & Pitts, 1998). In an attempt to place moral reasoning within a broader decision-making perspective, Rest (e.g., Rest, 1983; Rest & Narvaez, 1994) suggested a model of moral choice that involves four components: ethical sensitivity to the situation (particularly concerning the consequences for all participants), judging alternatives in terms of the most ethical course of action, weighing both moral and nonmoral considerations in deciding what to actually do, and following through with the chosen behavior once a decision has been made.

Rest's four components are not independent of one another but interactive, and they should not be viewed as simply sequential in their operations. However, they do represent an attempt to focus discussion of moral development within the context of everyday decision making. They also provide a useful framework for discussion of the literature on moral development in later life (Pratt & Norris, 1994). Accordingly, we begin by reviewing the evidence regarding aging with respect to each of these components in turn.

COMPONENT 1: SENSITIVITY TO THE SITUATION

The first component describes individuals' tendencies and capacities to gather information about the needs and circumstances of the various parties involved in the context of moral decision making. Several capacities are relevant here, but one of the most central is certainly "perspective-taking" skills (Rest, 1983). These skills involve the tendency to both distinguish and integrate the perspectives of self and other on the same information or situation (e.g., Selman, 1980). There is much evidence that such skills become increasingly sophisticated across childhood and adolescence. It is also well established that childhood and adolescent levels of development in perspective taking are formally parallel and closely coordinated with capacities to reason regarding the Kohlberg moral stages (Selman, 1980). For example, attainment of specific perspective-taking stages has been shown to be a necessary condition for forward movement to a next stage in moral reasoning, using an experimental approach to testing these hypotheses about the coordination of moral development and perspective taking (Walker, 1980).

Research on perspective taking in later life is much less extensive, but a number of cross-sectional studies have been conducted. In general, these have suggested that older adults may perform at lower levels on such measures than do middle-aged adults (e.g., Chap, 1986; Cohen, Bearison, & Muller, 1987). Similarly, Hogg and Heller (1990) found that adults in their seventies performed more poorly than did younger adults (those in their sixties) on an index of "understanding" the problems of older adults in several standard vignettes.

Because these studies were cross-sectional, they were subject to a number of alternative, non developmental interpretations of any age differences. Recently, however, we reported a longitudinal study of this same issue, following 50 middle-aged and older adults across a 5-year period (Pratt, Diessner, Pratt, Hunsberger, & Pancer, 1996). In this research, members of our two groups, those between the ages of 30 and 55 and those between 60 and 80, were well educated and in good health, living in a community in eastern Canada. We used a four-level index developed by Chap (1986), which was based on Selman's model (1980) of perspective taking. The lowest level in this index represents seeing the issues of the dilemma in only one way. Level 2 entails seeing more than one view but failing to recognize any compatibility between them. At Level 3, two or more views are expressed and it is argued that one needs to understand the other, and at Level 4, a full reciprocity between competing views is acknowledged (Chap, 1986). Our results indicated that the two age groups of our study were initially equivalent on this measure (scoring approximately 2.5 on average on this 1–4 scale). Five years later, older adults' scores had declined significantly on average (to approximately 2.0), whereas the middle-aged group's scores remained unchanged from the first testing.

These findings provide longitudinal evidence that older adults may demonstrate some degree of loss in such perspective-taking skills over time. Because they are drawn from a small sample and are based on a perspective-taking index scored directly from the same Kohlberg dilemmas, we believe it is important to replicate these findings with a larger sample, using a different perspective-taking index. Using the same data for several different measures can be problematic because of rater biases or halo effects. Thus, we are currently studying a sample of 130 Canadian adults (age range, 18–75 initially), using standard dilemmas from Selman's Interpersonal Negotiation Strategy Index with adolescents (Selman, Beardslee, Schulz, Krupa, & Podorefsky, 1986), adapted for an adult population. So far, we have observed a significant but modest negative relation between age and perspective taking in this sample ($r = -.19$), primarily due to the lower scores of older women. A longitudinal follow-up of this sample is planned.

A number of social and cognitive predictors of different trajectories of change in perspective-taking performance were identified in our first longitudinal study (Pratt et al., 1996). In particular, greater levels of education, better health, and more self-reported availability of support all served as buffers against declines in perspective taking over time, broadly consistent with findings from a number of studies on general cognitive changes over time in later life (e.g., Baltes, 1993; Schaie, 1989). In our longitudinal follow-up, we want to pursue both social and biological cognitive variables (specifically, declines in "working memory" resources) as possible predictors of individual differences in perspective-taking changes in later life (e.g., Salthouse, 1992). Previous research has shown that gains in working memory resources can predict improved performance on role-taking tasks among children (Lapsley & Quintana, 1989), and so it seemed of interest to test whether this is a useful model for possible losses in role-taking during later adulthood as well.

Some years ago, we reported differences in the information-gathering preferences of adults of different ages regarding moral issues (Pratt, Golding, Hunter, & Norris, 1988). We found that older adults, when given a choice of information to help them resolve a standard moral dilemma from Kohlberg, preferred less specific information about particular dilemma characters than did younger adults. For example, in dealing with one of the Kohlberg dilemmas about euthanasia, younger adults reported wanting to know about the particular consequences in the life of a doctor for choosing to help a dying woman to end her life, whereas older adults were more concerned about the general implications of such a course of action for society as a whole (Pratt, Golding, et al., 1988). We replicated this finding in a second, unpublished study with a life span sample of adults (Pratt & Norris, 1989).

This result may represent a strategic adaptation of older adults in the direction of avoiding cognitive and memory overload by focusing less on demanding informational details for processing while deliberating about moral issues. Such differences could represent a type of compensation used by the older adult to maintain performance on the primary task of moral decision making. It certainly describes a selection difference in the way that Rest's first component (1983) appears to operate for older adults, but these findings need to be replicated longitudinally to establish their developmental nature. It is also possible that this pattern of lower use of specific information is linked to the less sophisticated levels of perspective taking shown by older adults as well. If perspective taking is a resource-demanding cognitive activity (Lapsley & Quintana, 1989), older adults may also prefer to use it less frequently as a strategy in deciding what to do about a particular moral problem.

This account then raises the question of the relations between perspective taking and moral reasoning in later adulthood. As noted, in earlier development, the correspondence between these two measures is strong (Selman, 1980; Walker, 1980). In our longitudinal study with adults, however, we found that relations between moral reasoning on the standard Kohlberg index and our measure of perspective taking were only modestly positive (Pratt et al., 1996), replicating the earlier findings of Chap (1986). An analysis of these relations within age group showed that the correlations were positive and substantial in the middle-aged sample ($r = .49$ at Times 1 and 2, respectively). However, among the older sample, both these correlations were low and nonsignificant ($r = .03$ and $-.21$, respectively). Thus, the relations between moral development and perspective taking may be less direct in later life. Moral judgments may rely less on perspective-taking activities among older adults, who may "compensate" for this in some other way in making moral decisions. Or perhaps, given the findings noted above regarding age and the generality of information sought, some older adults may simply decide to follow general rules in deciding moral dilemmas, without making the effort to contemplate the specific perspectives of others in a situation. We have more to say on this point in the section on collaborating with others later in this chapter.

COMPONENT 2: JUDGING AND EVALUATING MORAL CONSIDERATIONS

Rest's second component forms the traditional core of moral reasoning research. Most research with respect to this component has been conducted within the Kohlbergian cognitive-developmental framework (Pratt & Norris, 1994). These studies involve interviews regarding standard ethical dilemmas that are scored following a manual for judgments at the various stage levels. A weighted average of these scores is then assigned overall to summarize the individual's current overall level of thinking (Colby & Kohlberg, 1987). This model is generally based in the presumption of gradual forward movement through Kohlberg's six-stage sequence in development during the earlier part of the life span (Colby & Kohlberg, 1987). Although research with younger persons has been quite consistent with this developmental hypothesis, it appears to be the case that gains in moral reasoning over time are much more limited in midadulthood than in childhood (e.g., Walker, 1989).

In fact, on the basis of Piagetian models of cognitive development in later life, some had raised the question of whether older adults might show actual regression in moral stage reasoning (Bielby & Papalia, 1975). Several cross-sectional studies have been reported in the recent literature with adults across the life span (e.g., Chap, 1986; Walker, Pitts, Henig, & Matsuba, 1995; White, 1988). We have also reported several such descriptive studies using the Kohlberg stage measure (e.g., Pratt, Golding, & Hunter, 1983; Pratt, Diessner, Hunsberger, Pancer, & Savoy, 1991). The results of these studies have been consistent in showing that there is little evidence for lower average levels of moral stage usage among adults up to age 75, compared with middle-aged adults, and controlling for educational background. Instead, this evidence points to stability of reasoning levels across mid- to later life, though longitudinal evidence is needed to support this. Several of these studies also suggested that middle-aged adults may score somewhat higher than young adults, consistent with hypotheses of growth until midadulthood (Pratt et al., 1983; Walker et al., 1995).

We have recently reported evidence with adults in the short-term longitudinal research described above (Pratt et al., 1996). In this study, older adults up to age 80 were found to show no evidence of average change in stage of moral reasoning over a 5-year period. Midlife adults (age range, 30–50) also showed evidence of stability in level of reasoning over this period. Unfortunately, a young adult group was not included in this study.

Despite findings of average stability in moral reasoning stage overall, there were, of course, individual differences in these patterns over time. Our results suggested that older adults who were in better health (by self-report) and who reported more social support, were more likely to maintain their levels of moral reasoning on the Kohlberg instrument over time, compared with those who were in poor health or more socially isolated (Pratt et al., 1996). More specifically, adults who rated themselves low on Krause and Markides's measure (1990) of the perceived availability of supportive relationships declined significantly over time on average (from a mean of 359 to one of 338 on the standard 500-point Kohlberg scale), whereas those whose scores were higher on this support measure showed no change over time (means of 356 and 355 for Times 1 and 2, respectively). These results are broadly consistent with the wider literature on cognitive aging, which suggests that resources such as health and social support can be moderators of the experience of growing old (Baltes, 1993).

Two further personality moderator variables (not reported in the 1996 article) are also relevant. One is right-wing authoritarianism (RWA), assessed by a 30-item questionnaire developed by Altemeyer (1988). The second is generativity, a personality "strength" first articulated by Erikson (1950) as the seventh of his eight stages of ego development across the life span and more recently studied by McAdams, de St. Aubin, and Logan (1993).

Individuals high in RWA are characterized by political conservatism, deference to authority, and a tendency toward simplistic, black-and-white thinking (Altemeyer, 1988). Previously, we found that these adults are also prone to think about social and religious issues in more "simplistic" ways (Pratt, Hunsberger, Pancer, & Roth, 1992). For example, these adults understand and explain the behaviors of children using less sophisticated analyses than do their nonauthoritarian peers (Pratt, Hunsberger, Pancer, Roth, & Santolupo, 1993). Perhaps not surprisingly given these previous results, analyses of our middle-aged and older sample of 50 participants showed that more authoritarian adults on Altemeyer's measure (1988) were significantly more likely to reason at lower levels on the Kohlberg moral stages as well ($r = -.53$). This result is noteworthy because older adults are generally found to show higher RWA scores than are their younger counterparts (Pratt & Norris, 1994). Thus, possible increases in authoritarian styles of thinking among some older adults may be an important factor in understanding patterns of moral reasoning in maturity. Of course, longitudinal data would be needed to establish this and to rule out cohort effects as an alternative explanation of differences on the RWA scale.

A second personality moderator was generativity, an index of adults' degree of investment in caring for the next generation as a legacy of the self, based on Erikson's seventh stage in the human life cycle (McAdams et al., 1993). McAdams et al. showed that generative concern and action tend to be especially salient in maturity (40–75), with lower scores among young adults (18–30). We expected that a more generative personality style in adulthood would be associated with more advanced levels of thinking about moral problems. Consistent with this, in our life span study of adult moral development, we found that more generative adults on the McAdams measure were significantly more likely to reason at higher moral stages on Kohlberg's measure ($r = .22$) (Pratt, Norris, Arnold, & Filyer, in press).

COMPONENT 3: INTEGRATING MORAL
AND NONMORAL CONSIDERATIONS

A further step in the decision-making process identified by Rest (1983) involves making judgments regarding the appropriate course of action in a situation. Here, the issue is how the person weighs various considerations in coming to a decision. Two people might have identical judgments regarding a situation in the "morally ideal" sense but make actual decisions differently, depending on how other nonmoral considerations, needs, issues, and values are judged to be relevant within any particular situation. Thus, moral analysis is only one aspect of decision processes and may be seen as more or less relevant to a particular set of life choices. For example, if a problem is not judged to be primarily moral in nature (see Component 1), it may be that nonmoral considerations are then likely to take precedence.

Several interesting topics have been explored in this regard within the moral development literature. With children, for example, Damon (1981) has shown that personal desires often overwhelm the child's hard-won reasoning about how to carry out equitable distributions between the self and others. In practice, those tempting goodies are just too much to resist, despite our best standards of justice! Similarly, Krebs, Wark, & Krebs (1995) argue that adults reason at lower-stage levels when they are in situations directly involving self-interest than when being tested for abstract "competence" on standard tasks.

A very important issue here is that of personal values (e.g., Brabeck, 1995; Feather, 1994). Individuals differ in the extent to which they identify with certain values, and these differences must be important in guiding the process of moral decision making. For example, Colby and Damon (1992) reported that their sample of extraordinary moral exemplars experienced little sense of struggle in their decisions to act in moral ways. This was apparently because their identities were so strongly invested in the moral sphere that they could not even imagine behaving nonmorally in the situation. Similarly, McAdams, Diamond, de St. Aubin, and Mansfield (1997) found that midlife adults who strongly valued generative concerns constructed their narrative identities differently than did others who were less generative. Generative adults told distinctive life stories characterized by a sense of "early blessing," "positive redemption of negative events," and "moral steadfastness," among several other qualities. However, research to date has neither explored the implications of such generative values for adult moral decision making directly nor specifically studied this question among older adults.

In a study that did focus on later adulthood, Rybash, Hoyer, and Roodin (1983) reported that older adults were somewhat more likely than were their younger counterparts to say that they could think of no moral dilemmas in their personal lives at all. This finding could be evidence that the criteria for deciding whether an issue is moral or not may differ among older adults, though of course other explanations are possible. Older adults, for example, may simply be less likely to report any problems in their lives, moral or not.

We have conducted two analyses relevant to the issues of how people decide whether personal problems are indeed to be viewed as primarily within the moral sphere. In one study, we found that individuals who reasoned at higher stages within the Kohlberg system were somewhat more likely to report that personal problems that they had chosen to describe were at least partly moral in nature. By contrast, lower-stage reasoning was associated with a tendency to argue that the problems discussed did not have a moral dimension and thus that moral considerations were not relevant to their resolution. Of course, this result was limited by the fact that individuals' choice of personal problems was left open-ended, and so dilemma content was likely confounded with reasoning stage. In a second investigation (Pratt & Norris, 1989), we studied men and women of different ages and moral preference levels, as assessed on the Defining Issues Test of Rest (1979). We asked participants to rate a standard set of dilemmas, varying across a range of topics, as more or less moral in nature, on a Likert-type scale of moral "typicalness."

In fact, in both of these studies, older adults were just as likely as were younger adults to report that their recalled personal dilemmas were moral in nature and just as likely to judge a standard set of dilemmas as more or less prototypically moral. Similarly, Walker et al. (1995) did not find differences between the types of everyday moral problems reported by younger (age range, 16–48) versus older adults (age range, 65–84). Overall, this research suggests that the processes governing the applicability of moral reasoning to analyses of real-life problems and decisions do not show major changes of a systematic nature in later life. The findings of Rybash et al. (1983) reported in this section may simply indicate a reluctance to report problems or difficulties of any type among older adults, rather than differences in deciding what is moral.

COMPONENT 4: REASONING-BEHAVIOR CONSISTENCY

Previous studies with young adults have suggested that those individuals reasoning at higher stages tended to show clearer and more persistent commitments to their decisions in the face of situational pressures (e.g., Kohlberg & Candee, 1984; Thoma, 1994). For example, some early work indicated that American soldiers who were more likely to resist pressures to massacre civilians during the Vietnam War were more likely to reason at higher stages than were those who complied. Overall, these stage-action correlations are weak, however (e.g., Blasi, 1980), and to date, there has been no systematic research on such consistency across the adult life span. In some earlier work, however, we did observe that older adults were more likely to show consistency across several different measures of moral reasoning (Pratt et al., 1983), though belief–action consistency was not studied.

Interestingly, moral "consistency" or belief–action integrity was the second-most important virtue in adults' reports of real-life moral exemplars in the study by Walker et al. (1995), following only "compassionate and caring." It would seem that integrity between one's beliefs and actions has appeal across the life span, since no age differences in these patterns were reported. Certainly a lack of such integrity in public officials is one of the most common themes in complaints about modern political life.

SUMMARY

It appears that age differences in later adulthood in moral decision making may be confined mainly to the first, information-gathering, component of Rest's

(1983) model. Older adults may, in later life, become somewhat less sensitive to the needs and perspectives of others. More broadly, they may be less likely to seek all sorts of detailed information in selecting issues for deliberation in resolving a moral problem. There is no evidence that older adults show substantial changes in their capacities for moral judgment or in their tendencies to see problems as warranting more or less specifically moral consideration in decision making. Whether older as opposed to younger adults are more consistent in following through on moral decisions is unknown.

What explains any possible changes in Component 1 in later life? Such changes could be related to cognitive biological "losses" in aspects of memory function, such as declines in working memory resources, but this explanation needs more study. Such changes may also be partly strategic and/or compensatory in nature, with older adults attempting to minimize the burdens of processing by assimilating specific problems to general frameworks in more routine ways than do younger adults (Pratt, Golding, et al., 1988) or by using active perspective taking less directly in their moral thinking (Pratt et al., 1996). At any rate, this raises the interesting question of how older adults maintain their moral reasoning levels while apparently showing some loss in perspective-taking performance.

Although such cognitive biological factors may well be involved, there is also evidence in our studies that social factors may play an important role in changes in later life (Pratt et al., 1996). Our results suggest that some older adults experienced an increasing sense of social isolation and that for them, losses in actual moral reasoning levels were more likely. Conversely, among those older adults who retained a substantial level of availability of social support, moral reasoning levels were maintained over time. Next, we discuss research suggesting how such possible compensatory effects might be understood in relation to the role of "collaborative cognition" with others in maturity.

COLLABORATING WITH OTHERS TO SOLVE EVERYDAY MORAL PROBLEMS

In this section, we report some new descriptive research on patterns of help-seeking regarding personal moral dilemmas in adulthood, conducted within the framework of sociocultural theory (e.g., Wertsch & Kanner, 1992). We show that such consultation with others is associated with a somewhat more sophisticated representation of moral problems, as well as with more satisfaction with their solution. We then describe factors that may influence such consultation patterns in adulthood and we interpret the meaning of these within the framework of research on collaborative cognition (e.g., Baltes & Staudinger, 1996).

Since the mid-1990s, there has been a good deal of interest in the possible role of collaboration with others as one way of coping with the cognitive demands of later life, perhaps at least partly imposed by losses in cognitive capacities (e.g.,

Baltes, 1997; Dixon & Gould, 1996). Interestingly, there is considerable evidence that in the earlier part of the life cycle, youngsters and adults typically collaborate in task performance and that such collaboration plays a decisive role in the child's development (Wertsch & Kanner, 1992). From the sociocultural perspective of Vygotsky (1978), cognition is often a joint activity of the dyad, carried out together or distributed between the partners as a "zone of proximal development" created to guide the child's learning and mastery of the skill or task (e.g., Pratt, Kerig, Cowan, & Cowan, 1988; Pratt & Savoy-Levine, 1998).

Researchers studying memory, storytelling, and decision making in later life have noted the utility of such a collaborative perspective on cognition as well. Several recent studies have suggested that older adults may use social collaboration to compensate for limitations in individual cognitive performance. For example, with regard to memory, Dixon and Gould (1996) reported that older couples do as well as their younger counterparts in remembering information, despite the well-known pattern of poorer recall among older individuals. They suggested that one interpretation of this finding is that older adult dyads are using "jointly" constructed recall processes to enhance their recollection. Similarly, Staudinger (1996) found that adults who experienced a dialogue with another and then were given an opportunity to think about this conversation performed better on wisdom-related advice-giving tasks than did those in a conventional paradigm who simply heard the problem and then "thought aloud" about it. Adults who imagined how valued others might think about the problem also showed benefits, though not as great as those in the overt dialogue condition.

Although Staudinger's results (1996) are interesting and well controlled, they concerned adults' performance on a set of standardized "wisdom" dilemmas. We were interested in exploring how adults might be using social consultation to respond to everyday problems in their own lives. To this end, we asked adults across the life span to report on their discussions with others about life problems for which they "didn't know what was the right thing to do," following a protocol originally devised by Gilligan (1982). A wide range of problems was reported, from selecting the colors of a room for painting to euthanasia issues, many involving dilemmas judged to be moral in nature. After discussing the problem following a standard interview protocol (e.g., Pratt, Pancer, Hunsberger, & Manchester, 1990), adults reported on how extensively, and with whom, they had consulted on a simple rating scale, from 1, low—"no one" to 5, high—"many others with different views."

Across two separate studies using this task (the studies of 50 and 130 Canadian adults discussed more fully in the section on Component 1 of moral development), we found that adults typically reported consulting with at least some other people about their personal problems (about 80% of the time overall). Thus, social consultation appears to be a common response to the experience of dealing with difficult life problems in adulthood. There were also two interesting patterns of findings. First, adults who talked more with others about a specific problem were likely to represent the problem in more complex ways than those who had not (Pratt, 1997). Second, those who consulted more were also more satisfied with the problem solutions that they selected.

As a measure of the character of people's representations of past experiences, we used a standard discourse index, integrative complexity (e.g., Suedfeld, Tetlock, & Streufert, 1992). Complexity is based on two component features: (1) the amount of differentiation or distinction made between various concepts or viewpoints on an issue and (2) the extent to which these components are integrated or related to one another in systematic ways. Complexity of any sustained discourse, such as personal writings, interview responses, public speeches and the like, can be assessed on a 1–7 rating scale (e.g., Suedfeld et al., 1992).

Previous research on cognitive complexity has indicated that greater or lesser levels of complexity are not unfailingly predictive of either good or bad outcomes or performance (Suedfeld et al., 1992). However, in our own past research, there has been evidence that less complexity of discourse about personal problems is linked to negative markers associated with problems in aging, including lower education levels and lower levels of social support (e.g., Pratt et al., 1996; Pratt et al., 1992). Thus, simpler, unidimensional views may not always be negative, but they are associated with lower levels of personal resources in maturity. In late life, losses in the complexity of personal correspondence are directly linked to the phenomenon of "terminal decline" as well (Suedfeld & Piedrahita, 1984).

How, then, was social consultation related to the complexity of representation of personal life events in people's interview descriptions of their problems in these two studies? In study 1, greater levels of consultation were positively related to more complex problem descriptions. A parallel set of findings was obtained for Study 2 ($r = .25$ and .24, respectively) (Pratt, 1997). Of course, these simple correlations are subject to many alternative explanations. Regression analyses in both studies showed that these relations remained after controlling for several extraneous variables, such as education and social support, but other types of studies obviously would be needed to test causal models.

We may at least speculate, however, about why adults who consult with others might then think about personal issues in more complex ways than do those who have not consulted. On the basis of the sociocultural perspective of Bakhtin (1981) and Wertsch (1991), it would seem that the activity of collaborating about issues and problems might well affect the way in which these issues are mentally represented by the individual. Past (or anticipated future) dialogue with others about an incident or problem might lead people to elaborate a more complex representation of it, by thinking about the "voices" or perspectives of important partners about the situation, as well as one's responses to these partners. All this material may then become part of one's problem representation (e.g, Tetlock, 1983).

Two other findings from this study attest to the importance of social collaboration. Adults who had consulted more were significantly more satisfied with dilemma solutions. This was true in both studies ($r = .35$ and $.23$, respectively) and specifically seemed to reflect an increased sense of confidence in solutions as rated by adults, given more discussion with others. Consultation thus seemed to give people a sense of validation for their decisions, as well as provide them with actual advice. Furthermore, as noted in the review of moral reasoning development in the preceding section, we also found that low levels of perceived support and advice from others about difficult issues were associated with a tendency for midlife and older adults to show a decline in their stage of moral reasoning over time (Pratt et al., 1996). Of course, this longitudinal correlation could be due to other factors and is not necessarily causal.

Overall, these findings support the view that perceptions of collaboration and support from others are associated with more complex thoughts about specific life problems, with a greater feeling of satisfaction about the outcome of such problems and with a capacity for maintaining one's moral reasoning skills over time. In this context, it is interesting to note that older adults in our studies also tended to feel that they experienced less supportive dialogue with others overall. Table 13.1 shows the pattern of relations between the extent of reported social consultation and several individual characteristics. In Study 1, social consultation about personal problems was more common among younger than older adults. Older adults were also more likely than the middle-aged to report feeling that they received less support from others in dealing with personal problems. In Study 2, age was not related to consultation patterns about specific dilemmas but was again negatively related to feelings of lower overall levels of support. Thus, there was some indication that older adults on average have a sense of less help from others in coping with personal moral problems.

Table 13.1 shows that consulting with others was also related to individual personality style variables, specifically the RWA measure in Study 1 and generativity in Study 2. Highly authoritarian adults were less likely to discuss issues with oth-

TABLE 13.1   Correlations of Consultation and Social Support with Age and Individual Difference Factors, Studies 1 and 2

Factor	Study 1		Study 2	
	Consult	Support	Consult	Support
Age in years	−.48**	−.43**	−.09	−.44**
Right-wing author	−.28*	−.50**	—	—
Generative concern	—	—	.18*	.38**

Consult = Reported Level of Dilemma Consultation (1–5 scale); support = Krause and Markides's Perceived Availability of Support Scale; right-wing author = Altemeyer's Right-Wing Authoritarianism Score; generative concern = McAdams' Loyola Generativity Scale Score.

$* p < .05$, $** p < .01$. $df = 48$ for Study 1, 128 for Study 2.

ers and felt that others were less supportive of their decision making. These patterns may indeed reinforce the tendency of more authoritarian thinkers to see the moral world in simplistic terms, which we have already noted. Such isolation from the diversity of opinions of others may represent one pathway selected by some as they grow older, in which the "voice" of a single authority (e.g., biblical scriptures) is privileged over all others in thinking about moral and personal issues and conflicting opinion is avoided. By contrast, nonauthoritarian adults appeared more likely to seek out other voices or perspectives in thinking about personal issues (Table 13.1).

Table 13.1 also shows that in the second study, more generative adults were more likely to consult with others and also more likely to feel supported in dealing with problems. Adults who were more invested in future generations in their personal dispositions, then, like those who were low on authoritarianism, seemed disposed to select a more "open" style of consulting with a multiplicity of others about their views about everyday problems. Of course, only a longitudinal analysis could directly address these ideas regarding such a process of selection of different pathways or goals for social interaction in the course of adult development. Causality may also flow the other way; socially isolated adults may gradually become more authoritarian and/or less generative in their views. Most likely, these relations between personality style and social interaction are reciprocal in nature. At any rate, a key differentiating aspect for adult development seems to be the extent of perceived social cognitive support or isolation, which predicted different patterns of change in adult moral reasoning, as already discussed, but also may be reflective of differences in the personality styles of authoritarianism and generativity, as we have shown here (see Table 13.1).

Consistent with this model of different personal "styles" in adult moral decision making, being highly authoritarian in views in Study 1 was associated with a distinct pattern of relations between stage of moral reasoning and perspective-taking capacities. Those adults high on the RWA measure showed no relation between their moral reasoning stage and their perspective-taking scores ($r = .12$). By contrast, those low on the RWA showed the more typical significant positive relations between these two measures ($r = .40$). This finding could indicate that gathering information about the perspectives of others is less relevant for highly authoritarian individuals, who see the moral world (as other things) in simple, black-and-white terms. These adults consult less with others and perhaps do not apply information about others' views to their moral deliberations even when they do obtain it. By contrast, their nonauthoritarian peers (who also consult more with others generally) show a different pattern, in which their skills in perspective taking are more directly linked to their moral reasoning performance. One account of the possible dissociation between moral reasoning and perspective taking in later life that we noted above, then, may be a tendency for some adults to become somewhat more authoritarian as they age (Pratt & Norris, 1994) and thus to use their perspective-taking skills less fully in reasoning about moral questions. Of course, the answer to the question of how these adults then make moral judgments remains uncertain.

Consultation with and support from others, then, may serve to characterize one style of coping with the cognitive demands of everyday issues as we age (and perhaps find some of our personal capacities more taxed). Conversely, simplifying decision making by privileging a single, "correct" voice and avoiding the views of others may be an alternative strategy selected for dealing with these challenges, compatible with more "closed" styles of aging, and typical of more authoritarian adults. Interestingly, Lonky, Kaus, and Roodin (1984) found that mature adults who retrospectively reported dealing with difficult personal losses in more "open," problem-focused ways were indeed likely to score higher in moral reasoning than were those who used more avoidant styles. These findings are compatible with the present formulation and also suggest that different pathways may be more or less promoting of moral growth overall, though longitudinal study would be needed to test this idea. Longitudinal work on social consultation and coping in later life is needed to study this proposal regarding successful aging and selectivity in the goals of one's social relations.

A story from a 70-year-old woman in one of our samples seems to illustrate well several of the points made above:

> The lady next door to me was a very dear friend, and I used to help her quite a bit because she couldn't go up and down the stairs. We became very friendly, and I enjoyed helping her because she was such a sweet soul. She moved away and when she went, I felt a great loss and it made me realize how thankful I was to be healthy and to be able to do those little things. ... I used to talk to her about things and she made me realize that my personal problems weren't (so bad) ... she made me see the other side of things. So she kind of balanced the situation and made me realize that this is why and that's why. ... And now when things come up, I don't just jump to the conclusion that this is what it's like. I think, Well, maybe this or that, and then decide.

SUMMARY

Research on later-life sociomoral development from a collaborative cognition perspective suggests that there may be important individual differences in the extent to which consultation with others is used as a strategy for decision making among mature adults. Greater use of such consultation is associated with more complex representation of personal life problems and with a feeling of more successful resolution of these problems as well. Personality styles are also linked to these patterns as well, with older adults who are high in RWA less likely to report such consultation and those who are high in generativity more likely to do so. Overall, then, more extensive social consultation may be associated with a pattern of more successful aging in the sociomoral domain, but only some individuals may select this style as a way of coping with the challenges of mature adulthood.

INDIVIDUALS' PERSPECTIVES ON THEIR
OWN MORAL DEVELOPMENT

So far, we have discussed moral development in later life from an observer's perspective. However, in this section, we want to explore the views of adults themselves on their own moral development and experiences. To study these questions, we asked those in our ongoing longitudinal study, 130 adults between the ages of 18 and 75, to tell us about an incident from their own lives that they perceived as having had a "central" or "critical" impact on their current thinking about values and morals (following the technique of Barnett, Quackenbush, & Sinisi, 1995). Such a narrative approach to morality has become increasingly popular in recent years (e.g., Pratt & Arnold, 1995; Tappan & Brown, 1989). The "critical incident" stories told were then analyzed to see if there were age-related differences, both in the quality and focus of people's narratives and in their understanding of their implications for development. Two broad patterns of age differences emerged. First, older adults, compared with younger individuals, were more likely to talk about their critical moral incidents with more positive affect and emotion. Second, older adults reported learning more "lessons" from their reported critical incidents than did the younger groups.

A first consistent finding in our analyses of adults' critical event narratives was that older adults described more positive events than did young adults. This was true in several ways in our data. Older adults' emotions, as displayed in the narrative, were judged by an independent rater as significantly more positive regarding their chosen events, both initially at the time of their experiences as well as at present, looking back on these events now. Older adults were also more likely to discuss positive social content than were younger adults and were less likely to describe negative content or to mention their own transgressions as a focus for the stories they told. Many of the positive stories told by older adults had religious themes, and indeed Jensen (1995) and Walker et al. (1995) have both recently noted the salience of religion and spirituality in adults' thinking about morality. Here is a narrative by a 65-year-old woman, rated very positively on our affect scales:

> When I was a small child, I remember it was my grandmother that started me going to Sunday school, because my parents didn't go to church, but my grandmother did. I used to enjoy going to church with her because she always had peppermint candies for me... I guess she knew that young children do get restless. So that started me off, and I enjoyed Sunday school very much... And then when I got married and had children of my own, I started to teach Sunday school and I enjoyed that very much... The way the children would listen to the stories that you tell them, that was very rewarding. And then later on when my husband and I separated, I found that I needed that religion, it was very important... (Why was this event so critical to your moral development?) When I was young, I was very shy and I felt maybe left out of things. Being with my grandmother and having her spend attention just on me, I felt very good about it. I think that helped a lot...

Our findings for older adults' more positive emotional tone in their narratives of critical moral events can be seen as consistent with the ideas of Carstensen

(1993) regarding "emotional selectivity" theory. Carstensen presents considerable evidence to show that older adults tend to focus social interactions on more immediate positive emotional goals than do younger adults. Such selectivity is seen as appropriate because longer-term goals may be less useful to adults who may have more limited opportunities for interaction in the future. Consequently, older adult couples, for example, may seek to maximize immediate positive experiences in their interactions (Carstensen et al., 1995). Similarly, the present set of findings suggests that in the social context of retelling a critical event narrative to an interviewer, older adults may seek to maximize the positivity of their experience and mood by telling more pleasant stories. Of course, older adults may also tell such stories because they enhance their personal sense of growth and development beyond the immediate situation. As the old song goes, "You gotta accentuate the positive." Indeed, immediate situational enhancement of positive mood may simply be a part of this general optimistic trend. Regardless, these findings likely demonstrate processes of both selection of positive past experiences and optimization of a sense of self by older adults in the moral domain.

As a second major trend, older adults viewed themselves as having learned more than others from the incidents that they reported. These data were obtained by asking individuals to rate the extent to which they had "learned a lesson" about 14 different issues from their critical incident on a brief questionnaire, adapted from the earlier work of Barnett et al. (1995). The issues included topics such as *justice, caring, friendship, religion, social issues,* and *the self.* Scores on these items were substantially intercorrelated, and it was thus appropriate to sum them to provide an overall index of lessons learned (Cronbach's alpha was .84 across all 14 items).

Correlational analyses showed that reporting having learned more lessons from one's critical moral experience was significantly positively associated (as would be expected) with more thought about one's dilemma and with more discussion with others about it, though not with education level or with memory scores. Learning more lessons was also associated modestly with gender (women reported learning more), with higher stage scores on the Kohlberg moral reasoning measure and with higher perspective-taking scores on Selman's measure. Finally, reporting learning more lessons was associated with higher scores on generative concern. In addition, however, there was an overall positive relation with age, such that older adults reported more learning than did both their middle-aged and young counterparts. Regression analysis showed that this age effect contributed an additional 7% to the prediction of lessons learned, after controlling for the set of variables just mentioned. Thus, it seemed quite clear that this was a substantial effect. Here is an example narrative from a 62-year-old woman who believed she had learned a great deal from her experience (this woman was rated as showing very positive affect about her experience as well):

> We had a wonderful Sunday school teacher and she taught me through from 10 until I was a teenager... And I stayed with her a year while I was going to high school before the bus service went in. So she taught me in her daily living, too. She was very, very kind. She just taught me by example to be honest and caring and to help others, and she brought out a

lot of my talents. I think she was really quite an outstanding person, and ... like she's still in
my mind today, and things that happened, I don't know why, but I see her and I think "I
wonder how she would have handled this," and I seem to be able to reason out things just
from the way she taught me... I think it made me a better wife and mother and grandmother.
(Why was this critical to your moral development?) I was brought up in rather a strict home
and yet there was a lot of love and kindness there, too. I think this was just an extension of
that and I saw it from another person, an outsider, and it stayed with me more, maybe...

Such a view of personal learning experiences seems like potential evidence for
an increasingly coherent sense of growth and development into later adulthood.
One interpretation of this may be suggested by the literature on reminiscence
(e.g., Butler, 1963). Often, though not always, older adults seem to use life review
and reminiscence about earlier events as a way of providing meaning and continuity in their lives, and positive life review is typically associated with a more
successful adaptation to the experience of aging (Butler, 1963; Wong & Watt,
1991). This has been seen as reflective of Erikson's final stage of ego integrity, as
older adults strive to achieve a meaningful interpretation of their life course. It
seems likely that the present findings on "moral lessons" in later life reflect the
role of such adaptive ego processes. To the extent that the older adult thus
achieves a sense of completion regarding moral growth, this seems a possible
example of successful aging and specifically, perhaps, of "optimization" as discussed by Marsiske et al. (1995).

SUMMARY

Descriptions of critical moral events reported by adults across the life span
were studied with an eye to understanding age differences in people's own views
of their moral development. Two broad trends were noted. First, older adults were
more likely to report events that were positive in emotional tone and content than
were younger adults. Second, older adults reported learning more lessons from
their critical events than did the young. Both of these age differences may reflect
adaptations that enhance older adults' sense of wellbeing and ego integrity.
Despite the potential for cognitive losses from the "observer's" perspective, as
noted in the preceding sections, the results found here suggest that older adults
focus their own views of personal moral experience in growth-enhancing ways
that serve to optimize a sense of the integrity of their moral development over the
life course. Longitudinal study of how these processes predict the actual course of
later aging should prove interesting.

SUMMARY AND CONCLUSIONS

In this chapter, we have described research on moral development in maturity based on a life-span perspective on social cognition. Our commitment to a
life-span framework has entailed ongoing efforts to integrate the body of devel-

opmental work on moral and social reasoning during the earlier part of the life span with a research agenda on adulthood and aging. In particular, we have drawn on both the cognitive-developmental approach of Kohlberg (1976) and the sociocultural perspective of Vygotsky (1978), both firmly based in developmental research with the young, to help us understand aspects of moral functioning in later life. By anchoring this work within a life-span metatheory of successful aging, however, we have sought to ensure that these interpretations are appropriately contextualized and relevant to adult developmental theory (Baltes, 1997).

We specifically drew on Baltes's "selective optimization with compensation" metatheory (1997) to help us guide our interpretation of findings with respect to specific theories of moral development. For example, a number of findings described in the second section with respect to Kohlberg's cognitive-developmental theory were suggestive with regard to the concept of *compensation*, such as the maintenance of moral reasoning levels in later life despite apparent losses in related perspective-taking skills (Pratt et al., 1996). Similarly, the role of social consultation within the framework of sociocultural theory in the third section may be seen as highlighting the importance of selectivity by personality and cognitive style, whereas older individuals' own sense of greater learning from critical experiences described in our last section could illustrate aspects of the optimization of a coherent moral self. Overall, we believe, with Marsiske et al. (1995), that this life span metatheory is valuable, both for specific interpretations and for guiding the further research needed to test these ideas more fully within specific theoretical models of moral development.

Some years ago, we suggested that three general themes characterize a research agenda for life-span social cognition (Pratt & Norris, 1994). First, researchers need to understand and attend to the perspective of older adults themselves on their own experiences and development. Second, adult development and change must be viewed within the context of substantial and meaningful individual variation in the pathways followed throughout the life course. Third, individual psychological development is inherently social and contextualized and is best understood in these terms across the life span (Pratt & Norris, 1994).

In many respects, the research reported here is an attempt at further broadening the classic Kohlbergian paradigm for understanding moral development in the individual along these three lines. Thus, the research on collaborative cognitive activity around personal moral problems is an attempt to conceptualize individual decision making within a more fully social context, whereas the work in the last section provides a more qualitative, narrative perspective on individuals' own views of their experiences of moral development. In all of this work, we have drawn on the potential role of individual difference factors (such as personality and cognitive style) as moderators of distinctive adult developmental pathways.

There are of course many other issues in adult development that have not been addressed here. For example, gender and cultural differences in adult moral experience are beyond the scope of this chapter, but they are important to study in any truly contextualized research agenda on this topic. Nevertheless, we believe that studying moral development across the life span in this integrated way is an important enterprise that can shed light both on general adult developmental processes (Cole, 1996) and on the meaning and implications of the moral domain as it is embedded within the entire human life course.

ACKNOWLEDGMENTS

Research for this chapter was supported by Social Sciences and Humanities Research Council of Canada grants to Michael W. Pratt, Joan E. Norris, and Mary Louise Arnold, and to Bruce Hunsberger, S. Mark Pancer, and Michael W. Pratt. We thank Mary Louise Arnold and S. Mark Pancer for comments on a preliminary draft of this chapter and for their ongoing collaboration in this work, and Rhett Diessner, Kim Ewing, Rebecca Filyer, Stuart Kamenetsky, Judy Manchester, Valerie Powell, Adelle Pratt, and Irene Yue for their help with data collection and scoring.

REFERENCES

Altemeyer, R. A. (1988). *Enemies of freedom: Understanding right-wing authoritarianism.* San Francisco: Jossey-Bass.

Antonucci, T., & Akiyama, H. (1995). Convoys of social relations: Family and friendships within a life span context. In R. Blieszner & V. H. Bedford (Eds.), *Handbook of aging and the family* (pp. 355–371). Westport, CT: Greenwood.

Bakhtin, M. (1981/1975). *The dialogic imagination.* Austin, TX: University of Texas Press.

Baltes, P. B. (1987). Theoretical propositions of life-span developmental psychology: On the dynamics between growth and decline. *Developmental Psychology, 23,* 611–626.

Baltes, P. B. (1993). The aging mind: Potential and limits. *The Gerontologist, 33,* 580–594.

Baltes, P. B. (1997). On the incomplete architecture of human ontogeny: Selection, optimization, and compensation as foundations of developmental theory. *American Psychologist, 52,* 366–380.

Baltes, P. B., & Baltes, M. M. (1980). Plasticity and variability in psychological aging: Methodological and theoretical issues. In G. E. Gurski (Ed.), *Determining the effects of aging on the central nervous system* (pp. 41–66). Berlin: Schering.

Baltes, P. B., & Staudinger, U. (1996). *Interactive minds: Life-span perspectives on the social foundations of cognition.* New York: Cambridge University Press.

Barnett, M., Quackenbush, S., & Sinisi, C. (1995). The role of critical experiences in moral development. *Basic and Applied Social Psychology, 17,* 137–152.

Bengtson, V. L., Burgess, E. O., & Parrott, T. M. (1997). Theory, explanation, and a third generation of theoretical development in social gerontology. *Journal of Gerontology: Social Sciences, 52B,* S72–88.

Bielby, D., & Papalia, D. (1975). Moral development and perceptual role-taking: Their development and interrelationship across the lifespan. *International Journal of Aging and Human Development, 6,* 293–308.

Birren, J. E. & Schaie, K. W. (Eds.) (1996). *Handbook of the psychology of aging* (4th ed.). San Diego, CA: Academic Press.

Blasi, A. (1980). Bridging moral cognition and moral action: A critical review. *Psychological Bulletin, 88,* 1–45.

Brabeck, M. (1995). Morality: Thoughts about the past, thoughts about the future. *Moral Education Forum, 20,* 3–9.

Butler, R. N. (1963). The life review: An interpretation of reminiscence in the aged. *Psychiatry, 26,* 65–76.

Carstensen, L. L. (1991). Socioemotional selectivity theory: Social activity in lifespan context. *Annual Review of Gerontology and Geriatrics, 11,* 195–217.

Carstensen, L. (1993). Motivation for social contact across the lifespan. In J. Jacobs (Ed.), *Developmental perspectives on motivation, Nebraska Symposium* (vol. 40, pp. 209–254). Lincoln, NB: University of Nebraska Press.

Carstensen, L. L., Hansen, K. A., & Freund, A. M. (1995). Selection and compensation in adulthood. In R. Dixon & Backman, L. (Eds.), *Compensating for psychological deficits and declines* (pp. 107–126). Mahwah, NJ: Lawrence Erlbaum Associates.

Chap, J. B. (1986). Moral judgment in middle and late adulthood: The effects of age-appropriate moral dilemmas and spontaneous role taking. *International Journal of Aging and Human Development, 22,* 161–171.

Cohen, F., Bearison, D., & Muller, C. (1987). Interpersonal understanding in the elderly. *Research on Aging, 9,* 79–100.

Colby, A., & Damon, W. (1992). *Some do care: Contemporary lives of moral commitment.* New York: Free Press.

Colby, A., & Kohlberg, L. (1987). *The measurement of moral judgment* (Vol. 1). New York: Cambridge University Press.

Cole, T. (1996). What have we "made" of aging? *Journal of Gerontology: Social Sciences, 50B,* S341–S343.

Damon, W. (1981). Exploring children's social cognition on two fronts. In J. H. Flavell & L. Ross (Eds.), *Social cognitive development: Frontiers and possible futures.* (pp. 154–175). New York: Cambridge University Press.

Davey, A. & Norris, J. E. (in press). Social networks and exchange norms across the adult life-span. *Canadian Journal on Aging.*

Dixon, R. (1992). Contextual approaches to adult intellectual development. In R. Sternberg and C. Berg (Eds.), *Intellectual development.* New York: Cambridge Press.

Dixon, R., & Gould, O. (1996). Adults telling and retelling stories collaboratively. In P. Baltes & U. Staudinger (Eds.), *Interactive minds* (pp. 221–241). Cambridge, UK: Cambridge University Press.

Elash, A. (1997, November 3). Older and needier. *Maclean's,* 66.

Erikson, E. (1950). *Childhood in society.* New York: W. W. Norton.

Feather, N. (1994). Human values and their relation to justice. *Journal of Social Issues, 50,* 129–151.

Ferraro, K. F. (1990). The gerontological imagination. In K. F. Ferraro (Ed.), *Gerontological perspectives and issues* (pp. 3–18). New York: Springer.

Ferraro, K. F., & Farmer, M. (1996). Social compensation in adulthood and later life. In R. Dixon & L. Backman, L. (Eds.), *Compensating for psychological deficits and declines: Managing losses and promoting gains* (pp. 127–146). Mahwah, NJ: Lawrence Erlbaum Associates.

Fredrickson, B. L., & Carstensen, L. L. (1990). Choosing social partners: How old age and anticipated endings make people more selective. *Psychology and Aging, 5,* 335–347.

Gilligan, C. (1982). *In a different voice: Psychological theories and women's development.* Cambridge, MA: Harvard University Press.

Gould, O. N., & Dixon, R. (1993). How we spent our vacation: Collaborative storytelling by young and old adults. *Psychology and Aging, 8,* 10–17.

Hogg, J. R., & Heller, K. (1990). A measure of relational competence for community-dwelling elderly. *Psychology and Aging, 5,* 580–588.

Jensen, L. (1995). Habits of the heart revisited: Autonomy, community and divinity in adults' moral language. *Qualitative Sociology, 18,* 71–86.

Kahn, R. L., & Antonucci, T. C. (1980). Convoys over the life course: Attachment, roles, and social support. In P. Baltes & O. G. Brim (Eds.), *Life span development and behavior* (vol. 3, pp. 253–286). New York: Academic Press.

Kohlberg, L. (1969). Stage and sequence: The cognitive-developmental approach to socialization. In D. A. Goslin (Ed.), *Handbook of socialization: Theory and research* (pp. 347–480). San Diego: Academic Press.

Kohlberg, L. (1973). Continuities in childhood and adult moral development revisited. In P. B. Baltes & K. W. Schaie (Eds.), *Life-span developmental psychology* (pp. 180–204). New York: Academic Press.

Kohlberg, L. (1976). Moral stages and moralization: The cognitive-developmental approach. In T. Lickona (Ed.), *Moral development and moral behavior.* New York: Holt, Rinehart, & Winston.

Kohlberg, L., & Candee, D. (1984). The relationship of moral judgment to moral action. In W. M. Kurtines & J. L. Gewirtz (Eds.), *Morality, moral behavior and moral development: Basic issues in theory and research* (pp. 52–72). New York: Wiley.

Krause, N., & Markides, K. (1990). Measuring social support among older adults. *International Journal of Aging and Human Development, 30,* 37–53.

Krebs, D., Wark, G., & Krebs, D. (1995). Lessons from life: Toward a functional morality. *Moral Education Forum, 20,* 22–29.

Lapsley, D. K., & Quintana, S. M. (1989). Mental capacity and role taking: A structural equations approach. *Merrill-Palmer Quarterly, 35,* 143–163.

Lawton, M. P. (1987). Environment and the need satisfaction of the aging. In L. Carstensen & B. Edelstein (Eds.), *Handbook of clinical gerontology* (pp. 33–40). New York: Pergamon Press.

Lonky, E., Kaus, C., & Roodin, P. (1984). Life experience and mode of coping: Relation to moral judgment in adulthood. *Developmental Psychology, 20,* 1159–1167.

Lowenthal, M. F. (1968). Social isolation and mental illness in old age. In B. Neugarten (Ed.), *Middle age and aging: A reader in social psychology* (pp. 220–234). Chicago: University of Chicago Press.

Marshall, V. W. (1980). *Last chapters: A sociology of aging and dying.* Monterey, CA: Brooks/Cole.

Marsiske, M., Lang, F. R., Baltes, P. B், & Baltes, M. M. (1995). Selective optimization with compensation: Life-span perspectives on successful human development. In R. A. Dixon & L. Backman (Eds.), *Compensating for psychological deficits and declines: Managing losses and promoting gains* (pp. 35–82). Mahwah, NJ: Lawrence Erlbaum Associates.

McAdams, D., de St. Aubin, E., & Logan, R. (1993). Generativity among young, midlife, and older adults. *Psychology and Aging, 8,* 221–230.

McAdams, D., Diamond, A., de St. Aubin, E., & Mansfield, E. (1997). Stories of commitment: The psychosocial construction of generative lives. *Journal of Personality and Social Psychology, 72,* 678–694.

Piaget, J. (1932). *The moral judgment of the child,* New York: Free Press.

Pratt, M. (1997, August). *Adults' consultation with others about life problems: Collaborative cognition and the character of recollection.* Paper presented at the 16th Congress of the International Association of Gerontology, Adelaide, Australia.

Pratt, M., & Arnold, M. L. (1995). Narrative approaches to moral socialization across the lifespan. *Moral Education Forum, 20,* 13–22.

Pratt, M. W., Diessner, R., Hunsberger, B., Pancer, M., & Savoy, K. (1991). Four pathways in the analysis of adult development and aging: Comparing analyses of reasoning about personal life dilemmas. *Psychology and Aging, 7,* 666–675.

Pratt, M., Diessner, R., Pratt, A., Hunsberger, B., & Pancer, S. M. (1996). Moral and social reasoning and perspective-taking in later life: A longitudinal study. *Psychology and Aging, 11,* 66–73.

Pratt, M. W., Golding, G., & Hunter, W. J. (1983). Aging as ripening: Character and consistency of moral judgment in young, mature, and older adults. *Human Development, 26,* 277–288.

Pratt, M. W., Golding, G., Hunter, W., & Norris, J. (1988). From inquiry to judgment: Age and sex differences in patterns of adult moral thinking and information-seeking. *International Journal of Aging and Human Development, 27,* 115–130.

Pratt, M. W., Hunsberger, B., Pancer, S. M., & Roth, D. (1992). Reflections on religion: Aging, belief orthodoxy, and interpersonal conflict in the complexity of adult thinking about religious issues. *Journal for the Scientific Study of Religion, 31,* 514–522.

Pratt, M. W., Hunsberger, B., Pancer, M., Roth, D., & Santolupo, S. (1993). Thinking about parenting: Reasoning about developmental issues across the lifespan. *Developmental Psychology, 29,* 585–595.

Pratt, M., Kerig, P., Cowan, P., & Cowan, C. (1988). Mothers and fathers teaching three-year-olds: Authoritative parenting and adults' scaffolding of young children's learning. *Developmental Psychology, 24,* 732–739.

Pratt, M., & Norris, J. (1989). Sex, age and stage differences in the structure of the moral domain. Unpublished research fellowship final report, Wilfrid Laurier University, Waterloo, Ontario, Canada.

Pratt, M. W., & Norris, J. E. (1994). *The social psychology of aging: A cognitive perspective.* Oxford: Blackwell.

Pratt, M., Norris, J., Arnold, M., & Filyer, R. (in press). *Generativity and moral development as predictors of value socialization narratives for the young across the adult lifespan: From lessons learned to stories told. Psychology and Aging.*

Pratt, M. W., Pancer, M., Hunsberger, B., & Manchester, J. (1990). Reasoning about the self and relationships in maturity: An integrative complexity analysis of individual differences. *Journal of Personality and Social Psychology, 59,* 575–581.

Pratt, M., & Savoy-Levine, K. (1998). Contingent tutoring of long-division skills in fourth and fifth graders: Experimental tests of some hypotheses about scaffolding. *Journal of Applied Developmental Psychology, 19,* 287–304.

Rest, J. (1979). *Development in judging moral issues.* Minneapolis: University of Minnesota Press.

Rest, J. (1983). Morality. In P. Mussen (Gen. Ed.), *Manual of child psychology* (4th ed., pp. 556–629). New York: Wiley.

Rest, J., & Narvaez, D. (1994). *Moral development in the professions: Psychology and applied ethics.* Hillsdale, NJ: Lawrence Erlbaum Associates.

Rest, J., Narvaez, D., Bebeau, M., & Thoma, S. (1996). *Development, domains, and culture in morality: A neo-Kohlbergian approach.* Unpublished manuscript, University of Minnesota.

Russell, B. (1991). Reflections on my eightieth birthday. In M. Fowler & McCutcheon (Eds.), *Songs of experience: An anthology of literature on growing old* (pp. 45–48). New York: Ballantine Books.

Rybash, J. M., Hoyer, W. J., & Roodin, P. A. (1983). Expressions of moral thought in later adulthood. *The Gerontologist, 23,* 254–260.

Salthouse, T. E. (1992). The information-processing perspective on cognitive aging. In R. Sternberg & C. Berg (Eds.), *Intellectual development.* New York: Cambridge Press.

Schaie, K. W. (1989). Hazards of cognitive aging. *The Gerontologist, 29,* 484–493.

Selman, R. (1980). *The growth of interpersonal understanding.* New York: Academic Press.

Selman, R. L., Beardslee, W., Schultz, L. H., Krupa, M., & Podorefsky, D. (1986). Assessing adolescent interpersonal negotiation strategies: Toward the integration of structural and functional models. *Developmental Psychology, 22,* 450–459.

Staudinger, U. (1996). Wisdom and the social-interactive foundation of the mind. In P. Baltes & U. Staudinger (Eds.), *Interactive minds: Lifespan perspectives on the social foundation of cognition* (pp. 276–318). New York: Cambridge University Press.

Suedfeld, P., & Piedrahita, L. (1984). Intimations of mortality: Integrative simplification as a precursor of death. *Journal of Personality and Social Psychology, 47,* 848–852.

Suedfeld, P., Tetlock, P., & Streufert, S. (1992). Conceptual/integrative complexity. In J. Atkinson, D. McClelland, & J. Veroff (Eds.), *Handbook of thematic analysis* (pp. 393–400). New York: Springer-Verlag.

Tappan, M., & Brown, L. (1989). Stories told and lessons learned: Toward a narrative approach to moral development. *Harvard Educational Review, 59,* 182–205.

Tetlock, P. (1983). Accountability and complexity of thought. *Journal of Personality and Social Psychology, 45,* 118–126.

Thoma, S. (1994). Moral judgment and moral action. In J. Rest & D. Narvaez (Eds.), *Moral development in the professions: Psychology and applied ethics* (pp. 199–211). Hillsdale, NJ: Lawrence Erlbaum Associates.

Vygotsky, L. (1978). *Mind in society.* Cambridge, MA: MIT Press.

Walker, L. J. (1980). Cognitive and perspective-taking prerequisites for moral development. *Child Development, 51,* 131–139.

Walker, L. J. (1989). A longitudinal study of moral reasoning. *Child Development, 60,* 157–166.

Walker, L., & Pitts, R. (1998). Naturalistic conceptions of moral maturity. *Developmental Psychology, 34,* 403–419.

Walker, L., Pitts, R., Hennig, K., & Matsuba, M. K. (1995). Reasoning about morality and real-life moral problems. In M. Killen & D. Hart (Eds.), *Morality in everyday life* (pp. 371–407). Cambridge, UK: Cambridge University Press.

Wertsch, J. V. (1991). *Voices of the mind.* Cambridge, MA: Harvard Press.

Wertsch, J., & Kanner, B. (1992). A sociocultural approach to intellectual development. In R. Sternberg & C. Berg (Eds.), *Intellectual development.* (pp. 328–349). Cambridge, UK: Cambridge University Press.

White, C. B. (1988). Age, education, and sex effects on adult moral reasoning. *International Journal of Aging and Human Development, 27,* 271–281.

Wong, P. T., & Watt, L. M. (1991). What types of reminiscence are associated with successful aging? *Psychology and Aging, 6,* 272–279.

14

THE ROLE OF TIME
IN THE SETTING OF
SOCIAL GOALS ACROSS
THE LIFE SPAN

SUSAN TURK CHARLES
LAURA L. CARSTENSEN

Department of Psychology
Stanford University
Stanford, California

INTRODUCTION

The concept of time is ubiquitous in psychology. It is evidenced in the chrono-logical foundations of virtually all developmental theories and is the tacit founda-tion of numerous psychological concepts, such as rumination, which involves dwelling on past events and feelings (Nolen-Hoeksema, McBride, & Larson, 1997); anxiety, which involves concerns and expectancies about the future (Reiss & McNally, 1985; Schmidt, Lerew, & Jackson, 1997); and more normative con-structs such as *self* or *identity,* which implicitly involve the sense of continuity across time (Cross & Markus, 1991; Markus & Wurf, 1987).

In this chapter, we address the ways in which construals of time influence social cognition, motivation, and behavior. We refer to "time" as the uniquely human ability to appreciate the passage of time and, thus, to monitor one's place in the life cycle. Our thesis is that people are always consciously or subcon-sciously aware of time and that this consideration of time is an essential component in human motivation, influencing the adoption, pursuit, and realization of goals across adulthood.

We argue that time is particularly related to life-span development. Because mortality places constraints on time, there are reliable age differences in time perspective. Older adults generally foresee a relatively limited future, whereas younger adults envision a relatively expansive one (Carstensen, 1993). Throughout life, especially in adulthood, various events provide subtle and not so subtle reminders that time is passing. For many people, a chronic illness such as high blood pressure or osteoarthritis is experienced for the first time. Deaths of friends or family members bring social endings and awareness of one's own mortality. Even experiences regarded primarily in positive terms can influence time perspective. For example, in the United States, certain types of events, such as watching a child graduate from high school or seeing him or her marry, bring into consciousness the fact that time is passing. Adults describe the reliable sense that time moves faster and faster with age.

Other influences on time perspective include the experience of off-time events. A terminal illness in early life transforms the time perspective of younger adults into one similar to that of elderly adults; indeed, we expect that simply living in a crime-ridden neighborhood changes time perspective in adolescents, many of whom believe that they may never survive young adulthood. Conversely, other events expand time perspective, such as medical breakthroughs that offer individuals suffering from potentially fatal illnesses additional years of life. We suspect that population changes in life expectancy has expanded the time perspective of older adults since the turn of the 20th century.

Socioemotional selectivity theory provides the theoretical basis for the work described herein. The cardinal tenet is that time perspective is importantly related to the selection and pursuit of goals. According to the theory, social behavior is motivated throughout life by a fairly stable constellation of goals, from protection and physical sustenance to psychological well-being. Throughout life, goals compete, and in situations in which multiple goals vie with one another, certain goals assume primacy. Socioemotional selectivity theory focuses on two main classes of psychological goals: One comprises acquiring knowledge, and the other, regulating and experiencing positive emotions. The theory posits that the perception of time determines which goals are selected in particular social conditions. When time is perceived as expansive, preparatory goals are more likely to be selected because they enhance flexibility in the future; when time is perceived as limited, emotional goals are selected because they are typically experienced in the moment of contact.

In this chapter, we review reliable age-related patterns of social interactions and traditional theories offered to explain them. Next, we return to the consideration of time in social cognition and elaborate specific postulates of socioemotional selectivity theory. We then report findings from empirical research designed to test them. Finally, we attempt to illuminate how consideration of time perspective places motivation at center stage and generates alternative hypotheses about a range of phenomena studied in social and cognitive aging.

MOTIVATION FOR SOCIAL CONTACT THROUGHOUT THE LIFE SPAN

All theories about human motivation and self-concept emphasize the importance of social relatedness throughout life. Most social scientists agree that the inclination to bond with others evolved over the millennia Deci & Ryan, 1991; James, 1890; Ryan, 1993; White, 1959). From the beginning of life, infants are socially oriented, displaying attentional biases for the human face (Fantz, 1963) and being soothed by human contact (Rothbart, 1994). There is widespread agreement, for example, that the social smile of infants is "hard-wired" because of the selective advantages of infants who bonded with caretakers. Even blind infants smile.

Early in life, children show a readiness to initiate social contact (Tronick, 1989), and this need for social connections continues throughout life. Social interaction is necessary for constructing and reaffirming the self (e.g. Markus & Wurf, 1987) and for ongoing assessment of accuracy, consistency, and self-enhancement of this self-representation (Fiske & Taylor, 1991). Group processes rely fundamentally on the human predilection to bond with others. Threats from external sources promote group bonding, cooperative behavior, and motivation to accomplish group goals (Sherif & Sherif, 1953). In short, social awareness and social bonding are universal.

The importance of social connectedness does not diminish with age. Among healthy older adults, social support is provided and received from others through support exchange. Interestingly, the amount of received and provided support is comparable across generations (Antonucci & Akiyama, 1987). Moreover, social connectedness remains important for psychological well-being into very old age (Lang & Carstensen, 1994). Among the frail elderly, social interaction often takes the form of instrumental support from friends, family, and professional caregivers who facilitate access to physicians and health-care compliance. For both healthy and frail older adults, the presence of social interaction and social support are associated with physical health status, health functioning, and even mortality (Antonucci & Jackson, 1987; Berkman & Syme, 1979; Blazer, 1982).

Yet despite the importance of social connections, the most reliable finding in social gerontology is that overall rates of social interaction diminish. Cross-sectional (Cumming & Henry, 1961, Gordon & Gaitz, 1976; Harvey & Singleton, 1989; Lawton, Moss, & Fulcomer, 1987), and longitudinal studies (Lee & Markides, 1990) document the reliable relationships among advancing age and decreasing social interaction. This decrease has been found to begin as early as young adulthood (Carstensen, 1992) and appears to accelerate from middle adulthood to old age (Palmore, 1981).

TRADITIONAL THEORIES OF SOCIAL
BEHAVIOR IN OLD AGE

Until recently, primarily two theories addressed this decrease in social activity with age, both of which are grounded in sociological perspectives: disengagement theory (Cumming & Henry, 1961) and activity theory (Havighurst, 1961, Havighurst & Albrecht, 1953; Maddox, 1963, 1965). Disengagement theory maintains that decreased social contact is a direct result of the general emotional disengagement experienced by the older adult coupled with the societal need to prepare for the loss of its member. According to this theory, older adults experience emotional dampening and focus more on self-reflection as a result of their subconscious awareness of the imminence of death. The process is viewed as adaptive, because both the older adult and society participate in a mutual withdrawal process in symbolic preparation for the approaching death. Researchers claim that decreases in social interaction in old age directly support this theory (Cumming & Henry, 1961).

The second theory commonly used to explain reduced rates of social interaction is activity theory. This theory maintains that older and younger people are comparably motivated to engage in social contact, but older people cannot realize social goals because societal and physical barriers render these goals unrealistic. Age-related physical problems, deaths of friends and loved ones, and societal practices such as mandatory retirement play a role in preventing social contact. In accordance with this theory, activity levels decline with age, and Western societies do treat older adults in ageist ways that limit opportunities (Pasupathi, Carstensen, & Tsai, 1995; Rosenwasser, McBride, Brantley, & Ginsburg, 1986; Waldman & Avolio, 1986). Instrumental barriers, such as the absence of public transportation, and physical conditions also impede access to social partners for older adults. Activity theory posits that it is the constellation of these factors that promote reduced rates of social interaction in old age. As a consequence, reduction in opportunities for emotional satisfaction is inevitable.

Despite the attention these theories have received in the social gerontology literature, the overall profile of empirical findings challenges their basic contentions. Both theories conclude that reduction in social contacts reflects reduced or diminished emotional states. For disengagement theory, emotions are dampened. For activity theory, reductions in social interactions lead to reductions in positive emotional experiences. However, empirical evidence shows that older adults do not have dampened emotional experiences. On the contrary, a growing body of literature indicates that, if anything, emotion assumes greater importance in old age. Older adults express subjective levels of emotional experience of equal intensity to those of younger adults (Carstensen, Gross, & Fung, 1997; Labouvie-Vief, Hakim-Larson, DeVoe, & Schoeberlein, 1989; Lawton, Kleban, Rajagopal, & Dean, 1992; Levenson, Carstensen, Friesen, & Ekman, 1991) and report equivalent, if not higher, levels of positive affect and lower levels of negative affect (Gross et al., 1997). In addition, emotional closeness to spouses, children, and grandchildren is, by self-report, even more satisfying in old age compared with earlier times in life. Indeed, interactions with family members and established friends—those emotionally close social partners that disengagement theory explicity predicts should decrease the most—are viewed as even more meaningful and satisfying over time (Field & Minkler, 1988; Carstensen, 1992). Moreover, older adults do not appear motivated to enlarge their social networks: interventions aimed at establishing friendships among older adults have yielded small and short-lived effects (Carstensen & Erickson, 1986).

Older adults are not suffering psychologically from decreases in overall rates of social interactions. Whereas older adults were presumed to be more depressed and socially isolated compared to younger adults in the mid-1970s (Gurland, 1976), empirical findings show that this is not the case. In large epidemiological studies, older adults have lower levels of almost every type of mental disorder—with the exceptions being dementia and other organic brain syndromes—than do younger adults (George, Blazer, Winfield-Laird, Leaf, & Fischback, 1988). Younger cohorts have higher prevalence and incidence rates of depression than do older cohorts (Wittchen, Knauper, & Kessler 1994) and report higher levels of general satisfaction with relationships than do college students (Herzog & Rogers, 1981).

Given the importance of social interaction to well-being for people of all ages, the profile of findings mentioned above appears on the surface, to be paradoxical. Socioemotional selectivity theory offers an explanation that reconciles the reduced rates of social interaction coupled with the overall high levels of emotional well-being among older adults. Unlike the traditional theories in gerontology that have focused on loss and societal barriers, socioemotional selectivity theory stresses the role of individual differences in motivation for social contact. According to the theory, social motivations operate throughout the life span; however, these motivations change as a function of place in the life cycle. For people who perceive themselves near the end of life, reduction in social partners reflects an active selection process of focusing on emotionally meaningful interactions and discarding less emotionally important social partners.

SOCIOEMOTIONAL SELECTIVITY THEORY

Socioemotional selectivity theory views reductions in social interaction as proactive selection processes that reflect changes in goals as a function of time left in life (Carstensen, 1992, 1993, 1995; Carstensen et al., 1997). The theory assumes that social interaction is motivated by fundamental human needs, such as hunger and sex, as well as psychological needs that regulate affective states. Social interaction allows individuals to meet many of these needs, such as information acquisition, the development and maintenance of self-concept, and the regulation of emotional states. According to the theory, the larger goal constellation can be condensed into two broad classes of psychosocial motives. The first class comprises the acquisition of knowledge about the self and social world, and the second class comprises the need for emotional gratification.

Knowledge-related social motives include information seeking, social comparison, identity strivings, and achievement motivation. Knowledge is obviously required for the development of expertise, occupational development, and other pursuits related to intellectual goals. Information seeking also includes learning about social norms, such as observations of social interactions (e.g., modeling) and direct acquisition of "facts" through contact with others. Emotional gratification includes motivation to derive emotional meaning from life, establish intimacy, experience satisfaction and contentment, and verify the self. The theory posits that the perception of time influences the course of these two trajectories throughout life.

Socioemotional selectivity maintains that the perception of time is essential to understanding how motivation and goals change throughout life. Whereas disengagement theory includes a discussion of a subconscious awareness of impending death for older adults as integral to its argument, socioemotional selectivity theory posits that the awareness of time is not unique for older adults. Rather, the conscious and subconscious awareness of time is present throughout the adult life span. Understanding general patterns of time perception among adult populations prepares a foundation from which to understand how emotional and knowledge-related social motives interweave and vary in importance at different times along the life span. In the next section, we provide an overview of how time is constructed in American culture. Although the examples we provide are culture specific, we argue that the basic cognitive developmental processes of young age and the awareness of death at the end of the life span are likely universal.

TIME PERCEPTION THROUGHOUT THE LIFE SPAN

Time perception is an important factor in social cognition and behavior throughout the adult life span, shifting predictably according to place in the life cycle. In early childhood, the understanding of time is a central cognitive developmental task, important for a variety of social skills, including the use of relational schemas. Although children show evidence of visual and auditory habituation and recognition immediately after birth (DeCasper & Fifer, 1980), delays of even seconds prevents memory encoding (Diamond, 1985). By 2–3 years of age, memory for past events appears (Fivush, Gray, & Fromhoff, 1987), and by 4 years of age, children understand the concept of past events (Nelson, 1992). The "future" appears to represent knowledge that events will happen more so than a future that can be shaped with planning and forethought. The result of this lack of time perception in youth is that until about the age of 12, children nearly always prefer smaller instantaneous rewards to bigger rewards following a time delay (Mischel, 1968). Social goals, like all other goals, are focused on the present. In short, very young children focus on the present and probably construe a tacit but ambiguous future.

By late adolescence, a clear understanding of future time appears. At this time, individuals' time perspective is influenced not by cognitive ability but by societal structure and social mores that in themselves structure time perspective. Certain goals for adolescents and young adults are limited only by age, such as the age for legal independence from a parent or guardian. Other goals include age as one necessary requirement, such as the ability to obtain a driver's license, vote, or open a checking account. The future is salient to adolescents and young adults, as time requirements play a role for many longed-for goals.

In middle age, people begin to place greater emphasis on past than future experiences (Whitbourne & Dannefer, 1985–1986). Events across adulthood mark the passage of time, priming individuals to consider their place in the life cycle. Although some individuals continue to alter their career paths, others begin to consider retirement and take steps to ensure long-term financial stability. Many adults become caregivers to frail parents and witness their deaths. For the first time in life, men and women find themselves the oldest in their households. Western society communicates in magazine articles, comic strips, and television programs a phenomenon termed *midlife crisis* centered about the realization of a limited future. Although researchers have found little evidence for a normative midlife crisis (Clausen, 1981; Neugarten, 1973), priorities nonetheless start to shift (Goffee & Scase, 1992). These priorities often include shifts in social goals. For example, one study found that a realization of a limited number of years left in a career shifted focus from career strivings to greater concerns about family (Goffee & Scase, 1992). According to socioemotional selectivity theory, motivation is guided by time, and the uniquely human ability to appreciate that life ultimately ends provides the cognitive capacity to plan and shift the relative importance of and motivations for emotion and knowledge-related goals.

THE KNOWLEDGE AND EMOTION TRAJECTORIES ACROSS THE LIFE SPAN

The influence of time perspective offers a relatively predictable pattern of the pursuit of emotional and knowledge-related goals along the life span. The theory states that knowledge is fundamentally future oriented in that it prepares people for the future. Social contact motivated by the pursuit of knowledge is most likely when knowledge is limited and time is expansive. Emotional goals are more likely to be present focused, as they relate to the regulation of current feelings. Figure 14.1 illustrates the emotional and information-seeking trajectory along the life span.

The critical developmental stage from birth to early adolescence is marked by high needs for both information and emotional goals. Social goals are centered around immediate attention and gratification of basic needs. Emotional attachment with significant caregivers is important for continual comfort and reassurance. Separation anxiety develops, and it serves to motivate intimacy with emotionally reinforcing caregivers. Emotional gratification is of paramount

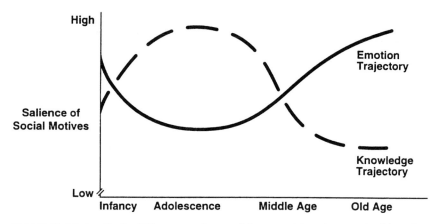

FIGURE 14.1   Idealized life course trajectory of the two social motives postulated in socioe-motional selectivity theory. (From Carstensen, Gross, & Fung, 1997, with permission.)

importance early in life, as children benefit from positive reinforcement and veri-fication of the self. In addition, information becomes vital for the assimilation and accommodation necessary for cognitive growth. Schemas are formed that provide a cognitive framework to assimilate and accommodate new information about the environment. Almost any social interaction provides young children with infor-mation, including how to perform instrumental tasks, social modeling for future interactions, and knowledge on which to base identity and value systems. The amount of social information gained within the first few years of life suggests that there is a readiness at birth for social learning that involves the motivation to seek contact with other people.

From late adolescence throughout early adulthood, the drive for information remains dominant. At this time, individuals learn information necessary for inde-pendent functioning and often assume responsibility for their own needs for the first time in life. Developmentally, the knowledge trajectory peaks during adoles-cence and early adulthood and gradually declines in middle and old age. During this period, social goals are often informational ones. By interacting with others, people gain a sense of cognitive control that aids in information gathering and helps with implementing plans gaining feedback, and reformulating life's chal-lenges (Fiske & Taylor, 1991). Even at a romantic level—which obviously involves satisfaction of emotional goals—prospective mates are often "tried out" so that individuals can learn about the types of people they prefer as a long-term partner and friends.

Across adulthood, the importance of gaining knowledge through social inter-action decreases at the same time that the importance of emotional goals increases. As adults develop expertise in their respective fields, information sources become more specialized. Whereas a novice can receive new information from almost anyone in his or her field of research, an ingrained, experienced practitioner gains information from only a specialized few. In addition, information pertaining to social goals, such as learning about social values and the type of people one likes and dislikes, has also become well learned over the years and is no longer enhanced by novel social partners. As a result, the information trajectory declines gradually as knowledge is gained and the future for which it is banked grows shorter. The decrease of informational goals in social interactions does not imply that information becomes less important with age. Rather, as people gain expertise in their fields of interest and knowledge about the world in general, it is more difficult to find people who can offer novel information. Knowledge obtained through nonsocial means (e.g. reading) no doubt continues. Rather, *social* partners are less likely to be sought for their informative potential.

For the first time since childhood, the motivation to satisfy emotional goals surpasses that of knowledge-based goals in the social context. This phenomenon is illustrated by patterns of frequency of interaction, emotional closeness, and satisfaction in six types of social relationships—acquaintances, siblings, parents, close friends, children, and spouses (Carstensen, 1992). Results indicate that as individuals move from early to middle adulthood, the number of reported acquaintances declines and satisfaction from these acquaintances declines (Figure 14.2). Interaction rates for people who provide emotional ties, such as spouses and close friends, remain constant or decline slightly, but the satisfaction of these interactions increases (see Figure 14.3 for an illustration of spousal interaction and satisfaction). Even when reductions are seen among interactions with family

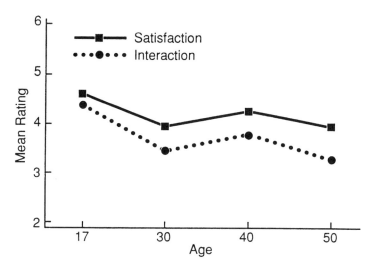

FIGURE 14.2   Rates of satisfaction and levels of interactions with acquaintances over time. (From Carstensen, 1992, with permission.)

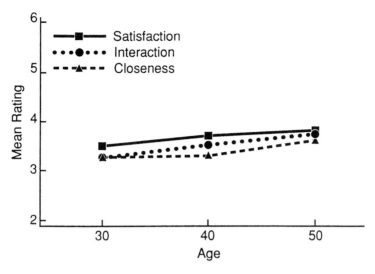

FIGURE 14.3   Rates of satisfaction and levels of interactions with spouses over time. (From Carstensen, 1992, with permission.)

members, these interactions are nonetheless regarded as important (Field & Minkler, 1988).

The trend of decreasing social interaction seen from young adulthood to middle age continues into old age. In old age, the frequency of interaction with grandchildren decreases over time, but the satisfaction associated with these relationships remains stable; for relationships with adult children, satisfaction and interactions increase over time (Field & Minkler, 1988). Older adults invest more in the emotional payoffs of social interactions than in the information gains. As a result, older adults are less likely to engage in social interaction with acquaintances and are more likely to prefer and interact with close friends and family members. Although overall interactions do decrease, this decrease in the total number of social partners is a direct result of older adults reducing contact with peripheral social contacts, not with familiar and emotionally close social partners. Older adults realize that their time is limited and prefer to maximize the interactions that fulfill emotional goals.

The above description of the relative emphasis of information and emotion-related goals over time does not imply that individuals are motivated exclusively by one dimension at any given life stage. Throughout life, both informational and emotional goals are present and constantly compete with one another. Emotion researchers have long held that the all individuals strive to avoid negative states and experience positive ones (Higgins, 1997; Tomkins, 1970); a principle that is not reserved only for older adults. In addition, the quest for information, whether it concerns geographical directions in a new city or information about health-care reform, does not disappear when people reach old age. Socioemotional selectivity posits that both classes of goals operate throughout life, yet their relative importance shifts with age.

TIME AND THE MENTAL REPRESENTATION
OF SOCIAL PARTNERS

Experience, as noted above, plays a role in goal selection, but socioemotional selectivity theory suggests that goals are prioritized on the basis of the perception of time. With a sense of limited time, present-oriented social goals—that is, emotional goals—are emphasized over long-term, informational goals. We hypothesized that this shift of goals would be evident in representations of social partners, such that younger and older adults would place relatively more or less emphasis along informational and emotional dimensions as a function of time perspective. Among older adults, potential partners would be represented along affective dimensions; among younger adults, cognitive representations would include more future potential and information-seeking dimensions.

We developed an experimental paradigm that we have used in several studies. We asked people to classify various social partners on the basis of perceived similarities (Fredrickson & Carstensen, 1990; Carstensen & Fredrickson, 1998). In our first study, participants included age groups ranging from adolescents to octogenarians. Subjects from all age groups were relatively healthy and living in the community, with one exception. In addition to our healthy older sample, we recruited an age-matched sample of older adults ($M = 80$ years) who were physically frail and living in a residential-care facility. The inclusion of this subsample provided us with the opportunity to examine differences determined by place in the life cycle rather than chronological age. In a second study, we recruited a larger sample composed of both white- and blue-collar workers who ranged in age from 18 to 88. African Americans comprised one third of the sample, and the rest were European Americans.

Research participants were presented with a set of 18 cards, each of which described a particular type of social partner. The cards contained a broad spectrum of people, some of whom are likely to provide novel information (e.g., "the author of a book you've read") in the course of social interaction and others who are more likely to yield emotional payoffs (e.g., "a close friend"). Participants were asked to sort the cards into as many or few piles as they wished according to how similarly they would feel interacting with the person. Thus, the participants' cognitive construals when making social judgments could be measured without the possible demand characteristics that might have been elicited by asking about specific feelings and thoughts regarding certain social partners.

Multidimensional scaling techniques revealed three primary dimensions that accounted reliably for most of the variance in the subjects' card sorts. The first dimension clearly represented the "affective potential" (i.e. a likeable/dislikeable dimension) of the social partners described on the cards. Both additional dimensions were consistent with knowledge-related qualities of social partners: One was interpreted as "future possibilities," or people from whom subsequent contact was either likely or unlikely, and the other as "information-seeking," or people from whom novel information was likely versus those from whom novel information was unlikely. The scaling techniques allowed us not only to identify the dimensions along which people perceive social partners but also to assess the weight specific age groups placed on these dimensions. In both studies, the pattern of findings was the same. As hypothesized, each successive age group placed greater weights on the affective dimension. Adolescents placed the greatest weight on the dimension of future possibilities. The change in emphasis on the affective dimension from adolescence to middle age mirrors the decrease in rates of social interaction with acquaintances (Carstensen, 1992). Oldest participants categorized social partners almost exclusively along the affective dimension. Importantly, the sample of frail elderly showed the strongest tendency to consider social partners in affective terms, even more so than did same-aged, healthy counterparts. The difference between these two older age groups confirmed our suspicions that time left in life—as opposed to chronological age—plays a role in social-partner preferences. Although older participants in this study were the same age, frail older adults, those with presumably shorter life spans, were even more likely than their healthier counterparts to perceive social partners along emotional themes. The second study replicated these age differences across diverse socioeconomic level and ethnicity (Carstensen & Fredrickson, 1998).

Findings from these two studies suggest that toward the end of the life, the affective potential of social partners becomes increasingly important. Socioemotional selectivity theory posits that the perception of time, which is correlated with but not determined by age, is responsible for this motivational shift. In a third study, we attempted to advance our efforts to decouple age from time. To test the postulate that a greater emphasis on emotional goals than on informational goals is a result of perceived endings and not age, we applied the identical research paradigm to a sample of relatively young men ($M = 37$ years) living with a terminal illness (Carstensen & Fredrickson, 1998). In this sample, some tested negative for human immunodeficiency virus (HIV), some positive for HIV but not symptomatic of acquired immunodeficiency syndrome (AIDS), and some positive for HIV and actively experiencing symptoms of AIDS. We hypothesized that men who were HIV positive and had AIDS symptoms would perceive social partners along the affective dimension just like the older adults in our earlier studies. Following the same logic, we hypothesized that those who were HIV negative would organize potential social partners least along emotional dimensions, relative to the other two groups. Participants were given the same 18 cards, using the same methods and analytical procedures as the studies described above. Results revealed the same affective and informational dimensions that were found in the previous studies. Those with the most limited time left in life—HIV positive and with symptoms of AIDS—mentally represented potential social partners along affective dimensions to a greater extent than did those who were HIV positive but without AIDS symptoms, followed by those who were HIV negative. Thus, findings across these very different samples support the contention that time left in life is an important factor in the representation of social partners.

TIME PERSPECTIVE AND EMOTION

The above findings indicate that individuals with a limited perceived future are more likely to cognitively represent potential social partners along affective dimensions compared with those who perceive an open-ended future. We suggest that this emphasis on affect is a result of motivation for certain goals. Individuals who foresee an open-ended future are more likely to engage in long-term goals, including information gain that can be banked for later use. For individuals who perceive constraints on time, short-term goals—those that maximize positive experiences—are most important. Socioemotional selectivity theory posits that motivation for emotional goals increases as a function of time perspective, such that those with perceived time limitations place higher priority on emotions across a range of experiences both within and outside of a social context, compared with those who perceive their time as expansive.

How do goal changes affect other cognitive processes? We expected that increased salience of emotion in goal-directed behavior might indirectly affect the type of information people attend to and process. In another study, we employed an incidental memory paradigm to explore the cognitive processing of emotional and neutral information (Carstensen & Turk-Charles, 1994). Eighty-three individuals between the ages of 20 and 83 years were randomly assigned to read one of two short selections from a popular novel. Each selection described a social interaction between two adults and had comparable amounts of emotional and neutral information. At the end of an hour during which participants responded to unrelated questionnaires, they were asked to recall all that they could about the passage. Responses were transcribed and parsed into units of either neutral or emotional material, and the proportion of emotional information to neutral information was calculated for each individual. Because age-related reductions in memory have been well established (Smith, 1996), we did not presume that older adults remember more emotional information overall than do younger adults. However, we did hypothesize that older adults process emotion more deeply and therefore a greater proportion of their recall would include emotional material. Indeed, the proportion of emotional information recalled increased with each age group (Figure 14.4). The proportional increase was due not to an increase in the absolute amount of emotional information recalled with age but rather to a decrease in the recall of neutral information.

According to socioemotional selectivity theory, enhanced attention to emotional states and greater value placed on emotionaly meaningful experiences results in better regulation of emotion. An increased ability to regulate emotions stems in part from interacting with well-known, emotionally meaningful social partners who provide relatively predictable emotional experiences. In addition,

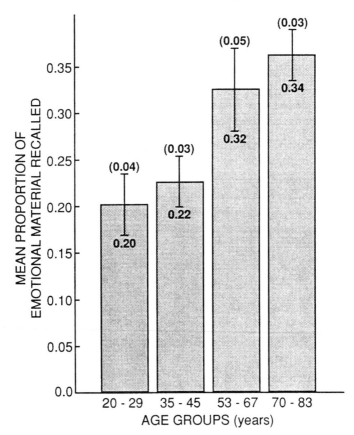

FIGURE 14.4   Mean proportion of emotional material recalled in four adult age groups. (From Carstensen & Turk-Charles, 1994, with permission.)

individuals who value emotional goals pay attention to the emotional quality of a situation and actively engage in strategies to optimize aspects of important social relationships. These strategies may include greater emotional regulation for social interactions that would be reflected in overall rates of positive and negative emotional experiences.

In another study, we examined affect, emotional regulation, experience, expression, and control in four ethnically and culturally diverse samples, each comprising a wide range of younger and older adults (Gross et al., 1997). The four groups included community samples of (1) African Americans and European Americans, (2) Chinese Americans and European Americans, (3) Norwegians, and (4) American nuns. We hypothesized that despite the diversity of the four groups, age-related differences in emotion would appear for each of the samples. Participants completed questionnaires that asked about various dimensions of emotional experience and expression. Consistent with previous findings on emotion, older adults from each of the samples reported greater emotional control and fewer emotionally negative experiences. Older adults also reported less emotional surgency compared to younger adults. These results support the greater use of emotional regulation as purported by the socioemotional selectivity theory. Because older adults are aware of a less expansive future than are younger adults, they strive to achieve short-term goals that include positive emotional experiences.

Emotional regulation, through careful selection of social partners, is one example of antecedent-focused emotional regulation, a strategy that entails constructing the environment to influence the type of emotions that will be experienced (Carstensen et al., 1997). This "front end" regulation strategy is presumed to increase in later life, whether it takes the form of discriminating among choices of social partners, managing actual interactions such that potentially damaging arguments are avoided, or using psychological processes such as cognitive reappraisal, self-enhancement, self-protection, and repair. In addition to antecedent emotion control, however, we have reason to expect that age is positively related to the ability to navigate difficult interactions such that their emotional tone is optimized.

In a very different line of research, we examined emotional expression and regulation in interactions between middle-aged and older married couples as they discussed emotionally charged topics (Carstensen, Gottman & Levenson, 1995; Levenson, Carstensen, & Gottman, 1994). Happily and unhappily married couples were equally represented in both age groups to avoid selection biases that no doubt contribute to the general finding of high marital satisfaction among older married couples. Spouses completed a questionnaire about the severity of various marital conflicts, identified a mutually agreed on conflict, and discussed this area of conflict for 15 minutes. Discussions were videotaped and coded for emotional expression and discussion content.

Results support the contention that greater emotional regulation is superior among older adults. Older couples rated problem severity lower than younger couples. In fact, none of the topics on the conflict list, which included money, children, and recreation, were more conflictual for older adults compared with younger adults; four were significantly less so. Moreover, observational data revealed that during the conflict discussion, older couples displayed less negative affect and incorporated less anger, disgust, belligerence, and whining than did middle-aged couples. They also displayed more affection to one another amidst these otherwise tense exchanges. Importantly, there was a main effect for age: even unhappily married couples expressed more affection to one another than did their unhappily married younger counterparts.

AGE DIFFERENCES IN SOCIAL PARTNER PREFERENCES

We have reviewed the way in which time perspective influences the mental representation of social partners. Individuals who perceive social endings perceive social partners along affective dimensions to a greater extent than do individuals who perceive an expansive future. We have also reviewed studies that suggest that a limited time perspective influences emotional goals in other areas as well, including memory for text and qualitative aspects of social interactions. The increased salience of emotion is compatible with other lines of research that suggest that developmentally, the ability to process emotional material increases with age.

We now return to the issue of why the size of social networks decreases among older adults. Recall from our introductory comments that the decrease in social network size is one of the most reliable findings in social gerontology. In fact, the research program that eventually led to socioemotional selectivity theory was originally prompted by efforts to understand the role motivation played in the narrowing of social spheres. Finding that older adults do appear to place greater importance on emotional experiences and emotional goals than do younger adults, we undertook a series of studies directly examining social network composition and social choices. Socioemotional selectivity theory predicts that limitations on time lead to decreases in social network size because social partners are selected to maximize positive emotional experiences and feelings of social connectedness (Carstensen et al., 1997). Because these partners are generally familiar social partners, the theory predicts that decreases in social network size are largely a function of the elimination of novel social partners and acquaintances. By contrast, younger adults are more focused on information gain than are older adults and therefore strive to maintain relatively larger and more diverse social networks that include a larger number of novel social partners and acquaintances.

Prior research had documented the reliable shrinkage of social networks with age. We conducted two studies to examine targeted reduction. Samples for each study were derived from participants from the Berlin Aging Study, a study of both community-dwelling and institutionalized older adults in West Berlin ranging from 70 to 104 years old. Participants were asked to define social partners into separate categories, classifying individuals as very close, close, less close, or not close. Results indicate that the reduction in social interaction seen with age is largely accounted for by reductions in acquaintances and less close social contacts. The number of interactions with long-term relationships is fairly stable across cohorts of old and very old adults (Lang & Carstensen, 1994). Thus, when the total number of social contacts is examined, age is associated with a greater proportion of time spent with close friends and families (Figure 14.5). The second study replicated the first and showed that this reduction in the number of peripheral partners remains even after controlling for personality variables (Lang, Staudinger, & Carstensen, 1997).

Of course, social network data provide only distal support for the presumed mechanisms posited in socioemotional selectivity theory. In a series of experiments, we manipulated time perspective to determine its influence in social partner selection. In each study, the methods were similar: Participants were phoned and asked to imagine that they had 30 minutes of free time and then were asked to

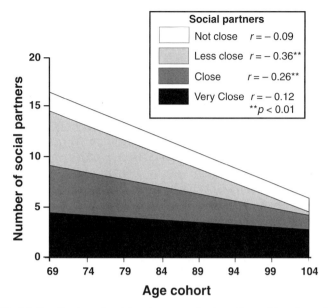

FIGURE 14.5   Number of social partners as a function of age. (From Lang & Carstensen, 1994, with permission.)

chose one person from a list of three with whom to engage in social interaction. The three choices represented each of the dimensions found in our previous work on mental representations of social partners: a member of your immediate family (the affective dimension), the author of a book you just read (the information dimension), and a recent acquaintance with whom you seem to have much in common (the future possibilities dimension). In one study, we phoned a large group of community residents, 384 people ranging from 11 to 92 years of age, and asked about their preferred social partners under two conditions (Fredrickson & Carstensen, 1990). In the first condition, participants were asked to choose a social partner, given 30 minutes of free time. Responses were consistent with the theory: older age coincided with a preference toward familiar over novel partners. For younger adults, preferences were distributed equally across the three options, representing no bias for a specific social partner.

In the second condition, older and younger adults were asked to imagine that they would be moving across the country, unaccompanied by either family or friends. By imaging this move, we imposed an "endings" condition among the participants to see whether the responses of younger adults would mimic those of older adults when time was perceived as limited. After this imagined scenario, participants were again asked to imagine 30 minutes of unencumbered free time and asked to choose among the three social partners listed above. Responses were similar for older adults: as with the first question, older adults preferred to interact with a member of their immediate family. For the younger adults, results varied from their previous response. Like the older adults, younger adults now demonstrated a preference for familiar social partners. By priming a social ending, younger adults became strikingly similar to older adults in their social preference.

We used the same experimental paradigm to study the role of time perspective in social preferences (Fung, Carstensen, & Lutz, in press). In this study, we expanded time perspective. Participants were first asked about social preferences without any additional instructions, just like the study described above. However, in the second condition, participants were asked to imagine that a new medical discovery had been found that would likely add 20 years to their life expectancies. Results confirmed the hypothesis. In the first condition, we replicated earlier findings: Older adults preferred the familiar social partners, whereas younger adults did not have a preference for any one choice. In the second condition, however, the preferences of the younger adults were the same, but preferences of the older adults shifted. For the first time, older adults' preferences for familiar social partners disappeared: They were as likely to choose a novel partner as a familiar one.

SOCIOEMOTIONAL SELECTIVITY THEORY AND THE BROADER LITERATURE ON SOCIAL AGING

Findings from socioemotional selectivity are consistent with a growing literature in life-span development that points to heightened attention to and strivings for emotional aspects of life. Labouvie-Vief and her colleagues proposed a cognitive–emotional integration theory to describe the development of emotion and cognition throughout adult development using a neo-Piagetian model (Labouvie-Vief & DeVoe, 1991; Labouvie-Vief, DeVoe, & Bulka, 1989). According to their theory, affective complexity and interpersonal perception, involving both self-and other-awareness, continue to develop into middle age. Affective complexity follows a pattern that begins with individuals experiencing emotions as global and polarized and then matures into a process in which individuals are able to experience several emotions simultaneously, recognizing and accepting contrasts. In the realm of perception of self and others, the course of development flows from a state in which individuals do not distinguish self from others and in which they place people into specific categories to a state in which both self and other are seen abstractly, as products of history and culture yet with distinct internal conflicts and contradictions. This advanced understanding of emotion and perception of self and others allows for greater insight into problem solving and perspective taking. According to their theory, mature individuals are able to perceive multiple emotions and viewpoints and integrate their cognitive and emotional abilities. Although this advanced complexity is related to cognitive and emotional development—most often measured by ego development—this measure correlates highly with age.

Labouvie-Vief and her colleagues have examined age differences in the processing of emotional material. In laboratory studies, they found that adults are more successful at understanding the emotional states of others (Labouvie-Vief et al., 1989). When asked to focus on their own emotional experiences, younger adults reported control strategies when regulating emotions that focused on distraction, such as redirecting one's thoughts or ignoring the situation. Older adults more often mentioned that they acknowledge and focus on their emotional reactions to the emotion-eliciting event or experience. In addition, when faced with conflict, older adults show greater impulse control and are more likely to appraise conflict situations positively (Diehl, Coyle, & Labouvie-Vief, 1996), whereas adults and adolescents express lower levels of impulse control and are more likely to display signs of aggression.

Labouvie-Vief and her colleagues also reported that older adults process information with a greater focus on subjective states and symbolic themes compared with younger adults (Labouvie-Vief, 1997). Several studies that have examined text have found that older adults focus more on psychological themes and offer metaphors when recalling and interpreting text (Adams, 1991; Adams, Smith, Nyquist, & Perlmutter, 1997; Labouvie-Vief & Hakim-Larson, 1989).

Findings regarding the role of emotion in cognitive processing are consistent with socioemotional selectivity theory, which posits that focus on emotional content is motivated by the satisfaction of emotional goals. Therefore, older adults are motivated to regulate their emotions and pay attention to situations, people, and events that will aid them in emotion regulation. Socioemotional selectivity theory does not deny the possibility that years of experience enable older adults to cope with emotions affectively; however, the theory maintains that time plays a fundamental role.

Blanchard-Fields has studied the role of emotions in social perception and problem solving (Blanchard-Fields, 1996, 1997). She and her colleagues evaluated problem-solving skills on the basis of emotional saliency of the problem in a group of people ranging from adolescents to older adults (Blanchard-Fields, 1986; Blanchard-Fields & Norris, 1994). They found that for problems low in emotional saliency, no age differences in problem solving occurred. Both younger and older adults used similar amounts of relativistic thinking in their problem-solving approach. However, for problems medium and high in emotional saliency, older adults used relativistic thinking more often than did adolescents.

In a further examination of problem solving for highly emotional events, younger, middle-aged, and older adults were asked to make attributions, either situational or dispositional, concerning the cause of interpersonal events (Blanchard-Fields, 1994; Blanchard-Fields & Norris, 1994). Results indicate that older adults use more interactive attributions, concluding that the event was caused by both the situation and the disposition of the primary character, than do younger adults. This interactional attribution style is considered to reflect more sophisticated understanding of social situations, allowing the adoption of multiple perspectives (Labouvie-Vief, 1997). However, older adults, compared with younger adults, are also more likely to blame the primary character for the outcome in negative interpersonal events. Blanchard-Fields and her colleagues interpreted the older adults' response as a reaction to the vignettes based on personal experience and values. Findings from our laboratory also concur: Older adults appear to weight emotion more heavily in cognitive processing. Findings are also consistent with the theoretical proposition that older adults make more frequent use of antecedent–response emotional regulation, selecting intimates over strangers and paying considerable attention to characteristics that may lead to negative emotions. Sensitivity to negative qualities in unfamiliar people allows older adults to prepare for possibly negative interactions or avoid them altogether.

SUMMARY AND CONCLUSIONS

Traditionally, the well-established decrease in social interaction seen in old age has been attributed to age-related deficits. Whether the deficit included societal constraints and biases or psychological or physical decline, the overall message has been that social interaction is not spared from age-related deficits. The assumption of age-related loss fits well with strong deficit models prevalent in gerontological research. Even positive adaption is often viewed as a coping strategy to precipitated loss. In contrast to these models, socioemotional selectivity maintains that patterns of age-related decrease reflect changes in motivations for social goals. These changes are not a result of age decrements but are explained by social cognitions concerning time perspective. Specifically, when people perceive their future as limited, affective goals are more salient than are informational goals, and social preferences are influenced by the increased emphasis on emotions. For people who perceive social endings, social goals more often focus on emotional gains and familiar social partners are preferred. Individuals who perceive time as limited place greater value on emotional information, pay greater attention to emotional material and regulate their social interactions to optimize emotional encounters. Socioemotional selectivity theory views human mortality as a fundamental constraint on time. However, the theory suggests that time is constrained in many other ways throughout the life span, such as geographical relocation or job changes. The advantage of taking a social cognitive perspective is that decreases in social interaction seen with advanced age or in other situations in which endings are primed are not misconstrued as maladaptive patterns. Instead, this social behavior represents individuals actively structuring their social environments to meet their social goals. Time perspective, critical to human identity, motivation, and behavior, plays an integral role in social preferences and social cognition.

ACKNOWLEDGMENTS

Support for this chapter was provided by National (NIA) grant R01-8816 to Laura L. Carstensen.

REFERENCES

Adams, C. (1991). Qualitative age differences in memory for text: A life-span developmental perspective. *Psychology and Aging, 6,* 323–336.

Adams, C., Smith, M. C., Nyquist, L., & Perlmutter, M. (1997). Adult age-group differences in recall for the literal and interpretive meanings of narrative text. *Journal of Gerontology: Psychological Sciences, 52,* P187–P195.

Antonucci, T. C., & Akiyama, H. (1987). An examination of sex differences in social support in mid and late life. *Sex Roles, 17,* 737–749.

Antonucci, T. C., & Jackson, J. S. (1987). Social support, interpersonal efficacy, and health. In L. L. Carstensen & B. Edelstein (Eds.), *Handbook of Clinical Gerontology* (pp. 291–311). New York: Pergamon Press.

Berkman, L. & Syme, S. L. (1979). Social networks, host resistance, and mortality: A nine year follow-up study of Alameda County residents. *American Journal of Epidemiology, 109,* 186–204.

Blanchard-Fields, F. (1986). Reasoning on social dilemmas varying in emotional saliency: An adult developmental perspective. *Psychology and Aging, 1,* 325–333.

Blanchard-Fields, F. (1994). Age differences in causal attributions from an adult development perspective. *Journal of Gerontology: Psychological Sciences, 49,* P43–P51.

Blanchard-Fields, F. (1996). Emotion and everyday problem solving in adult development. In C. Magai & S. H. McFadden (Eds.), *Handbook of emotion, adult development, and aging* (pp. 149–165). New York: Academic Press.

Blanchard-Fields, F. (1997). The role of emotion in social cognition across the adult life span. In K. W. Schaie & M. P. Lawton (Eds.), *Annual Review of Gerontology and Geriatrics* (Vol. 17, pp. 238–265).

Blanchard-Fields, F., & Norris, L. (1994). Causal attributions from adolescence through adulthood: Age differences, ego level, and generalized response style. *Aging and Cognition, 1,* 67–86.

Blazer, D. (1982). Social support and mortality in an elderly community population. *American Journal of Epidemiology, 115,* 684–694.

Carstensen, L. L. (1992). Social and emotional patterns in adulthood: Support for socioemotional selectivity theory. *Psychology and Aging, 7,* 331–338.

Carstensen, L. L. (1993). Motivation for social contact across the life span: A theory of socioemotional selectivity. *Nebraska Symposium on Motivation, 40,* 209–254.

Carstensen, L. L. (1995). Evidence for a life-span theory of socioemotional selectivity *Current Directions in Psychological Science, 4,* 151–156.

Carstensen, L. L., & Erickson, R. E. (1986). Enhancing the social environments of elderly nursing home residents: Are high rates of interaction enough? *Journal of Applied Behavior Analysis, 19,* 349–355.

Carstensen, L. L., & Fredrickson, B. F. (1998). Socioemotional selectivity in healthy older people and younger people living with the human immunodeficiency virus: The centrality of emotion when the future is constrained. *Health Psychology, 17,* 494–503.

Carstensen, L. L., Gottman, J. M., & Levenson, R. W. (1995). Emotional behavior in long-term marriage. *Psychology and Aging, 10,* 140–149.

Carstensen, L. L., Gross, J., & Fung, H. (1997). The social context of emotion. In K. W. Schaie & M. P. Lawton (Eds.), *Annual review of geriatrics and gerontology, 17,* 325–352. New York: Springer.

Carstensen. L. L., & Turk-Charles, S. (1994). The salience of emotion across the adult life course. *Psychology and Aging, 9,* 259–264.

Clausen, J. A. (1981). Men's occupational careers in the middle years In D. H. Eichorn, J. A. Clausen, N. Haan, M. P. Honzik, & P. Mussen (Eds.), *Present and past in middle life* (pp. 321–351) New York: Academic Press.

Cross, S., & Markus, H. (1991). Possible selves across the life span. *Human Development, 34,* 230–255.

Cumming, E., & Henry, W. E. (1961). *Growing old: The process of disengagement.* New York: Basic Books.

DeCasper, A. J., & Fifer, W. P. (1980). Of human bonding: New borns prefer their mother's voices. *Science, 208,* 1174–1176.

Deci, E. L., & Ryan, R. M. (1991). A motivational approach to self: Integration in personality. *Nebraska Symposium on Motivation, 40,* 209–254.

Diamond, A. (1985). Development of the ability to use recall to guide action, as indicated by infants' performance on AB. *Child Development, 9,* 133–150.

Diehl, M., Coyle, N., & Labouvie-Vief, G. (1996). Age and sex differences in strategies of coping and defense across the life span. *Psychology and Aging, 11,* 127–139.

Fantz, R. L. (1963). Pattern vision in newborn infants. *Science, 140,* 296–297.

Field, D., & Minkler, M. (1988). Continuity and change in social support between young-old, old-old, and very-old adults. *Journal of Gerontology, Psychological Sciences, 43,* P100–P106.

Fiske, S. T., & Taylor, S. E. (1991). *Social cognition* (2nd Ed). New York: McGraw-Hill.

Fivush, R., Gray, J. T., & Fromhoff, F. A. (1987). Two-year-olds talk about the past. *Cognitive Development, 2,* 396–409.

Fredrickson, B. F., & Carstensen, L. L. (1990). Choosing social partners: How old age and anticipated endings make us more selective. *Psychology and Aging, 5,* 335–347.

Fung, H. H., Carstensen, L. L., & Lutz, A. M. (in press). The influence of time on social preferences: Implications for life-span development. *Psychology and Aging.*

George, L. K., Blazer, D. F., Winfield-Laird, I., Leaf, P. J., & Fischback, F. R. (1988). Psychiatric disorders and mental health service use in later life: Evidence from the Epidemiologic Catchment Area Program. In J. Brody & G. Maddox (Eds.), *Epidemiology and Aging* (pp. 189–219). New York: Springer.

Goffee, R., & Scase, R. (1992). Organizational change and the corporate career: The restructuring of managers' job aspirations. *Human Relations, 45,* 363–385.

Gordon, C., & Gaitz, C. (1976). Leisure and lives. In R. Binstock & E. Shanas (Eds.), *Handbook of aging and the social sciences* vol. 1, (pp. 310–341). New York; Van Nostrand Reinhold.

Gross, J. J., Carstensen, L. L., Pasupathi, M., Tsai, J., Skorpen, K., & Hsu, A. Y. C. (1997). Emotion and aging: Experience, expression, and control. *Psychology and Aging, 12,* 590–599.

Gurland, B. (1976). The comparative frequency of depression in various adult age groups. *Journal of Gerontology, 31,* 283–292.

Harvey, A. S., & Singleton, J. F. (1989). Canadian activity patterns across the life span: A time budget perspective. *Canadian Journal of Aging, 8,* 268–285.

Havighurst, R. J. (1961). Successful aging. *Gerontologist, 1,* 8–13.

Havighurst, R. J., & Albrecht, R. (1953). *Older people.* New York: Longmans.

Herzog, A. R., & Rogers, W. L. (1981). Age and satisfaction: Data from several large surveys. *Research on Aging, 3,* 142–165.

Higgins, E. T. (1997). Beyond pleasure and pain. *American Psychologist, 52,* 1280–1300.

Howe, M. L., & Courage, M. L. (1993). On resolving the enigma of infantile amnesia. *Psychological Bulletin, 113,* 305–326.

James, W. (1890). *The principles of psychology* (vol. 1 and 2). New York: Holt.

Labouvie-Vief, G. (1997). Cognitive-emotional integration in adulthood. In K. W. Schaie & M. P. Lawton (Eds.), *Annual Review of Gerontology and Geriatrics, 17,* 206–237.

Labouvie-Vief, G., & DeVoe, M. (1991). Emotional regulation in adulthood and later life: A developmental view. *Annual review of gerontology and geriatrics, 11,* 172–194. New York: Springer.

Labouvie-Vief, G., DeVoe, M., & Bulka, D. (1989). Speaking about feelings: Conceptions of emotion across the life span. *Psychology and Aging, 4,* 425–437.

Labouvie-Vief, G., & Hakim-Larson, J. (1989). Developmental shifts in adult thought. In S. Hunter & M. Sundel (Eds.), *Midlife myths* (pp. 69–96). Newbury Park, CA: Sage.

Labouvie-Vief, G., Hakim-Larson, J., DeVoe, M., & Schoebarlein, S. (1989) Emotions and self-regulation: A life span view. *Human Development, 32,* 279–299.

Lang, F. R., & Carstensen, L. L. (1994). Close emotional relationships in late life: Further support for proactive aging in the social domain. *Psychology and Aging, 9,* 315–324.

Lang, F. R., Staudinger, U. M., & Carstensen, L. L. (1997). Perspectives on socioemotional selectivity in late life: How personality and social context do (and do not) make a difference. *Journal of Gerontology: Psychological Sciences, 53,* P21–P30.

Lawton, M. P., Kleban, M. H., Rajagopal, D., & Dean, J. (1992). Dimensions of affective experience in three age groups. *Psychology and Aging, 7,* 171–184.

Lawton, M. P., Moss, M., & Fulcomer, M. (1987). Objective and subjective uses of time by older people. *International Journal of Aging and Human Development, 24,* 171–188.

Lee, D. J., & Markides, K. S. (1990). Activity and mortality among aged persons over an eight-year period. *The Journals of Gerontology: Social Sciences, 45,* 39–42.

Levenson, R. W., Carstensen, L. L., & Friesen, W. V., & Ekman, P. (1991). Emotion, physiology, and expression in old age. *Psychology & Aging, 6,* 28–35.

Levenson, R. W., Carstensen, L. L., & Gottman, J. M. (1994). Marital interaction in old and middle-aged long-term marriages: Physiology, affect, and their interrelations. *Journal of Personality and Social Psychology, 67,* 56–68.

Maddox, G. L. (1963). Activity and morale: A longitudinal study of selected elderly subjects. *Social Forces, 42,* 195–204.

Maddox, G. L. (1965). Fact and artifact: Evidence bearing on disengagement theory from the Duke Geriatrics Project. *Human Development, 8,* 117–130.

Markus, H., & Wurf, E. (1987). The dynamic self-concept: A social psychological perspective. *Annual Review of Psychology, 38,* 299–676.

Mischel, W. (1968). *Personality and assessment.* New York: Wiley.

Nelson, K. (1992). Emergence of autobiographical memory at age four. *Human Development, 35,* 172–177.

Neugarten, B. L. (1973). Adult personality: A developmental view. In D. C. Charles & W. R. Looft (Eds.), *Readings in psychological development through life* (pp. 356–366). New York: Holt, Rinehart, and Winston.

Nolen-Hoeksema, S., McBride, A., & Larson, J. (1997). Rumination and psychological distress among bereaved partners. *Journal of Personality & Social Psychology, 72,* 855–862.

Palmore, E. (1981). Social patterns in normal aging: Findings from the Duke Longitudinal Study. Durham, N. C: Duke University Press.

Pasupathi, M., Carstensen, L. L., & Tsai, J. (1995). Ageism in interpersonal settings. In B. E. Lott & D. Maluso (Eds.), *The social psychology of interpersonal discrimination* (pp. 160–182). New York: Guilford Press.

Reiss, S., & McNally, R. J. (1985). The expectancy model of fear. In S. Reiss & R. R. Bootzin (Eds.), *Theoretical issues in behavior therapy* (pp. 107–121). New York: Academic Press.

Rothbart, M. K. (1994). Emotional development: Changes in reactivity and self-regulation. In P. Ekman & R. J. Davidson (Eds.), *The nature of emotion: Fundamental questions* (pp. 369–372). Oxford: Oxford University Press.

Ryan, R. M. (1993). Agency and organization: Intrinsic motivation, autonomy, and the self in psychological development. *Nebraska Symposium on Motivation, 40,* 1–58.

Schmidt, N. B., Lerew, D. R., & Jackson, R. J. (1997). The role of anxiety sensitivity in the pathogenesis of panic: Prospective evaluation of spontaneous panic attacks during acute stress. *Journal of Abnormal Psychology, 106,* 355–364.

Sherif, M., & Sherif, C. W. (1953). *Groups in harmony and tension.* New York: Harper & Row.

Shmotkin, D. (1991). The role of time orientation in life satisfaction across the life span. *Journals of Gerontology: Psychological Sciences, 46,* P243–P250.

Smith, A. D. (1996). Memory. In J. Birren & W. Schaie (Eds.) *Handbook of the psychology of aging* (pp. 236–250). San Diego: Academic Press.

Tomkins, S. S. (1970). Affect as the primary motivational systems. In M. B. Arnold (Ed.), *Feelings and emotions* (pp. 101–110), New York: Academic Press.

Tronick, E. Z. (1989). Emotions and emotional communication in infants. *American Psychologist, 44,* 112–119.

Waldman, D. A., & Avolio, B. J. (1986). A meta-analysis of age differences in job performance. *Journal of Applied Psychology, 71,* 33–38.

Whitbourne, S. K., & Dannefer, W. D. (1985–1986). The "life drawing" as a measure of time perspective in adulthood. *International Journal of Aging and Human Development, 22,* 147–155.

White, R. W. (1959). Motivation reconsidered: The concept of competence. *Psychological Review, 66,* 297–333.

Wittchen, H., Knauper, B., & Kessler, R. C. (1994). Lifetime risk of depression. *British Journal of Psychiatry, 165,* 16–22.

15

SOCIAL COGNITION AND A PSYCHOLOGICAL APPROACH TO AN ART OF LIFE

URSULA M. STAUDINGER

Max Planck Institute for Human Development
Center for Lifespan Psychology
Germany

The reader may be surprised to find a concept life *art of life* in the title of a scientific chapter. *Art of life* is an ancient topic in philosophy that, through the ages, has repeatedly gained attention. Endeavors range form Aristotle's considerations about the "good life" to Michel Foucault's writings about ethics and the art of life. Quite often, the notion of an art of life is discredited by linking it to hedonism and optimization of the pleasures in life (cf. Schmid, 1991). Thus, it does not come as a surprise that over the last several centuries—and even now—the art of life has been primarily a topic for popular books with a "how to…" focus rather than for scientific investigations. It has seemingly been forgotten that originally—that is, in ancient Greece and in Roman times—the notion art of life (*ars vivendi*) aimed at providing guidance on how to lead and compose one's life, a topic that is ideally suited for psychological investigations.

From a sociology of science perspective, it may also not be surprising that the quest for an art of life has resurfaced again. The discussions around postmodernity and deconstructivism (Welsch, 1995) have demonstrated that we live in times in which traditional ethical and moral systems no longer provide guidance and answers to the existential questions that arise in a fast-changing and increasingly complex world.

To avoid potential misunderstandings, I must point out that in this chapter *art of life* is not used in the sense of how to master societal rules (e.g., Verly, 1957) or in the sense of survival rules (Bruckner & Finkielkraut, 1981; Vaneigem, 1980). Rather, I explore what psychological research primarily of a developmental social cognitive nature has to offer with regard to knowledge and strategies that may be helpful in leading and creating our own lives in a fulfilling manner.

Rediscovering the notion of an art of life seems worthwhile for still another reason that is related to the aesthetic aspects implied by the term. These aesthetic aspects may add an epistemological dimension to psychological inquiry that—quite in contrast to philosophical epistemology—has been underdeveloped. Kant, for instance, in his *Kritik der Urteilskraft,* introduced and acknowledged the epistemological importance of three kinds of rationality: the aesthetic, the moral, and the cognitive. In the ancient Greek tradition, insight, perspicacity, sagacity, and estimation by the eye were basic constituents of rationality. The senses were not devalued as nonrational but rather seen as indivisible aspects of human rationality. This is in line with current philosophical discourse that argues for the interrelatedness of Kant's three rationalities, the aesthestic, the moral, and the cognitive (e.g., Plato, Nietzsche, Adorno, Gehlen, Bourdieu). Thus, rather than compromising the scientific quality of psychological inquiry, investigating a construct like *art of life* may add aesthetic rationality as another epistemological dimension. Based on the original Greek meaning of the word *aesthetic rationality* refers to the epistemological potential of sensory perceptions and intuitions.

When aiming at a psychological art of life, it may be useful to consider life as the unit of psychological investigation. Traditionally, the individual, action, personality, cognition, or development have been chosen as units of psychological analysis. Selecting human life as the unit of investigation may sound very bold. I hope, however, to succeed in illustrating its advantages. What do I mean by "life as unit of investigation"? It can imply many different kinds of studies, from following a whole life longitudinally through analyzing one difficult life decision to exploring narrative accounts of real and virtual lives. In this chapter, I summarize this approach to psychological investigation by the term *life perspective,* then outline seven characteristics that further delineate the life perspective. Taking a life perspective may help us aggregate available psychological evidence in a new manner and arrive at new conclusions that contribute to a psychological art of life. Indeed, the history of psychology, especially in the anthropological–existential and the personal psychology area, holds a rich tradition of choosing the individual life as a topic of psychological considerations. For instance, Bühler (1933), Dilthey (1894/1968), Klages (1937), Lewin (1946), Rothacker (1938), and Stern (1930), used life as a central concept of their psychologies. Another tradition can be traced back to the beginnings of psychosomatic medicine in which endeavors to procure an art of life revolved around the dissolution of the distinction between body and soul (e.g., Sohni, 1973). In current psychology, we find a number of concepts that use the prefix *life,* such as *life satisfaction* or *life course.* It seems, however, that the use of the term *life* in such contexts does not necessarily relate to human life as the unit of psychological investigations but is rather used synonymously with *person/self* or *development* (cf. Wollheim, 1984).

This chapter focuses on conveying the basic idea of a life perspective and its contribution to building a psychological art of life. I illustrate these notions primarily by referring to my own work. I hope, however, to also stimulate readers to think about how their own work and other work they know may fit the presented framework.

In taking a life perspective, I distinguish between two broad domains of psychological inquiry. One is called *life insight* and deals with what people know about life and how they evaluate it. The other is labeled *life composition* and refers to how individuals shape their lives in interaction with life contexts and how they are shaped by such contexts. Arriving at a good and satisfactory life lies at the heart of what an art of life is all about. It seems that evidence of knowing about life and how to evaluate it (i.e., life insight) as well as of mastering life in one's actions and reactions (i.e., life composition) may be useful building elements of a psychological attempt at delineating an art of life.

Before I proceed to describe the constituents of a life perspective, I must at least mention three theories that seem to quite "naturally" converge into a life perspective and thus have been very influential in my thinking about a life perspective: lifespan psychology (e.g., Baltes, 1997; Baltes, Lindenberger, & Staudinger, 1998), action theory (e.g., Boesch, 1971; Brandtstädter, 1998), and phenomenology (e.g., Graumann, 1960; Spranger, 1947). I will return to each of those as I further develop my argument.

When I combine these three theoretical influences in consideration of a psychological art of life, my interest has developed such that I focus not on *development* or *action* or any other particular *phenomenon* but rather on human life as the most comprehensive unit of investigation. What is it, then, that we should understand by the term *life?* Philosophers have told us that one should not even try to provide a comprehensive definition, as human life is so overdetermined that any such definition can only result in loss of meaning (Simon, 1974). Nevertheless, some of the guidelines of my conceptualization should be presented.

In my thinking about a life perspective, the energetic aspects of human life are important, but by no means should the term *life* be reduced to its biological meaning. Life is also understood in its biographical and autobiographical sense but, again, is not confined to only that one sense. Both the subjective and objective level of analysis are included in the life perspective presented here. Human life is to be considered a process as well as a product: It is actively shaped by us (e.g., Lerner & Busch-Rossnagel, 1981), but it also happens to us (e.g., Brandtstädter, 1984).

SEVEN CONSTITUENT FEATURES
OF A LIFE PERSPECTIVE

The following seven constituent features are combined in a unique fashion when taking a life perspective in psychology: (1) the individual as an active part of a larger whole, (2) inherent diachronicity, (3) the joining of different domains of psychological functioning, (4) ecological relevance, (5) methodological richness, (6) a continuous search for reserve potential and meaning, and (7) an embracing of the ontology of the first and the third person. When taking a life perspective, we profit from the fact that these features are necessarily implied, whereas when investigating the individual or an action, we need to pay special attention to addressing these aspects.

I am not arguing that these seven aspects are new and have not yet been discussed in psychology. Rather, my argument is that human life can serve as a useful integrating framework for such features. Further, it may be the case that—as is quite convincingly argued in Gestalt psychology—the whole is more than the sum of its parts; in this sense, a life perspective may have even more to offer. Using human life as the unit of aggregation, observation, and integration of psychological inquiry may allow us to ask new questions that otherwise would not have arisen. For example, what would it imply if cognitive psychology were to seriously take a life perspective? It might lead to efforts at understanding cognitive structures and procedures reflecting structures of life, such as permission, obligation, or cheating. Work on pragmatic and domain-specific reasoning schemas may serve as a sample case (e.g., Cheng & Holyoak, 1985; Gigerenzer, 1996). This research has shown that when cognitive tasks reflect such life structures (e.g., permission, obligation, cheating) rather than Aristotelian logic, participants commit fewer reasoning mistakes. Another example is investigations that have highlighted the fact that our knowledge is organized not only around semantic categories or schemas and scripts but also around important people in our lives (cf. Staudinger & Baltes, 1996). In one study that is described in more detail in the next section, we demonstrated that asking participants to consider what people important to them might say to a given problem served as a highly effective stimulus for the activation of reserves in wisdom-related knowledge and judgment.

THE INDIVIDUAL AS AN ACTIVE PART
OF A LARGER WHOLE

When life is the target unit of psychological research and theorizing, the individual does play a central, active role, but at the same time, the individual is only part of the larger whole—"life." Thus, individuals can eventually be understood only by taking into consideration the larger whole—that is, the social and physical contexts in which individuals are embedded and embed themselves during the life course. This is exactly what lifespan developmental psychology and ecological developmental psychology have suggested (e.g., Baltes et al., 1998; Bronfen-brenner & Morris, 1998; Elder, 1998).

The social and physical contexts of life form a complex interlocking and hier-archically ordered system and range from proximal influences, such as the social and material contexts with which the individual directly interacts, to distal influ-ences, such as societal structures and historical constellations. Climatic and geo-graphical conditions also exert influences, though more indirectly. These levels of social and material contexts are interrelated and influence each other. Bronfen-brenner (e.g., Bronfenbrenner & Morris, 1998) has called them *micro-, meso-, exo-,* and *macrosystems.*

A number of extant concepts, such as life structure (Levinson, 1978) or devel-opmental tasks (Havighurst, 1948), also reflect these theoretical ideas. Levinson defines life structures as the combination of personal goals and contexts in which an individual is embedded at a given point in time. Further concepts that address the contextualized and social-interactive nature of human existence are Erikson's psychosocial crises of development (Erikson, 1959) and Havighurst's develop-mental tasks (Havighurst, 1948). Especially for Havighurst's notion of develop-mental tasks, the interaction among biology, person, and social–material context is constitutive.

Research Examples from the Field of Life Composition

In this vein, the investigation of the goal system, for instance, reflects the demands of *internal and external developmental contexts.* Personal life invest-ment can be considered as one facet of our goal system. It is assessed by asking individuals to what degree they think about and take action in each of 10 central life domains—for example, health, family relations, finances (e.g., Staudinger, 1996a; Staudinger & Fleeson, 1996; Staudinger, Freund, Linden & Mass, 1999). In accordance with the developmental tasks characterizing the respective age periods, in young adulthood the domains *work* and *friends* rank highest in invest-ment. In midlife, it is *family* and *work* and in old age, *health* and *family* that out-rank the other domains. Also, the adaptivity of personal life investment patterns depends on developmental contexts. For instance, higher degrees of overall life investment are not always—as one may be inclined to expect—related to higher levels of subjective well-being. Rather, in old age—and particularly under condi-tions of high health-related constraints—quite the opposite is the case; that is, lower levels of life investment are related to higher levels of well-being. Follow-up analyses showed that lower levels of investment were primarily brought about by selectively investing a lot in a few domains and very little in the others, rather than by lowering the investments across all domains. Selective investment seems adaptive, given a highly constraining developmental context (Staudinger & Flee-son, 1996; Staudinger et al., 1999).

Contextualized adaptivity is also a central finding in studies on coping. In old age and under conditions of strong health-related constraints, coping mechanisms such as "giving up" or "feeling desperate" or "wishing for someone to take over" lose their maladaptive function and may to a certain degree even support adaptivity (e.g., Aldwin & Revenson, 1987; Holahan & Moos, 1987; Lazarus & Golden, 1981; Staudinger & Fleeson, 1996; Thomae, 1994). These findings contradict coping theories that have categorized those coping styles as generally maladaptive (e.g., Haan, 1977). It seems that the adaptivity of self-regulatory mechanisms such as coping behaviors and life investment patterns is not absolute and universal but rather is determined by combining them with life contexts (see also Magnusson & Stattin, 1998).

Research Examples from the Field of Life Insight

In a similar way, the development of life insight, the other element that may—as we will see—eventually contribute to a psychological art of life, is highly *context dependent*. It has been demonstrated that when life insight is operationalized as knowledge and judgment in the fundamental pragmatics of life (e.g., Baltes, Smith, & Staudinger, 1992), professional context (i.e. training and practice in a profession dealing with life and life problems) contributes to higher levels of knowledge and judgment in the fundamental pragmatics of life—that is, in wisdom-related knowledge and judgment (e.g., Smith, Staudinger, & Baltes, 1994; Staudinger, Smith & Baltes, 1992). In these studies, clinical psychologist was chosen as a profession that by virtue of training and practice may lead to a higher exposure to difficult life issues and their potential solutions. Most likely, similar effects could be found when comparing, for example, family judges, personnel managers, or counseling ministers with control professionals.

So that wisdom-related knowledge and judgment could be assessed, participants came to the lab and were trained in thinking aloud before they were presented with the life dilemma of a fictitious person described in a short vignette and were asked to think aloud about that problem. Subsequently, the transcribed thinking-aloud protocols were rated by a trained expert rater panel on five criteria that had been theoretically defined to index wisdom-related knowledge and judgment (rich factual and procedural knowledge about life, lifespan contextualism, value relativism, awareness and management of uncertainty; for an extensive description of procedure, see Staudinger et al., 1994).

Please note that the higher levels of wisdom-related performance observed in clinical psychologists were not simply due to a professional bias in the wisdom theory applied. This was demonstrated in another study that compared clinical psychologists and people nominated as wise according to lay theories of wisdom. Wisdom nominees demonstrated significantly higher wisdom-related performances than did clinical psychologists in the most difficult life dilemma (Baltes, Staudinger, Maercker, & Smith, 1995). Thus, people (nonpsychologists) nominated as wise independent of our "psychological" theory of wisdom ranked highest in the scoring according to the theory's five wisdom criteria.

The studies comparing clinical psychologists with other professionals also allowed a first look at the interaction between internal and external context. Clinical psychologists were found to be characterized by a personality profile that distinguished them from the control groups. Unfortunately, cross-sectional data do not allow differentiation between self-selection into a profession and the potential personality changes taking place due to being in the profession. Analyzing the unique and shared parts of the variance that personality and experiential context (i.e., professional specialization) contributed to the prediction of wisdom-related performance, however, demonstrated that experiential contexts preserved unique predictive variance even after personality was partialed out, but not the other way around (Staudinger, Maciel, Smith, & Baltes, 1998).

The importance of experiential contexts is also supported by the investigation of the wisdom nominees just mentioned. In this study, it was found that the wisdom nominees were characterized by biographies full of challenging and threatening events and that they had also lived through a historical period that was highly conducive to such events (Third Reich in Germany and World War II). Findings supporting the impact of experiential contexts and historical periods on life insight also stem from research studying Holocaust survivors (e.g., Kruse, 1996).

So far, the effects of rather distal contexts on life insight (e.g., professional settings, historical period) have been discussed. Proximal social and material contexts have also been found to be highly influential with regard to social cognitive processes such as life insight. Wisdom-related performance, for instance, was enhanced by about one standard deviation when allowing participants to discuss the presented difficult life problem with a partner they had brought to the laboratory and to think by themselves about the discussion before they gave their own responses. A similarly strong effect was obtained by asking participants to consider, before responding, what people whose advice they value might say about the problem (Staudinger & Baltes, 1996; this study is discussed in more detail in a later section). Finally, proximal-material contexts, such as the use of notebooks or photographs, have also been found to facilitate social cognitive performance levels (e.g., Dixon & Bäckman, 1995; Haight & Webster, 1995).

To summarize, the point made in this section has been that when taking a life perspective on the study of psychological functioning, one has no alternative but to study the whole system of interlocking social and material contexts and their interaction with individual performance and/or characteristics. Evidence from the areas of life composition and life insight were used to illustrate this point.

INHERENT DIACHRONICITY

Besides paying natural tribute to the hierarchical order of the socioecological system and its effects on social cognition, a life perspective also acknowledges the importance of the chronological and lifetime dimension of psychological functioning (e.g., Bühler, 1933; Lewin, 1926). Not only synchronic but also diachronic processes are constitutive for human life (e.g., Bergius, 1957; Boesch, 1991; Heidegger, 1979/1927; Jaspers, 1932; Mead, 1929). How is the past reconstructed and how does it influence current actions and nonactions as well as projections into the future—and vice versa? What are the conceptions of the future and how do those influence the present and the reconstruction of the past? The mental representations as well as the objective effects of the temporal extension of human life (diachronicity) become a natural part of psychological inquiry when one concentrates on human life as the unit of investigation.

Again, this notion of the inherent temporality of human existence is not new. It is part of a number of theoretical and empirical efforts in the literature. A very prominent example is the Lewinian notion of life space *(Lebensraum)*, which by definition is diachronic and in addition distinguishes between a "real" and an ideal level of analysis (Lewin, 1946). Lewin introduced the notion of life space to integrate what he viewed as the two basic dimensions of human experience and action—that is, time and space. From a developmental perspective, he was interested in how the perception, differentiation, and usage of this life space—comprising a past, a present, a future, and the ideal—changed with age.

Both subjective and *objective aspects* of the diachronicity of human life can be distinguished. Some empirical examples may illustrate this distinction. Real physical time, for instance, is a feature of all longitudinal studies of psychological functioning. Instead of studying life constellations at a given point in time, investigators study types of life trajectories (e.g., Eichhorn, Clausen, Haan, Honzik, & Mussen, 1981; Maas & Kuypers, 1974). Thus, this long-standing method of developmental research takes into account the objective (physical) diachronicity of human life (e.g., Stern, 1910; Tetens, 1777; for historical review, see Baltes & Nesselroade, 1979).

An extreme case of the objective facet of the temporality of human life is its evolutionary basis. The subdiscipline of evolutionary psychology asks how evolution (i.e., selection, survival of the fittest) may have shaped our current way of experiencing the world and behaving. The empirical endeavors in this subdiscipline have demonstrated how stimulating it can be to consider this extreme dimension of the diachronicity of human life (e.g., Barkow, Cosmides, & Tooby, 1992; Gigerenzer, 1996; Magnusson, 1996). Human life is shaped not only by the present, the near past, and the near future but also by very distant times. For instance, it seems that our intellectual functioning has been shaped by evolutionary selection such that we do possess reasoning structures that make it easy to detect cheating (e.g., Gigerenzer, 1996). Another example is the fact that the set point of subjective well-being is located in the moderately positive range (e.g., Diener & Diener, 1996). Chances to reproduce and survive might have been higher for those individuals who had the capacity to regulate their assessments of well-being back to a moderately positive set point even after highly traumatic events (e.g., becoming paraplegic, cancer diagnosis, constraining financial conditions), as well as after highly positive events (e.g., gaining a lot of money).

The notion of life experience *(Lebenserfahrung)* is a prototypical example of the *subjective side* of the inherent diachronicity of human life (e.g., Staudinger & Dittmann-Kohli, 1994). Life experiences are crystallizations of events and event sequences that extend across minutes, hours, days, months, or years. Thus, one may say past events are condensed into the present. This crystallization is not, however, a one-to-one recording of what happened; rather, through processes of evaluation and categorization, it reflects our reconstruction of the past, our evaluation of the present, and our projections into the future (wishes, hopes). In some early psychological and education writing, life experience was indeed identified as a centerpiece of human development and the construction of meaning (e.g., Spranger, 1947). Both life insight (i.e., knowledge and judgment about life) and life composition (i.e., leading a life) are informed by our life experiences.

Research Examples from the Field of Life Insight

It is social cognitive processes like life review (e.g., Butler, 1963, Dilthey, 1968/1894; see also Haight & Webster, 1995; Staudinger, 1989) and life planning (e.g., Rawls, 1971; for review see Smith, 1996) that help us understand how individuals reconstruct the past and design the future. Life review and life planning are, for instance, useful tools in accessing individual's life insights (e.g., Staudinger, 1989; Smith & Baltes, 1990). In our studies of wisdom-related knowledge and judgment, we ask participants to engage in life review or life planning for a fictitious person who is facing a review or a planning dilemma that is briefly described in a task vignette. When participants develop the review or the plan for the hypothetical person, their knowledge and judgment about difficult life matters become visible. When such ecologically relevant *social* cognitive processes—that is, life planning and life review—are used to assess cognitive performance of the pragmatic type in old age, old individuals do not show the usual declines identified in cognitive functioning of the mechanic type (e.g., Lindenberger & Baltes, 1994; Salthouse, 1994). Rather, stability and sometimes increases in performance are observed. The fact, that it is not primarily age-related increases in life insight that are observed, however, supports an ontogenetic model that specifies a complex pattern of preconditions that need to be fulfilled for life insight and eventually wisdom to evolve; this pattern is discussed in more detail in a later section (cf. Baltes & Smith, 1990; Staudinger & Baltes, 1994).

Research Examples from the Field of Life Composition

Besides providing us with access to people's life insights, the social cognitive processes of life planning and life review also direct our life (Staudinger & Dittmann-Kohli, 1994). Both aspects make them important elements of a psychological art of life: How do people reconstruct disappointment, failures, and successes? Are they able to identify consistencies and inconsistencies in their own behavior? Is a person's life planning characterized by the "right" mixture of flexibility and commitment to minimize frustrations and waste of psychological energy?

Finally, with regard to life composition, the diachronicity of human life has also been identified as a reserve. The diachronicity of human life represents a potential that may be useful in times of challenges and stress. The social cognitive process of temporal comparison can be called on to illustrate this point. It has been demonstrated, for instance, that individuals refer to earlier or hoped-for successes to master current difficulties (for review, see Staudinger, Marsiske, & Baltes, 1995). It has been found that in old age, remembering past instances of mastery facilitates coping with present threats and challenges (e.g., Aldwin, Sutton, & Lachman, 1996; Staudinger et al., 1999), But hoping for a better future may also aid in managing the present (e.g., Cross & Markus, 1991). Work on the concept of *delay of gratification* further illustrates the point (cf. Mischel, Shoda, & Rodriguez, 1989).

COMBINING MULTIPLE DOMAINS OF
PSYCHOLOGICAL FUNCTIONING

The life perspective not only links individual and context or past, present, and future but by definition it also links different domains of psychological functioning that otherwise are often studied in separation. To understand human life, we need to study thinking, wanting, feeling, and doing conjointly. Using a different terminology, we need to pool our understanding and investigations of intelligence with those of self, personality, and—ideally—actual behavior. Such a wholistic approach perfectly fits the tradition of Gestalt psychology (e.g., Krueger, 1953; Wertheimer, 1925), except that rather than focusing on the either–or of elements and the whole, a life perspective supports a both–and focus. In fact, it may be exactly this combination of an elementaristic and wholistic approach that makes room for new insights into psychological functioning.

Whenever one discusses the linkages between cognition, motivation, and emotion, a fundamental terminology problem arises. Using the terms *cognition, motivation,* and *emotion* does not imply that these are three systems that operate independently of each other. The possibility that motivation and emotion are cognitively mediated, for instance, should not be excluded; neither should the fact that some emotions are regulated by the hormonal system—as suggested by evolutionary considerations—and thus are triggered independently of cognitions (e.g., Hansell, 1989; Kuhl, 1983). At present, it seems that interactive and systemic models of combining cognition, emotion, and motivation are most adequate (e.g., Kuhl & Goschke, 1994; Leventhal & Scherer, 1987; Magai & Nusbaum, 1996).

If the goal is to better understand human life from a psychological perspective, it does not seem particularly useful to study either cognition, emotion, or motivation by itself. Instead, the question of interest becomes how these domains of functioning act together to provide us with the ability to gain insight into life and to compose our lives. This systemic–wholistic approach, which attempts to study cognition, emotion, and motivation conjointly, is illustrated by work on pragmatic reasoning schemas or domain-specific reasoning (e.g., Cheng & Holyoak, 1985; Cosmides, 1989; Gigerenzer & Hug, 1992). The study of such reasoning schemas combines the investigation of the cognitive mechanics with prototypical patterns of experiences such as obligation or cheating, which involve emotions and motivation at the same time. Further, work in the neo-Piagetian tradition that is concerned with the characteristics of mature thought belongs to that category. The neo-Piagetian tradition investigates how cognition, emotion, and motivation may become integrated across the life span (e.g., Blanchard-Fields & Hess, 1996; Labouvie-Vief, 1980, 1994; Sternberg & Berg, 1992).

Finally, the investigation of indicators of life insight such as wisdom-related knowledge and judgment may serve as an example of that category (Staudinger, Lopez, & Baltes, 1997; Staudinger, et al., 1998). In one of our studies of wisdom-related knowledge and judgment, working with a very heterogeneous sample recruited through a survey company, we showed that our measure of wisdom-related performance was weakly related to measures of the cognitive mechanics, somewhat more strongly to facets of personality, and most strongly to measures, such as creativity and cognitive style, located at the interface between personality and intelligence (Staudinger et al., 1997). As predicted by the historical wisdom literature as well as by implicit theories of wisdom, wisdom-related knowledge and judgment are related to a hybrid of intellectual and personality-related abilities and characteristics. I should add that the selection into and/or exposure to certain experiential contexts plays an important role as well (Staudinger et al., 1998). Thus, it seems that knowledge and judgment about difficult and uncertain matters of life are less related to Aristotelian logic as represented, for instance, by measures of the cognitive mechanics than to a "logic of life" or a "socio-logic" (Goodwin & Wenzel, 1981) that incorporates emotions and motivations with cognitions.

Unfortunately, no longitudinal evidence on the development of wisdom related knowledge and judgment is yet available that would allow us to better understand causal connections between cognition, emotion, motivation, and wisdom-related knowledge and judgment. We do know that chronological age is not only a facilitator (Staudinger, in press). In fact, with increasing chronological age, many processes work against age-related increases in life insight. Decline in the fluid mechanics of the mind, for instance, undermines the application of accumulated experiences, and age-related declines in openness to experience counteract wise responses (Staudinger et al., 1997). Obviously because we used cross-sectional data, we cannot rule out the presence of cohort effects. The lack of age differences in life insight, such as wisdom-related performance, may be due to the fact that young adults nowadays have many more opportunities for anticipatory socialization; that is, they can indirectly experience the problems of life periods to come by reading or watching TV, etc. Thus, anticipatory socialization helps them to make up for a lack of personal experiences (see Staudinger et al., 1992).

On the basis of theoretical considerations (e.g., Staudinger & Dittmann-Kohli, 1994; Staudinger & Baltes, 1994), we may assume that the accumulation of life insights depends on the successful integration of cognition, emotion, and motivation. Only individuals who have attempted to reflect on the strength and weaknesses of human beings and are motivated to change beliefs given counterevidence may succeed in building wisdom-related knowledge and judgment from experiences, thus learning from new experience rather than perpetuating beliefs once formed.

Recently, very interesting evidence on the developmental sequencing of and need for integration of cognition and emotion emerged from studies of the development of emotions in early childhood. In one study, Dunn (1995) demonstrated that early ability to explain the behavior of others was actually related to worse socioemotional adjustment 3 years later, whereas the opposite was the case with early understanding of others' emotions. Unfortunately, no interrelations in this study between the understanding of emotions and behavior was reported.

In sum, a life perspective leads to the study of constructs such as wisdom-related knowledge and judgment, which entail the joint study of cognition, emotion, and motivation. Results from such studies may be conducive to producing evidence that may help shape a psychological art of life.

IMPLIED ECOLOGICAL RELEVANCE

Human life as a unit of consideration almost by definition implies a phenomenological approach and the ecological relevance of the questions under study. The study of life insight and wisdom, for example, emerged from the attempt to identify ecologically relevant forms of adult intellectual functioning (e.g., Labouvie-Vief, 1985). Cognitive developmental psychology was confronted with the dilemma that as early as 25 to 30 years of age, adults show decline in fluid tests of intelligence. The very same adults, however, manage their everyday life perfectly and, in fact, govern our economy and society. This initiated the search for domains of cognitive functioning that more adequately tap into such intellectual competencies (e.g., Baltes, Dittmann-Kohli & Dixon, 1984; Staudinger, 1989). The areas of life management, life planning, and life review seemed appropriate, as were everyday problem solving or the development of professional expertise (cf. Dixon & Baltes, 1986; Poon, Rubin, & Wilson, 1989; Sternberg & Wagner, 1986). Do we increase in our ability to deal with difficult life problems and uncertainties? Do we get better at solving the more mundane problems of everyday life? Do we use the insights that we gain through our professional activities? Such work has been subsumed under the headings of cognitive pragmatics (Baltes et al., 1984), life pragmatics (Staudinger & Pasupathi, in press), and social cognition (e.g., Blanchard-Fields & Abeles, 1996; Hess, 1994). Especially with regard to the study of everyday problem solving, it is important to repeat an argument by Labouvie-Vief (1985): Quite rightly, she has emphasized that when studying ecologically relevant intellectual functioning, it is not enough to change only the content of a task form abstract to concrete everyday terms; it is also necessary to change the logical structure of the task.

When it comes to the investigation of processes of life composition more and more studies select samples of people who have faced or are currently facing certain life events or life tasks. Thus, processes of self- and developmental regulation—or, as I prefer to say, life composition—are studied almost *in vivo* (e.g., relocation to a retirement home [Showers & Ryff, 1996]; diagnosis of cancer [Filipp, 1999]; striving for academic and social success [Cantor & Blanton, 1996]; combining family and career planning [Wiese, Freund, & Baltes, 1998]). Selecting certain samples is one approach to ecological relevance with regard to life composition; the selection of the construct under study is another. I have recently developed and started to work with a construct called personal life investment (PLI). This construct has been developed as an indicator of the motivational system that determines how people distribute their psychological energies across central domains and themes of life (e.g., Staudinger et al., 1999). Initial results are promising, as it seems that people's life tasks are reflected in the assessment of their PLI patterns (Staudinger, 1996a).

METHODOLOGICAL PLURALISM AND RICHNESS

The close connection between a life perspective and ecological relevance should not be mistaken to mean that only qualitative methods and field research can be used to investigate questions emerging from a life perspective. On the contrary, I would like to maintain that the heterogeneity of human life should be mirrored by the heterogeneity of the methods employed to study it. Methods should range from anthropologically oriented qualitative research to the quantitative methods of the more natural-science type. The challenge in studying ecologically relevant topics lies exactly in the creative use of the whole set of psychological methods.

For instance, in our study of the concept of wisdom from the field of life insight, a concept with a long ideational history that many believe defies scientific investigation, we combined methodology that had originally been developed for the study of expertise (e.g., Chi, Glaser, & Farr, 1991; Ericsson & Smith, 1991) with our study of the historical wisdom literature. The empirical evidence we collected using this paradigm demonstrated that by creating a differentiated rating and training system, we succeeded in developing a paradigm that constitutes one approach to the reliable and—as far as this is testable—valid measurement of a concept as complex and rich as wisdom (Baltes et al., 1992; Staudinger & Baltes, 1994).

A life perspective that poses questions of ecological relevance may also promote the development of new methods. For example, the inherent social and interactive nature of human life (e.g., Cole, 1996) leads to a search for assessment methods that do justice to that characteristic. Consideration of the social nature of human beings has a long and rich theoretical tradition (e.g., Bartlett, 1923; Mead, 1934, Vygotsky, 1978). In the 1990s, this topic drew new attention (e.g., Baltes & Staudinger, 1996; Cranach, Doise & Mugny, 1992; Levine, Resnick & Higgins, 1993; Sternberg & Wagner, 1994; Wozniak & Fisher, 1993).

In one of our studies of life insight and wisdom, we were interested in developing a paradigm that would allow us to capture the collective character of wisdom and the everyday ecology of dealing with life dilemmas. To study an individual in isolation—which still is the prevalent measurement paradigm in psychology—would hardly do justice to that social nature. Social interactions and collectivity play a role with regard to ontogenesis but also with regard to microgenesis of wisdom-related knowledge and judgment and the assignment of wisdom (Staudinger, 1996b). In a similar way as linguistics have argued that language is too complex and large a knowledge system to be completely stored in one head (cf. Klein, 1996), we also believe that the body of knowledge and judgment related to the fundamental issues of life does not "fit" into one head. Such considerations lead us to hypothesize that providing the opportunity to discuss wisdom problems with another person (with whom one usually discusses life problems in everyday life) should facilitate wisdom-related performance better than would settings that test the individual in isolation. However, study of the rich literature on group problem solving in social psychology (e.g., Hill, 1982) makes it obvious that social interaction is not only supportive of higher levels of performance but may also result in performance decreases (Staudinger, 1996b). Thus, it seems crucial to identify the conditions under which the strengths of social interaction can unfold and its weaknesses are minimized. On the basis of such considerations, we developed performance conditions that varied in ecological relevance and the degree to which they involved social interaction.

Two main findings from this study should be highlighted (Staudinger & Baltes, 1996). It became clear that human beings do have wisdom-related potential that can be activated given the right performance conditions. Performance level was increased by one standard deviation in two conditions. One successful performance setting was constituted by combining the discussion of the wisdom task with a natural partner with having some time to think alone before responding individually. In the other facilitative condition, participants were asked to think about the wisdom task and, while doing so, to consider what people whose advice they value might have to say about the problem. Thus, this condition used not real but rather virtual dialogues as a means of promoting individual performance levels. The voices inside our head seem to be powerful modulators of our performance (see also Wertsch, 1991). Needless to say, the interactive-minds paradigm is not confined to the study of wisdom; it has also been used in studying memory performance or basic cognitive development in children (e.g., Dixon & Gould, 1996; Rogoff & Chavajay, 1995).

Certainly, the use of interactive assessment paradigms is not limited to investigations in the area of life insight. Interesting studies could be conducted using interactive-minds paradigms in the area of life composition. For instance, one could study coping much more interactively than is currently done when asking about social support. Coping is a deeply interactive process, from how the challenging or threatening situation is defined to which strategies are chosen and eventually carried out. The results of Berg and her colleagues on coping with everyday problems underscore this interactive nature (e.g., Berg, Stroug, Calderone, Sansone, & Weir, 1998).

Another example from our work on wisdom illustrates the use of experimental methods to study ecologically relevant and complex constructs. We have developed a method that uses the recognition rather than the free production of wisdom-related knowledge and judgment (Staudinger, Braß, & Frensch, 1998). In this study, on the basis of responses collected in earlier studies and our theoretical framework, we constructed short response units (3–4 sentences each) that each represent one of four performance levels. This was done for each of five wisdom-related criteria. These 20 response units were presented to participants on a computer screen using two different conditions. Under one condition, participants had to react immediately and judge the wisdom-related quality of the response unit. Under the other condition, participants had 2 minutes to think before they entered their evaluations into the computer. This study enabled us to relate free-production and recognition measures of wisdom. As expected, we found a satisfactory but by no means perfect relation of $r = .40$. Besides the basic relationship between a free-production and a recognition measure of life insight, we wanted to test a hypothesis from the expertise literature. We were interested whether life-insight experts, because of their level of automaticity, would be faster in making decisions than novices would be (cf. Ericsson & Smith, 1991). Somewhat in contrast to our expectation, the more expert participants did not show larger performance superiority under the short response time condition. Rather, the difference between novices and experts was largest when participants had 3 minutes to think about their response. Multiple interpretations seem possible. For instance, it might have been the case that the level of expertise present in the sample was not high enough to observe the automaticity effect postulated in the expertise literature.

These two study examples may suffice to illustrate that experimental methods can be very helpful in furthering our understanding of ecologically relevant phenomena (see also Blanchard-Fields & Abeles, 1996; Hess, 1994).

I would like to stress that my focus on the use of quantitative and experimental methods for the study of ecologically relevant phenomena does not imply that narrative methods have no room in studies guided by a life perspective. However, it seems more crucial to provide evidence that experimental methods can be put to use in examining ecologically relevant phenomena as well. With narrative analysis, there has been a growing interest in developing methods that allow the replicable evaluation of narrative interviews (e.g., Staudinger, 1984; Straub, 1989). Using such methods as the narrative interview, on the one hand, provides materials that reflect the richness and systemic complexity of human life in a way that is hardly achievable with quantitative methods (e.g., Gergen & Gergen, 1988; Middleton, in press). Also, narratives have been found to be powerful in shaping reality (Staudinger & Pasupathi, in press). On the other hand, narrative interviews will never provide the same precision on certain select aspects of a person's life. Thus, the complementary use of both types of methods seems desirable.

Another investigative tool that seems ideally suited to study human life is the diary method (e.g., Wheeler & Reis, 1991), which uses not only diaries that are kept personally but also those that are kept according to a researcher's instructions (e.g., daily, weekly, or beeper guided). This method comes as close as possible to continuous observation of human beings in their natural settings) and has been exercised more commonly and proficiently by anthropologists than by psychologists (e.g., Heath, in press; Shweder, 1991). High-frequency assessment of one person on certain dimensions of functioning—as is possible when using a diary method—allows us to approximate processes of adaptation in the area of life composition as well as to study the development of knowledge and judgment in the area of life insight.

For instance, Nesselroade and colleagues conducted a series of studies using high-frequency assessments of characteristics ranging from indicators of physical functioning (e.g., Nesselroade, Featherman, Aggen, & Rowe, 1995) to depressivity (Nesselroade & Featherman, 1991) and world views (Kim, Nesselroade, & Featherman, 1996). The evidence accrued in these studies implies that short-term fluctuations are not merely noise to be ignored and statistically controlled but rather information studied in its own right. The magnitude and profile of intraindividual variability seems to have predictive power above and beyond information collected in one-time measures.

Richness in methods does not refer only to methods of data collection; it refers also to methods of data analysis. The complexity and system characteristics of human life may make it necessary to question the assumption of linearity that is essential for most of the standard statistical methods used in psychological research. For instance, with regard to research on life insight, we have found evidence in our studies on wisdom that fluid intellectual abilities may show a very weak relationship with wisdom-related performance as long as a certain level of fluid functioning is maintained. Once performance drops below this level, however, the relationship between fluid ability and wisdom-related performance becomes much stronger. Thus, this seems to be a relationship that follows a threshold model rather than a linear trend (Baltes et al., 1995).

Another example of alternative methods of analysis, from the field of life composition, is research on developmental risks and resilience. This research has focused on types of individuals or types of pathways rather than on the relationship between continuous dimensions (e.g., Caspi, 1998; Rutter, 1996; Smith & Baltes, 1997; Staudinger et al., 1999). Indeed, it seems that the complexities of risk and protective networks are better approximated that way. Magnusson, Anderson, and Törestad (1993), for instance, reported that only by analyzing the pattern of risk conditions in adolescence rather than individual risks could they successfully differentiate adults with alcohol problems from those without. It is reassuring to see that such methodological trends have been picked up by top statisticians as well (Van der Maas & Molenaar, 1992).

CONTINUOUS SEARCH FOR RESERVE POTENTIAL AND MEANING

A life perspective encourages the search for the reserve potential and meaning of human existence. It is quite common to ask ourselves how our lives might have been different and what new forms they may take in the future or in the best of all possible worlds (ideal).

The assessment of reserve potential has been an important characteristic of the lifespan approach to development (e.g., Baltes et al., 1998; Lerner, 1984). At least three different ways of investigating reserves can be distinguished. One way is to test reserves experimentally. This method has a long tradition in research on intellectual functioning. Using various training procedures, participants approach their maximal performance levels (e.g., Kliegl & Baltes, 1987). Another way is to assess reserves cross-sectionally or, ideally, longitudinally by investigating people's reactions under threatening or challenging life circumstances. This method is primarily employed in research on resilience (e.g., Masten & Coatsworth, 1995; Rutter & Rutter, 1993; Staudinger et al., 1995). Finally, reserve potential can also be conceptualized as the subjectively conceived amount of potential in various domains of life. Research has demonstrated that participants can report on this realm of potentiality and that it serves adaptive functions (Cross & Markus, 1991; Hooker, 1992; Ryff, 1991).

Let us return once more to the two categories life insight and life composition to illustrate the experimental assessment of reserves. When considering *life insight,* wisdom, as one construct studied under that heading, is a prototypical example for the study of potential. Wisdom has often been proposed as the ideal of human development (e.g., Assmann, 1994; Erikson, 1959; 1982). In the previous section, I described the interactive-minds paradigm that has uncovered wisdom-related potential, that is performance increases of one standard deviation, given the right performance conditions (Staudinger & Baltes, 1996). These results encouraged us to search for other interventions that access and activate wisdom-related potential. Thus, in a wisdom study currently under way, we are interested in how the possibility of keeping notes while thinking about a difficult life problem would enhance performance levels (Staudinger & Baltes, in preparation). We will compare the differences in performance increase when given the opportunity to write something down during a 10-minute thinking period versus 10 minutes' thinking time without notes and 10 minutes' thinking time during which participants are asked to think what other people whose advice they value might have said about the problem. On the basis of the cognitive aging literature, we would expect an age interaction such that older participants would profit more (compared to baseline assessment) from the note-taking conditions than would younger participants, as older participants may profit more from the related working memory relief. In the second study, we developed a knowledge-activating memory strategy, based on the method of loci (Yates, 1966), that was meant to specifically foster value-relativistic knowledge and judgment (Böhmig-Krumhaar, Staudinger, & Baltes, 1999). This strategy took people on an imaginary journey around the world while sitting on a cloud. The journey had four stops represented by four landmarks: Berlin (Brandenburg Gate), Italy (Leaning Tower of Pisa), Egypt (the Great Pyramid of Cheops), and China (Great Wall of China). After creating a vivid image of people's life at the respective four places, participants were asked to solve a life dilemma at each of the four locations. This was done for two training problems. In the next session, participants of the training group were asked to think about the journey on the cloud while responding to the presented test problems. The training group showed higher performance as compared with baseline and with a control group that was tested only twice.

Another approach to the study of wisdom-related potential has been the development of more and more difficult tasks. Thus, in one study, we developed a task dealing with a fictitious suicide situation. The topic of suicide addresses the limits of human existence, which have been claimed to be especially suited to activate human reserves (Jaspers, 1932). Indeed, we showed that only a group of wisdom nominees did well on this task, whereas less positively selected groups had a lot of difficulties with it (Baltes et al., 1995). In sum, we have been searching for a collection of internal and external performance conditions that may facilitate wisdom-related performance and thus activate wisdom-related performance potential.

The second way to investigate reserve potential—that is, the activation of reserves in real life—is exemplified in research examples from the realm of *life composition*. In work based on data from the Berlin Aging Study and from the John D. and Catherine T. MacArthur Foundation Network on Successful Midlife Development, I was interested in analyzing the reserve potential of individuals in difficult life circumstances (e.g., Staudinger & Fleeson, 1996; Staudinger, Fleeson & Baltes, 1998; Staudinger et al., 1999). Which are the coping styles, the patterns of PLI, and the time experience patterns that contribute to resilience? How do people under extremely constraining health and/or financial conditions manage to still report moderately positive levels of adaptivity? We demonstrated that social cognitive processes such as coping styles, social comparison, readjustment of level of aspiration, and rearrangement of life priorities allow individuals to show resilience in the face of threatening and challenging events (e.g., Staudinger et al., 1999). Such investigations, however, also made clear that life circumstances may exist—for instance, in very old age—that are too constraining and thus cannot be counterbalanced by available reserves (see also Smith & Baltes, 1997). Thus, as postulated by lifespan psychology (e.g., Baltes, 1987, 1997), the limits of reserves did become visible.

The life perspective introduced in this chapter, however, leads us beyond people's internal reserves to also explore their external reserves (see also Baltes & Carstensen, 1999; Lawton, 1991; Rutter & Rutter, 1993). Internal reserves, as just discussed, refer, for instance, to increases in power, effort, intellectual investment, changes in life goals, and aspirations. External reserves comprise, for instance, social support (emotional and instrumental) and support through technology. On the basis of the assumptions of lifespan psychology, we can maintain that the use of external resources is highly important in old age. Indeed, the employment of external resources may follow a shallow U-shaped function (high need for external resources very early and late in life and moderate use in midlife [Staudinger, 1996a]), whereas internal resources may show the complementary inverted U-shaped function. Returning to the title of this chapter, it may constitute one important feature of an art of life to know how to access one's potential and one's internal and external reserves in life insight and life composition.

Finally, the third way of studying reserves is to investigate subjective perceptions of potentiality and their predictive power. This means, for example, to study a person's conceptions of their own possibilities and ideals. In Lewin's notion of life space, this ideal level of analysis played an important role (Lewin, 1946). In research on the self, the investigation of possible and ideal selves has gained importance since the 1980s (e.g., Fleeson & Baltes, in press; Higgins, 1996; Markus & Nurius, 1986; Oettingen, 1996; Ryff, 1991). Which are the adaptive and maladaptive functions of ideals and fantasies about one's life (e.g., Baltes et al., 1998, pp. 1107–1109; Colvin & Block, 1994)?

Taking a macroanalytical perspective, one may also ask which are the societal structures that optimize or undermine the potential to compose our lives. Thus, when striving to optimize old age, Western industrialized societies may have to rethink some of their values such as youthfulness, quickness, or progress and may also have to come to accept new forms of productivity that result not in direct but rather in indirect increases of the gross national product (Baltes & Montada, 1996; Staudinger, 1996a).

The search for reserve potential that is part of taking a life perspective also includes asking for the right measure, the right direction, and the right time. It encompasses the classic Aristotelian search for a "good life." The quest for meaning in life is a very complex issue that can only be touched on here (for more comprehensive coverage, see Staudinger & Dittmann-Kohli, 1994). There is a long philosophical tradition of discourse about the good life (for review, see Kekes, 1995; Rentsch, 1994), but the topic has attracted a number of researchers in psychology also (e.g., Baumeister, 1987; Dittmann-Kohli, 1995; Kruse, 1995; Reker & Wong, 1988). Studying the meaning of life from a psychological perspective makes it clear that the goal cannot be to determine absolute criteria of meaning but rather must be to describe different forms of meaning of life in different subgroups of society and different cultures and relate those to indicators of adaptivity. The construction of meaning is influenced, for instance, by religious, individualistic, future-oriented, or health-oriented interpretations of life (e.g., Shotter & Gergen, 1989). To ask the question about the meaning of life and to find satisfactory answers (there does not have to be only one answer) seems to constitute one of the centerpieces of an art of life.

In sum, I argued in this section that a life perspective implies the search for reserve potential and meaning. This was illustrated by research examples from the area of life insight and life composition. At the same time, insight into the activation of reserves and the identification or construction of meaning both constitute important elements of an art of life.

EMBRACING OF THE ONTOLOGY OF THE FIRST AND THE THIRD PERSON

What do I mean by the ontology of the first and the third person? This notion is borrowed from philosopher John Searle (e.g., 1992). Ontology of the first person is knowledge and insight into life based on self experience, whereas the ontology of the third person is the view of life based on an observer's perspective. Linked to the first-person perspective is this question: How does a person view and lead his or her *own* life? This is the avenue that most of the developmental theories have taken (e.g., Bühler, 1933; Erikson, 1959; Havighurst, 1948). The other avenue, the third-person perspective, is to ask about insights about life *in general* (beyond the individual life). What does an individual know about life from an observer's point of view? What kind of knowledge about life is represented on a societal level? How do both of these two ontologies influence the understanding and composing of our lives?

There are a number of studies in the area of self-regulation that document how societal norms about development are reflected in individuals' conceptions about their own development (e.g., Heckhausen, 1999). Such research reveals that knowledge about life in general (third-person perspective) has a strong impact on how we compose our own lives (first-person perspective). For instance, we compare our own life with those of others (e.g., Wood, 1996), and life events take on different meanings depending on whether the event is considered normative (i.e., statistically frequent) for a given age or not (e.g., Hultsch & Plemons, 1979).

The distinction between first- and third-person knowledge takes on specific relevance when we consider the development of life insight or wisdom. It seems that the dynamic between first- and third-person knowledge and judgment about life may be at the heart of eventually attaining wisdom. Unfortunately, with the exception of work on the development of autobiographical memory (e.g., Nelson, 1992), there is no research—to my knowledge—dealing with the development of knowledge about one's own life. There is work on the development of self-conceptions and of personality characteristics, but I am not aware of investigations of how knowledge about our own life develops. When it comes to the third-person perspective—that is, knowledge about life in general—research on theories of mind is relevant. Research on theories of mind refers to the early precursors of our general knowledge about life (e.g., Flavell, 1978; Perner, 1991; Wellmann, 1990). With regard to the later periods of life, our work on wisdom-related knowledge and judgment applies. We are interested in the quality and quantity of people's knowledge and judgment, starting in adolescence, about difficult life issues. The development of knowledge and judgment about one's own life is clearly understudied. In the future, it will be useful to develop procedures that focus specifically on the assessment of first person—that is, personal wisdom—to be able to investigate the dynamics between first and third-person knowledge and judgment. Very rarely in the literature on wisdom is this distinction between first and third person drawn. For instance, in the writings of Erikson, it is left open whether he refers to self-related wisdom, to general wisdom, or to both. However, given the fact that in his theorizing he was concerned with personality development, one might argue that it is more likely that without specifying it, he talked about self-related wisdom (first person) rather than general wisdom (third person). The Oxford dictionary, for instance, defines *wisdom* as good insight, judgment, and advice regarding difficult and uncertain life matters. Again, a distinction between general and self-related wisdom is not drawn, but it seems that general rather than self-related wisdom is implied by this definition. An understanding of the dynamics between first- and third-person wisdom seems central for the building of a psychological art of life.

SOCIAL COGNITION AND AN ART OF LIFE: FUTURE DIRECTIONS

In this closing section, I offer a conceptual framework that may help in pursuing a life perspective in the future and I summarize the status quo of psychological efforts toward creating an art of life.

LIFE AS DYNAMIC SYSTEM

The previously introduced characterization of a life perspective on psychological inquiry requires an organizing theoretical framework. It seems that dynamic systems theory may be one such framework (cf. Prigogine & Stengers, 1984). Originating in physics and biology, dynamic systems theory currently has many different interpretations and is not nearly as homogenous as its constant label may make us believe (e.g., Barton, 1994). In this short summary of dynamic systems theory, I refer only to some of the existing adaptations for psychology (e.g., Ford & Lerner, 1992; Lewis, 1995; Sameroff, 1995; Thelen & Smith, 1994).

Applying terminology from dynamic systems theory, human life can be considered as a dynamic system consisting of hierarchically ordered and interacting elements and levels of analyses. However, these levels of analyses are not perfectly linked by causal relations and thus cannot easily be reduced to one another. On a descriptive as well as an explanatory level, the system is more than the sum of its parts. In the case of human life, the following levels of analysis can, for instance, be distinguished: the biological, the psychological, the sociocultural, and the historical level. Each of these levels of analysis comprises various elements. On the biological level, for example, the elements are genes, cells, and organs. On the psychological level, they are, for instance, the distinction among cognition, motivation, and emotion. On the sociocultural level, they are different social and material contexts that are more or less proximal to the individual. Elements of each level but also of different levels are related by recursive interactions. Using this terminology, we can describe human life as a dynamic system comprising hierarchically ordered elements that in interaction with changes on the various levels of analysis continuously reorganizes and restabilizes.

Is this more than playing with words? I argue that applying dynamic systems theory to a life perspective in psychology implies the epistemological advantage that insights gained from general dynamic systems theory can be used to generate hypotheses about human life (e.g., Höger, 1992; Kelso, Mandell & Schlesinger, 1988). Especially in developmental psychology, there is already quite a history of making use of dynamic systems theory to conceptualize developmental processes (cf. Magnusson, 1996). Our insight into motor development, for instance, has profited enormously from the dynamic systems approach (see Thelen & Smith, 1994). In the future, so may our knowledge about the interaction between cognition and emotion (see Lewis, 1995). In cognitive psychology, too, there are examples such as the conceptualization of problem solving in complex systems (e.g., Reichert & Dörner, 1988) and action regulation when dealing with chaotic systems (e.g., Höger, 1992).

In the following, I will illustrate the meaning of the three central characteristics of dynamic systems when applied to a life perspective in psychological inquiry: nonlinearity, self-organization, and self-stabilization.

Nonlinearity

Human life is not necessarily linear, but neither is it pure chance. I mentioned before the example of the nonlinear relationship between fluid cognitive functioning and wisdom-related performance. Using methods based on the general linear model (GLM), we identified no significant relationship; however, when a critical threshold of fluid cognitive functioning was missed, the relationship between fluid intelligence and wisdom-related performance became very strong (Baltes et al. 1995).

Self-organization

To illustrate the consequences of conceptualizing human life as a self-organizing system, evidence from the field of self and personality seems well suited (e.g., Baltes et al., 1998; Lewis, 1995). Self-organization implies that interaction between elements of another level may result in new and unpredictable forms. Such knowledge may reconcile seemingly contradictory evidence on stability and change of personality. In this interpretation, the Big Five (e.g., Goldberg, 1993; McCrae & Costa, 1997) are considered as elements of a self-organizing system. On the one hand, the Big Five form a stable structure. On the other hand, when interacting with certain contexts and/or other elements of the dynamic system "human life," they can also lead to new forms of experience and behavior and thus change. Such stable structures are highly functional and play a crucial role in development. In the cognitive literature, stable structures and their contribution to adaptive flexibility and phenotypic discontinuity have been acknowledged and discussed under the heading of *constraints* (e.g., Keil, 1981).

Self-stabilization

Finally, the self-stabilizing characteristic of dynamic systems implies that dynamic systems have a tendency to react to disturbances by homeostatic (returning to a set point) or homeorhetic feedback loops (returning to a set trajectory [e.g., Sameroff, 1995]). Evidence from the area of self-regulation provides very rich empirical evidence to illustrate that characteristic (e.g., Baltes et al., 1998; Brandtstädter, 1998; Blanchard-Fields & Abeles, 1996; Gollwitzer & Bargh,

1996; Staudinger et al., 1995). Take, for example, the regulation of subjective well-being. Many studies have demonstrated again and again that objectively threatening and challenging life circumstances, such as extreme health constraints or social marginalization, are not at all or hardly reflected in the afflicted individuals' subjective well-being (e.g., Diener & Diener, 1996). It seems that self and personality have available a rich set of regulatory processes, such as changing the aspirational level or the comparison group or concentration of psychological energies, to almost always return to moderately positive levels of subjective well-being (e.g., Baltes & Baltes, 1990; Brandtstädter & Greve, 1994; Carstensen, 1995; Filipp, 1996; Heckhausen & Schulz, 1995; Staudinger et al., 1995).

The phenomenology of human life may be more comprehensively reflected in a dynamic systems approach than within the general linear model. Currently, one obstacle in applying the dynamic systems approach more widely is the resulting high level of complexity in conceptualization and methodology. In the long run, however, dynamic systems theory and related methodology may hold the potential to fruitfully reconcile qualitative ideographic and quantitative nomothetic approaches in psychology.

FROM LIFE INSIGHT AND LIFE COMPOSITION TO AN ART OF LIFE?

Finally, I would like to return to the topic of the beginning of this chapter and discuss the possibilities of a psychologically informed art of life. To clarify, a psychological art of life is not meant to be something elitist that only the rich and well educated may have the liberty to indulge in. Rather, a psychological art of life is meant to be a body of knowledge and strategies that any human being needs and may use. The term *art of life* should remind us that human life is based not only on analytical rationality but on aesthetic and moral rationality as well. A scientific psychological approach to creating an art of life needs to accommodate that. The human ability of self-reflection seems to be central to a psychological approach to an art of life. Evidence on life insight and life composition recommend these processes as useful elements in building such a psychological art of life.

Knowledge and strategies regarding life composition can be derived, for instance, from longitudinal evidence on predictors of adaptive outcomes. Such a collection of developmental "wild cards" may be considered elements that contribute to an art of life. Such wild cards of adaptive development—or general-purpose mechanisms (Karmiloff-Smith, 1992), as they have been called in cognitive psychology—are, for example, a certain level of frustration tolerance (cf. Mischel et al., 1989), the right amount of self-efficacy and internal control belief (e.g., Seligman, 1991), conscientiousness (Friedman et al., 1993), and selective flexibility in coping behavior (Staudinger & Fleeson, 1996). There is abundant evidence that these "tools" support individuals in consciously and unconsciously (automatized) managing and composing their lives. It seems that in contrast to the area of cognitive functioning, these general-purpose mechanisms of life composition often refer to a "right measure at the right time" algorithm rather than a fixed expression of a self-regulatory mechanism or a personality characteristic.

Another source informative for the theme of life composition is recent models of successful development (e.g., Baltes & Carstensen, 1996; Baltes & Baltes, 1990; Brandtstädter & Greve, 1994; Heckhausen & Schulz, 1995). For example, Baltes and Baltes (1990) maintained that the three processes of selection, compensation, and optimization (SOC) are central to successful adaptation across the life span. In other models of successful development, the critical processes are primary and secondary control (Heckhausen & Schulz, 1995) or assimilation and accommodation (Brandtstädter & Greve, 1994). In all these models, the art seems to consist in arriving at the right combination between the multiple processes at the right place and time—in finding the right time to give up a certain goal to avoid serious disturbances of life's balance and the right time to still try harder.

Life insight, the other suggested component of an art of life, may be of help in selecting the right behavior, the right context, and the right time. One may, for instance, try to derive such guiding principles from linking the five-criteria model of wisdom-related knowledge and judgment with models of successful development, such as the SOC model. Why should that be helpful and what might that look like? Any art of life has to abstain from prescriptions. Psychologists do not want to prescribe the right life. This creates the dilemma that most of the models of successful development have specified their mechanisms at a metalevel of analysis. No algorithms are described that allow exact determination of when to select or compensate, or to assimilate and accommodate, or to exert primary or secondary control. By combining strategies of life composition with the five wisdom criteria (rich factual, and procedural knowledge about life, lifespan contextualism, value relativism, awareness and management of life's uncertainties [see Baltes et al., 1992 for extensive description]) some guidance on these decisions may be provided without prescription. Orienting their thinking along the lines of the five wisdom criteria may support individuals in identifying the right decisions for their own lives. For instance, the criterion of lifespan contextualism may help to solve internal conflicts between life domains by setting time-bound priorities. Value relativism may help to find the appropriate behavior in an interpersonal conflict.

Combining life composition and life insight in that manner implies the extension of the wisdom paradigm to capture knowledge and judgment about life—that is, the insights and strategies individuals mention when problems of their own lives are concerned. There is reason to believe that in general it is harder to have good knowledge and judgment about one's own life than about life in general, as whenever our own life is concerned, we are "burdened" by our own involvement (hot cognitions) and our own value priorities and "blind spots." It is much more difficult to abstain from such predilections when it comes to our own lives than when life in general is concerned. The distance and flexibility characteristic of wise judgment is much harder to attain with regard to our own lives.

There has been some speculation about the possible ontogenetic paths that both forms of wisdom may take and about their interdependency (Staudinger &

Dittmann-Kohli, 1994). Are they very much independent or inextricably intertwined with each other? Is it possible to conceive of persons who are wise about their own life but not at all able to judge wisely about life in general? Or is it possible to imagine people who are wise about life in general but not wise when it comes to their own lives? Both seem possible, but the latter may have a higher probability than the former. Therefore, I would hypothesize that if there are interdependencies, it is that general wisdom is more likely given personal wisdom than the other way around.

It would be a very exciting research project to identify the self-regulatory and structural personality characteristics that distinguish people who have some general *and* personal wisdom from those who have only some general but very low personal wisdom. Such research would, at the same time, be crucial in providing further evidence that can be used to build a psychological art of life.

Suffice this to illustrate that psychology already offers precious materials that can be used in shaping a psychological art of life. In my view, we are closer to creating a psychological art of life than the "exotic" sound of the term may suggest. A psychological art of life begins with the creative aspects of composing and managing one's life, which comprise processes of continuous generation, revision, and deletion. This composition process is initiated by the individual and subsequently interacts with proximal (e.g., interacting lives of others) and distal (e.g., societal life scripts) contexts. Consistencies emerge in the style of the composition rather than the selected tunes. The various processes subsumed under the headings of *life insight* and *life composition* may qualify to serve as potential notes in this composition. For a psychological art of life to succeed scientifically, it seems crucial, however, to reduce the phenomenological complexity and dynamics of life to a still convincing but simpler framework. In this chapter, I have tried to argue that some of the building materials for a psychological art of life are theoretically and empirically already available awaiting their composition; by taking a life perspective, we may allow the composition to flow more easily.

ACKNOWLEDGMENTS

I acknowledge the many valuable discussions with colleagues from the Max Planck Institute for Human Development (Center of Lifespan Psychology), the Berlin Aging Study, and the John D. and Catherine T. MacArthur Foundation Network on Successful Midlife Development. For helpful comments on an earlier version of this paper, I thank Susan Bluck. Address correspondence to the authors at Max Planck Institute for Human Development, Lentzeallee 94, 14195 Berlin, Germany, or Staudinger@mpib-berlin.mpg.de.

REFERENCES

Aldwin, C. M., & Revenson, T. A. (1987). Does coping help? A reexamination of the relation between coping and mental health. *Journal of Personality and Social Psychology, 53,* 337–348.

Aldwin, C. M., Sutton, K. J., & Lachman, M. (1996). The development of coping resources in adulthood. *Journal of Personality, 64*, 837–871.

Assmann, A. (1994). Wholesome knowledge: Concepts of wisdom in a historical and cross-cultural perspective. In D. L. Featherman, R. M. Lerner, & M. Perlmutter (Eds.), *Life-span development and behavior* (vol. 12, pp. 187–224). Hillsdale, NJ: Lawrence Erlbaum Associates.

Baltes, M. M., & Carstensen, L. L. (1996). The process of successful ageing. *Ageing and Society, 397–422*.

Baltes, M. M., & Carstensen, L. L. (1999). Social psychological theories and their applications to aging: From individual to collective social psychology. In V. L. Bengtson & K. W. Schaie (Eds.), *Handbook of theories of aging* (pp. 209–226). New York: Springer.

Baltes, M. M., & Montada, L. (Eds.). (1996). *Produktives Leben im Alter* [Productivity in old age]. Frankfurt: Campus.

Baltes, P. B. (1987). Theoretical propositions of life-span developmental psychology: On the dynamics between growth and decline. *Developmental Psychology, 23*, 611–626.

Baltes, P. B. (1997). On the incomplete architecture of human ontogeny: Selection, optimization, and compensation as foundation of developmental theory. *American Psychologist, 52*, 366–380.

Baltes, P. B., & Baltes, M. M. (Eds.). (1990). *Successful aging: Perspectives from the behavioral sciences*. Cambridge: Cambridge University Press.

Baltes, P. B., Dittmann-Kohli, F., & Dixon, R. A. (1984). New perspectives on the development of intelligence in adulthood: Toward a dual-process conception and a model of selective optimization with compensation. In P. B. Baltes & O. G. Brim (Eds.), *Life-span development and behavior* (vol. 6, pp. 33–76). New York: Academic Press.

Baltes, P. B., Lindenberger, U., & Staudinger, U. M. (1998). Life-span theory in developmental psychology. In R. M. Lerner (Ed.), *Handbook of child psychology. Vol. 1: Theoretical models of human development* (5th ed., pp. 1029–1143). New York: Wiley.

Baltes, P. B., & Nesselroade, J. R. (1979). *History and rationale of longitudinal research*. New York: Academic Press.

Baltes, P. B., & Smith, J. (1990). Toward a psychology of wisdom and its ontogenesis. In R. J. Sternberg (Ed.), *Wisdom: Its nature, origins, and development* (pp. 87–120). New York: Cambridge University Press.

Baltes, P. B., Smith, J., & Staudinger, U. M. (1992). Wisdom and successful aging. In T. B. Sonderegger (Ed.), *Nebraska symposium on motivation* (vol. 39, pp. 123–167). Lincoln, NB: University of Nebraska Press.

Baltes, P. B., & Staudinger, U. M. (Eds.) (1996). *Interactive minds: life-span perspectives on the social foundation of cognition*. New York: Cambridge University Press.

Baltes, P. B., Staudinger, U. M., Maercker, A., & Smith, J. (1995). People nominated as wise: A comparative study of wisdom-related knowledge. *Psychology and Aging, 10*, 155–166.

Barkow, J. H., Cosmides, L., & Tooby, J. (Eds.). (1992). *The adapted mind: Evolutionary psychology and the generation of culture*. New York: Oxford University Press.

Bartlett, F. C. (1923). *Psychology and primitive culture*. Cambridge, UK: Cambridge University Press.

Barton, S. (1994). Chaos, self-organization, and psychology. *American Psychologist, 49*, 5–14.

Baumeister, R. F. (1987). How the self became a problem: Psychological review of theoretical research. *Journal of Personality and Social Psychology, 52*, 163–176.

Berg, C. A., Stroug, J., Calderone, K. S., Sansone, C., & Weir, C. (1998). The role of problem definitions in understanding age and context effects on strategies for solving everyday problems. *Psychology and Aging, 13*, 29–44.

Bergius, R. (1957). *Formen des Zukunftserlebens*. Munich: Barth.

Blanchard-Fields, F., & Abeles, R. A. (1996). Social cognition and aging. In J. E. Birren & K. W. Schaie (Eds.), *Handbook of the psychology of aging* (4th ed., pp. 150–161). New York: Academic Press.

Blanchard-Fields, F., & Hess, T. M. (Eds.). (1996). *Perspectives on cognitive change in adulthood and aging*. New York: McGraw-Hill.

Boesch, E. E. (1971). *Zwischen zwei Wirklichkeiten: Prolegomena zu einer ökologischen Psychologie*. Bern: Huber.

Boesch, E. E. (1991). *Symbolic action theory and cultural psychology.* Heidelberg: Springer-Verlag.

Böhmig-Krumhaar, S., Staudinger, U. M., & Baltes, P. B. (1999). Development of a memory strategy that activates value-relativistic knowledge and judgement. Unpublished manuscript. Berlin: Max Planck Institute for Human Development.

Brandtstädter, J. (1984). Personal and social control over development: Some implications of an action perspective in life-span developmental psychology. In P. B. Baltes & J. O. G. Brim (Eds.), *Life-span development and behavior* (vol. 6, pp. 1–32). New York: Academic Press.

Brandtstädter, J. (1998). Action perspectives on human development. In R. M. Lerner (Ed.), *Handbook of child psychology* (vol. 1, pp. 807–863). New York: Wiley.

Brandtstädter, J., & Greve, W. (1994). The aging self: Stabilizing and protective processes. *Developmental Review, 14,* 52–80.

Bronfenbrenner, U. & Morris, P. A. (1998). *The ecology of developmental processes.* In R. M. Lerner (Ed.), *Handbook of child psychology: Vol. 1. Theoretical models of human development* (5th ed., pp. 993–1028). New York: Wiley.

Bruckner, P., & Finkielkraut, A. (1981). *Kleines Handbuch der Alltagsüberlebenskunst.* Munich: Wilhelm Fink Verlag.

Bühler, C. (1933). *Der Lebenslauf als psychologisches Problem.* Göttingen, Germany. Hogrefe.

Butler, R. N. (1963). The life review: An interpretation of reminiscence in the aged. *Psychiatry, 26,* 65–76.

Cantor, N., & Blanton, H. (1996). Effortful pursuit of personal goals in daily life. In P. M. Gollwitzer & J. A. Bargh (Eds.), *The psychology of action: Linking cognition and motivation to behavior* (pp. 338–359). New York: Guilford Press.

Carstensen, L. L. (1995). Evidence for a life-span theory of socioemotional selectivity. *Current Directions in Psychological Science, 4,* 151–156.

Caspi, A. (1998). Personality development across the life course. In N, Eisenberg (Ed.), *Handbook of child psychology: Social emotional, and personality development* (5th ed., vol. 3, pp. 311–387). New York: Wiley.

Cheng, P. W., & Holyoak, K. J. (1985). Pragmatic reasoning schemes. *Cognitive Psychology, 17,* 391–416.

Chi, M. T. H., Glaser, R., & Farr, M. J. (Eds.). (1991). *Toward a general theory of expertise.* Hillsdale, NJ: Lawrence Erlbaum Associates.

Cole, M. (1996). Interacting minds in a life-span perspective: A cultural/historical approach to culture and cognitive development. In P. B. Baltes & U. M. Staudinger (Eds.), *Interactive minds: Lifespan perspectives on the social foundation of cognition* (pp. 59–87). New York: Cambridge University Press.

Colvin, C. R., & Block, J. (1994). Do positive illusions foster mental health? An examination of the Taylor and Brown formulation. *Psychological Bulletin, 116,* 3–20.

Cosmides, L. (1989). The logic of social exchange: Has natural selection shaped how humans reason? *Cognition, 31,* 187–276.

Cranach, M. V., Doise, W., & Mugny, G. (Eds.). (1992). *Social representations and the social bases of knowledge.* Lewiston, NY: Hogrefe & Huber.

Cross, S., & Markus, H. (1991). Possible selves across the life span. *Human Development, 34,* 230–255.

Diener, E., & Diener, C. (1996). Most people are happy. *Psychological Science, 7,* 181–185.

Dilthey, W. (1968/1894). *Der Aufbau der geschichtlichen Welt in den Geisteswissenschaften.* (vol. 7). Stuttgart: Teubner.

Dittmann-Kohli, F. (1995). *Das persönliche Sinnsystem: Ein Vergleich zwischen frühem und spätem Erwachsenenalter.* Göttingen, Germany. Hogrefe.

Dixon, R. A., & Bäckman, L. (Eds.). (1995). *Compensating for psychological defects and declines: Managing losses and promoting gains.* Mahwah, NJ: Lawrence Erlbaum Associates.

Dixon, R. A., & Baltes, P. B. (1986). Toward life-span research on the functions and pragmatics of intelligence. In R. J. Sternberg & R. K. Wagner (Eds.), *Practical intelligence: Origins of competence in the everyday world* (pp. 203–235). New York: Cambridge University Press.

Dixon, R. A., & Gould, O. N. (1996). Collaborative memory for narratives in adulthood. In P. B. Baltes & U. M. Staudinger (Eds.), *Interactive minds: Life-span perspectives on the social foundation of cognition* (pp. 221–241). New York: Cambridge University Press.

Dunn, J. (1995). Children as psychologists: The later correlates of individual differences in understanding of emotions and other minds. *Cognition and Emotion, 9,* 187–201.

Eichorn, D. H., Clausen, J. A., Haan, N., Honzik, M. P., & Mussen, P. H. (Eds.). (1981). *Present and past in middle life.* New York: Academic Press.

Elder, Jr., G. H. (1998). The life course and human development. In R. M. Lerner (Ed.), *Handbook of child psychology. Vol. 1: Theoretical models of human development* (5th ed., pp. 939–991). New York: Wiley.

Ericsson, K. A., & Smith, J. (Eds.). (1991). *Toward a general theory of expertise: Prospects and limits.* Cambridge, MA: Cambridge University Press.

Erikson, E. H. (1959). *Identity and the life cycle.* New York: International University Press.

Erikson, E. H. (1982). *The life cycle completed: a review.* New York: Norton.

Filipp, S.-H. (1996). Motivation and emotion. In J. E. Birren & K. W. Schaie (Eds.), *Handbook of the psychology of aging* (pp. 218–235). San Diego: Academic Press.

Filipp, S. H. (1999). A three-stage model of coping with loss and trauma: Lessons from patients suffering from severe and chronic disease. In A. Maercker, M. Schützwohl, & Z. Solomon (Eds.), *Posttraumatic stress disorder: A lifespan developmental perspective* (pp. 132–164). Seattle: Hogrefe & Huber.

Flavell, J. H. (1978). Metacognitive development. In J. M. Scandura & C. J. Brainerd (Eds.), *Structural/complex models of complex human behavior* (pp. 213–245). Alphen a.d. Rijn: Sijthoff & Noordhoff.

Fleeson, W., & Baltes, P. B. (in press). Beyond present-day personality assessment: An encouraging exploration of the measurement properties and predictive power of subjective lifetime personality. *Journal of Research in Personality.*

Ford, D. H., & Lerner, R. M. (1992). *Developmental systems theory: An integrative approach.* London: Sage.

Friedman, H. S., Tucker, J. S., Tomlinson Keasey, C., Schwartz, J. E., Wingard, D. L., & Criqui, M. H. (1993). Does childhood personality predict longevity? *Journal of Personality and Social Psychology, 65,* 176–185.

Gergen, K. J., & Gergen, M. M. (1988). *Narrative and the self as relationship.* (vol. 21). San Diego: Academic Press.

Gigerenzer, G. (1996). Rationality: Why social context matters. In P. B. Baltes & U. M. Staudinger (Eds.), *Interactive minds: Life-span perspectives on the social foundation of cognition* (pp. 317–346). Cambridge: Cambridge: University Press.

Gigerenzer, G., & Hug, K. (1992). Domain-specific reasoning: Social contracts, cheating, and perspective change. *Cognition, 43,* 127–171.

Goldberg, L. R. (1993). The structure of phenotypic personality traits. Sixth European Conference on Personality (1992, Groningen, Netherlands). *American Psychologist, 48,* 26–34.

Gollwitzer, P. M., & Bargh, J. A. (Eds.). (1996). *The psychology of action: Linking cognition and motivation to action.* New York: Guilford Press.

Goodwin, P. D., & Wenzel, J. W. (1981). Proverbs and practical reasoning: A study in socio-logic. In W. Mieder & A. Dundes (Eds.), *The wisdom of many: Essays on the proverb* (pp. 140–159). New York: Garland.

Graumann, C. F. (1960). *Grundlagen einer Phänomenologie und Psychologie der Perspektivität.* Berlin: de Gruyter.

Haan, N. (1977). *Coping and defending: Processes of self-environment organization.* New York: Academic Press.

Haight, B. K., & Webster, J. D. (Eds.). (1995). *The art and science of reminiscing.* Washington, D. C.: Taylor and Francis.

Hansell, J. H. (1989). Theories of emotion and motivation: A historical and conceptional review. *Genetic, Social, and General Psychology Monographs, 115,* 429–448.

Havighurst, R. J. (1948). *Developmental tasks and education.* New York: David McKay.

Heath, S. B. (in press). Culture: Contested realm in research on children and youth. *Journal of Applied Developmental Sciences.*

Heckhausen, J. (1999). *Developmental regulation in adulthood: Age-normative and sociostructural constraints as adaptive challenges.* New York: Cambridge University Press.

Heckhausen, J., & Schulz, R. (1995). A life-span theory of control. *Psychological Review, 102,* 284–304.

Heidegger, M. (1979/1927). *Sein und Zeit.* Tübingen, Germany: Niemeyer.

Hess, T. M. (1994). Social cognition in adulthood: Aging-related changes in knowledge and processing mechanisms. *Developmental Review, 14,* 373–412.

Higgins, E. T. (1996). The "self digest": Self-knowledge serving self-regulatory functions. *Journal of Personality and Social Psychology, 71,* 1062–1083.

Hill, G. W. (1982). Group versus individual performance: Are N+1 heads better than one? *Psychological Bulletin, 91,* 517–539.

Höger, R. (1992). Chaos-Forschung und ihre Perspektiven für die Psychologie. *Psychologische Rundschau, 43,* 223–231.

Holahan, C. J., & Moos, R. H. (1987). Personal and contextual determinants of coping strategies. *Journal of Personality and Social Psychology, 52,* 946–955.

Hooker, K. (1992). Possible selves and perceived health in older adults and college students. *Journal of Gerontology: Psychological Sciences, 47,* P85–P95.

Hultsch, D. F., & Plemons, J. K. (1979). Life events and life-span development. In P. B. Baltes & J. O. G. Brim (Eds.), *Life-span development and behavior* (pp. 1–37). New York: Academic Press.

Jaspers, K. (1932). *Philosophie II: Existenzerhellung.* Berlin: Springer.

Karmiloff-Smith, A. (1992). *Beyond modularity: A developmental perspective on cognitive science.* Cambridge, MA: MIT Press.

Keil, F. C. (1981). Constraints on knowledge and cognitive development. *Psychological Review, 88,* 187–227.

Kekes, J. (1995). *Moral wisdom and good lives.* Ithaca, NY: Cornell University Press.

Kelso, J. A. S., Mandell, A. J., & Schlesinger, M. F. (Eds.). (1988). *Dynamic patterns in complex systems.* Singapore: World Scientific.

Kim, J. E., Nesselroade, J. R., & Featherman, D. L. (1996). The state component in self-reported worldviews and religious beliefs of older adults: The MacArthur successful aging studies. *Psychology and Aging, 11,* 396–407.

Klages, L. (1937). *Der Mensch und das Leben.* Jena, Germany: Diederichs.

Klein, W. (1996). Essentially social: On the origin of linguistic knowledge in the individual. In P. B. Baltes & U. M. Staudinger (Eds.), *Interactive minds: life-span perspectives on the social foundation of cognition* (pp. 88–108). New York: Cambridge University Press.

Kliegl, R., & Baltes, P. B. (1987). Theory-guided analysis of development and aging mechanisms through testing-the-limits and research on expertise. In C. Schooler & K. W. Schaie (Eds.), *Cognitive functioning and social structure over the life course* (pp. 95–119). Norwood, NJ: Ablex.

Krueger, F. (1953). *Zur Philosophie und Psychologie der Ganzheit.* Berlin: Springer.

Kruse, A. (1995). Entwicklungspotentialität im Alter. Eine lebenslauf—und situationsorientierte Sicht psychischer Entwicklung. In P. Borscheid (Ed.), *Alter und Gesellschaft* (pp. 63–86). Stuttgart: S. Hirzel.

Kruse, A. (1996). Alltagspraktische und sozioemotionale Kompetenz. In M. M. Baltes & L. Montada (Eds.), *Produktivität und Altern* (pp. 290–322). Frankfurt/Main: Campus.

Kuhl, J. (1983). *Motivation, Konflikt und Handlungskontrolle.* Berlin: Springer-Verlag.

Kuhl, J., & Goschke, T. (1994). A theory of action control: Mental subsystems, modes of control, and volitional conflict-resolution strategies. In J. Kuhl & J. Beckmann (Eds.), *Volition and personality: Action versus state orientation* (vol. 1, pp. 93–124). Göttingen, Germany: Hogrefe.

Labouvie-Vief, G. (1980). Adaptive dimensions of adult cognition. In N. Datan & N. Lohmann (Eds.), *Transitions of aging* (pp. 3–26). New York: Academic Press.

Labouvie-Vief, G. (1985). Intelligence and cognition. In J. E. Birren & K. W. Schaie (Eds.), *The handbook of the psychology of aging* (2nd ed., pp. 500–530). New York: Van Nostrand Reinhold.

Labouvie-Vief, G. (1994). *Psyche & eros: Mind and gender in the life course.* New York: Cambridge University Press.

Lawton, M. P. (1991). Functional status and aging well. *Generations, 15,* 31–34.

Lazarus, R. S., & Golden, G. Y. (1981). The function of denial in stress, coping, and aging. In J. L. McGaugh & S. B. Kiesler (Eds.), *Aging: biology and behavior* (pp. 283–307). New York: Academic Press.

Lerner, R. M. (1984). *On the nature of human plasticity.* New York: Cambridge University Press.

Lerner, R. M., & Busch-Rossnagel, N. A. (1981). *Individuals as producers of their development: a life-span perspective.* New York: Academic Press.

Leventhal, H., & Scherer, K. (1987). The relationship of emotion and cognition: A functional approach to a semantic controversy. *Cognition and Emotion, 1,* 3–28.

Levine, J. M., Resnick, L. B., & Higgins, E. T. (1993). Social foundations of cognition. *Annual Review of Psychology, 44,* 585–612.

Levinson, D. J. (1978). *The seasons of a man's life.* New York: Ballantine Books.

Lewin, K. (1926). Untersuchungen zur Handlungs—und Affektpsychologie: II Vorsatz, Wille und Bedürfnis. *Psychologische Forschung, 7,* 330–385.

Lewin, K. (1946). Behavior and development as a function of the total situation. In L. Carmichael (Ed.), *Manual of child psychology* (pp. 791–844). New York: Wiley.

Lewis, M. D. (1995). Cognition-emotion feedback and the self-organization of developmental paths. *Human Development, 38,* 71–102.

Lindenberger, U., & Baltes, P. B. (1994). Aging and intelligence. In R. J. Sternberg (Ed.), *Encyclopedia of intelligence,* (vol. 1, pp. 52–66). New York: Macmillan.

Maas, H., & Kuypers, J. (1974). *From thirty to seventy: A forty-year longitudinal study of adult life styles and personality.* San Francisco: Jossey-Bass.

Magai, C., & Nusbaum, B. (1996). Personality change in adulthood: Dynamic systems, emotions, and the transformed self. In C. Magai & S. H. McFadden (Eds.), *Handbook of emotion, adult development, and aging* (pp. 403–420). San Diego: Academic Press.

Magnusson, D. L. (Ed.) (1996). *Individual development over the life span: Biological and psychosocial perspectives.* Cambridge, MA: Cambridge University Press.

Magnusson, D., Andersson, T., & Törestad, B. (1993). Methodological implications of a peephole perspective on personality. In D. C. Funder, R. D. Parke, C. Tomlinson-Keasey, & K. Widaman (Eds.), *Studying lives through time: Personality and development* (pp. 207–220). Washington, D. C.: American Psychological Association.

Magnusson, D., & Stattin, H. (1998). Person-context interaction theories. In R. M. Lerner (Ed.), *Theoretical models of human development. Volume 1: Handbook of child psychology* (pp. 685–759). New York: Wiley.

Markus, H. R., & Nurius, P. (1986). Possible selves. *American Psychologist, 41,* 954–969.

Masten, A. S., & Coatsworth, J. D. (1995). Competence, resilience, and psychopathology. In D. Cicchetti & D. Cohen (Eds.), *Developmental psychopathology. Vol. 2: Risk, disorder, and adaptation* (pp. 715–752). New York: Wiley.

McCrae, R. R., & Costa, Jr., P. T. (1997). Personality trait structure as a human universal. *American Psychologist, 52,* 509–516.

Mead, G. H. (1987/1929). Das Wesen der Vergangenheit. In H. Joas & G. H. Mead (Eds.), *Gesammelte Aufsätze* (vol. 2).

Mead, G. H. (1934). *Mind, self, and society.* Chicago: University of Chicago Press.

Middleton, D. (in press). *Social remembering.* London: Sage.

Mischel, W., Shoda, Y., & Rodriguez, M. L. (1989). Delay of gratification in children. *Science, 244,* 933–938.

Nelson, K. (1992). Emergence of autobiographical memory at age 4. *Human Development, 35,* 172–177.

Nesselroade, J. R., & Featherman, D. L. (1991). Intraindividual variability in older adults' depression scores: Some implications for developmental theory and longitudinal research. In D. Magnusson,

L. Bergman, G. Rudinger, & B. Torestad (Eds.), *Problems and methods in longitudinal research: Stability and change* (pp. 47–66). London: Cambridge University Press.

Nesselroade, J. R., Featherman, D. L., Aggen, S. H., & Rowe, J. W. (1995). *Short-term variability in physiological attributes of older adults: The MacArthur successful aging studies.* Unpublished manuscript. Charlottesville: University of Virginia, Department of Psychology.

Oettingen, G. (1996). Positive fantasy and motivation. In P. M. Gollwitzer & J. A. Bargh (Eds.), *The psychology of action: Linking cognition and motivation to action* (pp. 236–259). New York: Guilford Press.

Perner, J. (1991). *Understanding the representation of mind.* Harvard, MA: MIT Press.

Poon, L. W., Rubin, D. C., & Wilson, B. A. (Eds.). (1989). *Everyday cognition in adulthood and late life.* New York: Cambridge University Press.

Prigogine, I., & Stengers, I. (1984). *Order out of chaos: Man's new dialogue with nature.* New York: Bantam.

Rawls, J. (1971). *A theory of justice.* Cambridge: Cambridge University Press.

Reichert, I., & Dörner, D. (1988). Heurismen beim Umgang mit einem "einfachen" dynamischen System. *Sprache und Kognition, 7,* 12–24.

Reker, G. T., & Wong, P. T. P. (1988). Aging as an individual process: Toward a theory of personal meaning. In J. E. Birren & V. L. Bengston (Eds.), *Emergent theories of aging* (pp. 214–246). New York: Springer.

Rentsch, T. (1994). Philosophische Anthropologie und Ethik der späten Lebenszeit. In P. B. Baltes, J. Mittelstraβ, & U. M. Staudinger (Eds.), *Alter und Altern: Ein interdisziplinärer Studientext zur Gerontologie* (pp. 283–304). Berlin: de Gruyter.

Rogoff, B. & Chavajay, P. (1995). What's become of research on the cultural basis of cognitive development. *American Psychologist, 50,* 859–877.

Rothacker, E. (1938). *Die Schichten der Persönlichkeit* (8th ed.). Bonn: Bouvier.

Rutter, M. (1996). Transitions and turning points in developmental psychopathology: As applied to the age span between childhood and mid-adulthood. *International Journal of Behavioral Development, 19,* 603–626.

Rutter, M., & Rutter, M. (1993). *Developing minds: Challenge and continuity across the life span.* New York: Basic Books.

Ryff, C. D. (1991). Possible selves in adulthood and old age: A tale of shifting horizons. *Psychology and Aging, 6,* 286–295.

Salthouse, T. A. (1994). How many causes are there of aging-related decrements in cognitive functioning? *Developmental Review, 14,* 413–437.

Sameroff, A. J. (1995). General systems theories and developmental psychopathology. In D. Cicchetti & D. J. Cohen (Eds.), *Developmental psychopathology. Vol. 1: Theory and methods* (pp. 659–695). New York: Wiley.

Schmid, W. (1991). *Auf der Suche nach einer neuen Lebenskunst: Die Frage nach dem Grund und die Neubegründung der Ethik bei Foucault.* Frankfurt/Main: Suhrkamp.

Searle, J. R. (1992). *The rediscovery of the mind.* Cambridge, MA: Cambridge University Press.

Seligman, M. E. P. (1991). *Learned optimism.* New York: Knopf.

Shotter, J., & Gergen, K. J. (Eds.). (1989). *Texts of identity.* London: Sage.

Showers, C. J., & Ryff, C. D. (1996). Self-differentiation and well-being in a life transition. *Personality and Social Psychology Bulletin, 22,* 448–460.

Shweder, R. A. (1991). *Thinking through cultures.* Cambridge, MA: Harvard University Press.

Simon, J. (1974). Leben. In H. Krings, H. M. Baumgarten, & C. Wild (Eds.), *Handbuch philosophischer Grundbegriffe* (vol.2, pp. 844–859). Munich: K#aosel.

Smith, J. (1996). Planning about life: A social-interactive and life-span perspective. In P. B. Baltes & U. M. Staudinger (Eds.), *Interactive minds: Life-span perspectives on the social foundation of cognition* (pp. 242–275). Hillsdale, NJ: Lawrence Erlbaum Associates.

Smith, J., & Baltes, P. B. (1990). Wisdom-related knowledge: Age/cohort differences in responses to life planning problems. *Developmental Psychology, 26,* 494–505.

Smith, J., & Baltes, P. B. (1997). Profiles of psychological functioning in the old and oldest-old. *Psychology and Aging, 12,* 458–478.

Smith, J., Staudinger, U. M., & Baltes, P. B. (1994). Occupational settings facilitative of wisdom-related knowledge: The sample case of clinical psychologists. *Journal of Consulting and Clinical Psychology, 62,* 989–1000.

Sohni, H. (1973). *Die Medizin der Frühromantik.* Freiburg: Schulz.

Spranger, E. (1947). *Lebenserfahrung.* Tübingen: Wunderlich.

Staudinger, U. M. (1984). *Lebensgeschichte: ein psychologisches Forschungsinteresse—und dann?* Friedrich-Alexander-Universität, Erlangen-Nürnberg.

Staudinger, U. M. (1989). *The study of life review: An approach to the investigation of intellectual development across the life span.* Berlin: Sigma.

Staudinger, U. M. (1996a). Psychologische Produktivität und Selbstentfaltung im Alter. In M. M. Baltes & L. Montada (Eds.), *Produktivität und Altern* (pp. 344–373). Frankfurt/Main: Campus Verlag.

Staudinger, U. M. (1996b). Wisdom and the social-interactive foundation of the mind. In P. B. Baltes & U. M. Staudinger (Eds.), *Interactive minds: Life-span perspectives on the social foundation of cognition* (pp. 276–315). New York: Cambridge University Press.

Staudinger, U. M. (in press). Older and wiser? Integrating results from a psychological approach to the study of wisdom. *International Journal of Behavioral Development.*

Staudinger, U. M., & Baltes, P. B. (1994). The psychology of wisdom. In R. J. Sternberg (Ed.), *Encyclopedia of intelligence* (pp. 1143–1152). New York: Macmillan.

Staudinger, U. M., & Baltes, P. B. (1996). Interactive minds: A facilitative setting for wisdom-related performance. *Journal of Personality and Social Psychology, 71,* 746–762.

Staudinger, U. M., & Baltes, P. B. (in preparation). *Wisdom-related potential: Comparing different types of contextual support.* Berlin: Max Planck Institute for Human Development.

Staudinger, U. M., Braß, M., & Frensch, P. A. (in preparation). *Recognition and free production of wisdom-related knowledge and judgement.* Berlin: Max Planck Institute for Human Development.

Staudinger, U. M., & Dittmann-Kohli, F. (1994). Lebenserfahrung und Lebenssinn. In P. B. Baltes, J. Mittelstraß, & U. M. Staudinger (Eds.), *Alter und Altern: Ein interdisziplinärer Studientext zur Gerontologie* (pp. 408–436). Berlin: de Gruyter.

Staudinger, U. M., & Fleeson, W. (1996). Self and personality in old and very old age: A sample case of resilience? *Development and Psychopathology, 8,* 867–885.

Staudinger, U. M., Fleeson, W., & Baltes, P. B. (in press). Predictors of subjective physical health and global well-being during midlife: Similarities and differences between the U. S. and the F. R. G. Berlin: Max Planck Institute for Human Development.

Staudinger, U. M., Freund, A. M., Linden, M., & Maas, I. (in press). Self, personality, and life management: Psychological resilience and vulnerability. In P. B. Baltes & K. U. Mayer (Eds.), *The Berlin aging study: Aging from 70 to 100.* New York: Cambridge University Press.

Staudinger, U. M., Lopez, D. F., & Baltes, P. B. (1997). The psychometric location of wisdom-related performance. *Personality and Social Psychology Bulletin, 23,* 1200–1214.

Staudinger, U. M., Maciel, A., Smith, J., & Baltes, P. B. (1998). What predicts wisdom-related knowledge? A first look at personality, intelligence, and facilitative experimental contexts. *European Journal of Personality, 12,* 1–17.

Staudinger, U. M., Marsiske, M., & Baltes, P. B. (1995). Resilience and reserve capacity in later adulthood: Potentials and limits of development across the life span. In D. Cicchetti & D. Cohen (Eds.), *Developmental psychopathology* (vol. 2, pp. 801–847). New York: Wiley.

Staudinger, U. M., & Pasupathi, M. (in press). Life-span perspectives on self, personality and social cognition. In T. Salthouse & F. Craik (Eds.), *Handbook of cognition and aging.*

Staudinger, U. M., Smith, J., & Baltes, P. B. (1992). Wisdom-related knowledge in a life review task: Age differences and the role of professional specialization. *Psychology and Aging, 7,* 271–281.

Staudinger, U. M., Smith, J., & Baltes, P. B. (1994). *Manual for the assessment of wisdom-related knowledge* (Technical Report No. 46): Max Planck Institute for Human Development and Education.

Stern, W. (1910). Über Aufgabe und Anlage der Psychographie. *Zeitschrift für angewandte Psychologie und psychologische Sammelforschung, 3,* 166–190.

Stern, W. (1930). *Studien zur Personwissenschaft, Erster Teil: Personalistische Wissenschaft.* Leipzig: Barth.

Sternberg, R. J., & Berg, C. A. (Eds.). (1992). *Intellectual development.* New York Cambridge University Press.

Sternberg, R. J., & Wagner, R. K. (Eds.). (1986). *Practical intelligence.* New York: Cambridge University Press.

Sternberg, R. J., & Wagner, R. K. (Eds.). (1994). *Mind in context: Interactionist perspectives on human intelligence.* New York: Cambridge University Press.

Straub, J. (1989). *Historisch-psychologische Biographieforschung: theoretische, methodologische und methodische Argumentation in systematischer Absicht.* Heidelberg: Asanger.

Tetens, J. N. (1777). *Philosophische Versuche über die menschliche Natur und ihre Entwicklung.* Leipzig: Weidmanns Erben & Reich.

Thelen, E., & Smith, L. B. (1994). *A dynamic systems approach to the development of cognition and action.* Cambridge, MA: MIT Press.

Thomae, H. (1994). Trust, social support, and relying on others: A contribution to the interface between behavioral and social gerontology. *Zeitschrift für Gerontologie, 27,* 103–109.

Van der Maas, H. L., & Molenaar, P. C. (1992). Stagewise cognitive development: An application of catastrophe theory. *Psychological Review, 99,* 395–417.

Vaneigem, R. (1980). *Handbuch der Lebenskunst für die jungen Generationen.* Hamburg: Association.

Verly, L. (1957). *L'art de vivre.* Paris: Gallimard.

Vygotsky, L. S. (1978). *Mind in society: The development of higher psychological processes.* Cambridge, MA: Harvard University Press.

Webster, J. L. (1993). Construction and validation of the reminiscence functions scale. *Journal of Gerontology: Psychological Sciences, 48,* 256–262.

Wellmann, H. M. (1990). *The child's theory of mind.* Cambridge, MA: MIT Press.

Welsch, W. (1995). *Vernunft: Die zeitgenössische Vernunftkritik und das Konzept der transversalen Vernunft.* Frankfurt: Suhrkamp.

Wertheimer, M. (1925). *Drei Abhandlungen zur Gestalttheorie.* Erlangen, Germany: Palm & Enke.

Wertsch, J. V. (1991). *Voices of the mind: A sociocultural approach to mediated action.* Cambridge, MA: Harvard University Press.

Wheeler, L., & Reis, H. T. (1991). Self-recording of everyday life events: Origins, types, and uses. *Journal of Personality, 59,* 339–354.

Wiese, B. S., Freund, A. M., & Baltes, P. B. (1998). *Selection, optimization, and compensation in day-to-day life: Orchestrating life-management in partnership/family and work/career domains.* Berlin: Max Planck Institute for Human Development.

Wood, J. V. (1996). What is social comparison and how should we study it? *Personality and Social Psychology Bulletin, 22,* 520–537.

Wollheim, R. (1984). *The thread of life.* Cambridge, MA: Harvard University Press.

Wozniak, R. H., & Fischer, K. W. (Eds.). (1993). *Development in context. Acting and thinking in specific environments.* Hillsdale, NJ: Lawrence Erlbaum Associates.

Yates, F. A. (1966). *The art of memory.* London: Routledge & Kegan Paul.

Index